Healthy Sexuality

Richard Blonna, ED.D, CHES
William Paterson University

Jean Levitan, PH.D.
William Paterson University

Morton Publishing Company

925 W. Kenyon Ave., Unit 12
Englewood, Colorado 80110

http://www.morton-pub.com

Book Team

Publisher:	Douglas Morton
Managing Editor:	Ruth Horton
Editorial Assistant:	Dona Mendoza
Production Manager:	Joanne Saliger, Ash Street Typecrafters, Inc.
Illustrator:	Kevin Kertz
Cover Design:	Bob Schram, Bookends
Cover Photo:	Sharon and Werner Hoeger. Used with permission from Fitness and Wellness, Inc., Boise, ID

Photo Models

Matt and Mike Bernstein, Alex, Heide, T. Michael, Richard, and William Blonna, Dan, Donna, and Ken Horvath, Erik Maas, Alonna, Brielle, and Jenna Nesto, Sam D. Pegues family

Special Photo Credits:

Chapter 1 — Sam Pegues, p. 4
Chapter 3 — Sam Pegues, p. 81, Dr. Betty Dodson, p 54
Chapter 4 — Dr. S.H. Biber, Trinidad, Colorado, p. 113, Harold Bernstein, p. 96
Chapter 7 — Werner Hoeger, p. 213
Chapter 9 — World Wide Associated Press, pp. 270, 272
Chapter 13 — Anthony Nesto, p. 403
Chapter 14 — Durex Consumer Products, p. 441,
　　　　　　　Cervical Cap (CXC) Ltd., www.cervcap.com, 408-395-2100, p. 447
Chapter 15 — Center for Disease Control (CDC), pp. 497-500, 507, 509, 511
Chapter 17 — World Wide Associated Press, pp. 564, 566

Printed in the United States of America
by Morton Publishing Company
925 W. Kenyon Ave., Unit 12, Englewood, CO 80110

10   9   8   7   6   5   4   3   2   1

ISBN: 0-89582-410-8

Preface

As an introductory text in human sexuality, *Healthy Sexuality* is based on the fundamental information and concepts that have evolved from the body of research in this field. We firmly believe in a psychosocial model of human sexuality. In this view, humans become sexual beings and evolve as a result of a continual interaction between biological and psychosocial forces.

We also believe that human sexuality is intimately tied to overall health and wellness. *Healthy Sexuality* examines how the components of wellness — physical, intellectual, emotional, social, spiritual, and environmental — influence sexual health. The book points out how the healthy expression of sexuality can improve one's level of health and well-being.

Essential to being healthy, people have to come to grips with themselves as human beings, to make sound sexual decisions and self-actualize their sexual selves. Although we do cover sexual health concerns and risks (unintended pregnancy, STDs, date rape, and so on), *Healthy Sexuality* takes a pro-sex rather than a problem-oriented approach to sexual issues.

Healthy Sexuality is intended to be practical and usable. Unlike some of the dry, technical introductory books in the field, readers will find this one to be friendly and enjoyable to read. We hope to engage the reader in this topic as the fascinating, relevant subject it truly is.

Features of the Text

- To orient the reader to the content of each chapter, a brief outline of the **Major Topics** is presented on the chapter introductory page.

- Also on the chapter opening page is a set of **Student Learning Objectives** to put the chapter's content into a meaningful framework.

- Throughout the text, **Key Terms** are highlighted and defined to clarify the content and give the student easy access to the meanings of vocabulary essential to their understanding.

- The **Health Hints** within each chapter are practical, step-by-step suggestions for achieving optimal sexual health and well-being related to the accompanying discussion.

- The **Perspectives** scattered throughout the text present unusual, interesting, and sometimes controversial material related to the discussion. They add interest and expand upon the basic topic.

- **Critical Thinking** features call the reader's mind into play, bringing up questions that readers have to answer for themselves. These questions have no right or wrong answers; they are an exercise in mental gymnastics — and represent possible topics for the instructor to consider for group discussion.

- Each chapter includes several **Case Studies**, bringing the book to life through real situations. Most of these are taken from the authors' own files. Although the names have been changed, the cases are authentic and point out dilemmas for which the counselees have sought professional assistance.

- Each chapter concludes with a **Wellness Synthesis,** tying the chapter content to the six dimensions of health and wellness — physical, intellectual, emotional, social, spiritual, and environmental.

- The **Student Study Questions** at the end of the chapter offer readers an opportunity to ask themselves what they have learned and to reinforce this knowledge by putting it in written form.

- To further personalize learning, the **Student Assessment** in each chapter is a tool by which readers can apply what they have learned to their own lives — and thereby improve their health and well-being.

- **World Wide Web sites,** with annotations, at the end of the chapter direct the reader to further, specific information related to the chapter topic. These entries are current and have been verified for authenticity.

- The **Note System** of documentation is used in preference to the tedious author/date citation method, which detracts from readability. This results in a more reader-friendly book while retaining the source data to which the reader may wish to refer.

- In the spirit of **diversity,** we have included information relative to differences between races and ethnic groups, as in the most current data generated by the Centers for Disease Control. We use the federally sanctioned usage in referring to these groups.

- We integrate issues of **sexual orientation** throughout the book wherever appropriate rather than presenting this as a stand-alone topic in a single chapter. In this way, we hope to project the view of sexual orientation as a mainstream issue rather than a separate topic.

- We incorporate data to support the textual presentation through **illustrative tables and figures** from the most current sources available, complemented by the classic studies by Kinsey, Masters and Johnson, Laumann and colleagues, and other respected researchers in this field.

- The judicious use of **photographs** illustrates important information under the principle that a picture is worth a thousand words.

- At the end of the book you will find a **Glossary** of the important terminology used in the book, along with a concise, clear definition of each term.

- A **Select Bibliography** lists the most important references underlying the book's development. It is not intended to include every resource we used but, rather, to highlight the sources of which the reader should be most aware pertaining to the field of human sexuality and related issues.

- An **Appendix** listing current resources to which the reader may refer for further information or assistance.

Ancillaries

To assist the instructor in presenting the course in an interesting and comprehensive way and for the student to get the most out of the class, the following ancillaries are provided without charge to qualified adopters. All are incorporated on one CD-ROM for easy access in Windows and Macintosh.

- An *Instructor Manual* contains the following information for each chapter:
    - Detailed outline of the text

- Suggested activities
- Quizzes
- Black-and-white pointer transparency masters
- WorldWideWeb sites

- *Microtest*, a computerized testbank with the following features:
  - More than 800 multiple-choice, true/false, and essay questions
  - Capability to add or edit test questions in any format
  - Explanations for why a question is true, false, correct, or incorrect
  - Ability to save and recall previously generated test to create a new version of the test, as the multiple-choice answers will rotate each time a test is printed
  - Allows tests to be generated using a LaserJet printer
  - Available in Windows and Macintosh

- Overhead color transparency masters of the book's most important graphics to facilitate class instruction and assist in explaining key concepts (within the Instructor Manual).

- Image Bank and PowerPoint presentation on CD-ROM:
  - Available in Windows and Macintosh
  - Includes PowerPoint viewer on CD-ROM, which allows instructors to use without PowerPoint program
  - Enables instructors who have PowerPoint to edit presentation to fit their lecture
  - Allows the instructor to go back to past chapters and to start at any chapter

Student Supplement

- *Student Interactive Study Guide*, to help the student study for tests and retain information learned in the course.
  - A fun CD-ROM to reinforce the content of each chapter
  - Key terms matched to the description
  - Review of chapter objectives
  - Quizzes that are different each time they are called up, as the questions rotate
  - A brief outline of the chapter that can be printed for notetaking during class
  - A game utilizing the full Glossary
  - Available in Windows and Macintosh

- *Issues in Human Sexuality: Current & Controversial Readings* with Links to Relevant WebSites that can be value-packaged with the text. This educational resource contains 34 current and controversial readings on topics in human sexuality with WebSites relevant to the issue discussed in the readings.

The features and ancillaries outlined here have resulted in a comprehensive course presentation that covers the content in a most expansive way. We developed this book with the student at the forefront. We hope readers will apply the information to their own lives in a positive way, leading to their optimal sexual health and overall wellness.

About the Authors

Richard Blonna, Ed.D, CHES, has been teaching the Human Sexuality course for more than 20 years. His initial work in the field was in education and control of sexually transmitted diseases. He served as an STD investigator, counselor, supervisor, and trainer for the New Jersey State Department of Health (NJSDH) STD Control Program. He also worked for the NJSDH as a Health Education Consultant for the AIDS and Family Planning Programs. He has taught Human Sexuality at Temple University and, most recently, William Paterson University, where he also teaches Health Counseling, Epidemiology, and Stress Management.

Jean Levitan, Ph.D., has been teaching Human Sexuality at the university level for more than 25 years. At William Paterson University she has taught in both the Community Health and the Women's Studies departments. Past activities include teacher training for human sexuality and evaluation of the Family Life Education Program for the City of New York. In addition to teaching Human Sexuality, she teaches Women's Health, supervises community health interns, teaches Racisim and Sexism in the United States, and currently is developing a course on reproductive rights.

To our loving families:
Heidi, Will, Mike, Matt, Mike, and Steve,
who put up with the stress of our deadlines and the time spent
locked in our offices working on the manuscript.

Acknowledgments

First, I acknowledge two people who were early influences in my development as a human sexuality professional. Drs. Richard Cross and Sandra Leiblum of the University of Medicine and Dentistry of New Jersey first opened my eyes to the field and my own sexuality many years ago in one of their intensive sexuality seminars for medical students and invited professionals. Their ease and professionalism in dealing with sexual matters left a lasting impression on me. They provided my first exposure to the scientific, professional study of sexuality and validated sexuality as a scientific discipline worthy of serious study.

I'd like to thank my mentor and role model, Dr. Marvin Levy of Temple University, for standing out as the epitome of what I consider a "healthy sexuality professional." With his rugged, athletic masculinity, scholarly wisdom, and health background, Marv created an image in my mind of someone able to place sexuality squarely in the framework of health rather than a series of problems to be addressed and feared. I was lucky to come under his influence at a crucial time in my life as a young husband and developing professional. I'm thankful for his guidance in both areas of my life.

Finally, I thank Clifford G. Freund, my mentor with the NJSDH. Cliff nurtured my early career as an STD professional and supported by initial interests in sexuality and education. He had the faith in my work and the wisdom to give me the freedom to explore issues and develop as a sexuality professional.   — RB

★   ★   ★

Though my graduate school experience was years ago, the training and learning that took place under the mentorship of Deryck Calderwood and the faculty of New York University, along with the incredible work accomplished with classmates, set the foundation for this text. Since then, the professional friendships developed through the scientific study of sexuality, and the research challenges presented at society meetings, have bolstered my grounding in healthy sexuality.

My gratitude and appreciation also go to the following people for their contributions to this text: Eva Goldfarb, Ernie Green, Bridget Finn, Konnie McCaffree, Janet Pollack, Donna Excroll, Arlene Scala, and Anthony Nesto.   — JL

★   ★   ★

We'd like to thank the following people at Morton Publishing: Mimi Egan for listening to our initial ideas and motivating us to submit the proposal; Doug Morton for offering us a contract to write the book; Ruth Horton for her support, help, and persistence in developing the actual manuscript; and Dona Mendoza for paying attention to and taking care of all of the myriad details involved in bringing the manuscript to publication.

To our reviewers — Lillian Cook Carter of Towson State University, Fern Goodhart of Rutgers University, James G. McGuire, University of Southern Mississippi, and Margaret Pepe of Kent State University — we extend thanks for their time, dedication to thoroughly review the text, and their thoughtful comments that enabled us to improve the manuscript.

Finally, we thank our colleagues in the Department of Community Health for their support on this project and for providing a wonderful work environment.

    — RB
    — JL

Contents

7 Human Sexual Response.... 201

8 Sensuality and Sexual Behavior 231

9 Atypical Sexual Behavior ... 263

10 Intimate Relationships.... 287

Introduction

1

Student Learning Objectives

After reading this chapter, students will be able to:

- Define *human sexuality*.

- Define *health* and *wellness*.

- Describe the key components of healthy sexuality.

- Explain how the six dimensions of health and wellness impact one's sexuality.

- Compare and contrast behaviors that enhance or inhibit healthy sexuality.

- Describe the key sources of sexual information.

- Evaluate sources of sexuality information.

- Describe the major findings of the key researchers of sexuality over the past 100 years.

- Describe the components of informed decision making.

- Compare the characteristics of healthy and unhealthy relationships.

Self-esteem
a way of looking at oneself;
may be high or low

As we begin the 21st century, students may be struggling to sort out the conflicting messages about "healthy sexuality." Sexuality remains a critical force shaping our lives. It is part of how we see ourselves and impacts our **self-esteem**. It is ever-present as we relate to others on both romantic and platonic levels. Students, as well as the population at large, are constantly confronted with media messages on enhancing sexuality through the use of various products. Sexual themes remain prominent in all forms of entertainment, including books, film, television, and music.

As health educators, we hold to the position that good decision making is grounded in having accurate information, an opportunity to develop a personal value system, and discussion of possible and probable outcomes of behavior. We advocate the accompanying opportunity to become aware of the variety of sexual lifestyles and concerns of those who are unlike oneself.

OUR SEXUAL CLIMATE

To try to figure out how best to make healthy personal decisions in a climate of contrasts is confusing and problematic. Americans talk about sex and sexuality all the time. It is a favorite subject of the media. Some conservative media pundits criticize our culture for its overemphasis on sex. They claim that sexual themes dominate our culture and the media and that the government has gone too far in allowing the free expression of sexuality. Some liberal commentators say exactly the opposite. They claim that our culture is sexually restrictive and downright puritanical. As examples of a restrictive culture, they cite the lack of uniform standards for sex education in the schools, conservative agendas for prohibiting the availability of RU486 (the "abortion pill"), and the prohibition of gay marriage. Still others claim that our culture sends mixed messages about sexuality. It is used to market and sell almost everything, yet most schools are not allowed to teach about it.

The reality is that both government and society have limited influence on our sexuality. We are sexual beings from conception to death. Our sexuality evolves and grows regardless of official sanctions or restrictions. We learn about sex whether we do or do not have sex education in our schools. It is not a question of whether we learn. Its more a matter of the *quality* of what we learn. A key to understanding sexual learning is to realize that we learn about sexuality and what it means to be a man or woman even if no one ever sits us down and has a heart-to-heart talk about the "birds and the bees." And that classic explanation of where we came from is only a small part of understanding ourselves.

Quality sexuality programs result from well thought out curricula, with goals and objectives for student learning. Curricula are based on accurate information, in which the pursuit of knowledge is encouraged rather than restricted. Students have a chance to examine their values and the factors that contribute to healthy and appropriate personal decisions. States that mandate sexuality education are Alabama, Arkansas, Delaware, the District of Columbia, Georgia, Hawaii, Iowa, Kansas, Maryland, Minnesota, Nevada, New Jersey, North Carolina, Rhode Island, South Carolina, Tennessee, Utah, Vermont, and West Virginia.[1] Mandates notwithstanding, what transpires within a classroom varies tremendously across the United States.

In many ways the sexual learning that takes place outside any classroom is far more influential, as it is constant, both verbal and nonverbal, and often insidious. Students can easily relate the types of misinformation they acquired from friends throughout their childhood and simultaneously often report that their parents didn't talk with them about sexuality issues. In reality, though, parents convey information, impart values, and serve as **role models** whether a formal, face-to-face, serious conversation ever takes place between parent and child. A frown or a raised eyebrow can convey disapproval just as a nod, smile, or laugh indicates support. To be silent on an issue, to omit sexuality from the daily discourse in our lives, to never bring up sexuality as part of the conversation around the dinner table sends a strong message about its being a taboo subject.

We learn about sex through assimilation regardless of whether we receive formal instruction from parents, school, or others.

Role model
a person whose behaviors are imitated by others

Some of what we see and learn, unfortunately, does not present the healthiest picture of sexuality. Sometimes our parents, caregivers, friends, teachers, and media figures do not provide us with the best role models or information for healthy sexuality. The sexual scripts we receive may not promote healthy relationships and in some cases may actually jeopardize our lives. For example, if women are taught that they must be thin to be sexually attractive, what connection might that "lesson" have to eating disorders such as anorexia and bulimia? If men are taught that they are entitled to sex and that women want to be dominated, what connection does that "lesson" have to dating violence and rape? Sometimes the very people and institutions charged with teaching us and nurturing us fail or, worse yet, sexually abuse us.

So what is human sexuality? **Sexuality** is a broad term that refers to all aspects of being sexual. Many people think human sexuality refers to sexual behavior — what people do, how often they do it, and so on. Although sexual behavior is an important part of being sexual, human sexuality encompasses much more than that. Sexuality involves our genetic inheritance, our anatomy and physiology, and the reality of being a sexual creature in a biological sense. It also encompasses our thoughts and feelings about our body and what it means to be a man or a woman. It involves our ethics, values, and the cultural mores we've assimilated through our family, ethnic group, and religious affiliation.

Sexuality
a broad term referring to all aspects of being sexual

Our sexuality extends beyond the self to encompass our friendships, intimate relationships, and sexual relationships. Last, our sexuality does not exist in a vacuum. It is influenced by and influences our environment. Our institutions (schools, governments, and so on), neighborhoods, communities, campuses, states, and countries, and their policies, help shape the person we are and our options as a sexual being.

FACTORS THAT CONTRIBUTE TO OUR SEXUALITY

Our sexuality is influenced by many factors throughout our lives, each impacting our development in similar or unique ways. No researcher or theorist has the widely accepted, definitive explanation for how each of us becomes who we are. Some rely heavily on biology, looking to our genetic inheritance as a prescription for how we will develop. Others hold the culture and the socialization process to be the critical forces that shape our lives. Some believe the psyche processes information as a result of experiences perceived as positive or negative, which in the end cause the individual to become the person he or she is. Finally, some maintain that the person we are is a result of the interaction of heredity/genetics, family socialization, culture, and personal experience.

Without being able to clearly determine which factor is most influential, we do know that we all receive strong and perhaps conflicting messages about sexuality from family, friends, school, media, religion, and the culture. **Sexologists**, those who study sexuality through various rigorous research methodologies, provide input into our knowledge base. Developing a healthy sexuality involves processing that information and, as individuals, internalizing that which is useful.

Sexologists
specialized researchers of sexual subjects from a variety of disciplines including psychology, biology, medicine, nursing, and health

Family

The nature/nurture argument about development can be challenged by examining the family environment. Are we the individuals we are because of our genetic material? From a biological perspective, family represents those to whom one is related "by blood" and, consequently, we may be like our parents and siblings. Or are we the persons we are because of how we were reared? In a social sense, the term *family* has taken on broader connotations as people's living arrangements take on a variety of forms. Divorce, remarriage, stepfamilies, blended families, and single families introduce other models. Reproductive technologies and adoption practices add still another dimension to the influence of parents.

Nuclear family
a family made up of the mother, father, and their children

The traditional **nuclear family**, consisting of a married man and woman and their biological children, represents less than half of all households in the United States today. The primary caregiver, thus, may assume a greater role in a child's development than previously. The challenge comes in trying to evaluate the impacts of various family arrangements on its members.

The impact of parental influence on sexuality is still open to debate. For example, the societal concern with homosexuality has led courts, almost exclusively until more recent times, to award children to heterosexual parents in custody cases resulting from divorce. The concern is that gay or lesbian parents will influence their children to be gay or lesbian. That the

Children learn about sex without it ever being mentioned.

heterosexual parents of the gay and lesbian adults were unable to influence their children's orientation is not given the same credibility.

The family influences the development of healthy sexuality in numerous ways. Through family, we learn gender roles and expectations, are taught about love and affection, learn patterns of touch, develop a sense of our physical selves, and develop patterns of social interaction. In each of these areas, our experiences can lead to healthy or unhealthy development. In some areas of parenting, a number of approaches can lead to healthy sexual development.

It is generally accepted that parents should be loving and supportive toward their children. Children who receive physical affection will, in turn, be more likely to be able to give affection to others. Embedded in such general advice, however, are individual patterns that may be criticized. For example, research has shown that boy children stop receiving physical affection earlier than girls, who may continue to be hugged and kissed throughout their lives. Does the change in the type of touch boys receive impact their adult patterns?

In terms of **gender role** expectations, most parents reinforce gender stereotyped behaviors very early on. Boys are expected to play aggressively, enjoy trucks, Legos™, action figures, and the like. Girls get socialized to plan for motherhood, beauty, and domestic tasks. The women's movement of the late 1960s and early 1970s questioned the impact of gender-stereotyping on the healthy development of boys and girls. Almost 30 years later, television commercials for children's toys reveal little departure from the traditional gender-role expectations. Toy manufacturers, in their defense, claim they are marketing to the children who will buy their products. When they have attempted to market toys in a more gender-neutral manner, their efforts have not been successful. Families have different views on what is socially acceptable and what toys they want to purchase, yet children seem to develop their own preferences regardless.

Gender role
the different behaviors and attitudes that society expects of females and males

Samantha, 4 years of age, preferred to play with the boys at nursery school. She also preferred boys underwear and was allowed to wear boys cartoon underpants to school. Should her parents and the school have discouraged this behavior so she could develop more "normally?" What values were taught to you about how you were to act? Look? Treat others?

Friends

One's peer group has always maintained a powerful role in shaping our attitudes and values about sexuality. Depending upon the friends with whom we socialize, we have various experiences at different ages. Teens may refer to others as "being in the fast crowd" — which may mean that more sexual activity and drinking take place. Kids may refer to others as "geeks" or "nerds" — meaning that, though smart, they seem to lack social

Case Study

Karen:
With Eyes Wide Open

I remember, as a kid, traveling with the "in crowd" in junior high school. A couple of girls were considered the "pretty ones" and they had the boyfriends. I always got invited to the parties but ended up being the last one to ever get kissed. I had one friend who my mother worried was a "bad influence." Her parents were divorced, her father was out of the picture, and she was living with her grandparents.

One weekend she invited me to join her on a visit to her mother's apartment in the city. Her mother had two different boyfriends, and in retrospect I realize that she slept with both of them. What is a clear memory of that weekend is her mother walking around the apartment in her underwear, sitting on one boyfriend's lap. Somehow I knew that my own mother would have been very upset if she knew what type of interaction I was witnessing.

skills. Regardless, peer pressure, social judgments, and opportunities all interact to influence healthy development. At the same time, those very influences can leave a negative mark dominated by low self-esteem, depression, and feelings of inadequacy.

Most students report that the bulk of their sexuality education comes from talks with friends. They say that some friends passed along accurate information and others spoke with authority while dispensing inaccurate information. Students have reported that, as children and teens, they saw sexually explicit pictures, magazines, and videos at a friend's home — all supposedly belonging to "my friend's dad." The sneaking around and the searching through hidden material conveys a message about sexuality.

As sexuality educators, we have volumes of accurate information available to children. Nonetheless, we have been confronted at times with, "What do you know?!" and, "Why do you have to have all this stuff around?"

Despite increasing amounts of good information available for parents, college students still report that the bulk of their information about sexuality comes from their friends. How similar are your values and experiences to those of your peer group? Do you remember friends providing you with accurate information?

Culture

Culture
sum of the learned set of rules governing the behavior of people, often focused on the influences of race, class, religion, and ethnicity

Anthropologists have defined **culture** as anything and everything that humans learn. Implied within that is a learned set of rules for appropriate behavior. In practice, when addressing issues of culture, what actually may be under study are influences of race, class, religion, and ethnicity.

How exactly would you define the environment and community within which you were reared? When we use the term "cultural conflict," what values are clashing?

All cultures have established rules to regulate sexual activity. Some are viewed as restrictive, and others are seen as permissive. Even though Western cultures share certain traditions and values — such as patriarchy, monogamy, having children within marriage — actual behavior varies from one group to another.

As the United States becomes an increasingly pluralistic society, it is forced to confront what may seem to be "foreign" practices. For example, female genital mutilation or female circumcision (discussed more fully with female anatomy and physiology in Chapter 3) is a custom practiced primarily in parts of Africa. Today, U. S. healthcare providers find themselves caring for girls and women who have undergone this mutilating experience.

The New York Times (October 18, 1997) reported on a couple living on the run in England. The woman was afraid that her father or brother was going to kill her because she had defied her culture by choosing her partner. Western ideas of falling in love, being able to decide whom to marry, and the like were in direct conflict with her Muslim upbringing, which dictated that the bride's father arranged the marriages with her input having little or no value.

Think about the cultural influences on the decisions you make? Does your race guide you in any particular way? How does being "middle class" versus "wealthy" versus "poor" affect your sexuality? If you grew up in a rural area, how would your options differ from what you learned about sexuality and yourself while living in an urban area?

School

Schools are charged as the institutions primarily responsible for transmitting knowledge and helping children learn about the world. As a logical extension, schools are to play a key role in sexuality education. Even so, the debate has raged for decades regarding the role schools should play, the depth of information they should convey, at what ages children should learn information about sexuality, and how, if at all, schools can teach in a "value-free" way. Programs that have been successful have been conducted by working closely with parents, clergy, and community leaders to develop curricula that are acceptable. The efforts in this regard far exceed those in other subject areas such as English or history. Research shows that most parents support sexuality education in the public schools.

In 1997, the federal government earmarked multimillion dollar grants to the states for development of **abstinence-based curricula** (see Figure 1.1).

Abstinence-based curricula
school programs that advocate not having sex before marriage

"Abstinence education" means an educational or motivational program which:

A. Has, as its exclusive purpose, teaching the social, psychological, and health gains to be realized by abstaining from sexual activity.

B. Teaches abstinence from sexual activity outside marriage as the expected standard for school-age children.

C. Teaches that abstinence from sexual activity is the only certain way to avoid out-of-wedlock pregnancy, sexually transmitted diseases, and other associated health problems.

D. Teaches that a mutually faithful monogamous relationship in context of marriage is the expected standard of human sexual activity.

E. Teaches that sexual activity outside of the context of marriage is likely to have harmful consequences for the child, the child's parents, and society.

F. Teaches young people how to reject sexual advances and how alcohol and drug use increases vulnerability to sexual advances, and

G. Teaches the importance of attaining self-sufficiency before engaging in sexual activity.

Source: Cited in the *Federal Register*, 62:49 (March 13, 1997).

Figure 1.1   Federal guidelines for abstinence education.

 Will the federal guidelines promote sexual health? Can you identify any biases, opinions, or inaccuracies in the guidelines?

These curricula, and other one-dimensional approaches to sexuality education, go against the recommendations of the major sexuality and educational professional organizations.

The Sexuality Information and Education Council of the United States (SIECUS) has developed comprehensive sexuality education guidelines, in conjunction with several major sexuality and health education organizations involved with the health and welfare of youth. These professional groups propose that comprehensive sexuality programs meet children's real, present, and future needs. A thorough appreciation of their development, variety, and backgrounds can lead to opportunities to promote sexual health.

 What do you remember learning about sexuality in school? Were you free to ask questions? Were any topics forbidden? Did you have an opportunity to honestly discuss sexual issues and explore decision-making? How would you like your learning to be different?

EVALUATING SOURCES OF INFORMATION

As we strive toward a personally healthy sexuality, a critical task for all of us is to evaluate the information we receive. Sexology, the scientific study of sexuality, is often conducted by researchers who also may be part of other recognized disciplines. Because the field of sexuality is truly interdisciplinary, research may be conducted by biologists, psychologists, sociologists, anthropologists, health educators, nurses, historians, physicians, and more. And, because disciplines have their own established perspectives, the research may have limitations or biases. Key criteria separate good research from poor research. Issues such as bias, sampling issues, honesty, and access all contribute to the quality of sexuality research findings.

When applying research findings to one's personal life, practical questions to consider include: Are you like most people? If not, how aren't you? If you are part of a sexual minority, such as bisexual people, how does this

PERSPECTIVES

Criteria Associated with Good Research

We are bombarded with sexual information every day. Countless studies and reports are released and presented by the media. "Experts" report new findings that challenge our notions about sexual issues. Here are some guidelines for evaluating sources of sexual information and research:

1. Evaluate the researchers
   - ❧ Who did the research?
   - ❧ Was the study done by reputable researchers?
     Reputable researchers are well-known in their fields, have some kind of university or agency affiliation, are members in good standing in professional organizations, and their research is not connected to or funded by for-profit businesses.

2. Evaluate the researchers' track record.
   - ❧ Have they conducted scientific studies before?
   - ❧ Is their previous research respected and accepted in the field?

3. Evaluate the sample. Two issues related to the population studied will tell you the most about the quality of the study — sample size and randomness.
   - ❧ How large is the sample? (In general, the larger the sample, the better the study.)
   - ❧ Were the samples chosen randomly? (subjects chosen at random from a larger pool of eligible) or were the subjects taken from a convenience sample (an intact group; students in a certain class — prison population, army recruits, subscribers to a certain magazine, etc.)?

4. Evaluate the methods.
   - ❧ How was information about the subjects obtained?
   - ❧ In general, first-person observable reports (person-to-person interview or direct observation) are better than other ways of gathering data (e.g., mailed questionnaires, telephone interviews). Sexuality research is unique, though. Anonymity protections in many situations will help to guarantee better results. Unfortunately, when facing a questioner, respondents may be sensitive to reactions to their answers and consequently give desired answers rather than honest ones.

5. Evaluate replication.
   - ❧ Has the study been replicated with a different population resulting in the same findings? (Studies that are replicated with different samples and come up with similar findings are more likely to stand the test of time.) Research linking smoking to lung cancer, for instance, has been replicated with samples from different countries over the past decade and yielded similar results.

6. Examine the impact.
   - ❧ Have other researchers in the field received the study well? (Examine reviews and reports of the study in reputable journals.)

affect your lifestyle? If some expert claims that a sexual behavior is problematic and you engage in it, will your behavior change? Should it? Who *is* this expert when it comes to making decisions about your sexuality?

One counselee was a mother who occasionally liked to bathe with her 2-year-old son. This was a fun time for both of them. Her husband happened to notice a letter to a "Dear . . ." column, from a father who was upset that his wife was bathing with their 2-year old son. The columnist replied that the father had every right to be upset, and that a parent's bathing with a child of that age, particularly of the other sex, is inappropriate. Do you agree with the columnist or the mother? Give your reasons.

WHO ARE THE EXPERTS?

Because of the interdisciplinary nature of the field of sexology, individuals and teams of researchers have conducted research exploring various aspects of sexuality. Some of the prominent names in the field have examined human sexual response and subsequently developed strategies to help people respond more fully and positively. Others have focused their work on patterns of behavior, differentiating for gender, race, and ethnicity, where possible. Theorists have worked on questions of gender and orientation. Others have looked at relationship patterns. Table 1.1 highlights some of the prominent researchers and theorists in the field.

A HOLISTIC APPROACH TO UNDERSTANDING SEXUALITY

One way to explain and understand our sexuality is to look at it from a holistic, multifaceted approach. All of the facets of our sexuality affect and are affected by each other. A person cannot study something such as body image, for example, without looking at issues related to individual personality, family and peer influences, and societal expectations. The focus of this textbook is on healthy sexuality and strategies for maximizing our sexual potential.

Healthy sexuality
the safe and open exploration and development of our potential as human beings

Healthy sexuality enables a person to develop to the fullest potential. It requires being knowledgeable. It involves personalizing information and using it to make informed decisions about your life and the world around you. Making good decisions about yourself and others is an essential part of healthy sexuality. It involves our personal level of well-being, the health of our relationships with others, and the nature of the environment in which everything occurs. The best way to conceptualize this approach to understanding human sexuality is to use a health and wellness model to describe it.

Human sexuality is best examined by using a holistic, multifaceted approach.

Health and Wellness Defined

In 1947 the World Health Organization (WHO) defined **health** as "the state of complete mental, physical, and social well-being, not merely the absence of disease.[2] WHO's definition was the first globally accepted conceptualization of health and stood the test of time for more than a decade.

Although multifaceted, this definition of health was flawed, according to members of a new movement called **holistic health.** The holistic health movement came into being in the 1960s as an attempt to expand the view of health that WHO had promulgated.

Health
total mental, physical, and social well-being, not merely the absence of disease

Holistic health
the process of moving toward optimal functioning across the physical, social, spiritual, emotional, and intellectual dimensions

Table 1.1 Contributions of Experts on Sex

Researchers	Research	Years	Comments
Alfred Kinsey and associates	Sexual Behavior in the Human Male Sexual Behavior in the Human Female	1948, 1953	A pioneer undertaking involving thousands of males and females interviewed about their sexual behavior.
William Masters and Virginia Johnson	Human Sexual Response Human Sexual Inadequacy	1966 to present	The first research efforts to photograph and physiologically record thousands of instances of sexual arousal, orgasm, masturbation, and coitus. Followed by brief effective treatment for sexual problems.
Morton Hunt	Sexual Behavior in the 1970s	1974	Showed consistencies and changes in sexual behavior a generation after the Kinsey findings.
Philip Blumstein and Pepper Schwartz	American Couples	1983	Study of sexual and affectional behavior of couples.
Shere Hite	The Hite Report on Female Sexuality The Hite Report on Male Sexuality Women and Love Good Guys, Bad Guys	1976 1981 1991	While statistically unrepresentative, an early attempt at qualitative research yielding valuable insights to behavior.
Various	Magazine surveys: Redbook, Cosmopolitan, Playboy	1980 1983 1987	Surveyed more than 100,000 readers; findings often apply more to magazine's readers than to all adults.
Richard Green	The "Sissy Boy" Syndrome	1987	Controversial study on the origins of homosexuality.
Edward Brecher	Love, Sex, and Aging	1984	One of the first large-scale scientific studies of sexuality in older people.
John Money	Gay, Straight and In-between	1988	Attempted definitions of the biological and psychological determinants of sex, sexuality, and gender.
Edward Lauman, John Gagnon, Robert Michael, Stuart Michaels	The Social Organization of Sexuality: Sexual Practices in the United States	1994	Comprehensive examination of practices within social settings and their meanings.
Vern and Bonnie Bullough	Sin, Sickness, and Sanity; Women and Prostitution: A Social History; Cross Dressing, Sex, and Gender	1957–present	Review of extensive historical data on a variety of subjects.

PERSPECTIVES   Diversity in Sex Research

One of the longstanding criticisms of many human sexuality studies is the lack of diversity in their subjects. Most of the classic studies in the field have focused on White, heterosexual, middle-class subjects. The two best known sexuality works — Kinsey's studies of male and female sexual behavior and Masters and Johnson's work on sexual response — are both based on such a sample. Both were conducted more than 30 years ago, when diversity received much less attention.

The lack of diversity seems to affect three distinct minority subgroups: lower socioeconomic populations, racial minorities (Blacks, Asians, and Hispanics/Latinos), and gays/lesbians/bisexuals. To complicate matters, although these three categories of populations are underrepresented in major studies of sexual response and behavior, they are overrepresented in other types of sex research, such as those focusing on sexually transmitted diseases (STDs) and teen pregnancy.

The problem may represent a lack of aggressive recruitment of non-White, non-middle class, non-heterosexual subjects in major sexuality research (particularly studies that are privately funded), and overreliance on sampling from public clinic populations (people with STDs, family planning), which tend to have higher minority representation.

Studies of gay, lesbian, and bisexual populations also have been clouded by methodological problems associated with sampling. Studies of gay men draw heavily from men who frequent gay bars, subscribe to gay publications, are incarcerated, or attend gay public events. Little is known about lesbian women. A true cross-sectional sample of gay men and lesbians representing various socioeconomic and racial/ethnic lines is needed.

Methodological issues related to sampling and sample size have been cited as the primary problems related to obtaining more diverse samples. It is harder to target recruitment efforts for lower SES, minority, and gay/lesbian populations. Targeting narrow segments of these populations (for example, gay men attending gay bars) is easier and has a higher-yield recruitment than mainstream sources such as newspapers, random digit telephoning, and the like. Narrowing the scope of recruitment, however, means that sampling may miss a true cross-section of the population targeted for study.

Can these studies accurately reflect human sexual behavior and response if they omit large segments of the population? Are there differences between and among various racial and ethnic groups, SES segments, and different sexual orientations that might lend greater insight into the true nature of human sexuality?

One of the early pioneers in the field, Halbert Dunn, believed that the WHO vision of health characterized it as a static state.[3] Rather than call health a state of well-being, Dunn preferred to view it as a continuum. Developing and maintaining a high level of health means moving toward optimal functioning. Health is a conscious and deliberate approach to life and being, rather than something to be abdicated to doctors and the health-care system. Like your health in general, your sexual health is viewed as moving along a continuum, reaching optimal states as a result of your decisions and behavior (see Figure 1.2).

In addition, Dunn recast the notion of well-being to revolve around functioning. How well does the organism function? Dunn viewed functioning as evidence of well-being. Although people will have setbacks in their quest for optimal functioning, the direction in which their lives are moving becomes an important criterion for evaluating their well-being. In this movement, daily habits and behaviors, and overall lifestyle, assumed primary importance.

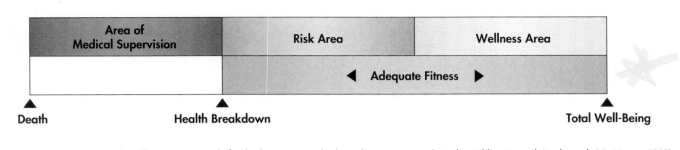

Source: *Personal Health: Perspectives and Lifestyles,* by Patricia A. Floyd, Sandra E. Mimms, and Caroline Yelding-Howard, (Englewood, CO: Morton, 1998).

Figure 1.2	Health as a continuum.

Originally, the scope of well-being was limited to three dimensions: physical, social, and mental. Adherents of holistic health argued that the mental dimension has two components — the intellectual (rational thought processes) and the emotional (feelings and emotions). Each of these domains deals with a different aspect of psychological well-being. A final dimension, the spiritual, was added because it was thought that humans could not function optimally in a spiritual vacuum. Therefore, the holistic definition of health has five dimensions: physical, social, emotional, intellectual, and spiritual.

In the 1980s and 1990s, the definition of health was expanded once again by the wellness movement.[4] Adherents defined **wellness** as the state of optimal well-being. With wellness comes vigor and vitality and the ability to live life to its fullest. Most recently, some adherents of the wellness approach have added a sixth dimension of health: environmental or planetary health.

A key element of the wellness model is striving for balance. When all of the six dimensions are at high levels and in balance, we have optimal health and well-being. When the dimensions are out of balance or one is severely lacking, we have lower levels of health and well-being. Figure 1.3 illustrates this concept.

The Six Dimensions of Wellness

The first dimension, **physical well-being,** is reflected in how well the body performs its intended functions. Absence of disease — although an important influence — is not the sole criterion for health. The physical domain is influenced by one's genetic inheritance, nutritional status, fitness level, **body composition**, and immune status, to name just a few.

Wellness
the state of optimal health and well-being

Physical well-being
a component of wellness reflected in how well the body performs its intended functions

Body composition
the fat and nonfat components of the human body; important in assessing recommended body weight

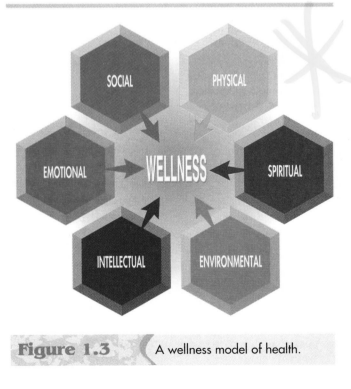

Figure 1.3	A wellness model of health.

The average college campus offers many opportunities to increase physical well-being.

Intellectual well-being
a component of wellness referring to the ability to process information effectively and rationally

Emotional well-being
a component of wellness that refers to being in touch with one's feelings, having the ability to express them, and being able to control them when necessary

Social well-being
a component of wellness that involves connection to others through various types of relationships

Spiritual well-being
a component of wellness that involves feeling connected to something beyond oneself

Environmental well-being
a component of wellness that reflects our ability to function in our immediate environment, such as home, school, and work, as well as being able to deal with the world at large

Intellectual well-being is the ability to process information effectively. It involves the capability to use information in a rational way to solve problems and grow. It includes issues such as creativity, spontaneity, and openness to new ways of viewing situations. To maintain a high level of intellectual well-being, one must seek knowledge and learn from one's experiences.

Emotional well-being means being in touch with one's feelings, having the ability to express them, and being able to control them when necessary. Optimal functioning involves the understanding that emotions are the mirror to the soul. Emotions help us get in touch with what is important in our lives. Our emotions make us feel alive and provide us with a richness of experience that is uniquely human.

Social well-being involves being connected to others through various types of relationships. Individuals who function optimally in this domain are able to form friendships, have intimate relationships, give and receive love and affection, and accept others unconditionally. They are able to give of themselves and share in the joys and sorrows of being part of a community.

Spiritual well-being involves feeling connected to something beyond oneself. One way to express spirituality is by participating in organized religious activities. This usually means believing in a supreme being or higher supernatural force and subscribing to a formalized code of conduct to live by. In a secular sense, spirituality could manifest itself through connection to something greater than oneself. Whether it is being part of a community, working to save the environment, helping to feed the needy, or being committed to world peace, the underlying feeling is a perception of life as having meaning beyond the self.

Finally, **environmental well-being** involves high-level functioning on two levels. The most immediate environment consists of school, home, worksite, neighborhood, family, friends, and associates. This environment greatly affects our health and personal safety by influencing whether we are at risk

During your college years the campus is a primary environment.

for and fear issues such as theft, crime, and violence. The quality of our air and water, noise pollution, overcrowding, and other issues that affect our stress levels are also affected. Our social support system is also part of this environment.

The level of well-being at a larger level — state, country, the world at large — also affects our wellness. The impact of things such as violence, war, international disputes, racism, sexism, heterosexism, ageism, and so on — all influence us to some extent. Decisions that our political leaders make, such as engaging in wars or determining where we store radioactive wastes, affect the way we think and live our lives. Our ability to stay focused and whole are constantly challenged by the media, which bring the entire world and its problems into our living rooms each night. We need to learn to think globally, act locally, and be happy despite the myriad of problems in the world.

Wellness and Human Sexuality

Our sexuality both contributes to overall health and well-being and is affected by it. High-level sexual health can be a positive force in our lives. It contributes to the full functioning of our body, mind, spirit, and social relationships. When we are engaged in healthy sexual activity and have a healthy outlook concerning our sexuality, we can maximize our potential as men and women. Conversely, our sexuality is affected by our overall level of health and well-being.

The important thing is to be moving toward optimal health, even if you never achieve it. If your current level of health is lower than you would like, the main thing is to take steps to improve. The experience and process of improving, the journey, is as important as the current level of functioning.

Many of us have limitations that keep us from achieving the high levels of health that others enjoy. A wellness perspective

Our level of sexual well-being contributes to our overall level of health. Conversely, our overall level of health influences our sexuality.

Health Hint

Making Informed Sexual Decisions

The following is a simple decision-making model that may help you make better decisions about your sexuality.

1. **Establish your goal.** Try to put in a broader context the decision you are making about an issue. ("How will this decision affect my goal?")

2. **List the pros and cons.** In two columns on a sheet of paper, list the consequences of saying either yes or no to the question you are trying to make a decision about. Don't scrimp. Put down all of them, no matter how trivial they might seem.

3. **Prioritize the pros and cons.** Rank the pros and cons from most important to least important.

4. **Weigh the pros and cons.** Although one column might be greater than the other (many more pros than cons, for instance), the top one or two items on the shorter list might carry much more weight.

5. **Ponder the results.** Examine the lists, and discuss them with one or two people whose opinions you value.

6. **Listen to your instincts.** Sometimes something may seem to be right for the average person but not feel like the best thing for you. Your rational/intellectual evaluation of your lists and your significant other's advice provides you with two pieces of information; your gut-level intuition provides you with another.

7. **Decide.** Action is important. You must make a decision and move on with your life.

8. **Give it time.** Once you make a decision, give yourself time to experience the effects of that decision. At first it may seem that you made the wrong decision. Only time will tell.

9. **Reevaluate.** Go through this model again to reevaluate your decision once a sufficient amount of time has passed.

10. **Don't beat yourself up!** You are human! Sometimes you will make the wrong decisions. Learn from your mistakes, and try not to make the same ones twice. Persecuting yourself and putting yourself down are not productive and will not help you make better decisions.

of health and sexuality helps us accept our limitations and maximize the potential within us. You may never have the body of the man or woman of your dreams, but you can enjoy healthy sexuality if you strive to be the best you can be.

High-level *physical well-being* can make us feel better about our bodies and provide the energy and capacity to maximize sexual pleasure and functioning. High-level cardiovascular fitness and muscle tone can enhance sexual functioning and pleasure. When our bodies are healthy and optimally functioning, we feel better about how we look and move and have higher self-esteem — two elements critical to healthy sexuality.

High-level *emotional well-being* can help us understand and cope with the myriad of feelings that being sexual creates. It helps us cope with the emotional roller coaster that most of us face when confronted with issues such as gender identity, sexual orientation, puberty, dating, and preventing unintended pregnancy. A high level of emotional well-being helps us understand and accept our emotions related to these and other sexual issues.

High-level *intellectual well-being* helps us process sexual information, think critically, and make sound decisions regarding our sexual health. The ability to sort through the often conflicting barrage of sexual information

Friendships are important to social well-being.

and advice requires an ability to seek out information, evaluate facts, seek clarification of unanswered questions, solve problems, and relate this information to our own needs, wants, and values.

High-level *social well-being* enhances our sexuality and provides a safe forum to explore it and share it with others. Having solid friendships, intimate relationships, and sexual partnerships with people we care about, love, and trust allows us to explore our developing sexuality in a safe way.

Our sexual health is based in our ability to form healthy relationships with others. Intimacy is the ability to be open and honest and to feel close with another person. Intimacy enhances relationships but is not part of all the relationships we form. For example, you may be open and honest with a college roommate with whom you live day to day. In contrast, you may not find it appropriate or feel comfortable discussing personal concerns

In assessing the health of a relationship:

⌣ Are you comfortable with yourself — knowing who you are, what you want, what you believe in? This is a critical first step toward being able to relate to others.

⌣ When you're with this person, do you feel good about yourself? Are you complimented? Praised? Do you feel you receive a lot of support?

⌣ Is your relationship based on shared interests? Are your personal values close enough in perspective to allow for becoming close? Do you have a sense of mutual respect?

⌣ Can you tolerate differences? If you two are different, are those differences critical? For example, can your relationship surpass differences in age, race, sexual orientation, money, political outlook?

⌣ Can you maintain a sense of individuality within the relationship?

with colleagues at work. Relationships that involve an obvious power dynamic — such as boss and employee — often dictate that we are prudent in what we disclose and how intimate we become.

The expression "blood is thicker than water" has been used to explain the support we often expect from family. Friends may come and go, but your family is always your family. In truth, some people have wonderfully intimate relationships with family while others have disengaged from their family or contact them only in times of need. For some people, friendships provide for the intimacy they need.

Someone once noted that if heterosexual women could relate to their male partners and hold them to the same expectations they have for their female friends, romantic relationships would be in a better state. This observation points to the subtle ways by which we change the script when we look toward developing healthy romantic relationships. Identifying what is unhealthy in someone else's relationship is often easier than seeing the weaknesses in one's own relationships.

High-level spiritual health connects us with a higher power. It puts our sexuality in a broader context, providing a different perspective from which to view ourselves and our behavior. It also links our lives with a broader purpose and historical continuity that reaches beyond the self and mere personal fulfillment. We feel as though we are part of something that transcends our present place and time.

High-level environmental health provides a safe context for our sexual development. An environment that is nurturing and protective, supportive, and nonexploitive enables everyone to grow to their fullest as sexual beings without fear of disease, persecution, or retribution. An environment that respects all people and safeguards the rights and safety of individuals allows us to develop and grow.

A safe sexual environment should protect us from rape, sexual abuse, sexual harassment, violence against people because of their sexual orientation, sexually transmitted diseases, unintended pregnancy, and other situations. It does this through a combination of constitutional rights, legal

Natural surroundings can create a spiritual setting.

sanctions, and social standards. It operates through both formal justice (the courts and police, for example) and social conscience (cultural attitudes, values, and behavior).

HEALTHY ENVIRONMENTS

A safe environment starts with a functioning family unit, which is the cornerstone for personal security. Our environment extends beyond the family and household into the immediate community. Community standards for safety and support vary from place to place. Official government, police, and school policies on diverse issues such as treatment of known sexual offenders, sexual harassment in the community, gay rights, sexual abuse, prostitution, prevention and treatment of sexually transmitted diseases, and so on — all influence one's sexual health. Unofficial community standards interact with official policies to create a climate within a community that either supports sexual development and expression or sets up barriers to it.

A primary environment for college students is the campus. Campus policies, especially for residential students, have a great impact on issues related to sexual health. Colleges are becoming increasingly aware of the necessity of formalizing policies on issues such as the prevention and treatment of students with HIV/AIDS, sexual harassment and assault, sexual health services, and so on. The American College Health Association provides guidance on developing these policy issues.[5] See Figure 1.4 for a sample college policy regarding AIDS.

Health Hint

Creating Healthy Environments

❧ To help create a healthy sexual environment within your community: Be a role model for healthy sexuality. Lead by example, whether through words or actions.

❧ Get involved in organizations that actively champion sexual rights. If you can't or don't want to get publically involved with them, support organizations financially. Make a contribution to acknowledge and support their work.

❧ Be an advocate within any organization in which you are involved, such as youth sports, church or temple, fraternity/sorority, and the like. If you see or hear things that work against creating or maintaining a healthy sexual environment, speak out.

The staggering implications of this country's most life-threatening disease, AIDS, have become part of our nation's consciousness. We must now make the necessary preparations to protect the rights of both those students who have been exposed to or infected by HIV as well as the noninfected members of our University community. Above all, we must train all members of the University community to have a humane, well-informed reaction to those whose lives have been compromised by being exposed to or infected by the virus.

AIDS Advisory Board

WPU responded to the AIDS crisis by creating a presidentially appointed 6-member AIDS Advisory Board in 1987. The primary goals of this committee are as follows:

1. To encourage the faculty to include discussions of the social, medical, and economic effects of AIDS in their classes.

2. To offer our students a comprehensive roster of referral sources for their own educational advancement and, if necessary, their own health concerns.

3. To train peer educators to address the social forces that promote behavior that could make them susceptible to HIV infection (alcohol abuse, drug abuse, STDs, etc.).

4. To provide speakers for educational programming.

Guidelines

1. The initial admission decision for applicants will not take into consideration whether the applicant has a positive test to the virus thought to cause AIDS (a + HIV antibody test).

2. Students with the HIV infection will be afforded the same living arrangement as are all other residential students, except in specific cases where the health of the infected student is in jeopardy. Since this virus can be transmitted only by intimate sexual contact and/or by sharing contaminated blood products, the University feels separate housing accommodations are not justified. Individual decisions will be made on a case-by-case basis. It should be noted that the infected student stands a far greater chance of having his/her health compromised by a non-infected roommate through the transmission of the common airborne viruses than would the non-infected student of acquiring HIV through casual contact with his/her infected roommate.

3. Students with HIV infection will be afforded normal classroom attendance, working conditions and participation in cocurricular and extracurricular activities in an unrestricted manner as long as they are physically and psychologically able to do so.

4. Students with HIV infection will have access to all public facilities open to the University community.

5. Programs will not be implemented to require screening of students with HIV infection.

Institutional Responsibility/ Confidentiality of Information

The American Council on Education (ACE) recommends that institutions have the responsibility to provide the following:

1. A comprehensive program of education about AIDS.

2. A training program that includes not only information about AIDS but a clear representation of the University's AIDS policy.

3. A system of encouraging people with the HIV infection to inform those who are appropriate of their condition.

4. A means of counseling people with the HIV infection about the facts of the disease and what has to be done to avoid transmission.

5. Regular assessment (every three months) of students with HIV infection to determine health status and psychological needs.

Although this University may be unaware that infected students may be unreasonably engaged in conduct that threatens the health of others, we will attempt to offer protection to the community at large while still protecting the rights of the person with HIV.

Section 504 of the Federal Rehabilitation Act of 1973 prohibits discrimination against individual(s) with disabilities. **No qualified student with disabilities at William Paterson University is to be excluded from participation in, be denied benefits of, or be subjected to discrimination under any program or activities of the university community.**

The knowledge that a given individual is carrying HIV could have such a profound and possibly irrational effect upon the recipient of this information who then might take steps that could easily compromise the campus life of the individual in question. The likelihood is that such information could not legally be placed in any non-medical files without the expressed written permission of the student, according to the **Family Education Rights and Privacy Act of 1974.** This Act would probably apply to any verbal communication as well, and thus confidentiality must extend to faculty, administrators, other students and even partners.

The diagnosis of HIV or AIDS would occur at a hospital as part of a complete medical work-up and then be reported to the New Jersey State Department of Health, which then should forward the information to the Centers for Disease Control in Atlanta. The hospital or the student may report back the results of such testing, which are confidential, as part of the student health record. Often, a student would continue outside health care and not report to the Student Health Service. Education and counseling are available through the health center and counseling center when requested.

Source: *Student Handbook,* William Paterson University, 1998–99. Reprinted with permission.

Figure 1.4   Excerpts from a university AIDS policy.

WEB RESOURCES

American Association of Sex Educators, Counselors, and Therapists

http://www.aasect.org/

Professional organization devoted to the promotion of sexual health by the development and advancement of the fields of sex therapy, counseling, and education. There is a selection of associated Web links and the "contemporary sexuality" section providing general items of interest on sexuality.

Go Ask Alice

http://www.goaskalice.columbia.edu/

Columbia University's Health Education Program, offering facts and questions (FAQ), information, and e-mail advice on sexual health, sexuality, communication, and relationships. The primary goal is to make health and wellness a life priority for students, staff, and professors.

Mayo Clinic Health Oasis on Sexuality

http://www.mayohealth.org/mayo/library/htm/sexual.htm

Mayo Foundation for Medical Education and Research site, Health Oasis Mayo Clinic, containing a search engine that provides reliable information for a healthier life. The articles found within the sexuality library contain many general topics on sexuality.

Sexuality Information and Education Council of the United States (SIECUS)

http://www.siecus.org/

National nonprofit organization that promotes comprehensive education about sexuality and advocates the right of individuals to make responsible sexual choices. This site details information on sexuality, contraception, and sexual abuse and assault.

Notes

1. SIECUS, *Advocates Report* 5:2 (1998).
2. "Constitution of the World Health Organization," *Chronicles of the World Health Organization*, 1 (1947), 29–43.
3. "High-level Wellness in the World of Today," *Journal of the American Osteopathic Association*, 61:9 (1962).
4. Don Ardell, *The History and Future of Wellness* (Dubuque, IA: Kendall/Hunt, 1985).
5. *Policy Guidelines for HIV/AIDS on Campus* (Washington, DC, 1996).

Student Study Questions

1. What is human sexuality? What are its components?

2. What is the definition of health according to the World Health Organization?

3. What complaints did the wellness movement have with the WHO conceptualization of health?

4. What is the definition of *wellness*? What are its six components?

5. Define healthy sexuality, incorporating the elements of wellness.

Student Assessment

Wellness Lifestyle Questionnaire

Because sexual health cannot be separated from overall health, we would do well to attend to all the dimensions of our well-being. As you answer the items, try to think about how each may have an impact on your sexual health.

Please circle the appropriate answer to each question and total your points as indicated at the end of the questionnaire. Circle 5 if the statement is ALWAYS true, 4 if the statement is FREQUENTLY true, 3 if the statement is OCCASIONALLY true, 2 if the statement is SELDOM true, 1 if the statement is NEVER true.

1. I am able to identify the situations and factors that overstress me. 5 (4) 3 2 1
2. I eat only when I am hungry. 5 4 3 (2) 1
3. I don't take tranquilizers or other drugs to relax. 5 4 3 2 (1)
4. I support efforts in my community to reduce environmental pollution. 5 4 (3) 2 1
5. I avoid buying foods with artificial colorings. 5 4 3 2 (1)
6. I rarely have problems concentrating on what I'm doing because of worrying about other things. 5 4 3 2 1
7. My employer (school) takes measures to ensure that my work (study) place is safe. 5 4 3 2 1
8. I try not to use medications when I feel unwell. 5 4 3 2 1
9. I am able to identify certain bodily responses and illnesses as my reactions to stress. 5 4 3 2 1
10. I question the use of diagnostic x-rays. 5 4 3 2 1
11. I try to alter personal living habits that are risk factors for heart disease, cancer, and other lifestyle diseases. 5 4 3 2 1
12. I avoid taking sleeping pills to help me sleep. 5 4 3 2 1
13. I try not to eat foods with refined sugar or corn sugar ingredients. 5 4 3 2 1
14. I accomplish goals I set for myself. 5 4 3 2 1
15. I stretch or bend for several minutes each day to keep my body flexible. 5 4 3 2 1
16. I support immunization of all children for common childhood diseases. 5 4 3 2 1
17. I try to prevent friends from driving after they drink alcohol. 5 4 3 2 1
18. I minimize extra salt intake. 5 4 3 2 1
19. I don't mind when other people and situations make me wait or lose time. 5 4 3 2 1

(Continued)

Student Assessment

Wellness Lifestyle Questionnaire (cont.)

20. I walk four or fewer flights of stairs rather than take the elevator.	5	4	3	2	1
21. I eat fresh fruits and vegetables.	5	4	3	2	1
22. I use dental floss at least once a day.	5	4	3	2	1
23. I read product labels on foods to determine their ingredients.	5	4	3	2	1
24. I try to maintain a normal body weight.	5	4	3	2	1
25. I record my feelings and thoughts in a journal or diary.	5	4	3	2	1
26. I have no difficulty falling asleep.	5	4	3	2	1
27. I engage in some form of vigorous physical activity at least three times a week.	5	4	3	2	1
28. I take time each day to quiet my mind and relax.	5	4	3	2	1
29. I am willing to make and sustain close friendships and intimate relationships.	5	4	3	2	1
30. I obtain an adequate daily supply of vitamins from my food or vitamin supplements.	5	4	3	2	1
31. I rarely have tension or migraine headaches, or pain in the neck or shoulders.	5	4	3	2	1
32. I wear a seat belt when driving.	5	4	3	2	1
33. I am aware of the emotional and situational factors that lead me to overeat.	5	4	3	2	1
34. I avoid driving my car after drinking any alcohol.	5	4	3	2	1
35. I am aware of the side effects of the medicines I take.	5	4	3	2	1
36. I am able to accept feelings of sadness, depression, and anxiety, knowing that they are almost always transient.	5	4	3	2	1
37. I would seek several additional professional opinions if my doctor were to recommend surgery for me.	5	4	3	2	1
38. I agree that nonsmokers should not have to breathe the smoke from cigarettes in public places.	5	4	3	2	1
39. I agree that pregnant women who smoke harm their babies.	5	4	3	2	1
40. I believe I get enough sleep.	5	4	3	2	1
41. I ask my doctor why a certain medication is being prescribed and inquire about alternatives.	5	4	3	2	1

Wellness Lifestyle Questionnaire (cont.)

42. I am aware of the calories expended in my activities. 5 4 3 2 1

43. I am willing to give priority to my own needs for time
and psychological space by saying "no" to others' requests of me. 5 4 3 2 1

44. I walk instead of drive whenever feasible. 5 4 3 2 1

45. I eat a breakfast that contains about one-third of my daily need
for calories, proteins, and vitamins. 5 4 3 2 1

46. I prohibit smoking in my home. 5 4 3 2 1

47. I remember and think about my dreams. 5 4 3 2 1

48. I seek medical attention only when I have symptoms or think
some (potential) condition requires checking, rather than
have routine yearly checkups. 5 4 3 2 1

49. I endeavor to make my home accident-free. 5 4 3 2 1

50. I ask my doctor to explain the diagnosis of my problem
until I understand all that I care to. 5 4 3 2 1

51. I try to include fiber (whole grains, fresh fruits and vegetables,
or bran) in my daily diet. 5 4 3 2 1

52. I can deal with my emotional problems
without alcohol or other mood-altering drugs. 5 4 3 2 1

53. I am satisfied with my school/work. 5 4 3 2 1

54. I require children riding in my car to be in infant seats
or in shoulder harnesses. 5 4 3 2 1

55. I try to associate with people who have a positive attitude about life. 5 4 3 2 1

56. I try not to eat snacks of candy, pastries, and other "junk" foods. 5 4 3 2 1

57. I avoid people who are "down" all the time
and bring down those around them. 5 4 3 2 1

58. I am aware of the calorie content of the foods I eat. 5 4 3 2 1

59. I brush my teeth after meals. 5 4 3 2 1

60. (*for women only*) I routinely examine my breasts. 5 4 3 2 1
(*for men only*) I am aware of the signs of testicular cancer. 5 4 3 2 1

(Continued)

Student Assessment

Wellness Lifestyle Questionnaire (cont.)

How to Score

Enter the numbers you've circled next to the question number, and total your score for each category. Then determine your degree of wellness for each category using the wellness status key.

Emotional health	Fitness and body care	Environmental health	Stress	Nutrition	Medical self-responsibility
6＿＿	15＿＿	4＿＿	1＿＿	2＿＿	8＿＿
12＿＿	20＿＿	7＿＿	3＿＿	5＿＿	10＿＿
25＿＿	22＿＿	17＿＿	9＿＿	13＿＿	11＿＿
26＿＿	24＿＿	32＿＿	14＿＿	18＿＿	16＿＿
36＿＿	27＿＿	34＿＿	19＿＿	21＿＿	35＿＿
40＿＿	33＿＿	38＿＿	28＿＿	23＿＿	37＿＿
47＿＿	42＿＿	39＿＿	29＿＿	30＿＿	41＿＿
52＿＿	44＿＿	46＿＿	31＿＿	45＿＿	48＿＿
55＿＿	58＿＿	49＿＿	43＿＿	51＿＿	59＿＿
57＿＿	59＿＿	54＿＿	53＿＿	56＿＿	60＿＿
Total＿＿	Total＿＿	Total＿＿	Total＿＿	Total＿＿	Total＿＿

Wellness Status

To assess your status in each of the six categories, compare your total score in each to the following key:

0–34 Need improvement; **35–44** Good; **45–50** Excellent

Male Sexual Anatomy and Physiology

2

Major Topics

External Male Sexual Structures
  Penis
  Scrotum
  Perineum
  Anus
  Breasts
Internal Male Sexual Structures
  Testes
  Epididymis
  Vas Deferens
  Seminal Vesicles
  Prostate Gland
  Cowper's Glands
Common Disorders of Male
   Sexual Anatomy
  Benign Prostatic
   Enlargement (BPH)
  Prostatitis
  Prostate Cancer
  Urethritis
  Phimosis and Balanitis
  Hydrocele
  Testicular Cancer
  Gynecomastia
  Male Breast Cancer
Wellness Synthesis
  Physical Well-being
  Intellectual Well-being
  Emotional Well-being
  Social Well-being
  Spiritual Well-being
  Environmental Well-being

Student Learning Objectives

After reading this chapter, students will be able to:

- Identify and locate key structures of the male sexual anatomy.

- Describe the main functions of the male sexual structures.

- Identify and describe the functions of the key male sex glands.

- Explain the erogenous potential of the key male sexual structures.

- Perform a testicular self-exam.

- Identify the signs and symptoms of, and treatment for, eight common male sexual disorders.

- Describe a variety of screening tests used to diagnose common male sexual disorders.

 One of the more interesting things about healthy sexuality is the great diversity we are capable of bringing to our sexual response. Whether we are straight or gay, male or female, our bodies are capable of responding in a myriad of pleasurable ways if we take the time to understand them and explore their potential. As the first step in understanding, we will focus on the male physiology in this chapter and the female physiology in Chapter 3.

Much of male sexual anatomy is external. Most men touch their genitals frequently during urination, and because of this, men tend to be familiar with the external parts. Even though men tend to be comfortable with their external sexual anatomy and physiology, sexual health extends to understanding the proper functioning of the internal structures also.

Many of the internal and external sexual structures of both men and women are capable of responding sexually. Proper stimulation can provide intense sexual pleasure. We vary tremendously in how we like to stimulate (and have our partners stimulate) these structures. We will discuss this further at various points in this and other chapters.

EXTERNAL MALE SEXUAL STRUCTURES

The external structures of the male sexual anatomy (see Figure 2.1) include the penis and scrotum, as well as the perineum, anus, and breasts. The last three, although not traditionally considered parts of sexual anatomy, are included here because of their potential as **erogenous** structures.

Erogenous
capable of producing sexual excitement

Penis

Like many structures in the human body, the penis has more than one function. Both sperm and urine pass through the penis on their way out of a man's body. The same organ used to pass liquid waste is capable of providing

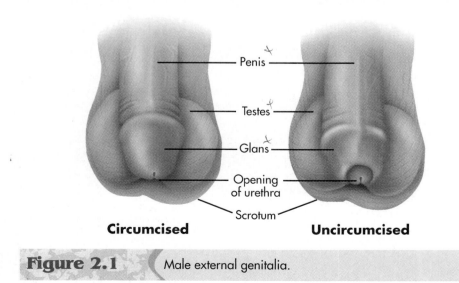

Penis

Testes

Glans

Opening of urethra

Scrotum

Circumcised   **Uncircumcised**

Source: *Personal Health: Perspectives and Lifestyles*, by Patricia A. Floyd, Sandra E. Mimms, and Caroline Yelding-Howard (Englewood, CO: Morton 1998), p. 92.

Figure 2.1   Male external genitalia.

exquisite sexual pleasure. This duality of function is often cited as a reason for feeling squeamish about engaging in **fellatio**.

Structure of the Penis

The penis (Figure 2.2) consists of two main parts: the shaft and the glans. The shaft of the penis consists of two cylinders of spongy tissue — the larger cavernous body (*corpora cavernosa*) and one smaller spongy body (*corpus spongiosum*) — wrapped in thick membrane sheaths. Similar to a common household sponge, this cylindrical tissue has many pockets of open space or cavities that are richly endowed with blood vessels, allowing them to fill with blood during sexual arousal. This is how a penis becomes erect during sexual arousal.

A key to understanding this is to visualize how a sponge expands as its cavities fill with water. Contrary to popular belief, the penis has no bone or cartilage and very little muscle tissue. Slang terms such as "boner" and "hard on" derive their origin from the firm, protruding nature of the spongiosum during erection. The spongy cylinders are held together by **connective tissue** attached to a loose wrapping of skin. The penis is capable of great expansion and changes in size because of its spongy tissue and loose covering of skin.

The *corpora cavernosa* run side by side along the entire length of the penis, attaching to the abdominal cavity by their roots, the *crura*. The cavernous body lies above the *corpus spongiosum* and wraps around it, appearing to create two cylinder-like structures on either side. The *corpus*

Fellatio
licking and sucking of the penis

Like a sponge that expands when absorbing water, the penis also enlarges as its cavities fill with blood.

Connective tissue
tissue that supports or binds other tissue

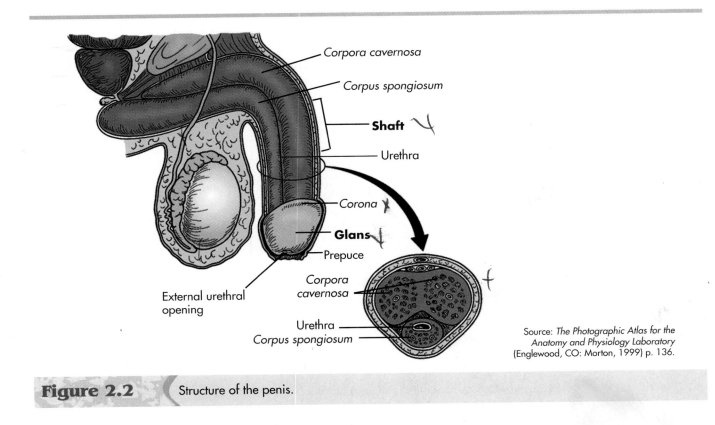

Source: *The Photographic Atlas for the Anatomy and Physiology Laboratory* (Englewood, CO: Morton, 1999) p. 136.

Figure 2.2 ❴ Structure of the penis.

Urethra
tube that transports urine and
ejaculate through penis

spongiosum also runs the entire length of the shaft, forming the head or glans penis. When the penis is erect, the *corpus spongiosum* is what gets hard and protrudes, forming a pronounced ridge along the underside of the penis. The **urethra** runs through the *corpus spongiosum*.

The entire penis is responsive to touch. The amount and type of touch that men like varies from man to man and sexual encounter to encounter. Even though the entire penis is responsive to touch, the greatest concentration of nerves is on the glans penis, illustrated in Figure 2.3. Two regions of the glans in particular — the coronal ridge and the frenulum — are the most richly endowed with nerve endings and capable of providing the greatest pleasure.

The *coronal ridge* forms the mushroom-like cap of the penis, separating it from the shaft. The *frenulum* is the triangular patch of tissue on the underside of the penis where the ridge pinches in to give the glans its distinctive shape. Both the corona and the frenulum are involved during arousal but are stimulated more precisely through oral sex and manual stimulation. The latter two forms of stimulation allow more individual control over the type and amount of pressure and stimulation than through intercourse.

The loose layer of skin that covers the shaft of the penis attaches at one end to the base of the penis near the abdomen and at the other end just behind the coronal ridge of the glans. The skin continues forward, extending beyond the glans penis, forming the prepuce or *foreskin*. In the unaroused state, the foreskin extends over the glans, covering and protecting it. During arousal, as the penis grows and expands, the foreskin retracts and stretches backward, exposing the glans for sexual activity.

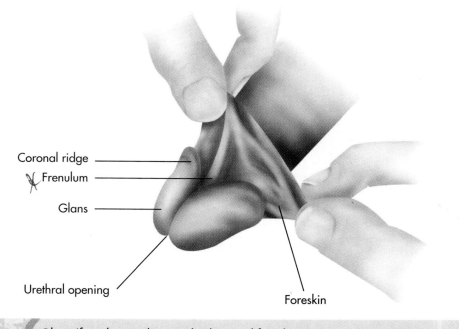

Coronal ridge

Frenulum

Glans

Urethral opening

Foreskin

Figure 2.3   Glans (frenulum and coronal ridge) and foreskin.

Circumcision

In most cultures and parts of the world, the foreskin is viewed as a normal part of male sexual anatomy, is left intact, and little attention is paid to it. In the United States, the foreskin is usually removed during the first few days following birth through the surgical procedure called **circumcision**. Two methods of circumcision are the clamp and the plastibell, shown in Figure 2.4. Removal of the foreskin leaves the glans penis exposed.

Most circumcisions done today are for religious, cultural, or aesthetic reasons. Circumcision is an important, required ritual in Judaic and Islamic religious practice.

Prior to 1971, the American Academy of Pediatrics, the nation's foremost pediatric professional organization, had recommended circumcision of newborn males for health concerns associated with smegma and its supposed links to cervical cancer in women and penile cancer in men. Smegma is a mixture of oily secretions from sebaceous glands on the skin of the

Circumcision
surgical removal of foreskin of penis

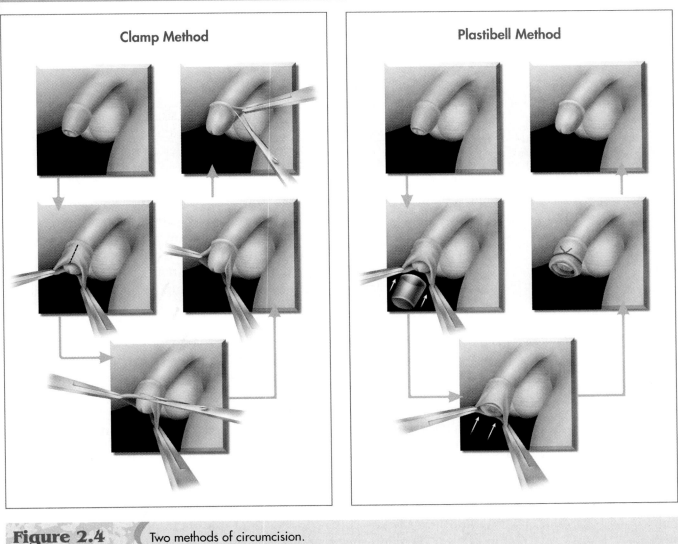

Clamp Method

Plastibell Method

Figure 2.4   Two methods of circumcision.

Health Hint

To Circumcise or Not to Circumcise?

Parents of newborn males must decide whether to have the infant circumcised. Recommendations about circumcision vary from state to state and medical facility to facility. In 1971 the American Academy of Pediatrics (AAP) removed its recommendation that male babies be routinely circumcised. The AAP now finds circumcision to be unnecessary to safeguard the health of newborn males except under special health circumstances.

Although the number and percentage of circumcisions has decreased since the AAP dropped its recommendation, most parents still opt for this procedure. The following facts are intended to help you make an informed choice about circumcision for your child.

1. Circumcision is not required as a routine procedure.

2. The American Academy of Pediatrics no longer recommends circumcision as a routine procedure.

3. As with any surgical procedure, circumcision involves a small risk for the newborn.

4. Research indicates that uncircumcised boys have a slightly higher rate than circumcised boys of urethral infection.

5. Many fathers prefer that their son's penis look like theirs.

6. No evidence is available that uncircumcised sons of circumcised fathers suffer any psychological distress over this difference.

7. If you opt to have the procedure done, you have the right to indicate who will perform your son's circumcision.

penis, dead epithelial cells, dirt, bacteria, and sweat. Smegma build-up is prevented through simple washing with soap and water and pulling the foreskin back to cleanse this area of the penis. It can be compared to other routine procedures such as washing behind the ears regularly.

Beginning with the 1971 edition of its procedures manual and reiterated in subsequent revisions in 1975 and 1983, the Academy's Task Force on Neonatal Circumcision found no absolute indication for routine circumcision. In 1989 the Task Force reexamined the issue in light of new research on circumcision status and urinary tract infections and sexually transmitted diseases. The Task Force concluded at the time that newborn male circumcision had potential medical benefits and advantages as well as disadvantages and risks.

The most recent report and recommendations of the Task Force on Neonatal Circumcision were released on March 1, 1999. This report follows 2 years of study of the most recent data available concerning neonatal male circumcision. The Academy report states that existing scientific evidence demonstrates potential medical benefits of routine newborn male circumcision; however, these data are not sufficient to recommend routine neonatal circumcision. Parents should determine what is in the best interests of their child.

Erection
filling of the penile spongy tissue with blood during vasocongestion, resulting a hard, erect, penis

Penis Size

The average penis is approximately 3 to 4 inches when flaccid (soft), and 6 inches when erect. Most of the variation in penis size occurs during erection. **Erection** has been called "the great equalizer" because smaller penises seem to grow more during erection than larger ones, so the extremes tend to equalize when erect.

There is a long history of obsession with penis size. Most young boys are curious about their penis size and use rulers and tape measures to actually measure their penises. They are concerned that their penises are smaller than their peers'. By late adolescence, most boys grow out of their fears and obsessions about the size of their penises.

Much of the adult male concern about penis size stems from the perception, promoted through inaccurate media coverage, that size equates to virility and sexual performance. Penis size is a central theme in both straight and gay erotica and pornography. Male pornographic actors are recruited as much for the size of their penises as their ability to act.

Researchers Masters, Johnson, and Kolodny found that penis size had little physiological effect on women's sexual response.[1] The vagina, Masters and Johnson pointed out, is capable of adjusting to penises of varying sizes from small to large. The inner depth of the vagina can be reached by a man with an average-size penis by using intercourse positions (such as rear entry) that facilitate deeper penetration. An unusually long penis can extend beyond the depth of the vagina. A slightly shortened vagina also can be the byproduct of a hysterectomy. Partners can accommodate for any discomfort by adjusting intercourse positions and avoiding those that facilitate deeper penetration.

The inner depth of the vagina, the area stimulated by the probing of a larger penis, is relatively devoid of nerve endings. The main musculature of the vagina responsible for contracting and gripping the penis is at the outer third of the vagina, thereby accessible to all sizes of penises. The most sensitive area

PERSPECTIVES

Penis Size Throughout History

People have been preoccupied with penises and penis size throughout time. Penis artifacts, ranging from pottery to temple decorations to statues with grinning characters possessing huge penises have been recovered across the globe. Nearly 2000 years ago the Romans worshipped Priapus, the God of Fertility. Priapus symbolized both passion and fertility. Although small in stature, Priapus had a huge penis. Every bride of the Roman aristocracy was supposed to lose her virginity by sacrificing it on the alter of Priapus.

In Greece, giant penises adorned the classic columns used to support its massive structures. In India, the temple of Kama Sutra is decorated with characters having oversized penises. The erotic pen-and-ink art of Japan has, as its focal point, couples lost in their passion, their elaborate silk robes parted, capturing

their genitalia. The men all possess oversized penises that they are thrusting into their enraptured lovers.

No wonder that men are convinced that the size of their penises determines their masculinity!

Case Study

Penis Size and Self-Esteem

Jordan is a 19-year-old college sophomore attending a large urban Northeast university. He says:

For the longest time I can remember being hung-up on the size of my penis. I remember, as a kid, getting my mom's tape measure and measuring the length and circumference of my penis. I never talked to my friends about size because I was convinced mine was smaller than theirs.

My dad used to kid me about how small mine was when he'd see me in the shower. I'd get intimidated by his because it seemed so big. I probably should have talked to him about it, but I couldn't. He wasn't so approachable and, like I said, he always seemed to be making fun of mine. Maybe this was his way of trying to break the ice and get a conversation going. I don't know. I doubt it.

Anyway, I guess I just kind of felt that mine was small and if I tried to bring it up with my friends, they'd laugh at me or, worse yet, I'd find out that theirs were really bigger than mine. I sent away for this stuff from the back of a magazine that was "guaranteed" to make your penis grow. The only thing it did was make my penis burn. It must have been some kind of liniment or something. I decided from that point on that I'd have to be satisfied with what I have.

for sexual stimulation is actually the clitoris, not the vagina. Clitoral stimulation is not contingent upon penis size (or even the presence of a penis) at all.

Among gay men, the importance of penis size in sexual satisfaction varies. From a purely scientific viewpoint in regard to anal intercourse, the length of the rectum and bowel is longer than the vagina, allowing for either deeper penetration or a longer penis.

Although penis size has little physiological relationship to sexual response, it can play a big part in one's psychological functioning. Men, whether straight, gay, or bisexual, who are overly concerned with or anxious about the size of their penis seem to be more likely to develop sexual disorders than men who don't share this concern.[2] Men who are overly concerned about their penis size can become anxious about sexual relations and develop sexual arousal disorders and even inhibited sexual desire.

Scrotum

Scrotum
a double-chambered pouch of tissue that hangs loosely from the base of the penis, containing the testicles

The **scrotum** is a sac or pouch with two chambers that house the testes. Each testicle is cradled in its own scrotal pouch, suspended by a *spermatic cord* and *cremaster muscle*. A midline, or *raphe*, divides the scrotum into left and right halves. The scrotum has a sparse covering of hair and is usually darker in pigmentation than skin elsewhere on the body.

The scrotum normally hangs loosely, away from the body. This provides an optimal temperature of about 93° F. for the testicles. In a sense, the scrotum acts like a thermostat, regulating temperature by pulling the testicles closer to the abdominal cavity in colder temperatures and letting them hang loosely and away from the body under warmer circumstances.

The scrotum is composed of a thin layer of muscle tissue called the *tunica dartos* covered by skin. The skin attaches to the body at the base of the penis. During sexual arousal, exposure to cold, or threat of physical harm, the tunica dartos contracts and works together with the cremaster muscle to pull the testicles closer to the abdominal cavity for warmth and protection. In doing this, the scrotal sac shrinks and becomes taut.

Like the penis, the scrotum is responsive sexually to various forms of stimulation and pressure. When stimulating the scrotum, care must be taken since each man varies in sensitivity to stimulation.

Perineum

The **perineum** is an area between the thighs, bounded in the front by the pelvis joint (symphysis pubis) and in the rear by the coccyx (tail bone). The perineum can be divided into two triangles of muscle tissue, the first containing the base of the penis and the scrotum and the second containing the anal opening. The muscular tissue is covered by a layer of skin. Although not normally considered part of male sexual anatomy, the perineum plays a part in the male sexual response because the entire area is endowed with nerve endings and responsive to stimulation. Again, the nature and intensity of stimulation to this area varies from man to man and encounter to encounter.

Perineum
the erogenous area of skin extending from the base of testicles to the anal opening

Anus

The **anus,** or opening of the bowel, is another body part with multiple functions. Although the primary function of the anus is to eliminate solid waste from the body, it also serves as a part of male sexual anatomy.

The anal canal is about 1⅕ inches long and is composed of two sets of sphincter muscles. The internal anal sphincter muscle is made up of smooth muscle tissue, and the external anal sphincter is composed of skeletal muscle. The anal sphincters act like the strings of a purse to open and close the anus. The anus is normally closed, except during defecation and sexual stimulation. Anal tissue is slightly elastic. The bowel or anus produces no natural lubrication.

The anus is richly endowed with nerve endings, can be stimulated manually or orally, and is enjoyed sexually by gay and straight men alike.

As a result of the AIDS epidemic, this behavior is being talked about more openly. Gay and straight couples have discovered that sex toys can be inserted into the anus to provide sexual pleasure that entails less risk than anal intercourse. We will discuss this in greater detail in Chapters 7 and 15.

Anus
opening of the bowel, through which fecal matter is eliminated from the body

Breasts

The breast is not usually discussed as a part of the male sexual anatomy. Although men's breasts are not typically thought of as erogenous, heterosexual women and gay men find the sight and feel of men's breasts to be sexually appealing. In addition, many men enjoy having their breasts stimulated manually or orally during sexual contact.

The standard for physical perfection is often difficult for young men to match.

Structurally, men's breasts have the same components as women's: nipple, areola, fat, and glandular tissue. Men's breasts, however, have much less underlying fatty and glandular tissue than women's do, and men do not lactate. Men's breasts normally do not enlarge during puberty. A small percentage of men develop a condition known as gynecomastia, which will be discussed in greater detail later in the chapter.

Breast size and concerns about other external sexual anatomy and body shape in general is a source of stress for many men. A "manly" torso, with well-developed pectoral (chest) muscles, broad shoulders, and a tapered waist is the ideal that the media and society present to us. Many men become obsessed with trying to achieve the perfect body and, toward that end, try everything from binging and purging to taking steroids. Separating good health from physical perfection is something we have to learn.

Case Study

Competing with Mr. America

Noredeen is a 45-year-old student returning to college to complete his second degree, this one in accounting. He says:

I remember being a kid and reading the ads in the back of comic books for muscle-building equipment. There was always this picture of some well-developed guy kicking sand in the face of a scrawny kid as this really foxy woman watched and laughed at the kid. The ad went on to describe how "you too can have a body like this and keep the bullies from kicking sand in your face."

I was that kid. I would die a thousand deaths every time I looked at it, because it rang so true for me. I did get picked on a lot by bullies, and I was small and scrawny. I was always embarrassed to take off my shirt and run around in a swimming suit. Needless to say, I didn't date much, and none of the sexy girls wanted to be around me.

I remember cutting out that picture and dreaming about saving enough money to send away for the muscle-building program that would transform me into the kind of man sexy women want. I really felt that if I could just have a body like that, I'd get respect and the girls would go crazy after me.

It was years before I realized that the muscles were nice but it was the person inside of the muscles that really mattered.

I eventually developed enough self-confidence to start asking girls out more often and I found that there actually were girls in high school who liked me for who I was, not who I wasn't. Eventually I became more interested in sport and fitness and filled out a little. It didn't seem to matter as much as it did when I was thirteen. I guess I never had the desire to invest the time it takes to build a body like the guy in the comic book.

INTERNAL MALE SEXUAL STRUCTURES

The internal male sexual structures are illustrated in Figure 2.5.

Testes

The **testes** are oval-shaped male **gonads** housed in the scrotum. During the third trimester of fetal development, the testes form inside the abdominal cavity and descend into the scrotum. The testes are held in place within the scrotal sac by the spermatic cord, which passes through the inguinal canal attaching to the wall of the abdomen and the cremaster muscle, which connects with the lower part of the internal oblique abdominal muscle (see Figure 2.6).

When one or both testicles have not descended by birth, the infant is diagnosed with **cryptorchidism**. In most cases the testicles will descend by the end of 5 years. If they do not descend by this time, surgical or hormonal treatment may be necessary to get them to fall into place. Undescended testicles are a risk factor for infertility, inguinal hernia, and testicular cancer.

The testes have two primary functions: sperm production and hormone production. Each oval-shaped (1.5 inches long × 1 inch in diameter) testis is divided into 300–400 cone-shaped lobules. Each lobule contains two to three tightly coiled *seminiferous tubules* and endocrine cells called *interstitial* or *Leydig cells*. **Spermatogenesis** occurs within the seminiferous tubules.

Testes
two almond-shaped male gonads responsible for sperm and hormone production

Gonads
male sex organs

Cryptorchidism
undescended testicle(s)

Spermatogenesis
sperm production

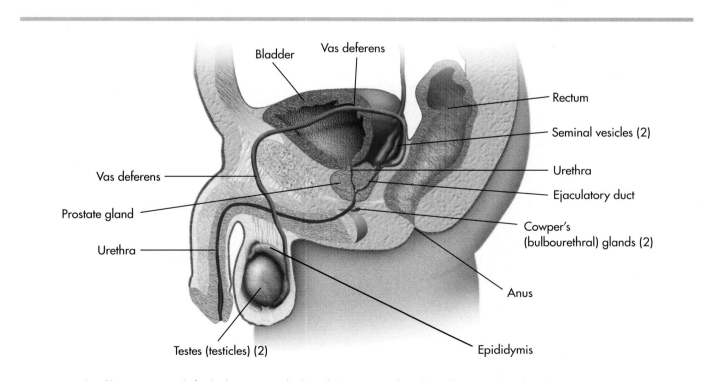

Source: *Personal Health: Perspectives and Lifestyles,* by Patricia A. Floyd, Sandra E. Mimms, and Caroline Yelding-Howard (Englewood, CO: Morton 1998), p. 93.

Figure 2.5 　 Male internal sexual structures.

The Leydig cells produce the male sex hormone testosterone. If laid end-to-end, the seminiferous tubules (each between 1 and 3 feet long) from both testicles combined would stretch almost 1/2 mile.

Sperm production begins at puberty and can continue until death, although the rate of production does diminish with aging. Some men fear "running out" of sperm. In fact, sperm are produced on an ongoing basis. Many things can interfere with sperm production, resulting in a low sperm count. Examples of the range of conditions that can lower sperm production as a result of damage to the testicles are injuries incurred during participation in sports and other circumstances, tight clothing, and exposure to toxic chemicals.

Testosterone, the main hormone associated with sexual desire, also is produced first during puberty, and its production ends with death. No evidence shows that sperm have anything to do with energy production and loss. Many men (including athletic coaches, trainers, and associated personnel) erroneously believe that depletion of sperm (through sexual activity) will weaken athletes and hamper their performance. Because of this, coaches sometimes sequester their teams before games or matches to prevent these

Testosterone
main male hormone associated with sexual desire

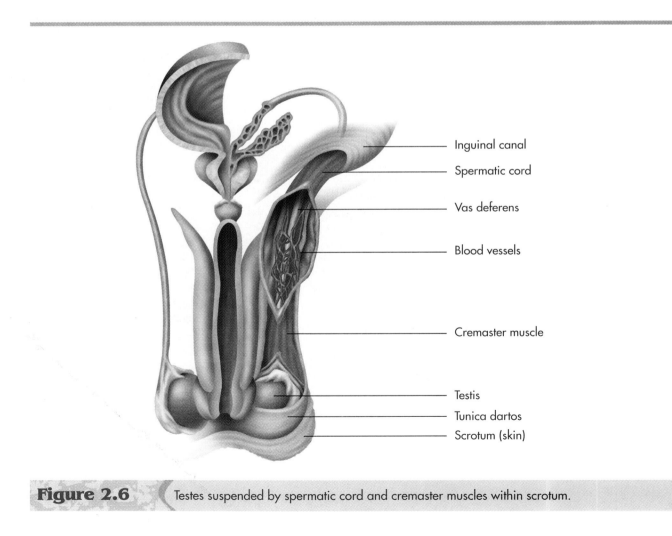

Inguinal canal

Spermatic cord

Vas deferens

Blood vessels

Cremaster muscle

Testis

Tunica dartos

Scrotum (skin)

Figure 2.6 Testes suspended by spermatic cord and cremaster muscles within scrotum.

athletes from having sex. We will discuss the influence of testosterone and other hormones on sexual response in greater detail in Chapter 4.

Epididymis

The **epididymis** is a C- or comma-shaped, coiled duct that sits on top of and extends along the back of each testis. Each of its heads merges the sperm-producing seminiferous tubules, and each tail connects with the vas deferens (*ductus deferens*). Within the coiled, 20-foot-long epididymis, immature sperm produced in the seminiferous tubules become motile and fertile. The journey of the sperm from head to tail takes about 20 days. During this time, the sperm receive nutrients and mature fully, and the inactive sperm undergo a quality control procedure. Defective and immature sperm are "weeded out" before they are able to be ejaculated. This helps to ensure that only healthy, viable sperm are available for potential fertilization of a ripe female ovum (egg).

Epididymis
comma-shaped structure that sits along top of each testicle and serves as storage chamber for immature sperm

Vas Deferens (ductus deferens)

The **vas deferens** are two long, thin ducts that originate in the base of the testis and extend up and around the bladder and into the prostate gland. There, they merge with the urethra. Each vas deferens is responsible for transporting mature sperm from the epididymis to the urethra. Each vas deferens joins the ejaculatory duct of the seminal vesicles just prior to entering the prostate gland.

The smooth muscle tissue of the vas deferens contracts during ejaculation, moving sperm as it does so. The sperm mix with secretions of the seminal vesicles, prostate gland, and Cowpers gland to form the milky white fluid released through ejaculation. Each ejaculate contains about 1 teaspoon of fluid.

During a **vasectomy**, the vas deferens are located, a piece is cut out of each, and the end is tied or burned off. This prevents sperm from mixing in the ejaculate. We will discuss this method of male sterilization more fully in Chapter 14.

Vas deferens
a tube extending from testicles to prostate gland, where it converts into urethra; responsible for transporting sperm and other ejaculatory fluid

Vasectomy
a male contraceptive method resulting in sterilization by cutting the vas deferens

Seminal Vesicles

The **seminal vesicles** are two saclike glandular structures located behind the urinary bladder. Each gland is about 2 inches long and tapers into a short duct that joins with the vas deferens to form the ejaculatory duct. The seminal vesicles produce an alkaline fluid that is high in the sugar fructose. The alkalinity helps neutralize the acidity of the urethra, protecting sperm as they pass through it. The fructose provides energy the sperm need to reach their ultimate destination, a mature female egg, or ova. Seminal vesicle fluid contributes 60% to 70% of the total amount of fluid ejaculated.

Seminal vesicles
small structures connected to vas deferens, which release fluids that nourish and buffer sperm as they are ejaculated

Prostate Gland

The **prostate** gland is about the size and shape of a chestnut. The prostate produces several enzymes that play a role in activating sperm. These enzymes

Prostate gland
chestnut-sized gland connected to neck of the bladder and vas deferens, which secretes alkaline fluid and enzymes that are part of ejaculatory fluid

are released in a milky-white alkaline fluid that mixes with seminal vesicle fluid and sperm to make up about 30% of the total fluid ejaculated.

The prostate is located immediately in front of the rectum, enabling digital (by finger) examination to detect any changes in shape and size. A routine prostate examination is recommended for all men over 40 years of age as part of their preventive health check-ups. Some men find stimulation of the prostate (through digital penetration or receptive anal intercourse) sexually arousing. Others find any contact with the prostate uncomfortable.

Cowper's Glands

Cowper's glands
bulbourethral glands, located below seminal vesicles, which produce preejaculatory fluid that lubricate vas deferens and urethra and protect sperm that are being ejaculated

The **Cowper's glands**, also known as the bulbourethral glands, are ducts that secrete a thick, clear mucus during the plateau stage of sexual arousal, prior to ejaculation. This clear, alkaline, preejaculatory fluid provides an additional buffer for sperm against the acidic environment of the urethra as the sperm make their way out of the body.

Advocates of birth control have long speculated that enough live sperm can be present in preejaculatory fluid to cause an unintended pregnancy. This has not been proven, however, in scientific studies of preejaculatory fluid. Two studies intended to determine the ability of preejaculatory fluid to transmit HIV found that the preejaculate was free of spermatozoa.[3] Some sperm may remain in the urethra following ejaculation. The two variables that contribute to the presence or absence of live sperm within the urethra are *time* (sperm live 3 to 5 days) and *urination* (urination flushes the urethra and the acidity kills sperm). If live sperm are present in the urethra before a man urinates, they possibly could get mixed into the preejaculatory fluid secreted by the Cowper's gland, and thus increase the risk of pregnancy.

COMMON DISORDERS OF MALE SEXUAL ANATOMY

The most common disorders of the male sexual anatomy are: benign prostatic enlargement, prostatitis, prostate cancer, urethritis, phimosis, and balanitis, hydrocele, testicular cancer, and gynecomastia

Benign Prostatic Enlargement (BPH)

BPH is a noncancerous enlargement of the prostate gland. Because the prostate gland surrounds the urethra, any prostatic swelling, irritation, or infection can obstruct the flow of urine. Men with BPH usually have problems with urination, such as a weak, hesitant, or interrupted stream of urine or an urgency to urinate, more frequent urination (especially at night), and leaking or dripping. In extreme cases, urination is impossible.

The risk for BPH increases with age. BPH occurs in about 10% of men by the age of 40, more than 50% of men by age 60, and close to 90% of men in their 70s and 80s.[4] The cause of BPH is unknown. Diagnosis is usually made by a rectal exam or measurement of urine flow using a flow meter.

In some cases **cystoscopy** is used to diagnose BPH. The urethra is anesthetized, and a cystoscope is inserted into the urethra. The instrument has a light and camera lens that allow the physician to observe the inside of the urethra and the bladder.

Treatment of BPH depends upon the size of the enlargement and the extent of complications. Up to one-third of all cases clear up spontaneously. Drugs can be used to help shrink a mildly enlarged prostate gland. Balloon dilation — a new treatment similar to what is used to open clogged coronary arteries — stretches the urethra and facilitates the passage of urine, alleviating the condition until the prostate can shrink. If no spontaneous shrinkage occurs, surgery is performed to remove the enlarged part of the prostate pressing against the urethra.

Cystoscopy
direct visual examination of interior of urethra, urinary bladder, and kidneys by inserting a cystoscope (optical viewing tube) into the urethra

Regular orgasm and ejaculation are related to healthy prostate functioning.

Prostatitis

Prostatitis is an inflammation of the prostate gland. The symptoms of prostatitis are lower back and pelvic pain, a sensation of heat and tenderness in the area, a thin discharge from the penis, and swelling in the genital area. The two types of prostatitis are infectious and congestive.

Prostatitis
inflammation and irritation of the prostate gland

1. *Infectious prostatitis* is caused by bacterial or viral infection. Treatment usually involves taking antibiotics.
2. *Congestive prostatitis* is associated with failure to ejaculate prostatic fluid. Prostate secretions are produced in response to a man's sexual behavior patterns. Reducing the frequency of sexual activity disrupts the pattern of production and removal of prostatic fluid. If prostatic fluid is not ejaculated, it begins to decompose and build up, causing congestion. Congestive prostatitis usually responds to warm baths and prostate massage.

Prostate Cancer

About 38,000 men die from prostate cancer each year. Prostate cancer is the second leading cause of cancer deaths (lung cancer is number one) among men.[5] The risk for prostate cancer increases with age. The two greatest risk factors for prostate cancer are being over age 65, and being Black Americans. One in nine Black men in the United States will develop prostate cancer. The disease is common in North America and Northwestern Europe and rare in Asia, Africa, and South America. This rate is 30% higher than for White men. The signs and symptoms of prostate cancer are exactly the same as those of prostatitis and benign prostate enlargement.

The probability of recovery from prostate cancer is excellent if it is caught early. The American Cancer Society recommends that all men older than 50 years of age have annual digital rectal prostate examinations (see Figure 2.7) and prostate-specific antigen (PSA) blood tests every year.[6] The blood tests check for the presence of antibodies that indicates prostate cancer. Men who are at high risk for prostate cancer (Blacks and men who have a history of prostate cancer in close family members) should consider beginning these tests at an earlier age.

Urethritis

Urethritis
inflammation and irritation of urethra

Dysuria
burning upon urination

Discharge
draining of pus from the urethra

Urethritis is the inflammation and irritation of the urethra. The two most common symptoms of urethritis are **dysuria** and **discharge**. Urethritis can be caused by a variety of things including mild injury, exposure to irritants, and infection. The urethra can incur mild injury from too vigorous masturbation or other sexual activity. The tissue is temporarily damaged and becomes sensitive to the passage of urine. The urethra also can become irritated from exposure to harsh soaps or other personal hygiene products. Mild injury and irritation usually resolve within a day or two without any special treatment.

Urethral infections can be sexually transmitted or nonsexually transmitted. We cover sexually transmitted infections in great detail in Chapter 15. Nonsexually transmitted urethritis is usually associated with poor personal hygiene and infection with microorganisms. Daily washing or bathing of the genitals will remove most microorganisms capable of causing urethritis. Uncircumcised men who do not practice normal daily hygiene have a slightly higher risk for infectious urethritis. Infectious urethritis is treated with antibiotics and responds rapidly to treatment.

Phimosis and Balanitis

Phimosis
a tight foreskin that cannot be retracted fully

Balanitis
inflammation of the glans penis

Glans penis
end of corpus spongiosum, which comprises head of penis and urethral opening

Phimosis is a condition of uncircumcised men who have a tight foreskin that is not fully retractable. **Balanitis** is an inflammation of the **glans penis**. By adolescence, more than 95% of all uncircumcised males have fully retractable

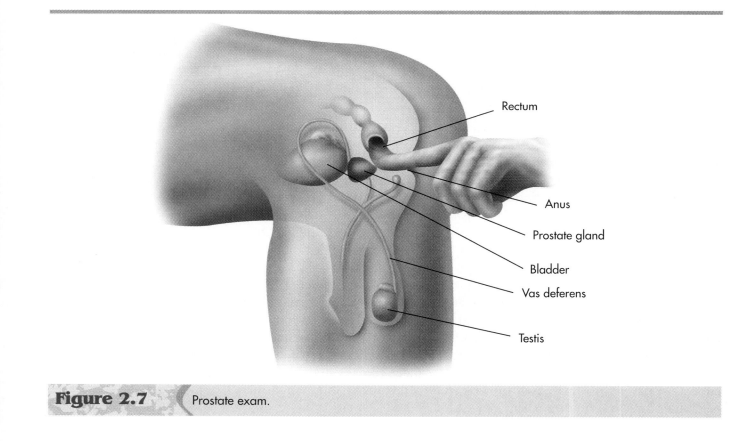

Figure 2.7 Prostate exam.

foreskins. Although it was once thought that all newborn males had fully retractable foreskins, studies in the 1960s and 1970s showed that fewer than half of newborn males had fully retractable foreskins.

Newborns and young, uncircumcised boys often have some degree of tightness in their foreskins. A tight foreskin usually is not a problem in pre-pubescent boys. As long as the urethral opening and urine flow remains unobstructed, this condition has no negative health risks. Phimosis that occurs in a young man who has gone through the physiological changes and growth of puberty can be corrected with a variety of treatments ranging from topical steroids to surgery designed to loosen the foreskin and separate it from the glans.

Uncircumcised newborns and young boys often have some tightness in their foreskins.

Phimosis also can be caused by infection. This is a possible complication of urethritis. The discharge associated with urethritis can get trapped under the foreskin, causing balanitis and inflammation of the foreskin, which results in increased tightness and difficulty retracting the skin. Because both conditions are associated with the infectious urethritis, antibiotic treatment of this infection usually reduces swelling and alleviates balanitis and phimosis. In rare instances, emergency circumcision is done to relieve the swelling and pain associated with infectious phimosis.

The larger, fluid-filled sacs characteristic of hydroceles often can be distinguished from the smaller, firmer lumps of testicular cancer through self-exam.

Hydrocele

A **hydrocele** is an accumulation of fluid in any saclike cavity or duct. Hydroceles are commonly found in the scrotum. Fluid accumulates in the *tunica vaginalis*, a small, closed sac that covers most of the testes. The condition is caused by an inflammation of the testis or epididymis or obstruction in blood or lymphatic fluid within the spermatic cord.

Hydrocele
accumulation of fluid in any sac, cavity, or duct

A hydrocele can develop as a result of congenital malformation or from injury during any period in a man's life. Hydroceles usually require surgical repair. In some cases the sac may be aspirated and the fluid removed. This usually is considered a temporary treatment because in most cases the sac will refill with fluid. A hydrocele is distinguished from the small, solid lump associated with testicular cancer; hydroceles are larger, fluid-filled sacs.

Testicular Cancer

Testicular cancer is a relatively rare form of cancer, representing less than 2% of all cancers). Still, it is the most common type of cancer in men 35 years of age. Most cases of testicular cancer affect men between the ages of 15 and 40 years. The risk for testicular cancer among White men is approximately four times greater than that of Black men in the United States.

If detected early, testicular cancer is one of the easiest cancers to cure and is rarely fatal.

Symptoms of testicular cancer are a painless lump on the side of a testicle, a swollen or enlarged testicle, and a sensation of heaviness or dragging in the groin or scrotum. If detected early, testicular cancer is one of the easiest cancers to cure and is rarely fatal.

Risk factors for testicular cancer include:

- family history of testicular cancer
- men who were born with undescended testicles
- injury to the testicle(s)
- history of childhood mumps
- history of maternal hormonal treatment during pregnancy

As a preventive measure, men should perform a testicular self-exam on a regular basis when they shower.

Gynecomastia

Gynecomastia
enlargement of one or both breasts in men

Gynecomastia, the abnormal swelling or enlargement of one or both of a man's breasts, is usually temporary and benign. If it occurs around the time of puberty, it usually is the result of a temporary hormonal imbalance. If it

---

Health Hint

Testicular Self-Exam

How do I do this examination?

Roll each testicle between your thumb and first three fingers until you have felt the entire surface (see illustration). The testicles should feel round and smooth, like hard-boiled eggs.

These are the things to be on the lookout for:

- Lumps

- Irregularities

- A change in the size of the testicle

- Pain in the testicle

- A dragging or heavy sensation.

How often do I have to do this exam?

Do it at least once a month. It helps to pick a regular day of the month — the day of your birthday, the first of the month, the first Sunday, or some other day that's easy for you to remember. You can do the exam more often if you like.

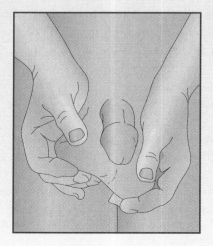

occurs later in life, it may be attributable to a tumor of the testis or pituitary, taking medications that contain estrogen or other steroids, or liver failure associated with cirrhosis or other causes. In cases where gynecomastia does not resolve spontaneously, corrective surgery may be necessary, especially if it is contributing to psychological stress and illness.

Male Breast Cancer

Breast cancer is primarily a disease affecting women; however, it does affect men. Male breast cancer accounts for less than 1% of the overall incidence and mortality of breast cancer. Even though men are at low risk of developing breast cancer, they should be aware of risk factors, especially family history, and report any changes in their breasts to a physician. Early detection improves the chances for successful treatment.

WELLNESS SYNTHESIS

Male sexuality is related to the six dimensions of wellness: physical, intellectual, emotional, social, spiritual, and environmental.

Physical Well-being

Physical well-being affects healthy sexuality from conception until death. As we will explore in more detail in Chapter 5, psychosexual development begins at conception. The male sexual anatomy begins to differentiate after the first 6 weeks of gestation. Internal and external structures continue to develop during the prenatal period. A mother's physical health and lifestyle affect the normal development of her baby. Factors such as prenatal nutrition, drug and alcohol use, and weight management can influence fetal development.

Parents must decide how they are going to handle the issue of circumcision. If they desire to have the procedure done, they have to make arrangements concerning who will perform the surgery. If they decide not to have it done, they need to make sure their obstetrician or midwife is aware of this and builds it into the birth plan.

To ensure optimal physical well-being, boys must be taught about their bodies and understand issues such as proper hygiene and protection of their genitals during sports and other activities. To protect the genitals against injury from trauma, all male athletes participating in contact sports should use a plastic protective cup within their athletic supporters.

As boys approach puberty, they need to be aware of the changes that will take place in their bodies and their sexual anatomy and physiology. They need to understand issues such as nocturnal emissions and ejaculation, increasing sexual desire, hygiene, prevention of sexually transmitted disease and unintended pregnancy, and testicular self-exam.

Fitness, proper nutrition, weight management, not smoking or abusing drugs and alcohol — all become increasingly important in sexual health as males age. Often, physical and other disabilities impact on physical well-being. Rather than respond to all disabilities in a stereotypical way, we need to understand the extent of any limitations the disability imposes and strive to maximize all remaining functions. In Chapter 4 we will go into greater detail about the relationship between physical well-being and sexual response.

Intellectual Well-being

Understanding how the body works and how to maintain the body for optimal performance is crucial for healthy sexuality. The proper functioning of the male sexual anatomy and physiology is directly related to the level of wellness. This involves learning about the body, staying current by reading about new information related to men's health, and being a critical consumer of sexual health studies and products.

Emotional Well-being

Issues related to sexual anatomy and physiology can provoke strong emotions. Body-image is often directly related to sexual anatomy and physiology and can be a source of shame, concern, obsessiveness and emotional distress or of joy, contentment, and emotional security.

Issues such as penis size and function, secondary sex characteristics, and onset of puberty can affect our emotional well-being. Our intellectual resources can provide objective information about our sexuality that might help us understand and control our emotions.

Social Well-being

Parents can be the greatest resource in understanding sexual anatomy and physiology and helping their sons develop healthy lifestyles that optimize sexual functioning. As the primary sex educators, parents can teach their sons about their bodies, how they work, and what to expect as they grow and age. A father or other older male can be an excellent role model for sexual health, exhibiting proper hygiene and a healthy lifestyle. Older brothers can serve the same function.

Other members of a man's social environment can help him understand his sexual anatomy and physiology. Partners, friends, peers, teachers, coaches, and others are often there to give advice, share information, and help put issues into a broader perspective. As males mature and form intimate sexual relationships, they learn about sexual anatomy and physiology from lovers and wives. These intimate partners share a concern for health and well-being and can be a source of information, comfort, and support.

Spiritual Well-being

Spirituality and religiosity influence sexual health and anatomy and physiology. Circumcision often is part of a religious tradition. Spirituality affects decisions regarding masturbation, sexual intercourse, use of contraceptives, abortion, and so on. Associated decisions influence the risks for acquiring STDs, producing an unintended pregnancy, and the like. Spirituality cannot be separated from morality and subsequent behavior.

Environmental Well-being

The environment can be health-enhancing, providing good role models, a free and open exchange of information and ideas, and access to health products and care. Conversely, poor role models, a closed, secretive environment, with limited access to information, products, and health care can detract from sexual health. Also, the work environment can expose people to unnecessary sexual health risks. Exposure to toxic chemicals or other carcinogens, for instance, can have a negative impact on sexual health.

WEB RESOURCES

Male Health Center

http://www.malehealthcenter.com/

First center in the United States specializing in male health. The center takes a holistic approach to health and covers impotence, prostate disorders, sexually transmitted diseases, vasectomy, cancer screening, and wellness.

Men's Health Network

http://www.menshealthnetwork.org/

An information and educational organization that recognizes men's health as a specific societal concern and is committed to promoting issues affecting men's health. See "Library" and "Men's Links" for 54 pages of links to magazines and journals, books, organizations, miscellaneous resources, and men's health resources.

Notes

1. W. H. Masters, V. E. Johnson and R. Kolodny. *Human Sexuality*, 6th ed. (New York: HarperCollins, 1996).
2. Masters, Johnson, and Kolodny.
3. Ilaria, G., Jacobs, J.L., Plosky, B., Koll, B., MacLow, C., Armstrong, D. Schlegal, P.N. (1992). Detection of HIV-1DNA Sequences in pre-ejaculatory fluid. Lancet340 (8833), pg. 1469; Pudney, J. Oneta, M., Mayer, K., Seage, G., Anderson, D. (1992). Pre-ejaculatory fluid as a potential vector for the transmission of HIV-1. Lancet 340(8833), pg. 1470.

4. P. A. Floyd, S. E. Mimms, and C. Yelding-Howard, *Personal Health*: *Perspectives and Lifestyles* (Englewood, CO: Morton, 1998); G. J. Tortora and N.P. Anagnostakos. *Principles of Anatomy and Physiology*, 5th ed. (New York: Harper & Row, 1987); J. S. Hyde, *Understanding Human Sexuality*, 5th ed. (New York: McGraw Hill, 1994).

5. American Cancer Society, www. cancer.org/statistics/off99/ selectedcancers.html.
6. American Cancer Society, www. cancer.org/statistics/off99/ selectedcancers.html.

Student Study Questions

1. Describe the nature of penile erectile tissue. How does it facilitate erection?

2. Discuss the pros and cons of circumcision. Would you have your son circumcised? Why or why not?

3. What are the functions of the scrotum?

4. a. What two major processes occur within the testes?

   b. In which part of the testes do these occur? Describe these structures.

5. What is the route of ejaculation from the testes to expulsion out of the penis?

6. What is the role of testosterone in male sexuality?

7. How can you reduce your risks for the six common male sexual disorders described in this chapter?

Student Assessment

Body Image: Males

Body image refers to our evaluation and perception of our body, specific body parts and their functioning. It includes the messages (positive and negative) that we tell ourselves about our bodies, our self-esteem and the behaviors and choices we make as a result. The following inventory will help males assess their body image:

Rate each body part listed below using the following scale:

Extremely satisfied 5   satisfied 4   neutral 3   dissatisfied 2   extremely dissatisfied 1

____ 1. eyes	____ 7. weight	____ 13. hands	____ 19. feet
____ 2. ears	____ 8. face	____ 14. height	____ 20. sex organs
____ 3. nose	____ 9. shoulders	____ 15. stomach	____ 21. overall body
____ 4. hair	____ 10. chest	____ 16. buttocks	
____ 5. teeth	____ 11. arms	____ 17. hips	
____ 6. mouth	____ 12. calves	____ 18. thighs	

Scoring:

105–80 very positive body image
60–80 positive body image
40–60 ambivalent about your body

20–40 negative body image
0–20 very negative body image

Rate each item below, using the following scale:

very comfortable 5   comfortable 4   neutral 3   uncomfortable 2   very uncomfortable 1

____ 22. looking at my nude body in the mirror

____ 23. performing self-examinations of my nude body

____ 24. being nude when I am alone

____ 25. being nude when I am with my lover

____ 26. being nude when I am around my kids

____ 27. sunbathing in the nude

____ 28. swimming in the nude

____ 29. walking around the house nude

Scoring:

32–40 very comfortable with nudity
21–32 comfortable with nudity
16–21 ambivalent about nudity

12–16 uncomfortable with nudity
0–12 very uncomfortable with nudity

Complete the following sentences:

30. The thing I like best about my body is _____

_____

31. The thing I dislike most about my body is _____

_____

Female Sexual Anatomy and Physiology

Major Topics

External Female Sexual Structures
Mons Veneris
Labia Majora
Labia Minora
Clitoris
Vestibule
Hymen and Introitus
Perineum
Anus
Underlying Structures
Breasts
Internal Female Sexual Structures
Vagina
Uterus
Cervix
Fallopian Tubes
Ovaries
Reproductive Physiology
Ovarian Cycle
Menstrual or Uterine Cycle
Common Disorders of
Female Sexual Anatomy
Endometriosis
Uterine Fibroid Tumors
Fibrocystic Breast Disease
Breast Cancer
Vaginitis
Cervical Cancer
Uterine Cancer
Ovarian Cancer
Premenstrual Syndrome
Dysmenorrhea
Toxic Shock Syndrome
Wellness Synthesis
Physical Well-being
Intellectual Well-being
Emotional Well-being
Social Well-being
Spiritual Well-being
Environmental Well-being

Student Learning Objectives

After reading this chapter, students will be able to:

- Identify and locate the key structures of the female sexual anatomy.

- Describe the main functions of the key female sexual structures.

- Identify and describe the functions of the key female sex hormones.

- Explain the erogenous potential of the female sexual structures.

- Perform a breast self-exam.

- Identify the signs and symptoms of, and treatment for, common female sexual disorders.

- Describe a variety of screening tests used to diagnose common female sexual disorders.

Many of the structures and functions of the female sexual anatomy are similar to those in males. Indeed, an underlying theme in this book is the emphasis on how men and women are more similar than different.

EXTERNAL FEMALE SEXUAL STRUCTURES

Vulva
the external female genitalia collectively

The formal term used to describe all of the external female genital structures collectively is the **vulva**. The vulva includes the mons pubis (also known as *mons veneris*), labia majora and minora, clitoris, hymen, introitus, and vestibule. These are shown in Figure 3.1

Mons Veneris

The mons veneris is named after the Greek goddess of love. In Latin, *mons veneris* means "the mound of Venus." The mons veneris, commonly called the pubic area, is the softly protruding cushion of fat, skin, and pubic hair that covers the pubis symphysis, the juncture of the pubic bones of the pelvis. Although it serves no reproductive function, the mons is sensitive to stimulation during sexual arousal. Its pad of fatty tissue provides a soft cushion to maximize pleasure during sexual activities, particularly those involving grinding circular movements.

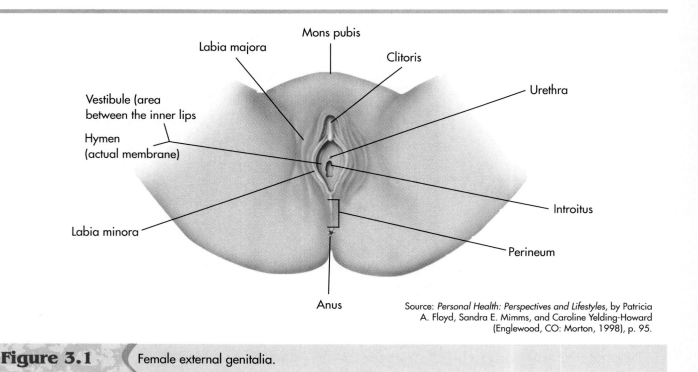

Source: *Personal Health: Perspectives and Lifestyles*, by Patricia A. Floyd, Sandra E. Mimms, and Caroline Yelding-Howard (Englewood, CO: Morton, 1998), p. 95.

Figure 3.1   Female external genitalia.

Labia Majora

The two **labia majora** form the outermost vaginal lips. The labia are folds of skin covering fatty tissue and are covered with hair on the outside. The inner portion of the labia majora is covered with numerous sweat and oil glands.

Labia majora
the larger, outer vaginal lips

In the unaroused state, the labia majora remain closed, providing protection for the vaginal opening and clitoris. The skin of the labia, like the male scrotum, is normally darker in color than the rest of a woman's body. During sexual arousal, underlying erectile tissue engorges with blood, causing the labia to swell, deepen in color, and open like "the petals of a flower" (see Betty Dodson's Art), exposing the vaginal opening and clitoris.

Good labial hygiene is similar to foreskin care in males: At least once a day, retract the skin and gently wash with warm soapy water.

The sweat and oil secretions of the labia majora are capable of producing a smegma-like material. Hygiene is comparable to uncircumcised male hygiene; daily washing of this area with soap and water can prevent unhealthy build-up of this material and ensure cleanliness.

Labia Minora

The **labia minora** are a second set of vaginal lips located within the larger labia majora. Thinner than the labia majora, the labia minora have spongy tissue containing oil and sweat glands and are richly endowed with blood vessels and nerve endings. The top portion of the labia majora fuse to form the clitoral hood, or prepuce. Unlike the labia majora, the minora are hairless. In the unaroused state they, too, remain closed, providing a second line of protection for the vaginal opening and clitoris.

Labia minora
the smaller, inner vaginal lips

The labia minora are highly sensitive to sexual stimulation and engorge with blood during sexual stimulation, opening up and exposing the vaginal opening and clitoris. Within the labia minora are **Bartholin's glands**, which secrete a mucouslike lubricating fluid during sexual arousal. The Bartholin's glands are homologous in structure and function to the bulbourethral (Cowper's) glands in males.

Bartholin's glands
small glands adjacent to the vaginal opening that secrete a mucouslike lubricant during arousal

Clitoris

The **clitoris** is a small structure made up of erectile tissue located at the top of the vestibule where the labia majora join. Like the penis, the clitoris has three parts; the glans, the shaft, and the root, or crura. The glans of the clitoris is exposed by retracting the prepuce or clitoral hood.

Clitoris
a small, highly sensitive, organ located at the top of the labia minora

Unlike the penis, the clitoris has no urinary or reproductive function. It is not involved in the passing of any body fluid. The sole function of the clitoris is to provide sexual pleasure. Because of this, many girls don't discover their clitoris until preadolescence or older. Figure 3.2 depicts the clitoris.

The clitoris is richly endowed with nerve endings. Although it is only a fraction of the size of the male penis, the clitoris has a comparable number

PERSPECTIVES

Betty Dodson's Art

The vulva has long been the subject of artistic expression. The vulva has often been portrayed as a flower, with the labia representing its petals, moist with the dew of sexual arousal, unfolding to reveal the secrets of love and lust contained within.

For more than 20 years, author, artist, and lecturer Betty Dodson has been celebrating female form and function. She has had over 100 exhibitions, and her artwork has adorned countless galleries throughout the world. Her sketches of the vulva capture the variety and uniqueness of female external genitalia. She combines artistic expression with sexual-health activism.

Her book *Liberating Masturbation* is a celebration of female sexuality. In the book, Dodson chronicles her own personal journey from a woman who questioned her own sexual response and ability to enjoy orgasm to a champion of women's sexual health. For a decade and more, Dodson has run workshops devoted to helping women become orgasmic by using masturbation to liberate their sexual energy. Her artwork adorns her book, illustrating the sensual nature of female sexuality.

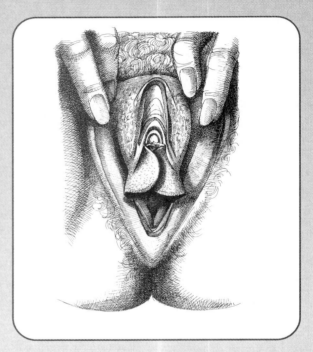

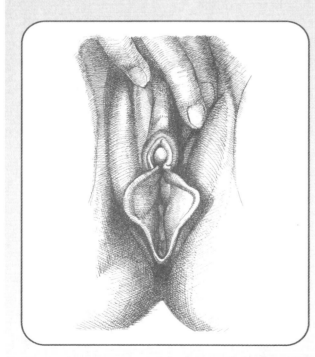

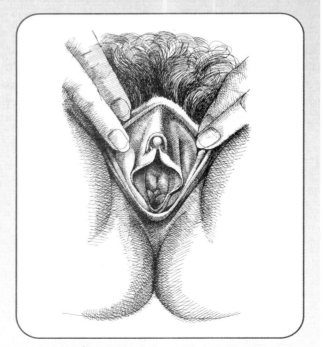

Dr. Betty Dodson's art pays homage to the beauty of the female vulva.

of nerve endings. Because of its dense concentration of nerve endings, the clitoris is sensitive to over stimulation and the prepuce will move forward to cover and protect it from excessive stimulation.

In the unaroused state, the clitoris is hidden by the prepuce. During sexual arousal, the spongy tissue of the clitoris engorges with blood, causing the clitoris to grow, become erect, and protrude from the prepuce, which retracts as the labia minora unfold. The clitoris is highly sensitive to sexual stimulation. Adequate clitoral stimulation plays a key role in female sexual response.[1]

Women often find that certain forms of sexual activity do not always produce the correct form and amount of stimulation necessary for them to reach orgasm. Manual, oral, and mechanical stimulation of the clitoris, as well as female-on-top intercourse positions, seem to be the most effective for clitoral stimulation.

For years, Masters and Johnson's pioneering discovery that the clitoris was the seat of sexual stimulation in women was criticized because of the fear that this discovery would end heterosexuality, marriage, and childrearing. Women would no longer need men for sexual satisfaction. After 30 years, we are happy to report that men and women

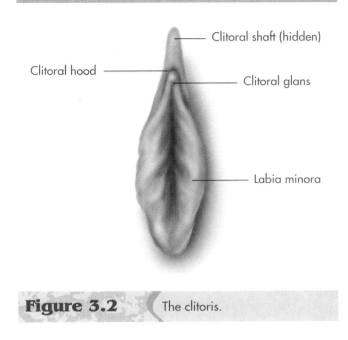

Figure 3.2　　The clitoris.

Labels: Clitoral hood — Clitoral shaft (hidden) — Clitoral glans — Labia minora

PERSPECTIVES

Genital Mutilation in the 1990s

The practice now best known as *female genital mutilation* (FGM) — a centuries-old tradition in some cultures — involves removing a girl's clitoris in part (clitoral circumcision) or totally (clitoridectomy) before puberty. This cultural and religious custom has been done to reduce females' ability to experience sexual pleasure and ensure marital fidelity. The cultures that practice FGM do not believe a woman should derive pleasure from sex. Genital mutilation is still done in some parts of Africa, the Middle East, and Asia.

In recent years many organized groups, most prominently the World Health Organization and the United Nations Children's Fund, have condemned this treatment of females and are continuing to pressure the countries and cultures that still practice genital mutilation to end it. U. S. representatives to the World Bank and other financial institutions oppose loans to countries that widely practice genital mutilation and have no anti-FGM educational programs.

In the United States, the Federal Prohibition of Female Genital Mutilation Act of 1995 passed in September, 1996, provides for prison sentences for anyone who performs this procedure on a female under 18 years of age. That law does permit the surgery if it is "necessary to the health of the person on whom it is performed." Other countries that outlaw the procedure include England, Canada, France, Sweden, and Switzerland.

U. S. health care professionals see the effects of genital mutilation on females emigrating to the United States. Dr. Terry Dunn, director of a women's clinic in Denver, Colorado, reported that the clinic sees about four cases at that clinic each year. Extrapolating this figure nationwide gives an indication of its prevalence among recent immigrants. Some states are introducing legislation to further refine the federal law.

have applied Masters and Johnson's discovery to enhance their sexual pleasure by focusing more attention on the clitoris.

Vestibule

Vestibule
the area within the labia minora that includes the hymen, introitus, and urethral opening

The **vestibule** is the area between the labia minora that is covered with the hymen and contains the openings to the vagina and urethra. In a sense, the vestibule represents the entrance to the vagina. During sexual arousal, the vestibule is sensitive to stimulation of all kinds. Like the labia and clitoris, it is richly endowed with nerve endings.

Hymen and Introitus

Hymen
membrane that lines the introitus

Introitus
vaginal opening

The **hymen** is a thin mucous membrane that covers the vestibule and **introitus** (vaginal opening). The hymen is intact at birth but typically becomes perforated by the time a young woman reaches puberty, allowing the passage of menstrual flow. Various activities ranging from sports and exercise to inserting fingers or other objects into the vagina during masturbation are capable of perforating the hymen.

Although the hymen is durable, its opening is capable of being stretched or enlarged through intercourse, masturbation, or insertion of a tampon. Some mothers discourage their daughters from using tampons for fear of ruining the hymen. Figure 3.3 illustrates the three main types of hymens.

The most common is the annular where the tissue surrounds the entire opening of the vagina and is open in the middle. The cribiform hymen has a web of tissue over the introitus and it has several small openings. The septate has a single band of tissue that divides the introitus into two parts. In rare occurrences, girls are born with the hymen completely covering the

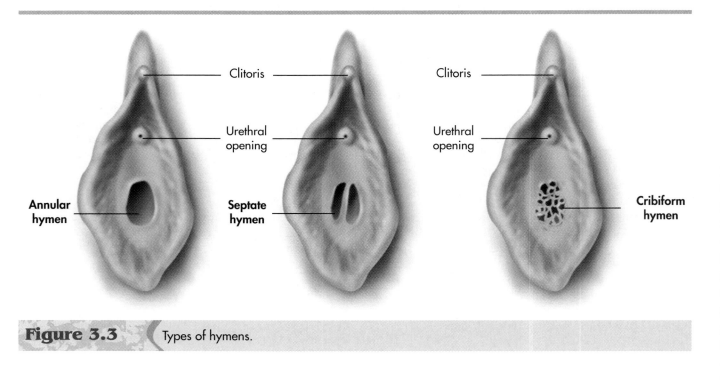

Figure 3.3   Types of hymens.

opening of the vagina, which is not discovered until she starts menstruating. This causes the fluid to build up in the vagina. When this happens, a physician must make a small opening to allow the menstrual flow. Many people believe that the presence of a hymen is proof of a woman's virginity. This is not true.

If the hymen is still present at the time of first intercourse, penetration by the penis can produce some discomfort or even bleeding if the hymen is torn. The hymen can be gradually widened by inserting fingers into the opening, or a physician may also cut the hymen or stretch it with dilators. Generally, there is little trouble inserting the penis through the hymen if the male is gentle with lubrication.

Perineum

The female **perineum**, as in the male, is an area between the thighs bounded in the front by the pelvis joint (the *symphysis pubis*) and in the rear by the coccyx (tailbone). The muscular tissue is covered by a layer of skin.

Although it is not normally considered part of the female sexual anatomy, the perineum plays a part in sexual response because the entire area is endowed with nerve endings and is highly responsive to sexual stimulation. As with men, the nature and intensity of stimulation desired in this area varies from woman to woman and encounter to encounter.

The major difference between the perineum in men and women is its role in childbearing. The perineum of pregnant women is subject to tearing of the skin and muscle tissue during childbirth. This is usually the time when they first become aware of this region. During delivery, pressure from the emerging fetus can exert a tremendous force on the perineum, first stretching, then tearing, the muscle and skin. The muscles and skin will heal, although some women report less sensitivity, as nerve endings can be injured and require additional time to recover. Jagged tears are more likely to result in scar tissue, which can reduce the sensitivity of nerves in the area.

Two schools of thought have emerged concerning how to minimize damage to the perineum during childbirth. To avert tearing, obstetricians often perform a surgical procedure called an **episiotomy** to enlarge the opening, which facilitates the birth of the fetus. We will discuss this procedure in detail in Chapter 6. Midwives try to avoid performing episiotomies whenever possible. They encourage pregnant women to massage the perineum with oil during pregnancy and labor to help deliver their babies without an episiotomy. Sometimes the massage will help minimize the tear.

Perineum
area of muscle and skin between vagina and anus

Episiotomy
a surgical procedure that facilitates childbirth by enlarging the vaginal opening through cutting the perineum

Anus

The anus in women is exactly the same as in men and, as such, is capable of similar responsiveness during sexual activity. Many women enjoy oral (anilingus) and manual stimulation, as well as anal intercourse. Some women use anal intercourse as an alternative to vaginal coitus because they think that by doing this, they can "preserve their virginity" and still enjoy sex.

Women's underlying structures respond to vasocongestion in a fashion similar to the male penis; they engorge with blood, enlarge, and deepen in color.

Underlying Structures

Underlying the structures of the vulva are a series of spongy bodies of erectile tissue. These vestibular bulbs, along with the crura of the clitoris, are responsible for the shape and color changes associated with sexual arousal. The structures (see Figure 3.4) engorge with blood during sexual arousal, causing the labia, clitoris, and vagina to enlarge, swell, and deepen in color. These changes can be compared to the changes associated with erection in men.

Breasts

Lactation
the process of producing and secreting milk from the breasts

Although the main function of the female breast is **lactation**, it has taken on added erotic and sexual significance in American and other cultures. Breast size and shape have become markers for attractiveness, sexiness, femininity, and motherhood, as well as disease. The breasts are composed of mammary glands, fatty tissue, the nipple and areola, and underlying muscle and ligaments.

Mammary Glands

Mammary glands
glands within the breasts that produce milk for lactation

The **mammary glands** are divided into 15–20 lobes or compartments separated by fatty tissue. Each lobe is made up of several smaller components called lobules. Imbedded in the lobules are milk-secreting cells called alveoli. Following childbirth, special hormones trigger the production and secretion of milk from the alveoli. Milk secreted from the alveoli are stored in chambers called mammary ducts and are drained through nursing.

Swelling of glandular tissue and storage of milk typically cause the breasts of nursing women to enlarge significantly. Breast size returns to

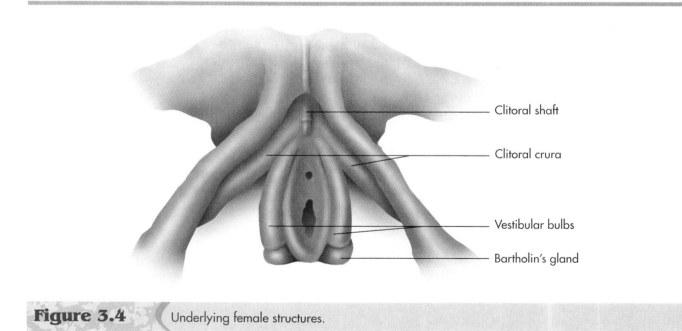

Clitoral shaft

Clitoral crura

Vestibular bulbs

Bartholin's gland

Figure 3.4   Underlying female structures.

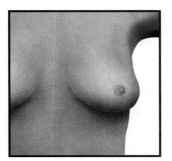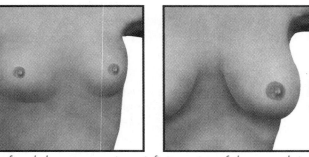

The female breast comes in an infinite variety of shapes and sizes.

normal after nursing ceases. We will discuss lactation and nursing more fully in the Chapter 13. Breast swelling, and in some cases painful tenderness, often precedes menstruation, as the breasts (like the uterus) prepare for potential pregnancy.

Fatty Tissue

Breast size and shape in a woman who is not nursing is determined primarily by heredity and the amount of adipose or fatty tissue present in the

Case Study

Breast Reduction

Denise, a 35-year-old continuing student is married, has two children, and is finishing her degree in psychology at night. She discussed her breast reduction surgery in a small group in human sexuality class.

I couldn't wait to get my breast reduction surgery. I could never understand why some women want large breasts. I've had them since puberty, and they've been nothing but a pain in the neck. Ever since middle school it seems that boys, and later men, would gawk at my breasts.

It's not like I ever did anything to invite this. I've always dressed conservatively and never flaunted my breasts (size 38DD), but it's hard to conceal them. Lord knows I've tried, but after a while I just got disgusted trying to hide them and figured there was nothing I could do about them until I got older and could think about surgery.

A lot of guys thought that just because I had big breasts, I was loose and interested in them sexually. That pretty much stopped after a couple of guys I

dated in high school got the word out that I wasn't "one of *those* girls."

Anyway, I met my husband in my junior year of high school, and we've been together ever since. We got married in our sophomore year in college and had kids right away. We decided that after the kids were out of diapers and we decided we didn't want any more, we'd talk about my surgery.

I breastfed each of my kids for more than a year, and that solidified my decision. My breasts were absolutely ponderous when I was nursing. As soon as our second child was three, we made the arrangements to get the surgery done. Everything went well, but the post-operative healing was a little painful and took longer than I expected. I even lost some sensation in my nipples and breasts for about a year. That's come back now, and I love my smaller, firmer breasts. I can jog and go braless — something I never did before the operation — and my husband still thinks my breasts are great. I'm happy I had it done.

breast. The amount of fatty tissue is influenced by heredity and overall percentage of body fat. Changing hormonal levels also can influence breast size. A common side effect of using hormonal contraceptive is a larger breast size.

Because of the cultural emphasis on breast size, surgical breast augmentation and reduction procedures have become much more common than before. In 1990, approximately 100,000 women had breast implant surgery. The overwhelming majority of those women had the procedure done for cosmetic purposes, to augment the size of their breasts. The number of procedures dropped to around 32,000 in 1992, the year the Food and Drug Administration (FDA) banned silicone implants because of the problems associated with leakage and the subsequent development of cancer and other health problems. Cosmetic surgeons began to substitute medically safe saline-filled forms for silicone.

Case Study

Breast Augmentation

Yolanda is a 21-year-old college senior, a health education student with a 1-year-old daughter. She lives with her boyfriend. Highly attractive, bright, and health-conscious, Yolanda came to us to discuss her desires for breast augmentation.

When Yolanda first came to the office, she seemed a little sheepish about discussing her concerns.

Yolanda: I'm a little unsure about how to say this, but I need to talk to you about something.

RB: Is it about sex?

Yolanda: Yes. I figured I could talk to you since you teach human sexuality and seem approachable.

RB: (Reassuring her that she could feel free to discuss any sexual matter with me).

Yolanda: I'm thinking about having my breasts enlarged. I'm kind of small, as you can see — a 32A — and I want to get up to a 32C. I've always felt good about my body except for my breasts. I'm very self-conscious about them being so small. I hate to wear bathing suits and can't wear some of the dresses and blouses that my boyfriend and I like.

RB: Is this something you want to do to please him?

Yolanda: Yes and no. I mean, I want to please him, but this is something I've wanted ever since puberty. He says he loves them the way they are, but if I really want them, he'll pay for the procedure. I've thought about it for a long time. I know it probably says something about my low self-esteem and all that, but I don't care. I've tried everything, and they just won't grow. I came to you to ask about any health risks I should know about. As long as the operation is safe, I want to have it done.

I talked to her and explained the controversy surrounding the older silicone implants, current technology, and post-operative healing. She thanked me and promised to come back after school break to show me the results.

When she came by in February, she was wearing a sweater and beamed, "Well, what do you think?" To tell you the truth, I couldn't tell the difference!

Breast augmentation and reduction procedures are not without problems. Both procedures carry a risk of scarring and loss of sensation in the nipples. Both procedures also can result in the inability to breastfeed. Major weight gain can influence both procedures and undo the effects of breast reduction.

Areola and Nipple

At the end of the breast is a ring of darker skin called the **areola**. In the center of the areola is the nipple. The areola is slightly rougher in texture than the rest of the breast because it contains oil glands that help lubricate the nipples during breastfeeding. The areola also contains small muscles and many nerve endings. This makes it highly responsive to sexual stimulation. Nursing mothers also report that suckling their babies can cause sensual feelings that can be a source of confusion.

The nipple is located within the areola and contains smooth muscle fibers, milk ducts, and many nerve endings. The nipples and areola are highly sensitive, and their smooth muscle fibers can contract upon stimulation, causing them to stiffen and become erect. Nipples also can stiffen and become erect in response to cold and nonsexual tactile stimulation.

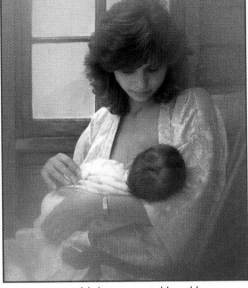

Nursing establishes a special bond between mother and child, as well as supplying all the food the newborn needs.

Areola
brownish or pink ring of tissue surrounding the nipple of the breast

Case Study

Cindy's Feelings About Nursing

Cindy, 25 years old, recently gave birth to her first child, Cara. After carefully reviewing the literature about the benefits and convenience, Cindy decided to breastfeed Cara. Recently she has been having some misgivings about her decision.

I guess it came as a shock that I would actually enjoy the sensations associated with nursing Cara. I had talked with other nursing moms, and they all raved about the special feelings of bonding and physical intimacy that came along with nursing. I definitely feel this. I don't think I've ever felt as close or nurturing as when Cara is nursing.

What I'm talking about, though, is different. It isn't a sexual feeling. Maybe sensual is a better way to describe it. My breasts swell and my nipples engorge, and the warm, tingly feeling of nursing is

very satisfying. It's not like when my husband plays with and sucks on my breasts. That's different. That gets me very excited and makes me want to have sex with him. I don't feel that way when I nurse, but I definitely enjoy the physical sensations as well as the nurturing part.

(Cindy was very troubled by these feelings at first and went to her midwife to talk about them.)

I was a little worried about this at first. I thought maybe something was wrong with me, you know, enjoying this so much. My midwife assured me that this is normal, and some women even experience orgasm while nursing. She explained that this is a special feeling nursing mothers experience. It is definitely sensual and normal.

INTERNAL FEMALE SEXUAL STRUCTURES

The internal structures of the female anatomy includes the vagina, uterus, cervix, fallopian tubes, and ovaries (Figure 3.5).

Vagina

Vagina
tubular organ connecting to the uterus, which serves both reproductive and erotic functions

The **vagina** is a thin-walled muscular tube, about 3 to 4 inches long, lying between the bladder and the rectum, which connects to the cervix at one end and opens up to the outside of the body at the other. The vagina is tilted upward at a 45-degree angle extending toward the small of the back.

The walls of the vagina contain an outer layer of muscular tissue and an inner layer of mucous membrane. The mucous membrane tissue produces a thin, clear, moderately acidic (pH 3.5–4) discharge that provides an efficient self-cleaning mechanism. During sexual arousal, these same tissues engorge with blood and weep, producing a thin, slippery lubrication that reduces friction and facilitates intercourse.

The outer third of the vagina contains the most muscle tissue and nerve endings. The interior and rear part, which connects with the cervix, is relatively devoid of nerve endings. In the unaroused state the vagina resembles a collapsed space similar to a balloon without

In the unaroused state the walls of the vagina represent a potential space similar to the sides of a balloon before it is blown up.

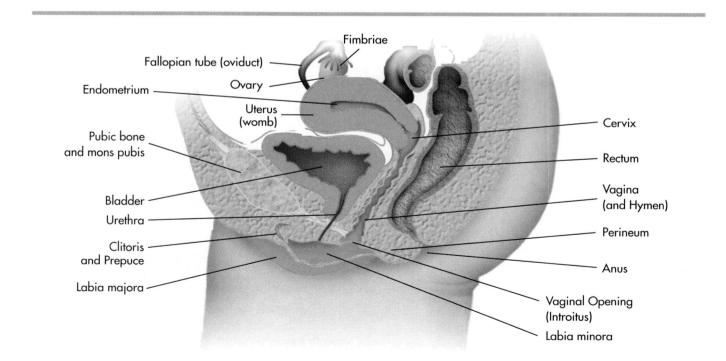

Source: *Personal Health: Perspectives and Lifestyles*, by Patricia A. Floyd, Sandra E. Mimms, and Caroline Yelding-Howard (Englewood, CO: Morton, 1998) p. 96.

Figure 3.5   Internal female sexual structures.

air in it. During sexual arousal the vagina expands, accommodating objects of varying sizes ranging from a tampon, penis, or sex toy to a newborn's head.

Myths and stories allude to male or female partners being incompatible: "He's too big for me," "she's to loose for him," and so on. Women can improve the tone of the vaginal and pelvic muscles used during sex by doing Kegel exercises.[2]

The vagina is also known as the birth canal because of its function as the exit point for the newborn during childbirth. The vagina has both reproductive and sexual-pleasuring functions. Unlike the penis, the vagina is not involved during urination. Urine is excreted through the urethra, whose opening is located above the vaginal opening in the introitus.

Uterus

The **uterus** is an organ that is sized and shaped like a pear. It is connected to the vagina at its narrow end. The end, or cervix, of the uterus is attached to the vagina and protrudes into the end of the vaginal canal. The wider end (the fundus) extends backward and is held in place by a broad uterine ligament. The uterus is tipped slightly forward.

The uterus is composed of three layers of tissue. The innermost layer is called the **endometrium**. The endometrium undergoes a cycle of transformation each menstrual period as it prepares for implantation of a fertilized egg. The endometrium is where a fertilized egg implants and grows during pregnancy. If fertilization does not occur, the endometrium breaks down and is shed during menstruation.

Uterus
womb

Endometrium
inner lining of uterus

Health Hint

Pelvic-Floor (Kegel) Exercises

You can practice contracting your pelvic-floor muscles to prevent or reduce sagging of the organs and urinary incontinence (losing urine when you cough, sneeze, or laugh), to strengthen your orgasms, and to prepare for childbirth. If done regularly, these exercises can help prevent prolapse of the uterus (falling uterus into a stretched vagina, which has lost its muscle tone), cystocele (a bulge of the bladder into the vagina) and rectocele (bulge of the rectum into the vagina).

A good way to locate these muscles is to spread your legs apart while urinating to start and stop the flow of urine. Your ability to do this is one indication of how strong your muscles are. Another method is to try tightening against a man's erect penis during intercourse (this will feel pleasant to him and can help to enhance your pleasure, too).

Begin exercising these muscles by contracting hard for a second and then releasing completely. Repeat this 10 times in a row to make up one group of exercises (this takes about 20 seconds). In a month's time, try to work up to 20 groups during one day (about 7 minutes total). You can do this at any time — sitting in a car or bus, talking on the telephone, or even as a "wake-up" exercise.

Some of us have noticed improved muscle tone (and occasionally increased pleasure during intercourse) in just several weeks. For more detailed instruction on Kegel exercises, consult your local childbirth group.

Source: "Sexual Function of the Pubococcus Muscle," by A. Kegel, *Western Journal of Surgery, Obstetrics, and Gynecology*, 60 (1952), 521–524.

Myometrium
muscular, middle layer of uterus

The next layer of tissue, the **myometrium**, makes up the bulk of the uterus. This is thick muscular tissue capable of providing the powerful contractions necessary to dislodge endometrial tissue during menstruation or deliver a developed fetus during childbirth. This layer is capable of expanding the size of the uterus from that of a pear, pre-pregnancy, to a small watermelon during pregnancy, and then returning to near its original size within 2 months after birth.

Often, the myometrial contractions associated with menstruation can cause dysmenorrhea, which results in severe cramping and pain. At the end of this chapter, we will discuss self-help strategies to reduce these and other symptoms associated with menstrual discomfort. The third and outermost layer of uterine tissue is called the **perimetrium**.

Perimetrium
outer lining of uterus

Cervix

Cervix
neck of the uterus, which extends into inner end of vagina

The **cervix** is described as the neck of the uterus. It resembles a small ring or button, the center portion tightly contracted and blocked with a plug of mucus. Running through the cervix is the cervical canal, a small passageway connecting the vagina to the uterus. It is filled with irregularly shaped spaces called crypts. The cervical opening, or *cervical os* remains closed and blocked with mucus during most of a woman's menstrual cycle. As a woman's fertile time approaches, the mucous plug thins, allowing a passageway through the cervix into the uterus. Figure 3.6 shows the cervix and related structures.

T-zone
transformation zone of cervix, where columnar epithelial tissue of uterus meets with squamous tissue of vagina

During adolescence the tissue of the cervix changes, or transforms. This transformation zone is referred to as the **T-zone**. Cervical tissue (columnar

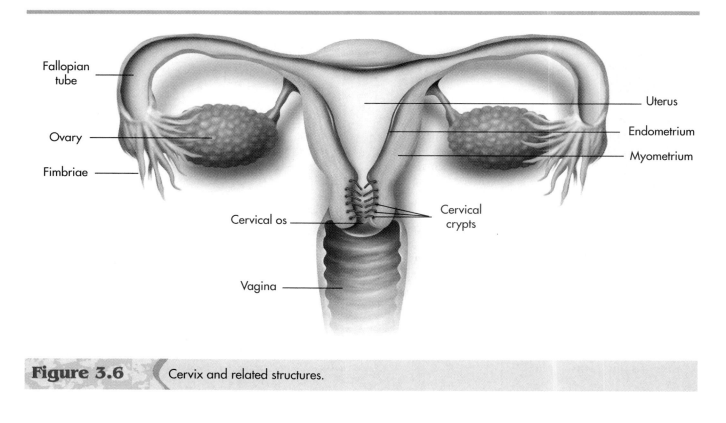

Fallopian tube

Ovary

Fimbriae

Uterus

Endometrium

Myometrium

Cervical os

Cervical crypts

Vagina

Figure 3.6 Cervix and related structures.

PERSPECTIVES

The Pelvic Exam: A View from the Other Side

For many women, the pelvic examination is a visit they don't look forward to. Draped from the waist down, lying on their back on the exam table with their feet in stirrups, legs spread wide apart, vulva completely exposed, they wait, feeling vulnerable.

Even when performed by the most sensitive of clinicians, the pelvic examination can be uncomfortable. The examination is designed to allow the clinician to visually and manually examine a woman's internal and external sexual anatomy. To facilitate this examination, a speculum is used to spread the walls of the vagina, and a light is used to illuminate the vaginal walls and cervix.

The examination consists of looking at the vulva and internal structures for any abnormalities — unusual growths, erosions, lumps, rashes, or discharges. After visually examining the area, the clinician manually probes the various structures, feeling for any changes in size or shape. A bimanual examination means using two hands to palpate structures such as the cervix, uterus, fallopian tubes, and ovaries. During this procedure, the clinician places one hand on the patient's abdomen and inserts two fingers from the other hand into the vagina. The clinician then feels for any abnormalities. Often these palpations will cause pain if disease is present.

Patient-centered clinicians take extra time and care to prepare patients for what is about to happen. They explain each procedure before it is done, helping the patient adjust to the probes and prods that are part of the examination. They also offer patients the option to see what is happening through the use of floor and hand-held mirrors. Little things such as warming a speculum before inserting it and helping patients relax with breathing exercises can go a long way toward making the examination less offensive.

epithelial tissue) is different from vaginal tissue (squamous mucous membrane tissue). During childhood, a young girl's cervix is covered with more columnar epithelial tissue than squamous tissue. As she matures, the amount of exposed columnar epithelial tissue decreases. The T-zone becomes smaller, encompassing the cervix and cervical canal. The T-zone is the area most commonly infected by gonorrhea, chlamydia, and other sexually transmitted diseases during unprotected vaginal sexual intercourse. Because columnar epithelial tissue seems much more susceptible than squamous tissue to STD infection, all women (particularly young women) who are having vaginal intercourse should protect this area with barrier contraceptives.

The cervix is also a common site for the development of cancer in women. STD infection of the T-zone in young women can be a precursor of cervical cancer in later life. This is particularly true of infection with viral organisms (human papilloma virus, herpes simplex virus) introduced into the cervix during adolescence. It literally lays the seeds for the development of cervical cancer that appears a decade or more later.

When viruses invade the cervix, they create a seeding effect for future changes in tissue.

Fallopian Tubes

The two **fallopian tubes**, also known as oviducts and uterine tubes, approximately 4 inches long, stretch from either side of the fundus of the uterus to the ovaries. Unlike the male vas deferens, which connects to the epididymis,

Fallopian tubes
also called oviducts, extending from fundus of uterus to ovaries. They serve as the passageway for the ova

the fallopian tubes do not actually connect with the ovary. Each fallopian tube stops just short of the ovary, and is held in place with ligaments that attach it to the peritoneum cavity. The open end of the fallopian tube is funnel-shaped, with fingerlike projections called fimbriae, which shroud but do not connect with the ovaries. The fallopian tubes are made up of smooth muscle tissue and are lined with hairlike projections called cilia.

During ovulation, an egg released from the ovary is drawn into the fimbriae of its surrounding fallopian tube. No one knows for sure how this happens, but once inside the tube, the egg is whisked along by a combination of smooth-muscle contractions and the wave-like action of the cilia. Figure 3.7 shows how the female egg develops and moves.

Fallopian-tube cilia are highly susceptible to destruction from infection. Destruction of these cilia is a common byproduct of infection with gonorrhea or chlamydia. Once the cilia are destroyed, they do not grow back. This can result in infertility or **ectopic pregnancy** because loss of cilia affects the speed and movement of ova. For the egg to be fertilized and implanted within the uterus, a ripe ova must reach a viable sperm within 24 hours.

Ectopic pregnancy
implantation of egg outside the womb

Ovaries

The **ovaries** are the size and shape of almonds. Each is located adjacent to a fallopian tube and is held in place in the peritoneum by connective tissue that anchors them to the broad uterine ligament. Like the male testes, the ovaries have two primary functions: fertility and hormone production. The ovaries produce ova (eggs), and the two important female sex hormones, estrogen and progesterone.

Ovaries
two almond-shaped structures that contain and release ova and secrete the hormones estrogen and progesterone

REPRODUCTIVE PHYSIOLOGY

Two distinct cycles — the menstrual (also known as uterine) and ovarian — work in concert to control reproduction. Each cycle is regulated by hormones secreted by various endocrine glands. These cycles and their respective hormones are introduced here, and described in greater detail in Chapter 13, Human Reproduction.

Ovarian Cycle

Unlike male sperm, which are freshly produced in unlimited numbers, women are born with approximately 400,000 immature ova in each ovary. The health and viability of the ova are affected by age and various environmental factors. Exposure to radiation, toxic chemicals, and other hazards can impair the health of the ova. In general, the viability of ova declines with age.

In a normal cycle, one immature egg matures, is released, and either is fertilized or dies and is discarded with the menstrual flow. This three-phased process is called the **ovarian cycle** (see Figure 3.8). Each cycle has a follicular, ovulatory, and luteal phase. In a typical 28-day cycle (cycles vary significantly; a 28-day average cycle was chosen for the purpose of illustration).

Ovarian cycle
a three-phased period of time covering maturation of a follicle, release of ovum, and secreting role of corpus luteum

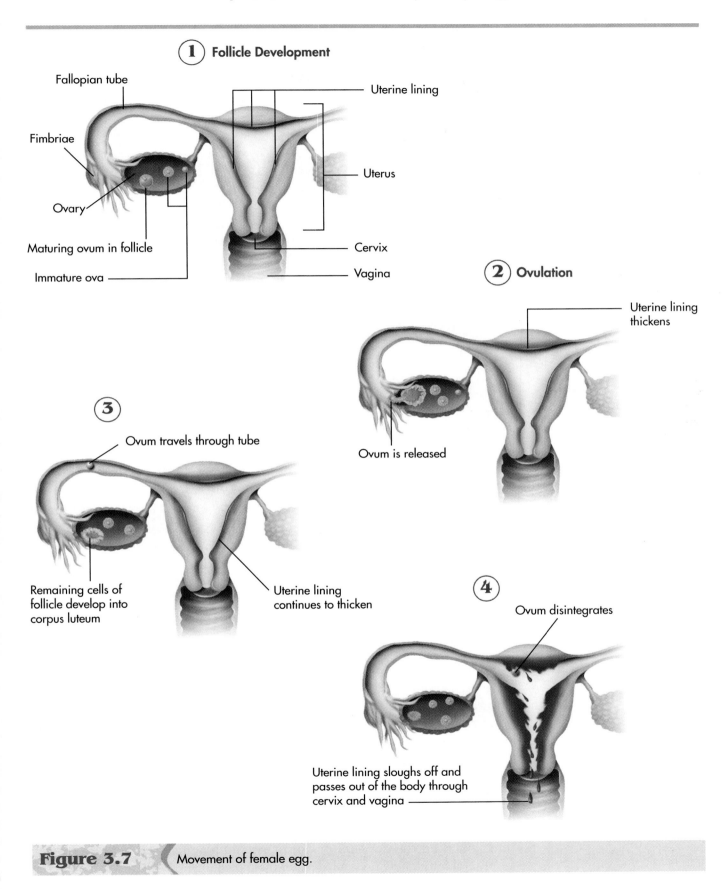

Figure 3.7   Movement of female egg.

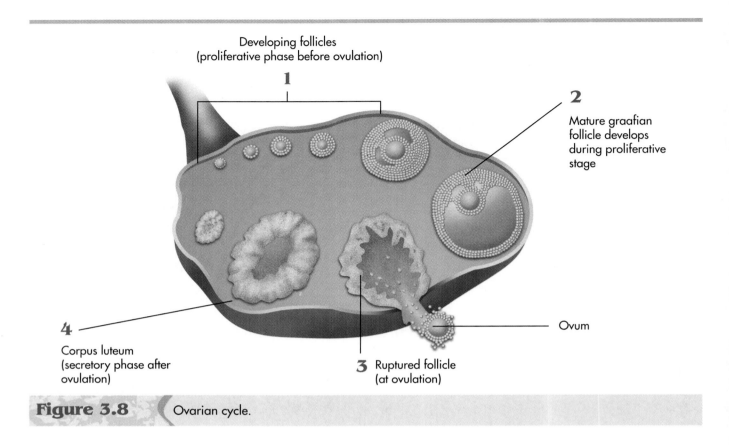

Developing follicles
(proliferative phase before ovulation)

1

2

Mature graafian
follicle develops
during proliferative
stage

Ovum

4

Corpus luteum
(secretory phase after
ovulation)

3 Ruptured follicle
(at ovulation)

Figure 3.8   Ovarian cycle.

Follicle
an egg sac in the ovary

Corpus luteum
the follicle after it has released its
ovum and begins to produce
progesterone

1. The *follicular phase* consists of the first 10 days. During this time a **follicle** grows, preparing to release a mature egg.

2. The *ovulatory phase*, days 11–14, consists of final preparation for and release of a mature egg.

3. The *luteal phase*, days 14–28, revolves around the activity of the **corpus luteum**. The corpus luteum's role of secreting progesterone to sustain the rich endometrial lining necessary for implantation varies depending upon whether fertilization occurs.

Menstrual or Uterine Cycle

Although the main function of the uterus is to house the implanted and developing embryo, the cyclic nature of reproduction allows this for only a few short days each month. The menstrual cycle coincides perfectly with the ovarian cycle to ensure the union of sperm and egg at the best possible time to enhance successful implantation in the endometrium. The phases of the menstrual cycle are depicted in Figure 3.9.

Menstrual Phase

During the menstrual phase, which lasts approximately 3 to 5 days, the uterus sheds its endometrial lining. The strong muscles of the uterus contract and slough off the rich network of tissue and blood vessels built up to support fetal implantation and development. The cervix dilates to allow the bloody menstrual flow to work its way out of the uterus and through the vagina, where can be absorbed by tampons or sanitary napkins.

Proliferative Phase

During this phase of the menstrual cycle, the uterine lining rebuilds. The endometrium literally proliferates with a rich network of tissue and blood vessels, preparing the uterus for pregnancy. To support a pregnancy, the lining must be thick enough and endowed with the complex network of blood vessels necessary to sustain successful implantation and development of an embryo for the 9 months of prenatal development. During the build-up the endometrium relies on a constant source of the hormone estrogen. This phase takes about 9 days and ends with ovulation.

Secretory Phase

The secretory phase begins with ovulation and lasts about 14 days or until the onset of the menstrual phase. The secretory phase is divided into two parts. During the first half of the phase, the uterus prepares for implantation of a fertilized ovum. Luteinizing hormone (LH), secreted by the pituitary gland triggers the ruptured ovarian corpus luteum to secrete high levels of progesterone. This extra progesterone mixes with estrogen, causing the endometrium to thicken even more and become engorged with blood vessels.

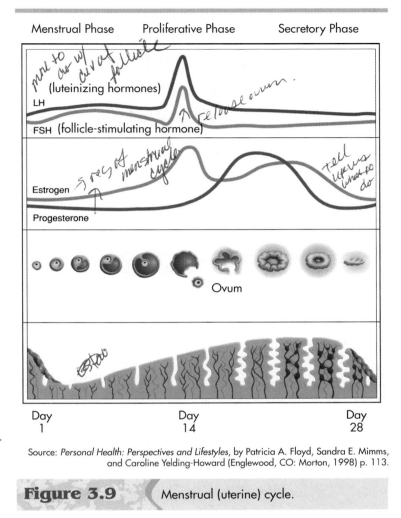

Source: *Personal Health: Perspectives and Lifestyles*, by Patricia A. Floyd, Sandra E. Mimms, and Caroline Yelding-Howard (Englewood, CO: Morton, 1998) p. 113.

Figure 3.9 Menstrual (uterine) cycle.

If fertilization does not occur, the second phase of the secretory cycle begins with a decline in estrogen, LH, and progesterone levels. The corpus luteum degenerates, and the endometrium begins to die, ultimately leading to its sloughing off during the menstrual phase.

COMMON DISORDERS OF FEMALE SEXUAL ANATOMY

A variety of disorders can affect female sexual anatomy and physiology. Among the most common are endometriosis, uterine fibroid tumors, fibrocystic breast disease, breast cancer, vaginitis, premenstrual syndrome (PMS), and dysmenorrhea. Some women develop cancer of the cervix, endometrium of the uterus, or ovaries, resulting in the removal of those structures. We consider menopause a normal part of a woman's aging process and not a disorder. Therefore, it is discussed within Chapter 6, Adult Sexuality.

Endometriosis

Endometriosis
a condition in which pieces of the endometrium migrate to the fallopian tubes, ovaries, or abdominal cavity

Cysts
an abnormal condition of fluid-filled sacs that can burst and cause pain and scarring

Adhesions
spiderweblike bands of scar tissue that painfully bind internal organs to each other or the abdominal wall

Laparoscope
a medical instrument made up of a tube with a light that permits examination of reproductive structures, requiring only a small abdominal incision

Endometriosis is a disorder of the endometrium resulting from migration of the byproducts of menstruation into the fallopian tubes, ovaries, and abdominal cavity. The shed endometrial tissue, called implants, adheres to these structures and continues to respond to the effects of hormones during the menstrual cycle. They swell, bleed, and may form **cysts** that can burst, resulting in scar tissue and painful **adhesions**.

The most common symptoms of endometriosis are sharp pain, cramps, and heavy bleeding during menstruation. Some women have chronic pelvic or low back pain or a feeling of pressure during sexual intercourse. If the endometrial implants spread to the bladder or bowel, this can cause painful elimination and blood in the urine or feces. In some cases, endometriosis can cause infertility.

Endometriosis is diagnosed through a combination of history of signs and symptoms and visual examination. An instrument called a **laparoscope**, a flexible tube with a light, is used to locate and examine the implants internally. The abdomen is inflated with carbon dioxide gas, a small incision is made near the navel, and the tube is inserted. The physician can examine the abdomen through the laparoscope, find the exact location of the implants, and determine the extent of the problem.

Several forms of treatment are available for endometriosis. They depend on the extent of the problem, the woman's age, and several other considerations. The least invasive treatments involve hormonal or drug therapies to temporarily halt ovulation and menstruation, resulting in the shrinkage and eventual disappearance of the implants. Surgical removal of the implants and the scar tissue is a more invasive treatment. In extreme circumstances, radical surgery is done to remove the uterus, ovaries, and fallopian tubes.

Uterine Fibroid Tumors

Uterine fibroid tumors
noncancerous solid growths on the endometrium

Hysterectomy
surgical removal of uterus. In practice, a hysterectomy often is accompanied by surgical removal of fallopian tubes, and sometimes the ovaries as well

Myomectomy
surgical procedure that removes fibroid tumors without removing the uterus

Uterine fibroid tumors are masses of muscle and connective tissue growing in the uterus. These noncancerous tumors are one of the most common disorders of female sexual anatomy in the United States. One in four women is affected, and uterine fibroid tumors are the reason for approximately 30% of all hysterectomies performed in the United States.[3] Women's health experts continue to debate whether **hysterectomy** is the best or only treatment option. A less radical procedure, **myomectomy**, involves removing the fibroids but preserving the uterus, thereby allowing for subsequent pregnancy.

Small tumors usually do not produce noticeable symptoms. As they grow, they begin to take up more space within the uterus and begin to produce symptoms. The most common symptom of fibroid tumors is unusually heavy menstrual bleeding, followed by pressure or pain in the abdomen. If the tumor gets very large (tumors can grow to be as large as a softball), it begins to put pressure on the bladder, causing urinary problems. The tumor can actually push against the stomach, making the woman look pregnant. Large tumors, and the heavy and prolonged bleeding they cause, can cause anemia, resulting in fatigue and other symptoms.

Uterine fibroid tumors are diagnosed in a variety of ways, depending upon their location and size. A routine pelvic exam can detect some fibroid tumors. Ultrasound, x-ray, laparoscopy, and a variety of other diagnostic procedures are used to diagnose the rest of the cases.

Treatment depends upon a variety of factors including the size of the tumor, its location, the woman's age, the woman's desire to bear children, and others. Small tumors often are removed through surgery. Some of the larger tumors cannot be removed. In these cases, hysterectomy is recommended. Drug therapies that block the production of estrogen also are used. These treatments mimic the effects of menopause, which seem to have a beneficial effect on fibroid tumors. Fibroid tumors may grow less rapidly and shrink during menopause because estrogen production ceases. Unfortunately, the tumors begin to grow back once the therapy is discontinued and estrogen production resumes.

Fibrocystic Breast Disease

Fibrocystic breast disease is a disorder involving the swelling, and resulting "lumpy" configuration, of breast tissue. The breasts, like the uterus, change as ovulation and menstruation approach. The secretory cells surrounding the mammary ducts secrete fluids that seep into the fibrous connective tissue in the lower parts of the breast, and breast tissue swells. This fluid sometimes creates pockets of fluid that appear to be cysts.

Normally, the fluid in these pockets drains from the breast tissue through the lymph system and **lymph nodes** under the breast. Fibrocystic breast condition occurs when the breasts are unable to fully drain this fluid. It results in swollen, firm, or hardened fibrous breast tissue.

Lymph nodes
the main drainage and filtration sites in the lymph system

Sometimes the inability to drain the breasts fully results in permanent cysts or tumors. Of all cysts and tumors, 80% are benign (noncancerous). Cysts, also known as **fibroadenomas,** are less common than tumors. These lumps are small, round, and move around freely under the skin. Even though fibroadenomas are noncancerous, they can be a source of distress for women because they are often confused with cancerous lumps. Depending upon their size and number, the lumps can cause symptoms ranging from tenderness and mild discomfort to severe discomfort.

Fibroadenomas
benign, solid tumors associated with fibrocystic breast disorder

Fibrocystic breast condition and fibroadenomas are diagnosed through physical examination and laboratory testing. All swelling and lumps should be approached as potentially cancerous until cancer is ruled out when the lumps disappear or biopsy and testing prove negative. This is often difficult for women to do because of the fear associated with breast cancer and the tendency to deny that the lumps exist, despite the fact that more than half of all women have them.

All lumps should be considered potentially cancerous until proven otherwise.

Breast Cancer

Breast cancer develops when cancerous cells proliferate, causing one or more tumors. Because breast cancer cells are of different types, the form of cancer a woman has may have more to do with her survival than how early or late her cancer has been detected. Tumors may metastasize, with malignant cells spreading throughout the body in lymph fluid and the bloodstream.

Breast cancer is the second leading cause of deaths from cancer in women, surpassed only by lung cancer. An estimated 175,000 new cases of breast cancer will be diagnosed in U.S. women in 1999, with 43,700 women dying of the disease.[4]

The major risk factors for breast cancer in women are: family history of breast cancer (mother or sister infected with the disease), family history of other cancers, and previous personal history of cancer. Other risk factors include late childbearing (first child after 30 years old), early onset of menstruation, late menopause, and a history of fibrocystic breast disease. Risk factors that are less strongly associated with breast cancer are: diet high in saturated fat, body composition (excess fatty deposits in waist and hips), excessive alcohol consumption, and hormone replacement therapy (HRT).

Within the past few years, the public has begun to hear that if a woman carries mutations of either BRCA1 or the BRCA2 gene, she may be at great risk for developing either breast or ovarian cancer. Although much more research is needed to clearly assess the contribution of these two genes to the incidence of breast and ovarian cancers, some women want to be screened. Genetic screening then can be followed by prophylactic mastectomy and hysterectomy, a radical attempt at maintaining health.

Women need to play an active role in maintaining the health of their breasts. Menstruation, pregnancy, and menopause can all affect how the breast appears and feels. To check for the possibility of breast cancer, women need to learn to conduct a breast self-exam (BSE). The American Cancer Society recommends that a BSE be conducted monthly, and that women 20–39 years of age have a clinical breast exam performed by a

---

Health Hint

Reducing the Risks for Breast Cancer

Although many of the risks for breast cancer (family history of cancer or breast cancer, age of onset of menstruation, menopause) can't be modified, you can do several things to minimize your cancer risk, regardless of your personal history.

1. Evaluate your family history of cancer (family members afflicted with breast and other cancers).
2. Evaluate your personal history (onset of menstruation, menopause, body composition).

3. Practice breast self-exam (early detection improves diagnosis, treatment, and survival).
4. Have a mammogram every year starting at age 40 if you have no major cancer risks or at age 35 if you are at high risk (have a history of mother/sister with the disease, symptoms or a history of fibrocystic breast disease, etc.).
5. Modify minor risk factors (reduce body and dietary fat; minimize alcohol consumption).

Health Hint

How to Examine Your Breasts

1

Lie down with a pillow under your right shoulder and place your right arm behind your head.

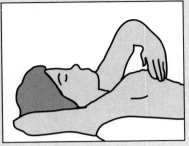

2

Use the finger pads of the three middle fingers on your left hand to feel for lumps in the right breast.

3

Press firmly enough to know how your breast feels. A firm ridge in the lower curve of each breast is normal. If you're not sure how hard to press, talk with your doctor or nurse.

4

Move around the breast in a circular, up and down line, or wedge pattern. Be sure to do it the same way every time, check the entire breast area, and remember how your breast feels from month to month.

5

Repeat the exam on your left breast, using the finger pads of the right hand. (Move the pillow to under your left shoulder.)

6

If you find any changes, see your doctor right away.

7

Repeat the examination of both breasts while standing, with your one arm behind your head. The upright position makes it easier to check the upper and outer part of the breasts (toward your armpit). This is where about half of breast cancers are found. You may want to do the standing part of the BSE while you are in the shower. Some breast changes can be felt more easily when your when your skin is wet and soapy.

For added safety, you can check your breasts for any dimpling of the skin, changes in the nipple, redness, or swelling while standing in front of a mirror right after your BSE each month.

*Please note that a breast self-examination should not be considered a substitute for a regular mammogram.

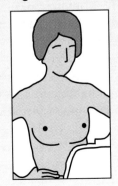
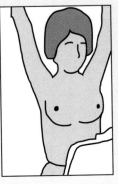

Source: American Cancer Society, Atlanta, GA. Reprinted with permission.

A mammogram can detect breast lumps too small to feel during breast self-exam.
Source: American Cancer Society Inc.
Reprinted with permission.

health care professional every 3 years. Mammograms, which are x-rays of the breast, are recommended annually for women 40 years of age and older.

If breast cancer is diagnosed, women should discuss the various treatment options with their physicians. More and more women are able to have a lumpectomy, which is removal of the tumor, rather than a mastectomy, which is removal of the breast. Both treatments may require radiation therapy and chemotherapy afterward to help prevent further spread of any errant cells.

Vaginitis

Vaginitis
inflammation and irritation of the vagina

In **vaginitis**, the vagina becomes inflamed, resulting in one or more of the following symptoms: discharge, dryness, burning upon urination (if the inflammation spreads into the urethral opening), and pain during intercourse. The discharge associated with vaginitis is often overlooked or mistaken for a woman's normal vaginal fluid. Three characteristics of vaginal discharge — quantity, color, and odor — can vary in response to vaginitis. The discharge associated with vaginitis is usually profuse (quantity), ranging from frothy white to greenish yellow (color), and changes from a woman's normal scent to a foul, even fishy-smelling odor. Sometimes vaginitis causes vaginal dryness instead of discharge. This unusual dryness results in pain.

The urethra can become inflamed either as a result of the discharge or unusual dryness. When the urethra is inflamed, urination is painful. Painful intercourse is another common symptom of vaginitis.

Vaginitis is diagnosed through a combination of clinical examination and laboratory tests. Various forms of vaginitis have different combinations of symptoms. An experienced clinician often can make the diagnosis based on the symptoms. Microscopic examination of vaginal fluids makes the diagnosis more precise and allows the clinician to treat the patient more effectively. In some cases a specimen is taken from the vagina or cervix and is grown on a biological culture plate, with the results available within 1 week.

Various prescription drugs and over-the-counter medications are available to treat the different forms of vaginitis. Antibiotics are used with vaginitis caused by bacteria (E-coli, gonorrhea). Antifungal agents are used to treat vaginitis attributable to yeast overgrowth (monilia, candida albicans). Other agents (*trichomonas vaginalis*) necessitate the use of other types of drugs. Self-treatment of vaginitis (especially involving douching) is not recommended without an accurate diagnosis of the condition.

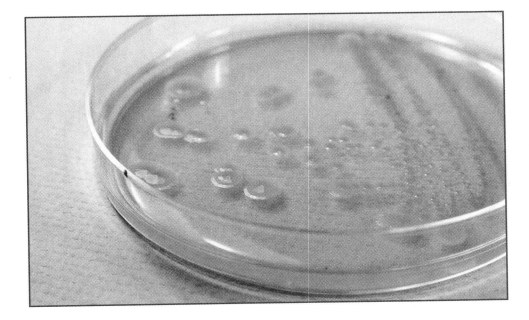

A culture plate serves as a growth medium for a variety of infectious agents.

Health Hint

Promoting Optimal Vaginal Health

1. Wash the vulva daily with warm, soapy water.
2. Avoid douching.
3. If you have to douche, use a vinegar in water solution.
4. Avoid using talcum powder on the vulva.
5. Be careful about what you insert into your vagina (make sure all sex toys and other objects are safe and clean before inserting them).
6. Do not progress from anal intercourse to vaginal intercourse (a common way to transfer germs from the rectum to the vagina) without first washing your partner's penis.
7. Never force vaginal penetration (make sure your vagina is well lubricated before inserting anything into it).
8. Become familiar with the amount, consistency, color, and odor of your normal daily discharge.
9. If the discharge changes, see a health care provider.

PERSPECTIVES

The Female Hygiene Industry

U. S. culture has spawned a multimillion-dollar business concerning vaginal care. Women have been convinced that they need to take special steps to ensure a clean and fresh-smelling vagina. The feminine hygiene industry has effectively convinced women (and men, too!) that the average vagina needs cosmetic help to be healthy and sexy. Nothing could be farther from the truth.

The vagina is actually a self-cleansing structure. To ensure vaginal health, the average, healthy woman needs to do nothing more than shower or bathe daily, (making sure to wash the vulva). She has no need to douche, wear mini-pads (if not menstruating), or use feminine hygiene sprays to perfume the vaginal area.

The walls of a normal, healthy vagina produce a thin, clear, slippery discharge that cleanses the vaginal lining. This discharge turns brownish when exposed to air. A small amount of this brownish discharge seeps out of the vagina and can be noticed on underwear. This does not indicate any problem. The discharge and the vagina in general have a characteristic musky odor. Sex partners often consider this odor erotic.

Changes in the amount, consistency, color, and odor can be used to assess whether you have a vaginal infection. If the amount of discharge increases, changes in color (from clear to yellow, green, or white), consistency (from thin and slippery to thick and curdish), or odor (becomes foul smelling), it could indicate a vaginal infection.

Ironically, feminine hygiene products can be a source of vaginal irritation and infection. Douches and vaginal perfumes alter the delicate balance of vaginal pH. This allows organisms such as monilia (yeast), which can normally live in the vagina, to overgrow and cause problems. Feminine hygiene products can wash away protective, lubricating vaginal secretions, causing the vagina to dry out.

Many women are allergic to the chemicals in feminine hygiene products and experience itching, burning, and irritation when exposed to them. A simple, inexpensive vinegar-and-water douche can be used if a health care provider deems necessary.

Cervical Cancer

Cervical cancer is the end stage of cervical dysplasia. Also known as cervical intraepithelial neoplasia (CIN), it is more common than both breast and uterine cancers. The good news is that it is almost 100% curable if detected early. Early detection of cervical cancer also can prevent its spread into the uterus. Early changes in the cells lining the cervix can be detected through a procedure called the Pap test. Pap test results are graded on the following 5-point scale;

Class 1: no abnormalities

Class 2: atypical benign symptoms of early CIN

Class 3: advanced CIN

Class 4: cancer *in situ*

Class 5: invasive cervical cancer

The Pap smear is the most reliable tool for detecting cervical cancer early. A Pap smear involves taking a specimen of cells from the cervix and usually is included as part of a routine pelvic exam. Cells are obtained by gently scraping the cervix with a small wooden spatula to dislodge the tissue and then smearing it onto a microscope slide. The slide is stained and examined under a microscope for abnormal cellular changes.

Health Hint

Reducing the Risks for Cervical Cancer

The major risk factors for cervical cancer are:

- early onset of intercourse (beginning in early adolescence)
- lifetime number of sexual partners (risks increase as numbers increase)
- history of STD infection (particularly viral STDs such as HPV and HSV)
- not using barrier contraception (condoms, diaphragm, etc.).

To lessen your risk:

1. Delay onset of intercourse (women who begin having intercourse after age 20 have a lower risk).
2. Reduce your number of total sexual partners (having one, uninfected sex partner is lowest risk).
3. Use barrier contraceptives (male and female condoms work best) to protect the T-zone.
4. Starting at age 18 or once you've begun having intercourse (whichever comes first), have an annual pelvic examination that includes a Pap test (this will ensure early detection and treatment of cancer).

Uterine Cancer

Uterine cancer usually affects the endometrial lining. Early symptoms include abnormal bleeding or spotting. An estimated 37,400 new cases will be diagnosed during 1999.[5] Risk factors for uterine cancer include estrogen replacement therapy (ERT) used during menopause, early menarche, late menopause, never having had children, and history of failure to ovulate. Pregnancy and the use of oral contraceptives provide protection against endometrial cancer.

The Pap test rarely detects endometrial cancer. Consequently, annual pelvic exams and the use of endometrial biopsy around the time of menopause are relied upon for diagnosis. If endometrial cancer is found, hysterectomy, radiation, and chemotherapy are the preferred treatments.

Ovarian Cancer

Even though ovarian cancer accounts for only 4% of all cancers among women, it results in more deaths than any cancer of the reproductive system because symptoms do not appear until later in its development. Women may experience abdominal enlargement and digestive disturbances such as persistent stomach discomfort and gas that cannot be explained by other causes.

An estimated 25,200 new cases were projected for U.S. women in 1999.[6] The early and well publicized experiences of comedienne Gilda Radner, a popular figure on the television program Saturday Night Live, did much to bring public attention to this disease.

As with breast cancer, current research is focusing on mutations in the BRCA1 and BRCA2 genes as risk factors for ovarian cancer. Pregnancy and the use of oral contraceptives are thought to reduce the risk of developing ovarian cancer. Once diagnosed, women undergo a hysterectomy, followed by radiation and various chemotherapy regimens.

Premenstrual Syndrome (PMS)

Premenstrual syndrome (PMS) is characterized by a myriad of physical and psychological symptoms that appear anywhere within 2 weeks of the onset of menstruation. Psychosocial symptoms include negative emotions such as anxiety, irritability, depression, anger, insomnia, confusion, or social withdrawal. Physical symptoms include fluid retention, breast tenderness, weight gain, headaches, dizziness, nausea, increased appetite, and craving for sweets. Because of the range of symptoms associated with PMS and the number of women affected (between 20% and 75%), many women's health experts are beginning to question whether the syndrome really exists or these are just the normal parameters of the menstrual experience.

Research into the causes, nature, and treatment of PMS lacks consistency. Although most PMS researchers believe that shifting hormonal balances play a key role in the condition, the specific hormones and exact mechanisms of action are unclear. The ratio of estrogen to progesterone has been implicated, along with the level of mineral corticoids that control fluid retention. Still other theorists postulate that the key hormones involved are those of the brain that influence mood.

Premenstrual syndrome (PMS) a condition preceding menstruation, characterized by a myriad of physical and psychological symptoms

Health Hint

Self-Help for PMS

Various treatments are available to help women who have PMS. For years, stress management and dietary changes have been advocated as part of a comprehensive PMS treatment program. Recently, prostaglandin inhibitors have been recommended. The following are some strategies that might work for you:

1. Eat a well-balanced diet high in complex carbohydrates, low in fat, and containing moderate protein. Eat at least three meals a day (it may be preferable to eat many smaller meals). This will provide the best fuel, and an even release of energy throughout the day.

2. Avoid excess sugar and snacks high in sugar and fat. This, coupled with #1, will help avoid the extreme high and low blood sugar levels associated with mood swings.

3. Avoid excess sodium intake (table salt and salt in food). This will help reduce bloating related to fluid retention.

4. Have an orgasm. This can help release pent-up vaginal and uterine muscle tension.

5. Try relaxation activities such as diaphragmatic breathing, imagery, meditation, and systematic muscle relaxation. These activities can help reduce stress and induce relaxation.

6. Have your partner (or a professional) give you a lower-back massage. It will help relieve muscle tension and induce relaxation.

7. Soak in a warm bath, jacuzzi, or hot tub, or apply heat to the abdominal area with a heating pad or water bottle. This will help you relieve muscle tension and induce relaxation.

8. Try antiprostaglandin medications. Prostaglandin inhibitors reduce the intensity and duration of cramps. Mild prostaglandin inhibitors include Ibuprophen (marketed as Motrin). Stronger prescription medications include naproxen (Naprosyn), naproxen sodium (Anaprox), and mefenamic acid (Ponstel).

An interesting aspect of PMS is the relationship between women's moods, attitudes, and emotions, and the physiological symptoms that characterize the syndrome. Researchers are still trying to ascertain whether negative emotions about menstruation and PMS are what trigger the hormonal and other physiological changes associated with the syndrome or whether the physical discomfort is what precipitates the psychological and social distress.

Dysmenorrhea

Often, the myometrial contractions associated with menstruation cause **dysmenorrhea**, which results in severe cramping and pain. As you might recall from our discussion earlier in this chapter, the myometrium is a thick layer of muscular tissue capable of providing the powerful contractions necessary to dislodge endometrial tissue during menstruation or expel a developed fetus during childbirth. Myometrial contractions are triggered by the release of powerful hormones called **prostaglandins**. Dysmenorrhea is often caused by excessively high levels of prostaglandins. This can cause more intense contractions that last longer than usual.

Dysmenorrhea
painful menstruation

Prostaglandins
hormones that can cause muscle contractions and have been associated with menstrual pain

Toxic Shock Syndrome

Toxic shock syndrome (TSS) is caused by infection with the *Staphylococcus aureus bacterium*, an organism that can live in the vagina without threatening a woman's health. Overgrowth of the bacteria, however, can result in TSS, which *is* life-threatening. Toxins produced from TSS infection produce initial symptoms including a sudden high fever (101°F or higher), headache, sore throat with swelling of the mucous membranes, diarrhea, vomiting, muscle aches, and a sunburnlike rash. If untreated, TSS can cause kidney or liver failure resulting in death in about 10% of all cases. If diagnosed early, TSS is easily treated with broad-spectrum antibiotics.

Initial research found that TSS was associated with tampons, especially the super-absorbent type. This led to the removal of Rely-brand tampons from the market. Subsequent studies found that cervical caps, diaphragms,

Health Hint

Reducing the Risk for Toxic Shock Syndrome

To reduce your risk for TSS:
1. Switch from high-absorbency tampons to regular ones.
2. If you have a history of TSS, avoid tampons altogether and switch to sanitary napkins.
3. If you use tampons, change them frequently (three or more times a day), and use sanitary napkins at least once during each 24-hour day you are menstruating.
4. If you have a history of TSS, do not use the sponge, cervical cap, or diaphragm during menstruation without a physician's permission.

and contraceptive sponges also pose a risk for developing TSS if they are used during menstruation. Since first being reported in 1980, the incidence of toxic shock syndrome has continued to decline.

WELLNESS SYNTHESIS

Female wellness, like male wellness, is associated with the six dimensions of wellness.

Physical Well-being

Physical well-being affects healthy sexuality from conception until death. Female sexual anatomy begins to differentiate after the first 6 weeks of gestation. A mother's physical health and lifestyle influence the normal development of her baby. Factors such as prenatal nutrition, drug and alcohol use, and weight management can influence fetal development.

Women often learn to associate health and prevention with sexual activity: "If I'm not sexually-active or pregnant, I don't need to see my physician or get a Pap smear." To ensure optimal physical well-being, girls should be taught about their body and understand issues such as proper hygiene and care and protection of their genitalia. As girls approach puberty, they need to be aware of the changes that will take place in their body and their sexual anatomy and physiology. They need to understand the changes associated with menstruation and fertility, increasing sexual desire, hygiene, prevention of sexually transmitted disease and unintended pregnancy, and breast self-examination.

As women age, fitness, proper nutrition, and weight management all become increasingly important in optimal sexual health. Throughout adulthood, proper functioning of female sexual anatomy, positive body image, and other sexual health issues are affected by the level of physical well-being.

Intellectual Well-being

Understanding how our body works and how to maintain it for optimal performance is critical in healthy sexuality. Women need to understand that proper functioning of the sexual anatomy and physiology is directly related to wellness. This involves learning about the body, staying current on issues related to women's health, and being critical consumers of sexual health studies and products.

Emotional Well-being

Issues related to sexual anatomy and physiology can provoke strong emotions. Our body image can be a source of concern and emotional distress or of contentment and emotional security. Breast size, weight, onset of puberty, and the like can have an impact on our emotional well-being, as well as propensity for conditions such as anorexia and bulimia. Our intellectual resources can provide objective information about sexuality to help us understand and control our emotions.

Mothers can be excellent role models of sexual health for girls.

Social Well-being

Parents can be the greatest resource in their children's understanding of sexual anatomy and physiology and developing healthy lifestyles to optimize sexual functioning. As the primary sex educators, parents can teach daughters about their body, how it works, and what to expect as they grow and age. A mother can be an excellent role model for sexual health for her daughter, by exhibiting proper hygiene and a healthy lifestyle. Older sisters can serve the same function.

Other members of a woman's social environment can help her understand her sexual anatomy and physiology. Friends, peers, teachers, coaches, and others give advice, share information, and help put issues into a broader perspective. As we mature and form intimate sexual relationships, we learn about our sexual anatomy and physiology from our lovers, husbands, and partners. These intimate partners share a concern for our health and well-being and can be a source of information, comfort, and support. These partners also can be harsh critics who undermine self-confidence and self-esteem with negative feedback. Women should confront those who undermine their self-esteem and seek help from those who care. Self-help groups and women's centers fill this need for women who lack a positive support system.

Spiritual Well-being

Spirituality and religiosity have a strong influence on our sexual health and anatomy and physiology. Our spirituality and religiosity also affect our sexual behavior, including decisions regarding masturbation, sexual intercourse, use of contraceptives, and abortion. The decisions we make influence our risks for acquiring STDs, having an unintended pregnancy, and so on. To separate spirituality from morality and subsequent behavior is difficult. Spirituality also helps us cope with issues related to loss, such as hysterectomy, breast cancer, and infertility. Spirituality and faith can make the difference between merely surviving losses or truly learning how to live again and feel whole once more.

Environmental Well-being

Environment can enhance health by providing good role models, a free and open exchange of information and ideas, and access to health products and care. This kind of environment optimizes sexual health.

Conversely, poor role models, a closed, secretive environment, and limited access to information, products, and health care can undermine sexual health.

WEB RESOURCES

American Medical Association — JAMA Woman's Health Information Center

http://www.ama-assn.org/special/womh/womh.htm

A resource for physicians and other health professionals, produced under the direction of an editorial review board of leading women's health authorities. This site has a large selection of readings and information including in-depth articles from major professional sources, abstracts from major articles published in the *Journal of the American Medical Association*, clinical guidelines, resources for contraception information, plus a collection of Web links.

OBGYN.net Women and Patients

http://www.obgyn.net/women/women.htm

Valuable information concerning all areas of women's health with links to many sites. Information covered in this site includes diseases and conditions, interactive tools, health information resources, forums, directories, organizations, publications, and international resources.

Notes

1. L. Barbach, *For Each Other: Sharing Sexual Intimacy* (Garden City, NY: Doubleday.
2. A. Kegel, "Sexual Functions of the Pubococcus Muscle," *Western Journal of Surgery, Obstetrics and Gynecology,* 60(1952), 521–524.
3. P. Floyd, S. Mimms, and C. Yelding-Howard, *Personal Health: Perspectives and Lifestyles* (Englewood, CO: Morton, 1998).
4. American Cancer Society, *1999 Facts and Figures* (Atlanta: ACS, 1999).
5. ACS.
6. ACS.

Student Study Questions

1. What is the proper term for the external female genitalia?

2. What are the components of the external female genitalia?

3. What is the nature of the hymen?

4. How are the clitoris and the penis alike and different?

5. What are the internal structures of the female sexual anatomy?

6. What are the characteristics of the vagina in the normal and aroused states?

7. What is the best way to ensure good vaginal health?

8. a. What are the cervical crypts and the transformation zone?

   b. Describe their significance in the transmission of STDs.

9. How are the ovaries and testes alike and different?

10. What are the phases of the menstrual cycle?

11. What is the role of female sex hormones in female sexuality?

Student Assessment

Body Image: Female

Body image refers to our evaluation and perception of our body, specific body parts and their functioning. It includes the messages (positive and negative) that we tell ourselves about our bodies, our self-esteem and the behaviors and choices we make as a result. The following inventory will help females assess their body image:

Rate each body part listed below using the following scale:

Extremely satisfied 5   satisfied 4   neutral 3   dissatisfied 2   extremely dissatisfied 1

____ 1. eyes	____ 7. weight	____ 13. hands	____ 19. feet
____ 2. ears	____ 8. face	____ 14. height	____ 20. sex organs
____ 3. nose	____ 9. shoulders	____ 15. stomach	____ 21. overall body
____ 4. hair	____ 10. breasts	____ 16. buttocks	
____ 5. teeth	____ 11. arms	____ 17. hips	
____ 6. mouth	____ 12. calves	____ 18. thighs	

Scoring:

105–80   very positive body image   20–40   negative body image
60–80   positive body image   0–20   very negative body image
40–60   ambivalent about your body

Rate each item below, using the following scale:

very comfortable 5   comfortable 4   neutral 3   uncomfortable 2   very uncomfortable 1

____ 22. looking at my nude body in the mirror   ____ 26. being nude when I am around my kids
____ 23. performing self-examinations of my nude body   ____ 27. sunbathing in the nude
____ 24. being nude when I am alone   ____ 28. swimming in the nude
____ 25. being nude when I am with my lover   ____ 29. walking around the house nude

Scoring:

32–40   very comfortable with nudity   12–16   uncomfortable with nudity
21–32   comfortable with nudity   0–12   very uncomfortable with nudity
16–21   ambivalent about nudity

Complete the following sentences:

30. The thing I like best about my body is _____

_____

31. The thing I dislike most about my body is _____

_____

Sexual Identity

4

Major Topics

Student Learning Objectives

After reading this chapter, students will be able to:

- Describe the components of gender development.

- Evaluate the impact of biological, psychological, sociological, and cultural factors on gender development.

- Evaluate the impact of biological, psychological, sociological, and cultural factors on sexual orientation.

- Analyze the similarities and differences in the development of a variety of sexual orientations.

- Discuss the more common forms of gender incongruities.

- Explain gender and sexual identity across different continua.

Biological/anatomical sex
categorizing individuals based primarily upon their reproductive organs, chromosome make-up, and hormone levels; traditionally, one sex is labeled male and the other female

Secondary sex characteristics
physical traits that develop during puberty and signal sexual maturity; examples are developed breasts, armpit and pubic hair, coarse facial hair

Gender identity
one's personal perception and sense of being male, female, or blended

Gender role
the ways we express our gender identity — including appearance, clothing, movement, and life choices

Sexual orientation
one's propensity for romantic and erotic attachments. Heterosexuality refers to attaching to a partner with different anatomy; homosexuality refers to a same-sex partner; bisexuality refers to attaching to both men and women

A basic philosophical question about sexuality is: Why are we the sexual beings we are? Some find a spiritual or religious answer to the question, looking toward their Supreme Being for the answer. Others turn to science and claim factual answers. Some question why, in the late 1990s and into the 21st century, researchers are still embroiled in the "nature versus nurture" controversy. Still others do not even appreciate why the question is being asked in the first place.

Sexual identity is a composite of several variables.

1. **Biological/anatomical sex,** which focuses on the anatomical parts associated most closely with reproductive capabilities and sexual arousal, specifically internal and external reproductive organs. Included as well are the influences of the endocrine system hormones, as reflected in **secondary sex characteristics** and the process of sexual differentiation in the brain.

2. **Gender identity** and **gender role,** the private sense of maleness or femaleness, and the exhibited and shared behaviors that reinforce gender. In the scheme of things, how we see ourselves and express ourselves is expected to correlate with our anatomy.

3. **Sexual orientation,** which defines romantic and erotic attachments in choice of partners. One can be drawn to male partners, or to female partners, or be receptive to both men and women.

Being better educated and respectful of people with diverse sexual identities promotes greater sexual health.

The question of why we are the sexual beings we are has no simple answer. Sexuality is complex, and our understanding of it continually grows. A number of questions have been, and are continuing to be researched:

- What factors contribute to the individuals we are? Can those factors be controlled? Altered?

- At what point, if any, is our sexual identity fixed? Is this locked in our genes?

- Are parents and other caregivers the principal forces in shaping our sexuality?

- How powerful are the actual experiences we have in determining how we see ourselves, and how we make decisions?

In this chapter we will explore the various dimensions of sexual identity, keeping in mind the following principles:

1. The research that has been conducted to date is not conclusive or definitive. Ongoing research from biologists, psychologists, sociologists, anthropologists, sexologists, the medical community, and others supports both sides of the nature/nurture argument. Most likely, the persons we are result from an interaction between a variety of forces.

2. The culture has forced a dichotomous view of sexual identity. A person is supposed to be either male or female, heterosexual or homosexual, masculine or feminine. In working toward a healthy sexual identity, we might, instead, think of issues along various continua.

3. The premise that sexuality "just is," and by some magical age one has evolved into a healthy, self-accepting, sexual being is false. The culture has defined rather narrowly what is deemed "acceptable," with an obvious preference for people to be heterosexual, attractive, able-bodied, and young. When we fall outside that norm — which for many is the reality — self-acceptance and acceptance or tolerance from others may be difficult to attain.

To be sexually healthy, we have to become introspective, examine our past, look for explanations and answers, and work through aspects of our sexual identity that are uncomfortable for us. To promote greater sexual health, society, too, has to become better educated and respectful of people with diverse sexual identities.

Our sexual identity develops as an interaction of heredity and environment. Genetic heritage, hormone levels of estrogen and testosterone, parental role modeling, and interactions with people outside our homes all influence the people we are, what we want, and how we live as sexual beings.

CONTINUA OF SEXUALITY

Sandra Bem and others have challenged the approach to sexuality that limits the individual to dichotomous choices about his or her sexuality.[1] You are either "male" or "female." You are either "masculine" or "feminine." You are either "heterosexual" or "homosexual." Needless to say, the culture at large seems to have mandated the dichotomy while simultaneously confusing issues of physical sexuality, gender identity, and sexual orientation. Greater sexual health may come from viewing identity along the continua described in this chapter.

Self-acceptance, as well as a more sophisticated and accurate assessment of others' sexuality, benefits from the recognition that three continua influence our sexual identity (see Figure 4.1). For each variable, the individual can place himself or herself at any point along the continuum. Permutations of the intersections are many. As a result, the tremendous diversity within sexuality becomes apparent.

For example, in the traditional model of female sexuality, the female has female reproductive organs — clitoris, vagina, uterus, and so on — that reflect female secondary sex characteristics such as developed breasts, broader hips, and narrow waist. To be viewed as an attractive female, the culture further prescribes an acceptable presentation of those characteristics. The female identifies herself as female, adopts the prescribed female role, enjoys feminine things, and behaves in feminine ways. She sees herself as heterosexual, making herself available to males in the culture. This person assumes positions at the extremes of the three continua.

Above and beyond fundamental questions regarding "feminine things and feminine ways" is the basic reality that the above description defines only certain females in the culture. According to the *gender continuum*, someone who is female can possess female reproductive structures but appear more "masculine" to others. A female could enjoy male clothing and be attracted to women. She could have both male and female reproductive

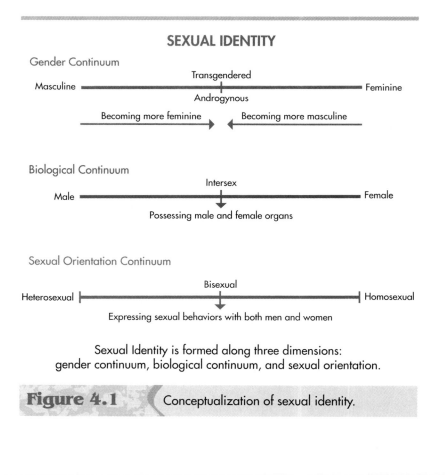

SEXUAL IDENTITY

Gender Continuum

Masculine ——————————————————— Feminine
                    Transgendered
                    Androgynous

Becoming more feminine →   ← Becoming more masculine

Biological Continuum

Male ——————————————————— Female
              Intersex
Possessing male and female organs

Sexual Orientation Continuum

Heterosexual |——————————————————| Homosexual
                    Bisexual
Expressing sexual behaviors with both men and women

Sexual Identity is formed along three dimensions:
gender continuum, biological continuum, and sexual orientation.

Figure 4.1   Conceptualization of sexual identity.

structures and enjoy relating to both men and women sexually. The possibilities and realities are numerous.

The *biological continuum* of identity is often thought to be separated clearly into "male and female," yet some individuals have reproductive structures from both. Previously referred to as *hermaphrodites* or pseudohermaprodites, these individuals have embraced the preferred label of **intersexual.**

The *sexual identity* continuum offers numerous points for placement. Individuals who consider themselves **androgynous** make choices about how they look and act without adhering to sexual stereotypes. Androgynous males might pierce their ears and wear pink clothing. Androgynous females may work on construction sites and avoid wearing dresses at all cost.

Placement along the *sexual orientation* continuum allows for erotic connections to males or females, or both. Exclusive **heterosexuality** involves erotic relationships with members of the other sex; males would connect with females and females with males. Exclusive **homosexuality** involves erotic relationships between members of the same sex — that is, males with males and females with females. **Bisexuality** is reflected by erotic connections in which the individual relates sexually to both males and females.

Bem's model enables an understanding that individuals may place themselves at different points along each continuum, and that those points may vary throughout the lifespan. These continua express the diversity of sexuality.

Biological Sex

Some researchers perceive that "biology is destiny"; biological influences are the strongest influences over our sexuality. At issue is not only one's anatomical parts but also the need to examine influences of hormones on the brain, particularly during gestation and puberty. For many years the prevailing wisdom held that "nurturing could override nature."[2]

John Money and Anke Ehrhardt wrote of the case of identical twin boys, in which, because of damage to one infant's penis during a circumcision repair, the child received sex reassignment surgery and was reared as a girl. Through strict feminine gender role experiences, the girl was thought to have a secure gender identity.[3] The child, though, began to realize that he was not biologically a girl, rejected playing with dolls, and attempted to urinate in a standing position. A suicide attempt in adolescence led to learning the truth, a cessation of female hormone treatments, and later extensive surgery to restore his masculinity. Today the man is married to a woman. This case gives support to those who argue that the brain has a fixed sexual identity resulting from genetic and gestational influences.

The biological dimension of sexuality leads toward a more dichotomous approach, yet in reality — like the other dimensions to be reviewed — one can evolve in varying ways. The process of **sexual differentiation** embraces the term "different." Males are different from females. If this is true, in what ways?

Sexual Differentiation

The moment of conception marks our beginning. The union of a sperm and an ovum represents the chromosomal level of development.

Intersexual
an individual possessing some degree of both male and female internal or external reproductive structures; the preferred term, replacing earlier labels of *hermaphrodite* and *pseudohermaphrodite*

Androgyny
expressing characteristics and traits considered stereotypically male and female

Heterosexuality
forming sexual relationships with members of the other sex

Homosexuality
forming sexual relationships with members of the same sex

Bisexuality
forming sexual relationships with both men and women

Sexual differentiation
the processes by which the embryo/fetus develops into a male or a female; internal and external genitalia develop in distinct ways, as does the brain

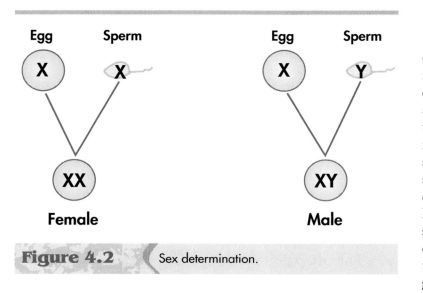

Figure 4.2   ⟨ Sex determination.

Gametes
the reproductive cells — sperm
and ova

Gonads
the ovaries and the testicles

Homologous structures
body parts that develop from the
same embryonic tissue (for
example, the female clitoris and
the male penis)

Chromosomal Level

Sperm and ova are known as **gametes**, each of which carries 23 individual chromosomes. Together they become the 23 chromosome pairs carrying the complex array of genes that define us. One of those pairs, the sex chromosomes, determine our biological sex. If a Y-bearing sperm fertilizes the ovum, the species presumably develops as a male with the gender chromosomes designated as XY; if the X-bearing sperm fertilizes the ovum, the species develops as female with the gender chromosomes designated as XX (Figure 4.2). The genetic material within the gender chromosomes then acts to shape the organism in a way that is consistent with that differentiation.

Figure 4.3 is useful toward understanding the many factors that influence identity. Chromosomes represent the beginning of a process that unfolds over many years, hopefully leading toward a clear identity.

In Utero Development

During the second and third months of pregnancy, the **gonads**, the primary reproductive organs, develop. We refer to the two testicles as male reproductive organs and two ovaries as female. Because these structures evolve from the same embryonic tissue, they are called **homologous structures.** If the embryo follows a male pattern of development, the Y chromosome causes the testicles to produce testosterone, helping to shape the structures that will develop. Specifically, the presence of the TDF gene — testis-determining factor — allows for male sexual differentiation. Without it, the fetus develops along female lines, regardless of chromosomes.

Estrogen and testosterone continue to play important roles in sexual development in utero as well as appearance and sexuality after birth. During development, the ratio of the two hormones will produce a child who is anatomically matched to the chromosomes and gonads. If the embryo is chromosomally XX, the ovaries will produce estrogen, which in turn will cause tissue to evolve into the internal and external reproductive organs associated with the female. If the embryo is chromosomally XY, testosterone will direct the tissue to developing into the internal and external reproductive structures of the male. Figure 4.4 shows the sexual differentiation of internal and external structures.

Hormones circulate throughout the developing fetus, affecting the brain, too, through a process referred to as neural encoding. Questions arise as to how the male brain may be different from the female brain. Researchers continue to debate whether the brain becomes encoded to later respond to the environment in a biologically predetermined way or whether the forces of socialization cannot be separated from identity. Although it has been reported that gonadal steroid hormones affect sexual differentiation of the brain in laboratory animals, the same case cannot be made for humans.[4] Researchers continue to examine the role of hormones on the brain during both gestation and puberty, working toward a better understanding of differences in male and female brains.

Questions continue, however, as development progresses in the areas of gender identity, gender role expression, and sexual orientation. The pituitary

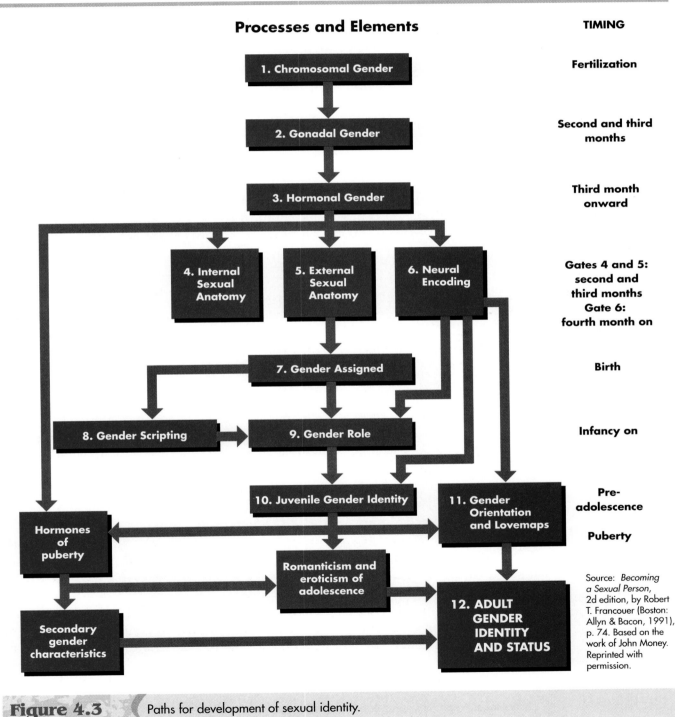

Figure 4.3   Paths for development of sexual identity.

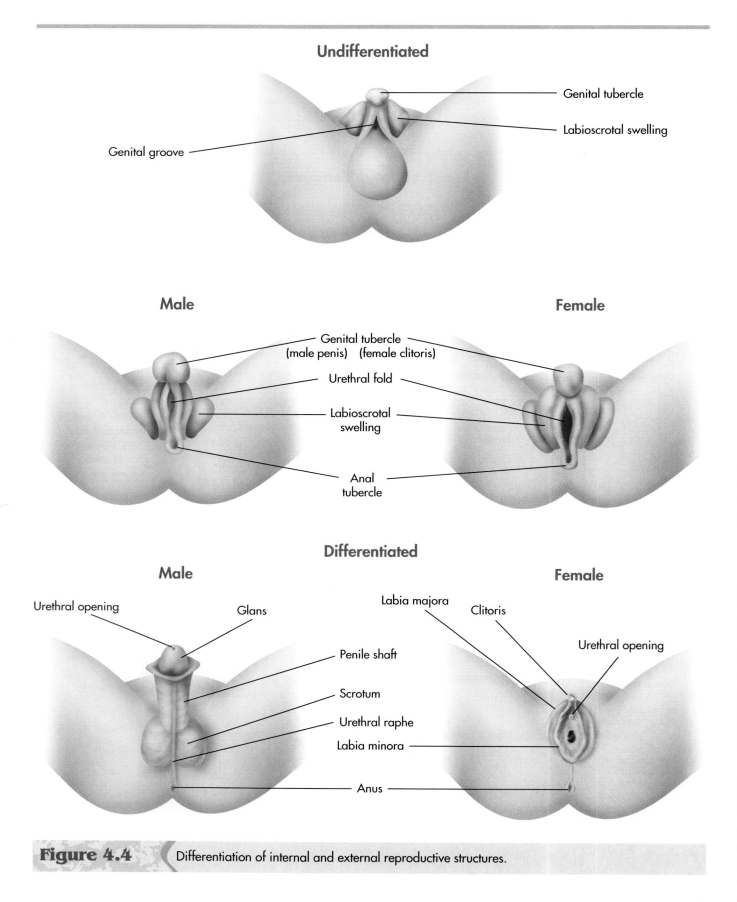

Figure 4.4   Differentiation of internal and external reproductive structures.

gland in the brain, and the hypothalamus interact to regulate the sex hormones estrogen and testosterone. One might ask whether the brain is set up to respond to the environment in a particular way, so that perhaps gender identity and sexual orientation evolve in a predetermined fashion.

Anthropologists, however, argue that gender identity, gender role, and sexual expression are not strictly a function of biology. Their studies of non-Western cultures challenge commonly held assumptions about the universality of sexual impulses, the importance of sexuality in human life, the private status of behavior, or its assumed reproductive nature.[5]

Birth

Traditionally, the next level of differentiation — gender assignment — is thought to occur at birth. Physicians, nurse midwives, and parents look at the external genitals of the baby and proclaim, "It's a girl!" or "It's a boy." In today's high-tech world of prenatal screening, many couples know the sex of the offspring months before the baby is born. Chorionic villus sampling and amniocentesis — two prenatal screening techniques discussed in greater detail in Chapter 13 — provide data about chromosomal abnormalities. In the second trimester of the pregnancy, prospective parents can be informed, if they are interested, as to whether the fetus is male or female. Sonograms have become routine in obstetrical practice, and they can yield pictures revealing the external genitalia. Thus, parents may be well aware of their child's gender before birth. In essence, they have time to begin gender socialization earlier than they could previously. Whether knowing the gender of the offspring prior to birth has any relevant impact on the development of sexual identity has yet to be researched.

Clearly, once we are born, those around us respond to us as "baby boy" or "baby girl." Think about your behavior when you are introduced to a baby. Do you say, "What a cute little baby!" If we have no gender markers to clue us in, do we ask, "Is it a girl?" "Is it a boy?"

Childhood

As soon as a baby begins to interact with the environment, the gender scripting and gender role learning begin. In Chapter 5 we examine psychosexual development in greater detail. Early childhood experiences play a pivotal role in a child's learning what being male or female means in a given culture. The classic work of Margaret Mead[6] conveys the concept that social scripts and gender roles are culture-specific.

Apart from primitive cultures, today's world is vastly connected through technology, and though cultural distinctions remain, men and women can have a clearer understanding of how people in other cultures may learn to be. As a result, the argument that males and females must behave in any one prescribed manner is becoming difficult to make. Reality stands testament to the wide differences in behavior.

Feminists in the United States during the late 1960s and 1970s argued that girls and women were oppressed by the stereotypical and limited scripts they were to learn and the roles they were to play. Sandra Bem proposed three lenses that frame our understanding of gender:[7]

Androcentrism
a position of viewing the world with the male at its center

Gender polarization
the belief that males and females are fundamentally different, with mutually exclusive gender scripts

Biological essentialism
the position that biology is destiny and our biology explains our nature

1. **Androcentrism,** defined as male centeredness
2. **Gender polarization,** the belief that males and females are fundamentally different and have mutually exclusive scripts for being male or female
3. **Biological essentialism,** which explains that androcentrism and gender polarization result from the fundamental biological differences in nature between males and females; when the individual attempts to carve out an identity that may be comfortable, deviation from society's script becomes problematic.

Sex-role stereotyping — in which girls were to be pretty, nurturing, and domestic to the exclusion of being independent and earning a meaningful

Cognizant of the criticism and research indicating better health through greater role flexibility, parents of the 1990s are given the theoretical choice to encourage their children to look and behave in ways they want. If you look around you, do you see evidence of social change in this regard? Watch television commercials for toys. Are toys marketed to one gender or the other? Visit a large toy store. Do children seem to show interest and purchase toys in any particular pattern?

Toys, games, and ideas of fun all affect our sexual development.

wage — is now thought to be damaging to women's overall health and survival. As an outgrowth of criticizing the female role, male health is questioned in its relationship to rigid, stereotyped roles.[8]

Dressing children and teaching them about life are roles of the parents, and the culture — television, schools, and other institutions — play a big part in how children learn about themselves. By 24 months of age, a child is usually able to distinguish between males and females, and by 3 years of age has developed a gender identity, a clear understanding of being male or female.

Children of the nineties do not experience the rigidity in gender role learning that those of previous generations did. It could be argued that the culture has changed somewhat in its tradition of "color coding" babies — that is, boys wear blue, and girls wear pink. Girls now wear blue, but can boys wear pink? The answer is still no. This may reflect the unspoken parental fear that putting a boy baby in pink clothes will feminize him. The color pink is purported to "sissify" boys, yet girls seem to have the ability to develop normally in spite of wearing blue clothes.

Boys and girls today can make freer choices for play and toys. Boys and girls can play with kitchen sets. Both can play with blocks and Legos™. Broader questions remain as to why children are drawn to certain types of toys and what kinds of play are fun versus what kinds of play are needed to reinforce established gender roles. The women's movement in the early 1970s called into question stereotyped gender roles and forced gender play. The prevailing wisdom was that both boys and girls would benefit from

Case Study

The Flower Boy

When my sister was planning her wedding, she asked us if our four-year-old son could be the flower boy. He would walk down the aisle just before the bride and throw rose petals along the path as he went. Though neither of us had ever seen or heard of a flower "boy," we thought that it was a wonderful idea. When we asked our son, he was excited about his important job.

It never occurred to us that there would be a problem until we started mentioning, in casual discussions, that our son was going to be the flower boy at the upcoming wedding. Reactions we got from family members and friends (not all, luckily) ranged from astonishment to disgust: "Boys don't throw flowers." "That is a girl's job." "How can you do that to your son? You will humiliate him." "You'll confuse him,"

and so on. Frankly, we could not believe the reactions people had. After all, we argued, we weren't planning to put him in a dress, and since when were flowers the sole purview of girls? Remember, we are talking about a four-year-old — a boy who happens to love picking flowers for his mommy and daddy.

In the face of scandal, we became even more committed to seeing this through. The day came, and our son, along with everyone else in the wedding party, was very excited and very nervous. As he came down the aisle, dressed in his tuxedo, a basket of rose petals in his hand, spontaneous "oohs" and "aahs" could be heard from those assembled. People saw not a radical, gender-bending experiment, but an adorable four-year-old spreading beauty and love. We were so proud of him!

Children are constantly being told in some way or other about expectations related to their appearance and behavior. If a child voices discomfort — "I want my hair cut" or "I don't like those clothes" — the reasons may or may not be asked for and listened to. How should parents react, for example, when children want to wear what they think of as gender-inappropriate clothing? If a son asks for a Barbie doll rather than G. I. Joe, is that cause for alarm?

broader choices based on interest and skill. Even though children in schools, for example, are no longer pushed to play in the "boys corner" or the "girls corner," evidence of gender preferences remains. Activities such as jumping rope, playing with dolls, and dressing up are more stereotypically female, whereas playing with toy guns, playing Star Wars, climbing trees, and so forth are more stereotypically male.

Regardless, examining play activity patterns in children remains only one piece of a complicated puzzle for identity development. A *persistent* preference for "gender-inappropriate" play or dress may be connected to various states of **gender dysphoria**, whereas greater gender role flexibility may be considered a sign of health.

Gender dysphoria
the condition wherein one's anatomy is inconsistent with one's gender identity

Dress-up dolls remain very popular with girls, with Barbie clearly dominating the market. Increasingly, the doll has been criticized for negatively impacting the self-perception of young girls. Barbie seems obsessed with clothes and has features that distort the female form. Yet, for close to 40 years, Barbie continues to be popular, with numerous versions available. In 1998, the manufacturer announced its plans to make Barbie's proportions more realistic; whether that adjustment will quiet the critics remains to be seen.

Barbie has remained popular for close to 40 years even though she has received much criticism.

Childhood also is the time when affectional patterns develop, and the basis for whom we find sexually attractive, what behaviors interest us, and with whom we want to romantically attach become set. Our sexual orientation defines whether the object of our attachment is male or female, or whether one becomes receptive to both males and females. In reflecting on their early childhoods, adults may remember being attracted to others in a particular pattern ("I always knew I was attracted to men"). Still, the concept of sexual orientation doesn't really take hold until adolescence and later.

John Money, internationally renowned researcher and clinician, coined the term *lovemaps* to refer to the patterns that develop in the brain, dictating what sexual behaviors will become arousing and pleasurable. His research highlights that lovemaps are formed in early childhood, underlying the power of this phase of development.

Adolescence

Puberty, marked by surges in estrogen and testosterone, represents another passage in gender development. Secondary sex characteristics develop in both males and females, and sexuality becomes eroticized. For boys, the surge in testosterone prompts an increase in body hair, specifically armpit and pubic hair. The pitch of the voice lowers, the male reaches adult height, muscles develop, and the genitals, both penis and testicles, increase to their adult size. For females, the hips broaden, breasts develop, hair grows on the mons pubis and in the armpits, and the uterus and ovaries begin to function to allow for menstruation and ovulation.

For some adolescents, hormones also have the undesirable impact of producing acne. Heredity also plays a key role in how we end up. To some extent, our adult physical selves reflect the genetic material passed down. If members of your family tend to be hairy, your hairy chest is more likely to reflect your heritage than to make a comment on your masculinity. If you

PERSPECTIVES

Body Image as a Lifelong Concern

Although adolescence is typified by self-absorption, self-assessment, and experimentation, it could be argued that, as we age, adults, too, become involved with questions of how acceptable we are as partners. As discussed earlier, body image is a lifelong issue. Hormonal changes can affect appearance at any time in life, with associated concern.

For example, with menopause comes a drop in estrogen levels, which may cause the development of coarse facial hair. Although the adrenal glands continue to produce estrogen, the amount in the body may not be at a level to suppress facial hair. Because estrogen and testosterone are present in both genders, their balance becomes important to external appearance. An older male may find that his breasts are growing as a result of aging or treatment for cancer. Some female cancer patients are given estrogen-inhibiting medications, and male cancer patients have been given testosterone-inhibiting medications. Although we take the medications to stay healthy, the resulting side effects do not always impact positively on our sexuality.

descend from large-breasted women, your large chest reflects that heritage rather than an unusually high estrogen level.

This phase of development is extremely powerful in its impact on self-esteem. Because of the many changes happening to the body, adolescents explore and play with appearance. A sense that we are acceptable as potential partners arises at this time: "Am I pretty? Am I thin enough? Are my breasts big enough?" "Are my muscles big?" Is my penis big enough? Am I too tall? Am I too short? Am I okay?

Adolescence is the time when sexual experimentation takes place for many teens. Social norms support the development of a heterosexual orientation — choosing a partner of the opposite sex. Males choose females, and vice versa. For teens who begin to struggle with confusing feelings, the social supports are less obvious. Gay and lesbian youth may find groups that help them clarify their orientation. On the other hand, in reflection, many gay and lesbian adults report "playing the game" during their junior high and high school years. They feigned crushes and dated opposite-sex partners to fit in with their peers.

Both determining for oneself and being open with others may or may not occur during adolescence. In an ideal world, individuals would be free to explore what makes them comfortable and happy. In reality, those who do not fit the norm, in whatever way, may find themselves lying, keeping secrets, and holding off from being who they are.

Adulthood

In the past, theorists would argue that, by the end of adolescence, one would be moving on to adulthood and, therefore, should embrace the tasks of adulthood. One's initial adult sexual identity should be complete. In reality, though, we all continue to struggle with questions of who we are, how we want to present ourselves, and what types of partners are most attractive to us. A key piece in adult happiness is having a clear sense of one's sexual orientation.

Sexual Orientation

In attempting to explain sexual orientation, theorists have often focused their efforts on explaining why some people identify as homosexual or bisexual. There is thought to be no need to explain heterosexuality, as that is the norm. That is what is expected. The strongest arguments for heterosexuality lie in the reproductive aspects of heterosexual behavior. Without heterosexuals, the argument goes, no children would be born. The species would die.

Some individuals look to their religious doctrines, citing passages that condemn behavior between same-sex individuals. There is the oft quoted, "If God wanted there to be homosexuals, he would have created Adam and Steve, not Adam and Eve." Still others perceive homosexuals as having a form of mental illness. And history is replete with violence, gay bashing, arrests, and even death for those thought to be homosexual. Consequently, homosexuals themselves have found their sexuality framed as a form of mental illness, a sin, or a form of illegal behavior.

While we appreciate the strength of various convictions, we take the position that sexual health requires accepting our sexual orientation, and that individuals who are comfortable with themselves are less likely to feel threatened by people who have orientations that are different from their own. The Gay and Lesbian Rights movement has often pointed out that, "We are everywhere. We are your children, your brothers and sisters, your parents, your friends." The issue is whether an individual can be open about his or her sexuality, and whether you are willing to know that aspect of those with whom you are close.

Theories of Sexual Orientation

Theories on sexual orientation abound, following different tracks. Biological theorists have looked toward genetic, hormonal, and structural differences in the brain to explain homosexuality. Psychological theorists propose psychoanalytic and learning constructs.

Biological Theories

Studies of sexual orientation among identical twins and fraternal twins show varying rates of being gay or lesbian, yet the rates are not 100%. In one study of gay men, with an admittedly small sample, 52% of the twins had a gay twin; among lesbians, the rate was 48%.[9] If the explanation for orientation were totally a genetic one, twins, particularly identical twins, would have to have the same sexual orientation. That is not always the case.

Research on hormonal influences during gestation have been conducted more carefully with rats than humans. Theorists look to the period of time when sexual differentiation occurs in the brain and the hypothalamus develops, arguing that hormonal imbalances may cause homosexuality (and gender dysphoria).[10] The hormonal imbalances may be a result of medications, steroid use, or high stress levels. A problem with the research in this area is the basic difficulty of carefully monitoring hormone levels in a large enough sample of pregnant women throughout their pregnancies and then being able to follow, in a longitudinal study, the development of their offspring. That kind of research has not been conducted.

Theorists also have looked to hormonal differences after birth, particularly from a "deficiency" perspective. This approach — which holds that gay men lack adequate testosterone and lesbian women lack adequate estrogen — smacks a bit of old stereotypes that gay men are effeminate and lesbian women are mannish. Most of the research in the area has been done on males, which also becomes a problem. The work conducted on males has not found any differences based on orientation.[11] At one time, treatment for male homosexuality involved testosterone therapy. Rather than changing orientation, that therapy just made patients "hornier and hairier."

The most publicized research on anatomical brain differences came from the work of Simon LeVay,[12] who dissected the brains of a small sample of gay men, and compared them to the brains of straight men and women. He found structural differences in a section of the hypothalamus of the gay men. The research has been roundly criticized for sample size, absence of lesbian women in the sample, and the complicating factor that the gay men had died of AIDS. The research sparked a lot of discussion but offered limited findings.

Psychological Theories

In looking to psychological theories, particularly psychoanalytic and learning theories, explanations of sexual orientation again have limited uses. In his *Three Essays on the Theory of Sexuality,* published in the early part of the 20th century, Freud spoke of the child as having an undifferentiated sexuality and having to learn appropriate responses as the child ages. Part of that learning would be to identify with the parent of the same sex, and to seek out a partner of the opposite sex. To be homosexual then could be construed as inappropriate identification. The female child, for example, would identify with her father and seek out women as partners.

For years, the field of mental health, led by psychiatrists, psychoanalysts, and psychologists, considered homosexuality a form of mental illness. Not until 1973 did the American Psychiatric Association remove homosexuality from its *Diagnostic and Statistical Manual of Mental Disorders* (DSM). Even with its removal, some professionals, as well as the lay population, still view homosexuality as a disorder.

Very popular for years was the notion that homosexuality in males resulted from a weak or absent father and a strong, domineering, overly intimate mother. In short, parental ways of interacting with their children and between themselves were responsible for the homosexuality of their children. In cases where such a relationship between the parents was found, however, the household also had heterosexual children. It becomes quizzical, to say the least, that the nature of the parental relationship would explain only homosexuality and not heterosexuality. Nonetheless, parents of gays and lesbians often struggle to understand their role in their child's homosexuality.

Learning theory as applied to sexual orientation can go in a variety of directions. A basic tenet is that the rewards and punishments associated with various behaviors and experiences channel sexual orientation in a certain direction. For example, negative reactions to heterosexual experiences could encourage later homosexual experiences. This line of thinking is supported by sex histories of lesbians who were sexually abused by their fathers in childhood. In contrast, positive childhood experiences could explain later homosexuality. This is exemplified by the adolescent male who had enjoyed oral sex with an older male cousin and develops into a gay adult whose partners are men.

One study extensively interviewed and compared responses from close to 1,000 gay and lesbian adults with those from a sample group of approximately 500 heterosexual males and females.[13] The interviewees were asked about their child and adolescent years. The results showed no patterns of family dysfunction, no prevalence of positive or negative sexual experiences to explain orientation, and, most important, predetermination of orientation before adolescence.

At the risk of oversimplification in describing various theories, it should become obvious that no one theory explains it all. Homosexual and heterosexual children can and do have the same biological parents, grow up in the same households, and end up differently along the continuum of sexual orientation.

Labels and Categories

Kinsey's work on male and female sexuality continues to provide a reference point for work on sexual orientation.[14] Along with his colleagues, he developed a 7-point scale that categorized sexual experience, shown in Figure 4.5.

After interviewing more than 10,000 people, Kinsey found it useful to categorize behaviors on a continuum based upon sexual experience with same-sex and other-sex partners. If one's behavior was exclusively with a member of the other sex, that person was referred to as a "Kinsey 0." A person whose behavior was exclusively with members of his or her own sex was labeled a "Kinsey 6." All other positions between 1 and 5 represented interest in both men and women.

Because the culture often seems to want to classify or label people regarding orientation, only "Kinsey 0's" would fit the definition of heterosexual. Individuals categorized as "Kinsey 6's" would be homosexual, and those falling within categories 1 through 5 would be bisexual or ambisexual.

Later researchers and theorists, as well as groups holding to one or more political positions, have objected to classifying individuals based only upon their behavior, as well as questioning the need to classify and label at all. Fred Klein pointed out the limitations of using behavior as the sole variable for labeling. Common sense dictates that *what we do* is only a part of *who we are* and what identity we have. Klein proposed that orientation be assessed on seven factors:[15]

1. *Sexual attraction*: To whom do we find ourselves attracted? Who turns us on? Do we respond only to women? Only to men? To both?

2. *Sexual behavior*: When you've engaged in sexual behavior, who have been your partners?

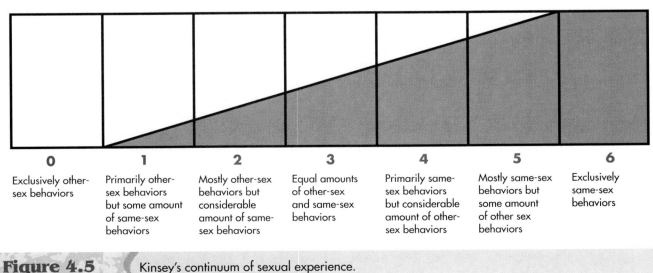

0	1	2	3	4	5	6
Exclusively other-sex behaviors	Primarily other-sex behaviors but some amount of same-sex behaviors	Mostly other-sex behaviors but considerable amount of same-sex behaviors	Equal amounts of other-sex and same-sex behaviors	Primarily same-sex behaviors but considerable amount of other-sex behaviors	Mostly same-sex behaviors but some amount of other sex behaviors	Exclusively same-sex behaviors

Figure 4.5   (Kinsey's continuum of sexual experience.

3. *Sexual fantasies*: When you fantasize or masturbate, what sex/gender is your partner?

4. *Emotional* or *affectional preference*: To whom do you connect on an emotional level? With whom do you "fall in love?"

5. *Social preference*: With whom do you prefer to socialize? With whom do you "go out?"

6. *Lifestyle*: In your community, with whom do you spend most of your time? Are your friends primarily lesbian or gay? Bisexual? Heterosexual?

7. *Self-identification*: How do *you* label yourself? Where do you place yourself on the Kinsey grid?

Important to consider is not only *what you have done* but *what you would like to be doing and with whom*. Another important aspect in sorting this is whether you find yourself enjoying the behavior. Some women and men, for example, claim to have been happily married, followed the heterosexual script, and had children. Later, they met someone of the same sex, fell in love, enjoyed lovemaking to an extent they hadn't before, and "came out." They don't feel the need to negate all of their past, nor do they claim that the sexual part of their relationship was dissatisfying but, rather, that

Case Study

Marcus's Story

Growing up the son of a professional football player, I was pretty sure that being attracted to other guys wasn't something I was ever going to talk about to anyone. For as long as I could remember, there was something there that I couldn't define. When I was a kid, there was no Ellen, nor the occasional gay character on a sitcom, and no Matt from Melrose Place. No one ever said that being attracted to guys was an okay thing for a guy to be. The only talking I ever heard about homosexuality was the constant tossing around of the word "fag" that was just used as a general, all-purpose term for anyone you were mad at. My older brother used to call me a fag all the time, not because I was unlike other guys in any way — that whole sissy-boy thing is pretty much a myth — but because he was my older brother and that's what older brothers do — torment their younger brothers.

I remember that homosexuality did come up once on a television show I was watching. A young man had a friend who had gone away to school and come back to tell him and everyone else that he was gay. The young man took it pretty badly and spent the first

fifty minutes of the hour-long show avoiding his old chum only to have it resolve nicely in the last five minutes. The old friend talked about how he had always had feelings for other guys and that he thought it was a phase he would eventually outgrow. Time passed and the phase didn't. He had to come to grips with it, and part of that process was to be honest.

As he talked with his friend, the young man admitted that when they were kids, he had had crushes on guys, too, but being gay wasn't what he was. His initial difficulty accepting his gay friend was because he related to what his friend had been through, and he was afraid that he was a little like him. The show was progressive for its time and made it clear that a lot of guys have same-gender crushes and for most of them, it doesn't mean they're gay. For me, however, it did.

I was like the old grade-school chum. I waited for the phase to pass, but it didn't. By the time I got to college, I was faced with the same dilemma the grade school chum had faced. I had to confront the fact that I was gay.

they have discovered an identity and a lifestyle that feels right.

It seems safe to say that society at large presumes people are heterosexual until proven otherwise. And then, if someone's gay or lesbian orientation becomes known, it is not unusual to hear someone remark, "Oh, I didn't know that person was gay."

Sexual orientation is determined by a number of factors, including those to whom you are sexually attracted, with whom you feel comfortable and sexually fantasize about, what you do sexually, and what you would like to be doing.

At one time in history, gays and lesbians were called "the invisible minority." The 1969 Stonewall Uprising in New York City, where a police raid of a gay bar was met with resistance, has been credited as the event that began the Gay and Lesbian Rights movement. That movement has led to more individuals feeling freer to be open about their sexual orientation, although many still report that to "come out" would leave them vulnerable to harassment, violence, and loss of jobs, housing, friendships, and family members. Some states (e.g., New Jersey) have included sexual orientation, along with race, creed, gender, ethnicity, military and veteran's status, and disability, as a basis for which one's civil rights must be protected.

It wasn't easy to handle at first. I admitted to myself that I was gay and that I would always be attracted to men. But, as a second-semester freshman, I swore that I would never act on it. I wouldn't think about guys. I wouldn't fantasize about guys. I wouldn't date guys. I would search out the perfect best friend, and the two of us would embark on a completely chaste relationship that would be mutually satisfying. Of course, no such guy existed, and several attempts to pin my flagging hopes on various friends of mine ended up in disaster. I had told myself that I would never do anything for which I would be ashamed.

After almost a full year of repressing all feelings of attraction for anyone, I came to realize that perhaps I could be happy and sexually active, and not end up living alone for the rest of my life. My feelings of self-hatred and shame, however, had run far too deep, and I started having anxiety attacks.

Over the next two-and-a-half years, I saw a therapist whose office was about a block off campus. I went not because I was sick but because I wanted to feel better about myself. Over those two-and-a-half years, I talked to the therapist about how I felt and who I was.

When I graduated, the therapist called my parents to settle up the final bills. When my mother hung up the phone, she had tears in her eyes. She said that my therapist shared how much he was going to miss talking to me each week and that, of all the students he had met, I was the only one he wished were his son.

Coming out is a long and hard process for many people, and my story is probably not all that unusual. Many of us still hear and see messages of hatred and spend some time hating ourselves. I'd hope that the positive images seen these days and supportive statements from various celebrities, magazines, books, and movies might make it much easier for gay people who are younger than I am. Some friends — whom I thought would never understand or accept me — have. Now, instead of admitting that I'm gay — as if it were something to be ashamed of — I can say with comfort and confidence that I, like that old school chum from that television show I watched as a kid, have accepted that I'm a gay man.

Health Hint

Advice on Coming Out

The decision to be open about one's homosexuality is a personal one, one that heterosexuals don't have to confront. It is almost as if lesbian and gay individuals have to explain to the world that they are not heterosexual, rather than "the world" having considered that possibility.

The risks a person takes for being open about sexual orientation depend on a variety of factors including age, geography, employment, and financial solvency, among others. Although civil rights protections are gradually being extended to people at the local and state levels, no constitutional amendment guarantees civil rights protection regardless of sexual orientation.

The following guidelines are adapted from the brochure, *Be Yourself* (PFLAG, 1998):

1. **Are you sure about your sexual orientation?** Don't raise the issue unless you're able to respond with confidence to the question "Are you sure?" Confusion on your part will increase your parents' confusion and decrease their confidence in your judgment.

2. **Are you comfortable with your gay sexuality?** If you're wrestling with guilt and periods of depression, you'll be better off waiting to tell your parents. Coming out to them may require tremendous energy on your part; it will require a reserve of positive self-image.

3. **Do you have support?** In the event your parents' reaction devastates you, there should be someone or a group that you can confidently turn to for emotional support and strength. Maintaining your sense of self-worth is critical.

4. **Are you knowledgeable about homosexuality?** Your parents will probably respond based on a lifetime of information from a homophobic society. If you've done some serious reading on the subject, you'll be able to assist them by sharing reliable information and research.

5. **What's the emotional climate at home?** If you have the choice of when to tell, consider the timing. Choose a time when they're not dealing with such matters as the death of a close friend, pending surgery, or the loss of a job.

6. **Can you be patient?** Your parents will require time to deal with this information if they haven't

Gay Pride parades take place in many cities across the United States.

considered it prior to your sharing. The process may last from six months to two years.

7. **What's your motive for coming out now?** Hopefully, it is because you love them and are uncomfortable with the distance you feel. Never come out in anger or during an argument, using your sexuality as a weapon.

8. **Do you have available resources?** Homosexuality is a subject most non-gay people know little about. Have available at least one of the following: a book addressed to parents, a contact for the local or national Parents and Friends of Lesbians and Gays, the name of a non-gay counselor who can deal fairly with the issue.

9. **Are you financially dependent on your parents?** If you suspect they are capable of withdrawing college finances or forcing you out of the house, you may choose to wait until they do not have this weapon to hold over you.

10. **What is your general relationship with your parents?** If you've gotten along well and have always known their love — and shared your love for them in return — chances are they'll be able to deal with the issue in a positive way.

11. **What is their moral societal view?** If they tend to see social issues in clear terms of good/bad or holy/sinful, you may anticipate that they will have serious problems dealing with your sexuality. If, however, they've evidenced a degree of flexibility when dealing with other changing societal matters, you may be able to anticipate a willingness to work this through with you.

12. **Is this your decision?** Not everyone should come out to their parents. Don't be pressured into it if you're not sure you'll be better off by doing so — no matter what their response.

Note: Be Yourself highlights the process that most parents go through when told that their child is gay. The stages include shock, denial, guilt, expression of feelings, personal decision-making, and true acceptance. It highlights that each family is unique, and offers suggestions of resources and support.

Source: *Read This Before Coming Out to Your Parents* by T. H. Sauerman, PFLAG Philadelphia, 1998. For ordering information: PFLAG Philadelphia, P.O. Box 176, Titusville, NJ 08560-0176. vrb@pupgg.princeton.edu.

How Many?

The subject of sexual orientation has often led to a need to document "how many." How many people are heterosexual? How many are lesbian and gay? How many are bisexual? As researchers attempt to count, a number of problems arise. What criterion will be used? How easily assessed is a sample, and can it be determined to be generalizable to the population at large?

Kinsey reported that 37% of males and 13% of females had engaged in adult same-sex behavior to the point of orgasm. He estimated that 2% of males and 1% of females could be categorized as Kinsey "6's."[16] A limitation of Kinsey's work, particularly as it pertains to the Heterosexual-Homosexual Rating Scale, is that behavior is emphasized without attending to the other factors that Klein identified.

When the National Health and Social Life Survey (NHSLS) results were reported,[17] the researchers addressed the difficulty they, or others, have in "counting" homosexuals. A primary problem lies with the definition of "homosexual." They point out that people change their behavior during their lifetime, that patterns of sexual desire and identification vary, and that, because of oppression, it can be difficult to get respondents to both identify themselves and honestly respond to questions.[18] As a result, a definitive picture of homosexuality in the United States becomes difficult to paint.

The NHSLS examined issues of attraction by asking respondents "In general, are you sexually attracted to . . . only women, mostly women, both men and women, mostly men, only men?" Appeal was measured by "How would you rate this activity: having sex with someone of the same sex . . . very appealing, somewhat appealing, not appealing, not at all appealing?" For self-identification, they asked, "Do you think of yourself as heterosexual, homosexual, bisexual, something else?" Figure 4.6 presents some of the findings.

The NHSLS researchers have claimed that their research represented a scientifically accurate survey of sex in the United States, representing nearly all adult U. S. men and women.[19] Although the researchers are not above criticism, they were able to interview and survey a wider range of people than other studies to date. For what it's worth "toward the count," they found that more people find others of the same gender sexually attractive than have homosexual sex.

Approximately 5.5% of women found the idea of having sex with another woman very appealing or appealing, with 4% reporting that they were sexually attracted to women. Less than 2% had had sex with a woman during the past year, yet slightly more than 4% reported having sex with a woman at some time in their lives.

About 6% of the men in the NHSLS study reported being attracted to other men, with 2% saying they had had sex with a man in the past year. By comparison to females, 9% reported having had sex with a man at least

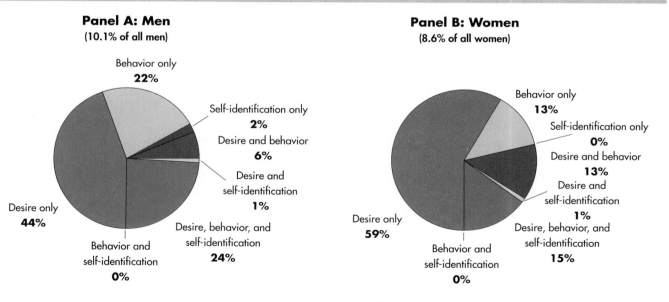

Source: *Sex in America: A Definitive Survey*, by R. Michael, J. Gagnon, and E. Laumann. Copyright © 1994 by CSG Enterprises, Inc. Little, Brown and Company. Reprinted with permission.

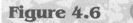 **Figure 4.6**   Interrelationship of three aspects of same-gender sexuality: desire, behavior, and self identification.

once since puberty. When respondents were asked to label themselves, only 1.4% of women thought of themselves as homosexual or bisexual and 2.8% of men identified themselves as homosexual or bisexual.

Why, if at all, is it necessary to count people based upon their sexual orientation? How do the numbers relate to me? If I fall somewhere within the majority or minority, does that help me better accept myself? If I know the sexual orientation of a colleague, will that change our relationship in any way? Will we be able to be friends if we differ in terms of sexual orientation?

ATYPICAL PATHS OF DEVELOPMENT

As the influences affecting sexual identity come into play, the question persists as to whether one is developing "normally." Regardless of one's definition of normal, what, if anything, is to be "done" when development varies? After birth, questions such as, "Is the child happy with himself or herself? "and "Are the parents happy with the child?" may be secondary to concerns expressed from family, physicians, and other outside observers.

Every year children are born who are not genetically, anatomically, or hormonally consistent with one sex or the other. Some situations are immediately apparent, as in ambiguous external genitalia. In other situations the chromosomal make-up may be abnormal, yet the impact of the genetic mosaic may not be obvious until childhood or adolescence. Table 4.1 charts the more common of variations.

U. S. culture traditionally has looked at atypical patterns as problems, and the medical community has become involved where possible to "fix" the child. The terms used to describe ambiguities are clinical. *Pseudohermaphrodism* described the conditions in which the child was genetically one sex, with mixed external and internal structures. Genetic females whose genitals are masculinized because of an accumulation of androgens from the adrenal glands is referred to as having *congenital adrenal hyperplasia* (CAH), also called adrenogenital syndrome. A condition with parallel outcomes — *androgen insensitivity syndrome* — is found in a genetic male whose body does not respond to the testosterone it produces, leading to female external genitalia. Adult individuals with these conditions have recently become more visible and political. They are asking to be referred to as intersexuals and demanding their civil rights.

The Intersex Society of North America (ISNA) is a support, education, and advocacy group founded by and for individuals who are intersexual. The organization opposes the predominant model of treatment that recommends emergency sex reassignment for infants, followed by hormonal treatments and gender role learning that reinforces that assignment. As a result of sharing their experiences, the intersexuals involved with ISNA claim that these early interventions, considered a form of genital mutilation, have impaired them in many ways.

If adult children are stating that their early experiences of surgery and hormonal interventions were damaging psychologically, that waiting until they have a clearer sense of their sexual identity before interventions take place is preferable, how do we retrain medical personnel? If your child were to be born with ambiguous genitalia, do you believe you could wait for treatment? Could you refer to your child as intersexual?

Table 4.1   Atypical Chromosomal and Hormonal Patterns

	Chromosomal Sex	Gonads	Internal Reproductive	External Reproductive	Secondary Sex Characteristics	Gender Identity
Chromosomal						
Klinefelter syndrome	Male	Testes	Normal male	Small penis and testes	Female secondary sex characteristics develop at puberty	Male
Turner syndrome	Female	Nonfunctioning or absent ovaries	Normal female except for ovaries	Underdeveloped genitals	No breast development or menstruation at puberty	Female
Hormonal						
Androgen-insensitivity syndrome	Male (46, XY)	Testes, but body unable to utilize testosterone	Shallow vagina, lacking normal male structures	Labia	Female secondary sex characteristics develop at puberty; no menstruation	Female
Congenital adrenal hyperplasia (pseudo-hermaphroditism)	Female (46, XX)	Ovaries	Normal female	Ambiguous, tending toward male appearance; fused vagina and enlarged clitoris may be mistaken for empty scrotal sac and beginnings of penis	Female secondary sex characteristics develop at puberty	Usually male

The ISNA has recommended a new model of treatment that avoids harmful or unnecessary surgery, requires family therapy by well trained mental health professionals, and asks that intersexual individuals be empowered to decide on treatment after fully understanding their status. For the overall health of the individual, they argue against genital surgery that is primarily rooted in cosmetic concerns.[20]

Other atypical patterns of development that fall along the gender identity continuum may not receive attention or any intervention until the child is older. Broad questions remain as to how strongly a child must identify with gender-appropriate appearance and roles and, indeed, what the list of "appropriateness" contains.

On the one hand is a movement away from enforcing rigid gender role stereotypes. Girls can have short hair; males can have long hair. When the

Case Study

Donna, a Transgendered Woman

I'm 40 years old. We can get into a whole list of identities — mother, daughter, lover, student. I see labels as political designations. You try them on to see which ones fit. Can you find "one" that encompasses a total human being? I don't think so. In the last five years I've taken "transgendered" as one of my primary identities. For me, what transgendered means is "crossing boundaries."

I've always been inappropriate. My mother was always into dressing me to be the pretty little girl, and in six seconds I would destroy her efforts. I wanted to climb trees, play in the dirt, and have fun — all sorts of things you can't do in a dress. By the time I was ten, I had pretty much won the battle, which meant that she bought me Tuff Stuff jeans and polos from Sears that I could wear to play in when I wasn't at school. For school I had to wear these horrendous polyester slacks — plaid or checked. I refused to wear dresses or skirts. My hair was always very long to please my mother. My way to manage that was to always keep it in pigtails.

Once on my own, I started dressing in drag. I came out to my family when I was 16, but to my painful surprise found the reception in the lesbian community most unwelcome. Being butch in the seventies was not politically correct. Looking like a man was as bad, perhaps even worse, than sleeping with one. Women sleeping with men were just preserving their

place in the power structure. Women perceived as trying to *be* a man were seen as appropriating that male power for themselves. My way of sorting through all that was to marry a man and try to live as a heterosexual woman. I was very successful at that game for close to twenty years.

As I look back at old photos, I realize that I really haven't changed much at all over the years. At my most stereotypically feminine, I received praise for my appearance for a look that was so artificial to me. Amusingly, when I was eight months pregnant, I was mistaken for a man even though I was wearing pink maternity clothes! Over time, it really hasn't mattered much what I had on. I've gotten more "How can I help you, sir's" than I can count.

Today it's a fifty–fifty shot as to whether people think I'm a man or a woman. I didn't choose to be a walking stereotype of a lesbian woman. I don't fit neatly into the transgendered community either. I don't have "gender dysphoria." My body is my body, and I accept it. I wear men's clothing primarily because it fits better, both body and psyche. I build muscle in "male-patterned" ways, my voice has gotten deeper over time, and my neck is thick. The blood tests I've had in the past all indicate "normal hormone parameters."

So here I am in the identity chapter. I'm clear on me. You deal with it.

girl wants a military-type crewcut or the male not only wants long hair, but wants to set it in curls, those choices move them away from stereotypes. Similarly, parents may not worry when little girls play aggressively, wear pants, climb trees, and are interested in sports.

It seems safe to say, however, that the girl "tomboy" is more easily accepted than the "sissy boy." The boy who wants to play with dolls, is interested in female clothing, and doesn't like sports, may become subjected to questions about both his gender identity and sexual orientation.

Recently, individuals whose gender identity and gender role encompasses both masculinity and femininity are referring to themselves as **transgendered**. The term may include individuals referred to as transvestites and transsexuals. The range of issues for these individuals varies. Being transgendered often gets confused with orientation issues, although being gay, bisexual, or heterosexual falls along another continuum. Some people crossdress in private, finding the process sexually arousing. Others crossdress for entertainment and are known for their skills at impersonation. Barbra Streisand is frequently a subject of impersonation. During her HBO concert in 1996, she joked that New York City is such a comfortable place for her to walk around; there were so many Barbra impersonators that she could pass without notice!

The essence of being transgendered is that one's gender identity falls somewhere away from the extremes of masculine or feminine. A person may desire to dress as the other sex does, move as the "other" sex does, and be treated as though one were a member of the other sex.

Gender dysphoria is the condition in which one's anatomy is inconsistent with one's gender identity. Someone who believes he or she is trapped in the wrong body suffers greatly and may even attempt genital mutilation to remove that which emphasizes the "mistake." Even though there are more male-to-female transsexuals, female-to-male transsexuals do receive treatment. More often, however, it is the male-to-female transsexual who seeks treatment and is given sex reassignment surgery.[21]

Sex reassignment surgery, along with the array of psychiatric, hormonal, and subsequent cosmetic surgeries, represents a long and painful process. Transsexuals first must be thoroughly evaluated to ensure that gender dysphoria is the correct diagnosis. Crossdressing is encouraged, followed by hormonal interventions to feminize male-to-female transsexuals or, conversely, masculinize female-to-male transsexuals. Changes in body hair, changes in the face, and fat deposits all move these individuals in their desired direction. These interventions are reversible if necessary and, for some, represent the extent of treatment that is both comfortable and affordable.

Surgical interventions are more complicated. The male-to-female transsexual will have the testicles and penis removed, and the skin of the penis is used to construct a vagina that can respond to sexual stimulation. A female-to-male transsexual will have a complete hysterectomy and a double mastectomy and will have a penis constructed. Because the clitoris is small and behind the penis, it can be left to improve the sexual response.

The personal adjustments required of transgendered individuals are many. Some have lost friends, family, and jobs as they attempt to find personal happiness. The following lyrics from the Broadway musical *La Cage*

Transgendered
preferred term to describe individuals whose gender identity and gender role encompasses both masculinity and femininity; previous labels were transvestite and transsexual

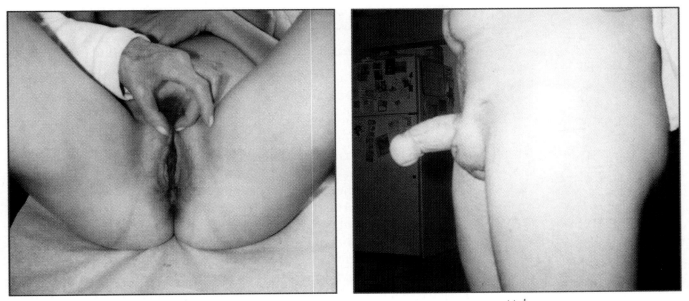

Female | Male

Post-operative transsexual genitalia.

Aux Folles (music and lyrics by Jerry Herman), are sung by one of the main characters, a gay, effeminate, often crossdressed man who demands to be accepted. Read the words and think of how they can apply to us all.

Lyrics to "I Am What I Am," from the musical *La Cage Aux Folles*, Music and Lyrics by Jerry Herman, 1983:

I am what I am. I am my own special creation.
So come take a look, Give me the hook or the ovation.
It's my world that I want to have a little pride in
My world and it's not a place I have to hide in.
Life's not worth a damn 'til you can say
"Hey world, I am what I am."
I am what I am. I don't want praise. I don't want pity.
I bang my own drum. Some think it's noise. I think it's pretty.
And so what — if I love each feather and each spangle
Why not try and see things from a different angle?
Your life is a sham 'til you can shout out loud
"I am what I am!"
I am what I am and what I am needs no excuses
I deal my own deck . . . sometimes the ace, sometimes the deuces.
There's one life, and there's no return and no deposit
One life, so it's time to open up your closet
Life's not worth a damn 'til you can say
"Hey world, I am what I am!"

WELLNESS SYNTHESIS

Sexual identity is associated with the six components of wellness.

Physical Well-being

The physical aspects of sexual identity come into play at many points. First, a pregnant woman should be sure to obtain the best prenatal care available and avoid medications and hormones that could impair normal development of the genitalia. If a baby is born with structural variations, these should be discussed thoroughly with competent medical and psychological personnel before undertaking any interventions.

As we age, particularly at puberty, our physical selves become a statement of gender. Heredity and hormones play a significant role in size, structure, and, to some extent, shape. Once we've matured, we make decisions about appearance — what clothes to wear, how to cut our hair, what we accentuate, what we hide. Through experimentation and feedback from others, we often take on an individual style that reflects our feelings about being male or female.

Good nutrition and exercise contribute significantly to physical health. What we eat has an impact on our skin and hair, in addition to our immune system. Exercise not only contributes to overall health and longevity but also to how we feel about ourselves. In the past several years, males and females alike have been using steroids as a way to increase muscle mass. The evidence is clear that steroids used in this way can be dangerous. Women body builders, for example, may have the desired large muscles but will notice diminished breast size, changes in the menstrual cycle, and more masculine contours to the face, not to mention increased facial hair. Males who use steroids may be excited by the size and strength of their muscles but unprepared for what is commonly called "roid rage," a pronounced and intense level of anger.

At various times throughout our lives, illness and disability also will influence the physical aspects of our identity. When cancer treatment results in the loss of a breast, testicle, prostate, ovary, or uterus, the repercussions are physical as well as psychological. Surgery and chemotherapy can alter hormone functioning, which in turn can affect physical appearance and sexual functioning. Disability may affect movement, which in turn may affect how we see ourselves and how others react to us.

Our physical body becomes the machine through which we express our sexuality and connectedness. Taking care of this machine and making it work for us, in whatever condition it is, is essential.

Intellectual Well-being

It is often said that "knowledge is power." In the area of sexual identity, it is helpful to know that theorists do not agree on why we are who we are. Parents should recognize where they can and cannot influence the sexual development of their children. Also the individual should know where to turn for more information.

The internet offers myriad opportunities to click into useful information. Prior to personal computers, however, groups still found ways to connect. Support groups are available for gay and lesbian youth. Boutiques provide clothing to transgendered men and women. Some hospitals conduct sex reassignment surgery. And most large bookstores today have sexuality sections and subsections where individuals can learn more about themselves and people they hold dear and care about.

Emotional Well-being

The cornerstone of emotional well-being is positive sexual self-esteem. Feeling good about ourselves and accepting who we are is vital to health. What is unique about emotional health is that it derives from the other dimensions of health. Feeling good about yourself may result from others liking you, or feeling good about yourself may depend upon your liking your body, or a combination of these.

All of us need to have realistic expectations about who we are. As the lyrics from "I Am Who I Am" highlight, though, "Life is not worth a damn until you can shout 'I am who I am.'" In essence, we all need to accept ourselves.

The road to positive self-acceptance is longer for some than others. If you cannot be open about who you are, secrecy and oppression take their toll. Support groups and mental health professionals trained in the area of sexuality can be extremely helpful to those who are struggling with identity issues, acceptance of their orientation, and figuring out how to negotiate environments that prove to be hostile.

Because our emotional health is also connected to others' behavior, we must focus attention on the need to reduce the hostility and discrimination faced by those who are perceived as "different." Improving the mental health of others and their ability to accept difference are critical factors in reducing oppression and permitting variations in lifestyle to co-exist.

Social Well-being

Social health depends upon making connections with others. We learn to do that by first making connections with our families, and then making friends and expanding our social groups. Our families affect our gender identity through the teaching of gender roles, although they are not the sole teachers. Once children interact in schools, turn on a television set, or take a trip to a shopping mall, they become exposed to the various ways that males and females appear and act. Comments of approval and disapproval shape our behaviors; they also can be the basis for whether we feel good or bad about ourselves.

The process to a clear and comfortable sexual identity is not always easy. For those who are gay, lesbian, bisexual, or transgendered, relationships with others may add risk in a way that heterosexuals don't experience: being thrown out of one's home, losing a job, or losing friends. Strong negative reactions to another's openness sever what were and could continue to be important relationships and, on a much broader level, diminish the humanity of our culture.

Although people do not segregate themselves socially based on sexuality, at times the ability to join a community of others like yourself becomes critical to one's health. That community may be on the internet, at a conference or gathering, in a therapeutic support group, and in the home. Urban areas offer more social opportunities than small towns regarding sexual identity. A number of cities (New York City and San Francisco, in particular) are known for their tolerance. Therefore, they have become places to which people purposely move to live a fuller life.

Spiritual Well-being

To achieve a sense of wholeness is a powerful experience. To recognize who you are and be free to express yourself are strong spiritual manifestations. Meditation and prayer have varying roles in people's lives, regardless of religious affiliation. Organized religion sometimes contributes to spiritual pain, yet more progressive religious groups are offering services to and welcoming people of varied orientations and lifestyles. Other groups that help people connect include centers and support groups that allow people to be with others who accept them.

Environmental Well-being

On an individual basis, we all must find a place to call home — a place that feels safe and secure and where we can be ourselves. The homes we grew up in may or may not have been places like this. Health and positive growth require that children be loved and nurtured and allowed to develop in their own unique way.

Some children live in environments that are threatening to their sexual development. Taunts and abuse from schoolmates, threats of, and real, violence from strangers, and, for some, self-abuse and suicide can result from identity issues. No longer should a child who is transgendered be mistaken as schizophrenic. No longer should a child be institutionalized in a mental hospital where shock treatments or other forms of aversive therapy are used to change sexual orientation. The medical community is better informed — though not necessarily better prepared — to deal with these issues.

Laws at the federal, state, and local levels have been slow to protect the civil rights of gay, lesbian, and transgendered individuals. The courts have made decisions about custody of children in divorce cases that usually favor the heterosexual parent. When gays or lesbians have tried to adopt children, their requests often have been denied, even if it means a child continues to live in an institution or a foster home. (Chapter 13 discusses the concerns of gay and lesbian parents in greater detail.) When the military adopted a "Don't ask, don't tell" policy, it was thought to be an improvement over denying gays and lesbians the right to serve in the armed forces. Media reports, however, show that individuals are still being investigated and discharged solely on the basis of their sexual orientation.

Creating environments where people can be who they are helps reduce the power of sexual difference and allows society to be enriched with citizens who can safely develop to their full potential. People learn that sexual identity is only one piece of a person's being, and that a person can form working relationships and even friendships, that allow for differences. Tolerant, respectful, and safe environments improve the opportunities for everyone.

WEB RESOURCES

Intersex Society of North America (ISNA)

http://www.isna.org/

A peer support, education, and advocacy group established for intersexuals, individuals born with anatomy or physiology different from cultural ideals of male and female. Available at this site are facts and questions (FAQ) of commonly asked questions with the ability to ask your own questions as well, a library to order books on the subject of transgender, and current information on a variety of health issues.

Kinsey Institute for Research in Sex, Gender, and Reproduction

http://www.indiana.edu/~kinsey/

Supports interdisciplinary research, scholarship, and study in the field of human sexuality, gender, and reproduction. The site lists professional organizations, articles, reference resources and a new link to Kinsey Institute Sexuality Research Information Service.

Parents, Families and Friends of Lesbians and Gays (PFLAG)

http://www.pflag.org/

A national, nonprofit organization supporting parents, families, and friends of lesbians and gays. The site provides resources, literature to assist in coping and to educate society to work to end discrimination and secure equal civil rights.

Renaissance Transgender Association

http://www.ren.org/

Provides comprehensive education and support to transgendered persons and those close to them. The association offers programs and resources for crossdressers, transvestites, and transexuals. The site offers articles from the International Congress on Sex and Gender.

Notes

1. "Sex Role Adaptability: One Consequence of Psychological Androgyny," *Journal of Personality and Social Psychology*, 31 (1975), 634–643; *Dismantling Gender Polarization: Shall We Turn the Volume Down or Shall We Turn the Volume Up?* Keynote address, 1995 Eastern Region Annual Conference, Society for the Scientific Study of Sexuality, West Atlantic City, NJ, April, 1995; also, C. Muehlenhard, Presidential address, Joint Meeting of American Association of Sex Educators, Counselors, and Therapists and Society for the Scientific Study of Sexuality, Arlington, VA, November, 1997.

2. Based on the work of J. Money and A. Ehrhardt, *Man and Woman, Boy and Girl* (Baltimore: Johns Hopkins University, 1972).

3. M. Diamond, "Sexual Identity, Monozygotic Twins Reared in Discordant Sex Roles and a BBC Follow Up," *Archives of Sexual Behavior*, 11:2 (1982), 181–186; M. Diamond and H. K. Sigmundson, *Archives of Pediatrics and Adolescent Medicine*, March 1997.

4. E. Coleman, L. Gooren, and M. Ross, "Theories of Gender Transpositions: A Critique and Suggestions for Further Research, *Journal of Sex Research*, 26:4 (1989), 525–538; M. Hines and M. L. Collaer, "Gonadal Hormones and Sex Differences," *Annual Review of Sex Research*, 4 (1993), 1–48.

5. C. Vance "Anthropology Rediscovers Sexuality: A Theoretical Comment," *Social Science Medicine*, 33:8 (1988), 875–884.

6. *Sex and Temperament in Three Primitive Societies* (New York: Morrow, 1935).

7. *The Lenses of Gender: Transforming the Debate on Sexual Inequality* (New Haven, CT: Yale University Press, 1993).

8. S. Bem, "Sex Role Adaptability: One Consequence of Psychological Androgyny," *Journal of Personality and Social Psychology*, 31 (1975), 634–643; R. LaTorre, "Gender Role and Psychological Adjustment," *Archives of Sexual Behavior*, 7:2 (1978), 89–96.

9. J. M. Bailey and C. Pillard, A Genetic Study of Male Sexual Orientation," *Archives of General Psychiatry*, 48 (1991), 1089–1096; J. M. Bailey, R. C. Pillard, M. C. Neal, and Y. Agyei "Heritable Factors Influence Sexual Orientation in Women," *Archives of General Psychiatry*, 50 (1993), 217–223.

10. L. Ellis and M. A. Ames "Neurohormonal Function and Sexual Orientation: A Theory of Homosexuality-Heterosexuality," *Psychological Bulletin*, 101 (1987), 233–258; L. Ellis, M. A. Ames, W. Peckham, and D. Burke, "Sexual Orientation of Human Offspring May be Altered by Severe Maternal Stress During Pregnancy," *Journal of Sex Research*, 25 (1988), 152–157.

11. A. Banks and N. K. Gartrell, "Hormones and "Sexual Orientation: A Questionable Link," *Journal of Homosexuality*, 28 (1995), 247–268.

12. "A Difference in Hypothalamic Structure Between Heterosexual and Homosexual Men," *Science*, 253 (1991), 1034–1037.

13. A. Bell, M. Weinberg, and S. Hammersmith, *Sexual Preference* (Bloomington: Indiana University Press, 1981).

14. A. Kensey, W. Pomeroy, and C. Martin, *Sexual Behavior in the Human Female* (Philadelphia: Saunders, 1948); A. Kinsey, W. Pomeroy, C. Martin, and P. Gebhard, *Sexual Behavior in the Human Female* (Philadelphia: Saunders, 1953).

15. *The Bisexual Option* (New York: Arbor House, 1978); F. Klein, B. Sepekoff, and T. J. Wolf, "Sexual Orientations: A Multivariable Dynamic Process," in *Bisexualities: Theory and Research*, edited by F. Klein and T. J. Wolf (New York: Haworth Press, 1985).

16. Kinsey et al., 1948 and 1953.

17. E. Laumann, J. Gagnon, R. Michael, and S. Michaels, *The Social Organization of Sexuality: Sexual Practices in the United States* (Chicago: University of Chicago Press, 1994).

18. R. Michael, J. Gagnon, E. Laumann, and G. Kolata, *Sex in America* (Boston: Little Brown, 1994).

19. Ibid.

20. Intersex Society of North America, *Recommendations for Treatment: Intersex Infants and Children* (San Francisco: ISNA, 1995).

21. S. Abramowitz (1986), "Psychosocial Outcomes of Sex Reassignment Surgery," *Journal of Consulting and Clinical Psychology*, 54 (1986), 183–189.

Student Study Questions

1. How are gender role, gender identity, and sexual orientation related?

2. What are the similarities and differences between heterosexual, homosexual, lesbian, and bisexual gender role, gender identity, and sexual orientation?

3. How do biological and psychosocial factors interact to influence gender development?

4. What is androgyny?

5. What are four major factors impacting on gender development?

6. How are men and women similar and different?

Messages About Gender

Our present thoughts and feelings concerning what being a man or a woman means have evolved over the years. A myriad of people and sources have contributed to our development. The purpose of this assessment is to trace the origin of many of the assumptions we all have about gender by examining the messages we received as children.

1. Describe in writing one specific message you received about expected male/female behavior during the following phases in your life that are applicable:

    a. preschool period

    b. elementary school period

    c. junior high/middle school

    d. high school

    e. college

    f. young adult (20s)

Continued

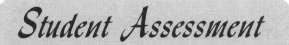

Student Assessment

Messages About Gender (cont.)

g. adulthood (30s–40s)

h. older adulthood

2. Describe the source of the message (parents, family, friends, etc.) and the context (where/when it was delivered)

3. Describe the immediate impact of the message on your gender identity/role

4. Describe the long-term impact of the message

Psychosexual Development: Childhood Through Adolescence

Major Topics

Personality Theories
  Behaviorism (Watson)
  Humanism (Maslow)
  Psychoanalytic Theory (Freud)
  Neo-Freudian Theory (Erikson)
Early Psychosexual Development
  Bonding
  Other Forms of Physical Intimacy
  Self-Exploration and Masturbation
  Nudity
  Toilet Training
  Other Early Tasks
Psychosexual Development in Early
  Childhood
Psychosexual Development:
  Childhood
Psychosexual Development in
  Preadolescence
Psychosexual Development
  During Adolescence
  Primary Sex Characteristics
  Secondary Sex Characteristics
  Adolescent Sexual Behavior
  Cultural Attitudes About
    Adolescent Sexuality
Retarded Sexual Development
  Consequences of Retarded Sexual
    Development
  Dealing with Adolescent Sexuality
Wellness Synthesis
  Physical Well-being
  Intellectual Well-being
  Emotional Well-being
  Social Well-being
  Spiritual Well-being
  Environmental Well-being

Student Learning Objectives

After reading this chapter, students will be able to:

- Compare and contrast a variety of theories of personality from birth through adolescence.

- Describe how the key aspects from various psychological theories impact psychosexual development.

- Discuss the effects of maternal and paternal bonding on healthy psychosexual development.

- Evaluate the impact of self-pleasuring and masturbation on psychosexual development.

- Describe the effects of childhood nudity on healthy sexual development.

- Describe the impact of toilet training on psychosexual development.

- Compare the biological consequences of puberty with the psychosocial aspects of adolescence.

- Describe the findings of a variety of studies concerning adolescent sexual behavior.

- Compare the adolescent sexual behavior of people in the United States with those from other cultures.

- Evaluate the positive and negative aspects of sexual intercourse during adolescence.

Psychosexual development
the blending of sexual aspects of one's development with other psychological factors

Psychosexual development is the process of becoming a sexual person. The term traditionally refers to the psychological aspects of sexual development. As we've mentioned throughout this text, though, to completely separate the psychological from the physical, intellectual, emotional, social, spiritual, and environmental facets of our sexuality is not possible. Because most discussions of psychosexual development present it as an outgrowth of personality, we will start by discussing personality and how it develops. We'll then move into a discussion of how some of the classical personality theorists explain psychosexual development.

PERSONALITY THEORIES

Personality
the collection of values, attitudes, and behavior that make us who we are

Personality is the entire collection of one's thoughts, attitudes, values, beliefs, perceptions and behaviors. Our personalities define how we see ourselves independently and within our environment. Personality is constantly evolving and is cumulative in nature. Your personality today is the sum total of all of the things you have experienced until this point in your life. Various theories have been proposed to explain how personality develops. Table 5.1 outlines four prominent theories of personality.

Our personality is constantly evolving and is cumulative in nature.

Behaviorism (Watson)

Behaviorism
a stimulus-response theory of personality development grounded in the belief that human personality evolves as a result of the interaction between exposure to stimuli and the responses that this exposure evokes in the person. Watson is credited with the theory, expanded later by Skinner

Behaviorism, developed by John Watson,[1] proposes that personality develops as a result of responses to general and specific stimuli. A stimulus-response model, it does not presuppose any innate human personality attributes. Behaviorists believe that at birth we are blank slates with no predetermined attributes. Our personalities evolve as the result of myriad interactions between stimuli (people, places, events, situations, images) and the responses they evoke. Responses can be either positive or negative and vary in strength. The more powerful the response, the more likely we will either embrace (positive response) or reject (negative response) whatever stimulus prompted it.

Table 5.1 Traditional Models of Personality	
Theory/Theorist	**Theme**
Behavioral (Watson)	Human responses to specific or generalized stimuli to explain human behavior
Humanism (Maslow)	Growth in response to inner needs
Psychoanalytic (Freud)	Growth as struggle between the unconscious-irrational and the conscious-rational mind
Neo-Freudian (Erikson)	Psychosocial aspects of growth

Let's use masturbation to explain how this stimulus-response model works. Imagine that when you were an infant, your mother caught you fondling yourself while lying on the rug in the living room in front of your grandmother. Your mother was upset and smacked your hand, saying, "Bad girl. Little ladies don't touch themselves down there." This negative reinforcement (slapping the hand away and saying "bad girl") in response to a stimulus (touching yourself) begins to shape how you feel toward masturbation. The specific context (in the living room, in a public setting, in front of grandma) also contributes to shaping the behavior.

If this response is repeated over time, in similar and different contexts, it can either extinguish (get rid of) the behavior of masturbation or drive it underground and surround it with shame and guilt. The person then might practice the behavior in private and associate it with negative feelings.

Other personality theories stress developmental stages and tasks. These theories propose that personality develops in stages that build upon each other.

Humanism (Maslow)

Maslow,[2] was one of the most influential humanists. The premise of **humanism** is that human beings are motivated by a desire for personal growth. Maslow believed that all humans are unique, and are capable of growth and reaching their utmost potential in all facets of their lives. Humans are essentially good and are capable of making choices about the direction their lives will take. Maslow believed that all people are capable of reaching their highest potential if they progress through a series of stages of development that meet various basic human needs. Figure 5.1 presents Maslow's hierarchy of needs. As you can see, they reflect the physical, social, intellectual, emotional, spiritual, and environmental domains that characterize present-day wellness theory.

Humanism
a theory of personality development proposing that human personality development is shaped by innate desire and need for maximizing personal growth

Few of us will fully self-actualize all of our potentials.

PERSPECTIVES

Characteristics of Transcenders

The following are characteristics of individuals who achieve self-actualization through transcendence:

- Transcenders have more "peak" or creative experiences than others.
- Transcenders are more responsive to beauty and more holistic in their perceptions of humanity and the world.
- Transcenders are innovators who are attracted to the unknown, embrace change, and see themselves as the instruments of their transcendence.

- Transcenders can fuse work and play. They are less attracted by the rewards of money and more motivated by the satisfaction of being true to who they really are and serving others.
- Transcenders are more likely to accept others with unconditional positive regard.

Source: *The Farthest Reaches of Human Nature*, by Abraham Maslow (Magnolia, MA: Peter Smith Publishers, 1983).

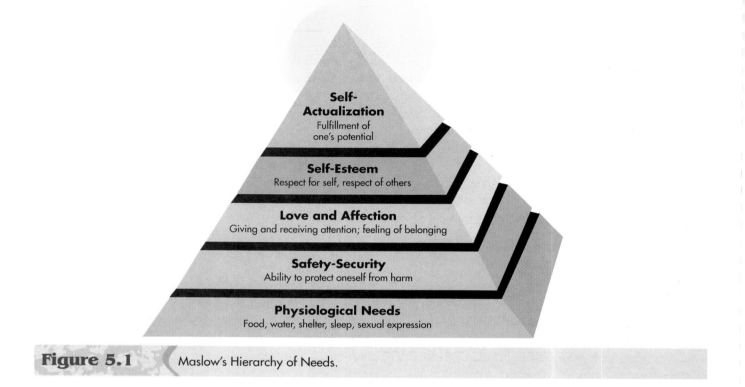

Figure 5.1   Maslow's Hierarchy of Needs.

Transcend
to rise above or extend beyond ordinary limits

Psychoanalytic theory
also known as Freudian theory (after its founder, Sigmund Freud), describes personality development as outgrowth of interaction of id (pleasure-seeking, guilt-free), superego (the conscience, influenced by society and parents), and ego (rational, analytical mind driven by logical thinking)

Ego
rational, analytical facet of human mind, according to Freudian theory

Superego
the conscience, influenced by society and family, according to Freudian theory

Id
pleasure-seeking, guilt-free facet of human mind, according to Freudian theory

Before people can develop loving, intimate relationships, they must meet their most fundamental needs for survival and safety that form the basis of the pyramid. To get to the top, one has to pass through all of the previous levels, successfully meeting the needs of each stage before preceding to the next. The top of Maslow's pyramid, self-actualization, represents the pinnacle of human development. People reaching the top are said to be fully self-actualized.

Maslow also believed that, as we work our way up this pyramid, we often encounter "peak experiences" — moments that crystallize what it means to be fully alive, to **transcend** mere existence. Maslow believed that these peak experiences help us feel connected to the world around us, to be one with our universe.

Psychoanalytic Theory (Freud)

Freudian **psychoanalytic theory** purports that personality develops as a result of a struggle between conscious and unconscious forces in our lives.[3] These forces are directed by our **ego** (the rational, thinking mind), **superego** (the conscience) and **id** (the pleasure-seeking life force). The ego is conscious and based in reality, interweaving sensory perceptions with thoughts and memories. The superego, which is partially unconscious, is judgmental; it factors in our beliefs about right and wrong.

The superego advises and sometimes threatens the ego. When the superego threatens the ego's judgment, this causes conflict and guilt. These forces struggle for control of our behavior with the id, the unconscious, irrational mind, which is driven by eros, a powerful life force motivated by the "pleasure principle." Freud called the fuel of this life force "libidinal energy." The id does not distinguish between right and wrong, good and evil. Whatever brings pleasure is good. The superego (in concert with the ego) is supposed to keep the id in check.

Freud believed that the transference of libidinal energy has direct consequences for our psychosexual development. According to him, libidinal energy is channeled into various centers of the body during different stages of human development, creating a set of needs that must be satisfied. Ultimately, when we reach adulthood, this libidinal energy resides in our genitals. Our personality, and our psychosexual development, develops in response to our ability to satisfy these libidinal needs. If we do not, we become fixated, or stuck, at various stages of life and develop neurotic personality and sexual traits. These traits carry over into the successive stages of development unless they are resolved at some point in time.

Oral Stage

The first, or oral, stage lasts from birth to the second year of life. During the oral stage, stimulation of the mouth through sucking, biting, and swallowing is the main source of erotic satisfaction. Inadequate satisfaction during the oral stage, according to Freud, would produce an "oral personality" — someone preoccupied with mouth habits such as overeating or smoking.

Anal Stage

During the second, anal phase, from ages 2 to 3, libidinal energy shifts to the anus. During this stage, the child derives pleasure from anal stimulation and being in control of defecation. This provides the child's first real opportunity to assert some independence from parental control.

This stage coincides with toilet training. Freud believed it is the holding back or letting go of bowel movements (personal control) that produces physical and psychological pleasure for the child.

Rushing a child through toilet training (thereby limiting the ability to derive anal pleasure) or making too big a fuss over soiling the diapers or making a mess could result in fixation at this stage. People who are fixated at this stage are either anal-expulsive (dirty, extravagant, wasteful) or anal-retentive (excessively clean, neat, cheap, and compulsive).

Phallic Stage

The third phase of development is the phallic stage, between the third and fourth years. During this time, libidinal energy shifts to the genitals and the child derives erotic pleasure through fondling and exhibitionism. Freud also believed that during this time the child develops a sexual attachment to the opposite-sex parent and becomes fearful of the parent of the same sex. Named the **Oedipal complex** (after the Greek legend in which Oedipus killed his father and married his mother), this attachment, if handled calmly and without undue concern or punishment, gradually subsides as the child moves into the next stage, latency.

Oedipal complex
a psychoanalytic term (named after Oedipus in Shakespeare's play) that describes the internal struggle that 3- to 4-year-olds face as they begin to identify more with their opposite-sex parent

Latency Stage

Freud believed that sexuality goes into a period of latency extending from age 5 until puberty. At this time, the child becomes more focused on nonsexual interests such as intellectual and social issues.

Genital

At puberty, genital sexuality reemerges, and the adolescent becomes sexually attracted to members of the opposite sex, a prerequisite for marriage and childrearing. Freud's theory is unabashedly heterosexist and is founded on the belief that marriage and heterosexuality are the hallmarks of normal psychosexual development.[4]

Neo-Freudian Theory (Erikson)

Neo-Freudians took issue with one or more aspects of Freud's developmental theory. Erik Erikson constructed a model of personality development that views it as the result of a struggle between opposing forces that present themselves in a series of stages that occur throughout our lives.[5] Figure 5.2 shows Erikson's eight stages of development. Instead of the struggle between the libidinal-driven id and the ego/superego, Erikson viewed development as a conflict between opposing psychosocial forces and qualities. According to Erikson, to continue to grow, we must resolve these crises.

Healthy personality development results from accomplishing the developmental tasks required for the stage and then moving on to the next one.

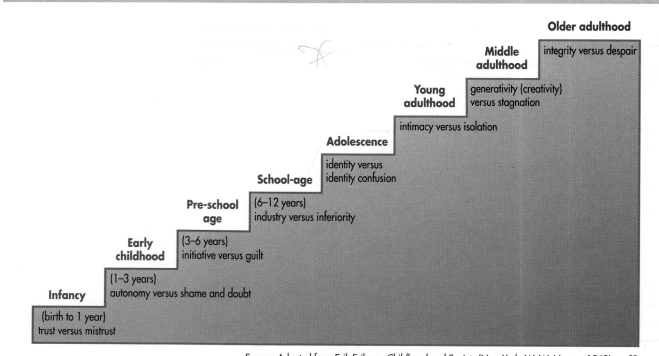

Source: Adopted from Erik Erikson, *Childhood and Society* (New York: W. W. Norton, 1963), p. 52.

Figure 5.2   Erikson's Developmental Stages and Conflicts.

In a sense, positive attributes win out over negative attributes, and the personality development moves to the next level. Inadequate task resolution results in thwarted development in that particular area. This leaves the person with a lack of certain skills and attributes that will be needed later in life.

For example, if, as an infant, one never successfully develops a sense of trust in oneself and others, the person will grow up with a stronger sense of mistrust. This stays with the person throughout life, limiting the ability to trust others, develop sustained loving relationships, and maximize the individual's potential as an adult. The inability to trust another person makes it difficult to develop intimate relationships based on faith, and sharing deeply personal emotions.

Compare the four theories discussed here. How do you relate them personally? Do you recognize any of the stages in your life?

EARLY PSYCHOSEXUAL DEVELOPMENT

Five common themes related to early sexuality transcend all of the theories about psychosexual development: bonding, other expressions of physical intimacy, self-exploration and masturbation, nudity, and toilet training. Even though theorists might differ in their interpretation and significance, most would agree that they exert a tremendous impact on psychosexual development. These critical psychosexual development issues surface during infancy and childhood and remain throughout life. How our caregivers initially handle these issues strongly influences the direction our psychosexual development takes.

The major task of infancy, according to Erikson, is to develop a sense of trust. For trust to win out over mistrust is essential to continuing healthy psychological development in all of us.

Bonding

One of the earliest behaviors that helps foster trust and satisfies our most primal physiological needs is bonding. **Bonding** is a process of developing a close physical and psychological relationship with one's primary caregiver. Bonding between mother and child begins almost immediately as the newborn and mother are brought together to share the first moments of life. Bonding continues as mother and child are brought together during feeding, diaper changing, and simple things such as smiling, talking to the child, and acknowledging the child when approaching him or her.

Fathers, too, can fulfill a bonding role. They can develop strong, close physical bonds with their children and share in their care and feeding. More and more fathers are taking advantage of this opportunity.[6]

Bonding
the close physical and emotional attachment between infants and their primary caregiver(s)

Bonding can take many forms. Here, a mom enjoys a splash in the pool with her new baby.

Thriving
pattern of normal weight gain, neuromuscular development, and other developmental attributes of infants

During the bonding process, infants learn to associate mother and father with fulfilling the most basic needs for sustaining life. Trust in the world as a whole begins by trusting in mothers and fathers. Infants respond positively to touch. **Thriving** — a term pediatricians use to describe physical and psychological growth — is enhanced by touch and bonding. Failure to thrive has been noted in infants who, among other things, have been deprived of sufficient physical nurturing during infancy. As children, these infants often lack the cognitive and motor abilities of their peers.

Other Forms of Physical Intimacy

In addition to bonding as a contributor to the development of sensuality and sexuality, other forms of touch play an important part. Beyond the basic need of touch for infants to thrive, touch is related to the development of sensuality. Our entire skin surface is capable of acting as an erogenous zone. It is sensitive to touch in all of its manifestations. Babies love to be held, stroked, and rocked. Although we can't interview them, we can tell this from the cooing sounds they make, their facial expressions, and their continued responsiveness to our stroking and hugging them. Our ability or inability to respond positively to physical intimacy is believed to be rooted in the time our parents spent touching and stroking us as infants.[7]

How we touch babies varies from generalized hugging and stroking to infant massage and baby exercise. Infant massage strokes are similar to those used with adults, but much gentler. Care must be taken to avoid sharp movements. Infants generally won't last through an entire full-body massage; they begin to wriggle and laugh. We should enjoy this lighthearted moment with them.[8]

Unfortunately, many parents feel awkward or uncomfortable expressing themselves through touch and physical contact. Some of us have grown up in households where touch was withheld or minimized. Sometimes parents worry that their feelings (or their child's) are sexual, not sensual. Even

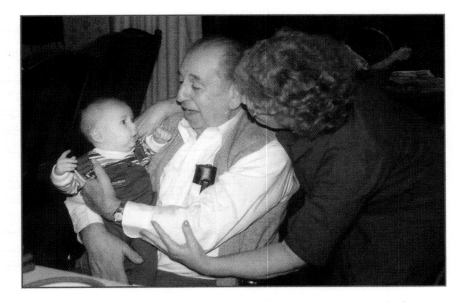

Grandparents can lavish love and attention on their grandchildren and bring extra sources of love and affection.

though infants are capable of experiencing erotic pleasure, sensual pleasure shared with your child and sexual desire are different. Mature, parental sensual pleasure associated with hugging and stroking one's child is vastly different from sexually desiring that child. There is no intention of genital sexual contact, nor is there any desire to experience such behavior.

An aversion to touch is a learned behavior. As such, you can unlearn it and not make the same mistakes with your own children. In sharing the joys of touch with them, you can relearn the joys of physical closeness and sensuality.

Self-Exploration and Masturbation

All infants discover the joys of genital pleasure inadvertently. They discover what it feels like to have their genitals rub against things in their immediate environment (crib, blanket, toys, diaper, clothing, their mother and father). If allowed to do so, infants between 6 and 12 months of age will touch their genitals. They will learn that they are capable of initiating the same pleasurable feelings they felt when rubbing against objects.

Sexologists have long debated whether this behavior should be considered **masturbation**, a form of "sexual" behavior. Although it is definitely sensual and erotic, it lacks the associated sexual connotations that older children and adults have concerning genital pleasuring. These associations are learned later. This genital play should be evaluated exactly for what it is — play.[9] It feels good, and children become frustrated if their hands are kept away from their genitals.

Infant self-exploration and masturbation also lay the foundation for developing a broad continuum of sexual feelings and behaviors. Masturbation is a normal developmental act, one of the earliest forms of sexual activity. Most children discover masturbation quite innocently as a physical, not sexual, act.

Boys' penile erections often occur as sexual reflexes in response to a variety of stimuli ranging from self-touching to breastfeeding. Girls experience clitoral erection and lubrication under similar circumstances.

Masturbation
individual or mutual stimulation of genitalia by hand or using other objects

These earliest attempts at self-exploration teach us about our body and the potential it has for providing pleasure. Conversely, the body has the potential for negatively influencing sexual development if parents overreact to their children's attempts at self-stimulation. Adults who punish children for masturbating may be denying them valuable opportunities for learning about self-pleasuring and setting the stage for negative attitudes (shame, guilt, fear) about sex. Parents who say nothing about masturbation send negative messages through their omission. Children learn that these omissions represent areas that are off-limits for discussion.

Yelling at a child, slapping his or her hand away, admonishing the child for doing something "dirty" — these adult responses to masturbation convey strong negative messages. Negatively reinforcing a behavior that is pleasurable — self-exploration — creates a confusing mixed message. If it is more related to the timing of these acts (little Billy always seems to play with his penis when Grandma is sitting next to him), gently moving the child to a crib or playpen in another room might help. When children become verbal, caregivers might explain to them that playing with themselves under private conditions (such as in their own rooms) is okay but it is not all right in more public settings where it might offend others (such as Grandma or the neighbors).

Masturbatory behavior is self-limiting.

Self-exploration, again, is normal. It cannot be carried to excess and is self-limiting if children are left alone. Adults should view it like other forms of play. It is amusing for a while, and then the child moves on to something else. If left alone, children will not sit in their rooms all day and play with themselves. Parents who cannot accept their children's self-exploration might discuss the matter with a counselor, priest, rabbi, minister, pediatrician, or sex therapist to get help in dealing with their feelings. Exploring their sexual fears and concerns will reassure them that this self-touching behavior will not misguide their children's sexual development.

Nudity

Infants and children are nudists at heart. Most infants and young children are perfectly comfortable lying and running around the house naked. They do not associate nudity with morality. To be naked to them is simply to be

Babies are sensual creatures. They like to be nude and feel the softness and textures of things such as this sheepskin throw.

without clothes. Parents and other caregivers (and, later, society at large) teach infants and children that nudity has sexual overtones.

Our culture, however, associates nudity with sexuality. In contrast, Scandinavian cultures have nude beaches that cater to families. Being naked with one's family is considered normal and healthy.

Unlike some other cultures that accept nudity as part of life and don't make a big deal about it one way or another, U. S. culture frowns upon most public displays of nakedness. We owe this to our puritan heritage. When they came to America, the puritans enacted many laws that attempted to curtail public displays of nakedness and sexual behavior. To this day, laws dating back to the early 1800s still are on the books concerning things such

The best way to handle nudity is to establish limits with which you and your spouse are comfortable.

as proper swimming attire. The rigid views concerning sex and nudity grew out of Victorian England of the 18th century. In that formal, rigid culture, visions of naked flesh were linked to uncontrolled sexual desire and giving into the will of the devil. In an almost comical adherence to covering their exposed limbs, the Victorians went to extremes such as putting "skirts" onto the legs of pianos and chairs lest they offend and tempt their owners to engage in lewd behavior.

Even though most states allow private displays of nudity in nudist colonies, this behavior is the exception rather than the rule. Community opposition to nude beaches, clubs, and public displays of nudity is still strong. Women seem to bear a heavier burden than men in our culture. Men are almost always allowed to go topless in public while female toplessness is considered lewd and almost always against the law.

Case Study

Experiences with Nursing

I grew up in a very puritanical household. My parents rarely touched or showed any kind of physical affection toward each other or my brother and me. I know they loved each other and us, but it just wasn't their way to express it physically, in public. Nudity also was not tolerated, and sex was never discussed.

I'm lucky to have made it through life with few ill effects from this kind of childhood. I think what saved me was meeting Michael. Michael has taught me how to be comfortable with my sexuality. He has been patient and loving and, most important, very physical. He has taught me that the physical expression of affection and love is a natural and positive thing.

It was Michael's idea to breastfeed our son Tommy. At first I was aghast at the idea. It seemed lewd

or immoral, but Michael persisted and helped me identify and accept the feelings I was having. He asked me to try it and give it some time. I found that I really enjoyed nursing Tommy. It created a special bond between us. Sometimes Michael would get in bed with us when we were nursing, and rub my back or stroke Tommy gently.

Nursing really set the stage for my accepting nudity and things like taking showers and bathing together. When Tommy got a little older, it also opened up opportunities to talk about things like "how boys and girls are different."

Given our puritanical heritage and history of opposition to nudity, most Americans not surprisingly feel more comfortable with their clothes on than off. This collective discomfort with nudity affects our comfort level with our own bodies and our ability to relax and be sensual and sexual with others.

Understanding nudity and how we deal with it with our infants and children has many facets. How we handle nudity plays a big part in the kind of foundation we lay for our children's psychosexual development. Many parents fear being nude with their children. Their fears range from their baby "having an accident" (unintentional urination/defecation) to transmitting the wrong message about sex. In actuality, letting your child be naked or being nude with your child is perfectly normal and healthy.

Bonding is enhanced by nudity. The warmth and close, physical contact that can be achieved from skin-to-skin contact is unparalleled. Even partial nudity, torso-to-torso, conveys a special closeness that cannot be achieved any other way. Allowing your children to be nude while establishing reasonable parameters for family nudity seems to be a prudent, middle-of-the-road approach to this issue.

We do not have the same accepting attitude toward nudity that we do concerning self-pleasuring.

Sol Gordon, renowned sexuality educator, believes that parents are taking on a relaxed attitude about nudity.[10] Further, Gordon believes that being nude with your child creates many "teachable moments" — those points in time when a child's curiosity about sexuality is given a natural outlet. Children will want to know why "mommy doesn't have a penis" or why "daddy's penis is bigger than juniors." These spontaneous questions provide opportunities to ask questions and explore basic sexual information and issues. In a way, it helps parents become more "askable." Taking advantage of teachable moments is

Skin-to-skin contact is something babies (and adults) enjoy.

Case Study

A Father's Bonding with His Son

I remember the first 6 months of my son's life vividly. My wife was breastfeeding, and we'd take turns getting up for Adam. When it was Susan's turn, she'd get up and go into Adam's room and nurse him while rocking in the chair in his room. When it was my turn (he normally nursed every 2 or 3 hours), I'd go in and get him and bring him to Susan. She'd nurse him, and I'd bring him back and put him down in his crib.

We took turns because sometimes Adam wouldn't go back to sleep without more rocking. We decided it would be more fair if we split the responsibility. At first I really resented it. I was so tired and felt like a zombie all day. I remember the first night I got over my initial resentment. I was sitting rocking Adam at two-thirty in the morning after getting two hours of sleep. I tried telling myself that we'd soon be through this stage and I may never experience this opportunity again, so I should try to relax and enjoy the moment.

I had just changed his dirty diaper, and after cleaning him off, I held him to my chest instead of putting on another diaper. I had my robe on, so I nestled him against my chest, partially covered by my robe. I rocked him as I cradled his head and looked into his eyes. He seemed so content, so peaceful. I continued to rock him and put his head on my shoulder while I gazed out his bedroom window. He was so soft, and he had that baby smell. I could feel his little heart beating against mine.

It was incredibly peaceful. I felt truly at one with Adam and the world around us. At that moment I felt truly in love with my wife for bringing me this son. I think that was a turning point in my life. From then on I no longer resented him and his demands on my life. Although I can't honestly say I looked forward to his two o'clock wake-up calls, I did begin to appreciate the time we spent together and the special closeness I felt with him, skin-to-skin, father to son.

a way to take advantage of children's natural curiosity and is preferable to forcing discussions about the "birds and the bees" at inopportune times.

Children naturally grow out of the desire to be nude around their parents. As they move into middle childhood and prepubescence, they become more independent and develop a personal sense of modesty. This is usually accompanied by their desire for more privacy and for other family members to be more fully clothed around the house.

Toilet Training

The mastery of toilet training is essential in completing the developmental tasks of toddlers, as well as building a solid foundation for sexual health and positive psychosexual development. Toilet-training is empowering for children. Along with mastering bowel control, they gain a measure of self-control, self-esteem, and independence. Wearing "big boy pants" is how one friend's son refers to his newfound freedom from diapers.

If parents or caregivers handle toilet-training properly and do not rush their children, they develop a sense of pride in accomplishing something important to them. Toilet-training is messy and involves a lot of time and work. Parents need to understand this and be careful not to punish their children or criticize them too harshly for the inevitable "mistakes" and soiled underpants they will encounter. Splitting the labor can help. When moms and dads (or other combinations of caregivers) work together, they each get a break from changing diapers and cleaning up messes.

Parents also need to accept that each child progresses through this stage on a different time schedule. When children are ready to give up diapers, they will. Adults can't rush the process or predict how long it will take. Trying to rush the child to fit someone else's timeline (for example, the day care center will take only toilet-trained children) may not be the best strategy. Following these simple guidelines, your children can develop those all-important feelings of self-control and self-esteem.[11]

Other Early Tasks

Another major developmental task of early childhood is learning to walk. Children who are helped with, but not overly protected from, the bumps and falls that are a normal part of learning to walk develop a sense of control

Health Hint

Becoming an Askable Parent

Becoming an askable parent is a lifelong process. A neon sign doesn't suddenly appear during adolescence signaling approachability. Being an askable parent is a reward earned after years of sending subtle messages about the desire to listen and willingness to help. The following are guidelines on how to be an askable parent:

1. *Start early.* Body language and nonverbal behaviors concerning bonding, nudity, and toilet training send messages about approachability.

2. *Don't worry about giving too much information.* Scientific evidence doesn't indicate that too much information too soon will overstimulate children. If a child is getting too much information, he or she will simply get bored, tune you out, and change the subject.

3. *Communicate even if you're not entirely comfortable about the topic.* If you are uncomfortable with a specific sexual issue, you can still address it openly and honestly with your children. The child might respond positively to your admission that you have difficulty talking about an issue.

4. *Admit your ignorance.* You don't know it all. Even the best teachers don't know everything about their subject. If your child asks a question you can't answer, admit it and offer to look it up. Better yet, look it up together.

5. *Realize that less is better.* Concise, simple answers that address the question at hand are better than long-winded answers.

6. *Don't worry about offering information that children can't understand.* If you make a mistake by being too technical, children will extract what they need or understand, and the rest will go over their head.

7. *Don't be afraid to make mistakes.* Everyone makes honest mistakes. Handle these as you would any other mistakes: Admit you were wrong and try to correct the mistake, if possible.

8. *Relate your values.* Children want to know how you feel about sexual matters. Take every opportunity to share relevant values with them.

9. *Have a sense of humor.* Lighten up. Sexuality education gives rise to opportunities to laugh and learn at the same time. Children feel less inhibited about an adult's talking about sexual matters if sex isn't always portrayed as a deadly serious topic.

over their environment. They learn about the literal "bumps and bruises" that are a normal part of achieving anything meaningful in life.

As children become more autonomous, they need to be able to explore their environment safely. To develop a sense of self-control and self-esteem they need to have hazard-free environments and the freedom to explore them autonomously. Children whose exploratory play is restricted or unsafe may even become fearful of being alone or taking a risk later in life. Children who are overly protected and shielded from even the most minor stumbles have a harder time becoming autonomous.

Parents have to realize that boys and girls alike need to develop this sense of autonomy and they are equally able to sustain the normal bumps and bruises inherent in developing autonomy. Traditional parents may feel a need to protect their daughters out of some ill-conceived notion of their frailty. Realizing that the skills essential for developing autonomy are also critical for healthy psychosexual development. Although they are not overtly sexual in nature, these skills help build self-esteem and self-confidence that will influence the child's, and later the adolescent's, ability to make good sexual decisions and minimize unnecessary risk-taking.

> *Skills that are central to developing autonomy are also critical for healthy psychosexual development.*

PSYCHOSEXUAL DEVELOPMENT IN EARLY CHILDHOOD

Self-exploration continues during early childhood (ages 3–5) and often extends to playmates. The more mobile child now begins to interact with other children more frequently. Games such as "doctor" and "nurse" typically provide opportunities for sex-play and exploration. The availability of playmates often influences the nature of play. Same-gender versus opposite-gender exploration is a function of who is available to play with rather than representing any adult sexual orientation (such as heterosexual or homosexual).

Children continue to gain freedom and begin to be exposed to a variety of people and experiences as they further explore their environment. The major task at this stage corresponds to Erikson's developmental initiative versus guilt (refer to Figure 5.2). Children's actions are more purposeful as they evaluate their own competencies and initiate behaviors consistent with these limits. Children's likes and dislikes at this stage are more firmly established, and their behavior is more purposeful. They know what they want and use their greater mobility and freedom to pursue these desires. When this pursuit puts conflicts with how significant others want them to behave, they begin to feel guilt.

Children at this level struggle with their overwhelming preoccupation with self as they are increasingly exposed to other youngsters in a variety of play and social situations. They find themselves in situations with other youngsters that force them to share, take turns, and accommodate others. This socialization is a vital and necessary developmental step that will prepare children for the kinds of social interactions necessary for their future success in school.

As we pointed out in Chapter 4, gender identity is already strongly established by this stage. Little boys and girls know what being masculine and feminine means, and they continue to explore and refine these roles. The more freedom they are given to explore behaviors and roles, the greater opportunity they will have in moving toward a more flexible gender identity. For instance, little girls who are allowed to play with boys and engage in active, physical play and sports might find that they enjoy this type of activity. Little boys who are allowed to play house and with dolls might find this an enjoyable addition to or replacement of more traditional rough-house activities.

PSYCHOSEXUAL DEVELOPMENT: CHILDHOOD

Children continue to explore and mimic gender-role behaviors and scripts they learn from their parents and the culture. "Playing house" is a common script for 5–7 year-olds. The boys play the "daddies" and the girls play the "mommies." Often these games include kissing, hugging, cuddling, and lying on each other. Children at this age talk about people they love and will marry someday. Children often have a "special friend" to whom they are attracted and for whom they have loving feelings. Elementary school children exchange valentines and other symbols of endearment.

Children at this age also begin to develop their own language and sense of sexual humor. Jokes about bodily functions are common. These children have a great deal of interest in sounds and smells associated with bodily functioning. Children of this age are amused by riddles and rhymes that often are crude and sexually coarse.

By 8 or 9 years of age, children begin to become more segregated in their play. Boys tend to play with other boys, and girls with their girlfriends. Although they still have the same interest in the opposite gender, the socialization process begins to segregate them more and more. Formal activities such as team sports and school-based extracurricular activities are often segregated, sometimes formally but usually informally. Little girls who might have played touch football with the guys last season may try out for cheerleading this year. Boys who played sandlot baseball with the neighborhood boys and girls may sign up for Little League while their female counterparts sign up for softball. Leagues in some towns, encourage mixed-gender participation.

In addition to cultural influences that help shape boys and girls and influence which direction they might take regarding sports, economic and political factors play a big part. Often, funding for girls sports and recreational activities does not equal that earmarked for boys. Consequently, girls haven't always been offered the same opportunities as boys to compete in youth sports. To attempt to rectify that, Title IX of the Civil Rights Act was passed to ensure parity in funding.

Title IX is the portion of the federal 1972 Education Amendments Act prohibiting sex discrimination in educational institutions that receive federal funds. The law declares that no person in the United States be excluded from participating in, be deprived of the benefits of, or be subjected to discrimination under any educational program or activity receiving federal financial assistance. Because the overwhelming majority of schools K–college receive federal funds in one form or another, the law covered almost all educational institutions.

The law refers to all benefits and activities available in schools. Most of the controversy regarding Title IX revolves around sports and athletic programs. Title IX has been instrumental in getting more girls and women involved in sports and athletic activities. In 1971, before the law was passed, 294,015 high school girls across the United States participated in high school sports. By 1973, a mere year after the law was instituted, that number had risen to 817,073, and in 1977 (5 years after its inception), more than 2,000,000 high school girls participated. In 1997, more than 3,000,000 girls participated in high school sports. Similar gains were reported for college women. Advocates are still unhappy, however, because of the continuing disparity in funding between men's and women's sports.

Most of the funding disparity is at the high school and college levels, where institutions traditionally spend much more money on men's sports than women's in everything from scholarships to equipment, travel, and training facilities. Football, in particular, has been singled out as the major culprit in funding disparity. In many instances, the football budget of an institution far outstrips spending on all other athletic programs combined.

Title IX advocates demand equal spending for men's and women's sports, even if it means dismantling football programs to achieve this goal. In 1997, Boston University's football program was discontinued, in part because of demands that the institution free up athletic dollars to comply with the mandates of Title IX. Opponents claim that eliminating a men's program to offer additional women's programs is discriminatory in itself. In addition, many alumni and college students think that big-time sports such as football add to the ambiance and tradition of college life and contribute to the institution's appeal.

Do you think this law is beneficial? Give reasons for your opinion.

PSYCHOSEXUAL DEVELOPMENT IN PREADOLESCENCE

Though Freud believed that children's sexual development goes underground roughly between the ages of 6 and 12, ample evidence is quite contrary to this belief. Studies show that although segregation of the sexes is more pronounced during this time, feelings of desire and affection are strong. Most boys and girls of this age view relationships with other preadolescents as important and something they desire. What seemed to be latent, or beneath the surface, to Freud is actually present but is really a work-in-progress.

Children in this age range are learning how to interact with members of the same and opposite sexes they find desirable. They are learning the scripts and rehearsing the behaviors necessary to make the transition from childhood to young adulthood. If adults make fun of pre-adolescents for doing this, they may be afraid to show an interest. Instead, they should be encouraged to have boyfriends or girlfriends.

Sixth-grade dances are good examples of this learning process. The room is filled with 11- and 12-year-olds who want to mix and mingle with girls and boys they are attracted to. What usually happens though, is that boys line up along one wall and the girls the other. They horse around and act goofy but rarely cross the line and ask someone to dance. This is a transition, a rite of passage in American culture. The next year or the year after that, they will begin to cross the line and ask each other to dance. Some will even bring partners to the dance. For now, it is a stepping stone, an opportunity to try out another script.

PSYCHOSEXUAL DEVELOPMENT DURING ADOLESCENCE

Adolescence
time period representing the psychosocial transition from childhood to young adulthood

Adolescence denotes a period of years (roughly between 12 and 18). The major task associated with adolescence is to develop a self-identity.[12] Adolescence can be a time of great excitement and joy as individuals literally move from childhood to adulthood. During adolescence, both the body and the mind change and grow. They outgrow not only their old clothes but often their old ideas as well, and sometimes their old friends, as they struggle to come to grips with who they are and where they are going.

Puberty
biological transition from childhood to young adulthood

Puberty is the time of myriad physiological events that characterize adolescence. It is a time of profound physiological change as the body matures and becomes "reproductively ready" with fully adult genitalia, a reproductive system, and hormones coursing through the bloodstream, sending messages to the brain of arriving sexually.

Psychosocial readiness for sexual activity with another person takes a while to catch up to reproductive readiness. Adolescents become caught in a state of confusion as the body sends the mind messages about sex that the adolescent may not be ready to handle psychosocially.

The media like to exploit this confusion and report about the problems and the failures associated with adolescence. We hear about teenage drug and alcohol misuse, HIV disease, teen pregnancy, satanic cults, and defiant behavior. Movies glorify adolescent rebelliousness and juvenile delinquency. But, as Michael Carrera, a respected adolescent sexuality expert, noted, most teenagers go through this time without major problems and emerge into young adulthood strong, competent, and whole. They try new things and expose themselves to new experiences that foster this discovery.

Psychosocial readiness for sex often does not coincide with reproductive readiness.

Figure 5.3 highlights the physiological changes associated with puberty. In general, these can be grouped into changes associated with primary and secondary sex characteristics.

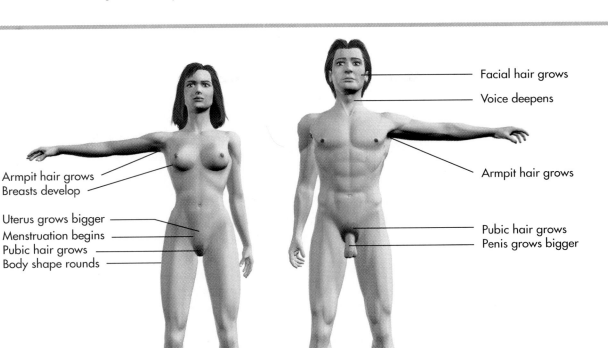

Armpit hair grows
Breasts develop

Uterus grows bigger
Menstruation begins
Pubic hair grows
Body shape rounds

Facial hair grows
Voice deepens

Armpit hair grows

Pubic hair grows
Penis grows bigger

Muscles develop

Figure 5.3   Changes associated with puberty.

Primary Sex Characteristics

Primary sex characteristics are associated with the full growth and development of the sex organs. A boy's penis and testicles grow and reach full adult size by the end of puberty. The testes begin to produce sperm and androgens, and first ejaculation signals the onset of reproductive readiness.

In girls the major internal (vagina, ovaries, uterus, and fallopian tubes) and external (labia, mons, clitoris) sexual structures reach maturity. First menstruation is the sign that puberty has arrived.

Primary sex characteristics growth of the sex organs

Secondary Sex Characteristics

Secondary sex characteristics are nongenital changes associated with puberty. Boys and girls both experience a growth spurt and begin to attain their subsequent adult height. They both grow pubic, underarm, and body hair. Although boys characteristically grow significantly more facial hair than girls do, this generally represents a continuum with a range of possibilities for boys and girls from relatively hairless to very hairy.

Body contours begin to develop. Girls naturally deposit more fat on their hips and breasts than boys do but, as with facial and body hair, there is a wide continuum of growth possibilities for both boys and girls.

Secondary sex characteristics nongenital changes associated with puberty; include growth of pubic, facial, and under-arm hair, breast development, increases in height and weight, and the like

The voice box in boys enlarges, creating a deeper, more resonating sound. The transition period involved in this change causes a squeaky quality to boys' voices.

By the end of puberty, the body has reached a stage of **reproductive readiness** with two major components: mature reproductive anatomy and hormonally influenced sexual desire. By the end of puberty, the sex organs are fully developed and capable of procreating as well as recreating. Not only are parts such as the penis and vagina fully mature and capable of responding to sexual desire, but ovaries and testes are also fully able to produce viable ova and sperm, respectively. This is often the time when a young girl discovers that her clitoris is capable of providing sexual pleasure.

In nature's eyes, humans are able and ready to propagate the species. Nature gives a boost in that our **gonads** (testes and ovaries), which have long been silent, now begin to produce hormones that stimulate sexual desire.

Androgens, primarily **testosterone**, stimulate sexual receptor centers in the brain, which trigger feelings of sexual desire. All of the cold showers in the world will not quell this sexual desire because, to a certain extent, it is fueled by hormones circulating in the bloodstream.

Adolescence has a profound impact on sexuality for the rest of our lives. Often our body image and initial impressions about our masculinity and femininity that were formed at this time color how we view ourselves for the rest of our lives. Old labels and images such as, "I'm not a good dancer" or "I'm shy" or "I'm not very good looking" influence our self-concept and stay with us for years to come.

Reproductive readiness
pubertal development resulting in full growth of genitalia and onset of fertility

> *By the end of puberty, the sex organs are fully developed and capable of procreation as well as recreation.*

Gonads
the primary endocrine glands in men (testes) and women (ovaries) that influence sexuality

Androgens
a group of naturally occurring steroid hormones produced by both men and women

Testosterone
the most notable androgen, recognized for fueling sexual desire and aggressiveness in males

Shaving is a pubertal ritual that most teenage boys eagerly anticipate.

Adolescent Sexual Behavior

The most common expression of adolescent sexual behavior is masturbation. Kinsey and his associates discovered that the rate of masturbation was different for boys and girls.[13] Among boys in that early study, the level of masturbation increased from 21% of 12-year-old boys to 82% of 15-year-old boys. Among girls, the level of masturbation increased from 12% of 12-year-old girls to 20% of 15-year-old girls. By the end of adolescence, more than 90% of the boys and about 35% of the girls had masturbated.

Other studies since Kinsey have shown that the level of masturbation for boys across adolescence is relatively unchanged but the rate among girls has risen. By the time they reach the end of adolescence, approximately 75% of all girls reported having have masturbated.[14]

Sexual Intercourse

As Laumann and colleagues point out, first sexual intercourse, especially for women, has traditionally been a symbol for loss of innocence, transition to adulthood, and assumption of responsibility for procreation for the next generation.[15] Over the past 40 years several interesting findings surfaced regarding adolescent sexual intercourse. The popular belief about the widespread level of premarital sexual intercourse is that this is a fairly recent phenomenon that is linked to social decay, a decrease in family values and the like. As Laumann et al. demonstrated, the drop in average age of first intercourse, and the increased level of adolescent sexual intercourse, has been at a fairly steady level over the past 40 years. Various studies have shown a general trend related to a decline in the average age of first intercourse and an increase in the number of sexual partners of adolescents.

By age 19, 20% of the girls and 45% of the boys in the Kinsey study had had intercourse. More than 20 years later, Sorenson reported a 25% increase (from 20% to 45%) in the percentage of female adolescents having intercourse and a 14% increase (45% to 59%) among males; using data from 1971 and 1976, Zelnick, Kanter, and Ford confirmed Sorenson's findings and added that the increases for Whites was two times greater than for Blacks.[16]

Nearly another 20 years later, Forrest and Singh and Sonenstein, Pleck, and Ku reported another increase in the level of adolescent intercourse.[17] Citing data from the National Study of Family Growth, Forrest and Singh demonstrated that the proportion of 15 to 19-year-old females having intercourse rose steadily in the 1970s and 1980s. In 1970, 28% of white and 45% of non-white girls were non-virgins. By 1988, 52% of White and 65% of non-White girls had experienced sexual intercourse. By 1988, 25% of all 15-year-olds and 75% of all 19-year-old girls had experienced intercourse.[18]

The National Survey of Adolescent Males (NSAM)[19] reported that approximately 30% of its 15-year-old subjects had experienced intercourse. By age 19, 86% of all the subjects had lost their virginity.

The National Health and Social Life Survey (NHSLS) found a slight trend toward earlier experiences of first intercourse for males and females. The NHSLS divided the sample into four birth cohorts: those who were high-school age between 1951 and 1960 (born 1933–1942); between 1961 and

1970 (born 1943–1952); between 1971 and 1980 (born 1953–1962); and between 1981 and 1985 (born 1963–1967). Figure 5.4 summarizes their findings.

Laumann et al. found a small decrease in the average age of first intercourse for both males and females and for both Whites and Blacks. Although the mean age declined for both men and women, women still had a slightly higher average age of first intercourse than men.

Figure 5.5 shows the curve for age of first intercourse for males and females ages 12–25 years of age. As you can see, a small percentage of the respondents experienced first intercourse by age 12, and the percentages begin a strong and predictable rise through the teen years. By age 25, more than 90% of all men and women have experienced intercourse.

A final study worth mentioning is the 1995 Youth Risk Behavior Survey of 10,904 high school students in grades 9–12.[20] The study found that approximately 53% of all the subjects had had sexual intercourse in their lifetime. Students in 12th grade (66% had intercourse) were more likely than students in 11th grade (59% had intercourse) and significantly more likely than 10th and 9th graders (48% and 37%, respectively, had intercourse) to have had sexual intercourse.

About 9% of the subjects in the Youth Risk Behavior Survey reported having had sexual intercourse before 13 years of age. Of these students, males (13%) were significantly more likely than females (5%) to have initiated sexual intercourse before the age of 13 years old. Black students (24%) were significantly more likely than White (6%) and Hispanic (9%) students to have initiated sexual intercourse before age 13 years old.

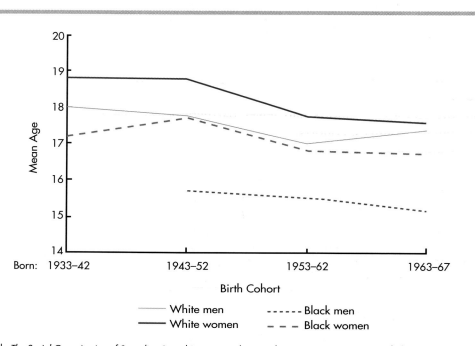

Source: E.O. Laumann et al., *The Social Organization of Sexuality: Sexual Practices in the United States*, © 1994, University of Chicago Press. Reprinted with permission.

Figure 5.4   Average age at first intercourse by four birth cohorts.

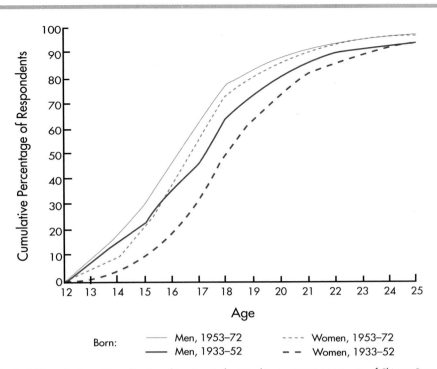

Source: E.O. Laumann et al., *The Social Organization of Sexuality: Sexual Practices in the United States*, © 1994, University of Chicago Press. Reprinted with permission.

Figure 5.5   Cumulative percentage of intercourse by age.

Another trend that has been continuing over the past 40 years is the increase in total number of sexual partners of adolescents. Laumann et al. discovered three interesting findings related to the number of sex partners adolescents have by age 18:

1. As the average age for the onset of intercourse drops, the average number of teenage partners increases.
2. Females from the oldest age cohorts had fewer partners before age 18 than women from the youngest cohorts.
3. Females are catching up to males.

Concerning the first finding, as teens are beginning to have sex at a younger age, they also are experiencing more partners. This is in contrast with teens over 50 years ago. At that time, teens who experienced first intercourse early (before 18 years of age) had fewer partners because they tended to marry their first sex partner. Often their first teenage encounter was as man and wife. Teens today rarely have first intercourse on their wedding night. Most of them have already had intercourse prior to this event.

Laumann et al. also found differences among the age cohorts regarding the number of partners before age 18. The females from earlier generations (born between 1933 and 1942) were much less likely to have had five or more partners by age 18 than the youngest cohort (born between 1963 and 1967). This relates to the last finding — that females are catching up to males in terms of overall number of sexual partners. The number of sex partners for males and females by age 18 is less variable for the youngest cohorts than for the oldest.

The Youth Risk Behavior Survey data support these findings. The study found that approximately 18% of students had had sexual intercourse with four or more partners during their lifetime. This was directly related to age and grade level. Students in 12th grade (23%) were significantly more likely than 9th or 10th graders to have had sexual intercourse with four or more partners.

Laumann et al. examined what motivated men and women to initiate first intercourse. Table 5.2 summarizes the reasons for first intercourse by gender.

Almost twice as many females as males reported affection as the primary motivation for first intercourse. Conversely, more than twice as many males than females reported curiosity as the underlying motivation for first intercourse. Contrary to popular belief, only a small percentage of males and females (4% and 3%, respectively) reported peer pressure as the underlying motivation for first intercourse. About 5% of subjects reported being forced to have intercourse the first time.

Data from the National Survey for Family Growth (NSFG), an ongoing study of women's and family health, reported a higher incidence of involuntary first intercourse. According to the study, approximately 8% of the 53,793 females ages 15–44 reported that their first intercourse was forced (categorized as either "rape" or "not voluntary").[21]

PERSPECTIVES

First Sex Among Lesbian/Gay Youth

Sexual behavior patterns in gay and lesbian youth are more complex because of the added dimension of coming to terms with a sexual identity that is different from their heterosexual peers and, in most cases, still unacceptable to mainstream American culture. Sexual behavior seems to be the fourth step in a five-step coming-out process that involves:

1. fear and suspicion that one's sexual desires and attraction are different (although still not clearly defined)

2. labeling of those feelings as homoerotic (sexual feelings for someone of the same sex)

3. defining oneself as gay or lesbian

4. having one's first gay love affair

5. becoming involved in the gay or lesbian subculture.

Source: *Introduction; Culture, History, and Life Course of Gay Men*, by G. Herdt and A. Boxer, in *Gay Culture in America: Essays from the Field*, edited by G. Herdt (Boston: Beacon, 1992); R. Troiden. *Gay and Lesbian Identity: A Sociological Analysis* (New York: General Hall, 1988).

Having sexual feelings for someone of the same sex (homoerotic feelings) almost always precedes sexual activity by several years among gay and lesbian people. Gay and lesbian youth today recognize feelings for same-sex partners and act upon them earlier than their peers of 20 years ago.

Source: "A Developmental, Clinical Perspective on Lesbian, Gay Male, and Bisexual Youth, by R. Savin-Williams and R. G. Rodriguez, *Adolescent Sexuality*, edited by T. P. Gullatta et al. (Newbury Park, CA: Sage, 1993).

Table 5.2   Reasons for Having First Intercourse by Sex

Attributed Reasons	Wanted First Intercourse		Not Wanted but Not Forced	
	Percent			
	Men	Women	Men	Women
Affection for partner	24.9	47.5	9.9	38.5
Peer pressure	4.2	3.3	28.6	24.6
Curiosity/readiness for sex	50.6	24.3	50.5	24.9
Pregnancy	.5	.6	0.0	0.0
Physical pleasure	12.2	2.8	6.6	2.1
Under the influence of alcohol or drugs	.7	.3	3.3	7.2
Wedding night	6.9	21.1	1.1	2.7

Source: E.O. Laumann et al., *The Social Organization of Sexuality: Sexual Practices in the United States,* © 1994, University of Chicago Press. Reprinted with permission.

Oral Sex

Patterns in oral sexual behavior among adolescents have mimicked the changes of adults in the United States. In general, changes in cultural acceptance of nongenital sexual behavior has led to increasing levels of all forms of oral sex among adults.[22] This pattern holds true for adolescents. Between 40% and 50% of all teenagers have engaged in oral sex by the time they finish puberty.[23] The true incidence might be even higher than that.[24] Laumann et al. found that twice as many males as females reported having oral sex at first intercourse.

A summary of the sexual techniques used during first intercourse is given in Table 5.3. As you can see, vaginal intercourse was the most common, followed by kissing and masturbation. Surprisingly, only slightly more

Table 5.3   Sexual Techniques Used During First Intercourse

	Men	Women			
		All	Wanted	Not Wanted/ Not Forced	Forced
		Percent			
Sexual technique					
Kissing	84.7	86.9	89.7	85.6	49.3
Manual stimulation of genitals	78.8	74.3	77.2	70.1	53.5
Oral sex	16.1	8.5	9.3	5.5	12.7
Anal sex	1.7	1.1	1.1	.7	2.8
Vaginal intercourse	95.1	95.9	95.9	96.3	95.8
Used birth control	33.8	37.9	43.1	28.4	7.1

Source: E.O. Laumann et al., *The Social Organization of Sexuality: Sexual Practices in the United States,* © 1994, University of Chicago Press. Reprinted with permission.

than a third of all respondents reported using birth control at first intercourse. This is disturbing considering the high rates of sexually transmitted diseases and unintended pregnancy rates in adolescents. It takes only one act of unprotected intercourse to become pregnant or infected with an STD.

Cultural Attitudes About Adolescent Sexuality

How does U.S. society view adolescent sexuality? It seems to view adolescent sexual behavior in general, and intercourse in particular, as a "problem" that will lead to negative outcomes (such as unintended pregnancy, sexually transmitted diseases including HIV, and sexual abuse, among others). A surprising finding of the NHSLS study was that, even though increasing numbers of study subjects reported engaging in intercourse by age 18, and having more partners, almost 80% of the respondents still think that teen sex is always or almost always wrong. These views are inconsistent with their own behavior. No wonder adolescents get mixed messages about sex!

Many other cultures view this matter entirely differently and celebrate this time in a young person's sexual life. Indeed, in some Pacific Island cultures, adolescent sexual behavior is encouraged, not merely tolerated. This is not to say that these cultures advocate promiscuity. Most have rules pertaining to adolescent sex.

The United States has a conservative sexual history. American culture evolved from devoutly religious, puritanical forefathers and mothers who

PERSPECTIVES

The Sexual Culture of Mangaia

In the 1950s, anthropologist Donald Marshall studied the sexual attitudes and activities of the people of Mangaia, the southernmost island in the Polynesian Cook chain. There, he found, the people were exposed to sexuality from early childhood. They listened to folk stories that included detailed accounts of sex acts and sexual anatomy, and they watched sensual ritual dances.

As adolescents, males underwent *superincision*, a surgical procedure in which the tissue at the end of the penis was cut and folded back, which exposed the glans. They were taught how to stimulate a woman's genitals and breasts with the mouth, how to bring female partners to orgasm, and how to control the timing of ejaculation. Mangaian girls were taught to be responsive and to participate actively during sexual activity.

In a practice called "night-crawling," a young male would sneak into the home of a young woman with the intent to have sexual intercourse. Because most homes had a single sleeping area, this act tended to be more public than private, though the other family members feigned sleep. The parents approved of night-crawling and listened for their daughter's laughter — a sign that she was happy with her partner. The parents encouraged their children to have more than one sexual partner before marriage, to find the most sexually compatible mate.

After marriage, couples in Mangaia continued to engage in sex more often than most Western countries. The emphasis, though, shifted from the number of orgasms during a single session to a goal of copulation every night. Throughout life, the emphasis for males and females alike was on pleasing the partner.

Source: "Sexual Behavior on Mangaia," by Donald Marshall, in *Human Sexual Behavior: Variations in the Ethnographic Spectrum*, edited by D. Marshall and R. Suggs (Englewood Cliffs, NJ: Prentice-Hall, 1971).

escaped persecution for their views in Europe by coming to this country. The American patriarchal culture emphasized the family and historically has viewed sex as something that occurs within the context of a marriage, with the primary function being procreation. A strong history, institutionalized formally in law and enforced informally through cultural taboos and parenting styles, perpetuates this. The United States is still a country where sex education is not universally taught in every school. Even when it is, it is mostly a course in reproductive anatomy.[25] In many states, nonprocreative sexual acts, including oral sex and anal intercourse between consenting adults (whether heterosexual or homosexual), is considered sodomy and is illegal.

Besides having a moral tradition that prohibits adolescent sexual education and experimentation, U. S. culture, like that of many industrialized societies, prolongs adolescent and young adult dependency. To succeed, adolescents, in most cases, need to further their education. For most of them, this means remaining indebted to their parents and pursuing additional training and education while either living at home or remaining financially obligated to their parents. In a sense, what this does is delay the transition from childhood to adulthood, and delaying with it adult privileges

PERSPECTIVES

Rites of Passage

Over the years, researchers have studied societies that recognize and celebrate the onset of puberty in adolescent boys and girls. Ford and Beach[1] found that more than 70 societies celebrated the onset of puberty in girls, and more than 65 in boys. In a sample of 192 societies, Schlegel and Barry,[2] found that

- ❧ 80 had no rites of passage
- ❧ 17 had ceremonies for boys only
- ❧ 39 had rites for girls only
- ❧ 46 had ceremonies for both sexes.

Larger societies, with intensive agricultural and manufacturing bases, and those with more complex forms of social organizations, tended not to have initiation rites.

Of the societies celebrating puberty in girls, these celebrations usually coincide with the onset of first menses and are directly related to the sexual significance of menstruation. Schlegel and Barry found that first menses signified fertility and the tribe's continued existence.

Often these ceremonies included seclusion of the young women, prohibiting any contact with men. In many instances the ceremonies included instruction

from older women in matters pertaining to sex and marriage. In some cultures, the young women were "deflowered" or subjected to piercing, tattooing, or genital adornment or mutilation. Often, the occasion was marked by a feast or celebration.

Schlegel and Barry found that segregation from males at this time is usually based on avoiding contact with menstrual flow, which is feared because of its supposed ability to weaken a hunter's abilities or contaminate the tribe's meat sources.

For boys, unlike with girls' first menses, no clear demarcation indicates that puberty has begun. Generally, boys are given the rites when evidence is sufficient (usually secondary sex characteristics) that they have reached puberty. Boys' ceremonies are similar to girls' in that they usually include some form of seclusion, instruction, and ritualistic physical sacrifice (often circumcision).

1. C. S. Ford and F. A. Beach, *Patterns of Sexual Behavior* (New York: Harper & Brothers, 1951).
2. A. Schlegel and H. Barry, "Adolescent Initiation Ceremonies: Cross-cultural Codes," *Ethnology*, 18(1979), 199–210; "The Evolutionary Significance of Adolescent Initiation Ceremonies, *American Ethnologist*, 7 (1980), 696–715.

such as sexual experimentation. In many other cultures adolescents are encouraged to begin to separate from their parents earlier, and this separation is often institutionalized in a formal rite of passage.

RETARDED SEXUAL DEVELOPMENT

The term "retarded sexual development" has been used to refer to the consequences of adolescent sexual development in the United States.[26] Martinson claims youths are not retarded in terms of sexual behavior, citing statistics concerning the average age of first intercourse, but, rather, in terms of their knowledge, attitudes, and values. They know significantly less about sexuality and place less value on issues such as consistent use of contraceptives and prevention of pregnancy than adolescents from other developed countries.

Martinson thinks this results from having grown up in a culture that fosters sexual naivete and guilt. These findings cut across all racial and ethnic groups. U. S. society is homogeneous in terms of how it views adolescent sexuality. The negative effects of sexual experience, Martinson claims, inhibits children's quest for knowledge and positive affirmation of a normal part of their development.

Martinson argues further that this combination of retarded sexual development and early onset of teenage intercourse is the root cause of this country's high adolescent pregnancy rate. In a multinational study of teenage pregnancy and sexuality, U. S. youth scored the lowest of five similar industrialized nations (Canada, Sweden, France, England, and the Netherlands) on tests of knowledge and attitudes concerning sexuality and conception.[27] Lack of basic information concerning sexual anatomy and physiology, contraception, and pregnancy were cited among other findings as indicators of what international experts would consider arrested sexual development.

Consequences of Retarded Sexual Development

Of the estimated 11 million unmarried, adolescent females who are having intercourse, about 1 million become pregnant each year. Of these 1 million pregnancies, about 50% result in live births, 40% are aborted, and the remaining 10% end in stillbirth or spontaneous abortion.[28]

Teen mothers are more likely to have pregnancy-related problems than women who delay childbearing until they are in their 20s. Adolescents are more likely to suffer from toxemia, hemorrhaging, and miscarriages than women who delay pregnancy. In addition, teens are more likely to have low birthweight babies, and they have an infant mortality rate that is 200% higher than that of older women.[29]

Most of the negative health outcomes associated with teenage pregnancy are believed to be caused by **biological immaturity**, women having children before their bodies are physiologically ready for them. Some evidence suggests that teenagers, given adequate prenatal care and proper nutrition, may have as good or better pregnancy outcomes than women who are older.[30]

Biological immaturity
the incomplete anatomical and physiological development associated with early adolescence or preadolescence

Unfortunately, obtaining adequate prenatal health care is the exception rather than the norm for most teens who get pregnant. Many are not under the care of a physician, midwife, or other health care provider for all three trimesters of pregnancy. As a result, routine testing and screening is delayed or is not done. When routine trimester examinations are not done, close monitoring of the size, weight, positioning, and vital signs of the fetus is not possible. In addition, these visits provide an opportunity for the health care provider to assess the health of the pregnant teen and talk about critical issues such as nutrition, substance use, and plans for delaying future pregnancies and adequately caring for their child if the pregnancy is going to be carried to full term. Approximately 95% of unmarried teenage mothers keep their babies.[31] Most of them continue to live at home and rear their babies with the help of their parents or grandparents while they try to cope with the realities of parenthood.

Case Study

James and Susan: Young Parents

James and Susan are 17-year-old high school seniors who decided to get married and keep their baby, Rebecca. Susan's parents let them live, rent free, in the apartment over their garage until they finish high school.

Although they are getting help from Susan's parents (in addition to providing the apartment, her mom watches Rebecca on the evenings Susan attends night school), they have been having a hard time adjusting to the demands of marriage and parenting and have discussed separation.

Both are in their last year of high school. James is attending during the day full-time while Susan watches Rebecca. Susan attends night school while either of their moms provides child care. Both James and Susan work 15–20 hours a week on weekends, and whenever they can fit in the hours during the week.

During a typical day, James and Susan get up about 6:00 a.m. (Rebecca is an early riser and wakes up at about 5:30, amusing herself in her crib until her parents get up). James showers and gets ready for school (he has to leave at 7:00 a.m.) while Susan feeds, washes, and changes Rebecca. At 7:30 Susan takes Rebecca along as she drives her mom and dad to their jobs. Susan then takes the family car and goes to the supermarket, library, pediatrician, or wherever she needs to go that morning. Around mid-morning, she puts Rebecca down for a nap and tries to do her homework from the previous evening. After she does her homework, she cleans her apartment and her mom's house and tries to catch up on the laundry.

Sometimes when Rebecca won't take her nap or is sick or just needs more attention, Susan gets tense, as all of her work gets backed up and she worries that she might not get it all done. On other days she feels so tired that she just lies down with Rebecca and rests, even though she knows this will put her behind in her work. On days when Rebecca has been up all night with a cold or some other problem, or has awakened several times during the evening, Susan is exhausted and stumbles through her day like a zombie.

When James' school day is over, he stops at home for 30 minutes to change into his work clothes (he pumps gas and is a mechanic-in-training at a local gas station) and grab a quick bite, then walks to work. He works until 7:00 p.m., when Susan has to leave for night school. Then James bathes Rebecca, reads her a story or plays with her for a while, then puts her to bed. James finally sits down, has dinner, and begins his homework, working until Susan gets home from night school.

After a long day, Susan and James try to relax, watch a little television, or rent a movie and make love, but they often find themselves falling asleep in front of the TV only to be awakened by Rebecca in the middle of the night. And the routine starts anew.

These unmarried, teenage mothers face a harder future than their peers who delay bearing children until they are older and married. Although keeping pregnant teens out of public school is illegal, most (approximately 80%) wind up dropping out and do not return.[32] Because of the twin burdens of the lack of a high school degree and the need for child care, these teens earn less, have less schooling, work in blue-collar professions and in general have a lower standard of living than their peers who delay marriage and childbirth.[33]

Other teens who become pregnant decide they aren't ready to become mothers and decide to use foster care or give up their babies for adoption. Foster care is designed to provide temporary help for mothers or parents who feel they can't take care of their child now but will be able to do it in the near future. Under foster care, mothers still have legal rights to their children, have formal visitation privileges, and are actively involved with their children. Women who give up their children for adoption permanently give over their rights as parents to another person or family.

Foster care and adoption offer viable options for teen mothers who are unable to cope with the demands of being a parent. Regardless of which of these options for coping with an unintended pregnancy is chosen, carrying the pregnancy to term and following through with giving up the baby can be extremely stressful. Many pregnant teens choose to terminate their pregnancies rather than be forced to choose between keeping their children, putting them in foster care, or giving them up for adoption. A significant number of American females who have abortions are young. More than 400,000 abortions are performed on females age 19 and younger. This accounts for almost 30% of all abortions performed in the United States.[34]

About 90% of all abortions are performed at or before 12 weeks of gestation. Early abortion is a relatively safe medical procedure. Risks associated with abortion include perforation of the uterus, hemorrhaging, and partial removal of the uterine contents. Studies show that abortions (during the first trimester) have little effect on subsequent fertility.[35] In some studies, the women who have had abortions have some initial anxiety or depression, but these feelings subside and give way to feelings of relief and eventual positive feelings about their choice.[36] Other studies show some long-term negative psychological effects. Whatever the medical and psychological consequences of abortion, being pregnant when a person didn't plan to be, deciding what to do, and terminating a pregnancy are potentially stressful.

A recent phenomenon that has been receiving national attention is the literal dumping of newborns by adolescent moms and dads. A case in New Jersey involved a college woman who gave birth in a motel room and, together with her boyfriend, also a college freshman, dumped the newborn in the motel trash dumpster. Another New Jersey case involved a high school senior who gave birth in the ladies room of the banquet hall at her high school prom. After disposing of her newborn in the garbage can, she returned to the dance floor and danced the rest of the night away. The case has raised questions concerning how people could have so little regard for human life that they could throw a baby in the dumpster and face being charged with murder.

Other negative health consequences are associated with retarded adolescent sexual development. Adolescents have higher rates than all other age groups of syphilis, gonorrhea, and pelvic inflammatory disease (PID). Adolescents also engage in sexual behavior that has high risk for HIV/AIDS.[37] Although the number of 13- to 19-year-olds reported infected with HIV is small (3,130 from 1981 through June 1998), many more young people are thought to be infected with HIV.[38] In addition, since one in five of all people diagnosed with AIDS is between 20 and 29 years of age (101,368 cases from 1981 through June 1998), and the incubation period for AIDS can last several years, many, if not most, of these people became infected when they were teenagers.

Dealing with Adolescent Sexuality

It is thought that the best way to deal with adolescent sexuality is to be honest with young people. If parents think their adolescent children would be better off to delay sexual intercourse or other forms of sexual activities with a partner, the best way for them to deal with it is to tell their children this and explain why. The healthy way to do this is to honestly admit to young people that sex is a powerful force in their lives and that, as parents, you would prefer adolescents to redirect that sexual energy from sexual intercourse into other, less risky sexual outlets, such as hugging, kissing, and masturbation. To deny the power of adolescent sexual urges, or worse, not mention it and hope the subject will never come up is unhealthy and dishonest.

Trivializing adolescent sexual desire with simplistic advice such as, "When you feel horny, take a cold shower" contributes to the mixed messages adolescents are already receiving about their sexuality. These mixed messages can be a real source of stress. On the one hand, their bodies are telling them, "yes, yes, yes," and on the other hand, adult society is telling them, "no, no, no." Media — music stars, television, movies — that target adolescents are telling them it is okay and a normal part of teenage rebelliousness to give

Moms can be a great source of comfort and advice to their sons.

into, even glorify, their sexual urges, yet parents tell them to take a cold shower and the urges will disappear.

To further complicate matters, federally funded abstinence-only sex-education curricula purport to reduce the incidence of unintended pregnancy and sexual intercourse. Parents can help their children by learning about and supporting comprehensive sexuality education programs in their local school districts.

Gay adolescents face an even tougher problem. Not only do they have to deal with the mixed messages and pressures associated with this part of

Case Study

Paul and Rich: Tumultuous Adolescence

Paul and Rich met as adults and compared their experiences of going through puberty and adolescence. Even though Paul is gay and Rich is heterosexual, their adolescent years had many similarities, and both had a tremendous amount of curiosity and guilt about their sexual desires.

Rich's adolescence was a fairly typical experience for a straight, lower middle-class young man growing up in urban America. His parents were high school graduates who worked in factories as piecework tailors. Although both were loving and attentive parents, neither was skilled at communicating openly with Rich about the issues he would face as an adolescent. Neither knew about the key developmental components of puberty and adolescence and weren't comfortable talking with Rich about these issues. Consequently, Rich's adolescence was a hit-or-miss, trial-and-error experience for which he was totally unprepared.

Rich remembers experiencing things such as wet dreams, his first "'true love," masturbation, his first ejaculation, and how puzzled he was trying to figure out how male and female genitalia come together during sexual intercourse.

Rich remembers agonizing about his first ejaculation, feeling as if perhaps he had injured himself or something had gone wrong because all of a sudden this liquid was coming out of the end of his penis. Rich had to be content with asking his friends or older brother about some of these things. Based on the responses he received, he knew that some of the answers were not the "right" ones.

It took Rich several years to get over much of the guilt and shame he had about his sexual feelings and

behavior during adolescence. He spent the better part of his 20s looking for the answers to unresolved questions and issues from his adolescence.

The major difference between Paul and Rich was in sexual orientation. Paul just never felt any sexual desire toward females. He played along when his friends talked about "getting laid" and carrying on with girls in general. Inside, however, Paul was troubled because he felt attracted to some of the boys in his class.

In addition, Paul's church had a stated position against masturbation, which created much confusion and guilt in Paul whenever he engaged in that activity. He did not dare to discuss his sexual feelings with anyone connected with his church. Further, as the only son of immigrant parents who did not discuss things of a sexual nature with him, he began to feel isolated.

All through his adolescence, Paul agonized over who or what he was. He tried dating girls but found it unsatisfactory. Paul suspected he was gay but didn't want to admit it and believed he had no one in whom he could confide or trust while exploring this facet of himself.

Paul coped with adolescence by suppressing most of his sexual feelings. He denied that they existed and spent most of his time immersed in studying. Not until he entered college as a pre-med student did he finally give in to his urges to explore this part of himself. Later, in medical school and a steady relationship with another male student, Paul was able to work through some of the pain and confusion that had marred his adolescence.

their lives, but they also face a wall of silence concerning their own emerging preferences. Gay adolescents usually learn early on that discussing their attraction to same-gender partners is taboo. Few social supports and people are available to turn to for these adolescents whose school guidance counselors and other community helpers are often either misinformed about how to help these young people or homophobic and a threat to the very youth they are being paid to care for. Many school districts forbid teaching that homosexuality is an acceptable lifestyle. Local chapters of Parents of Lesbians and Gays (PFLAG) and other gay and lesbian organizations are excellent places to find help and information about resources.

WELLNESS SYNTHESIS

The wellness domains apply to psychosocial development throughout the lifespan.

Physical Well-being

Psychosexual development is strongly influenced by physical forces. Sexuality begins at conception and continues throughout life. We discover sensual pleasure during infancy and early childhood through inadvertent (the sensuous feeling of rubbing against warm, soft, blankets, our parent's skin, and so forth) and directed (conscious manipulation of our own bodies) physical stimulation. This discovery is the basis of further exploration, which continues throughout childhood. Mastery of physical tasks such as toilet training and walking contribute further to our psychosexual development.

During puberty, the gonads begin providing the hormones that fuel continued physical development and sexual desire. Puberty represents one of the major physical contributions to psychosexual development.

Intellectual Well-being

Individuals begin to learn about sexuality from the day of birth. Infants and children learn symbolically. They learn about what feels good through direct physical exploration. They learn about what is taboo by the reactions of significant others. Caregivers shape psychosexual development through a series of rewards and punishments and by creating opportunities for exploration and growth.

Children continue to grow as they become more verbal and are able to communicate by asking questions and seeking clarification. Development takes shape according to the answers received and the nonverbal messages attached to the information. If children grow up in a household where sexual questions are allowed and teachable moments are capitalized, the natural curiosity about sex is satisfied.

This learning continues through childhood and adolescence. What differs is the sheer quantity of information to which people are exposed and the sources from which it is derived. Infants and young children receive sexual information mostly from parents and other caregivers. By the time of adolescence, sexual information flows in torrents from sources ranging from parents to mass media to the Internet.

Today, more than ever before, many excellent sources of information about sexuality are available — books, recordings, educational television shows, Web sites, and more. Unfortunately, many poor sources of information and negative gender roles also bombard us daily. The ability to process all of this information and make sense of it is aided by our ever growing intellectual development and rests on a foundation of "askable parents" and a school environment and curriculum that encourage questions and makes information readily available.

Emotional Well-being

Infant and childhood emotional development forms the foundation for much of our adult emotional make-up. Basic personality constructs such as self-esteem, trust, happiness, and optimism begin to take shape during infancy and childhood.

As Maslow and other developmental theorists point out, the ability to fully self-actualize as adults requires people to meet basic emotional needs early in life. It's harder to love others as adults if a person was not loved as an infant and if pieces of one's emotional development were left scattered on the floor of childhood and adolescence. Nurturing infants, children, and adolescents, attending to their needs, and providing a safe haven and outlet for their desires are all essential for their continuing emotional development and healthy sexuality.

Social Well-being

Physical development takes place within a social context provided initially by mother, father, and other primary caregivers. They set the social context in which tasks such as toilet training and self-pleasuring take place. They set the ground rules for the evolving physical development. For example, everyone eventually becomes toilet-trained, but the age at which this occurs, the rewards and punishments associated with it, and the associated emotions vary according to parameters our caregivers establish within the social dimension of infancy and early childhood.

As we age, peers become increasingly influential regarding our values and subsequent behavior. We learn what it means to be boy/man, girl/woman from friends, peers, and associates. As we try out roles and responsibilities, we refine these initial impressions. Intimate playmates, dates, and girlfriends/boyfriends teach us about intimacy, affection, love, and sexual response.

Spiritual Well-being

Although we are not always cognizant of it as infants and children, we begin to develop a sense of connectedness or disconnectedness during this stage. Probably the earliest manifestation of spirituality is the bonding with primary caregivers. This is a powerful connection not only to other human beings but also to the world as a whole. Developing a sense of trust in ourselves, others, and the world as a whole begins with the skin-to-skin nurturing we receive from our parents in times of need.

Parents and caregivers often describe the feeling of bonding and nurturing of an infant as one of the most profoundly spiritual feelings they have ever experienced. Many rediscover a sense of awe and faith in the power of love by connecting with and nurturing our children.

Environmental Well-being

As Maslow pointed out, people can't evolve and meet higher-level needs and tasks if the basic physiological and shelter needs are not met. To survive, we need a roof over our head, food in our stomach, and clothes on our backs. To really thrive, we need all of that plus a safe home and neighborhood where we can play and learn, and question and challenge and grow as individuals. We also need safe spaces to learn about ourselves and our emerging sexuality, and the freedom to develop into the sexual beings we were meant to be.

WEB RESOURCES

Advocates for Youth

http://www.advocatesforyouth.org

Creates programs and promotes policies that help young people make informed and responsible decisions about their sexual and reproductive health with the purpose of preventing pregnancy and sexually transmitted diseases including HIV. Large selection of links as well as links to minority youth sites. One section addresses contemporary issues that affect society and the way in which we live; and changes monthly.

Coalition for Positive Sexuality

http://www.positive.org/

A grassroots volunteer group started in 1992 to respond to the health crisis among Chicago teenagers. Teens receive information needed to make healthy decisions about sex, condom availability, and sex education. This site has FAQ with links to answers, national weblinks, and information on sexuality, health issues, and birth control.

Freud Net: Abraham A. Brill Library
of New York Psychoanalytic Institute

http://plaza.interport.net/nypsan/index.html

Links to psychoanalytic theory and Sigmund Freud, articles on psychoanalysis, and network resources in mental health.

Learning Theories

http://curriculum.calstatela.edu/faculty/psparks/theorists/501learn.htm

Summarizes major learning theories impacting education today. Behaviorism theory gives information on B. F. Skinner and Robert Gagne. Constructivism theory talks about Jean Piaget, Seymour Papert, Jerome Bruner, Lev Vygotsky, and John Dewey. Humanism theory recounts the works of Carl Rogers and Abraham Maslow. In a separate category is Erik Erikson's theory.

Notes

1. J. Watson, *Behaviorism* (New York: W. W. Norton, 1970).
2. A. Maslow, *Motivation and Personality*, 2d edition (New York: Harper & Row, 1970).
3. C. S. Hall. *A Primer of Freudian Psychotherapy* (New York: Mentor, 1954).
4. D. P. Schultz, *A History of Modern Psychology* (New York: Academic Press, 1969).
5. E. Erikson, *Childhood and Society*, 2d edition (New York: W. W. Norton, 1978).
6. D. Roberts and B. Mosley, "A Father's Time," *Psychology Today* (June/July 1978), pp. 48–70.
7. A. Montague. *Touching*, 3d edition (New York: Columbia University Press, 1986).
8. G. Inkeles and M. Todris, *The Art of Sensual Massage* (San Francisco: Straight Arrow Books, 1972).
9. H. S. Kaplan. *The New Sex Therapy* (New York: Brunner Mazel, 1974).
10. S. Gordon and J. Gordon, *Raising a Child Conservatively in a Sexually Permissive World* (New York: Simon & Schuster, 1983).
11. Gordon and Gordon.
12. Erikson.
13. A. C. Kinsey, W. B. Pomeroy, C. E. Martin. *Sexual Behavior in the Human Male* (Philadelphia: Saunders, 1948).
14. R. Sorenson, *Adolescent Sexuality in Contemporary America* (New York: World, 1983); L. Sarrel and P. Sarrel, *Sexual Turning Points: The Seven Signs of Adult Sexuality* (New York: Macmillan, 1984).
15. E. O. Laumann, J. H. Gagnon, R. T. Michael, and S. Michaels. *The Social Organization of Sexuality: Sexual Practices in the United States* (Chicago: University of Chicago Press, 1994).
16. M. Zelnick, J. Kanter, and K. Ford. *Sex and Pregnancy in Adolescence* (Beverly Hills CA: Sage, 1981).

17. J. D. Forrest and S. Singh, "The Sexual and Reproductive Behavior of American Women 1982–1988," *Family Planning Perspectives*, 22 (1990), 206–214; F. L. Sonenstein, J. H. Pleck, and L. C. Hu. "Sexual Activity, Condom Use, and AIDS Awareness Among Adolescent Males," *Family Planning Perspectives*, 21:4 (1989), 152–158.
18. Forrest and Singh.
19. Laumann et al.
20. Centers for Disease Control and Prevention, *Youth Risk Behavior Surveillance — United States, 1995, Morbidity and Mortality Weekly Report*, 45 (1996), SS–4, 1–86.
21. J. C. Abma, A. Chandra, W. D. Mosher, L. Peterson and L. Piccinino. "Fertility, Family Planning, and Women's Health: New Data from the National Survey of Family Growth," *National Center for Health Statistics, Vital Health Statistics*, 23:19 (1997).
22. S. M. Wilson and N. P. Medora, "Gender Comparisons of College Students: Attitudes Towards Sexual Behavior," *Adolescence*, 25 (99), 615–627.
23. S. M. Young, "Attitudes and Behavior of College Students to Oral-Genital Sexuality," *Archives of Sexual Behavior*, 9 (1986), 61–67; S. Newman and J. Udry. "Oral Sex in Adolescent Populations," *Archives of Sexual Behavior*, 14 (1988), 41–16.
24. W. H. Masters, V. E. Johnson, and R. C. Kolodny, *Human Sexuality*, 4th edition (New York: HarperCollins, 1992).
25. J. D. Forrest and J. Silverman, "What Public School Teachers Teach About Preventing Pregnancy, AIDS, and Sexually Transmitted Diseases," *Family Planning Perspectives*, 21 (1989), 65–72.

26. F. M. Martinson, "Against Sexual Retardation," *SIECUS Report*, 10:3 (1982), 3.
27. J. Dryfoos, "What the United States Can Learn About Prevention of Teenage Pregnancy from Other Countries," *SIECUS Report*, 14:2 (1985), 1–7.
28. M. McGrew and W. Shore, "The Problem of Teenage Pregnancy," *Journal of Family Practice*, 31 (1991), 17–25.
29. McGrew and Shore.
30. J. Trussel, "Teenage Pregnancy in the United States," *Family Planning Perspectives*, 20 (1988), 262–272.
31. C. Steven-Simon and M. White, "Adolescent Pregnancy," *Pediatric Annals*, 20 (1991), 322–331.
32. S. White and R. DeBlassie, "Adolescent Sexual Behavior," *Adolescence*, 27 (1992), 183–191.
33. Masters, Johnson, and Kolodny, p. 233.
34. Masters, Johnson, and Kolodny.
35. Masters, Johnson, and Kolodny.
36. P. Dagg, "The Psychological Sequalae of Therapeutic Abortion Denied and Completed," *American Journal of Psychiatry*, 148 (1991), 578–585; R. Hatcher, J. Trussel, and F. Stewart, et al., *Technology*, 16th edition (New York: Irvington, 1994).
37. J. B. Jemmott, L. Jemmott, and G. T. Fong. "Reductions in HIV Risk-associated Sexual Behaviors Among Black Male Adolescents: Effects of an AIDS Prevention Intervention," *American Journal of Public Health*, 82:3 (1992), 372–377.
38. Centers for Disease Control and Prevention (CDC). AIDS information: http://www.cdc.gov/nchstp/hiv_aids/stats/cumulati.htm, June 2, 1998.

Student Study Questions

1. What are five factors that help shape personality?

2. What are the behaviorist, humanist, Freudian, and Ericksonian theories concerning personality development?

3. What three common childhood developmental issues transcend all theories and their potential impact on psychosexual development?

4. What is bonding, and what is its relationship to adult sexuality? Are both mothers and fathers able to bond with their infants?

5. What are the effects of masturbation on childhood and later adult health?

6. Describe psychosocial and reproductive readiness for sex. How do the two relate to each other?

7. What are the pros and cons of sexual intercourse during adolescence?

Rites of Passage

U. S. culture has been criticized for lacking traditional rites of passage that help adolescents make a smoother transition from childhood to adulthood. The purpose of this assessment is to help you explore rites of passage in our culture and others by reflecting on your own experiences. This will enable you to understand why adolescence is often troubling for youth in the United States.

1. Read the "Rites of Passage" Perspective in this chapter.

2. Describe, in writing, your own thoughts and feelings about this reading.

3. How do you think these rites of passage would be accepted in the United States?

4. List and describe any cultural rituals that you have experienced while growing up that could be considered rites of passage and explain how they differ from the examples in the reading.

Adult Sexuality

6

Student Learning Objectives

After reading this chapter, students will be able to:

- Describe the normal psychosexual developmental tasks associated with young adulthood through older adulthood.

- Relate the findings of a variety of studies concerning the sexual behavior of college students and young adults.

- Assess a variety of living arrangements of the college years and young adulthood.

- Examine the major psychosexual developmental tasks associated with adulthood.

- Relate the findings of a variety of studies concerning the sexual behavior of adulthood and older adulthood.

- Assess a variety of sexual lifestyles in adulthood.

- Explain the impact of aging on sexual response and behavior.

- Describe the normal developmental course of long-term straight and gay relationships.

- Identify the major sources of marital and long-term unhappiness in relationships.

- Discuss the effects of divorce and widowhood on adult sexuality.

Intimacy
a gradual process of sharing one's innermost feelings with another

The primary task we face as young adults, according to Erik Erikson, is the development of **intimacy** — forming committed, intimate, loving relationships.[1] We begin to move away from the adolescent focus on ourselves toward exploring mutually satisfying relationships. This stage emphasizes commitment, both in intimate relationships and in work.

This is an exciting time of life. We meet new friends, explore intimate, loving relationships, and test the waters for work and career possibilities. This is the first time many college students are living apart from their parents. It is a time of unparalleled freedom. Students who have mastered the developmental tasks of adolescence and childhood enter this period in their lives ready and eager to sample all that life has to offer.

FORMING FRIENDSHIPS

New adult friendships form the basis of intimate relationships for many college students. Intimacy grows out of friendships as we become more trusting and comfortable with each other. In his book, *Friendship*, Joel Block contends that humans are "wired" with a basic desire for contact with others.[2] Our friendships, Block believes, are what make us whole. He says that friends enrich our existence and bond with us to form a conspiracy against the world. We like one another, understand each other, share interests, and have similar lifestyles or problems in life.

Although college literally throws people together (dorm pairings, class scheduling, and so on), what is it that draws friends together? Many friendships grow out of meeting people who share similar interests and experiences. We meet fellow students who have the same major, take the same classes, and join the same organizations. These similarities provide the initial attraction. If the attraction is strong enough, it provides the basis for spending more time together. As the friendship progresses, the friends share more time and experiences, reinforcing their commonality, deepening their

Friendships fill a special place in our lives.

bonds, and enriching their lives. Many people form their deepest friendships in college during young adulthood.

Friendship is a unique bond. Although it is fraught with entanglements that also characterize romantic relationships — competition, jealousy, and betrayal — it offers what Block called "psychological space." Friendships are more open-ended than relationships with family, mates, or lovers. Unlike these other, more intimate relationships, our friendships provide separate lives that allow time off and away from entanglements. Consequently, friends develop a greater tolerance for growth and change. We are most truly ourselves with our friends.

Friends are much more forgiving than lovers.

DATING AND INTIMATE RELATIONSHIPS

Whereas friendships may be casual, intimacy by definition is deeply personal and trusting. Intimate relationships are characterized by sharing deep personal information. Intimacy grows out of friendship and usually is nurtured through dating. We'll cover intimacy in detail in Chapter 10, on Relationships.

Every society has some rituals or norms for pairing and courtship. Although the "rules" for dating and courtship vary from culture (and subculture) to culture, every society has traditions that it passes along from one generation to the next. Adults who came of age in the late 1960s and early 1970s in the United States vividly remember the differences between the rigid rules of the 1950s and the more liberated 1960s. Prior to the cultural revolution of the 1960s, a young woman would not even consider asking a man out for a date. Men were expected to ask women out, pay for the evening's activities, and be responsible for picking up and dropping off their dates. Women were expected to wait for men to call them, even if a woman was interested and wanted to

Intimacy takes time to develop and does not necessarily involve sex.

Health Hint

To develop a lasting friendship with someone you care about:

- Start with someone you feel close to or *want* to feel close to.

- Learn trust. It's tough to face possible rejection when you let someone in on your deepest secrets, but a true friend will love and accept you regardless of your flaws.

Developing a Lasting Relationship

- Be willing to share your most personal thoughts and feelings, as well as your time, your possessions, and other things that are important to you.

- Spend plenty of time together; it's what helps you develop closeness. If you have to, adjust your schedule.

- Be a good listener. Your friend needs a confidant, too.

Dating provides an opportunity to find out things about each other.

initiate contact. The popular media played out these and other traditional dating scenarios, and mothers and fathers passed them on to their daughters and sons. Everyone was assumed to be heterosexual, and sex was not a part of the evening's activities.

The face of dating in the 1990s looks dramatically different. Dating behavior allows more freedom. A woman can initiate a date, pick up her date, and pay for herself. Straight, gay, and bisexual men and women have their own clubs, organizations, and dating services that make finding a partner easier and safer. In the past, bars and clubs for gay and lesbian women were disguised and subject to harassment from bullies and the police. Today they are more accepted and open.

Although the rituals and rules of dating change over time, the purpose of dating hasn't changed much. Dating is a mechanism for developing intimate relationships. Intimate relationships, in turn, influence both sexual behavior and living patterns.

COLLEGE SEXUAL STANDARDS

Many people equate intimacy with sexual activity and love, yet they are three separate entities. A person can be intimate and sexual with another person but not love that person or be sexually involved with another person. And a person can be sexual with another person but neither love nor be intimate with that person. In a survey of more than 10,000 adults, most respondents agreed that the best possible combination of all three would be to be sexual with someone toward whom you feel both intimate and loving.[3]

Research on college sexual mores has found three standards of behavior: traditional, sexually moderate, and sexually liberal or permissive.[4]

1. *Traditional students* believe that intercourse should occur only when the partners are in love and committed to marry. Heavy petting and other forms of sexual expression are allowed, but intercourse is accepted only when marriage plans are clearly established.

2. *Sexually moderate students* believe that intercourse is acceptable if the couple love each other. The couple need not commit to marriage or even discuss it.

3. *Sexually permissive students* believe that intercourse is a logical outcome of friendship and intimacy. They do not think being in love or planning to marry are prerequisites for intercourse.

The double standard, which posits that men can be sexually aggressive and experienced while women have to be passive and inexperienced is still alive, to some extent, among today's college students.

Sexual Behavior Among College Students

The trends we discussed in Chapter 5 regarding adolescent sexual behavior seem to continue into the college years. Specifically, evidence suggests increasing levels of sexual activity among college students over the past two decades, and women seem to be catching up to men in terms of the number of partners, level of sexual activity, and activities engaged in. Data concerning the sexual behavior of college students is difficult to extract from large-scale studies. Often, it is reported in studies of adolescent or teenage sexual behavior because the teen years extend into the first year or two of college. College students are also merged into studies of adult sexual behavior.

In their comprehensive study of sexuality in the United States, Laumann et al. include data on 18–29-year-olds.[5] Table 6.1 shows the number of sexual partners in the past 12 months for 18–29-year-olds by marital status. As you can see, the percentages of men and women who did not report any sexual partners in the past 12 months were similar for all categories of respondents. The men, however, were much more likely than the women to have had more than two sexual partners during the past 12 months.

In reporting the number of sexual partners during the past 5 years, the percentages of men and women reporting from none to four partners were fairly comparable (see Table 6.2).[6] The figures begin to change dramatically, however, when we examine the percentages of men and women who report 5–10, 11–20, and 21+ partners during the past 5 years. The percentages of these categories for men are twice those of women respondents.

Frequency of sexual activity for men and women aged 18–29 is compared in Table 6.3. From these data, women aged 18–29 seem to enjoy a slightly higher level of sexual activity. Table 6.3 illustrates the percentages of men and women engaging in various levels of sexual activity over a 12-month period.

Other interesting findings from Laumann et al. regarding the sexual behavior of 18–29-year-olds were related to masturbation and oral sex. An analysis of those behaviors is presented in Tables 6.4, 6.5, and 6.6.

Approximately 41% of the men and 64% of the women reported that they currently did not masturbate. Of those who masturbated, approximately 30% of the men and only 10% of the women did so at least once a week.

Men and women in the 18 to 24-year-old age group were similar in their levels of both active and receptive oral sex. Approximately 72% of the

| Table 6.1 | Number of Sex Partners During Past 12 Months |

Age and Partner Status	Cohabiting Status			Marital Status		
	Not Cohabiting	Cohabiting, Unmarried	Married	Never Married	Married	Formerly Married
			% Distribution			
Women						
18–29:						
No partners	14.3	0.0	0.0	12.9	0.0	2.0
1 partner	51.3	76.8	96.0	56.6	96.0	58.8
2–4 partners	27.7	18.8	3.0	24.2	3.0	33.3
5 or more partners	6.7	4.4	1.0	6.2	1.0	5.9
30–44:						
No partners	30.4	2.2	1.3	37.3	1.3	18.9
1 partner	45.8	86.7	96.4	42.4	96.4	58.3
2–4 partners	21.7	11.1	2.1	17.8	2.1	21.7
5 or more partners	2.0	0.2		2.5	0.2	1.1
45–49:						
No partners	61.3	†	7.3	64.9	7.3	54.1
1 partner	29.7	†	91.3	27.0	91.3	36.1
2–4 partners	8.4	†	1.4	8.1	1.4	9.0
5 or more partners	0.6	†	0.0	0.0	0.0	0.8
Men						
18–29:						
No partners	16.1	0.0	0.8	14.6	0.8	†
1 partner	35.8	67.3	90.9	40.7	90.9	†
2–4 partners	33.2	24.5	5.8	30.5	5.8	†
5 or more partners	15.0	8.2	2.5	14.2	2.5	†
30–44:						
No partners	22.7	0.0	0.6	23.1	0.6	14.0
1 partner	30.1	73.7	93.3	34.0	93.3	40.2
2–4 partners	39.4	23.7	5.6	35.4	5.6	39.2
5 or more partners	7.9	2.6	0.6	7.5	0.6	6.5
45–49:						
No partners	42.1	†	3.7	†	3.7	30.1
1 partner	35.5	†	91.5	†	91.5	45.2
2–4 partners	22.4	†	3.7	†	3.7	23.3
5 or more partners	0.0	†	1.2	†	1.2	1.4

Source: *The Social Organization of Sexuality: Sexual Practices in the United States*, by E. Laumann et al. (Chicago: University of Chicago Press, 1994). Used with permission.

men and 70% of the women reported ever performing oral sex on their partners. Of this group, 28% of the men and 19% of the women reported performing oral sex during their last sexual encounter with their partners. Similar percentages for men (75% ever and 29% last encounter) and women (75% ever and 24% last encounter) were reported for receiving oral sex.

A study of college students found that the total number of sex partners, for both the previous year and total lifetime, has increased for both college men and women.[7] The average number of total sexual partners for college women was 5.6, and the men reported an average 11.2 partners.

Similar percentages of male and female college students were found for the following behaviors: vaginal intercourse (68% for men and women), masturbation (men 78%, women 71%), performing oral sex (60% men, 68% women), receiving oral sex (64% men, 71% women), anal intercourse (6% men, 10% women), and using pornography (58% men, 37% women).[8]

Table 6.2 ⟩ Number of Sex Partners During Past 5 Years

Social Characteristics	No. of Sex Partners					
	0	1	2–4	5–10	11–20	21+
	% Distributions					
Total population	8.0	53.3	25.8	8.6	2.7	1.7
Gender:						
Male	7.1	45.7	27.7	12.0	4.2	3.3
Female	8.7	59.4	24.3	5.9	1.4	0.4
Age:						
18–29	16.2	59.5	74.7	29.9	12.5	7.1
30–44	18.3	180.5	72.1	21.6	4.5	2.9
45–59	33.5	216.5	40.5	7.3	0.7	1.4
Marital status:						
Never married, not cohabitating	19.2	16.0	34.8	19.7	6.4	3.9
Never married, cohabitating	0.8	31.0	43.4	15.5	5.4	3.9
Married	2.4	78.6	14.8	2.6	0.9	0.7
Divorced/separated/ widow, not cohabitating	13.3	32.1	41.1	9.9	2.5	1.1
Divorced/separated/ widow/cohabitating	4.4	34.1	47.2	12.1	2.2	0.0
Education:						
HS graduation equivalent	9.0	54.0	27.5	6.8	1.9	0.9
Finished college	6.6	52.2	26.4	9.2	2.5	3.1

Source: *The Social Organization of Sexuality: Sexual Practices in the United States*, by E. Laumann et al. (Chicago: University of Chicago Press, 1994). Used with permission.

Living Arrangements of College Students

Living arrangements of college students include: single and cohabitating.

Single

Many college students are single and live off-campus, either at home with their parents or in shared living environments. In 1991, the overwhelming majority of young adults lived at home. More than 30% between the ages of 24 and 29 lived at home, according to 1992 statistics from the

| **Table 6.3** | Frequency of Sex Intercourse During Past 12 months |

Master Status Variables	Frequency of Sex in the Past Year (%)				
	Not at All	A Few Times per Year	A Few Times per Month	Two to Three Times a Week	Four or More Times a Week
Men					
Total population	9.8	17.6	35.5	29.5	7.7
Age:					
18–29	21.4	35.9	54.9	64.2	23.8
30–44	23.2	46.2	119.1	93.2	18.3
45–59	36.2	64.1	120.0	67.2	12.3
Marital status:					
Never married, not cohabitating	22.0	26.2	25.4	18.8	7.6
Never married, cohabitating	0.0	8.5	35.6	37.3	18.6
Married	1.3	12.8	42.5	36.1	7.3
Divorced/separated/ widow, not cohabitating	23.8	22.5	28.5	20.5	4.6
Divorced/separated/ widow, cohabitating	0.0	8.3	36.1	44.4	11.1
Education:					
HS graduate equivalent	10.1	15.1	34.4	31.7	8.7
Finished college	9.0	15.8	43.9	25.8	5.4
Women					
Total population	13.6	16.1	37.2	26.3	6.7
Age:					
18–29	15.7	26.4	69.6	65.6	22.7
30–44	33.5	47.8	118.5	82.3	17.8
45–59	76.2	59.2	110.6	46.2	7.7
Marital status:					
Never married, not cohabitating	30.2	23.5	26.0	13.3	7.0
Never married, cohabitating	1.4	6.9	31.9	43.1	16.7
Married	3.0	11.9	46.5	31.9	6.6
Divorced/separated/ widow, not cohabitating	34.3	23.2	21.9	16.8	3.7
Divorced/separated/ widow, cohabitating	0.0	9.4	39.6	39.6	11.3
Education:					
HS graduate equivalent	10.8	15.9	37.7	29.6	6.0
Finished college	12.5	18.3	33.5	29.7	6.1

Source: *The Social Organization of Sexuality: Sexual Practices in the United States*, by E. Laumann et al. (Chicago: University of Chicago Press, 1994). Used with permission.

Census Bureau. This is in stark contrast to the living arrangements of men and women in this age group in the 1950s, when most men and women of this age range were married and out of their parents' houses.

Among the many factors that have contributed to this change are: trends in delaying marriage, increasing percentage of never-marrieds, high cost of housing, and the need for more people to continue education.

Cohabiting

According to the Census Bureau, about 6.3 million people in the United States cohabited in 1998. Of those, approximately half were under 25 years of age. No accurate numbers have been forthcoming regarding the actual number of college students who cohabit. **Cohabitation** is distinguished from having roommates of the opposite gender by the nature of the sexual interaction between cohabitors. Cohabitors are lovers who live together but are not married. Cohabitors initially describe their relationship as intimate and affectionate but not necessarily as leading to marriage.

Cohabitation
living together without being married

PERSPECTIVES

Cohabitation Facts

- An estimated 6.3 million Americans were in cohabitation relationships as of March 1998. That is up from about 5.3 million as recently as 1995.

- The age breakdown is as follows:
   15.5% of men and 22.1% of women under 15–24;
   38.7% of men and 37.2% of women 25–35;
   21.8% of men and 23.1% of women 35–44;
   23.9% of men and 17.5% of women 45+

- 4.2% of the female (approximately 134,000) and 1.7% of the men (approximately 55,000) cohabitors are students.

- 37% of college-educated women had lived in a cohabitating relationship, and that number is rising.

- Most cohabitations are short-lived and the couple either separates or marries.

- Divorce rates are higher among those who cohabited before marriage.

Source: U.S. Bureau of the Census, "Current Population Survey," Center for Demography and Ecology (University of Wisconsin, Madison, 1998).

ADULT SEXUAL BEHAVIOR

The most recent large-scale study of adult sexual behavior is the NHSLS conducted by Laumann et al. We will extend the discussion of sexuality during the college and young adult years into adulthood and old age.

Masturbation in Adulthood

Adult masturbation is often viewed as a second-class sexual experience and is inversely related to the availability of a steady partner.[9] The common belief is that masturbation is primarily motivated by the relief of sexual tension. This

Table 6.4 Frequency of Masturbation

Master Status	Frequency (%)			
	Not at All		Once a Week	
	Men	Women	Men	Women
Total population	36.7	58.3	26.7	7.6
Age:				
18–24	41.2	64.4	29.2	9.4
25–29	28.9	58.3	32.7	9.9
30–34	27.6	51.1	34.6	8.6
35–39	38.5	52.3	20.8	6.6
40–44	34.5	49.8	28.7	8.7
45–49	35.2	55.6	27.2	8.6
50–54	52.5	71.8	13.9	2.3
55–59	51.7	77.6	10.3	2.4
Marital status:				
Never married, not cohabitating	31.8	51.8	41.3	12.3
Never married, cohabitating	15.8	54.9	36.8	12.7
Married	42.6	62.9	16.5	4.7
Divorced/separated/widow, not cohabitating	30.2	52.7	34.9	9.6
Divorced/separated/widow, cohabitating	41.2	50.9	17.6	12.7
Education:				
HS graduate equivalent	45.1	68.4	20.0	5.6
Finished college	24.2	47.7	33.2	10.2
Master's/advanced degree	18.6	41.2	33.6	13.7

Source: *The Social Organization of Sexuality: Sexual Practices in the United States,* by E. Laumann et al. (Chicago: University of Chicago Press, 1994). Used with permission.

belief grows out of a Western cultural viewpoint that masturbation is juvenile sexual behavior, almost preintercourse in its development. We join Laumann et al. in taking issue with this notion. In Chapter 7 we provide a detailed overview of masturbation throughout the life cycle.

Laumann et al. examined masturbation in light of its relational context. They believe that masturbation, like all forms of sexual expression, is driven by a variety of social and biological factors throughout the life cycle and can have complementary, supplementary, or independent status with reference to partnered sex. This means that masturbation can enhance partnered sexual activity. It also can be an additional source of sexual expression within the context of the relationship, and last, it can serve as a solitary source of sexual pleasure independent of partnered sex.

Table 6.4 illustrated the frequency of masturbatory behavior by age and other selected demographic variables. Results were not segregated by sexual orientation. Laumann et al. emphasized one of the key findings of the table: The level of masturbation is not related to relationship status. Although the table does show a decline in the level of masturbatory behavior among married people, it does not show a similar pattern among those who are single but cohabit. This group tended to be younger overall than the married sample.

Rather than reinforce the stereotype that masturbation is a substitute for partnered sex, this finding shows that this isn't necessarily so. The frequency of individual masturbation is as likely to be a function of social factors and a variety of reasons as it is the availability of alternative outlets. Table 6.5 gives some of the reasons for masturbation, cited by gender.

Table 6.3 presented the frequency of sexual intercourse in the past year. Laumann et al. summarized the three main levels of sexual activities for adults: About 35% have sex with a partner two or more times per week; about 35% have partnered sex one to a few times per month; and the remaining 30% have partnered sex only a few times a year. These rates were fairly consistent across all racial, ethnic, and religious groups. About 7%–8% of the respondents had partnered sex four or more times a week, and about 10% reported having had no sex at all during the previous year. This, the researchers point out, paints quite a different picture of adult sexual behavior than the one portrayed in the popular media. The sexual activity of most Americans is much more modest than the frequency and expectations created by the media.

Table 6.5 Reasons for Masturbation		
	Gender of Respondent (%)	
Reasons for Masturbation	**Men**	**Women**
To relax	26	32
To relieve sex tension	73	63
Partner unavailable	32	32
Partner doesn't want sex	16	6
Boredom	11	5
Physical pleasure	40	42
Go to sleep	16	12
Fear of AIDS/STD	7	5
Other	5	5

Source: *The Social Organization of Sexuality: Sexual Practices in the United States,* by E. Laumann et al. (Chicago: University of Chicago Press, 1994). Used with permission.

An additional finding concerning partnered sexual activity related to the number of sex partners during the past year. As Table 6.1 pointed out, the number of different sex partners in the past year declines with age. In general, the largest percentage of respondents in each age cohort reported only one sex partner during the past year. Two moderating factors seem to be marital and cohabiting status. Young, single, noncohabiting men and women were much more likely than all other groups to report two or more different partners during the previous year.

Adult Oral Sex Activity

Table 6.6 illustrates the frequency of oral sexual activity among adults. The table does not segregate by sexual orientation. Straight and gay men and lesbian and heterosexual women are lumped together. The proportion of men reporting having had oral sex performed on them during their lives was similar to that of women reporting ever having had cunnilingus performed on them — roughly 75%. This percentage drops dramatically, however (about 50%), when oral sexual behavior is reported at latest sexual experience. Laumann et al. interpreted this as meaning that, although the majority of American men and women have experienced oral sex, it isn't as much a staple in their sexual repertoire as vaginal intercourse and kissing.

Laumann et al. viewed the increased frequency of oral sex as one of the basic changes in U.S. sexual behavior during the past century. They reported that the current incidence is probably an outgrowth of a trend that began in the 1920s. Kinsey et al. publicized oral sex in the late 1940s and it has continued to work its way into the fabric of American sexual behavior.

Table 6.6   Frequency of Oral Sex

			Sexual Practices						
	Mean Frequency of Sex per Month		Occurrence of Active Oral Sex (%)				Occurrence of Receptive Oral Sex (%)			
			Men		Women		Men		Women	
Master Status Variables	Men	Women	Life	Last Event	Life	Last Event	Life	Last Event	Life	Last Event
Total population	6.5	6.3	76.6	26.8	67.7	18.8	78.7	27.5	73.1	19.9
Age:										
18–24	7.2	7.4	72.4	27.7	69.1	19.1	74.2	28.9	74.7	24.2
25–29	7.6	7.5	84.8	32.0	76.2	23.8	84.8	33.7	79.8	24.3
30–34	6.7	6.8	78.9	29.6	76.6	19.1	78.9	32.2	83.1	22.3
35–39	6.6	6.1	82.3	30.4	71.3	21.0	87.5	29.8	73.7	23.3
40–44	5.9	5.5	84.0	31.2	72.7	16.9	85.7	28.9	76.8	12.6
45–49	6.2	5.5	73.4	21.2	65.2	21.6	77.4	22.1	72.7	18.3
50–54	5.5	4.6	60.0	16.1	48.5	11.7	66.0	13.8	59.4	12.6
55–59	4.4	3.5	58.4	9.9	38.9	5.5	58.0	14.1	44.3	6.9
Marital status:										
Never married, not cohabitating	5.6	5.3	66.7	28.9	59.4	21.0	70.3	32.8	67.7	26.8
Never married, cohabitating	8.6	8.8	85.7	30.2	72.2	21.5	89.3	34.0	76.4	22.7
Married	6.9	6.5	79.9	25.2	70.7	16.9	80.4	23.0	73.9	16.9
Divorced/separated/ widow, not cohabitating	5.4	5.1	81.5	30.1	64.1	25.4	88.1	34.5	73.1	24.2
Divorced/separated/ widow, cohabitating	8.0	7.6	80.0	29.7	79.6	16.3	80.0	37.8	85.2	20.4
Education:										
Less than high school	6.5	6.3	59.2	16.4	41.1	10.1	60.7	16.4	49.6	13.2
High school graduate or equivalent	6.9	6.3	75.3	30.1	59.6	16.4	76.6	25.3	67.1	18.5
Some college/ vocation	6.6	6.3	80.0	31.1	78.2	20.7	84.0	31.0	81.6	22.2
Finished college	6.0	6.4	83.7	23.7	78.9	22.9	84.6	31.1	83.1	20.7
Master's/advanced degree	6.1	5.1	80.5	20.6	79.0	28.8	81.4	30.4	81.9	27.0

Source: *The Social Organization of Sexuality: Sexual Practices in the United States,* by E. Laumann et al. (Chicago: University of Chicago Press, 1994). Used with permission.

Adult Anal Sexual Activity

Unlike oral sex, anal sex has yet to make a serious entry into the basic fabric of American sexual behavior. The overall level of heterosexual anal intercourse in the past year was around 9%. Only 2% of those ever having anal intercourse reported engaging in this activity at last sexual encounter. As with other forms of sexual activity reported in the NHSLS, anal intercourse seems to be reported across all categories of respondents and is not limited to certain racial, ethnic, or religious groups.

Some evidence indicates that a small segment of adolescent and college women view heterosexual anal intercourse as an acceptable alternative to vaginal penetration. We, too, have received similar anecdotal reports from students engaged in internships in family-planning agencies and from other health care providers serving young women.

A small segment of young women view anal intercourse as a behavior (along with oral sex) that doesn't involve losing one's "virginity." These women think that as long as the vagina is not penetrated, they technically remain "virgins." They also believe this is an acceptable form of contraception. What do you think?

ADULT RELATIONSHIPS

One of the major developmental tasks of adulthood is the continuation and deepening of the commitment to relationships that began in young adulthood. For most Americans this means a commitment to marriage and a family. For many, the commitment to someone else does not involve marriage but, instead, cohabitation. This is a period frequently marked by divorce or the death of a spouse. In the remaining part of this chapter we'll examine the changing nature of adult relationships.

Singlehood

A significant percentage of Americans are choosing to remain single for life. Reasons for remaining single include changes in sexual standards, greater financial independence for women, changing economic times, and changing conceptions of marriage. Sometimes, postponing marriage results in an inadvertent slide into permanent singlehood.[10] As people postpone marriage, they often realize that they can live satisfying lives being single. There is less urgency to marry, especially if they feel no desire to have children.

Regardless of the reasons, most people who chose to remain single for life in one study reported that they were quite happy. Contrary to popular beliefs, most singles are not lonely, and they develop alternative social patterns based on friendships and nonmarital love relationships.

Most singles are not lonely, and they develop alternative social patterns.

The satisfaction that singles derive from these relationships and their careers is more than adequate for their happiness.[11]

Dating and Single Adults

The two most stressful issues for single people are how to handle dating and others' expectations that they should marry.[12] The United States is a "couples-oriented" society that puts a premium on adults interacting socially as part of a heterosexual couple. The prevailing assumption is that everyone expects to get married someday. This puts inordinate pressure upon single people, especially when friends and associates are continually trying to "fix them up." Singles typically find themselves having to defend their position. Old friendships also tend to disappear when a friend marries and starts a family.

Gay single people find themselves in a double-bind. People are continually trying to fix them up with members of the opposite sex so they can "find someone" and settle down. When gay singles finally do "find someone," they usually don't feel comfortable sharing their relationship with their straight friends.

Cohabitation

Unmarried adult couples who live together are not much different from married couples. They share, argue, quarrel, make decisions about money, sex, household labor, and so on. The reasons for adults living together but not marrying are many and varied. Generally speaking, three forms of cohabitation are: casual or temporary involvement, preparation or testing for marriage, and a substitute for or alternative to marriage.

Marriage

The vast majority of Americans want to marry, although they are postponing it longer than in the past. The median age at first marriage has been rising for the past three decades. Even though it is an integral part of most cultures, marriage takes many forms and assumes many different purposes throughout the world. In the United States, most people take the following issues for granted concerning marriage: a legal bond, having children, permanence, heterosexuality, sexual exclusivity, emotional exclusivity, and **monogamy**.[13]

Monogamy
married to only
one person at a time

The U. S. culture also expects more from marriage than many other cultures do. Historically, marriages were intended to provide a stable economic unit in which to rear children. Today, people expect marriage to fulfill their social, emotional, financial, and sexual needs. When people marry, they find that many of these expectations are unrealistic and cannot be fully realized. This can lead to frustration, disillusionment, separation, and divorce. They also find that marriage is hard work. Even under the best of circumstances and with a good match in a partner, successful marriage requires continual assessment, communication, commitment and willingness to change.

Americans tend to expect marriage to fulfill all of their needs.

Weddings still symbolize hope and lifelong love.

The Developmental Course of Marriage

Berry and Williams proposed a developmental model of marriage across adulthood, shown in Figure 6.1. In the early, honeymoon phase, marriage is at its most intense. The two spend considerable time together, talking, sharing interests and leisure, establishing their roles within the relationship, arguing and making up. As the honeymoon phase begins to wind down and the couple settle into a routine, the intensity of the honeymoon phase diminishes and along with it, marital satisfaction. A big reason for this is the birth of children. Children result in less time available for the mate and the relationship.

Marital happiness reaches its lowest point during the mid-life phase of the relationship, which also coincides with adolescence of the couple's children. A myriad of problems, ranging from financial issues to coping with teenagers to changing roles for husband and wife — contribute to the unrest.

Happiness begins to rebound when the children leave home as adults. This frees up time and money, and the couple have rediscovered privacy to reestablish the things in their relationship that provide pleasure, as well as investigate new things together.

Marital happiness continues to rise in the later adult years and carries over into retirement. Depending upon a number of factors ranging from health to retirement income, the couple continue to enjoy their freedom, and in some cases relationships with their children's families and their grandchildren.

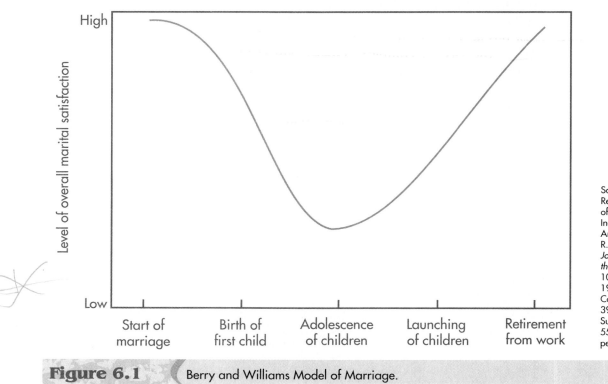

Source: "Assessing the Relationship Between Quality of Life and Marital and Income Satisfaction: A Path Analytic Approach," by R. E. Berry and E. Williams, *Journal of Marriage and the Family, 47* (1987), 107–116. Copyrighted 1987 by the National Council on Family Relations, 3989 Central Avenue NE, Suite 550, Minneapolis, MN 55421. Reprinted with permission.

Figure 6.1   Berry and Williams Model of Marriage.

Obviously, not all couples fit the Berry and Williams model. Other variables, such as physical illness, children living at home into their 30s, and loss of jobs, strain the relationship. In some cases children growing up and leaving the nest magnify problems in the relationship that lead to divorce. Not all relationships flourish in retirement. Sometimes work serves as a buffer between a couple and their problems.

Caring for children can be both demanding and rewarding.

Sexual Satisfaction and Happiness

Sexual satisfaction and happiness in marital and other partnered relationships have two dimensions: physical satisfaction and emotional happiness.[14] The relationship between the two is complex. Highly satisfying physical relationships usually bring with them high emotional happiness. High levels of emotional satisfaction, however, don't necessarily indicate high levels of physical satisfaction.

Overall, a fairly high proportion of men (47%) and women (41%) described their partnership as extremely physically pleasurable. Satisfaction seems to vary with age. Among men, the level of physical satisfaction was high to begin with and increased with age. Among women however, high

PERSPECTIVES

Mid-Life Crisis or Middle Age Myth?

You have heard the story before. A happy, successful 45-year-old businessman quits his job, leaves his wife and kids, and runs off to Tahiti with his 25-year-old secretary. Or, perhaps it is the 40-year-old mother of two facing the "empty nest" who jumps into her convertible BMW with her 20-year-old tennis instructor and heads west into the sunset in a torrid blaze of passionate sex.

These and other "midlife crises" that have been popularized by the print and film media make interesting stories and pose a romantic solution to many of the difficult issues that appear during middle age. In real life, however, relatively few people experience such catastrophic, radical changes. New information fueled by long-term research on aging is showing that middle age is the very best time of life. It is a developmental stage unlike most others, because it is not tied particularly to changes in the body, such as early childhood, adolescence, and old age. Midlife is characterized more by psychological adaptations and is reality-based.

By midlife, many of the stressful questions that faced us as young adults are answered, such as: Will anyone ever love me? Will this marriage work out? Will I ever find a job? What kind of lifestyle can I afford to lead?

By midlife, most people have found love. If they are married, they are more likely to stay married (the overwhelming majority of divorces occur within the first 6 to 8 years of marriage). They have settled into a job and have a pretty good idea of where they are headed (most professionals who are going to "make it" have made it by this time). They have a good sense of their earning capacity and therefore can gauge the kind of lifestyle they can expect.

Although the myth of midlife is that this period is characterized by unrest, discomfort, dissatisfaction, and upheaval, the reality is that it is a comfortable, satisfying time. It is a time to enjoy the rewards of 10 to 20 years of scuffling. It is a time to push a little easier at work, to get off a little early to watch your kid's Little League game. It is a time to focus on vacations and social gatherings, to take a class to learn how to paint, or improve your backhand. It is a time to lighten up a little.

Midlife is a period of gradual adjustment, not tumultuous change. It gradually unfolds and is based on several adjustments to reality. For most people it is based in reality, not fantasy. Those most likely to experience a true crisis (about 5%) are people who generally have experienced similar crises in all developmental stages of their lives. Their lives are based on unrealistic (therefore unrealized) notions and expectations. One of the major criticisms of earlier studies of midlife is that they were based on small numbers of case studies of atypical populations (mostly affluent, professional, and White). In the recent cross-sectional studies of more representative samples of Americans, researchers found that the average person's midlife adjustment is based on reality. People gradually adjust their expectations to fit the reality of their lives. By the time they settle into midlife, they have learned to make the best of what they have and are not constantly longing for things that are beyond their reach.

Source: *Coping with Stress in a Changing World*, by R. Blonna (New York: McGraw-Hill, 1996), p. 537.

levels of physical satisfaction dropped significantly after age 55. Findings are similar regarding emotional satisfaction. Laumann et al. accounted for this by explaining that men in their 50s and older are more likely than similar-aged women to acquire new sex partners after divorce.

Sources of Marital Problems

The potential sources of trouble over the lifespan of a marriage range from loss of initial sexual passion to economic instability in retirement.

Continuing romantic love is not a realistic expectation.

Many relationships are doomed from the start because they are based on an ideal that never can be fulfilled. Many expectations are unrealistic as a result of immature or romantic perceptions. The continuing intensity and bliss of romantic love cannot be expected to continue throughout marriage. Bliss

Case Study

Lynn: Juggling Life's Responsibilities

Lynn is 40 years old. She's been married for 15 years and has four children, ages 13, 11, 10, and 7. Lynn got married right out of junior college and never worked full-time in her field of preparation, accounting. She's done some part-time bookkeeping and child care in her home over the years, but for the most part she's been a full-time mother and housewife.

Lynn is excellent at what she does. She's managed to rear four children, keep her house clean, and get involved in a number of school, church, and community organizations. She's been a good mom, den mother, Sunday school teacher, and school board member. Although a little frazzled at times, Lynn has managed to care for her family well.

Lynn is ready for a change, though. Money has been more than a little tight lately. A few years ago her husband had decided to go back to school in the evening to get his master's degree so he could keep pace in his profession. Tuition costs have greatly eroded the family's meager savings. The kids all have needed braces, and the youngest had to have a congenital heart defect repaired.

Lynn went back to work 6 months ago. Her youngest child is in all-day kindergarten, and her husband was able to work flex hours to be able to pick up the kids at the after-school program. Lynn tried to work as a bookkeeper but found that she didn't like it any more. She always wanted to get into retail, so she

landed a sales job at one of the more fashionable women's department stores at the new mall nearby.

Lynn has done exceptionally well in retail. In 6 months she was promoted to assistant manager of her section (women's evening wear) and really likes it. She thrives on the personal contact, the fashion, getting dressed up, attending sales meetings — everything. She's decided to go back to school to get her bachelor's degree in retail management. Her company offers a special distributive education program through a local state college, where she can go to class and earn credit for her retail sales work. In 3 years she will have enough credits to graduate and, with a little luck, a position as a sales manager with her present company.

It hasn't been easy. Juggling the demands of motherhood, housework, school, and work has been trying at times. Her husband has been supportive and has learned to cook and clean so he can pull his weight around the house. The kids are pitching in wherever they can, and everyone tries to respect mom's "quiet time" when she is studying. Lynn's house is not as clean as it once was, her husband's shirt collars could be ironed better (he's learning), and the kids' lunches occasionally get mixed up, but it's working. Lynn has made a successful passage into another phase of her life that will help keep her and her family a dynamic, growing entity.

Health Hint

Lessons from Happy Marriages

In a happy marriage:

1. The partners find their prime source of joy in each other but maintain separate identities.

2. They are generous and giving out of love, not because they expect repayment or are keeping score.

3. The partners enjoy a healthy and vigorous sexual relationship.

4. The partners "fight" in a constructive way, airing feelings and frustrations without attacking or blaming the other.

5. The partners communicate with each other openly and honestly.

6. The partners trust each other.

7. Both talk about their future together. They have mutual goals.

The best marriages tend to be ones in which the partners are similar in:

— ethnicity
— locality (geography; urban or rural)
— maturity (emotional and social)
— goals and ideals
— intelligence levels
— amount of education
— economic level and financial resources
— social strata
— value system
— religious beliefs.

turns to boredom and aggravation, passion to comfort, and happiness to times of sadness. This does not mean that love is dead. Romantic love should be expected to transform into mature love.

Further, communication problems can sabotage a relationship. These problems may be rooted in a lack of assertiveness in which one or both members of the couple are unable to stand up for themselves. Communication problems also can arise when the partners are unable to express positive and constructive thoughts and feelings. Many people grow up in an environment where communication revolves around problems and the expression of negative emotions. Relationships can wither from a lack of expressions of recognition, caring, tenderness, and compassion.

Communication problems can be summarized as stemming from a lack of communication skills or the lack of desire to communicate, or both. The easier problem to remedy is the skill-based one. If one or both members of the relationship do not know how to communicate clearly and effectively or don't know how to fight fairly, they can learn — assuming they have the desire. If either or both don't have the desire to work things out, no amount of skill will improve the situation.

Communication problems usually involve a lack of skill or the desire to communicate, or both.

Loss of desire to talk and work things out is a warning sign of a deteriorating relationship. Sometimes a vicious cycle begins in which a lack of skill in communicating leads to a deteriorating relationship, which feeds a loss of desire. Low levels of desire keep the cycle going by not having the interest in talking about problems in the relationship. In the last case, one or both members may want to try to communicate in general but think the

Health Hint

Fighting Fairly

- Use "I" rather than "you." Instead of saying, "You're insensitive," say, "I feel hurt when you ignore me."

- Don't argue without good reason. Think before you speak.

- Don't fight in front of other people, including your children. The issue involves only the two of you.

- Don't make personal attacks — name-calling, put-downs — that you will regret later.

- Be specific. Don't generalize.

- Focus on only the issue that precipitated the argument.

- Learn to use active listening skills so your partner will know he or she is being heard.

- If you cannot agree after a "fair fight," agree to disagree or to renew the discussion later.

- Take responsibility for your own behavior. Avoid blaming.

- Obviously, do not resort to physical attacks or any form of violence.

problem is too difficult to talk about. Or they may want to try to communicate more effectively but lack the energy and commitment necessary to work out their problems.

Couples who want to resolve their problems but don't know where to start can benefit tremendously from couple's counseling. Sometimes, problems that seemed insurmountable before counseling seem workable after seeing a therapist.

Another factor, money — or more precisely what money means to each partner — is a major source of stress in long-term relationships. If the two differ in their perceptions and values surrounding money, this could create problems within the relationship. For instance, one partner may view money as relatively unimportant, only a means to obtain the things necessary for survival. The other, however, perceives money as important — a ticket to a better life, higher status, more luxuries, and so on. This couple is in trouble because their core values concerning money are the opposite. Often this is reflected in how much they spend and what they buy. If one partner perceives that the other is spending too much and making unnecessary purchases, it is bound to lead to problems.

Or one person may view credit as a fundamental economic necessity and have no problem with outstanding balances on credit cards, loans, and home-equity lines. Meanwhile, the other may not be comfortable even with a mortgage or a car loan, preferring to delay all purchases until they can be paid for in cash. The problem is compounded by the easy access to credit and aggressive marketing.

The perception of money affects everything from long-term planning to daily quality of life. It also involves the perception of gender roles as couples decide if one or both partners will work, whose job is more important, if one of them is to leave a career to take care of the children, and so forth. If one partner has a traditional gender role concerning money and the other doesn't, this could be a major source of marital discord. Couples need to discuss these issues and develop creative approaches to deal with their own money and the "couple's" money.

Unrealistic expectations about sex within the marriage also can lead to dissatisfaction. The partners might have differing expectations about the frequency of sex, use of protection, level of desire, and a host of other variables. These differing and unrealistic expectations about sex can be a sign of sexual incompatibility. Often, couples who cohabit in preparation for marriage do so in an effort to gauge sexual compatibility before they enter into a marital relationship. Unfortunately no evidence is available to suggest that couples who do this are more likely to stay together and have marital satisfaction than noncohabitors.[15]

Marital problems are often based on unrealistic ideals and expectations.

Once people leave the single life and pair off in either cohabiting or marital relationships, sex changes. It no longer is as frantic or as segmented from the rest of one's life as it was when the couple lived separately. While sexual pleasure is not sacrificed, sex becomes integrated into the ebb and flow of the couple's life. It is balanced with other needs and responsibilities

Case Study

Tom and Susan: Dealing with Finances

Tom and Susan have an interesting way of dealing with family finances. Having met in graduate business school, where they were pursuing their MBAs, they were in their late 20s when they met. Both had lived by themselves for a few years and had several years of work experience behind them. Each had a savings and checking account.

In discussing marriage, both were concerned about financial independence and protecting their savings, income, and spending patterns. Tom was a saver. He had banked well over $20,000 in savings before he met Susan, and he wanted to preserve this money. He was disciplined and always paid cash, even for his personal automobiles.

Susan was a spender. She believed in credit and never saw a catalog she didn't like. Saving was something people did once they turned 50 and began to think about retirement. For as long as she could remember, she has had outstanding balances on her credit accounts and eventually pays them off.

Being so different concerning money, but so alike in a number of other ways, Tom and Susan decided that after they were married, they would have three

separate accounts — his, hers, ours. The "ours" account would be used for all joint bills (rent, food, joint vacations, and childrearing (if it came up). Susan had wanted other expenses covered from this account, such as car purchases and retirement savings, but Tom, knowing she was a spender and he'd wind up contributing more than she, did not accept this arrangement. Speaking of contributing, the amount of money each would contribute to the joint account would be equal despite their individual salaries. If one made more money than the other, he or she would be allowed to do with it whatever the partner wanted.

Despite some stress, things have worked out okay for Tom and Susan. He's still a saver and has over $20,000 in his bank account. She's still a spender and has a $15,000 car loan and credit card debts exceeding $3,000. Tom considered helping her out with some payments but decided against it, as he thought she'd never learn if he were to bail her out.

Some of their friends think they're a little eccentric and that their marriage seems more like a business than a loving partnership. In any case, it seems to work for them.

More than half of all married couples report that they are extremely satisfied with their sexual relationship with their partner.

— an important developmental task in this stage of the relationship.[16] If a partner is unable or unwilling to communicate about sexual concerns and problems, the problems invariably worsen and become a source of stress within the relationship. Partners who cannot adjust become sexually dissatisfied and may turn to extramarital sex or divorce.

As we've reported, the frequency of sexual intercourse declines as relationships age. Sexual activity peaks within the first year of marriage and then begins to drop off. The frequency of sexual relations is highly correlated with marital satisfaction. In one study, 9 of 10 married couples who were having sex three or more times a week reported satisfaction with their relationships.[17] Conversely, only half of couples having sex one to four times a month were satisfied with their relationships. A more recent study found a similar relationship between the frequency of marital sex and level of satisfaction with the relationship.[18]

Many factors affect the level of sexual activity within a relationship. Work and other responsibilities affect the level of energy people have. Sexual desire may change in response to stress. Sometimes people have common sexual dysfunctions (such as situational erectile dysfunction in men) that lessen sexual frequency and pleasure.

Parenting and Marital Satisfaction

Children can be a major source of marital stress. Whether married or cohabiting, straight or gay, children change a couple's established patterns of interaction. As we've seen from the Berry and Williams analysis of marital happiness and adult developmental phases, satisfaction within a marriage reaches its lowest point about the time the children reach adolescence. Even though this seems to indicate that adolescents are responsible for their parent's stress, the demands of parenting pose formidable stressors at all stages of child development.

Parenting requires a tremendous amount of time and effort. The specific demands change with the child's stage of development, but the responsibility remains. Newborns require constant supervision. Even when they are sleeping, parents learn to sleep lightly, ready to react to their children's cries for help in the night. Young children need help with everything from getting washed and dressed to cutting the food on their plates. Older children need parents to spend time helping them with everything from doing their homework to getting them safely to and from friends' houses. Parents of young adolescents spend countless hours car-pooling their kids all over the place, and parents of older teens stay up all hours of the night waiting for the safe return of their teenager and the family car.

Children decrease up to half the amount of time parents have to share activities with each other.[19] This can disrupt everything from a couple's sexual relationship to the time they spend pursuing hobbies or other activities. In addition to the stress associated with the sheer time demands of children, children's needs are unpredictable. From early-morning feedings of babies, to car-pooling, to waiting for an adolescent to return home from a date, children pose unpredictable demands on the time, temperament, financial resources, and parents sexual desire.

Divorce

Not all marriages progress completely through the Berry and Williams phases described earlier in the chapter. More than half of all first marriages end in divorce. Raw numbers are misleading when interpreting divorce statistics. The divorce *rate*, which examines numbers of divorces in relation to numbers of marriages, rose steadily for twenty years, reaching a high of 5.3 divorces per 1000 Americans in 1981, then began declining (see Figure 6.2).

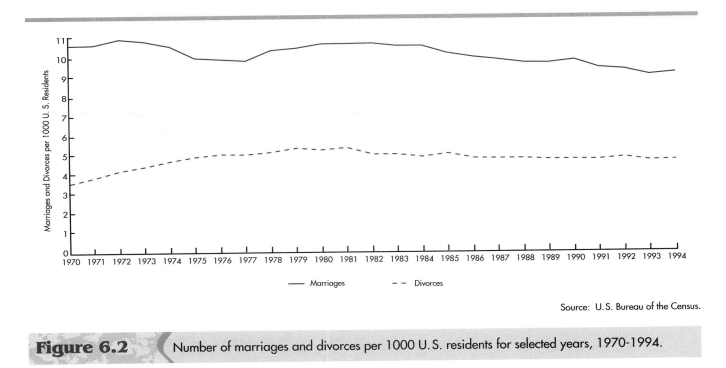

Source: U.S. Bureau of the Census.

Figure 6.2 Number of marriages and divorces per 1000 U.S. residents for selected years, 1970-1994.

Most people marry with the hope that the relationship will last forever. Divorce, therefore, often represents a loss of this hope. This often is accompanied by the loss of economic status (particularly for low and middle-income women), lifestyle, security of familiarity, friends, and sometimes children. The psychological effects of divorce can be compared with those of the grieving process associated with death of a loved one. First, shock sets in: ("Is this really happening to me?"), followed by disorganization ("Everything feels topsy-turvy"). Volatile emotions, then guilt ("It's my fault") usually follow. Loneliness, too, often accompanies divorce. Finally, after several months to a year, these feelings are replaced by a sense of relief and acceptance.

The grieving process leads to healing, a cleansing of wounds, which allows divorced people to move on with their lives. If, after a year or so, the divorced person hasn't gotten over the divorce and begun to accept what has happened, counseling and psychotherapy may be helpful.

Approximately three in four divorced persons remarry, most within 3 years after their divorce. Although most remarried people report that their second marriage is better than their first, the likelihood that this marriage also will end in divorce is greater than that among first marriages. No one

Health Hint

Dealing with the Grief of Loss

Grief is the nearly universal pattern of physical and emotional responses to separation and loss. It is natural, essential to healing. The classic expert on loss and grieving, Elisabeth Kübler Ross, identified a pattern of six stages:

1. Denial: disbelieving that the loss occurred
2. Anger: strong displeasure over the loss, directed at anyone or anything
3. Bargaining: trying to "deal" with God or oneself ("I'll change and be like. . . .") to reverse the loss
4. Depression: intense sorrow over the loss
5. Acceptance: accepting the inevitable
6. Hope: faith in the future

To heal following a loss, one must successfully work through each of the stages of grief. The grieving process cannot be rushed. The amount of time needed to grieve following a loss ranges from 18 to 24 months on the average but can last for years. The amount of time people need to fully recover from the loss of a loved one varies. Trying to rush the grieving process can result in not thoroughly working through each stage in succession.

To help in coping with grief and loss;

- Keep things in your life as status quo as possible. The loss of a loved one is a major source of stress, so do what you can to cut down on other stressors (a new job, for example.)
- If you can, postpone making decisions that can wait until later.
- Keep in touch with other people; social support is especially important now.
- Avoid the temptation to use alcohol or drugs.
- Get plenty of rest. Take naps if you need to, and try to maintain your normal sleeping pattern at night.
- Eat a balanced diet.
- Drink plenty of fluids, but steer away from alcohol, caffeine, and drugs.
- Exercise regularly.

Source: *Wellness: Guidelines for a Health Lifestyle,* by Brent Hafen and Werner W. K. Hoeger (Englewood, CO: Morton, 1998).

knows why this is so for sure, but some of the reasons given are less willingness to stay in the second marriage when they are embittered, closer scrutiny of the second marriage, financial problems (such as alimony and child support), and the trauma of divorce is less threatening after having experienced it once.

The psychological effects of divorce are similar to grieving the death of a loved one.

SEXUALITY IN OLDER ADULTS

In Erik Erikson's final stage, old age, our major developmental task is to maintain integrity in the face of death. This last stage begins in older adulthood with the growing awareness of the nearness of death. This is a time for facing our mortality and accepting the worth and uniqueness of our lives.

Maintaining integrity entails evaluating our lives and accomplishments. In a sense, we are verifying our existence and seeking its meaning. We do this by looking back at where we've been, what we've accomplished, whom we have touched.[20] This often involves reminiscing with family, friends, and others.

Sexual Response and Aging

Sex doesn't necessarily get better or worse as we age; it just gets different. Many myths have arisen in regard to sexual response and aging. The following

Sex doesn't necessarily get better or worse with aging; it's just different.

Health Hint

Changes in Sexual Response Associated with Aging

Women

The following changes are associated with sexual response in women who have gone through menopause:

1. The vagina is less elastic and not able to expand as much.
2. Physiological responses to sexual stimuli take more time.
3. Vaginal lubrication takes longer and may be less effective in reducing vaginal irritation.
4. The clitoris is smaller but not less responsive.
5. The intensity of orgasmic contractions diminishes slightly.
6. The ability to have multiple orgasms does not change.

Men

The following physiological changes have been observed in men older than age 55:

1. Arousal takes longer and may require manual stimulation of the penis.
2. Erections tend to be less firm.
3. Less semen is ejaculated.
4. There is less need to ejaculate to enjoy sexual activity.
5. The intensity of orgasmic contractions is slightly diminished.
6. More time is necessary to get another erection.

three are common ones that usually surface during classroom discussions in our classes:

- Once you start to get old (over age 50), you lose interest in sex.
- Older people aren't sexually attracted to each other.
- Older people can't perform sexually or have orgasms.

Physiologically, most men and women change very little during their 30s and early 40s. The most noticeable changes in sexual response in women are associated with menopause. They begin to experience a syndrome called the **female climacteric** between 45 and 55 years of age, as a result of a drop in levels of estrogen production associated with menopause. Common symptoms are hot flashes, irritability, inability to concentrate, and declines in sexual desire. The climacteric ends with menopause, which is the cessation of ovulation and loss of fertility. About one-fourth of women experience menopause before age 45, half from 45 to 50, and the remaining fourth after the age of 50.[21]

The changes in sexual physiology among most men in their 40s and 50s are less noticeable. Although sperm production slows down after age 40, it continues into the 80s and 90s. Similarly, though male sexual hormone levels decline gradually after age 55, most men have no noticeable drop-off in sexual desire. About 5% of men older than 60 experience the **male climacteric,** which produces symptoms similar to those of menopause. Men do not lose their fertility as a result of the climacteric as women do when they experience menopause.[22]

These physiological changes, in men and women, which basically revolve around the sexual response slowing and the intensity of response lessening slightly are more than offset by greater comfort about sexuality, no fear of pregnancy, familiarity with one's partner, and extending the sex act.

Changing Relationships

Older age is often affected by the changing nature of relationships and family life as the commitment to relationships that began in young adulthood continues and deepens. For many, this is a period marked by divorce or the death of a mate or lover. Duvall developed an often-cited eight-stage theory of the family life cycle given in Figure 6.3.[23] Stage 8, the postparental years, generally coincides with late adulthood and old age. Many events blend during this time: menopause and other physiological changes of aging, retirement, older children leaving the nest, and grandchildren, to name just a few. Although often characterized negatively as a time of loss and failed health, it also is a dynamic period in which newfound freedom, psychological and social stability, and wisdom can be a springboard to greater happiness for couples.

Most older couples today have grown old together. The average couple can expect at least 15 years of living together after the last child leaves. This is quite different from the turn of the century, when death affected half of all marriages before the last child left the house.[24]

Studies have revealed mixed findings concerning marital satisfaction and happiness in the older years. In general, most of those who remain married

Female climacteric
a syndrome experienced by women between 45 and 55 years of age as a result of declining levels of estrogen production associated with menopause

Male climacteric
a syndrome experienced by about 5% of men in their 40s and 50s, characterized by diminished interest in sex, loss of appetite, fatigue, and inability to concentrate

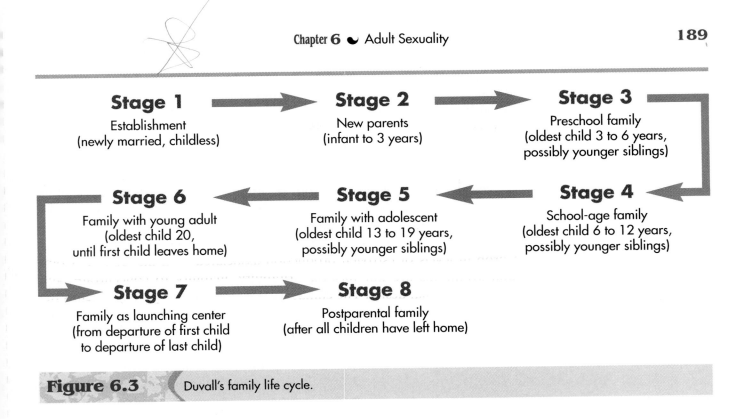

Figure 6.3   Duvall's family life cycle.

report high levels of marital satisfaction in their older years, but divorce among older people has doubled since 1960 and is predicted to be more prevalent in future populations over age 65.[25]

Marital Satisfaction and Aging

As married couples reach mid-adulthood, happiness that was at an all-time low in their early 40s begins to rebound when the adult children leave home.[26] Children's moving out free up time and money. The couple finds they have the time, money, and privacy to reestablish the things in their relationship that provide pleasure, as well as investigate new things together.

Marital happiness continues to rise in the later adult years and carries over into retirement. Depending upon a number of factors ranging from health to retirement income, the couple continue to enjoy their freedom, and in some cases relationships with their children's families and grandchildren.[27]

Most of us know couples who have celebrated their 50th, or golden, wedding anniversary. We marvel at their longevity and wonder about the secret to their success. Researchers have studied this issue, and the findings are inconsistent. Part of the problem lies with defining happiness. Older couples differ from younger ones in their standards for happiness. They share a history that includes memories of the Great Depression, world wars, and more traditional roles for marriage and marital satisfaction. Their marital happiness and contentment may be based on a different set of standards than those of younger married people.

A long-term study of 17 happily married couples found that the most significant factor related to marital satisfaction was their ability to adapt to change and "roll with the punches."[28] These couples had the ability to adapt to changing circumstances that normally might be interpreted as stressful and potentially damaging to the relationship. They might view a serious illness, for instance, as an opportunity for caring and closeness rather than anger and alienation.

DIVORCE IN OLDER COUPLES

In many cases, marital dissatisfaction in older adulthood is not related to any age-specific cause but, rather, resurfaces after years of being subordinated by issues related to childrearing. With the children grown and out of the house, old tensions and discontent surface and become a source of stress. Dependency is a key issue in the level of marital satisfaction in older couples.[29] The extent of dependence of one mate on the other seems to be related to the strength of the relationship and its ability to last. When dependence is mutual and the level is relatively equal for both partners, relationships are strong and close. When dependence is not equal and one partner's needs are much greater than the other's, marital conflict is much more likely.[30] When dependence is not equal or mutual, one partner may perceive normal developmental issues such as retirement and relocation as threatening and, therefore, it becomes a source of resentment, discontent, and stress. Other issues that dampen marital happiness in old age include health problems, caring for sick parents and children, and financial problems.

Dependency is a problem in a relationship when it is neither equal nor mutual.

Divorce is particularly distressing to older adults because of the long time invested in another's personal and practical life. In general, the longer the marriage, the greater is the trauma. In many cases an elderly person's identity is closely wrapped up in being another person's husband or wife. Loss of this status often results in loss of economic status and lifestyle, friends (who often choose sides), and self-concept.[31]

Divorce carries a much greater stigma for elderly people than for young people. Because of this, many elderly people underreport their status as divorced when filling out forms, applying for services, and the like.[32] Divorce in an elderly person, particularly a woman, also may account for much greater loss than for a younger adult because of retirement, the empty nest, and relocation of family. Whereas younger divorced persons still have a job to report to, children to care for and interact with, and friends and family in the vicinity, elderly people often face the loss of these important connections.

WIDOWHOOD

Widowhood
period of time between loss of spouse and remarriage

Although a person can become widowed at any time during a marriage, it is much more likely later in life. **Widowhood** is more common for women; more than half of all women over age 65 are widows, whereas just 15% of men are widowers at that age. The two main reasons are that men have a shorter average life expectancy than women and women tend to marry men older than themselves. Consequently, most married women in the United States can expect to live between 10 and 12 years as a widow if they choose not to remarry.[33]

Widowhood can be stressful in a number of ways besides ending a partnership. U.S. society does not have well-defined social roles for widowed people. Therefore, they often are left alone by family and friends who don't know how to respond to them. Widowed individuals also may feel awkward as single people trying to fit into their previously coupled world.

Men are generally older than women when they become widowed. Men are thought to be less able to cope with the death of their wife than women are by the loss of their husband. This may be a result of the way men are reared; the wife's having been the husband's only close confidant; the lack of experience of most men in cooking, cleaning, doing the laundry, and so forth; and the tendency of men to be more socially isolated than women.[34]

Women may be able to cope better because they have more extensive social networks and are better equipped to live alone, as most are able to maintain a household and take care of themselves. At the same time, women's widowhood behavior patterns seem to be more variable than men's.

Not all women find widowhood equally stressful or stressful at all. In studying more than 300 widows in Chicago, Lopata found six different behavior patterns in women after the deaths of their husbands:[35]

1. "Liberated wives" were able to grieve the loss of their spouse and move on to live full productive lives.
2. "Merry widows" went on to live lives of fun, dating, and various forms of entertainment.
3. "Working widows" continued their career or took a new job.
4. "Widows' widows" continued to live alone, were independent, and enjoyed the company of primarily other widows.
5. "Traditional widows" moved in with their children and took an active role in the lives of their grandchildren.
6. "Grieving widows" were unable to work through their loss and willingly isolated themselves from others.

The death of a loved one can lead to feelings of helplessness, hopelessness, and a sense of emptiness that can precipitate a variety of physical and mental illnesses. Cohen and Syme studied 4,500 adults over age 45 who had lost a spouse to premature death.[36] Their study became known as the "broken heart" study because they found that nearly 40% of the surviving spouses died of heart problems during the 6 months following the death of their spouse. The percentage of deaths dropped steadily after this time and returned to that of the control group after five years. Other studies have confirmed these findings and have indicated that one of the factors mediating a return to normal risk of death is remarriage of the surviving spouse.[37]

LONG-TERM GAY, LESBIAN, AND OTHER LONG-TERM RELATIONSHIPS

Most of the research regarding relationships relates to married heterosexuals. Comparatively little has been written regarding long-term gay and lesbian relationships. A prospective study of 65 gay and 47 lesbian long-term relationships found that the duration of the relationship was a predictor of satisfaction.[38] Gay and lesbian subjects in relationships of longer than an 8-year duration reported greater satisfaction than relationships of shorter duration. Further, lesbian couples reported higher levels of relationship satisfaction than gay men.[39]

Another study found that as homosexuals aged, those in close, committed relationships were the happiest.[40] Variables related to happiness in relationships, such as commitment, companionship, intimacy, and fulfillment of needs, were the same for homosexual and heterosexual couples.

The stereotypical picture of old age for gay men and women is one of unhappiness and loneliness. In actuality, it is quite the opposite. As a rule, homosexual men and women may be better prepared for the demands and challenges of old age than many traditional heterosexual couples. Because of stereotypical male and female gender roles, traditional heterosexual marriages are more likely to be built upon dependency. In traditional heterosexual relationships, husbands rely upon wives for certain activities, and wives are more dependent upon husbands for other activities.

Each partner has been socialized to be self-reliant. In the absence of social norms for gay male or female relationship roles, gay and lesbian relationships are, of necessity, more egalitarian. The lack of hard-and-fast gender-role stereotypes forces homosexual men and women to communicate more effectively and to be more flexible and creative in meeting relationship needs. Gay men and women are more willing to communicate, experiment, and be more attentive to detail in their sexual behavior.[41]

Stages in Homosexual Relationships

In one of the most extensive, long-term prospective studies of male homosexuals to date, McWhirter and Mattison followed 156 gay couples for more than 20 years.[42] The subjects were gay couples who had been together approximately 9 years before enrolling in the study. The researchers found that gay relationships, like those of their heterosexual counterparts, went through a series of stages.

1. *Stage one*, "blending, "characterizes the first year of the relationship. As with heterosexual couples, this year has the highest levels of sexual activity, strong love and passion, and a merging of personal interests.

2. *Stage two*, "nesting," takes place during years 2 to 3, emphasizing relationship-building and starting a home together. Ambivalence, problems, and doubts about the relationship are most likely to begin to surface at this stage.

3. *Stage three*, "maintaining," is characterized by a decline in passion and frequency of sexual activity, with an emphasis on conflict resolution and reassertion of some of the individuality subverted during the initial stages of the relationship.

4. *Stage four*, "building stage," occupies years 6 through 10 and is marked by increased personal productivity and independence but also enhanced

collaboration and developing sense of trust and dependability between the partners.

5. *Stage five*, "releasing" from years 11 to 20, is characterized by merging of money and other assets and beginning to take each other for granted. Sexual activity drops off noticeably in this stage.

6. *Stage six*, "renewing," extends beyond 20 years together and is marked by personal security and a restored sense of partnership based on remembering shared experiences and good times together.

Because of better planning throughout their relationship, homosexual men and women may be better prepared for dealing with losses such as the death of their partner and retirement. Many homosexuals have planned for their own financial support and have consciously developed supportive social networks. They also may be better prepared to cope with hardship, having lived a life of adversity as a member of a stigmatized group. This combination of attitude, social and financial resources, and self-reliance may help gay men and women cope with the demands of aging.

Grief and Loss in Nontraditional Long-Term Relationships

In a study of grief and loss among those in **nontraditional relationships** (extramarital affairs, cohabitation, and homosexual relationships), the normal stages of grief were compounded by the nontraditional nature of the relationships studied.[43] In the homosexual and other relationships, conflicting needs compound the healing process of grief. A need to declare and demonstrate sorrow and affection for the loved one is tempered by a need to maintain secrecy and fear that the relationship will be disclosed. Some hospitals, for instance, restrict access to "husbands or wives" or "immediate family." The need for social support, and to grieve with the other mourners, is countered by a sense of social isolation and distancing. These compounding factors are minimized for homosexual couples who are not maintaining a secret relationship. Being active in the gay community has helped gay couples develop social support networks that enabled them to cope more effectively with a variety of issues associated with aging.[44]

Nontraditional relationships
any relationships other than a monogamous, legal marriage between a man and a woman

A major issue in long-term gay and lesbian relationships is the denial of death benefits such as pension benefits and social security, to the surviving partner. This has been a hotly debated issue and one of the reasons cited for not recognizing gay marriages. What do you think about this?

WELLNESS SYNTHESIS

In this chapter we have explored sexuality in young adulthood, adulthood, and old age. Young adulthood is a time for separating from one's parents and beginning to take responsibility for oneself. It is a time for forming intimate relationships and making commitments.[45] These relationships continue and deepen in adulthood. As our level of commitment expands, the work we put into our relationships, jobs, and interests builds the legacy we will leave. It is a measure of our generativity and integrity.[46] As we age, we confront the major task associated with this stage: maintaining integrity in the face of despair. We look back on our lives to assess what we have accomplished and look forward for fresh challenges and new meanings.

Physical Well-being

As we enter young adulthood, we become fully responsible for maintaining and enhancing our physical well-being. Most of us are on our own, living apart from our parents, making our own decisions. The choices we make, behaviors we adopt, and lifestyles we live will either enhance or undermine our sexuality. Abusing our bodies and letting our physical well-being decline will have a negative impact on our sexuality. Everything from body image to sexual response to overall energy level will decline. This will impact negatively on our social relationships with lovers, spouses, employers, and others.

The choices we make as young adults set the stage for our level of physical well-being as we age. If we continue to physically decline as adults, our health will diminish and we will set the stage for premature disability and death. If we choose, in contrast, positive health behaviors and achieve high levels of physical well-being, our sexuality will evolve more positively. Better body image, sexual response, and energy level will help us meet the demands of our ever-changing sexuality. This not only will enhance our personal functioning but also will influence our relationships positively.

Intellectual Well-being

The ability to gather information, critically analyze it, and make good decisions are hallmarks of high-level mental functioning. Rational thinking and logical reasoning can help us understand the nature of our ever-changing sexuality as we pass through young adulthood into adulthood and old age. Having reasonable expectations about our sexuality, based on solid information, can guide us in decision making. It also can help us avoid unrealistic expectations about relationships and sexuality that are likely to lead to personal unhappiness and dissatisfaction with partners.

Emotional Well-being

High-level emotional well-being can help us understand and cope with the demands and challenges of adulthood and aging. We can acknowledge the full range of emotions associated with our roles and responsibilities and realize that they will change as we evolve. We acknowledge the changing nature of our roles as lovers, mates, parents, and caregivers to our parents, realizing that with each new role comes fresh challenges, experiences, and emotions that make us uniquely human. We seek to understand these emotions and challenges and do our best to meet them head on.

Social Well-being

Social well-being is a critical component of healthy sexuality from young adulthood through old age. Most of the major developmental tasks associated with the stages of our lives are social issues: forming intimate relationships, committing ourselves to others and to our work, being productive (in relationships, work, and so on). The social skills and issues critical in enhancing social well-being are communication skills, fighting fairly, negotiating, and the like.

The social legacy we develop and leave behind can be one of caring child, loving partner, devoted parent. We can move through the stages of our relationships eagerly anticipating the changes and tasks that await us. Others move through life and their relationships with a self-centeredness that obscures all propensity for caring, sharing, and nurturing. Adulthood and old age are viewed as opportunities for greater and greater self-indulgence. For some people, this is a period of taking and not giving back. These people resent the challenges of relationships, seeing them as infringements on the self. They leave behind a legacy of self-centeredness that might have been productive materially but empty socially.

Spiritual Well-being

Adulthood and old age are potentially a time of great spiritual awakening and renewal. For most people this is a time of developing intimate, loving relationships, making permanent (sacramental) commitments, having children, caring for sick and dying parents, and coming to terms with our own mortality. We are forced to examine these issues, all of which have a spiritual dimension. Understanding the meaning of these events, coping with them and their universality, help us develop a sense of connectedness with something other than ourselves. If we allow ourselves to look beyond the self and gain strength through connecting with others, we can enhance our spirituality, which can help us lead more satisfying and productive lives.

Environmental Well-being

Our environment can provide a context for the development of healthy sexuality in adulthood and old age. It can provide support systems within college, neighborhood, and worksite. Healthy environments have access to people and services that facilitate our growth and development as sexual adults. College offers services ranging from contraception to counseling to child care. Community professionals are valuable providers of information, services, and support, if needed.

WEB RESOURCES

Dating, Love, Marriage, and Sex

http://www.cmhc.com/psyhelp/chap10/

Mental Health Net, a guide to mental health, psychology, and psychiatry online. This home page enables you to search any subject. Dating, Love, Marriage, and Sex is a chapter from its online search. This article starts out with meeting, dating, and selecting a partner; the nature of attraction and love; predicting and improving marital success; books about selecting a partner; marriage and love; handling marital problems; additional sources of help with marital problems; coping with divorce; remarriage and step-parenting; sex and cultural taboos; choosing your sexual lifestyle; premarital sex; sex in a committed relationship; dealing with specific sexual problems; homosexuality; and sources of information about special sexual problems.

National Institutes of Health

http://www.nih.gov/

Using their search engine, "Sexuality," NIH posts an article on aging and sexuality, addressing the impact of various illnesses and surgeries on sexuality.

Notes

1. A discussion is contained in Erikson's book, *Childhood and Society*, 2d edition (New York: W.W. Norton, 1978).
2. The complete title is *Friendship: How to Give it, How to Get it* (New York: Macmillan, 1980).
3. P. Blumstein and P. Schwartz, *American Couples* (New York: William Morrow, 1983).
4. F. Christopher and R. Cate, "Factors Involved in Premarital Decision-Making," *Journal of Sex Research*, 20 (1984) 363–376; L. A. Peplau and S. D. Cochran, *Sex Differences in Values Concerning Love Relationships*, paper presented at annual meeting of American Psychological Association, Montreal, Canada, 1980; R. Sherwin and S. Corbett, "Campus Social Norms and Dating Relationships," *Journal of Sex Research*, 21:3 (1985), 258–274.
5. E. Laumann et al., *The Social Organization of Sexuality: Sexual Practices in the United States* (Chicago: University of Chicago Press, 1994).
6. Laumann et al.
7. J. M. Reinisch, *The Kinsey Institute New Report on Sex* (New York: St. Martin's Press, 1992).
8. E. S. Person, *Women — Sex and Sexuality* (Chicago: University of Chicago Press, 1989).
9. Laumann et al.
10. J. C. Cavanaugh, *Adult Development and Aging* (Belmont CA: Wadsworth, 1993).
11. D. E. Phillis and P. J. Stein, "Sink or Swing? The Lifestyles of Single Adults," in *Changing Boundaries: Gender Roles and Sexual Behavior*, edited by E. R. Allegeir and N. B. McCormick (Palo Alto, CA: Mayfield, 1983).
12. Cavanaugh, p. 348.
13. R. E. Berry and E. Williams, "Assessing the Relationship Between Quality of Life and Marital and Income Satisfaction: A Path Analytic Approach," *Journal of Marriage and the Family*, 49, (1987), 107–116.
14. Laumann et al.
15. W. H. Masters, V. E. Johnson, and R. C. Kolodny, *Human Sexuality*, 4th edition (New York: HarperCollins, 1992), pp. 248–249.
16. Masters, Johnson, and Kolodny, p. 250.
17. Blumstein and Schwartz.
18. Laumann et al.
19. Cavanaugh, p. 357.
20. Erikson.
21. C. Kart. *The Realities of Aging: An Introduction to Gerontology* (Boston: Allyn & Bacon, 1994).
22. Masters, Johnson, and Kolodny.
23. E. M. Duvall, *Family Development* (Philadelphia: Lippincott, 1977).
24. Kart, p. 248.
25. Kart.
26. Berry and Williams.
27. Cavanaugh.
28. S. Weishaus and D. Field, "A Half Century of Marriage: Continuity or Change?" *Journal of Marriage and the Family*, 50 (1988), 763–774.
30. Cavanaugh, p. 347.
31. Cavanaugh, p. 353.
32. Kart, p. 249.
33. Cavanaugh, p. 355.
34. Cavanaugh, p. 356.
35. H. Z. Lopata, *Widowhood in an American City* (Cambridge, MA: Schenkman, 1973).
36. S. Cohen and S. L. Syme, *Social Support and Health* (Orlando, FL: Academic Press, 1985).
37. B. Q. Hafen, K. J. Frandsen, K. J. Karren, and K. R. Hooker, *The Health Effects of Attitudes, Emotions, and Relationships* (Provo, UT: EMS Associates, 1992), p. 370.
38. L. Kurdack, "Relationship Quality of Gay and Lesbian Cohabiting Couples," *Journal of Homosexuality*, 15: 3–4 (1989), 93–118.
39. Kurdack, 1989.
40. A. Lipman, "Homosexual Relationships," *Generations*, 10:4 (1986), 51–54.
41. L. Kurdak, "The Allocation of Household Labor in Gay, Lesbian, and Heterosexual Married Couples," *Journal of Social Issues*, 49:3 (1993), 127–139; Masters, Johnson, and Kolodny.
42. D. McWhirter, A. Mattison. *The Male Couple* (Englewood Cliffs, NJ: Prentice Hall, 1984).
43. K. J. Doka, "Silent Sorrow: Grief and Loss of Significant Others," *Death Studies*, 11:8 (1987), pp. 455–469.
44. J. K. Quam and G. S. Whitford, "Adaptation and Age-related Expectations of Elder Gay and Lesbian Adults," *Gerontologist*, 32:3(1992), 367–374.
45. Erikson.
46. Erikson.

Student Study Questions

1. What are some of the major developmental tasks of college students? Compare these to the major developmental tasks associated with adolescence.

2. Compare and contrast sexual behavior during the college years with that of middle adulthood. What are the differences?

3. What is Berry and Williams' model of marital satisfaction? Identify the stages.

4. What are the similarities and differences between long-term heterosexual relationships and lesbian and gay unions of a similar duration?

5. What factors contribute to satisfaction and happiness in long-term relationships?

6. What changes in sexual response are associated with aging?

Relationship/Marriage Contract

Relationships are fluid. Even marital relationships vary tremendously from couple to couple. The purpose of this assessment is to help you examine the nature of your intimate relationships. A secondary purpose is to help you realize that you have the ability to structure your relationships any way you want.

   Fill out the following relationship contract. There are no right or wrong answers. Just jot down your thoughts and feelings regarding the various categories. You may wish to ask your instructor for the opportunity to go over your contract with other students in a small group.

Name:

Should the wife take on the husband's last name? _____

Should the husband take on the wife's last name? _____

Should both take on a hyphenated last name? _____

Should both take a new name? _____

Should both keep their own name? _____

What will the children's surname be if there are any? _____

Birth Control:

What kind? _____

Whose responsibility? _____

Household Duties:

Who does what? _____

Leisure Time:

Should evenings and weekends be spent together? _____

Who decides what to do? _____

Should vacations be spent together? With children? Separate? _____

Living Arrangements:

Where will the couple live? _____

What kind of privacy do you need? _____

Shared bedroom? _____

Continued

Student Assessment

Relationship/Marriage Contract (cont.)

Do you want to live with others? _____

What will you and your partner do if you want to live in different places because of jobs or for any other reasons? _____

_____

Money:

Will both partners work? _____

If so, will you pool your money? _____

Or will each keep own salary? _____

Or will the cost of living expenses be shared equally and the rest kept for yourselves? _____

Sexual Rights:

Commitment to monogamy? _____

Who initiates sex? _____

Is either partner free not to respond? _____

Children:

How many? _____

When? _____

Adopt? _____

Who will take primary responsibility for rearing the children? _____

Will one partner have to quit a job? _____

Other Relationships:

Are you and your partner free to make relationships with other people? _____

With those of the same sex? _____

With those of the opposite sex? _____

What is to be the extent of these relationships? _____

Do you include each other in these relationships? _____

Human Sexual Response

Student Learning Objectives

After reading this chapter, students will be able to:

- Identify the key brain structures involved in the human sexual response.

- Describe how the nervous and endocrine systems interact during sexual response.

- Explain how psychological and physiological factors interact during sexual response.

- Compare and contrast a variety of sexual response theories.

- Diagram and describe the four phases of the Masters and Johnson sexual response cycle.

- Define *aphrodisiac* and evaluate the effects of aphrodisiacs on sexual response.

- Describe factors that enhance vasocongestion and sexual response.

If you were to ask the average person which part of the body is the most important for controlling sexual response, the answer most likely would be "the penis" or "the vagina." Most people equate sexual response to genital functioning. In reality, sexual response begins and ends in the brain. The brain, not the genitals, is the seat of human sexual response. Human sexual response originates with the brain's perception of desire. What makes you want to respond? What allows you to become comfortable and relax so the response will happen? In this chapter we'll examine sexual response and try to answer these and many other questions.

The brain is the seat of sexual pleasure.

PHYSIOLOGY OF SEXUAL RESPONSE

Sexual response is the result of a complex interaction between psychological and physiological factors originating in the brain and spreading through

Case Study

Sexual Response: John & Michelle

John is working on his computer in the apartment he shares with Michelle, his steady girlfriend of 3 years. Michelle is out with friends, having agreed to give John some quiet time to work on a paper he is writing. From his desk, he can gaze out onto the street in front of his apartment. His mind is busy trying to piece together the words that ultimately will make up his paper on Shakespeare for his English Literature class. His fingers move quickly over the keyboard, his eyes riveted on the screen and his attention on his work.

As he works on the computer, he senses a car pull up, its doors swing open, and someone gets out. Without taking his eyes off the screen, John senses that this might be Michelle. He looks out the window and sees Michelle. She is wearing a short, silky, summer dress that sways with her long, athletic legs. He hears her laughter as she and her friends say their goodbyes as they drive off.

Michelle enters their apartment and, although he can't see her yet, he hears the rustling of her skirt, and a trace of Michelle's perfume wafts through the door. He hears her voice call out, "John, I'm home." The sound of her voice and the smell of her perfume cause

his mind to wander and his body begins to respond. He feels his penis begin to get erect. Although he tries to fight it, his mind continues to wander, drifting from his writing to his erection, to thoughts of Michelle's warm body and past lovemaking and back to his writing again.

Realizing that he'll never finish his writing if he allows his thoughts to keep wandering like this, John focuses his attention on his paper, and his brain begins to shut down his sexual response. After about 10 minutes, Michelle enters the room and, with a sexy smile, wanders over to John's desk and interrupts his concentration.

"Interested in taking a little break?" she asks, as she takes his glasses off his nose, wraps her arms around his shoulders, and begins to nibble on his ear. He turns, gives her a kiss, and feels his body respond to her warmth and softness.

After a couple of kisses, John decides to stop trying to fight his brain's urges and allows his body to take over. He picks up Michelle, carries her over to the bed, and they proceed to make love, both deciding that Shakespeare can wait a couple of hours.

various body parts and systems. We'll trace the sexual response, describing the key components and mechanisms of action that control it.

Brain

The brain has four parts (see Figure 7.1):

1. cerebral cortex
2. diencephalon
3. limbic system
4. brain stem.

The entire surface of the brain is irregular, with ridges and shallow and deep grooves, and is divided into two halves called **hemispheres**. The cerebral hemispheres form the outermost part of the brain and are divided into sections called lobes. The frontal, parietal, occipital, and temporal lobes of each hemisphere are responsible for controlling a variety of **motor, sensory,** and **associational brain functions**, which are directly involved in sexual response.

Cerebral Cortex

The conscious awareness of sensations (sight, sound, smell, taste, and touch) is controlled by the parietal, occipital, and temporal lobes of the cerebral cortex, the thinking part of the brain. These sensations, in some combination, enter one's consciousness through the sensory areas of the cerebral cortex and are interpreted as sexual. The cortex picks up the message, and the associational areas interpret them.

Hemispheres
the two halves of the cerebrum; each controls the functions of the opposite side of the body

Motor
relating to nerve impulses going out to muscles

Sensory
relating to nerve messages coming into the brain

Associational brain functions
connecting together individual sensory inputs

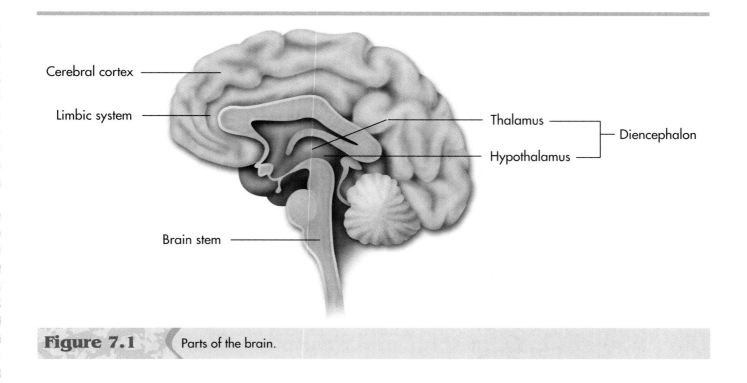

Figure 7.1 Parts of the brain.

Flirting is often perceived as a sign of sexual interest.

Although each sensory stimulus is entered as a distinct, separate entity, they are quickly assimilated, sorted out, deciphered, and combined as a potentially sexy signal. This interplay relies upon stored memories (whether real or imagined) of past experiences that influence the person's assessment of the present incoming stimuli and expectations of what is to follow.

Diencephalon

The diencephalon forms the central core of the brain and contains the **thalamus** and **hypothalamus**. This area plays a crucial role in the continuation of sexual response that begins with the interpretation of an incoming stimulus as sexual.

The thalamus, a hidden region of the brain, might best be described as the relay center for all inputs to the cerebral cortex. The hypothalamus is located directly beneath the thalamus at the end of the brain stem. Despite its small size, the hypothalamus exerts a tremendous amount of control over body functioning. It works in concert with the nervous and endocrine systems, sending its messages via direct nerve transmissions and chemicals called **hormonal releasing factors**.

The nervous and endocrine systems provide the main pathways of human sexual response. The hypothalamus instantaneously sends electrical (direct nerve transmissions) and chemical (hormones) messages to switch on the body parts responsible for initiating the sexual response. The heart, responding to electrical and chemical stimulation, increases the volume of blood pumped throughout the body by increasing its rate and pressure. This increased pumping of blood is necessary for supplying the extra oxygen and energy used during sexual activity.

Blood vessels supplying the genitals, brain, and skeletal muscles dilate, allowing greater blood flow to the areas involved in sexual response.

Thalamus
part of the brain that relays all inputs to the cerebral cortex

Hypothalamus
part of the brain that correlates activities between the nervous centers and the pituitary gland

Hormonal releasing factors
chemicals secreted by the hypothalamus that trigger the pituitary to release specific hormones

The lungs respond instantly by increasing the rate and depth of breathing. The airways expand, allowing maximum intake of air so its vital oxygen is mixed with the blood. The skeletal muscles began to contract and build tension.

Limbic System

The limbic system is a complex arrangement of nerve tissue that links the emotional brain with the thinking, rational brain (cerebral cortex). In this way, the limbic system establishes a relationship between our thoughts and our feelings. Sometimes this relationship is clear-cut and appropriate, and other times it is not. Sometimes our emotions get the best of us so we don't think clearly. We might interpret someone's verbal communication, body language, or behavior as conveying interest in having sex when they really are not. The cerebral cortex does have the ability to shut down sexual response through conscious control of behavior at any point.

Sometimes the relationship between our thoughts, feelings, and desires is not clear-cut.

A person can shut down the sexual response through conscious control of behavior, despite feelings.

Case Study

Jorge: Mistaken Perceptions

Jorge is a 19-year-old college sophomore. He shared a story about mistaking a date's expressions of affection as an invitation to have sexual intercourse. Jorge started by saying:

I'm a little embarrassed about talking about this, but I think it's exactly what we were just talking about in class. I dated a girl last semester who was really fine. I was instantly attracted to her when I saw her at the student center. I went up to her, and we hit it off, so I asked her out. We went to one of the jazz concerts on campus and hung out afterward. We walked around campus, and after a while she kind of snuggled up against me on one of the benches by the auditorium. She smelled real good, and it felt great having my arm around her. We started to kiss and make out. Everything seemed to be going great. We were laughing and snuggling, having a great time.

It started to get late, so I suggested I walk her back to her room. Her roommates had gone home, so she invited me in, and we started making out again. I really thought she wanted to have sex. I mean, she

was hot and rubbing up against me. By now I had an erection, and I started to unbutton her blouse. When I got about halfway she stopped me and said, "No."

I said, "No what?" She said, "Listen, I like you a lot, but I really don't want to have sex."

I must admit, I was shocked and upset. In the past I had never gotten this far without having sex. I wasn't sure what to do. My penis was throbbing, and I really was horny. I said, "Can you take care of me?"

She said "I'm really sorry. I just don't want to do this any more. Could you please leave?"

I really didn't know if she was serious or not, so I asked her, "Are you serious?"

She said she was, and I got myself straightened up and left. I was surprised, but by the time I got out of her dorm and started to walk back to my place, I had lost both my erection and my desire. I found out the next week that she had just broken up with her boyfriend that day, and I guess I came along at the wrong time. I never could bring myself to call her again.

Brain Stem

The structures of the brain stem produce the autonomic functions necessary for our survival, in addition to serving as the pathway for connections between the higher and lower brain functions. A key part of the brain stem, the reticular activating system (RAS), is a collection of neurons running through the three regions of the brain stem. It is responsible for both arousing the brain and filtering out unnecessary information. During arousal the RAS is responsible for magnifying and increasing our awareness of specific stimuli. It allows us to home in or focus on details of the stimulus.

The RAS also acts as a filter. Although we don't realize it, the RAS filters out a tremendous number of stimuli, allowing us to attend to only the important information. The RAS disregards more than 90% of all familiar, repetitive, or weak sensory stimulation as unimportant while allowing new, unusual, or strong stimuli to penetrate. This helps us to focus our attention on important stimuli.

> Think about a time when your attention was riveted on someone who really caught your attention. Did you notice how everything else seemed to fade out of consciousness? It seems like every fiber of your being is riveted on the image.

Central nervous system
the brain and spinal cord

Peripheral nervous system
all nerves coming off of the spinal cord

Somatic nervous system
the part of the peripheral nervous system under voluntary control

Autonomic nervous system
the part of the peripheral nervous system that is automatic and involuntary

Nervous System

The human nervous system is composed of two parts: the central nervous system and the peripheral nervous system. The **central nervous system** is made up of the brain and spinal cord. The **peripheral nervous system** consists of all other nerves and connects the spinal cord to various target organs, glands, and tissue. Figure 7.2 shows the nervous system.

The peripheral nervous system is made up of two divisions: the **somatic nervous system** and the **autonomic nervous system**. The initial information in the sexual response is passed along as electrical impulses from the brain, through the spinal cord to the peripheral nervous system, and ultimately to the specific glands, organs, and tissues involved in sexual response.

Endocrine System

The endocrine system is responsible for the production and secretion of potent hormones that

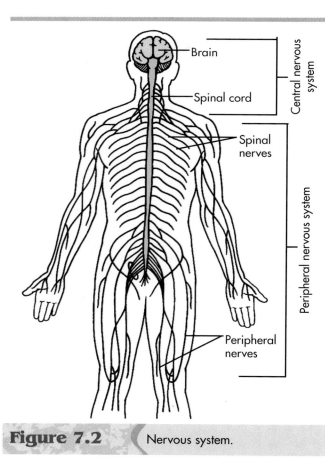

Figure 7.2   Nervous system.

initiate and perpetuate the sexual response, in addition to a variety of other functions ranging from the stress response to growth. The endocrine system is made up of the pituitary, thyroid, parathyroid, adrenal, pancreas, thymus, and pineal glands, as well as the ovaries and the testes. These are illustrated in Figure 7.3.

The endocrine system works on the principle of feedback, with the hypothalamus acting as a thermostat that senses the level of a hormone circulating in the bloodstream. Just as the thermostat in your home senses the level of heat and turns on the heating or cooling system to regulate the temperature, the hypothalamus senses the level of circulating hormones in your bloodstream. If the level of a hormone is too low, the hypothalamus secretes specific releasing factors that travel through the bloodstream to the target endocrine gland, prompting it to begin producing hormones.

Sex Hormones

The role of sex hormones in human sexual response is tremendously confusing. Part of the problem stems from categorizing "male hormones" as androgens and "female hormones" as estrogens. In fact, the primary "male hormone," testosterone, is produced in both males and females. In addition, the primary "female hormone," estrogen, is similarly produced in males and females. What varies is the level of each hormone and their sites of production.

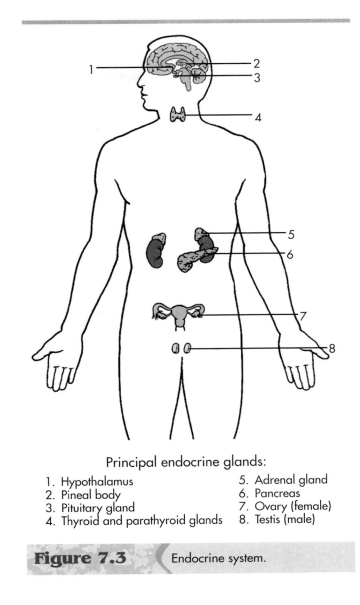

Principal endocrine glands:

1. Hypothalamus
2. Pineal body
3. Pituitary gland
4. Thyroid and parathyroid glands
5. Adrenal gland
6. Pancreas
7. Ovary (female)
8. Testis (male)

Figure 7.3   Endocrine system.

Testosterone Testosterone is the hormone that seems to exert the most dramatic effect on sexual response. It is the main hormone associated with sexual desire in both men and women. The average man produces between 6 and 8 mg of testosterone daily. Most of the male testosterone (about 95%) is manufactured in the testes, and the remainder is produced in the adrenal glands. The average woman produces about .5 mg of testosterone daily, manufactured in the ovaries and adrenal glands. Prior to puberty, testosterone is produced in similar quantities in boys and girls, in the adrenal glands.

Although men produce much more testosterone than women daily, women seem to have a lower threshold for testosterone sensitivity; they need less in circulation to derive the effects of this potent hormone. Regardless of the overall level of testosterone in men or women, deficiencies of this hormone result in a drop-off in sexual desire. Patients treated for low sexual desire associated with stress also had low levels of testosterone.[1]

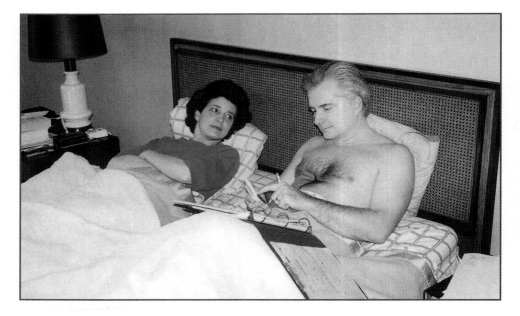

Overwork can diminish our interest in sex.

Overwork, worry over bills, and a variety of other stressors can lower testosterone production. When these patients learned how to cope with their stress, their testosterone production increased and sexual interest returned. Another study produced similar results associated with fluctuating levels of testosterone production and sexual desire.[2]

Men are especially dependent on testosterone levels for sexual performance. When testosterone levels drop, they have difficulty obtaining and maintaining erections. Women's sexual performance does not seem to be affected as much by testosterone levels. When their levels of testosterone drop, they still are able to experience lubrication, orgasm, and other changes associated with sexual performance.[3]

Estrogens Although commonly referred to as "female hormones," estrogens are also produced by men. Women manufacture estrogens in their ovaries, whereas men produce it in their testes. Estrogen levels also are related to sexual response. Estrogens play a role in maintaining vaginal lubrication, thus facilitating intercourse.

Women who have had their ovaries removed through hysterectomy and other procedures do not experience a reduction in sexual drive, although they may experience vaginal dryness and subsequent pain, which can diminish their interest and desire in sex. Women with high levels of estrogen do not experience heightened (or reduced) levels of sexual desire. Men also do not seem to be affected by too little estrogen. Excessive estrogen in men can have a "feminizing" effect that includes breast enlargement and erectile difficulties.

Progesterone Progesterone is another major female sex hormone produced in the ovaries. It seems to play a primary role in reproduction by ensuring the viability of the endometrium. Its role in sexual desire and functioning is not understood very well. It may actually suppress the sexual interest of men and women alike.[4]

MODELS OF SEXUAL RESPONSE

Four models of sexual response are discussed here. By far the best known is the one by Masters and Johnson, pioneers in the study of sexual response.

Masters and Johnson Phases

In 1966 Masters and Johnson published their ground-breaking work, *Human Sexual Response.*[5] The book was ground-breaking for several reasons. Although previous researchers (Kinsey being the most notable) had published reports concerning self-reported sexual behavior, Masters and Johnson's was the first large-scale study of sexual response. Masters (a gynecologist) and Johnson (a psychologist) were the first researchers to study sexual response in a laboratory setting. They were the first mainstream scientists to apply the scientific rigor necessary to quantify and qualify a very private act. Their work provided a graphic depiction of the actual sexual processes in action.

Masters and Johnson invented the technology and instruments necessary for studying our most intimate body parts. They devised clear, plastic, penis-shaped cameras to photograph things such as changes in vaginal lubrication. They invented electromyographic devices to measure the most intimate of all muscular contractions, those of the penis, vagina, and anus.

Imagine for a moment that a team of professors from your college is going to begin a study of sexual response among college students (singles and couples) at your school and on other campuses across the country. They are recruiting volunteers to participate in the study. You are curious about this and agree to be contacted by the team to see if you meet the study's subject protocols. They give you some preliminary reading material about the study to examine before you come in for the interview.

The material explains that the team is interested in studying the sexual response of college students to see how it has changed since the days of Masters and Johnson's research. They will be studying the sexual responses of gay and straight students under the following conditions:

- viewing erotic films alone
- viewing erotic films in a co-ed group
- solitary masturbation
- shared masturbation
- vaginal intercourse
- oral intercourse
- anal intercourse

They explain that every attempt will be made to conduct the study under the strictest standards of confidentiality. Members of the team, however, will view sexual responses through two-way mirrors and will record the responses through various instruments including videocameras. The literature explains that this is necessary for the team to review the subjects' responses later.

Would you like to participate in this study?

What are some of the specific things you might find objectionable about participating in this study?

Do you think the average student would volunteer to participate?

Do you think these issues create subject bias in this study?

Many of these instruments and methods also were used to treat sexual dysfunction. The Masters and Johnson Institute in St. Louis became world-renowned for the study and treatment of sexual dysfunctions.

Besides the technology, they operationally defined **orgasm**. An operational definition was a prerequisite for experimental research of the phenomenon. They created a language of sexuality that included words such as orgasm, vasocongestion, myotonia, and others that allowed professionals in the field to communicate with each other and disseminate their research findings.

Orgasm
the stage of sexual response characterized by ejaculation in males and involuntary muscular contractions followed by relaxation in both males and females

Masters and Johnson were the first researchers to divide sexual response into phases that blend into one another as sexual response continue. They identified four phases:

1. excitement
2. plateau
3. orgasm
4. resolution

G-Spot
an area in the upper, rear section of the vagina named after Ernest Grafenberg, who claimed it to be an erogenous zone

This sequence was the same regardless of the nature of sexual stimulation (masturbation, intercourse, and so forth) or sexual orientation (heterosexual, homosexual, bisexual) studied. The four stages are depicted in Figure 7.4 for men and Figure 7.5 for women.

Finally, Masters and Johnson discovered that the seat of women's sexual response is the clitoris, not the vagina. This broke new ground for understanding and conducting future research concerning women's sexual response. It opened the door for future research concerning issues such as the **G-spot**, differences in response

Masters and Johnson's findings concerning female sexual response opened the door for future studies in this area.

PERSPECTIVES   # The G-Spot

One of the more controversial topics of the past decade is the G-spot, named after Dr. Ernest Grafenberg. Grafenberg claimed that the G-spot is a mass of erectile tissue located on the front wall of the vagina, midway between the introitus and the cervix. He claimed that the G-spot is an erogenous zone capable of being stimulated during sex play. Once stimulated, the G-spot is purported to be capable of triggering orgasm and ejaculation. Between 10% and 40% of women ejaculate after sufficient stimulation of the G-spot.[1] Masters and Johnson claimed that this female ejaculate may come from the skene's glands near the bladder, which develop from the same embryonic tissue as the male prostate.

Critics of this research claim that female ejaculation is rare and that the fluid ejaculated is actually urine released from the bladder in response to deep penetration of the vagina that some intercourse positions create. Whipple and associates respond to this criticism by claiming that, although the fluid contains traces of urine, it is not urine but, rather, a new liquid released by stimulation of the G-spot.

Other critics point to the inability of researchers to isolate G-spot tissue. They claim that no one has been able to identify and biopsy tissue from the part of the vagina that is dissimilar to the squamous tissue that is normally present.

[1] A. Ladas, R. Whipple, and T. Perry, *The G-Spot* (New York: Holt, Rinehart, and Winston, 1982)

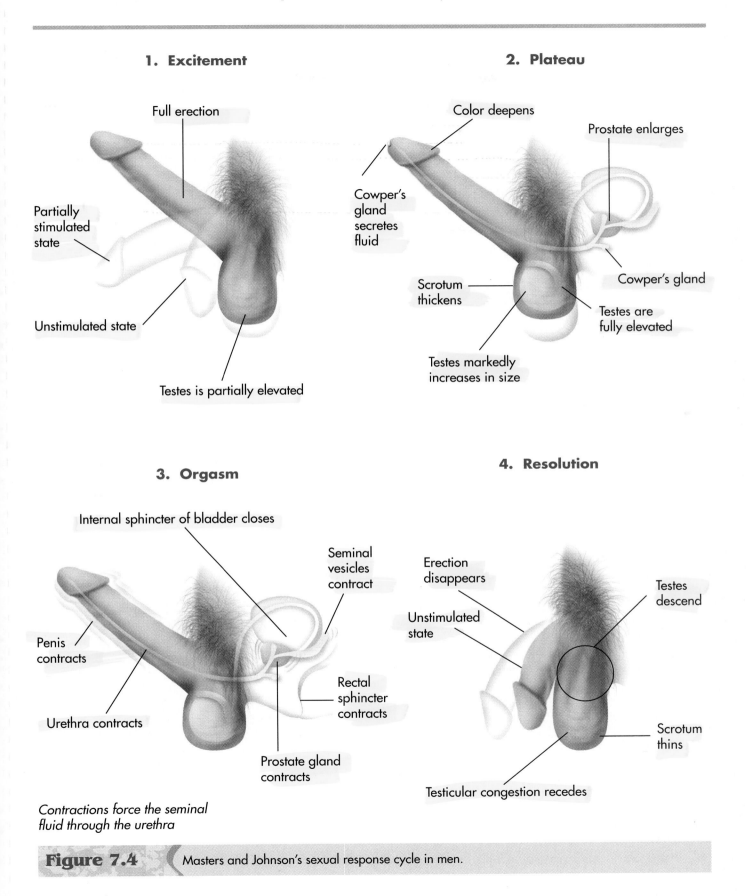

1. Excitement

Full erection

Partially stimulated state

Unstimulated state

Testes is partially elevated

2. Plateau

Color deepens

Prostate enlarges

Cowper's gland secretes fluid

Cowper's gland

Scrotum thickens

Testes are fully elevated

Testes markedly increases in size

3. Orgasm

Internal sphincter of bladder closes

Seminal vesicles contract

Penis contracts

Urethra contracts

Rectal sphincter contracts

Prostate gland contracts

Contractions force the seminal fluid through the urethra

4. Resolution

Erection disappears

Unstimulated state

Testes descend

Scrotum thins

Testicular congestion recedes

Figure 7.4 Masters and Johnson's sexual response cycle in men.

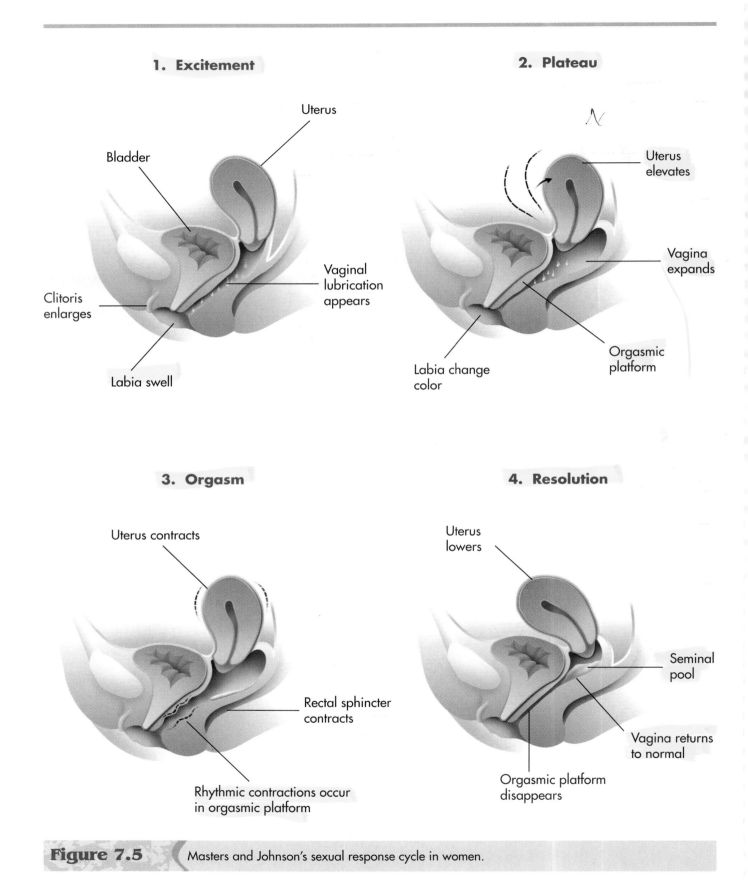

Figure 7.5 Masters and Johnson's sexual response cycle in women.

patterns in women before and after a hysterectomy, and a host of other areas.

Heterosexual and lesbian women (as well as their partners) have had the opportunity to apply Masters and Johnson's discoveries to enhance their sexual pleasure by better understanding their sexual functioning.

Excitement

During the first stage of Masters and Johnson's human sexual response, excitement, sexual arousal is initiated. Excitement can be triggered by a limitless array of cognitive and sensory stimuli ranging from viewing erotic films to listening to romantic music or getting a whiff of a familiar cologne or perfume.

The excitement stage is characterized by engorgement of erectile tissue in the genitals and a build-up of muscle tension throughout the body. The brain processes sensory and motor stimuli as being sexual in nature and passes a message to the hypothalamus, which initiates the nerve and hormonal sexual response.

Many cardiovascular changes are set into motion during excitement. The heart rate increases and blood vessels throughout the body constrict, increasing blood pressure. Blood vessels in the genitals dilate, resulting in increased blood flow to the genitalia. The increased blood flow fills up the spongy tissue that makes up this region. Blood flow into the genitals is greater than outflow. As this tissue fills with blood, it becomes engorged, enlarging in size, deepening in color, and increasing in sensitivity. Masters and Johnson called this engorgement process **vasocongestion.** In men, the major changes associated with vasocongestion are erection of the penis and deepening of the color of the genitalia. In women, vasocongestion is responsible for labial swelling, deepening of the color of the vulva, vaginal lubrication, and increased size and sensitivity of the breasts.

Vasocongestion
the movement of blood flow into the genitals at a resulting in a variety of responses including erection in men and lubrication in women

Cardiovascular fitness can enhance vasocongestion.

Transudation
the production of vaginal lubrication because of sweating of vaginal tissue engorged with blood during vasocongestion

Myotonia
involuntary skeletal muscle contractions

Prior to Masters and Johnson's research, sex researchers believed that vaginal lubrication was caused by sweat and oil glands within the vagina. Masters and Johnson discovered, and documented through special intravaginal photography, that lubrication is a byproduct of vasocongestion. Vaginal mucosal tissue becomes engorged with blood and produces a clear, slippery fluid that empties from the cells directly into the vagina. They called this process **transudation** and discovered that it was directly linked to the level of sexual excitement. Masters and Johnson found that insufficient lubrication is often the result of too little foreplay and low levels of excitement or anxiety.

The second characteristic associated with excitement is **myotonia**, the gradual build-up of tension in the skeletal muscles throughout the body. Unlike the muscle tension associated with stress, myotonia is a gradual build-up that is progressive and pleasurable. Employing specially developed instruments and methods, Masters and Johnson were able to quantify the level of

Health Hint

The Effects of Aphrodisiacs

People are always searching for a magic potion that will enhance their sexual response and enable them to respond quicker, last longer, and become rearoused quicker. This has enabled a multimillion-dollar aphrodisiac market to flourish. Certain foods, nutrients, and other aphrodisiacs are promoted as aids to sexual response. But do they work? The answer is yes and no.

Although no true aphrodisiac (potion that increases desire and performance) exists, if you think it's helping, it probably is, as is the case with any placebo. Because the mind and the body work together in initiating and perpetuating sexual response, it makes sense that if a person perceives that a substance will help to promote sexual response, it just might.

Physiologically, however, the effects of aphrodisiacs are mixed. In general, they can be categorized by the way they work: provide energy, increase blood flow to the genitals, decrease the sensitivity of genital tissue, and increase desire in the brain.

Various "pep pills" are promoted as increasing energy levels. These are featured in fitness and "muscle" magazines and claim to enhance sexual desire by increasing overall energy levels. Though we believe that sexual desire is enhanced through high-level well-being, we think this should emanate from a healthy lifestyle, not a "pep pill."

Other aphrodisiacs, in the form of salves and creams, claim to work by enhancing vasocongestion

(firmer erections, more responsiveness) — sending more blood to the genital area. In reality, vasocongestion is a result of dilation and constriction of blood vessels and changes in blood pressure, not extra surface blood in the smaller capillaries.

Still other aphrodisiacs claim to work by decreasing sensitivity, which hypothetically allows men to "last longer." These topical creams and ointments often inflame sensitive genital tissue, creating painful irritation. Using a condom to cover the head of the penis is a better way to decrease sensitivity.

Psychoactive drugs and alcohol work by altering perception. Alcohol deadens the parts of the brain that controls conscious thought. This can reduce negative thoughts and feelings that might inhibit sexual response. Other drugs, such as marijuana, heighten sensations such as touch and smell. Enhancing the ability to perceive sensations can heighten enjoyment of sexual activity and promote sexual response.

The best "aphrodisiacs," in our opinion, are summarized as the following.

- Become physically fit.
- Develop healthy eating habits.
- Reduce stress through relaxation techniques and behavior management.

muscle tension in various parts of the body during sexual arousal. This was done by placing electrodes on strategic parts of the body to measure **electromyographic** activity during sexual arousal.

During excitement in men, the testes elevate, moving closer to the body. In women, the inner two-thirds of the vagina expands and the uterus is pulled backward.

Plateau

In the second phase of Masters and Johnson's sexual response cycle, called the plateau, processes set into motion during the excitement phase reach their maximum levels. Vasocongestion creates peak levels of engorgement, color changes, and lubrication, and muscular tension also reaches its maximum level.

In men, the testes become fully elevated, and the prostate gland enlarges. The Cowper's gland releases clear, slippery, pre-ejaculatory fluid (we will discuss the sperm-carrying capability of this in Chapter 14). In women, the labia reach their maximum size, the vagina forms the "orgasmic platform," and the clitoris retracts under its protective hood. Both men and women experience a "sex flush," a rash-like reddish tinge to the skin of the chest and back associated with dilation of the blood vessels and increased blood flow in these areas.

Masters and Johnson found that the plateau was the most variable stage in terms of time. More experienced couples, for instance, were able to prolong the plateau if they desired, whereas younger, less sexually experienced subjects had much shorter plateau periods.

Orgasm

The third phase of Masters and Johnson's response cycle, orgasm, is characterized by the dramatic release of tension and other physiological processes (heart rate, blood pressure, increased breathing, and so on) associated with the excitement and plateau stages. During orgasm most of the male and female sexual structures undergo rhythmic, muscular contractions. These are responsible for the release of pent-up muscular tension in men and women and ejaculation in men.

Masters and Johnson found that women have a one-step orgasm, whereas it is a two-step process in men. The first step in men is called **ejaculatory inevitability.** During this step men sense the release of tension and feel the inevitability of ejaculation. During the next step, **emission** contractions of the vas-deferens and other structures move sperm and other ejaculatory fluids through the vas deferens and out of the urethra. Masters and Johnson found that women did not ejaculate during orgasm.

Prior to Masters and Johnson, researchers studying sexual response used much more subjective criteria for determining whether an orgasm had or had not occurred. Masters and Johnson quantified the muscular contractions, fluid expulsions (in men only), and physiological reversals associated with the release of tension as a result of orgasm.

Electromyographic
refers to measurement of muscle tension through electrical sensors at skin surface

Ejaculatory inevitability
the first step in male ejaculation; beginning of smooth-muscle contractions that trigger release of ejaculate

Emission
release of secretions from various organs and glands that produce male ejaculate

Masters and Johnson were the first to operationally define orgasm.

PERSPECTIVES

Tantric Sex

For most Americans, orgasm is the whole point of sexual activities. As a culture, we're obsessed with orgasm. We keep track of orgasms like box scores for baseball: number of at-bats (sexual encounters), number of hits (orgasms), and whether they are singles (okay), doubles (slightly better orgasms), triples (really good orgasms), and home runs (really, really, great orgasms). We are not only obsessed with our own orgasms but we also want to know about our partner's orgasms. "Was it good for you?" we ask. Our ultimate criterion is to achieve simultaneous orgasm with our partner — the ultimate, two home runs at the same time!

None of these scoring measures correlates perfectly with sexual satisfaction or healthy sexuality. Frequency, intensity, and mutuality of orgasms vary in their relationship to sexual satisfaction for people. One can even enjoy sex without orgasm. The idea of

having intercourse but intentionally not having an orgasm may seem strange, but that's exactly the point of Tantric sex: conserving orgasm. The energy that emanates from sexual arousal is shared with one's partner and transcends the couple's sexual union to help bring the two closer to spiritual oneness with a higher power. Tantric sex is part of the spiritual form of yoga. The spiritual form of yoga is practiced to achieve a transcendent state of being.

In the United States, disciples of Tantric sex view it as a spiritual activity that unites partners in transcendence and also as a technique to enhance sexual intensity. Couples focus on sexual pleasuring, not the outcome of orgasm. This deemphasis on orgasm allows couples to relax and enjoy the sensations without being so goal-directed. Some organizations run Tantric sex training programs and retreats.

Resolution

The last phase of the sexual response cycle is resolution, return of the body to the unaroused state. Masters and Johnson found that after orgasm, the two key physiological processes — vasocongestion and myotonia — reverse. Orgasm triggers the brain to normalize the dilation of blood vessels, heart rate, and blood pressure, allowing blood flow to return to normal and vasocongestion to reverse. With this reversal, the erection begins to shrink, lubrication ceases, and color changes disappear. In addition, the build-up of muscular tension followed by contractions stops, and muscle tissue returns to normal.

Masters and Johnson coined the term **refractory period** to describe the time required after an orgasm before a person could enter the excitement stage again.[5] They found tremendous variability in this time between men and women, and among individual men. They found that women did not have a refractory period. Women did not need recovery time to get excited again and reach orgasm.

Vasocongestion and lubrication could remain at optimal levels if the source and intensity of stimulation and interest in maintaining activity with the partner were to continue. The significance of this finding was that it proved that women could have multiple orgasms without a refractory period. This is both a difference between men's and women's sexual response patterns and a significant finding in terms of women's ability to extend and enjoy sexual relations if they desire. For most women in Masters and Johnson's study, however, sexual stimulation ceased after their

Refractory period
the time from last orgasm to the next beginning of excitement

partner's orgasm. Often, this is because of pre-set agendas that couples have about trying to achieve orgasm simultaneously or a "me first, then you" pattern in achieving orgasm. In follow-up studies, Masters and Johnson found that most male partners did not realize that they could continue to stimulate their partners (if desired, through pubic contact or manual/oral stimulation), even if they were to lose their erection.[6]

Unlike women, men need a certain amount of down time before they can achieve another erection. The amount of time varies significantly. Among the variables related to the amount of time needed to obtain another erection, the most significant were age and time since last orgasm. In general, the younger the man, the shorter the refractory period. The longer the duration since the last orgasm, the shorter the refractory period. Thus, a younger man who hadn't had an orgasm in some time would become rearoused much more quickly than an older man who recently had an orgasm. Other variables, such as overall level of health, stress, and obesity, were also found to be related to the length of refractory period.

Figures 7.6 and 7.7 show the patterns in sexual response that Masters and Johnson discovered for the men and women in their study. Figure 7.6, their classic cycle for men, shows a steady build-up in excitement followed by a moderate level of plateau. The level of stimulation in the plateau stage reaches its zenith with orgasm. This is followed by the cessation of stimulation and a rapid dropoff into resolution.

Figure 7.7 diagrams multiple orgasms in women. The pattern is similar to that in Figure 7.6 except that following orgasm, stimulation continues and the woman is able to achieve multiple orgasms before entering the resolution phase.

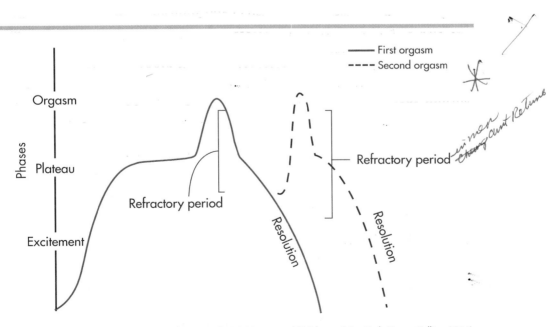

Source: *Human Sexual Response* by W. Masters and V. Johnson (New York: HarperCollins, 1966).

Figure 7.6 Masters and Johnson's pattern of sexual response in males.

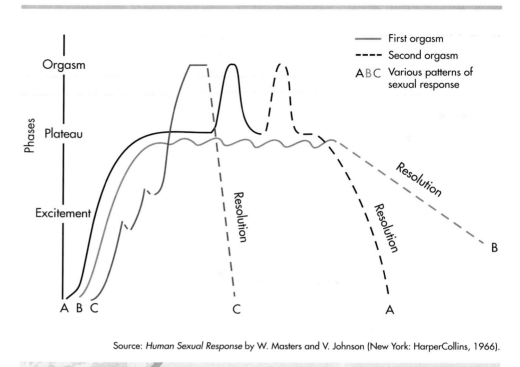

Source: *Human Sexual Response* by W. Masters and V. Johnson (New York: HarperCollins, 1966).

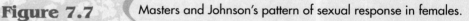

Figure 7.7   Masters and Johnson's pattern of sexual response in females.

Pattern B in Figure 7.7 shows what happens when the level or type of stimulation is insufficient to trigger orgasm. Excitement builds with the stimulation, and plateau is achieved. The level or type of stimulation, however, lacks the intensity (or stops before it can build to high enough levels) to trigger orgasm, which is responsible for reversing the effects of vasocongestion. This results in a protracted resolution stage until the pelvic area and genitals return to their unaroused levels. This phenomenon in men has been called "blue balls." Although no equivalent slang term applies to women, females experience similar effects: pelvic congestion, swollen genitalia, throbbing pelvic area, and so on.

Although Masters and Johnson's findings added valuable information about the objective experience of sexual response, the analysis is physiological and is open to a more subjective interpretation. For instance, even though an orgasm, according to Masters and Johnson, is characterized by a certain number of muscular contractions at a certain intensity and other physiological parameters, a person could have an enjoyable sexual experience without having an official Masters and Johnson orgasm.

What operationalizing a concept such as orgasm does is to allow us to study it more rigorously. For instance, if researchers want to study the effects of alcohol on orgasm, their research will be easier and more accurate if they are able to operationally define orgasm. The same kind of rigor need not enter into our human relations.

You can have a satisfying sexual experience without having an official Masters and Johnson orgasm.

People have described some ways an orgasm feels like.

- ◟ Like a mild explosion
- ◟ Like I was soaring in the sky
- ◟ Throbbing
- ◟ Like an avalanche
- ◟ Like pulsating bursts of energy
- ◟ Like a dive into a pool
- ◟ Exhilarating
- ◟ Intense and earth-shattering
- ◟ Like small, self-contained moments
- ◟ Like a cork popping out of a champagne bottle
- ◟ Like a warm rush from my toes to my head

What does an orgasm feel like to you?

Singer-Kaplan's Triphasic Model of Sexual Response

Helen Singer-Kaplan disagreed with Masters and Johnson's four-phase sexual response cycle. She argued that the model neglects the importance of sexual desire in human sexual response. Further, she agreed with others in the field who claimed that the plateau stage is really indistinguishable from excitement and the two stages would more appropriately be merged together.[7]

Singer-Kaplan's original model had two stages: excitement and orgasm. She modified it, however, after her work with dysfunctional individuals and couples revealed that many of them had problems with low levels of interest in sex. She then proposed a triphasic model of sexual response that included the phases of desire, excitement, and orgasm. She placed most of the emphasis on desire and the role of the brain in initiating sexual response.

Desire

During the desire phase, some activating thought, emotion, fantasy, or sensation arises in the cortex or limbic system and triggers the activation of neural and hormonal sexual stimulation. The emphasis here is on the key role the cerebral cortex plays in initiating sexual response, and the subjective, emotional nature of arousal. As we mentioned at the beginning of this chapter, the brain is the sexiest organ in the body and plays the key role in determining whether the sexual response continues.

Excitement

Singer-Kaplan accepted Masters and Johnson's findings concerning the physiology of sexual arousal. She agreed that vasocongestion is the key physiological process involved in *excitement*. Singer-Kaplan disagreed, however, with the idea of separating the plateau from excitement. She argued that the plateau is really nothing more than end-stage excitement or culmination of the excitement phase. When excitement peaks, the person reaches the plateau, or level of maximum arousal. As such, however, to clinically distinguish plateau from excitement is next to impossible, and, therefore, the two phases should be merged.

Orgasm

Once again, Singer-Kaplan accepted Masters and Johnson's findings concerning the physiology of orgasm. She also described *orgasm* as the one phase that is clearly distinguishable for most people. Unlike the transition from desire to excitement, which is hard to pinpoint, the onset of orgasm is an event most people readily identify.

Walen and Roth's Model of Sexual Response

Walen and Roth developed a cognitive model of human sexual response that emphasizes the importance of perception and cognitive factors in the

PERSPECTIVES   Expanding Your Perception of Lovemaking and Orgasm

Sex is a goal-oriented activity for many people. It seems they view sex as a race with both partners competing to see who crosses first with an orgasm. Even better, both partners cross at the same time and have the ultimate prize — mutual orgasms. The prize is the perfect orgasm, achieved together. The ultimate victory is the quest for perfect sex.

Is this really the best sex? Is sex best viewed as a competition, a race? We like to think of sex as more of a multi-course gourmet meal. With each course the couple anticipates something special, a unique taste delight.

A before-dinner appetite sets the mood for the evening and whets the appetite for the next course. Appetizers delight the palate. They come in an infinite variety, each with its own special ability to please.

Next comes a soup, followed by a special salad. Each tickles the taste buds and is savored for its uniqueness. Between these courses we pause and have a refreshing sorbet to cleanse the palate. We stop and sit back, savoring the exquisite gastronomical delights we've already sampled, and we eagerly anticipate the rest of the meal to follow. We enjoy good conversation and admiring looks.

The entree comes next — not too much food, just enough to satisfy our cravings and delight our palate.

We pause again to savor our meal before dessert is served. Dessert provides just a taste of sweetness to round off our meal.

Finally, we sit back, sipping our after-dinner brandy. This brings our meal to a close.

When we eat a meal such as this, who can argue that the entree is the only or most important part of the meal? Sometimes the entree isn't as special as the other parts of the meal, and we only sample it.

We can view lovemaking as a feast, a multi-course meal that first involves the build-up of desire through kissing, hugging, massage, and noncoital foreplay. The lovemaking continues with a variety of techniques including oral sex, vaginal intercourse, and so on, extending the plateau as long as we desire. We pause frequently to talk, laugh, touch, have a drink, and the like. We continue into and through orgasm, and finish by staying coupled and basking in each other's pleasure until we go limp.

If we envision sex as a feast for the senses rather than a race, perhaps we will enjoy our orgasms more when they occur and not feel as though we've missed something if we don't have them once in a while.

initiation and perpetuation of sexual response.[8] Although accepting much of Masters and Johnson's physiology of sexual arousal, Walen and Roth argued that a sexual stimulus is potentially erotic only until it is perceived as such. Something that is capable of turning on a person may not do so in all situations and under all circumstances. A person first must evaluate the stimulus positively. Walen and Roth's model, in short, explains that it is not just the sexual stimulus that creates the turn-on; our perception and acceptance of it are what allow our body to become sexually aroused.

Case Study

Steve and Tracy: What Good Sex Means to Us

Steve is a 26-year-old senior, majoring in Small Business Administration. He took some time off after high school and worked in construction before starting college. Tracy is a 23-year-old senior education major. She is a fifth-year senior, having worked her way full-time through college.

Steve: Good sex to me is being able to relax with my partner. With Tracy, I don't have to worry about anything. I trust her.

Tracy: Yeah, that's it — trust. Before I met Steve, I went through a lot of one-night stands or real short relationships where I think the guys just wanted to get laid. I never felt I could trust any of them.

Professor: What do you mean by "trust them?"

Tracy: I guess I mean trust them about *anything*. Would they respect me and my wishes? Would they have my interests at heart or just their own? I also was worried about pregnancy and disease. Could I trust them to be disease-free, wear a condom, those sort of things? Oh yeah, I also wanted to be able to trust that they'd respect my privacy. I didn't want them to go bragging to their friends about me or tell other people the most intimate aspects of my sex life.

Steve: I feel the same way. I like to be able to let down my guard in order to enjoy sex. I guess you could say that, for me, it's sexy to be vulnerable with a woman. With Tracy, I can tell her about my desires,

concerns, fears, and trust her to act in my best interests. I remember telling one woman I had sex with that I liked it when she played with my anus during sex but that I always worried that this might mean I was gay. I later found out she had told this to a sorority sister, and before long everyone in the house knew, as well as some members of the fraternity they were little sisters to.

Professor: How does trust affect your sexual response?

Tracy: For me, it allows me to let down my guard and relax. I trust Steve completely, and that allows my mind and body to relax. I've never been as responsive with anyone else as I am with Steve. I can get sexually aroused and have orgasm with very little effort.

Steve: I feel the same way. With Tracy, I feel so relaxed that things just naturally happen. I remember with other women worrying that I might not perform up to their standards, and that made it real difficult to get excited and erect. I know I can please Tracy, and even if I have an off-night, she'll understand and not use it against me.

Tracy: I hope I don't make it seem that because I'm so relaxed, there's no spark or sexual tension between Steve and me. Nothing can be farther from the truth. Even though I'm completely relaxed in bed with him, I can get aroused just thinking about sex with him. I hope this never changes.

Once arousal has begun, Walen and Roth accept Masters and Johnson's physiological explanation of the process of excitement Once again, though, the role of perception plays a part. In each of our brains is a stored bank of perceptions concerning sexual arousal. We expect and anticipate certain things to happen once we begin to get sexually aroused or engage in getting our partner aroused.

Walen and Roth propose that our perception of arousal plays into the continuation of our arousal and sexual response. Once things begin to heat up, we look for certain indicators to let us know whether everything is proceeding as planned. We ask ourselves questions ("Is my erection firm enough?" "Is my partner responding to my touch?" "Will I be able to keep this up?") to check out our expectations. If everything is proceeding as expected and planned, we can relax and our sexual response continues.

If we don't perceive arousal positively, our response can be short-circuited. Our brain can literally get in the way of our body. If negative thoughts and emotions such as fear, mistrust, or anger are part of our perception, they can short-circuit our sexual response or result in less enjoyment or lack of orgasm.

Perceptions are a problem especially when they create sexual expectations that are illogical or irrational. People who are too critical or who have

Case Study

Alyssa:
A Case of Fear and Mistrust

Alyssa is a 20-year-old college junior. She recently broke up with Ed, her boyfriend of 2 years. She and Ed had been having sexual intercourse for about 1½ years. Alyssa has had little sexual desire and problems having an orgasm ever since she broke up with Ed about 3 months ago.

Counselor: Tell me about what's been troubling you.

Alyssa: I've been having a hard time having an orgasm lately when I have intercourse. I seem to be able to get excited, but something seems to keep me from being able to come.

Counselor: Have you ever had this kind of problem before?

Alyssa: No, I never had problems coming when I was going out with Ed.

Counselor: When did you break up with Ed?

Alyssa: About three months ago.

Counselor: How many times have you had sex since then?

Alyssa: I still masturbate about twice a week, but I've had intercourse only four or five times — once with a guy I met at a fraternity party and the other times with a guy from one of my classes. In each case I didn't have sex on the first date, only after we went out a couple of times.

Counselor: Do you achieve orgasm when you masturbate?

Alyssa: Yes. Always.

Counselor: Tell me about your feelings toward these two guys.

Alyssa: The first guy, Jim, is fun to be around. He's a real party guy, likes to dance, go to karaoke bars. . . . We have a good time together, but I worry about his past. I try to talk to him about his past sex life,

too high expectations for performance can become spectators in their own sexual activity, literally sitting back and observing their (and their partner's) behavior rather than being fully involved. It's almost as if they step out of their body to critically examine what's going on. Ongoing critical evaluation can lead to unsatisfying perceptions of one's sexual response and begin to affect it adversely.

Zilbergeld and Ellison's Sexual Response Model

Zilbergeld and Ellison proposed a five-phase sexual response cycle that also emphasizes the role of cognitive factors in sexual response.[9] Like Singer-Kaplan, they separate the desire phase of sexual response from the excitement phase. They name their first phase *interest/desire* and, like Walen and Roth, stress the impact of the cognitive perception of potentially sexual stimuli. Once interest and desire are present, a person proceeds to the next phase, *arousal*, which is the initial stage of readiness for sexual activity. If aroused sufficiently, the individual proceeds to *physiological readiness*, characterized by lubrication in women and erection in men. Physiological

but he kind of blows it off. It's hard to talk about this stuff. One of my girlfriends told me that she heard that Jim has had a lot of different sexual partners in his life. This worries me. I don't want to get AIDS.

Counselor: What are you doing about this?

Alyssa: I insisted that we use a condom until we get to know each other better. It basically worked. He wore it, but I got the sense that he didn't really want to. He's never said as much, but I could pick it up from his attitude. It didn't make for great sex. I kind of anticipated that it was going to be a problem, so it put a damper on things for me. I never really relaxed. I didn't come.

Counselor: Tell me about the other guy.

Alyssa: The other guy, Tom, is very nice. I know him from class last year, and he's in my psychology class this semester. He asked me out when he found out I broke up with Ed. He was very tender and understanding. He encouraged me to talk about Ed and get a lot of things out. We've had sex a few times, but I still haven't been able to come.

Tom has a real temper. I've seen him almost lose it a couple of times over silly things like getting cut off by another driver on the highway. He seems to respect me, but I worry about him going ballistic on me if I ever get on his bad side. I can't fully relax around him when we're in bed. I've heard of date rape and I'm afraid if I ever refuse him because I'm not in the mood for sex, he might force me. Not a real good way to start a relationship, huh?

readiness sets the stage for initiation of *sexual activity*. The next phase, *orgasm*, is similar to that of Masters and Johnson's cycle.

The last stage, *satisfaction*, is completely different from the other theories. Unlike the other stages (particularly, readiness and orgasm), satisfaction is entirely subjective. Good sex or satisfaction reflects the individual's personal level of enjoyment or fulfillment in the sexual encounter.

WELLNESS SYNTHESIS

Although the sexual response is an obvious function of the physical domain, each of the other components of wellness has a large influence as well.

Physical Well-being

Physical well-being contributes directly to healthy sexual response. When we are physically fit, our bodies respond and perform better sexually. High-level cardiorespiratory endurance can facilitate maximum blood flow and staying power. Vasocongestion hinges on efficient blood flow through the blood vessels to the genitals. Atherosclerosis, the narrowing and hardening of blood vessels, can inhibit maximum blood flow. Smoking also can speed up atherosclerosis and lead to constriction of blood flow. This affects overall health and also sexual response. Increasing the overall level of fitness (particularly, cardiorespiratory fitness and flexibility), improving the diet (minimizing fats and cholesterol), limiting use of alcohol and other illicit drugs, and maximizing body composition can increase overall physical well-being and improve sexual response.

Although being fit doesn't ensure good sex, it can enhance the physiological (body strength and endurance, increased blood flow, and the like) and psychological (higher self-esteem, positive outlook, enhanced body image) components of good sex. Conversely, having a disability or illness or being unfit doesn't necessarily preclude sexual satisfaction. People with disabilities and chronic illnesses that impact their sexual response can learn to maximize their sexual potentials and abilities, whatever they are. People who do not have the highest levels of fitness still can have good sex as they work their way toward becoming fit.

Intellectual Well-being

Knowing what to expect concerning sexual response can make the difference between allowing ourselves to relax and let things happen or becoming overly concerned with the process and worry that it won't happen. Knowing that our sexual desires and responses vary from day to day will help us understand the differences and enable us to relax and go with the changes. Understanding that our needs and responses won't always perfectly mirror our partner's can help us devise ways to work around these and other differences.

Understanding the effects of drugs, fatigue, stress and other substances on our sexual response empowers us and helps us moderate their effects.

Knowledge also can prepare us for the future, by enabling us to anticipate the changes in sexual response associated with aging.

Knowing how our perceptions can influence our sexual response opens the door to relearning things about our sexuality that until now might have been barriers to our sexual fulfillment. If we believe in the cognitive basis of sexual response, we can unlearn negative sexual information and learn new, healthy ways of viewing ourselves and our sexuality.

Knowing about the sexual response patterns in men and women and the areas that are most responsive to stimulation can make us better lovers, regardless of whether we are straight, gay, lesbian, or bisexual. Knowing our limitations and capabilities, how to work around certain disabilities and health conditions, can help us improve our sexual response and maintain our self-respect and self-esteem.

Emotional Well-being

Good sexual response hinges on emotional well-being. Because sexual response involves both physiological and psychological variables, we have to be in the right frame of mind for vasocongestion to happen. When we are nervous, angry, sad, worried, or in a number of other negative emotional states, we have trouble relaxing enough to allow our brain to trigger efficient vasocongestion. Even if we allow ourselves to become sexually excited, we may not be able to have an orgasm.

The best sex is usually when we are able to let down our guard, free our mind, and relax. High-level emotional well-being allows us to do this. We are in control of our emotions; they don't control us. We feel good about ourselves and our partners, and we trust ourselves and our partners enough to relax and let the sexual response happen.

Social Well-being

The quality of our social relationships plays a big part in our sexual response. Being able to relax, feel secure, and trust our partner is crucial for good sex. Another key to good sex is open communication. Getting to know your partner requires time. Intimacy builds over time as a result of shared experiences and open communication about our innermost thoughts, feelings, needs, and wants.

Other relationships can help us enhance our sexual response. By talking with people other than our sex partner about our body and how it works, we can learn things, share information, and, relieve anxiety (you find out you're not the only one who thinks that way). Having friends, family, a counselor, or someone to talk to can help.

Spiritual Well-being

Most theories emphasize the physical, emotional, intellectual, and social dimensions of sexual response. Even though each of the theories in this chapter presents a unique framework for studying human sexual response, all omit the spiritual dimension of sexual response. We believe the transcendence that orgasm offers is inherent in our sexual response and not totally reliant on our emotional connections to another. We also believe, however, that sex and orgasm with someone we love and are committed to gives a heightened level of spirituality.

By definition, spirituality revolves around transcending ourselves and connecting with something greater than ourselves. Whether we believe our spirituality connects us with God, some higher power, or all other living things, transcendence of the self is the key to spirituality. We've often heard people describe orgasm in terms of feeling "uplifted," "out-of-this-world," or "at one with the universe."

- Do you think sexual response, particularly orgasm, has a spiritual component?
- What are your spiritual thoughts and feelings about orgasm and sexual response?
- Does your spiritual connection vary according to the emotional nature of your relationship (sex with someone you love, like, are indifferent about)? If so, how does it differ. Why?

Sharing an intense orgasm with another person can, at times, make you feel instantly at one with the universe. If one positive human experience is capable of linking all of us together, it just might be orgasm. Humans and other animals seem to share the ability to respond sexually to one another.

Sexual activity with a partner, by its nature, connects us to someone else in a unique way. A high level of spiritual well-being can help us form sexual relationships based on caring and mutual respect instead of exploitation and disrespect.

Environmental Well-being

Feeling secure and being safe are essential to healthy sexuality. Our sexual response depends upon a safe and comfortable environment. If we can't relax and feel safe and secure, we won't be able to relax enough to let the sexual response flow.

Have you ever been in a strange house as a guest and felt uncomfortable having sex? Think about being in a strange environment (your boyfriend's/girlfriend's fraternity/sorority house, a tent in a campground, a bed and breakfast with thin walls, your partner's parent's house) and how it feels to try to fully relax and let your sexual response flow.

Even meeting potential sex partners requires a safe environment. Think about going out to a bar, club, or other public place and feeling that people there don't like you or want you around, or having to suppress your natural urges to hold hands, dance, or make out. This is what many gay and lesbian people face every day in trying to meet potential friends and lovers.

WEB RESOURCES

Intimacy Institute Sexuality Database

http://www.sexualitydata.com

Database for information concerning sexual response and other areas of sexuality, written by the Sinclair Intimacy Institute staff. Provides answers to frequently asked questions through an up-to-date sexuality database with access to additional online resources.

HealthGate Healthy Sexuality

http://www.healthgate.com/healthy/sexuality/index.shtml

Features different articles on women's and men's health each day of the week. Weekly Friday feature articles on different areas of sexuality from biology of attraction to disorders of desire.

Notes

1. Helen Singer-Kaplan, *The New Sex Therapy* (New York: Brunnel/Mazer, 1974).
2. J. Bancroft, "Hormones and Human Sexual Behavior," *Journal of Sex and Marital Therapy*, 10 (1984), 3–21.
3. Bancroft, 1984.
4. Bancroft, 1984.
5. A decade later, Masters and Johnson published *The Pleasure Bond* (New York: Bantam Books, 1976).
6. *Disorders of Sexual Desire* (New York: Brunnel/Mazer, 1979).
7. Singer-Kaplan, *The New Sex Therapy*.
8. "A Cognitive Approach to Sex Therapy," in *Theories of Human Sexuality*, edited by J. H. Geer and W. T. O'Donohue (New York: Plenum, 1987).
9. "Desire Discrepancies and Arousal Problems in Sex Therapy," in *Principles and Practice of Sex Therapy*, by S. Lieblum and L. A. Pervin (New York: Guilford, 1980), pp. 65–104.

Student Study Questions

1. How do the various regions of the brain process potentially arousing sexual stimuli and initiate sexual response?

2. How do the nervous system and the endocrine system work during sexual response?

3. What are some of the things that made Masters and Johnson pioneers in the field of sexual response?

4. What are vasocongestion and myotonia?

5. Compare and contrast the physiological changes in men and women during Masters and Johnson's sexual response cycle.

6. Compare Masters and Johnson's model of sexual response to the other models presented in this chapter.

7. Evaluate the effectiveness of common "aphrodisiacs" on sexual response.

Things That Turn Me On

People become aroused in a variety of ways. Each of us has our own unique sights and sounds that get us in the mood. The purpose of this assessment is to help you take a personal inventory of your personal turn-ons and give you the opportunity to share them anonymously with your classmates.

Describe in detail the things that turn you on in the following categories:

● Sights (visual images that are arousing to you):

● Sounds (types of music, words, conversation that you find stimulating):

● Tastes (food, drink, body fluids, or other tastes that are arousing):

● Smells (perfume, cologne, body smells, other odors you find stimulating):

● Touches (types, body parts, motions you find stimulating):

Sensuality and Sexual Behavior

Major Topics

Developing Sensuality
Types of Sexual Behavior
 Celibacy and Abstinence
 Nonpenetrative Sexual Activity
  Kissing
  Hugging/Rubbing
  Massage
  Masturbation
 Sexual Intercourse
  Vaginal Intercourse
  Anal Intercourse
  Oral Sex
Sexuality and Disability
Wellness Synthesis
 Physical Well-being
 Intellectual Well-being
 Emotional Well-being
 Social Well-being
 Spiritual Well-being
 Environmental Well-being

Student Learning Objectives

After reading this chapter, students will be able to:

❧ Compare and contrast sensuality and sexuality.

❧ Compare and contrast celibacy and abstinence.

❧ Describe a variety of nonpenetrative sexual behaviors.

❧ Know how to give a sensual massage.

❧ Evaluate the myths associated with masturbation.

❧ Compare and contrast a variety of positions for vaginal intercourse.

❧ Identify the factors associated with healthy anal sexual behavior.

❧ Describe a variety of oral sex behaviors.

What makes a person sensual? Is it the richness and texture of her features (thick, long hair, distinct, angular nose, high cheek bones, long, exotic nails, tantalizing perfume/cologne, self-assured body language)? Is it his attitude (a deep thinker, caring/loving personality, down-to-earth simplicity)? Could it be her appreciation of life (enjoys great food, appreciates music, enjoys nature, enjoys physical activities)? Isolating attributes that are sexual from those that are sensual is difficult. Although they are intimately related, sexuality and sensuality are different.

Sensuality is the quality of being sensual, of experiencing life fully through all of the senses. **Sexuality**, you will remember, is a broad term that refers to all aspects of being sexual, encompassing a variety of biological, psychological, and cultural variables. Sensuality is a part of our sexuality. Sensual people have a heightened awareness of sight, sound, taste, touch, and smell. They use this increased sensitivity to, and appreciation of, the senses to experience life through all of these senses whenever possible. They approach each experience, every day, through this context or frame of reference. A walk in the woods or down a bustling city street is a symphony of sounds, colors, scents, tastes, and textures.

Sensual people bring this context to their lovemaking. The heightened awareness of all the senses enhances lovemaking. Sensual lovers delight in all aspects of their partners and their surroundings, making sex a feast for the senses. Sex isn't just a genital-driven quest for orgasm. It is a five-course gourmet meal that may include climax as the entree.

Sensuality
experiencing things through all five senses

Sexuality
broad term that refers to all aspects of being sexual

Heightened sensuality enhances sexual enjoyment.

DEVELOPING SENSUALITY

William Burnham, a pioneering educational psychologist, believed that all humans are born as sensual creatures.[1] As newborns, we experience life

Think about how toddlers play in the grass. They roll around in it, close their eyes, lie back in it and listen to the sounds the wind makes as it blows through the high blades. They pull out handsful of grass, throw them up in the air, and watch the blades fall to earth. They take a blade of grass and examine it carefully, rolling it around in their fingers, maybe even against their cheeks with their eyes closed. As they squeeze the grass between their fingers, they notice that oils are secreted. They smell this oil and taste it. Satisfied that they know what grass is all about, they move on to the next activity.

Do you still revel in something as simple as this? Along the course of our lives, we lose this integration, this ability to experience life with all of our senses. We pay less and less attention to anything other than sight, sound, and occasionally smell. Why does this happen? What transforms the sensual child into a constrained adult? Are we afraid of what others would think if they were to see us rolling in the grass at age 18 or 28 or 48 years? Or have we "been there, done that?" Are we too jaded to enjoy the simple, free, sensual delights that surround us?

through all of our senses. Burnham referred to this as being "fully integrated." Little separates our intellect and our senses.

Losing the ability to be sensual can greatly affect our ability to experience sexual pleasure and experience eroticism through all of the senses. In Chapter 12 we describe several methods for restoring lost sensuality and ways to enhance sexual response. For the rest of this chapter, we will explore sexual behavior and its relationship to sensuality.

TYPES OF SEXUAL BEHAVIOR

One way to present the many forms of sexual behavior is to place them on a continuum from celibacy to oral/anal sex. This presentation is useful in understanding safer sex options, as well as choices in fertility control.

PERSPECTIVES

Celibate Passion

Most of us have a hard time understanding the concept of celibacy. We have less of a problem with situational abstinence. Abstaining from sex makes good sense at various points in our life. Celibacy presents us with an entirely different picture. It's hard to understand how, or why, someone would want to impose such a hardship on themselves. In a fascinating account of Benedictine Monks, Kathleen Norris examined what she described "the hidden rewards of quitting sex." Norris questioned the popular notion that celibacy constitutes a hatred or denial of sexuality. She debunked the myth that celibate people are perverse, their lives somehow stunted by their rejection of sexual activity.

In her 10-year association with Benedictine Monks, she cultivated deep friendships with celibate men and women. Rather than deny their sexuality, Norris found that these men and women are fully aware of themselves as sexual beings but consciously choose to "sublimate their sexual energies toward another purpose than sexual intercourse and procreation."

She found that, among the monks, "the constraints of celibacy have somehow been transformed into an openness. They exude a sense of freedom." They are free, as Norris noted, to pursue the kind of commitment to community life that can't be attained given the demands inherent in sustaining sexual and other paired relationships. They are free to commit themselves 100% to community and "friendship."

Friendship takes on a special meaning with the celibate. According to Norris, "I have never had a monk friend make an insinuating remark along the lines of, 'You have beautiful eyes' (or legs, breasts, knees, elbows, nostrils), the kind of remark women grow accustomed to deflecting. A monk is supposed to give up the idea of possessing anything, including women."

This understanding of complete friendship minus the need to possess anyone is a revelation. Norris claims that this helped her appreciate the true nature of friendship and what being married means. "They [the monks] have helped me recognize that celibacy, like monogamy, is not a matter of the will disdaining and conquering the desires of the flesh, but a discipline that many people think of as undesirable, if not impossible — a conscious form of sublimation. It's helped me better respect the bonds and boundaries of marriage."

Celibacy is not holiness, not an accomplishment put on a resumé. Celibacy is a form of ministry, the ability to make oneself available to others, body and soul, with no ulterior motive or hidden agenda. What celibacy allows, according to Norris, is the ability of the celibate person to create a special kind of friendship, one that makes others feel appreciated, enlarged.

Source: "Celibate Passion," by Kathleen Norris, in *Utne Reader*, Sept–Oct 1996, pp. 51–53.

Celibacy and Abstinence

Celibacy
abstaining from sexual
intercourse

Celibacy is defined as abstaining from sexual intercourse. Although the formal definition of celibacy refers specifically to abstaining from sexual intercourse and never marrying, many people assume that celibacy and abstinence mean total avoidance of all forms of sexual release and the absence of sexual desire. Celibacy may or may not include masturbation and fantasy as forms of sexual release. Celibate people also have varying degrees of sexual desire. Not all celibate people lack sexual interest and desire though; they merely choose to channel that energy and desire into different avenues of expression.

Celibacy is usually associated with a spiritual or religious sacrifice and is considered to be a lifelong commitment. Priests and nuns, for instance, declare a vow of celibacy so they may devote themselves fully to serving God and never marry. It is a conscious, willful diversion of sexual energy into nonsexual activity. Kathleen Norris uses the phrase "celibate passion" to describe how celibate monks are able to transform sexual energy into a sense of deep caring and love that she found to be unique among celibate people.[2]

Not all people who choose celibacy, however, do so as part of a religious commitment. Actually, all of us choose to wait before we engage in intercourse. Many people choose celibacy because they are not ready to begin having intercourse, and they satisfy their sexual needs through other behaviors. We all develop at our own pace, and some of us are simply not ready as soon as others are.

We sometimes choose celibacy because we need time to recover or grieve from relationships that have ended. We need time to heal emotionally and are not interested in forming sexual relationships at the time. Others choose celibacy because they do not have the time or energy to sustain a commitment (sexual or otherwise) with another person. They think they

Case Study

Susan:
Choosing to be Celibate

I've been celibate for the past year and a half. I'm thirty-one years old, have a seven-year-old daughter, work full-time, and go to school full-time. Things just never worked out with my daughter's father, and ever since I've been back to school, I haven't had the energy to even think about sex. My schedule is crazy, and I don't have much free time. When I have time off, I prefer to spend it with my daughter. I don't have the time to spend on cultivating a relationship. I really

want to finish school and get good enough grades to get into graduate school someday.

I don't miss intercourse. It's not that I don't like sex. My sex life with my daughter's father was really great, but since we split up, I've been burned out on the idea of starting a new relationship.

I masturbate a couple of times a week and prefer to deal with my sexual needs that way. I can see this changing someday, but I'm not looking for a relationship now.

Health Hint

10 Good Reasons for Choosing Abstinence

Abstinence has gotten a bad rap over the years. It's almost politically incorrect to talk about abstaining from sexual intercourse (and penetrative sex, if you're a lesbian). Here are 10 good reasons to choose abstinence:

1. To retain your virginity for someone special.

2. To get to know your partner better (you want to become more comfortable with your partner and come to trust him or her).

3. To ascertain your partner's STD/HIV status (you'd rather wait to have intercourse but might consider other safer-sex options).

4. To wait to be in the mood (you'd rather be doing something else).

5. If you're heterosexual, to avoid pregnancy if neither of you has contraception (you might consider a low-risk sexual outlet other than intercourse).

6. To find a suitable partner (sure you've had offers, but nobody really turns you on).

7. To recuperate from an illness or surgery (you're not feeling very sexy or are feeling downright lousy).

8. To get a medical opinion on unusual genital symptoms (these might represent an STD).

9. To get some sleep (you're tired and need sleep, not sex).

10. To adhere to your personal moral code (regarding premarital, extramarital, or other sexual taboos that make up your personal set of ethics).

What are other good reasons for abstaining from sexual intercourse at a given time?

need all of their energy for school or work, especially if they are beginning a new career or starting school. They don't want to divert time and energy from these areas.

The generic definition of **abstinence** is self-restraint or self-denial. Sexual abstinence, therefore, refers to self-restraint or self-denial of sexual activities. Many people assume that abstinence means denial of all forms of sexual behavior. Actually, one can choose to abstain from unprotected intercourse but not other forms of sexual behavior.

Abstinence usually is not discussed as a lifelong spiritual or religious commitment. It is more situational; a person can abstain for a day, a week, a month, a semester, and so on. It doesn't have to be an all-or-nothing proposition. Most of us have voluntarily chosen to abstain from sexual intercourse at various times during our lives. Once abstinence is viewed as a situational choice and not a lifetime commitment, it becomes easier to accept and understand as a viable sexual option. We also believe that, although abstinence is a valid option for people, it is not the only option.

Abstinence
self-restraint or self-denial, as in not engaging in sexual activity

Abstinence is situational in nature.

Nonpenetrative Sexual Activity

Nonpenetrative sexual activities offer a wide variety of pleasurable behaviors that can be carried out to the point of orgasm and involve little risk of pregnancy or disease. This activity has been called "outercourse" and includes options ranging from kissing and hugging to using sex toys. To us, nonpenetrative sexual activity includes any sexual behaviors that do not involve genital-to-genital or mouth-to-genital sexual contact.

Kissing

Kissing can provide intense sensual and sexual delight. The sucking, licking and rubbing, and tongue probing associated with kissing is pleasurable and carries no risk for pregnancy. Volumes have been written about kissing.

As we age, we seem to become more genitally focused and lose some of our interest in kissing. Kissing becomes an ancillary activity associated with the real objective — orgasm — rather than a satisfying activity in and of itself.

Hugging/Rubbing

Kissing is usually associated with hugging and rubbing. These activities, once commonly called petting, can take on new meaning if we can visualize them as viable forms of sexual expression. Hugging and rubbing, even with one's clothes on, can be intensely pleasurable and can be carried to the point of orgasm with no risk of pregnancy or disease. These activities also can serve as a prelude to other noninsertive forms of sexual activity such as masturbation and use of sex toys. A delightful way to use rubbing as a safe sexual release is to rub against your partner to the point of orgasm. Typically this is done with both partners fully clothed. You rub your penis or

PERSPECTIVES

Variations on Kissing

We asked our students to talk about kissing — their likes, dislikes, the role it plays in their relationships. Here's what they had to say:

Marcia (sophomore, age 19): "I love kissing. I especially like long, deep, french-kissing with my boyfriend. I really enjoy deep tongue-thrusting, you know, like when he tries to run his tongue all the way down my throat — what a turn-on."

Mary (freshman, age 18): "I like gentle kissing. I like lighter pressure — soft pecks, nuzzles, gentle tongue-probing. I hate it when a guy tries to ram his tongue down my throat. It's disgusting. Oh, and I hate hickeys. Why do some guys feel compelled to leave their mark on my neck? I never go out with a guy again if he tries to lay a hickey on me. How gross."

John (junior, age 20): "I like kissing. It's kind of like a game, tongues darting back and forth, in and out. There's almost a rhythm or method to kissing. I

like to work my tongue around my girlfriend's whole mouth."

Sonja (junior, 20): "I personally think french-kissing is overrated. I prefer lip action. I like to nip and suck, just using my lips. I like it when my boyfriend nibbles on my lips and when we just use the tips of our tongues around our lips and the outer parts of our mouths. I find this kind of darting tongue action preferable to all of that deep tongue-thrusting. That makes me gag."

Glen (returning senior, 41): "At this point in my life, I find that my wife and I are more gentle in our kissing. We still get into all the deep french-kissing every once in a while, but most of our kissing is more affectionate than passionate. Don't get me wrong — our sex is great and intercourse is usually pretty passionate. We just seem to kiss more as an expression of love and affection. Kissing during sex is less frequent than when we were in our 20s."

Kissing is an almost universal form of sexual expression.

vulva against your partner's groin, leg, arm (or another convenient body part) to the point of orgasm.

You control the pressure, rhythm, and intensity. Although students sometimes call this "dry-humping," it doesn't have to be either. You can enhance your enjoyment by doing it with your clothes off and adding oil or lotion to the equation. Try spreading lotion on your partner's breasts or chest. Take your clothes off, lie on your back, and let your partner rub your penis or vulva back and forth and up and down between her breasts or his chest until you come. Try spreading some lotion or oil on your partner's buttocks and small of his or her back. Straddle the backside and ride back and forth to the point of orgasm. If this seems too messy, try rubbing your penis or vulva through your partner's hair and against his or her head and neck. You can use hugging and rubbing in many ways to enjoy a highly erotic sexual episode without fear of disease or pregnancy.

Massage

Nongenital massage is one of the greatest sensual delights you can share with your partner. Massage can be a stand-alone sensual activity or be part of activities culminating with orgasm. Sex therapists often prescribe nongenital massage for clients as a way to help them reestablish touching each other's bodies again. Massage allows us to explore every nook and cranny of our partner's bodies in a relaxed, sensual way.

Separating our sensuality from our sexuality is sometimes difficult when it comes to massage. The only time many of us touch others in such an intimate way is when we are being sexual. Massage is not an inherently sexual activity. It *is* sensual, though. Kneading, stroking, and manipulating another person's flesh requires us to be in tune with the sensation of touch. We must be acutely aware of pressure and motion when we give a massage. Also, many of the massage oils available are scented and bring into play our sense of smell. Visually, the sight of exposed flesh has the potential for arousal.

The ability to enjoy giving and getting a massage and viewing these as sensual delights that don't have to lead to sexual activity may take time. Of course, giving a massage with the intent to sexually arouse your partner is a natural way to initiate erotic activities if that is the intention. Being able to give and receive sensual pleasure without sexual release is excellent training in becoming a compassionate lover.

Giving a massage is a natural behavior. Instinctively, we believe that if it feels good to us, it will feel good to the person we are massaging. Usually, giving a massage is easier if you use some form of lubricating oil. Some people prefer powder to reduce friction, and they like the sensation of powder. Most people, however, prefer oil. Oil should be warm or at room temperature. Cold oil on the skin can get the massage off to a bad start. The oil should sit at room temperature or be warmed in the container under hot water in the sink before starting. The oil should be poured into the hands and rubbed onto the body rather than squirted directly onto the person's skin.[3]

Have you ever had a massage? If so, how would you describe it? If you have not, how do you think massage would affect you?
Are sensuality and sexuality necessarily related? Could you separate the two?

Most important in giving a massage is to take your time.

Massage should be done with sufficient room to get completely around the person without having to lean on or jump over him or her. When straddling a person, you should not sit directly on him or her. You should be able to position yourself over the person so you can apply firm pressure during some strokes. A massage table or high bed is ideal because it allows you to stand while giving a massage. You also could kneel next to the person receiving the massage. It allows the person to lie comfortably with the face down, facilitating easy access to the neck, shoulders, and head. A professional table isn't necessary though. You could place a pillow under the person's head for support and have him or her rest the head gently to the side.

Most important in giving a massage is to take your time. The other person will sense if you feel obligated to do this and are rushing through it. Giving a massage is an act of kindness and must be done slowly, lovingly, with no expectations for getting anything in return.

Several types of strokes can be used in giving a massage. All of them require maintaining contact with the partner as much as possible while moving from one body part and stroke to the next. The strokes should merge to form a sense of continuous motion with the muscles. A visual image of the muscular system may help. Figure 8.1 shows the human skeletal muscular system.

The strokes should be rhythmic and symmetrical and will get better with practice. The whole hand should be used to effectively master all of

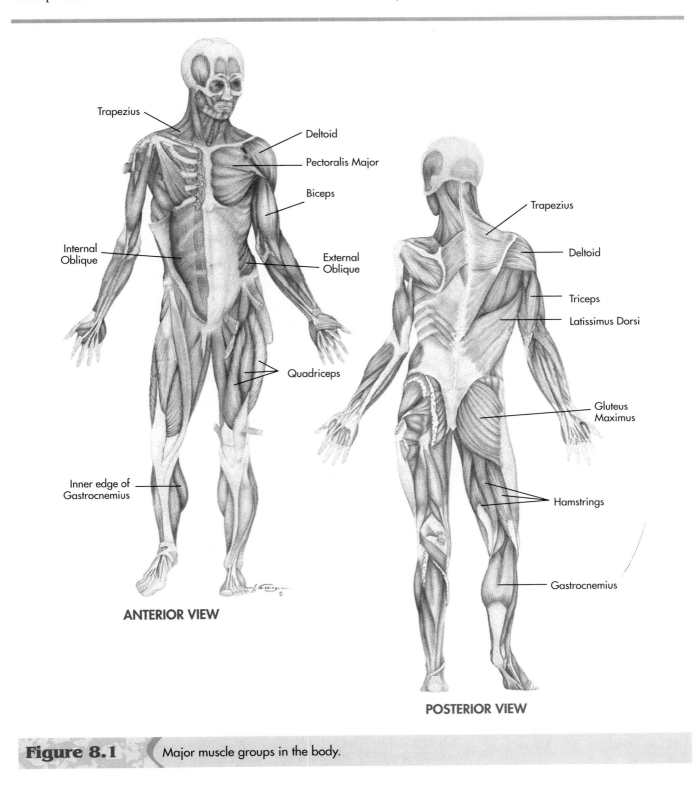

Trapezius

Deltoid

Pectoralis Major

Biceps

Internal Oblique

External Oblique

Quadriceps

Inner edge of Gastrocnemius

ANTERIOR VIEW

Trapezius

Deltoid

Triceps

Latissimus Dorsi

Gluteus Maximus

Hamstrings

Gastrocnemius

POSTERIOR VIEW

Figure 8.1   Major muscle groups in the body.

Case Study

Chrissy & Ken: Sensual Massage

Chrissy and Ken are seniors. They have been dating and having sex for 2 years and are planning to get engaged sometime before graduation in June. They have worked massage into their sexual lifestyle.

Chrissy: Ken and I got into massage after a vacation we took last year. The hotel we stayed in had a massage service and we each took advantage of it. It was a great stress and tension remover.

Ken: Yeah, after the massage we'd feel relaxed and contented. It seemed natural to want to extend it and not stop at the genitals. The next day I tried some of the massage strokes they used at the spa but finished up by massaging Chrissy's breasts and vulva.

Chrissy: It was very erotic. I felt so pampered. Ken was really patient. I didn't feel rushed or that the purpose of the massage was to get me excited for sex.

Ken: That's what I was worried about. We got into massage as a way to relax and enjoy the sensual part of it. I didn't want Chrissy to think the only time she'd get a massage was when I wanted to have sex.

Chrissy: We talk about what our needs are. If we want just a massage, we know this going into it, and that's what we do. If we're feeling sexy, we sometimes use massage to feel more sensual and get excited. We spend a lot of time massaging each other's erogenous zones.

Ken: I really get excited when Chrissy uses oil to massage my toes. I also love it when she uses long, slow strokes up my inner thighs and gently kneads the skin there.

Chrissy: I really go wild when Ken uses small, circular strokes around my temples or kneads the base of my skull. I start to get wet when he spends a few minutes doing that.

the strokes. The fingers, palm, heel, and fist all come into play. The types of strokes are as follows.[4]

1. *Kneading.* In kneading, you grasp the flesh with all four fingers of both hands and rotate your thumbs in opposite directions. Kneading works beautifully with the muscles of the arms, legs, hands, feet, back, and shoulders. You can practice kneading by making homemade bread and working on the dough. Figure 8.2 illustrates kneading the back.

2. *Pressing.* Pressing involves pushing against the body with the heel of the hand. For extra pressure you can use your other hand to apply pressure against the heel of the hand involved in the pressing. Pressing can be used in long strokes or in a circular motion and is effective with thicker muscles such as those in the back.

3. *Stroking.* Stroking is done with the fingertips, either pushing away from you in circles or drawing toward you. Stroking also can employ all five fingers gently drawing flesh toward you. Stroking is good with the scalp, neck, and inner thighs and also works well as a long continuous motion along the back, torso, arms, and legs.

4. *Pulling.* Pulling is similar to stroking toward you except that it involves more pressure. Whereas stroking movements glide over the skin, pulling involves grabbing hold and gently tugging. You can pull with just your fingers or with an entire hand, or both hands. Pulling is well suited for the head, hands, fingers, toes, feet, arms, and legs.

5. *Lifting.* In some cases, actually lifting a part of the body, such as the head, torso, or leg, and supporting it in your hands is relaxing. When lifting, the hands are cupped to cradle the part being elevated.

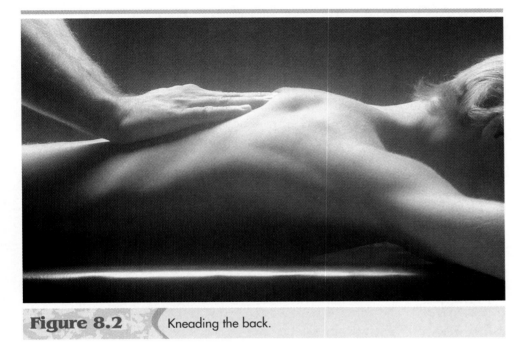

Figure 8.2 　 Kneading the back.

Health Hint

Giving a Massage

You can give full-body or partial massages. Sometimes just a back massage or a foot massage will do the trick. At other times, a full body massage, complete with scented candles, is preferred. When giving a full body massage:

◗ Start anywhere. Wherever you start, move in the direction toward the heart to facilitate venous blood flow.

◗ Start with the feet, work up to the head, and finish at the hands. Or work in the reverse order. Or start at the abdomen, as it is the center of the body and, when stressed, is the place where blood pools. Cover the entire body in a systematic

way. Don't jump around from feet to head to toes. Finish a part thoroughly, then move on to the next.

◗ Massage both hands/arms or feet/legs before moving to the next body part.

◗ After a massage, allow the person some quiet time to savor the results — and maybe even offer to reciprocate.

Massage can be a prelude to other forms of sexual activity. In sensual massage, the focus shifts to providing more direct contact with the genitals and other erogenous zones.

6. *Pounding*. Making a fist and gently pounding a body part can release accumulated tension. Pounding isn't for everyone or every body part. It is most effective on the back.

Masturbation

Masturbation
the manual stimulation of the genitals to provide sexual pleasure

One of the first activities linking our sensuality to sexual behavior is **masturbation**. Masturbation usually evolves out of sensual exploration of our own body. We notice that it feels good when we unintentionally or intentionally rub (or rub up against) our genitals. In her book, *Liberating Masturbation*, feminist writer, artist, and sex educator Betty Dodson describes masturbation as "our primary sex life, our sexual base."[5] According to Dodson, all other forms of sexual expression are a result of socialization. The expression of healthy sexual relationships between individuals begins with self-exploration of sensual and sexual pleasure from the time of birth.

As described in Chapter 5, most of us learn the joy and security of cuddling, hugging, and warm, caring touch early in our lives, from contact with our parents and other caregivers. Although our earliest bonding experiences with our mother and father are not sexual in nature, they provide a sensual connection that leads to healthy sexuality.

Besides laying the foundation for developing trust and self-esteem, physical bonding with, and nurturing by, parents sets the stage for recognition and acceptance of our own body as a potential source of pleasure. Solitary sexual behavior, or masturbation, provides our first, and usually lifelong, source of sexual pleasure. Too many of us, however, associate masturbation with sinful, inappropriate behavior.

Masturbation usually is the first source of sexual pleasure.

Masturbation can be a solitary sexual behavior, or can be enjoyed with a partner. As a solitary behavior, masturbation may or may not be accompanied by sexual fantasy and other autoerotic activity. Couples can masturbate each other simultaneously, take turns pleasing each other, or masturbate themselves simultaneously.

Male Techniques In her study of male sexuality, Shere Hite reported the following male masturbatory techniques in order of preference: (1) stimulating the penis by hand, (2) lying down on the stomach rubbing against a bed, and (3) with water in the shower.[6]

Few men choose to masturbate using sex toys such as vibrators, dildos, plastic sleeves, penile pumps, and inflatable dolls, although these devices are readily available. Though still relatively uncommon, proponents of these sex toys claim that they can enhance sexual pleasure, provide a change of pace from routine masturbatory practices, and add variety to safe-sex options.

Masters and Johnson found that many men masturbate by rubbing, stroking, or pumping the shaft of the penis with one hand.[7] The tempo of movement usually builds gradually in response to the increase in arousal. Slow, deliberate touch gradually gives way to more forceful, rapid movements, often accompanied by increases in pressure and tension. A small percentage of men studied spend time stimulating the frenulum on the underside of the glans of the penis.

Uncircumcised men seem to spend more time stimulating the glans and frenulum through pulling the foreskin back and forth. Ejaculation varies more, some men preferring to slow down and relax their grip and others desiring to increase pressure, squeezing out the last drops of semen. Figure 8.3 illustrates male masturbation.

Because the male penis is not lubricated, and masturbation usually involves a build-up of heat and friction, most men use some form of lubrication while masturbating. Body lotion and baby oil are two commonly used lubricants.

Female Techniques Masters and Johnson noted that women exhibit much greater variation in masturbatory behavior. Even when women had a similar style of stimulation, the tempo, timing, and approach to masturbation varied. The most common form of female masturbation is to stimulate the clitoris, labia, and mons by hand through stroking, pulling, or rubbing.[8]

Most women prefer to masturbate while lying on the back. A smaller percentage chooses to sit or stand while stimulating the genitalia. Between 5% and 10% of women prefer to masturbate while lying on their stomach, either placing a hand between their legs to stimulate the clitoris or rubbing the vulva against a pillow or some other object.[9] Figure 8.4 illustrates female masturbation.

Masters and Johnson reported the following patterns of masturbatory behavior in order of preference: (1) manually stimulating the vulva, (2) using a vibrator to stimulate the clitoris/vulva, (3) inserting something into the vagina, (4) rubbing up against an object, (5) pressing the thighs together, (6) using water massage, and (7) all other methods. About half of the younger

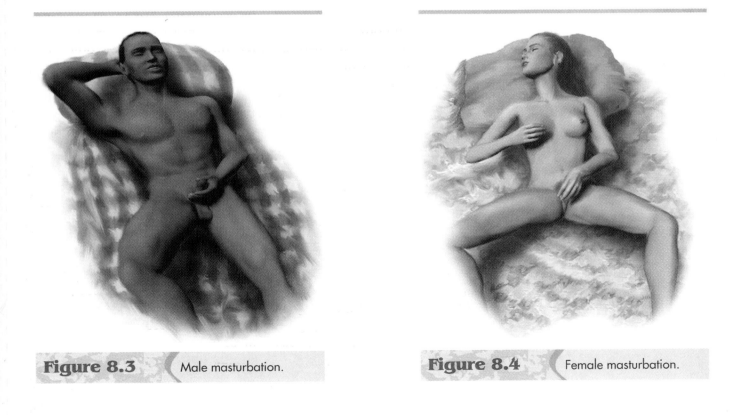

Figure 8.3 ⟨ Male masturbation.

Figure 8.4 ⟨ Female masturbation.

women reported using sex toys (vibrators, dildos, or other devices) to masturbate, choosing either to insert these or to use them to apply external vibration. A smaller percentage reports using these devices in a similar fashion to stimulate the anus during masturbation. The variety and complexity has increased markedly as more women (and their partners) express interest in these products.

Health Aspects of Masturbation Early critics of masturbation posed pseudo-scientific charges that masturbation was neither "healthy" nor "normal." In fact, masturbation has no adverse health consequences. It does not cause any physical problems. It carries no risk for any physical or psychological illness. Most safe-sex educators encourage their students to masturbate to relieve sexual tension or to enjoy an orgasm whenever they want one. It is also an excellent way to learn what feels good and how their own body responds.

From a physiological perspective, a person cannot masturbate to excess. It is a self-limiting behavior; we ultimately lose our interest in it. As long as people follow basic hygienic precautions (clean hands, toys, and so on) and have adequate lubrication, they can masturbate as often as they want to. Rather than being a source of problems, masturbation is a healthy outlet for sexual desire, can reduce risk for sexually transmitted diseases in people who don't have safe sexual partners, and is an alternative to having sex with prostitutes or anonymous partners.

> *Rather than being a problem, masturbation is a healthy outlet to satisfy sexual desire.*

Patterns of Masturbatory Behavior Masturbation is a form of autoerotic behavior. **Autoeroticism** is the dimension of the sex life defined by sexual desire or gratification, or both, experienced by a person without the direct participation of another.[10] Even though autoerotic activities lack a sex partner, sexual fantasies always include the imaginary presence of another person. In addition, autoerotic activity follows a specific social script appropriate to the individual, even if he or she never wishes to act out the fantasy.

Autoerotic activities differ from partnered activities because they do not require coordination with another person, can avoid many of the reality-based features of sex with a partner, and are limited only by the person's imagination. A surprising finding of Laumann et al. was the lack of imagination and repetitiveness of pornographic and fantasy themes. Table 8.1 gives the most common autoerotic themes that accompany masturbation. These common themes permeate various autoerotic media (adult books and magazines, films, CD Roms, videos, telephone and computer sex) and behaviors (use of sex toys, vibrators, dildos). Table 8.2 illustrates the use of autoerotic materials by gender.

Autoeroticism
the dimension of the sex life defined by sexual desire and/or gratification experienced by a person without the direct participation of another

Table 8.1	Common Autoerotic Themes		
Fantasy Content		**% Men**	**% Women**
Intercourse with loved one		75	70
Intercourse with stranger		47	21
Sex with more than one person of the other sex		33	18
Sexual activities that would not be done in reality		19	28
Forcing someone to have sex		13	3
Being forced to have sex		10	19
Homosexual activity		7	11

Source: *Sexual Behavior in the 1970s*, by Morton Hunt (Chicago: Playboy Press, 1974).

Table 8.2 ❭ Autoerotic Activity by Gender

	% Distributions	
	Men	Women
Thinking about sex		
More frequently	54	19
Less frequently	43	67
Never or rarely	4	14
Autoerotic material		
X-rated movies or videos	23	11
Go to a club that has nude or seminude dancers	22	4
Sexually explicit books or magazines	16	4
Vibrators or dildos	2	2
Other sex toys	1	2
Sex phone numbers	1	0
Any of the above	41	16

Note: *Rarely* or *never* refers to "less than once a month" or "never"; *less frequently* refers to "a few times a month" to "a few times a week"; *more frequently* refers to "every day" or "several times a day" *Fantasy* is measured by the frequency with which the respondent reported thinking about sex.

Source: *The Social Organization of Sexuality: Sexual Practices in the United States,* by E.O. Laumann, J.H. Gagnon, R.T. Michael, and S. Michaels. © University of Chicago Press. Reprinted with permission.

Case Study

Masturbation: Student Reports

Although masturbation is a generally accepted form of sexual expression for our students, their feelings about it vary considerable. Some are completely accepting and open about their masturbatory behavior. Others still feel guilty masturbating and hide their behavior from their partners, and friends. Here are a few reports from our students concerning masturbation:

Tom (freshman, age 18): I would say I masturbate once or twice a week. I'm a little nervous masturbating in my room because I can't really relax, having a roommate. I'm never sure when he's going to walk in. When I go home on weekends I enjoy it more because I can lock my door, look at my magazines, and "get off" in private. My parents have never said anything, but I think they know I do it.

Susan (senior, age 21): I masturbate a couple of times a month, usually when I'm stressed out. I used to feel a little guilty about it, but I've found I can deal with things a lot better if I can get rid of my tension.

Usually my boyfriend and I make love when we see each other on the weekend, but sometimes he's away on business and we miss a week. I'll usually go home and take a nice bath, relax, and make myself come. My parents were very strict when I was growing up, and masturbation was a definite no. I don't think they could imagine that I do it, and I guess that's why I still feel guilty about it.

Ed (senior, age 25): I masturbate about two times a week. Sometimes my fiancee and I will watch x-rated films and then masturbate each other. She'll do me, and then I do her. Other times, if either one of us isn't horny, we'll masturbate the other to orgasm. Sometimes we won't even have intercourse. We masturbate each other and finish off with oral sex. I never have had any inhibitions about masturbation. My parents always told me it was normal and okay as long as I keep it private. I don't view it as second best to intercourse, just different.

Even though the content of <u>sex fantasies is similar for men and women,</u> <u>the most important finding in this area by Laumann et al. is the great dis-</u> <u>parity in levels of autoerotic activity between men and women. Men are</u> <u>much more likely to engage in autoerotic activities and to associate masturba-</u> <u>tion with these activities.</u> Laumann et al. attribute this to the continuing social

Health Hint

Safe Fantasy

Sexual fantasy serves several important functions. They help us expand our sexual scripts. They help us to explore and expand our sexual repertoire. Sexual fantasies are a healthy sexual outlet. Coupled with masturbation, they provide a safe, exciting release of sexual tension. Sexual fantasy provides a "practice arena" to work through sexual scripts and encounters that we eventually may want to enact in real life. This safe practice carries none of the interpersonal or health risks of an actual encounter. Fantasies allow us to experience activities that turn us on but are not things we want to experience in real life. Fantasies do not necessarily represent what we really want in reality.

Sometimes, however, the lure of living out our sexual fantasies is strong. When is turning a fantasy into a reality a good idea? The following criteria may help you determine when you may appropriately cross that line.

1. the nature of the fantasy
2. the strength of the turn-on
3. the social context of the fantasy
4. the nature of your partner(s)
5. your level of control over the specific situation
6. whether the person is willing to lose the fantasy (sometimes living out a fantasy makes it lose its fantasy appeal).

The nature of the fantasy refers to how unusual, bizarre, or dangerous the fantasy is. The more bizarre or dangerous the fantasy, the more cautious you should be about wanting to turn it into a reality. If you can control for some of the other variables (items 3, 4, and 5) and safety, you might want to act it out. If you can't control these variables, you're probably better off leaving it as a fantasy.

The strength of the arousal exerts a powerful influence on whether to act out the fantasy. If a strong desire isn't there, you may not want to turn it into reality at this time.

The social context of the fantasy refers to the setting in which the fantasy plays out. For example, many people are turned on by the fantasy of having sex in a public place. Public places range from semi-deserted beaches (where the likelihood of discovery is minimal) to the elevator at your favorite hotel (where the chance of discovery is high). Combining the risk of exposure with the consequences of being discovered (being arrested, losing your job, public stature, and the like) will help you evaluate the social context of acting out the fantasy. Some fantasies are based on giving up control. The turn-on with dominance and submission lies in being vulnerable and letting someone have control over you. Other fantasies are more amenable to control. The greater the control, the safer is the fantasy. In general, the less control you have in the situation, the greater is your need to act out the fantasy with a trusting partner in a familiar, safe environment.

The last warning concerns losing the turn-on after you act it out. Some sexual experiences are better left as fantasies. They provide a strong turn-on that is satisfying. When you turn this into reality, however, you run the risk that the reality won't be as exciting as the fantasy. When this happens, the fantasy often loses its appeal and its ability to turn you on.

The nature of your partner(s) will help you evaluate the safety and confidentiality of acting out your fantasy. Asking your wife to tie you to the bedpost and then acting out a dominatrix scenario in the safety of your own bedroom is vastly different from going downtown to Mistress Helga's illegal place and allowing her to put manacles on you. Fantasies acted out with a well-known partner whom you can trust are much safer than those with strangers and prostitutes.

Source: *The Social Organization of Human Sexuality: Sexual Practices in the United States*, by E.O. Laumann, J.H. Gagnon, R.T. Michael, and S. Michael (Chicago: University of Chicago Press, 1994).

context of masturbation among men. Masturbation is a socially acceptable concept among adolescent males and almost completely absent in the social context of adolescent females.

A final finding of Laumann et al. concerning autoerotic activity is the lack of association between autoerotic behavior and not having a primary sex partner. In fact, higher levels of autoerotic activity were associated with higher levels of partnered sexual activity. Rather than being a way to compensate for the lack of a sex partner, autoerotic activity seems to be a source of additional sexual pleasure. Laumann et al. found that individuals with higher levels of autoerotic activity were more likely than those with lower levels to engage in a broader range of sexual activities. In a sense, they have a much more elaborate set of sexual scripts. The development of sexual scripts or scenarios is influenced by a variety of sources of information, including autoerotic activities.

Autoeroticism is highly correlated with an increased incidence of techniques such as fellatio, cunnilingus, and anal intercourse.[11] Men and women who reported the highest levels of autoerotic behavior were more likely to engage in these behaviors than their peers who had lower levels of autoerotic activity.

Sexual Intercourse

Many people think that being a good lover means being particularly adept at sexual intercourse. Actually, being a good lover means having certain skills (knowing how to arouse your partner, using various sexual behaviors, and so on), as well as having good psychosocial skills (knowing how to communicate, when to initiate, and the like). In this section we will focus on a variety of intercourse positions.

Vaginal Intercourse

Vaginal intercourse, also known as **coitus,** is one of the most common forms of sexual activity. Vaginal intercourse is primarily a heterosexual activity, although sexual paraphernalia (artificial penises, harnesses, and the like) are available for lesbian women to practice this activity if they desire. The three starting points for vaginal intercourse are: face to face, side by side, and rear entry. We call these starting points rather than positions because each starting point offers a limitless array of positions depending upon how you place the rest of your body (arms, legs, torso, and so on).

Coitus
vaginal intercourse

Face-to-Face Face-to-face positions have two variations: man on top and woman on top.

Man on Top. The man-on-top position, illustrated in Figure 8.5, is also known as the "missionary position." It is the most commonly used intercourse position in the United States. In this position, the partners stimulate each other until they are sufficiently aroused. The man then moves on top of the woman. Either partner spreads the female's vaginal lips and inserts the penis into the vagina. The man supports his weight on his elbows, hands, knees, or across his partner's entire body as his penis moves in the vagina.

Figure 8.5　Man-on-top.

The most typical penile movements involve thrusting in and out as the female either remains still or moves her hips in concert with her partner's thrusting. These motions provide direct sexual stimulation of the male's penile nerve endings (on the shaft, glans, and corona). The woman's clitoris usually is stimulated as the clitoral hood (top of the labia minora) pulls back and forth over it or the man's pubic area rubs against it. The vagina is stimulated as the penis slides in and out. The deeper recesses of the vagina (cervical area) may or may not be stimulated depending upon the depth of the strokes and the positions.

Being a good lover involves physical and psychosocial skills.

An option to thrusting in and out is a circular motion, known as grinding, which involves more pubis-to-pubis contact and stimulates the female's clitoris differently. This provides more direct and intense stimulation of the clitoris and the base of the man's penis and can be done even if the man has ejaculated. If he hasn't withdrawn the penis before it has become limp, he can continue stimulating his partner with the circular motion. Sometimes this can go on through his refractory period, and he can achieve another erection without removing his penis. This allows his partner to be stimulated and have additional orgasms even though he has climaxed. Many men find this type of stimulation enjoyable even though they have a limp penis and already have had an orgasm.

Variations of this starting point involve changing the position of the legs and arms. The woman on the bottom can experience a variety of different sensations and depths of penetration by wrapping her legs around the partner's ankles, legs, or waist. Or she can throw her legs over her partner's shoulders as he thrusts in and out, which affords the deepest penetration.

One of the advantages of this position is that it allows the partners to look into each other's eyes and communicate. It also allows the partners to rub and caress each other's chest and shoulders. Further, it allows use of the hands to enhance stimulation by touching or rubbing the partner's genitals during intercourse.

The woman may enjoy stretching her arms over her head, arching her back. This allows her partner better access to caress the breasts and nipples. She may enjoy having the partner pin her arms back over her head. This mild form of domination/submission allows her to "lose control" in a safe way. Individuals should participate in domination/submission only with someone they trust and must understand that "no means no" if either partner wants the activity to stop.

Safe domination and submission involves partners who know each other very well and trust each other completely.

Woman on Top. The woman-on-top position, shown in Figure 8.6a allows women greater control in the depth, pace, and motion of penile thrusting. It allows the woman the greatest control in clitoral stimulation and is the easiest intercourse position for manual clitoral stimulation. Orgasm rates are better for this position than any other. This position is also good for helping male partners control premature ejaculation. The woman can get to this position in two ways: Start with the man on top and roll over into this position or start with the man on his back and move on top. In the latter case, the partners must have enough room on the bed so they won't find themselves rolling off the bed and onto the floor.

When starting with the man on his back, the woman kneels over him with one knee on either side of his legs. Either partner can part the vaginal lips as the woman lowers herself onto the erect penis, guiding it in with a free hand.

With the penis inside, the woman can rock or thrust her hips or move them in a circular fashion. The rocking and thrusting motions allow maximum penile penetration, whereas the circular grinding motion stimulates the clitoris more directly. Each of these three creates entirely different sensations.

The man can either be passive and allow the woman to control all movements or move with her, synchronizing his motion with hers. The man also can initiate thrusting and grinding if the woman becomes tired or wants him to.

In this position the woman also has more freedom to use her hands in ways similar to those of the man-on-top position. From this position she can caress and manipulate either her partner or herself. One option that the woman-on-top position offers is the ability to rotate her torso, while still being penetrated by her partner's penis, so that her back faces him. In this position she can lean forward or sit back and achieve different depths of penetration and sensations. In this position her partner can fondle her buttocks and back while maintaining penetration.

One final, interesting variation of the woman-on-top position is to move from kneeling or lying on her partner to actually sitting on him (Figure 8.6b). Once she is sitting on him, he can sit up with her on top of him. By sitting on her partner, the woman-on-top position affords maximum

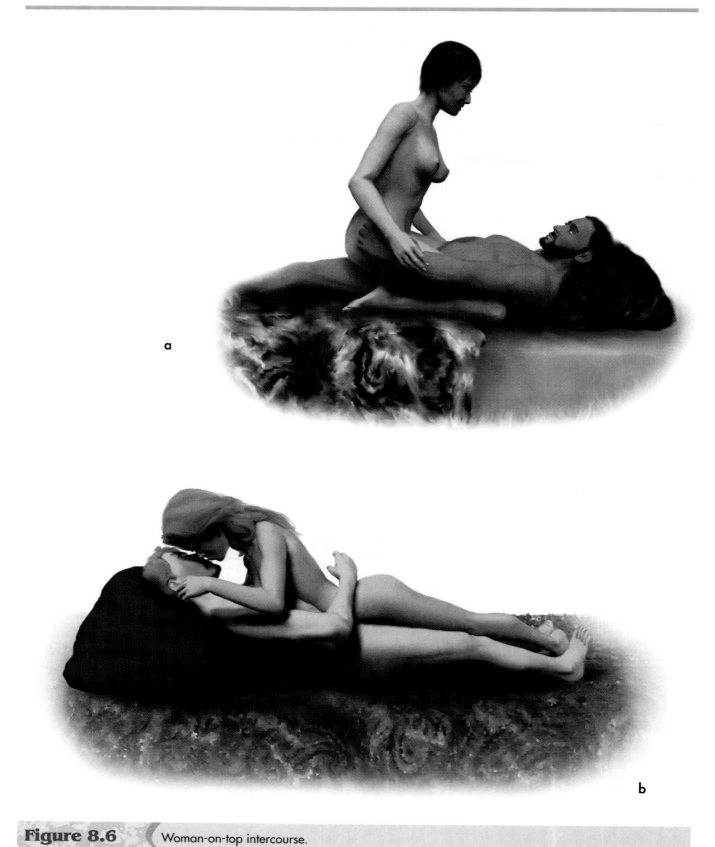

a

b

Figure 8.6   Woman-on-top intercourse.

penetration and intimacy as the couple can embrace, kiss, and talk. A common motion used in the sitting position is to gently rock back and forth, similar to being on a rocking horse, as the man's penis slides in and out.

Rear Entry The rear-entry starting point (Figure 8.7) is also known as "doggie style" because it is the way in which dogs and most other animals have intercourse. In rear-entry positions the man enters the woman's vagina from behind. This usually is accomplished with the woman kneeling on her hands and knees and the man kneeling behind her, either between or straddling her legs. Either partner parts the vaginal lips and guides the penis in.

This position creates deep vaginal penetration but little direct clitoral stimulation. For this reason, either the man or the woman stimulates the clitoris manually. This position also offers stimulation of the anus and perineum through pressure and friction from the man's pubis rubbing or grinding against it. Once engaged, the woman can lower her head and raise her hips higher to achieve maximum penetration.

Two other rear-entry position variations are: (1) The couple can lie down with the man on top of the woman, or (2) they can lie on their sides. The latter is commonly known as the "spoon" position. One disadvantage of this position is that the partners do not face each other, which makes communication and kissing more difficult.

Figure 8.7   Rear-entry intercourse.

Side to Side The side-to-side vaginal intercourse can involve face-to-face positioning (Figure 8.8) or rear-entry positioning. Because neither partner is bearing the full weight of the other, the side-to-side position is ideal for leisurely lovemaking or the rest period between more vigorous sessions. The easiest way to get into the side-to-side position is by rolling into it from the man-on-top or woman-on-top or the rear-entry position.

Besides being a comfortable position for leisurely lovemaking, the side-to-side variation has many advantages. It also is good for obese people, as it minimizes weight-bearing. The rear-entry variation (Figure 8.9) is good for pregnant women whose developing fetus and protruding abdomen make the man-on-top position impossible. The side-to-side position also facilitates good communication and kissing while leaving the hands free for hugging and forms of manual stimulation.

Figure 8.8   Side to side intercourse (facing).

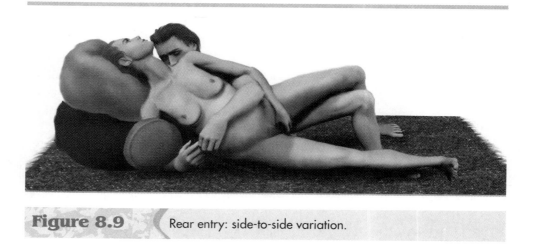

Figure 8.9   Rear entry: side-to-side variation.

Case Study

Delores: Sex in Pregnancy

Delores is 26 years old and the mother of a 6-month-old son, Greg. Delores describes her sexual experiences during her pregnancy.

Before I got pregnant, I was very concerned about the effects it would have on my sex life with my husband, Joe. We were married for three years and had a very satisfying sex life. I was worried about that changing. I've always liked sex, and I've kept in shape through running and lifting weights. I was concerned about gaining weight and my body changing shape. But I decided that I wouldn't limit my weight gain and make the baby suffer.

During the first trimester, my sex drive dropped a lot. I wasn't as horny as I normally was, and I had terrible morning sickness. Actually, I had morning, afternoon, and evening sickness and could hardly keep any food down. Other than that, though, nothing much changed. The frequency of sex dropped in half, but the kinds of things we did — positions — didn't change.

During the second trimester my morning sickness disappeared and I felt much better. I had put on some weight, but it really didn't affect our intercourse. I was concerned about bouncing around too much and things like rolling off the bed, but for the most part we didn't change our behaviors. The good news was that my sex drive returned to normal.

During the third trimester things changed again. I had put on over 20 pounds and had a big belly. I was really concerned about deep penetration. I worried that it might hurt the baby, but my doctor reassured me that everything would be okay. I didn't have much energy, so we made love less often. We couldn't use any man- or woman-on-top positions. I've always liked the woman-on-top position with me sitting on my husband's lap, and I had to give that up, too.

I found that the only position we could use was the spoon [side-by-side] position. That allowed us to have full-body contact without putting pressure on my belly. It also allowed my husband to massage my breasts and belly. I had no desire for him to perform oral sex on me, but sometimes I liked to satisfy him that way, particularly on those days when I didn't have much energy. Overall, I think our sex life survived my pregnancy very well.

Anal Intercourse

In anal intercourse a man inserts his penis into his partner's rectum. Heterosexual and homosexual couples both practice anal intercourse. Like vaginal intercourse, anal intercourse can take place from the three starting points: side-to-side, rear-entry, or face-to-face. The advantages and disadvantages associated with these starting points for vaginal intercourse are similar for anal intercourse. Rear entry is the most commonly used starting point for anal intercourse, although anal penetration can be accomplished through all of the positions previously described.

Oral Sex

Oral sex, also known as oral-genital sex, mouth-genital sex, giving head, and going down, is the stimulation of the partner's genitals with the lips, mouth, tongue, and face. The three main types of oral sex are fellatio (mouth-to-penis contact), cunnilingus (mouth-to-vulva contact), and anilingus (mouth-to-anus contact). All three are common forms of sexual expression for straight, gay, and bisexual people.

Fellatio
licking and sucking the penis

Fellatio Also known as a "blow job," **fellatio** involves licking and sucking a man's penis. The term is derived from the Latin word *fellare*, which means "to suck." During fellatio, the partner begins by licking and sucking the flaccid penis while holding it. As the penis begins to grow, a man usually enjoys having his penis move in and out of his partner's mouth. The man can accomplish this by gently thrusting his hips, driving the penis in and out of his partner's mouth. The partner can do this by moving his or her head up and down, moving the penis deeper into the mouth and then letting it slide back again.

Health Hint

Reducing Health Risks Associated with Anal Intercourse

Although the anus is richly endowed with nerve endings and has erogenous potential, it differs from other body parts and requires a few special considerations. One major difference between the tissue of the anus and rectum and that of the vagina concerns the blood vessels that supply the area. The blood vessels of the anus and rectum are very close to the surface. Any minor tearing or scraping of this tissue will result in bleeding and exposing these blood vessels to germs that could enter the bloodstream in this way.

Another major difference involves lubrication. Unlike the vagina, anal and rectal tissue does not produce natural lubrication as a product of vasocongestion. Therefore, care must be taken to adequately lubricate the anal opening and rectum with some other product. Saliva or a commercial water-based sterile lubricant are advisable. Saliva is not as slippery as most commercial products, such as K-Y jelly, but it is free and can be used at any time. Because petroleum-based products can erode the latex in condoms, these products, such as Vaseline, should not be used in conjunction with a condom.

Lubricants should be spread liberally on the penis and the anus. Gently inserting a lubricated finger into the rectum will lubricate this area and relax the sphincter that keep the anus closed. (Make sure your fingernails are trimmed!)

The lubricated penis is inserted gently and begins controlled thrusting to work the penis deeper into the rectum. Once the penis is inserted comfortably into the rectum, the couple can decide on the nature and intensity of pelvic thrusting. From this rear-entry starting point, couples can try most of the positions described in the section on vaginal intercourse.

Sex involving the anus and rectum also carries an increased risk for transmitting a range of infections ranging from hepatitis B to HIV. Organisms that are transmitted through contact with fecal matter or blood are easily transmitted through insertive or receptive anal intercourse or anilingus.

To reduce the likelihood of disease transmission and to enhance the sexual response associated with anal activities:

1. Do not engage in anilingus or anal intercourse with an anonymous (don't know at all) or a casual (don't know that well) partner.

2. Before engaging in anal activities, be sure your sex partner is HIV-negative and free of other STDs. This means getting to know your potential partner better, and sometimes being tested.

3. With disease-free partners, shower normally with soap and water before having sex to provide adequate hygiene.

4. Always use a water-based lubricant when anal penetration is involved.

5. Do not insert foreign objects (other than specially designed dildos, vibrators, and the like) into the rectum. Be careful not to let things you insert slip past the anal sphincter muscle. The object can get "lost" in the rectum and may require surgical removal.

6. If your partner's STD/HIV status is unknown, use a condom for anal intercourse. Using two condoms ("double-bagging") is recommended for maximum protection.

The sliding motion is accompanied by sucking, which can vary in intensity depending upon the man's preference. The tongue is used to lick, flick, or swirl around the penis as it moves in the mouth. Using these tongue motions to stimulate the glans and the coronal ridge (particularly the underside where the shaft meets the glans) provides maximum stimulation for the man.

These movements, if continued, usually provide enough stimulation to trigger orgasm. Many men find that a combination of oral and manual stimulation is necessary to provide enough stimulation for orgasm. The partner can grasp the penis at its base or along the shaft and pump it while simultaneously stimulating it with the mouth and tongue. Grasping the penis in one hand while licking and sucking it can also give the partner a sense of control over the depth and intensity of the man's thrusting.

When the penis is thrust into the throat, it typically initiates a gag reflex, which can be minimized by using your hand to control the depth of the partner's thrusting. To minimize this, the partner can relax the throat muscles and control the depth of thrusting by holding the penis.

Couples need to discuss their feelings about ejaculation. As discussed in Chapter 2, the male ejaculate is typically about 2½ tablespoons of fluid when he comes. The ejaculate is milky-white in color, has a slippery texture resembling egg whites, and leaves a salty aftertaste.

Most men enjoy the sensation of ejaculating into the partner's mouth. This also can be enjoyable to the partner. If the partner finds swallowing ejaculate distasteful, an alternative is fellatio to the point of orgasm, then to withdraw the penis and ejaculate outside of the partner's mouth, or to switch to some other form of sexual behavior prior to the point of orgasm.

Cunnilingus The oral stimulation of a woman's vulva through licking, sucking, and nibbling or rubbing with the face is called **cunnilingus**. It is a common sexual practice of straight, lesbian, and bisexual men and women. Although cunnilingus (from the Latin words cunnus [vulva] and lingere [to lick]) by definition refers to oral stimulation of the vulva, often the perineum and outer parts of the vagina are also stimulated during this act.

Cunnilingus typically begins as the partner kisses and licks the partner's inner thighs, abdomen, and mons area. The partner then gently parts the labia majora and uses the tongue to lick, flick, or swirl around the vaginal lips, clitoris, and introitus. Pressure can be applied by pressing the tongue against the vulva with greater force. Circular motions are often used to stimulate the vulva in a somewhat different fashion. Care must be taken not to apply too much pressure directly to the clitoris, as it is the part of the female sexual anatomy that is most richly endowed with nerve endings.

The mouth can be used to gently suck on the vaginal lips and clitoris. Gently sucking one or more lips into one's mouth can provide intense pleasure. The clitoris also can be sucked on gently. Some women find it arousing to have their partner gently nibble the vaginal lips and clitoris. The tongue also can be used to penetrate the vagina with thrusting motions.

The face (chin, cheeks, and forehead) can become involved in cunnilingus while the mouth and lips are busy providing stimulation. A partner can intentionally use the face to provide additional stimulation through direct

Cunnilingus
licking and sucking the vulva

pressure or circular motion. For instance, the bridge of the nose can provide clitoral stimulation while licking or sucking on the labia.

As with fellatio, cunnilingus can be performed with or without manual stimulation. Many women derive pleasure from having their partner insert a well-lubricated finger into their vagina or anus while performing cunnilingus. Saliva or vaginal lubrication can be used to make the fingers slippery. The partner also can stimulate the woman's clitoris with manual stimulation while licking or sucking on another part of the vulva.

Anilingus   licking and sucking the anus

Anilingus   Although it isn't as common as fellatio or cunnilingus, **anilingus**, also known as rimming, is another form of oral sex practiced by people of all forms of sexual orientation. During anilingus, a person kisses, licks, or sucks the partner's anus. The motions and activities of anilingus are similar to both cunnilingus and fellatio.

Performing anilingus affords a good opportunity to stimulate the perineum, an area richly endowed with nerve endings. Some men and women enjoy having their partners insert their tongues into their anus during anilingus. Others prefer that their partner insert a well-lubricated finger into the rectum. When performing anilingus on a woman, care must be taken to avoid spreading E-coli bacteria into the vagina. The tongue or fingers never should be inserted directly from the anus to the vagina without first being washed.

Another concern is the spread of hepatitis and other sexually transmitted disease (STD) organisms through anilingus. We do not recommend performing anilingus with a casual sex partner or someone whose STD status is unknown, as this could result in ingesting disease-causing organisms. This is discussed in greater detail in Chapter 15.

Mutual Oral Sex   The term used to describe simultaneous cunnilingus and fellatio is "sixty-nine." This usually is accomplished in the side-to-side starting point, with each partner's head at the other's genitals (see Figure 8.10). From this position, both partners have easy access to their partner's genitals. From the side-to-side starting point, it is easy to roll into the man or woman on either the top or bottom positions. By being on the top or the

Figure 8.10   Mutual oral sex.

bottom, a person can control for deeper penetration of the tongue when performing cunnilingus, or the penis during fellatio.

SEXUALITY AND DISABILITY

People with physical disabilities or illnesses can maximize their sexual potential by being creative despite their limitations. Although they may have some restrictions concerning what they can do, they still can enjoy robust sexual activity and satisfying relationships. In this book we cannot describe all of the potential variations in lovemaking associated with a full range of physical disabilities. We suggest that people with disabilities use the information in this chapter as a starting point to experiment with different forms of sexual behavior. They may find that accessories such as chairs or stools can be helpful when trying various positions. Communication with the partner is of primary importance, to ensure that the erotic and safety needs of both are being met.

WELLNESS SYNTHESIS

Our level of sexuality and sensuality depends on our well-being in all of the six areas of wellness.

Physical Well-being

High level physical fitness can enhance sexuality, and nowhere is this more evident than in relation to sexual behavior. High-level physical well-being enhances everything related to sexual behavior. Fitness influences our ability to perform sexually. Although the goal is not to become a sexual acrobat, a high level of fitness will increase our strength, flexibility, and endurance — all elements that can enhance sexual ability and creativity. People with physical disabilities or illnesses, too, can maximize their fitness level to achieve their sexual potential despite their limitations.

Physical well-being implies the absence of sexually transmitted diseases, which can severely curtail sexual activity and pleasure. Physical well-being also includes daily hygiene and health behaviors, both of which play a role in enjoying sexual behavior.

Intellectual Well-being

Intellectual well-being provides the objective basis for understanding sexual behavior. It allows you to separate fact from fiction, truth from myth, science from theology. It empowers you to gain access to information and make informed choices that are free from dogma and outside pressures. Many excellent textbooks and lovemaking manuals are available describing how to improve sexual technique.

Emotional Well-being

Emotional well-being allows you to understand your emotions without being overwhelmed by them. Often, our sexual desires and behavior are intertwined with our emotions. Sometimes, because of past experiences and learning, we are ashamed, embarrassed, confused, or anxious about our current desires and behavior. People who are emotionally healthy realize that sexuality is normal, and they try to work with their emotions rather than to suppress them or feel worse because of them. They talk about these issues with their partner and seek help if they need it.

Social Well-being

The quality of social relationships plays a big part in sexual behavior. The foundation of social well-being is a solid relationship with your sex partner. This relationship is built on caring, trust, mutual respect, equality, and openness. Within this type of relationship, sexual communication and experimentation will flourish. It allows you and your partner to explore and understand your sexuality in a safe, caring, disease-free way.

Spiritual Well-being

Sexual behavior with another person can either elevate us to a higher level of spiritual well-being or disconnect us from others. When our sexual relationships are based on respect, mutuality, and caring, our union with another person creates something that we cannot experience as individuals. In contrast, when our sexual relationships are based on exploitation, power, mistrust, fear, or other destructive intentions, we become disconnected from others, mere sexual mercenaries, out for ourselves only. Regardless of whether we are religious, we each have a moral code, a sense of right and wrong that can enhance our connectedness to others or destroy it. Those with high-level spirituality view their sexual relations with others with integrity and morality.

The college campus is the main environment for many of us. Is it safe? Can men and women, gay or straight, walk it without fear? Is it a place where people can relax and be themselves without harassment? Does it provide safe opportunities for meeting, socializing, having sex? Is it a place where relationships seem to be built predominantly on respect and mutuality or exploitation and dominance? Are there places where students can go for information, advice, counseling, contraceptives? If any of the answers to these questions is no, you can become proactive in changing your environment. You can make your needs known to the college administration. Start with the Director of Student Services and the Provost. These people are employed to enhance students' social and academic experiences on campus. You are a consumer and have every right to know how your tuition dollars are being spent.

From a larger perspective, is your state permissive or repressive? Are sodomy laws still enforced? Do young adults have access to sexual information and services? Are the courts supportive or punitive regarding sexual behavior? Do the schools teach sex education? The answers to these and similar questions provide fodder for spirited debate.

Environmental Well-being

We act out our sexual behavior within the context of our environment — the people and physical settings that make up our day-to-day landscape for sexual behavior. It influences who we meet, where we interact, our social parameters, and a host of other factors. It can either enhance or denigrate our sexuality.

WEB RESOURCES

The Celibate FAQ

http://mail.bris.ac.uk/~plmlp/celibate.html

A personal web page with frequently asked questions and answers on celibacy. The site gives reasons for celibacy, advantages and disadvantages, plus booklists and other resources. Questions raised include: What kind of people are celibate? What are the advantages/disadvantages of celibacy?

National Abstinence Clearinghouse

http://www.abstinence.net

An alliance of nationally known educators formed to promote the practice of abstinence. The NAC provides a resource center and training for educators and parents. Many links for related topics in the area of abstinence.

Notes

1. *The Wholesome Personalty* (New York: Appleton Century, 1932).
2. "Celibate Passion," *Utne Reader*, Sept–Oct, 1996, pp. 51–53.
3. Good Arts, *Sensual Massage*, available http:www.goodarts.com.
4. Inkeles, G., and Austin, K. K., *The New Sensual Massage* (Bayside, CA: Arcata Arts, 1992).
5. *Sex for One: The Joy of Selfloving* (New York: Crown Publisher, 1996).
6. *The Hite Report on Male Sexuality* (New York: Knopf, 1981).
7. W. H. Masters, V. Johnson, and R. Kolodny, *Human Sexuality* (New York: HarperCollins, 1993).
8. *The Hite Report: A Nationwide Study of Female Sexuality* (New York: Dell Books, 1976).
9. *The Hite Report: A Nationwide Study of Female Sexuality.*
10. E. O. Laumann, J. H. Gagnon, R. T. Michael, and S. Michaels. *The Social Organization of Human Sexuality: Sexual Practices in the United States* (Chicago: University of Chicago Press, 1994).
11. Laumann et al.

Resources

Barbach, Lonnie. (1984). *For Yourself: The Fulfillment of Female Sexuality*. New York: New American Library. One of the best women's self-help sexuality books. Describes how to maximize sexual pleasure.

Barbach, Lonnie. (1984). *For Each Other: Sharing Sexual Intimacy*. A follow-up targeted to couples.

Comfort, Alex. (1994). *The New Joy of Sex*. New York: Crown. Similar in nature to the *Joy of Sex* but targeted to the sexual needs of gays and lesbians.

Rubin, David. (1969). *Everything You Always Wanted to Know About Sex; But Were Afraid to Ask*. The first popular self-help book about sex; offers practical, nonthreatening answers to the most common questions about sexuality.

Silverstein, C. and Picano, F. (1993). *The New Joy of Gay Sex*. New York: Harper Perennial Library. An updated edition targeted to gay and lesbian sexual activity.

Vatsyayana. (1883). *The Kama Sutra*. Available online, translated by Sir Richard Burton. http://www.bibliomania.com/nonfiction/vatsyayana/kamasutra. The timeless Indian sex manual that merges yoga, spirituality, and sex.

Westheimer, Ruth (1994). *Dr. Ruth's Guide to Good Sex*. The famous Dr. Ruth at her best. Witty, irreverent, warmly engaging. This is a fun book about good sex for everyone.

Student Study Questions

1. What is sensuality? What does "sensual lover" mean?

2. What is Burnham's concept of integration? What contributes to adults losing this capacity?

3. What are some guidelines for giving a massage?

4. What is the difference between celibacy and abstinence? When are each appropriate?

5. What are five nonpenetrative forms of sexual activity?

6. What are the pros and cons of the man-on-top and woman-on-top intercourse positions?

7. What are the advantages of the side-by-side and rear-entry intercourse positions?

Favorite Sexual Behaviors

People satisfy their sexual needs in a variety of ways. We each engage in unique activities and behaviors to satisfy our sexual desire. The purpose of this activity is to illustrate how different positions satisfy different sexual needs. This will enable you to take a personal inventory of your personal turn-ons and have the opportunity to exchange them anonymously with your classmates.

1. Which autoerotic sexual activity do you find most enjoyable, and why? (If you do not engage in autoerotic activity, simply state this.)

2. Which partnered sexual activity do you find most satisfying? Why? (You could also include masturbation in this category.)

3. Describe your favorite sexual position within this category (for instance, if you enjoy vaginal intercourse most, which starting point and position do you find most enjoyable?)

Continued

Student Assessment

Favorite Sexual Behaviors (cont.)

4.　Describe your favorite sexual fantasy. (If you do not fantasize, simply state this.)

[The instructor distributes these anonymously to the class and leads a group discussion.]

Atypical Sexual Behavior

Student Learning Objectives

After reading this chapter, students will be able to:

- Distinguish between normal, atypical, and paraphiliac sexual behavior.

- Describe the four typical measures used to assess normalcy.

- Assess their own attitudes, values, and beliefs about what is normal.

- Describe the key characteristics of a variety of paraphilias.

- Evaluate the paraphiliac risks associated with the internet.

- Evaluate the health risks associated with body piercing.

- Differentiate transvestic fetishism and transsexualism (gender identity disorder).

- Describe the origins of atypical sexual behavior and paraphilias.

- Evaluate various ways of treating atypical sexual behaviors and paraphilias.

Normative behavior can be classified as sociological, biological, psychological, and statistical. Sexual behavior that is *sociologically* normal falls within the laws, mores, and customs of a society. Most of this behavior is culturally defined and passed from one generation to the next as a result of socialization. *Biologically* normal behavior is characterized as healthy and natural and helps to perpetuate the species in positive ways. *Psychologically* normal sexual behavior is sexual activity that does not result in emotional distress or in neurotic or psychotic functioning. Last, behavior that is considered *statistically* normal is sexual behavior in which the majority of people engage.

Given these four categories of "normality," defining abnormal sexual behavior might seem easy. Anything falling outside of the parameters established by these four categories would be considered "abnormal."

The words "normal" and "abnormal" are commonly used labels because they characterize sexual behavior in easy-to-understand, stereotypical patterns. Furthermore, dichotomizing normal and abnormal makes it easier to stigmatize and discriminate against people who are not in the norm. A more commonly accepted term to describe behaviors that the majority of the population do not practice is "atypical" sexual behavior. Atypical sexual behavior is described as behavior that is not statistically typical. The term "atypical" does not carry the same pejorative tone as "abnormal."

When describing unusual sexual practices, atypical *is a much less stereotypical term than* abnormal.

Upon closer examination, we can see how seemingly clear distinctions between "normal" and "abnormal" can get blurred. Consider these questions:

- Does sociological health refer to sexual mores and customs that the majority culture engages in and hands down, or does it refer to the customs and behaviors of individual minority groups within the total society?

- Does sociological health mean conforming to what society expects in terms of one's partners — opposite sex, same race, close in age, and so on?

- What about the various subcultures within majority and minority groups?

- If a person behaves within the accepted standards of these minority or subcultures but strays from the dominant culture, is his or her behavior "abnormal?"

- Is heterosexual vaginal intercourse biologically "normal" if the participants use contraception?

- ❧ Is it psychologically abnormal to engage in intercourse with one's spouse while fantasizing about being with another person, or to feign interest when a person is not really interested in making love?

- ❧ How much distress constitutes emotional distress?

- ❧ Does one's motivation for sex determine what is normal and healthy?

- ❧ Is it normal to use sex for power as well as pleasure?

- ❧ If the statistical average for intercourse for newlyweds is four times a week and you and your spouse make love only 2.5 times per week, are you abnormal, even if both of you are satisfied with your pattern of love-making?

- ❧ Is making love more than four times a week excessive, abnormal, or compulsive?

PARAPHILIAS

Paraphilias are atypical or unusual sexual behaviors that become the focal point for an obsessive preoccupation or need. The paraphilia is almost always the central focus of the person's sexual repertoire, and arousal and orgasm are difficult, if not impossible, in the absence of the paraphilia.

Paraphilias generally revolve around three common themes: (1) non-human objects, (2) suffering or humiliation involving oneself or one's own partner, and (3) children or other nonconsenting persons. In addition, to qualify as a paraphilia, a behavior has to occur over a period of at least 6 months and cause clinically significant distress or impairment in social, occupational, or other important areas of functioning.[1]

The fourth edition of the *Diagnostic and Statistical Manual of Mental Disorders* (DSM) lists eight categories of paraphilias and one catch-all category. The eight officially-recognized categories are:

- ❧ exhibitionism
- ❧ voyeurism
- ❧ fetishism
- ❧ frotteurism
- ❧ pedophilia
- ❧ sexual masochism
- ❧ sexual sadism
- ❧ transvestic fetishism

The catch-all category "not otherwise specified" includes the following paraphilias, which are less common and don't meet the criteria to be included in any of the other eight categories:

- ❧ telephone scatologia (obscene phone calls)
- ❧ necrophilia (sex with a corpse)

Paraphilia
an unusual or atypical sexual behavior that becomes the focal point for an obsessive preoccupation or need

- ❧ partialism (focus on certain parts of the body)
- ❧ zoophilia (sex with animals)
- ❧ coprophilia (contact with feces)
- ❧ klismaphilia (enemas)
- ❧ urophilia (undue attention to urine)

A person often exhibits more than one paraphiliac behavior.[2] Also, someone who exhibits true paraphiliac behavior and someone who casually experiments with atypical behavior are different. True paraphilia creates almost obsessive recurring, intense sexually arousing fantasies, urges, and behavior, and is the main focal point for sexual arousal.

Occasionally engaging in atypical sexual behaviors is not the same as a full-blown paraphilia.

In addition, the person recognizes that the paraphilia causes significant enough emotional, social, occupational, or other distress to interfere with daily functioning. Someone who casually experiments with episodic paraphiliac behavior (such as occasionally liking his lover to tie him to the bedpost) and does not suffer negative emotional or other consequences is considered a person who simply enjoys occasional atypical sexual behavior.

Exhibitionism

Exhibitionism
deriving sexual pleasure from exposing one's genitals to unsuspecting strangers

The paraphiliac focus in **exhibitionism** involves deriving sexual arousal by exposing one's genitals to unsuspecting strangers. The overwhelming majority of people with this paraphilia are men between 18 and 40 years of age. Sometimes the person masturbates while exposing himself or fantasizing exposing himself.[3] Often the sexual gratification is derived from the sheer shock value of the act and the reaction from the victim. The greater the reaction, the more the person has proven his masculinity.

Men who reveal exhibitionism tend to be shy, passive, and sexually inhibited. Exhibitionism is generally perceived to be unrelated to rape or sexual assault. In some instances, the man with this paraphilia believes that his victim will be sexually aroused by his nakedness and it will provoke a sexual encounter with her.

Exhibitionism is often confused with "mooning" (baring one's buttocks to unsuspecting passersby). Generally, those who moon do not derive sexual gratification from the act, and it usually is a prank typically associated with adolescents. In a sense, exhibitionism is culturally disparate. Male and female exotic dancers get paid to expose themselves. Nude or partially nude dancing and other forms of exotic entertaining are designed to be sexually arousing and are legal, yet streaking, which is not sexual, is illegal.

Voyeurism

Voyeurism
deriving sexual pleasure from observing unsuspecting individuals undressing or engaging in sexual activities

The paraphiliac focus of **voyeurism** is exactly the opposite of exhibitionism. The voyeur derives sexual excitement and pleasure from observing unsuspecting people (usually strangers) who are naked, disrobing, getting dressed, or in the act of having sex. The pleasure is derived from the act of "peeping" and is not intended to lead to an encounter with the unsuspecting stranger. Sexual release usually occurs through masturbation either while peeping or later with the voyeuristic memory of the encounter. The person may fantasize having sex with the stranger.[4]

Voyeuristic behavior can be depicted along a continuum. At the extreme is the person who can achieve sexual release only by observing others having sex. At the other end of the continuum is the person who watches others to augment sexual pleasure with a partner. This person might get turned on by watching exotic entertainers to fuel a sexual episode with a partner.

Voyeurs derive pleasure from watching others and have no desire to confront them.

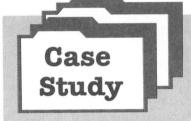

Case Study

Greg: Exhibitionism or Mooning?

Greg was the first client assigned to Dr. Blonna during the supervised clinical training component of the master's degree in Counseling. Greg, a 20-year-old, was on probation as a first-time sex offender convicted of exhibitionism. As a condition of parole, Greg had to seek counseling for a proscribed period of time.

In Dr. Blonna's words:

I'll never forget Greg. I was a 25-year-old man, not too much older than Greg. I was still working through issues related to my own sexuality and found Greg quite a challenge. He was referred to counseling because he had been arrested for exposing himself to a young woman.

It was hard for me to understand the significance of exhibitionism. I had been raised as a typical man of the 1950s and 1960s and viewed exhibitionism with amusement more than a clinician's understanding of it as a paraphilia. Indeed, I was only a few years removed from engaging in mooning and streaking as fraternity pranks. In time, my work with Greg crystallized the significance of his behavior and the furtive nature of exhibitionism.

Greg was a reluctant client at first. He did not want to be in counseling, and the first couple of sessions were almost totally devoid of any conversation. Gradually we began to establish a relationship and Greg started to talk about his exhibitionism. It became quite evident after that point that Greg's behavior was vastly different from mooning and other juvenile sexual

behavior that, although offensive, has an entirely different motivation. Mooning, streaking, and other prank public displays of nudity are not intended to serve as sexual come-ons. Greg's behavior had an entirely different purpose.

Greg was immature — both socially and sexually retarded. He was painfully shy, could not communicate with women effectively, and had limited dating experience. His sexual experience was limited to autoerotic activities and a handful of sexual liaisons with prostitutes. He lacked self-esteem and self-confidence and had a hard time maintaining eye-contact. He also admitted, while in counseling, that he was a voyeur and had masturbated several times while watching a few women in his neighborhood get undressed. He had a couple of peeping vantage points that allowed him to peer into the windows of apartment buildings in his neighborhood.

After seeing Greg for several sessions, it was obvious that exposing himself was his way of coming on to women sexually. He really believed that women, upon seeing his nakedness (and throbbing erection) would literally throw themselves at his feet and perform oral sex on him or ask him back to their place to have intercourse. He believed that his "manhood" would speak for itself and make traditional forms of establishing a sexual relationship unnecessary. In reality, Greg lacked the conversational and other social skills necessary to meet women and establish a sexual relationship.

Fetishism

Fetishism
deriving sexual pleasure from
inanimate objects

The paraphiliac focus of **fetishism** is deriving sexual arousal and gratification from nonliving objects. The overwhelming majority of people with fetishes consists of men who derive sexual pleasure from items of women's clothing such as underwear, bras, stockings, shoes, and boots. Typically, the man with paraphiliac fetishism masturbates while holding, stroking, smelling, or licking the object. To a lesser extent, the person may ask his partner (or pay a prostitute) to wear the item of clothing while they engage in sex or he masturbates.[5]

A person with a true paraphiliac fetish usually strongly prefers and needs the object to experience sexual desire. Often, a person with a fetish is unable to obtain or sustain an erection without the object being present. Fetishes often are linked to significant childhood experiences and are in place by adolescence.[6]

Frotteurism

Frotteurism
deriving sexual pleasure from
rubbing up against unsuspecting
and unwilling victims

The paraphiliac focus of **frotteurism** is deriving sexual arousal and pleasure from rubbing one's genitals against an unsuspecting, nonconsenting person. The male rubs his genitals against his victim's buttocks and thighs while simultaneously fondling her breasts or genitalia, or both. This typically occurs in crowded public places such as busy sidewalks, subways, buses, and other public places where the perpetrator can make a quick escape and avoid arrest.[7]

Pedophilia

Pedophilia
engaging in sexual activity with,
or fantasizing about,
prepubescent children

The legal aspects of **pedophilia** are discussed in detail in Chapter 16. The paraphiliac focus of pedophilia is fantasizing about engaging in sexual activity with a prepubescent child. Those sexually attracted to girls, in general, prefer 8–10-year-olds. Those attracted to boys favor slightly older children. The two subtypes of pedophilia are (1) exclusive (individuals who are sexually attracted to children only) and (2) nonexclusive (individuals who are sexually attracted to both adults and children.[8]

Individuals with pedophilia show a wide range of sexual activity with their victims. Not all pedophiles are child molesters. According to the law, a pedophile is an individual who fantasizes about sexual contact with children, whereas a child molester actually commits that act in some form.[9]

Most pedophiles masturbate while watching their victims undress, fondle themselves, or engage in sexual activities with another child or an adult. These activities can be live (paying children to perform in person or observing live sex shows broadcast over the internet), or available through print (magazines, newspapers, and the like), and other electronic media (including movies, videotapes, and CD ROMs).

Child molesters engage in a variety of sexual activities with their victims. This may consist of rubbing or fondling the child. Other child molesters penetrate the child's mouth, vagina, or rectum with their fingers, penis, or a foreign object. Some people with pedophilia obtain these sexual favors by gaining their victims' trust, affection, or loyalty. Others use physical force and psychological pressure and terror to obtain sex and control their victims.

Since 1977, no fewer than five federal laws have made the possession of any sexual image of kids under age 18 illegal. Nonetheless, the underground market for all forms of child pornography and prostitution is thriving.[10] Pedophiles have victimized their own children, stepchildren, foster children, or relatives' children. Less often victims are children adopted through foreign services, bought through underground slave trade, or exchanged with other pedophiles.

PERSPECTIVES    # The Internet & Pedophilia

The internet and the World Wide Web (WWW) have become a major source of concern for law enforcement officials around the world trying to stem the tide of child pornography and pedophilia-related abductions and murders that originated in chat and other services available on the WWW. The cases of Marc Dutrox of Belgium and Ronald Riva of California are just two of many that have brought attention to the problem of pedophilia and its many manifestations on the internet.

Dutrox was convicted of kidnapping and murdering young girls in Belgium. The suspected head of a Europe-wide pedophile sex ring, Dutrox used the internet to meet and lure his victims.

Riva, an unemployed truck driver, former prison officer, and father of four, was discovered when the mother of one of his victims (a 10-year-old girl) pressed charges of child abuse against him. The girl claimed that Riva had abused her when she stayed overnight at a slumber party for one of his daughters.

The case broke wide open when detectives discovered that Riva's house contained equipment (similar to that used in video-conferencing) that was set up to broadcast live "photo shoots" on the internet. Police also discovered computer files containing child pornography and links to another man, Melton Lee Myers, who had similar equipment.

The investigation ultimately linked the two to a worldwide pedophile ring with members based in the United States, Finland, Australia, and Canada. The group was abusing children as young as 5 years old and broadcasting pictures and live child-sex shows on the Internet.*

The WWW and internet have made it almost impossible to control kiddie-porn, and the number of federal "cybercops" (federal agents who scour the internet for such material) has increased from a handful to more than 100 operating in the United States alone.** Besides having a voracious appetite for pornography, which has contributed literally tens of thousands of child-sex visual images to the internet, pedophiles and child molesters have taken advantage of sophisticated broadcasting techniques to stay ahead of the law. Child pornographers often "morph" the head of one child on the body of another, making identification of the child and proof of sexual abuse almost impossible. The naked images of adults in child pornography are limited almost exclusively to shots from the torso down.

Additional obstacles to tracking pedophiles, child molesters, and child pornographers include the sheer volume and worldwide scope of their activities. Keeping abreast of new sites, linking perpetrators, and identifying victims is indeed difficult. Often, just as investigators are making progress, a site closes down and relocates with a new WEB address or country of origin.

One potential inroad being explored is forcing service providers to sever relationships with sites that have been known to contain child porn. A key component of the Communications Decency Act, which the U. S. Supreme Court struck down as unconstitutional in 1997, was the provision to hold providers (such as America Online) liable if their customers could gain access to obscene and indecent material. At present, a global effort is under way to come up with a way to control access of child pornography via the internet.

*J. Cusack, "The Murky World of Internet Porn: The "Orchid Club" Shakes Up the Law," *World Press Review*, 43:11 (1996), 8–10.
**D. E. Kaplan, "New Cybercop Tricks to Fight Child Porn: Police Struggle Against an Online Onslaught," *U. S. News and World Report*, 122:20 (1997), 29.

People with pedophilia have been known to use extraordinary means to obtain child pornography or actual live victims. In 1995 a man made headlines by arranging an encounter with a child while posing as an adolescent on an internet chat service.[11]

Pedophilia usually is chronic and is more difficult to treat than other paraphilias. The recidivism rate for men attracted to boys is more than twice that of men attracted to girls.[12]

Sexual Masochism

Sexual masochism
deriving sexual pleasure from being humiliated or forced to suffer pain

The paraphiliac focus of **sexual masochism** is deriving arousal and pleasure through being beaten, bound, humiliated (physical or mental), or being made to suffer in some other fashion.[13] Although fantasizing about being the victim of masochistic acts is common, true paraphilia involves engaging in the behaviors.

Many different masochistic acts typically are sought with a partner. These include being bound (physical restraint involving being tied, strapped, taped, chained, or handcuffed), spanked, bitten, paddled, whipped, beaten, shocked with an electrical current, cut, or pierced/pinned (infibulation). Another common masochistic desire is to be humiliated by being urinated or defecated on, to be forced to crawl and bark like a dog, and to be verbally abused. **Infantilism** involves being treated like an infant and forced to wear a diaper.

Infantilism
deriving sexual pleasure from being treated like an infant

Hypoxyphilia
deriving sexual pleasure from activities that involve oxygen deprivation

The last category of masochistic paraphilia involves **hypoxyphilia,** or oxygen deprivation, by noose or wire (ligature), chest compression, plastic bag, mask, or chemical (such as amyl nitrate, a powerful vasodilator that reduces the flow of oxygen to the brain). This is particularly dangerous

S & M objects run the gamut from studded dog collars to leather manacles and whips.

because mishap in applying these procedures for sexual arousal could result in death. It is estimated that between 250 and 1,000 deaths per year are caused by this behavior.[14]

Sometimes, individuals with sexual masochism engage in masochistic acts by themselves. They self-inflict pain and humiliation through pinning, binding, shocking, or engaging in hypoxyphilia. Men with sexual masochism often concurrently have fetishism, transvestic fetishism, or sexual masochism.[15] The practice of body piercing has its etiology in sexual masochism. Piercing erogenous body parts such as the labia, nipples, and scrotum by paraphiliacs represents self-mutilation associated with masochism and the desire to humiliate and injure oneself. Most body piercers, however, have the procedures done for personal adornment, a reflection of style.

Health Hint

Reducing the Health Risks Associated With Body Piercing

Body piercing, like other forms of adornment such as tattooing, branding, and ear piercing, carries some risk. The risks vary and are related to the body part being pierced, the piercing equipment, sterilization procedures used (or lack thereof), and the skill of the provider. The following hints can help reduce the risks associated with body piercing:

1. Think long and hard about your motivation for getting your body pierced. Make sure you understand the risks associated with the procedure.

2. Talk with people who have had piercing done. Ask what kind of experiences they had.

3. Before getting pierced, ask your physician about vaccination for hepatitis B, a bloodborne infection passed through contaminated needles.

4. Do not pierce yourself or let an inexperienced person (such as your best friend, who pierced her own ears) pierce you.

5. Go to a reputable piercing parlor that has been in business for some time. Ask for references from former customers.

6. Make sure the piercing parlor you choose uses an autoclave (a tabletop sterilizing device that uses heat and pressure to kill germs) to sterilize equipment. Ask to see the certificate verifying that the autoclave has been recently inspected. If only boiling water is used to clean equipment, head for the door.

7. If a tattoo artist uses individually sealed, sterile needles, ask him or her to open these in front of you. Request the same for the containers of ink being used for your tattoo.

8. Talk to your physician to learn about special considerations concerning the body part being pierced. Particularly risky parts (because of increased likelihood of infection or permanent damage) are the eyelids, the tongue, the nipples, the clitoris, and the frenulum of the penis.

9. Don't have piercing done if you are pregnant or nursing.

10. Follow after-care instructions to the letter. If you suspect infection, consult a doctor immediately.

11. Wear only jewelry that is 14K gold, niobium, or surgical-grade stainless steel. These contain fewer alloys and are less likely to cause allergic reactions.

Source: M.S. Baum, "A Piercing Issue," Health State, 14:3(1996), 1–7.

The body piercing used today for sexual adornment has its origins in the masochistic practice of self-mutilation.

Sexual Sadism

Sexual sadism
deriving sexual pleasure from inflicting pain or humiliation

The paraphiliac focus of **sexual sadism** involves deriving sexual arousal and pleasure by inflicting physical or psychological pain and suffering upon another person. The person may engage in sadistic activities with either a willing victim (usually someone with sexual masochism) or a nonconsenting victim.[16]

Sexual sadism incorporates a range of acts including all of those discussed previously under the topic of sexual masochism. In extreme cases, people with sexual sadism seek sexual arousal through extreme brutality, torture, mutilation, and murder. Typically, they engage in such behavior with nonconsenting victims and have had the condition for several years. The fantasies of sexual sadism usually are present in childhood, and the behavior begins in early adulthood and becomes chronic.

Transvestic Fetishism

Transvestic fetishism
deriving sexual pleasure from wearing women's clothing

Transvestic fetishism differs from other forms of fetishism in that the fetishist derives sexual arousal by crossdressing (dressing up as a female or wearing an article of female clothing). The transvestic fetishist typically masturbates to orgasm while dressed in that clothing.

The disorder is known only in males. It runs the full spectrum of behavior from routinely wearing a single item of female clothing (such as silk panties) under the male clothing to spending thousands of dollars on customized gowns and make-up and participating in the transvestic subculture.[17]

Case Study

Oliver, a Transvestite

While working as a counselor in a public STD clinic in Newark, New Jersey, Dr. Blonna met Oliver. He was a 25-year-old black genetic male in the middle stages of transsexual reassignment surgery. He had undergone full-body electrolysis, had crossdressed in public full-time for more than 6 months, and was on estrogen treatment to make his body more "feminine."

He was Dr. Blonna's first transsexual case of STD. He came into the clinic for a check-up because one of his sex partners had syphilis. At that time Dr. Blonna did not know Oliver was really a male. He still had a penis and testicles, but he also had breast implants and a long, flowing wig.

Oliver was actually quite stunning. S/he had flawless cafe-au-lait skin, perfect make-up, breasts spilling out of her/his halter top, and legs that went on forever. Oliver however, still had the well-defined arm muscles, broad shoulders, and muscle density, which belied his former history as a fairly good high-school football player, and a throaty male baritone voice.

As it turned out, Oliver was infected with syphilis and Dr. Blonna conducted several interviews over the next two years. Dr. Blonna was initially surprised that Oliver was a man, and Oliver explained that *most* people were surprised. He actually earned a living as an exotic dancer and prostitute. He considered himself a woman and had sex with men for money. Oliver explained that he needed an additional $15,000 dollars to complete the sex reassignment process, and after that time he'd find a man, stop soliciting, and just dance for money.

Dr. Blonna asked whether his customers knew he was a man and how he managed to work as a female exotic dancer (aka stripper) while still having a penis and testicles. He explained that most people didn't know he was a man.

He said he taped his penis back and used a bushy wig to cover the area. His breast implants were realistic. With his routine, he keeps moving and uses a lot of feathers and lights.

Oliver wanted to be beautiful, a beauty queen. He liked to shop and periodically dropped by the clinic, bringing samples of his/her latest outfits (shoes, sequined mini-skirts, and the like). S/he extended the invitation to Dr. Blonna to come to one of the clubs.

Transvestites are turned on by dressing up as women.

PERSPECTIVES　　The Underground World

In the 1970s Lou Reed, avant garde artist and lead singer for the Velvet Underground, sang about taking a walk on the wild side. The wild side that he sang about was the underground world of transsexuals — a world replete with its own bars, clubs, magazines, and clothing outlets.

Today you still can experience this underground world on certain streets in every major city in the United States, from New Orleans to New York City to San Francisco, and find a world filled with all of the transpeople — transsexuals, transvestites, and the transgendered. You'll find boutiques catering to transsexuals that carry everything in "women's" clothing from panties to feather boas in sizes designed to fit the average truck driver. You'll also find shoestores that cater to spiked heels in sizes 10, 11, and 12 in every

width. At night these districts come alive as club-goers of all sexual persuasions flock to see their favorite female impersonators, although some of the actors and actresses already have gone through sex reassignment surgery and can hardly be called impersonators.

The World Wide Web has opened the globe to the transcommunity. You now can view entire catalogs of merchandise on your computer, and shop from the privacy of your own home. There are social organizations, self-help groups, political action committees, legal aid societies, chat rooms, list-serves, travel clubs (they find the best places for transpeople to vacation), auto clubs, discount purchasing cooperatives, and the list goes on and on. The amazing thing is that most of these people, places, and services operate outside of the realization of mainstream society.

Men with transvestic fetishism do not have gender identity disorder (think they are really females), and most are heterosexual in sexual orientation.

Men with transvestic fetishism do not necessarily have gender identity dysphoria.

When not crossdressed, men with transvestic fetishism look like the average man. Men who do not have transvestic fetishism but occasionally like to put on articles of female clothing often do so with the willing participation of their female partners.

GENDER IDENTITY DISORDER

Transsexualism
(a gender identity disorder)
a strong and persistent
cross-gender identification

Gender identity disorder is also known as **transsexualism**. Gender identity disorder is characterized by four criteria:

- a strong and persistent cross-gender identification
- persistent discomfort with his or her sex or a sense of inappropriateness in the gender role of that sex
- the absence of any genetic or physical abnormality (intersex condition such as androgen insensitivity)
- significant accompanying clinical psychological distress and impairment in social, occupational or other functioning.

A strong and persistent cross-gender identification has several markers for children. The following evidence a strong and persistent cross-gender identification:

- a repeated stated desire to be, or insistence that he or she is, the other sex

◡ in boys, a preference for dressing in female attire or simulating girls' clothing; in girls, wearing only stereotypical boys' clothing

◡ a strong and persistent preference for cross-gender sex roles in make-believe play or fantasy

◡ desire and participation in the stereotypical games and pastimes of the other sex

◡ a strong preference for playmates of the other sex.

In adolescents and adults, the criteria for a strong and persistent cross-gender identification are met by the following symptoms:

◡ stated desire to be the other sex

◡ frequent passing as the other sex

◡ desire to live or be treated as the other sex

◡ conviction that he or she has the typical feelings and reactions as the other sex.

Supporting the second criterion is discomfort and inappropriateness with one's gender role. Boys strongly and persistently assert that their penis and testes are disgusting and wish they would disappear. They also have a strong aversion to typical rough-and-tumble play and stereotypical boys' toys, games, and activities. Girls have a strong and persistent resistance to sitting while urinating and assert that they do not want to grow breasts or menstruate. They also have an aversion to feminine clothing.

Transsexuals feel that they were born the wrong sex.

Adults with gender identity disorder are preoccupied with ridding themselves of their primary and secondary physical sexual characteristics through hormone therapy and surgery. Transsexuals feel, and have always felt, that they were literally born the wrong sex, as if nature had made some mistake with their genitals.

PERSPECTIVES — Jan Morris — A Conundrum

Jan Morris started out in life as John Morris, later to be knighted and become Sir John Morris. John Morris — man, husband, father, athlete, soldier, explorer, writer, world traveler, climber of Mt. Everest — was the epitome of every man's fantasy. He had power, prestige, wealth, and fame. Beautiful women wanted to be around him. He held the world in his hands.

John Morris had everything he wanted except for one thing: He really wanted to be a woman. He'd gladly have given it all up (and did) to become the woman he always wanted to be. In his book, *Conundrum*, one of the first of its genre, Jan Morris explains the crux of what being a transsexual means — feeling as though nature made a mistake. Morris recalls early recollections of feeling literally trapped within the wrong body. Her whole life, up to the point of having sex reassignment surgery, consisted of trying to do things to convince herself that maybe she actually did belong in that body. Ultimately she realized that she didn't, and she had the surgery necessary to become a female.

THE ORIGIN AND TREATMENT OF ATYPICAL SEXUAL BEHAVIOR

Many different theories abound about the causes and treatment of atypical sexual behavior and paraphilias. Implied in "atypical" is the need to fix something that is wrong. Therefore, we reemphasize the difference between individuals who occasionally engage in behaviors that are atypical and cause no harm to another person and individuals who have paraphilias that cause themselves and others pain and suffering. The difference lies in the psychological distress and impairment in social, occupational, and other functioning between the two types of behavior.

Ethical Considerations

Society has an ethical and moral obligation to protect paraphiliacs and their victims from harm, even if they do not realize they are at risk. A sexual masochist, for instance, should be protected from the violence and suffering that may co-exist with that paraphilia.

The need for treatment is less clear with problems such as gender identity disorder. Is this really a psychological disorder? Is the condition really a problem that requires treatment, or should their desire to be the other sex be respected? Many question the essential duality of maleness and femaleness. As mentioned in Chapter 4, gender is best viewed as a continuum rather than an absolute value (100% male versus 100% female).

The difference between engaging in atypical sex and true paraphiliac sexual behavior is the lack of obsession and emotional distress.

The ethics of sexual reassignment surgery (surgically removing the genitals and reconstructing the genitalia of the desired, opposite sex) has been the subject of much debate. Should people who have gender identity disorder be allowed to have sex reassignment surgery? Would it make more sense to try to help these people learn to accept both the fact that they have the genitalia of one gender and the identity of another? Why do we have to fit them into only one neat niche? These and other questions related to the diagnosis and treatment of atypical and paraphiliac sexual behavior are still being debated and may never be fully resolved.

Etiology

Many explanations have been set forth for the causes of atypical sexual behavior and paraphilias. Three of the more commonly accepted views revolve around a psychoanalytic appraisal, a behaviorist explanation, and an eclectic etiology.

Psychoanalytic Appraisal

A classic psychoanalytical explanation for atypical or paraphiliac sexual behavior is the fixation of libidinal energy at a specific point in development. An individual becomes "stuck" and, with advancing age, constantly regresses to that point in psychosexual development. The immature level of sexual development is a result of not having been allowed the full expression and passage of libidinal energy at the age-appropriate stage.

Sexual masochists' need to be humiliated by having their partner urinate or defecate on them, for instance, is attributed to unresolved issues at the anal stage. Perhaps this person was rushed through toilet training or belittled for soiling his underpants. Whatever the specific issue, the unresolved transition through this period results in the fixation of sexuality at this stage of development.

Behaviorism

The behaviorist focuses on some facet of learning and argues that atypical sexual behavior and paraphilia stem from some associative learning

Case Study

The Marv Albert Case

The sporting world was shocked when Marv Albert, a long-time radio and television sportscaster, was arraigned in Virginia on charges of forced sodomy and a variety of other lesser charges. Albert's 30-year career as the play-by-play announcer for NBC and other networks made him a celebrity, and his trademark "Yessss!!!" following key baskets during New York Knicks broadcasts was known across the USA.

Albert's accuser, a long-time lover, charged him with biting her in several places on the back and forcing her to perform fellatio on him. She claimed that Albert's behavior was in response to his disappointment in the woman's unwillingness to bring a third partner in a *menage a trois*, another man, to a rendezvous at a local hotel. The woman further asserted that she had a long history of such trysts with Albert, even several years ago while he was still married. Further, she claimed that Albert had a penchant for crossdressing, watching x-rated videos, and biting during sex.

Albert countered by claiming that the woman liked "rough sex" and the biting was part of their sexual repertoire. He confirmed their long-term relationship but claimed that he never had forced her to do anything. Her accusations, Albert asserted, were in response to his informing her that he would be getting engaged and married and would be ending their relationship.

During the investigation a second woman, a hotel manager from Washington, DC, surfaced, claiming that Albert had tried to force her to have sex with him also. She claimed that Albert had placed a call for room service and when she arrived, Albert met her at the door wearing only women's panties and a garter belt. He had an obvious erection and tried to force her to have sex with him. She said she fought him off and left the room.

The case ended with Albert's and the woman's attorneys working out a plea bargain in which the sportscaster agreed to a lesser charge of assault (a misdemeanor) in exchange for dropping the forced sodomy charge (a felony). Albert eventually received a suspended 12-month sentence with a promise to expunge his record of all charges if he would seek counseling and honor all of the conditions of his probation.

The case sent shock waves throughout the United States, touching off a flurry of talk show programs concerning rough sex, biting, crossdressing, and other paraphiliac behavior. Included in the debate was a discussion of whether someone like Albert could ever be "rehabilitated." Experts testified claiming that the goal of Albert's treatment would be to teach him how to control his urges to engage in such behavior in public with strangers or nonmarital partners. Albert is now back on the airwaves.

experience. Perhaps it was extremely harsh parental punishment for some minor sexual act such as observing mother in the shower or being caught masturbating. Or it may be pairing an act (observing a woman undressing, for instance) with a pleasurable sexual experience (such as masturbation) that is positively reinforcing. This type of behavior is likely to be repeated.

Eclectic Perspective

John Money posed an eclectic explanation to atypical sexual behavior and paraphilia.[18] He developed a biosocial theory of sexual and gender development (see Chapter 4) based on what he called "lovemaps" ("templates" in the brain for patterns of eroticism and love). These templates, according to Money, are developed between 5 and 8 years of age as a result of biological and psychosocial forces.

During this period of development, Money believes children begin to link sex, love, and lust. The child usually develops a normal, healthy connection between romantic love and lust (sexual desire). Each of us has a unique lovemap based on a combination of biology (genetic inheritance, gonadal and hormonal influences) and psychosocial learning (parental and other models of love and affection). Healthy lovemaps are imprinted in our brain and create our idealized lover, love affair, and erotic imagery.

Atypical sexual behavior and paraphilia, according to Money, are a result of a distorted or "vandalized" lovemap that does not make a healthy connection between romantic love and lust. Love and lust are imprinted as disparate entities. Because the two are not linked, sexual desire (lust) is not attached to normal romantic involvements but, rather, becomes attached to the inanimate objects, humiliating behavior, and the like that evolve into paraphilias. Sexual desire is something apart from intimacy and affection. Lovemaps can become distorted for a variety of reasons including incest, physical abuse, extremely harsh parental punishments for normal sexual activity in childhood, repressive parental attitudes, and lack of displays of affection between parents.

Treatment

Most paraphiliacs in treatment enter as a result of being arrested for their behavior. They do not seek treatment on their own or enter willingly. Paraphilias are extremely difficult to treat, and "cure rates" are low. Regardless of which view one holds regarding the etiology of paraphilias, most experts agree that atypical and paraphilia behavior originates early in life, manifests itself in fantasy and desire, and evolves into full-blown behavior and lifestyle by young adulthood. As such, the person has a long history of behavior that has been reinforced over time through pleasure (masturbation or other sources of orgasm). The prognosis for eliminating such behavior is not good.

Biomedical Treatment

One way to treat people with paraphilia is to attempt to lower their level of sexual desire through chemical (drugs) and surgical (castration) procedures. Drug therapy consists of administering drugs that either inhibit the production of testosterone or block its effects on the brain. As we discussed in Chapter 3, testosterone is the main androgen linked to sexual desire in men and women. Drugs such as cyproterone acetate (CPA) and medrohxyprogesterone (MPA; Depro Provera) interfere with the effects of progesterone. They have been shown to have limited effectiveness in treating pedophiles, rapists, and other male sex offenders.[19] Up until the 1980s, castration was used to reduce the sexual desire of sex offenders. The surgical removal of the testicles eliminates the production of most testosterone but does not prevent sexual excitement and erection.

Although decreasing testosterone levels lowers sexual desire, it does not eliminate desire entirely. Also, no evidence is available to show that reducing testosterone levels, and thus sexual desire, has any permanent effect on the focus of sexual behavior. Testosterone, as discussed in Chapter 2, is linked with sexual desire, not sexual orientation or the focus of sexual activity. Drug therapy seems to work by lessening the compulsion to engage in paraphiliac behavior.[20] It doesn't eliminate the desire but, in conjunction with other approaches invoking the patient's support system, helps to control the desire enough to allow intervention.

Behavior Modification

Behavior modification is used to desensitize paraphiliacs to their paraphilias and sensitize them to new, aversive stimuli. **Aversion therapy** is a behavior modification technique that pairs an aversive stimulus (such as electric shock) with the behavior that is targeted for change.

Covert sensitization is a type of aversion therapy sometimes used with paraphiliacs. In **covert sensitization**, an aversive fantasy (not behavior) is paired with the paraphiliac fantasy in an attempt to extinguish it. For example, a voyeur is asked to visualize a past fantasy that accompanied one of the voyeuristic episodes. As the person visualizes the pleasing fantasy (say, peeping on an unsuspecting woman), the therapist introduces an aversive fantasy image (such as vomiting uncontrollably). By pairing the new aversive image (the vomiting) with the previously arousing image (peeping at the victim), the therapist links the negative image to the paraphilia.

Aversion therapy
a behavior modification technique that pairs an aversive stimulus with the behavior targeted for change

Covert sensitization
a type of behavior modification in which an aversive fantasy is paired with the paraphiliac fantasy in an attempt to extinguish it

Skills Training

The focus of skills training is to enhance interpersonal skills. Paraphiliacs often rely on the paraphilia because of their inability to engage in satisfying interpersonal sexual relationships. Often they lack the self-esteem, confidence, and behavioral skills to meet potential sex partners and cultivate sexually satisfying relationships.

In skills training they learn a variety of behaviors ranging from communicating (how to initiate conversations, meet new people, and the like) to coping with stress. As individuals become more proficient with these skills, they can learn to rely less and less on their paraphilia for sexual arousal.[21]

WELLNESS SYNTHESIS

Sexual behaviors, like all behaviors, relate to all six components of wellness. A larger question in determining the level of wellness relates to what is "normal."

Physical Well-being

The continuum of atypical sexual behavior, as we've discussed, ranges from the relatively benign (occasional use of a fetish object) to the very dangerous (sadistic beatings and torture). As we've mentioned throughout this text, healthy sexuality promotes physical well-being and behaviors that enhance health. Engaging in many of the atypical sexual behaviors can put your physical health in jeopardy. It is crucial to follow all of the warnings associated with these behaviors. There are ways to reduce the physical health risks associated with atypical sexual behavior. Don't jeopardize your long-term physical health for a fleeting sexual moment.

Intellectual Well-being

Much of what we just said concerning emotional well-being applies to intellectual well-being also. High-level intellectual functioning can help a person know when an atypical behavior pattern represents a true paraphilia. Knowledge can help people understand that they have a problem and how to seek help in dealing with it. Paraphilias, however, tend to have such a strong hold over people that knowledge alone usually isn't enough to motivate them to seek help. Even so, knowledge can play a part in helping them learn how to live with their obsession and channel it into more acceptable forms of expression.

Emotional Well-being

The difference between someone who engages in atypical sexual behavior and the true paraphiliac is in the emotional distress and social dysfunction the latter experiences. An individual or couple can engages in almost all of the atypical behaviors of paraphiliacs without this representing a paraphiliac sexual condition. A person can be emotionally healthy and still enjoy an occasional walk on the wild side. Actually, some people engage in atypical sexual activities to add a spark to their sex lives. When the behavior becomes an obsession, however, and carries with it emotional distress and social dysfunction, it becomes a paraphiliac sexual disorder.

Social Well-being

People who engage in atypical sexual activity (particularly partnered activities) can be socially healthy. They may engage in atypical activities to add spice to their sex lives. Most people with full-blown paraphilias, however, are not doing well socially. Their paraphilia often originated from disordered social functioning and learning. The paraphilia takes the place of functional adult social and sexual relationships. Many paraphiliacs experience sexual release through solitary masturbation in the presence of their paraphiliac object of desire.

Spiritual Well-being

When discussing spiritual well-being, we must take care to separate people who engage in occasional atypical sexual behavior from paraphiliacs. Because spirituality emphasizes the interconnectedness of people and treating all people with respect and dignity, they cannot be spiritually healthy if they engage in paraphilias such as sadism, masochism, and pedophilia — which are based on disrespect. Seeking gratification by inflicting pain or humiliating or dominating others represents an absence of spirituality. It also points to the need to infuse spiritual development into treatment modalities for certain forms of paraphilia.

Environmental Well-being

The overwhelming majority of paraphiliacs are harmless, and as long as their behavior is private, and with consenting adults, it does not represent a threat to society. In other instances it does. Legislation was passed in New Jersey and California, for example, to protect children from sex offenders in their communities.

The New Jersey legislation, "Megan's Law," was enacted in response to the brutal murder of a young girl, Megan Kanka, by a neighbor who was a known sex offender. Essentially, the new law requires that neighbors be notified that a convicted sex offender has moved into their neighborhood. The hope is that such notification will enable parents and other neighbors to protect their children by keeping them away from the sex offender.

In 1994, 12 new laws were enacted in California specifically targeting sex offenders. Provisions of these laws include, among others, a state-maintained toll-free phone number that alerts people to registered sex offenders living in their area, stiffer penalties for first-time offenders convicted of child molestation or rape, and the barring of unsupervised visits of sex offenders to their children.

WEB RESOURCES

Continuing Medical Information

http://www.mhsource.com/edu/psytimes/p960627.html

An article from *Psychiatric Times* by Dr. Martin Kafka, on "Therapy for Sexuality: The Paraphilias and Paraphilia-Related Disorders." Paraphilias, sexual impulse disorders, and pharmacotherapy are discussed.

Human Sexuality from University of Missouri at Kansas Site

http://www.umkc.edu/sites/hsw/issues/para.html

Site of graduate students enrolled in Theories and Practice of Sexual Counseling. Presents a wide range of sexual issues and solutions from erectile dysfunction and female genital mutilation to marital infidelity. Included is a general sex education section and a section of sexual issues affecting health.

Sexual Compulsives Anonymous (SCA)

http://www.sca-recovery.org

A fellowship of men and women who desire to stop having compulsive sex. It is not allied with any sect, denomination, politics, organization, or institution. Using the 12-step Alcoholics Anonymous program, SCA helps members overcome sexual compulsiveness. Resources for other sexual recovery programs are listed along with literature about recovery.

Notes

1. American Psychiatric Association, *The Diagnostic and Statistical Manual of Mental Disorders*, 4th edition (Washington, DC: APA, 1994), p. 525.
2. APA, p. 524.
3. APA, p. 525.
4. APA, p. 532.
5. APA, p. 526.
6. APA, p. 526.
7. APA, p. 527.
8. APA, p. 527.
9. L. Davis, M.D. McShane, and F.P. Williams "Controlling Computer Access to Pornography: Special Conditions for Sex Offenders," *Federal Probation*, 59:2(1995), 43–48.
10. D.E. Kaplan, "New Cybercop Tricks to Fight Child Porn: Police Struggle Against an Online Onslaught," *U.S. News and World Report*, 122:20 (1997), 29.
11. Davis et al.
12. Davis et al.
13. APA, p. 529.
14. S.M. Innala, and K.E. Ernulf, Asphysixiophilia in Scandinavia, *Archives of Sexual Behavior*, 18, 181–190.
15. APA, p. 529.
16. APA, p. 530.
17. APA, p. 530.
18. In J. Money and M. Lamacz, *Vandalized Lovemaps* (New York: Prometheus, 1989).
19. J. Wincze, S. Bansal and M. Malamud, "Effects of Medroxprogesterone Acetate on Subjective Arousal, Arousal to Erotic Stimulation, and Nocturnal Penile Tumescence in Male Sex Offenders," *Archives of Sexual Behavior*, 15(1986), 293–306; A.J. Cooper, "Progesterone in the Treatment of Male Sex Offenders: A Review," *Canadian Journal of Psychiatry*, 31(1986), 73–79.
20. S. Walen and D. Roth, "A Cognitive Approach," *Theories of Human Sexuality*, edited by J.H. Geer and W.T. O'Donohue (New York: Plenum Press, 1987).
21. Zilbergeld, B. (1992).

Student Study Questions

1. What are some of the many facets of "normal" sexual behavior?

2. What does "atypical" sexual behavior mean?

3. When does atypical sexual behavior become a paraphilia?

4. How do a person's morality and ethics influence atypical sexual behavior?

5. How have the media treated some of the more common paraphilias such as voyeurism and exhibition?

6. What is the difference between a true transsexual and someone with transvestic fetishism?

7.   What are the origins of paraphilias?

8.   What are three treatment approaches for paraphilias?

Values Continuum

Instructions: For each of the 10 sexual behaviors below, mark the appropriate spot on the continuum indicating your level of approval/disapproval.

1. Heterosexual vaginal intercourse.

   strongly disapprove ◄─────────────────────────────────► strongly approve

2. Being tied to a bed, chair or other structure during sex.

   strongly disapprove ◄─────────────────────────────────► strongly approve

3. Being spanked or paddled during sex.

   strongly disapprove ◄─────────────────────────────────► strongly approve

4. Being pinched or bitten during sex.

   strongly disapprove ◄─────────────────────────────────► strongly approve

5. Masturbating or having sex with the aid of a special object (shoes etc.)

   strongly disapprove ◄─────────────────────────────────► strongly approve

6. Being totally submissive during sex (must follow your partner's instructions or be punished).

   strongly disapprove ◄─────────────────────────────────► strongly approve

7. Being totally dominating during sex (your partner must follow your instructions or be punished).

   strongly disapprove ◄─────────────────────────────────► strongly approve

8. Watch someone else (or a couple) get undressed or have sex.

   strongly disapprove ◄─────────────────────────────────► strongly approve

9. Intentionally get undressed or have sex in public view (shades open, etc.)

   strongly disapprove ◄─────────────────────────────────► strongly approve

10. Masturbate while looking at pictures of children.

    strongly disapprove ◄─────────────────────────────────► strongly approve

There is no right or wrong answer for the 10 statements. By examining your position on the 10 different continua you can get a sense of where your values lie regarding atypical sexual behavior. The important point is understanding your values and sharing them with your sex partner. You may wish to have your partner take this assessment and discuss your results with each other.

Intimate Relationships

Major Topics

Student Learning Objectives

After reading this chapter, students will be able to:

- Describe the key elements of healthy relationships.

- Define *intimacy* and trace its development in relationships.

- Define *love* and describe how it develops in relationships.

- Identify the impacts of unsuccessful relationships.

- Examine a variety of ways to end unhappy relationships.

- Compare a variety of theories regarding love.

- Evaluate a variety of barriers to intimacy.

- Describe various techniques used to overcome barriers to intimacy.

Intimacy
connectedness to another person characterized by mutual caring, openness, self-disclosure, honesty, attentiveness, sharing, commitment, trust, empathy, and tenderness

The ability to form healthy relationships is something we learn and practice.

Our quality of life depends to a large extent on the types of relationships we develop. Relationships define our connectedness to others and provide opportunities for **intimacy**. Intimate relationships are characterized by honesty, caring, sharing, trust, commitment, empathy, and tenderness. Forming healthy relationships with others is a skill a person *develops* and *practices*. For relationships to be intimate, we have to be ourselves and let others be who they are. Good relationships derive from good role models and require giving thought to the outcome of our actions.

As we age, we form social relationships with others on many levels — family, friends, working colleagues, neighbors, and partners. Although this chapter focuses primarily on partner relationships, we have to realize that becoming sexually intimate with someone does not necessarily mean that we automatically have an emotionally intimate relationship.

We learn patterns of relating to others from our families, friends, and past experiences. Some people are extroverted and outgoing, and enjoy having many different types of relationships. Developing relationships is easy for them. Other people are introverted and enjoy doing many things alone. They develop fewer relationships in their lives, and may have difficulty forming new relationships. Regardless, human contact is essential for health and wellness.

ESTABLISHING RELATIONSHIPS

The dynamics of forming close, intimate relationships with friends are different from the dynamics of developing intimate relationships with sexual partners. A look at the shelves of a bookstore quickly reveals rows of books offering advice on how to find a partner, keep a partner, satisfy a partner, and be satisfied with a partner. (Figure 10.1 humorously depicts the dilemma.) But you won't find rows and rows of books on how to make and keep friends. The same holds true for music. The lyrics of country, rock, and blues passionately describe the ups and downs of emotions related to love relationships. The intensity of feelings related to platonic friendships just doesn't compare.

Friends share activities, thoughts, and feelings. They help each other out. When a life experience tests a friendship, we often hear the comment, "That really let me know who my true friends are!" With friends, we are relaxed and able to "be yourself."

Now switch the scenario to a boyfriend, girlfriend, partner. A healthy romantic relationship, one that is founded on intimacy, requires the same expectations, yet we may find ourselves not being authentic with our thoughts and feelings, second guessing the other person, and sometimes tolerating behaviors we would never accept from our friends. The erotic piece of the puzzle is what changes the interaction. We often become self-conscious in ways we hadn't anticipated, and we might lose our identity in pursuit of the relationship. Healthy relationships are based on being able to clearly identify who we are, what we want, how we want to be treated, how we want to live, and recognizing that we deserve to want what we want.

Meeting People ⚔

The first step toward developing an intimate relationship is connecting with a potential partner. People can meet in many ways, not all equally comfortable or familiar. College is sometimes viewed as an ideal place to meet someone and form an intimate relationship, yet some students graduate without experiencing a serious dating relationship. Unlike years past, when many college women in particular had been told that they had four years to earn their "Mrs. degree," students today are likely to feel less pressure to be married upon graduation. Even when students do not have marriage as a goal, though, they have the desire to form intimate relationships.

Relationships start with being able to clearly see who you are and what you need.

Before looking at issues of where and how to meet people, they have to be ready for a relationship. Are they open to a relationship? Are they comfortable

Source: CATHY © Cathy Guisewite. Reprinted with permission of Universal Press Syndicate. All rights reserved.

Figure 10.1 ❭ Do you give men a chance?

Intimacy implies connectedness to someone else.

with themselves? If they were hurt in a previous relationship, they may not have let go of the "old baggage." Too often people approach a new relationship with defensiveness, negative past associations that become expectations with a new partner, and patterns of relating that prevent new relationships from developing.

Feeling comfortable when meeting people and forming relationships is a social skill, and, as such, is behavior that is modeled, taught, and practiced. People have to feel comfortable enough with themselves to believe they are worth getting to know — fundamental to self-esteem. People who consider themselves "shy" may find social settings very intimidating. They may not be able to identify the behaviors and words needed to make social contact with others.

Shyness

Zimbardo's classic work on shyness provides a framework for understanding what is a nearly universal experience of being shy at some point in one's life.[1] More than 80% reported feeling shy at some time, 25% described themselves as chronically shy, and 4% described themselves as being shy all the time, in all situations, with virtually all people. The ability to overcome shyness is essential to forming relationships.

Shyness is revealed in a number of ways. People who are shy may experience or demonstrate one or more of the following characteristics:

- speaking softly
- not making eye contact
- being reticent/reluctant to relate to others
- blushing
- experiencing "butterflies" in the stomach
- feeling embarrassed
- feeling self-conscious.

Although everyone has those experiences and feelings at times, shyness becomes a problem when the level and frequency of those experiences impedes the development of relationships. Shy individuals might be operating from a negative script in which they deem themselves unacceptable and unworthy, and they typically lack the social skills of knowing how to initiate conversation and make connections. Zimbardo found that overcoming shyness is possible if individuals are willing to work on making changes in the way they think about themselves and others and in how they behave.

Another impediment to forming intimate relationships is the fear of being rejected. Some people enter social situations with an expectation that they will be rejected. They become anxious about being rejected, expect to be rejected, and overreact to what may be ambiguous behavior in others.[2] Again, having a frame of mind that allows one to approach others in a positive way, without worrying about rejection, is more likely to lead to better interactions and a possible relationship.

"Pack" Dating

Reports from some colleges and universities reveal that students do not date in traditional ways; they prefer to socialize in groups rather than pair off.[3] Traveling with a small circle of five or six friends, they go to movies, parties, and dinner, feeling safe within their group. This is an excellent way to discover what types of people you enjoy being with and what you are looking for in a partner.

In a study of 9,100 undergraduates from campuses across the United States, students reported a preference for casual sex rather than deeply committed emotional relationships. Increasingly, sexual liaisons result from partying, drinking, going to someone's room, and then having little contact

College is an ideal setting for meeting someone with whom to form an intimate relationship.

with that person later. The term "hooking up" defines that experience for all its ambiguity: Two people can kiss and fondle extensively, sleep together fully clothed, or have sexual intercourse. Developing a long-term relationship is another matter. Some students explain their reticence for developing committed relationships by their lack of witnessing successful relationships among their parents and other adults they know.

Where and How to Meet People

As our lifestyles become busier, "meeting someone" can become a project of sorts. College life affords a variety of situations for students to meet other students — classes, student centers, clubs, and so on.

On an individual basis, a student spends many hours at school, and that setting is an obvious place to meet a potential partner. If you meet someone who lives in your dormitory who seems attractive, what would you do? If you are taking a class and someone across the room makes eye contact, begins to flirt, and suggests you both go to the Student Center to get something to eat, how would you react? Weighing the costs and benefits of developing dating relationships is not an easy task.

College offers a comfortable social environment in which to form relationships. Academic classes, clubs, parties, sorority and fraternity functions, rallies, student newspapers and yearbooks, and the like involve students in activities while simultaneously providing environments to meet others.

If similarities in race, culture, or religion are important, campus organizations whose members align themselves with the relevant similarities may be places to meet. Because of issues of "coming out" and the added burden of attempting to determine someone's sexual orientation, lesbian, gay, and bisexual students may want to meet through organizations in which sexual orientation is the foundation for the group.

As a result of the Anita Hill versus Clarence Thomas hearings related to sexual harassment, the culture has started to redefine and pay attention to settings where developing romantic attachments is deemed inappropriate and, at the minimum, adds complications, obvious and subtle. Consequently, although dating someone in your class can become awkward if the relationship doesn't work out, dating someone with whom you work can be more complicated, as work situations often involve competition and power. Sexual harassment laws and policies usually define work-based relationships and those that could develop with a professor or supervisor as prohibited and actionable under the law.

Outside of the school environment, you may find that dating becomes more of a project than you had anticipated. Work hours, busy schedules, and a desire to avoid the bar scene have led to technological interventions for dating. Personal advertisements, which used to be a feature in select newspapers and magazines, now have worked their way into mainstream newspapers (see Figure 10.2), cable television, and the internet. Sophisticated video dating services, in which registered members can review tapes of people they might want to meet, have flourished in some areas. Hefty membership fees and promises made by some dating services, however, have sometimes resulted in dissatisfied consumers suing for fraud.

Choosing a Partner

When asked to describe what makes someone attractive to them, students have responded with a combination of physical attributes and personality characteristics. Some responses are specific, and others are more general. A sampling from the authors' files includes the following.

- I like a guy who is not overly muscular, has a hairy chest, and nice buns.

- I like big breasts, a round butt, and long hair.

- He must be clean, have good teeth, and not smoke.

- The smile is important to me. And eyes — I can tell a lot from the eyes.

- I like to bike and mountain-climb. I need a partner who likes the outdoors and has a sense of adventure.

- She has to have some brains, not be too skinny, and like sports.

- I always like blondes — blond hair, blue eyes.

- My partners have always been dark — dark skin, dark eyes, dark hair.

- He has to be nice, have a good sense of humor, and enjoy family.

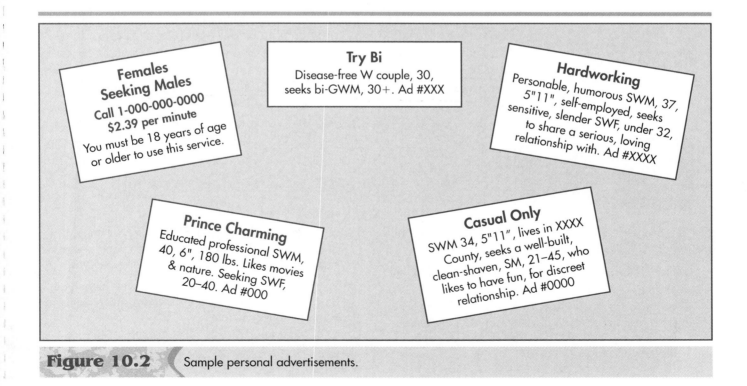

Females Seeking Males
Call 1-000-000-0000
$2.39 per minute
You must be 18 years of age or older to use this service.

Try Bi
Disease-free W couple, 30, seeks bi-GWM, 30+. Ad #XXX

Hardworking
Personable, humorous SWM, 37, 5"11", self-employed, seeks sensitive, slender SWF, under 32, to share a serious, loving relationship with. Ad #XXXX

Prince Charming
Educated professional SWM, 40, 6", 180 lbs. Likes movies & nature. Seeking SWF, 20–40. Ad #000

Casual Only
SWM 34, 5"11", lives in XXXX County, seeks a well-built, clean-shaven, SM, 21–45, who likes to have fun, for discreet relationship. Ad #0000

Figure 10.2 Sample personal advertisements.

- I'm very involved with my church and want to wait to have sex until I'm married. I find it hard sometimes to meet people at school who share my views. I'm attracted to religious, virginal types.

- I like them all. My partners have all been different. Looks don't matter that much to me. It's what's inside their head that counts."

Adjectives such as "nice" and "good" point to the subjectivity of attraction. Some of us have qualities that do not allow someone a chance. Some males refuse to get interested in females who are taller than they are, and some females refuse to get involved with males who are too short. Gay men who work out with weights and value large muscles might ignore men who don't exercise regularly. And lesbians who embrace looking natural could reject a woman who uses cosmetics and make-up.

Research on partner choice and attraction leads to certain generalizations. Most people are drawn to partners from similar backgrounds and form relationships with people who are close in age, race, ethnicity, and social status. Table 10.1 presents findings of the National Opinion Research Center (NORC), in which race, education, age, and religious background were found to be similar in a significant number of couples.[4]

The authors reported that about 90% of couples were of the same race. Having similar educational backgrounds was also the predominant pattern as individuals chose sexual partners. Men who had less than a high-school education seldom had a partner who had gone to college, and men with a college degree almost never reported having sex with women who had much less or much more education than they did.[5] Similarly, 81% of the women who did not finish high school chose men with a high-school degree or less, and women who had graduate degrees reported never choosing partners who had not finished high school.

Religion and age comparisons also yielded choices based on similarity. The authors of the NORC study concluded that couples with more marked differences in background tend to be the exception rather than the rule. Most people choose partners and marry someone who is the same race, same educational background, same religion, and within 5 years of their age.

Health Hint

Developing a Lasting Relationship

Here are some things you can do to develop a lasting friendship with someone you care about:

- Start with someone you feel close to or *want* to feel close to.

- Learn to trust. It's tough to face possible rejection when you let someone in on your deepest secrets, but a true friend will love and accept you regardless of your flaws.

- Be willing to share your most personal thoughts and feelings, as well as your time, your possessions, and other things that are important to you.

- Spend plenty of time together; it's what helps you develop a closeness. If you have to, make adjustments in your schedule.

- Be a good listener. Your friend needs a confidant, too.

| Table 10.1 | Partnerships in Which the Two Partners are Similar in Social Characteristics |

Type of Similarity	Type of Partnership			
	Marriage	Cohabitation	Long-term Noncohabiting	Short-term Noncohabiting
	Percent			
Racial/Ethnic	93	88	89	91
Age	78	75	76	83
Educational	82	87	83	87
Religious	72	53	56	60

Notes: (1) Observations are partnerships, including all sexually active partnerships in the past 12 months. Excluded are marriages or cohabitations that began more than 10 years before the interview date. Respondents with more than one sex partner in the past 12 months are represented more than once (up to a maximum of nine partnerships may be included for any one respondent). Short-term noncohabiting partnerships are those lasting less than 1 month and where no more than 10 sexual episodes occurred. Long-term noncohabiting partnerships include those lasting more than 1 month and/or involving more than 10 sexual episodes. (2) Age similarity is defined as no more than 5 years between partners' ages. Educational similarity is defined as a difference of no more than one educational category where the categories include: less than high school, high school graduate, some college or vocational training, 4-year college, and graduate degree. Race/ethnicity categories include: White, Black, Hispanic, and Asian. Religions include: none, mainline Protestant, conservative Protestant, and Catholic.

Source: *Sex in America*, by Robert T. Michael et al. Copyright © 1994 by CSG Enterprises, Inc., Little, Brown and Company. Used with permission.

Sometimes when a person tells you, "You're really nice, but I like you just as a friend," you feel rejected. When you meet people, what is it that makes you respond "Hmm . . . he's really cute" or, "I'd really like to go out with her?" What is it that makes us respond to someone as a potential romantic partner instead of a friend?

How important are race, religion, age, and educational background in your attraction to someone? By what means and to what extent do you check out someone's background before allowing yourself to get to know him or her better?

Our society tends to be structured in segregated ways. Consequently, where you live, work, and with whom you socialize have an influence on your choice of partner.[6] Figure 10.3 highlights where people met their partners.

Problems of definition exist in overvaluing the NORC findings. The topic of race alone is so complicated that critics of traditional demography recommend dispensing with that social classification altogether. Anthropologists have documented hundreds of races, so to describe groups using a few traditional categories — White, Black, Hispanic, Asian — is of limited value. For example, discussion of race has been part of many articles on pro golfer Tiger Woods; though some consider him "Black," his background is so diverse that "multiracial" seems to be the most accurate description.

Attraction

Many researchers have concluded that people prefer romantic partners who are physically attractive, and that there is some cultural consistency in what is deemed attractive.[7] An image of the ideal female and male physique emerges from the media and advertising, and though it may be hard to attain in reality, the standard is set in many people's minds. How we each think we measure up to cultural ideals also may influence our sexual self-esteem. Are we acceptable? Are we attractive? We have found in our classes that just as students can identify what they find attractive in others, they

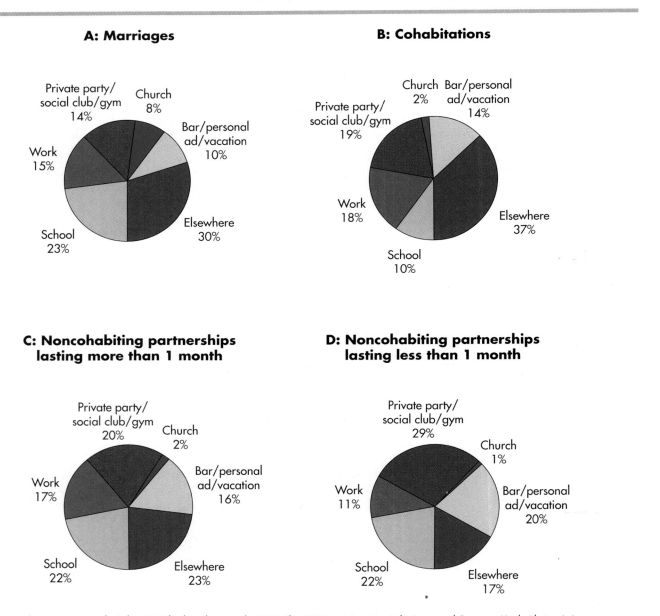

A: Marriages

Private party/social club/gym 14%
Church 8%
Bar/personal ad/vacation 10%
Work 15%
Elsewhere 30%
School 23%

B: Cohabitations

Church 2%
Bar/personal ad/vacation 14%
Private party/social club/gym 19%
Work 18%
Elsewhere 37%
School 10%

C: Noncohabiting partnerships lasting more than 1 month

Private party/social club/gym 20%
Church 2%
Bar/personal ad/vacation 16%
Work 17%
Elsewhere 23%
School 22%

D: Noncohabiting partnerships lasting less than 1 month

Private party/social club/gym 29%
Church 1%
Bar/personal ad/vacation 20%
Work 11%
Elsewhere 17%
School 22%

Source: *Sex in America,* by Robert T. Michael, et al. Copyright © 1994 by CSG Enterprises, Inc., Little, Brown and Company. Used with permission.

Figure 10.3   Where partners first met.

can identify aspects of themselves they deem attractive, as well as characteristics they do not like. Individuals will become sexually healthier when they can accept themselves or make constructive changes that allow them to interact in a healthier way.

Research on attraction has indicated different values between the sexes. Males place more emphasis on physical attributes than females do. Females value interpersonal warmth, personality, and earning potential over appearance.[8] Regardless, looks alone do not define attractiveness, nor can looks sustain a relationship. Most of us have admired someone for their looks only to discover that this person had a voice that detracted from their appearance or thoughts and values that we found objectionable, making that person unappealing after all. Over time, looks diminish in importance, as we develop loving feelings toward our partners and accept them "warts and all."

Social psychologist Donn Byrne developed a theory of attraction focusing on rewards and punishments.[9] He postulated that we tend to like people who reward us by making us feel good about ourselves and tend to dislike people who punish us and are nasty. Relationships can develop and function well when we get along with our partners. Although this sounds like common sense, too many people invest time and energy in relationships that are not working, with people who do not treat them well, and where they do not feel good about themselves.

Sexual Chemistry

Many times friends and family offer to "fix up" a person with someone they're "sure you'll like." A man may be told, "She's attractive, very nice, interested in a lot of different things." Or a woman may be told, "I have just the man for you! He's smart, handsome, talented, and has a great sense of humor." So, with such glowing testaments, they agree to a blind date (see Figure 10.4). They go out. They have an okay time but can't see anything romantic developing. They don't disagree about their date's attributes; he or she is objectively attractive, has a nice personality, and so on but just doesn't excite the other person. The explanation to the matchmaker is, "Well, there was just no chemistry — no spark."

Despite a host of attractive traits, chemistry may be lacking. People respond to the smell of others and bad breath may turn us off. Certain colognes, perfumes, and aftershaves are designed to turn us on. On an unconscious level, we may be responding to **pheromones**, which are sex-attractant chemicals, more familiar in lower animal forms. For example, a female dog "in heat" puts out an odor that male dogs can pick up from some distance. Even though human attraction is not founded so heavily in reproductive issues, odors may have a larger role than previously thought.[10]

Studies have begun to look at the impact of chemicals in male sweat and female vaginal secretions, examining their role in increasing attraction between a male and a female; their role in same-sex couples has yet to be assessed. The intense feelings associated with the early phases of a relationship, when we feel excited and caught up with the newness of the relationship, may have a chemical connection to higher levels of phenylenthylamine (PEA) and possibly dopamine and norepinephrine, stimulants the body

✗ **Pheromones**
body chemicals that attract potential sexual partners

produces. As a consequence, we literally can be on a "romantic high" that can be explained through chemistry.[11]

Compatibility

In the long run, what makes a relationship work is how compatible the two individuals are. A healthy relationship allows two people to be who they truly are, with no attempt to change the partners. The values and lifestyles of the two, therefore, must mesh closely.

Popular books abound, offering advice on finding the right partner and making the relationship work. One popular author whose approach works well from a wellness model is Barbara DeAngelis, author of *Are You the One for Me? Knowing Who's Right and Avoiding Who's Wrong.*[12] DeAngelis advises her readers to develop a compatibility checklist along 10 dimensions, identifying qualities that are important to them in each category. When two people are in an actual relationship, assessing compatibility takes time, as some things are learned early in a relationship and others over a period of months, if not longer.

Source: CATHY © Cathy Guisewite. Reprinted with permission of Universal Press Syndicate. All rights reserved.

Figure 10.4   Blind date.

PERSPECTIVES

Compatibility List

Barbara DeAngelis wrote "Your Compatibility List can help you understand what is and what isn't working between you and your mate, and make it easier to decide whether it's time to separate. If you're looking for a new relationship, your Compatibility List acts like a shopping list, directing you toward partners who are right for you and helping you avoid partners you don't need and who will be a waste of time."

Directions: Use the following 10 categories to identify qualities you possess and those you want in a partner. Being as specific as possible will make the list more useful. When comparing results, you need to keep in mind how flexible you can be, how frequently you need traits to be exhibited, and which aspects of a relationship may work even if you two don't match.

1. **Physical style**: appearance, eating habits, personal fitness habits, personal hygiene.

   Example: I exercise regularly. I would want a partner who likes to work out and exercise.

2. **Emotional style**: attitudes toward romance and affection, expression of emotions, approach to relationships.

   Example: I'm very affectionate and need a lot of support. I would want a partner who would be affectionate and care about my interests.

3. **Social style**: personality traits, ways of interacting with others.

   Example: I'm very outgoing and love to have family and friends around. I would not want a partner who only wanted to be with me and stay at home.

4. **Intellectual style**: educational background, attitude toward learning, world affairs.

   Example: I'm a college graduate and read the newspaper daily. I also love books, both fiction and nonfiction. I would want a partner who is aware of what is going on in the world and also loves to read. My partner would have to at least have an associate's degree, although I would prefer someone who has finished a four-year college program.

5. **Sexual style**: attitudes, skill, ability to enjoy sex.

   Example: I love to try new things and be adventurous. I would want a partner who enjoys sex and is creative.

6. **Communication style**: patterns of communication, attitude toward talking, other forms of expression.

   Example: I know that I tend to scream when I'm angry. My family is a bunch of screamers. While I may need to

work on that behavior, I'd need someone who would understand that the screaming is more style than substance and wouldn't let the volume get to him [her].

7. **Professional/financial style**: relationship with money, attitudes toward success, work, and organizational habits.

   Example: I work hard and budget my money carefully, never owing more than a couple hundred dollars on a credit card. I couldn't be with someone who gambles and is always in debt.

8. **Personal growth style**: attitudes toward self-improvement, ability to be introspective and change, willingness to work on a relationship.

   Example: I tend to think a lot about what I value and how I came to be who I am. If a relationship is important to me, I would do anything — even seek professional help if necessary — to make it work. I wouldn't want a partner who couldn't look at how we were getting along and work on the relationship.

9. **Spiritual style**: attitudes toward a higher power, spiritual practices, philosophy of life, moral views.

   Example: I'm very involved with my church, working with youth groups and helping at local shelters. My partner wouldn't have to be exactly the same faith but would have to respect my beliefs and have a sense of his or her own.

10. **Interests and hobbies:**

    Example: I love to travel, and I do my best to take at least one exciting vacation to some place new each year. I would want a partner who also likes to travel, or at least would be willing to travel.

After reviewing your list, think about how open you are to changing any of your answers. If you are without a partner, thinking about your interests becomes valuable in assessing how well you two match. As you get to know someone, finding dissimilar answers and styles in too many areas highlights a lack of compatibility. Most important, not all areas are equally important.

Excerpted and adapted in format from *Are You The One for Me? Knowing Who's Right and Avoiding Who's Wrong,* by Barbara DeAngelis (New York: Dell, ©1992, a division of Random House, Inc.), pp 366–369. Reprinted with permission.

MAINTAINING
HEALTHY RELATIONSHIPS

In plain language, a healthy relationship is one that is good for you. Finding a compatible partner is part of the process, yet the number of relationships that break up and marriages that end in divorce indicate that initial assessments can change or be wrong in the first place.

Relationships that are good for you make you happy most of the time. They are fun, sources of strength and support, and connections that improve the quality of your life. You can be who you are and be appreciated for your uniqueness. If you are unhappy, depressed, sad, and feeling that you are hiding your true self, those feelings should serve as a barometer to the health of the relationship. Putting your needs and self aside to "keep a relationship going" is not good, as it fosters imbalance of power and interest in

Case Study

Cheryl's Story

Tim and I met senior year at a party hosted by mutual friends. We lived in a small town outside Boston, where I was attending the regional Catholic high school and he the public one. I had seen him at some high school basketball games, but it wasn't until that party that we actually had a chance to talk. We dated each other exclusively from that moment on, spending Christmas with each other's families, going out alone or with friends every weekend, and sharing a very romantic senior prom. Graduation was both joyous and sad, as now we would be going away to different colleges.

At the end of August, we talked about our feelings for each other and decided to make the best of the distance between us. We wouldn't date anybody at school and would remain faithful to each other. All freshman year we talked twice a week by phone, wrote back and forth by e-mail, and managed to see each other one weekend a month. I enjoyed being away at school but missed Tim. I was often asked out but turned away all potential dates. I just wasn't interested in meeting any other guys. Tim was busy with his studies and working, so I wasn't worried that he was going out.

That summer we were together, and things were wonderful. Sophomore year was like freshman year

— lots of friends, a few parties — and again I didn't have any interest in dating. Tim was the man I loved, and I kept focused on the summer, when we would be together again. Little did I know what lay in store.

I still get knots in my stomach thinking about the summer of '95. One week Tim said he loved me. The next he wasn't sure. We would fight. I would cry. He would apologize. We'd be fine for a while, and then the cycle would start up again. My parents tried not to interfere, but they could see how miserable I was. At the end of August, we decided to break up and date other people.

Junior year was a quiet one for me. I still thought of Tim a lot, although I did try to focus on my major. Tim called occasionally and then asked if we could have dinner during winter break. Of course, I agreed. Seeing Tim again was awkward at first, but then we got back into our familiar banter. He told me how much he had missed me, and I realized how much I loved him. We decided to give the relationship another try.

We were "together," although physically apart, for the rest of junior year and senior year. I was looking into graduate school programs, and Tim was planning to go to work. When he accepted a job in California, I followed him there. I would go to grad

the relationship. Other people often can identify relationships as unhealthy when those in the relationship cannot.

Patterns of physical and mental abuse are obvious markers of an unhealthy relationship. Both forms of abuse may develop slowly but tend to increase as the relationship becomes more involved. Being put down, insulted, blamed for a partner's problems ("It's your fault . . ."), or being pushed, shoved, or beaten, are all forms of abuse.

Typically, the abuser has been abused himself or herself and has learned inappropriate ways of dealing with feelings of anger and frustration. Some abusers have violent personalities, and others have no respect for their partner's right to think and behave independently. Regardless, without the abusive person's getting professional help and being willing to change, the abuse will continue and the "relationship" will be between an abuser and a victim, rather than two adults in a healthy relationship.

school, we'd each have our own place, but we could finally live again in the same place.

Things were pretty good the first year. We saw each other when we could and functioned as a couple. Then his company transferred him to Chicago, and I was left in California to finish my program. Since I had put all my energy into studying and Tim, I found that I didn't have a lot of friends. That last year of school was quiet, but I knew if I could find a job in Chicago, we could be together again.

Tim encouraged me to move to Chicago. He bought a house there and had me move in. All this time my parents were rather reserved in their support. They weren't happy that I kept following Tim and now planned to live with him without our being formally engaged. I don't think they liked him or trusted him either, although they never said that — with words, anyway. I wasn't worried, because we were in love. I didn't even care that the house was Tim's, I just assumed that after we got married, it would be ours together.

Luck was on my side. I found a job in Chicago! The move went easily, and we set up house. I made friends at work, as had Tim. Slowly, however, tensions grew. I was cleaning the house, preparing meals, and taking care of "our" dog. Tim was busy and often liked to go out with the guys after work. I realized how lonely and depressed I was becoming. It was one thing to miss Tim because we were living apart. It was another thing to miss Tim when we were living together.

It took me the whole year to realize how unhappy I was. Tim and I seldom saw each other. When we did, he would often criticize me in some way — my hair was a mess, I looked fat, the house was dusty. It didn't take much to annoy him. Despite it all, I still loved him, yet was finally realizing that we didn't have a good relationship. Tim's telling me at Christmas that he wasn't sure if he loved me or not was the last straw. I resigned from my job, called home, and within one week I was packed and back with my family.

That was a few years ago. The memories are very strong, yet finally the anger has subsided. I was angry at Tim. And angry at myself. As the saying goes, I "couldn't see the forest for the trees." I invested a lot of time with one person and lost myself too much in the process.

Jealousy

Feelings of jealousy, particularly if out of control and increasingly intense, can spell the end of a relationship. The news too often announces murders committed by a jealous lover, current or from the past. Jealousy can result from a number of factors: low self-esteem, fear of loss, bruised pride, insecurity, and in some cases, a sense of "lost property."[13] Individuals may react with feelings of jealousy in response to behaviors they find threatening. For example, a woman may get upset at seeing her boyfriend be kissed by a female friend. Another woman may not care about gestures of affection but not be able to handle a current boyfriend even having a cup of coffee with a woman he used to date.

Men and women have been found to respond to feelings of jealousy in different ways. Jealous women are more likely to focus on the emotional involvement of their partner with another person, whereas, men may focus on the sexual activity of their partner with another person. Men are more likely to respond with rage and violence, and women are more likely to blame themselves and display more possessive behavior.[14]

When asked in a classroom setting, college students have voiced the opinion that some amount of jealousy is good for a relationship and shows love for the partner. In actuality, the foundation for jealous feelings is not based on love, nor are these feelings likely to be healthy for a relationship.

Love

Tina Turner made famous a song with the lyrics "What's love got to do with it?" The emotion of love is tied closely to our emotions and expectations from relationships and has been a topic for songwriters and researchers. Studies on love have attempted to classify the emotion, develop theory,

Shared interests are important to a relationship.

examine love styles, make cross-cultural comparisons, and recognize the complexity of the emotion.

Finding a comfortable definition of love is not easy. Some advise of the need to differentiate "love" and "lust." Others talk about being able to tell the difference between "love" and "infatuation." Hatfield and Rapson distinguish between passionate love and and companionate love.[15] **Passionate love** is "a hot, intense emotion, sometimes called a crush, obsessive love, lovesickness, head-over-heels in love, infatuation, or being in love." It is further defined as "an intense longing for union with another," and if it is reciprocated, there is fulfillment and ecstasy. If the love is unrequited, the person has feelings of emptiness, anxiety, or despair. Passionate love carries the desire to form a sexual union with the object of the love.

In contrast, **companionate love** is what we ideally experience as relationships endure. It is characterized by feelings of deep attachment, commitment, and intimacy. Companionate love encompasses feelings of affection and tenderness we feel for those with whom our lives are deeply connected.

Theories of Love

Robert Sternberg developed a theoretical model for examining love.[16] Shown in Figure 10.5, love is conceptualized as a triangle with three faces: passion, intimacy, and commitment. Each person within a love

Passionate love
feelings characterized by intense longing for another, infatuation, ecstasy when reciprocated, and emptiness when not shared by the other

Companionate love
feelings that include deep attachment, commitment, and intimacy

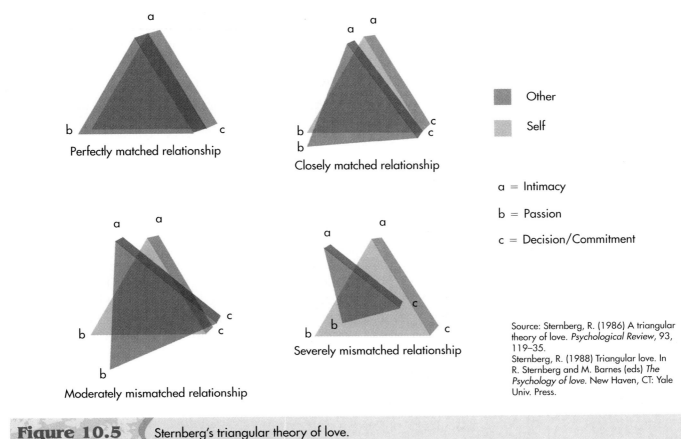

Perfectly matched relationship

Closely matched relationship

Moderately mismatched relationship

Severely mismatched relationship

■ Other
▢ Self

a = Intimacy

b = Passion

c = Decision/Commitment

Source: Sternberg, R. (1986) A triangular theory of love. *Psychological Review*, 93, 119–35.
Sternberg, R. (1988) Triangular love. In R. Sternberg and M. Barnes (eds) *The Psychology of love*. New Haven, CT: Yale Univ. Press.

Figure 10.5 Sternberg's triangular theory of love.

relationship brings his or her triangle to that relationship, albeit with varying dimensions. When two people are well matched, they tend to find satisfaction within their relationship.

Sternberg identified six different kinds of love that evolve in response to the varying dimensions.

- *Liking.* Intimacy only, such as may be found between friends.
- *Infatuation.* Passion only, with high physical and emotional attraction.
- *Romantic love.* A combination of intimacy and passion, similar to liking with the addition of physical attraction.
- *Companionate love.* A combination of intimacy and commitment; may have had romantic components, but the key element is the emotional bond between the two people.
- *Fatuous love.* A combination of passion and commitment, which may lead to two people quickly living together but over time realizing that they lack a deep, emotional intimacy.
- *Consummate love.* Ideal love, combining passion, intimacy, and commitment. Though we may strive to achieve this, it is hard to sustain over time.

Another typology for examining styles of love is credited to John Lee.[17] Recognizing that some styles can be combined, Lee described six styles of love:

- *Eros.* Focuses on physical beauty and has a strong sensual component.
- *Mania.* Characterized by a lot of roller-coaster emotions, with anxiety and ecstasy at the extremes.
- *Ludus.* Love for fun and play — nothing too serious.
- *Storge.* Marked by much affection, gradually deepening into love.
- *Agape.* Type of love that is undemanding, patient, and does not expect reciprocation.
- *Pragma.* Practical love; lovers carefully assess compatibility in background, values, and interest to find a good match.

From Theory to Practice

Most of us want to find a partner with whom we can make a relationship work. Not all relationships function in exactly the same way, yet some characteristics predict a greater likelihood of "success." The style of love may change as people age. The style of love may improve with experience. The style of love may interfere with one's getting into and sustaining the kind of relationship desired. Recognizing your values, style, and how well you "match" to your partner, therefore, becomes valuable as you seek out love and a partner.

Recognizing your values, your style, and how well you "match" to your partner becomes valuable as you seek out love and a partner.

Researchers have found differences in love styles based on gender.[18] In a survey of an extremely diverse

Health Hint

Guidelines for Healthy Relationships

Both people in a relationship have the right to:

- Ask for what they want
- Be accepted for who they are
- Be treated with respect
- Express their thoughts and feelings
- Not be forced to do anything
- Feel safe when alone with each other
- Give and receive expressions of affection
- Make some mistakes and be forgiven
- Say "no" and not feel guilty
- Have fun

No one in the relationship has the right to:

- Tell the other person where and when he or she can go out.
- Act like a boss and order the other person around.
- Degrade and humiliate the other person, either in public or private.
- Isolate the other from friends and family.
- Pressure the other to give up interests and goals.
- Read the partner's personal materials without permission, search private property, or follow the other around.
- Physically intimidate and harm the other person.

group of college students, females tended to be more manic, storgic, and pragmatic than males, who seemed more ludic and erotic. Women were found to be more conservative in their views toward love and relationships, incorporating concerns over finding a mate who would be a good provider and partner. Males, on the other hand, tended to respond early on to beauty and the playful aspects of relationships, and were less concerned with commitment.

SEXUAL ORIENTATION AND RELATIONSHIPS

Love and relationships among gay, lesbian, and bisexual adults have been subject to many myths. Perhaps one of the biggest problems lies in the secrecy involved. To be open about the relationship poses barriers that heterosexual couples seldom face. This translates into day to day losses such as relating stories of weekend fun with co-workers on Monday and the larger risk of losing one's job if co-workers find out about the gay or lesbian orientation.

Research comparing heterosexual couples and gay and lesbian couples has revealed some differences, although the similarities, such as valuing communication, sharing experiences, and laughing together, far outweigh the differences identified. The differences in values one brings to a love relationship are tied more closely to gender than sexual orientation.[19]

Perhaps because gay and lesbian marriages aren't sanctioned, or perhaps in response to the realization that gender role stereotyping is problematic when both partners are of the same sex, same-sex relationships tend to reject the traditional marriage model. (Increasingly, though, heterosexuals

Case Study

José's Story

Marco and I just celebrated our fifth anniversary together, yet few outside our circle of friends know about our relationship. His aunt knows we're a couple, and my sister and cousin know, yet we can't be "out" to our families — not yet, anyway.

I'm the only son in my family, and until recently was the middle child. My older sister was married, and my younger one is single. When my older sister died, my younger sister Selena and I felt increased pressure from my parents to provide grandchildren. My mother, in particular, is very religious and goes to church every day. She prays for her family, and her faith helped her deal with my sister's death. Now she prays to be blessed with a grandchild. Only one of us is going to be able answer those prayers — and Selena doesn't even have a boyfriend.

I get angry at my situation sometimes, and realize that things might be easier if I would come out to my parents. On the other hand, my mother is very religious, and the church hasn't been all that welcoming.

My father never gets into deep conversations, and I fear his disappointment. They've met Marco but just think he's one of my good friends. Since they live in Oklahoma and I'm in San Francisco, it's easier to maintain the lie. Marco and I have Caller ID on the phone, so we usually can tell who's calling before answering. The "right" person answers the phone.

My parents think I live alone and just have had little success dating women. I took a female friend to my senior prom, but other than her, I've never introduced my family to a girlfriend. They seem to be comfortable accepting my stories, although my mother tells me I should "settle down" and make a family.

When my sister died, it was hard to go home and not have Marco with me. And it continues to be hard to visit family without my partner. Straight people don't have to play these games. I'm getting sick of the secrets and know that I cut myself off from family because I expect them not to like me if they knew. I may be wrong, but I'm just not ready to take the risk.

aren't following that model either). Compared to heterosexual couples, gay and lesbian relationships are more egalitarian, in sharing household responsibilities and finances.[20]

Another reported difference has been greater openness to sexual relationships outside the primary one, although that pattern is more prevalent among gay men than lesbian women. The ability to separate sex and love theoretically diminishes feelings of jealousy. It could be easily argued, however, that couples who have an emotional investment in each other do not welcome outside involvements, regardless of sexual orientation.

BREAKING UP AND ENDING RELATIONSHIPS

Just as relationships can be formed in healthy ways, they can be ended in ways that are not destructive. When feelings are mutual, both parties realize that the relationship is not working, and the break-up may not be as difficult. The experience of having a partner break up with you without your awareness of any problems, however, is quite another matter. Ending a relationship in any case is emotionally difficult and painful for most of us.

For at least one of the partners, the relationship wasn't working. The best thing is to let it end and both move on. Mourning the loss and allowing

Health Hint	**Unhealthy Behaviors After Ending A Relationship**

Though some behaviors can be expected following a break-up, others become increasingly problematic if they persist. If the break-up is disrupting your life, get some help from a counselor or therapist. These symptoms indicate a problem:

꩜ Sleeping too much or too little

꩜ Using drugs and alcohol excessively

꩜ Inability to eat

꩜ Inability to concentrate on work

꩜ Inability to study

꩜ Wanting to drop classes

꩜ Wanting to drop out of school

꩜ Driving recklessly

꩜ Making harassing phone calls to the ex-partner

꩜ Following the ex-partner around

꩜ Harassing any new partner

꩜ Being violent toward the old partner or his/her property

꩜ Wanting to commit murder or suicide.

yourself time to recover before attempting a new relationship is generally a good idea. Sometimes talking to friends and family is helpful. In other cases, seeing a professional counselor may help.

WELLNESS SYNTHESIS

Relationships enhance our overall well-being. Connections with others have a positive influence on physical, intellectual, emotional, social, spiritual, and environmental health.

Physical Well-being

Relationships enhance physical health in many ways. Being in love energizes a person and may actually boost the immune system. Because the partners want to please each other, they may take better care of themselves.

Having intimate relationships usually means that someone is physically there for us, sharing daily experiences and also caring for us. Traditional marriage vows speak to "in sickness and in health"; couples in commitment ceremonies also vow to be there for each other in the good times and bad. A partner can help the other be healthier as well as manage illnesses that come along.

Intellectual Well-being

Self-identity contributes to intellectual well-being. Being in a partnership can be intellectually stimulating. It can be a vehicle to reciprocally exchange views, teach and learn new things, and broaden horizons.

Emotional Well-being

Emotional health is aided by involvement with others. As young children, most of us learn to trust and form loving relationships. As we get older, we have the opportunity to develop our own partner relationships. Having someone with whom to share thoughts and feelings, who will love us for who we are, who can give constructive feedback and support — all contribute to emotional well-being.

Plenty of evidence also indicates that unhealthy relationships can have a negative impact on emotional well-being. Being depressed about a partner, being the recipient of anger, and being rejected can all poke holes in self-esteem.

Social Well-being

Dating and being in relationships provide opportunities to broaden one's social network, to meet new people and make new connections. Being with others and forming intimate relationships is critical to social well-being. We all need people we can count on, who are our friends, and who see us through the good times and bad. Sharing activities with others is part of social health. To be alone all the time is not healthy.

Spiritual Well-being

Feelings of love and connectedness go hand in hand with great spiritual power. To be able to be yourself and be loved for who you are fills spiritual needs. The intensity of love feelings becomes apparent when we experience loss. Loss of a loved one tops stress scales, and the emptiness we feel highlights how much the loved one contributed to our lives.

Environmental Well-being

People are key players in the living environment. The quality of relationships formed in families, at work, at school, and with partners makes our environment a healthy (or unhealthy) place to be. People have to be able to feel safe in loving relationships. This "home" should be a secure place in which to develop and grow.

WEB RESOURCES

Dating, Love, Marriage, and Sex

http://www.cmhc.com/psyhelp/chap10/

A chapter from *Psychological Self-Help* by Calyton Tucker-Ladd, Mental Health Net. Discussion ranges from meeting potential partners to being happily married for a lifetime, or going through a divorce and remarrying. Other topics include sexual adjustment, sexual problems, and homosexuality.

Mayo Clinic's Health Oasis

http://www.mayohealth.org/mayo/9902/htm/sex2k_sb.htm

Answers to common questions on sexuality for couples by Dr. David Osborne, a psychologist at Mayo Clinic, Scottsdale, Arizona. At the end of the article, the reader can take a sex quiz, receive information on obsession with sex, midlife sexuality and women, sexual satisfaction in men, the role of aging on sexuality, sexual behavior in children, and Viagra.

SUNY Buffalo, Counseling Center

http://ub-counseling.buffalo.edu/Relationships/index.html

A selection of topics on relationships including common questions, starting a new relationship, communication, coercion, rape, relationships involving men, women, lesbian, gay, bisexual, and transgendered people, and breaking up and letting go.

University of Illinois at Urbana Champaign, Counseling Center

http://www.odos.uiuc.edu/Counseling_Center/comrel.htm

An article, "Committed Relationships and School," by the Counseling Center discussing areas of expectations, communications, boundaries, frequent concerns in the areas of money, rat-racing, communication breakdowns, and flexibility of roles.

Notes

1. P. G. Zimbardo, *Shyness* (Reading, MA: Addison Wesley, 1977).
2. Geraldine Downey and Scott I. Feldman, "Implications of Rejection Sensitivity for Intimate Relationships," *Journal of Personality and Social Psychology,* 70:6 (1996), 1327–1343.
3. T. Gabriel, "Pack Dating: For a Good Time, Call a Crowd" (Education Supplement), *New York Times,* Jan. 5, 1997, pp. 22–23, 38.
4. R. T. Michael, J. H. Gagnon, E. O. Laumann, and G. Kolata, *Sex in America* (New York: Little, Brown, 1994).
5. Michael et al., p. 47.
6. Michael et al., p. 72
7. E. Berscheid and E. Walster, "Physical Attractiveness," in *Advances in Experimental Social Psychology,* Vol. 7, edited by L. Berkowitz (New York: Academic Press, 1974); D. Byrne, O. London, and K. Reeves, "The Effects of Physical Attractiveness, Sex, and Attitude Similarity on Interpersonal Attraction," *Journal of Personality,* 36(1968), 259–271; K. L. Dion and K. K. Dion, "Belief in a Just World and Physical Attractiveness Stereotyping," *Journal of Personality and Social Psychology,* 52 (1987), 775–780; E. Hatfield and S. Sprecher, *Mirror, Mirror . . . The Importance of Looks in Everyday Life* (Albany: State University of New York Press, (1986).

8. J. Bailey, S. Gaulin, Y. Agyei, and B. Gladue, "Effects of Gender and Sexual Orientation on Evolutionary Relevant Aspects of Human Mating Psychology," *Journal of Personality and Social Psychology,* 66(1994), 1091–1093; J. Nevid, "Sex Differences in Factors of Romantic Attraction," *Sex Roles,* 11(1984), 401–411; S. Sprecher, Q. Sullivan, and E. Hatfield, "Mate Selection Preferences: Gender Differences Examined in a National Sample," *Journal of Personality and Social Psychology,* 66(1994), 1074–1080; M. Wiederman and E. Allgeier, "Gender Differences in Mate Selection Criteria: Sociobiological or Socioeconomic Explanations?" *Ethology and Sociobiology,* 13(1992), 115–124.
9. J. Hyde, and J. DeLametar, *Understanding Human Sexuality,* 6th edition (New York: McGraw Hill, 1997).
10. J. V. Kohl and R. T. Francouer, *The Scent of Eros: Mysteries of Odor in Human Sexuality* (New York: Continuum Publishers, 1995).
11. D. Botting and K. Botting, *Sex Appeal* (New York: St. Martin's Press, 1996).
12. (New York: Dell, 1992).
13. E. Hatfield and R. L. Rapson, *Love and Sex: Cross Cultural Perspectives* (Boston: Allyn & Bacon, 1996).
14. Hatfield and Rapson, p. 175.

15. *Love, Sex, and Intimacy: Their Psychology, Biology, and History* (New York: HarperCollins, 1993; *Love and Sex,* 1996), p. 3.
16. "A Triangular Theory of Love," *Psychological Review,* 93(1986), 199–135; and "Triangulating Love," *The Psychology of Love,* edited by R. Sternberg and M. Barnes (New Haven, CT: Yale University Press, 1988).
17. "The Styles of Loving," *Psychology Today,* 8(1974), 43–51; and "Love Styles," *The Psychology of Love,* edited by R. Sternberg and M. Barnes (New Haven, CT: Yale University Press, 1988).
18. S. Hendrick, F. J. Foote, and J. Slapion-Foote, "Do Men and Women Love Differently?" *Journal of Social and Personal Relationships,* 1(1984), 177–180, 184, 193–195.
19. L. A. Peplau, "What Homosexuals Want in Relationships," *Psychology Today,* March 1981, 28–34, pp. 37–38.
20. Peplau.

Student Study Questions

1. What is intimacy? How can a person be intimate but not have sex with a partner or have sex with someone but not be intimate?

2. What are three barriers to intimacy? Does gender role impact on our ability to form intimate relationships? If so, how?

3. Explain Sternberg's model of love.

4. Give an example of a love mismatch, according to Sternberg.

5. How does romantic love differ from consummate love?

6. What are three characteristics of happy couples?

7. What are three common problems that lead to break-ups and divorce?

How Jealous Are You?

Purpose: One feeling that often causes conflict between two people is jealousy, perhaps because men and women often experience and express jealousy in different ways. If partners are unable to communicate openly about an issue, a conflict may result. The following exercise is designed to help bring to light your experiences with jealousy so you may better understand yourself and your partner. If you currently do not have a partner, simply respond to the questions in terms of your last relationship or a hoped-for future one.

Directions: Read each statement carefully, then respond YES or NO in the blank following the statement.

1. You have found at times that you actually like feeling jealous. _____

2. Your spells of jealousy seem to follow a pattern, one after another. _____

3. Sometimes you get so jealous that you lose your appetite or you overeat. _____

4. When you hear about, or think about, your partner's former lovers, you are jealous. _____

5. You avoid close relationships with people other than your partner because such situations may cause your partner to be jealous. _____

6. You are very jealous of your partner's friends, yet you tell people you are not the jealous type. _____

7. You are apt to display fits of jealousy with no apparent cause. _____

8. You are often jealous of your partner's friends even when you know your partner has no romantic feelings toward them. _____

9. At social gatherings you are aware of every move your partner makes. _____

10. Jealousy has led you to spy on your partner. _____

11. You want to know where your partner is at all times. _____

12. It would definitely be a crisis if you were to discover that your partner had one sexual encounter with another person. _____

13. The feeling of loneliness is common to you. _____

14. You have thought of taking revenge on a person you felt was a rival. _____

15. You feel that jealousy is proof of your love for your partner. _____

16. You are jealous of your partner's hobbies. _____

Continued

Source: *Your Sexuality: A Self Assessment*, 2d edition, by R. Valois and S. Kammermann, New York: McGraw-Hill, 1992, pp. 111–112. Reprinted with permission.

Student Assessment

How Jealous Are You? (cont.)

Scoring: If you have responded YES to *more than five of these statements,* you are allowing jealousy to control your life. To continue in this way is to leave yourself open to considerable pain and anguish. When jealousy arises, talk about it and reaffirm your commitment to your partner. You need to listen to each other.

Reactions: Use the space provided to respond to the following questions.

1.   Which statements, to which you responded YES, are of most concern to you? After discussing them with a friend or partner, explain what you plan to do differently.

2.   Do you feel you are trying to control this person who is important to you? Why or why not?

Sexual Communication

11

Major Topics

Metacommunication
Transactional Analysis
Forms of Communication
   One-Way Communication
   Two-Way Communication
   Verbal Communication
   Nonverbal Communication
Initiating Skills
   Nonverbal Initiating Skills
   Verbal Initiating Skills
Listening Skills
Responding Skills
   Open-ended Statements
   Paraphrasing
   Mirroring
   Yes/No Questions
Barriers to Sexual Communication
   Failing to Initiate
   Inappropriate Time and Place
   Lack of Specificity
   Failing to Listen Actively
   Lack of Assertiveness
   Gender and Cultural
    Considerations
Models of Communication
   The DESC Model
   Rational Emotive Therapy (RET)
    and Irrational Thinking
Wellness Synthesis
   Physical Well-being
   Intellectual Well-being
   Emotional Well-being
   Social Well-being
   Spiritual Well-being
   Environmental Well-being

Student Learning Objectives

After reading this chapter, students will be able to:

- Compare a variety of communication models.

- Describe some of the key elements that make sexual communication different and difficult.

- Assess the importance of communication in sexual relationships.

- Describe a variety of verbal sexual communication techniques.

- Describe a variety of nonverbal sexual communication techniques.

- Compare and contrast verbal and nonverbal sexual communication techniques.

- Describe some barriers to effective sexual communication.

Communication is the foundation of healthy sexuality. It is essential to obtaining sexual information for oneself as well as communicating information to others. Sexual communication poses unique challenges because of the difficulty of communicating in general, plus the personal nature of sexuality. Communicating effectively requires skill, patience, and commitment as well as an understanding and mastery of sexual information. Honest and accurate sexual communication is essential in developing and maintaining good relationships and fostering healthy sexuality.

Communicating effectively requires skill, patience, and commitment.

Communication
the process by which information is exchanged between individuals through a common system of symbols, signs, and behaviors

Communication is defined as the process by which information is exchanged between individuals through a common system of symbols, signs, or behaviors. It involves all the modes of behavior that an individual uses to affect another person. It encompasses spoken and written words as well as nonverbal messages such as gestures, facial expressions, bodily messages or signals, and artistic symbols.[1]

METACOMMUNICATION

Communication also includes the interpersonal relationship between communicators. When we are in the presence of others, it is impossible not to communicate.[2] Activity and inactivity, speech and silence — all communicate messages. Communication occurs at two levels — the *content* level (what is actually being said) and the *relationship* level (what is going on between the communicants). This second relationship level is referred to as

Case Study

Susan: An Awkward Communication Circumstance

Susan, a gay professor, is attending an out-of-town conference with some friends. She is sitting at the bar in her hotel, waiting for friends to come down and go out to dinner with her. She is nursing a drink, trying to relax.

A man seated two stools to her right tries to draw Susan into a conversation he is having with a group of his friends about the sexual differences between men and women. Susan doesn't know any of these people. She finds them not only a little drunk but also pretentious, shallow, and untrustworthy. She immediately feels uncomfortable. Susan feigns interest in what they are talking about, nodding her head while

looking over their shoulders to try to spot her friends. She politely adds a comment here and there but can't relax around them as they carry on about a variety of issues she doesn't care about and trade barbs with each other. She also feels uncomfortable talking about this subject with a group of strangers who don't realize she is gay. These are characteristics of a complementary relationship.

Eventually Susan's friends arrive and she quickly excuses herself and joins her friends. She is able to let down her guard, be herself, and enjoy the rest of the evening in symmetrical conversation among peers she respects and feels comfortable around.

metacommunication, or communication about communication. **Pragmatics** refers to the relationship between communicators, and relationships are of two types — symmetrical and complementary.[3] **Symmetrical relationships** are based on equality. Each communicator treats the other in a like fashion, minimizing differences and conflict. Symmetrical relationships are comfortable and facilitate communication. When we are involved in symmetrical relationships, we are relaxed, our conversation is not forced, and we perceive periods of silence as comfortable and not awkward.

Complementary relationships are based on differences. Communicators maximize their differences, causing inequality and disharmony. Complementary relationships crackle with the tension in the air. Communication is forced and periods of silence seem interminable. Complementary relationships often result in stress.

Metacommunication
communication about communication

Pragmatics
the relationship between communicators

Symmetrical relationships
relationships based on equality

Complementary relationships
relationships based on differences

TRANSACTIONAL ANALYSIS

Eric Berne's **transactional analysis (TA)** model examines relationships that are either symmetrical or complementary.[4] Berne proposed that all of us have three sources of behavior, or ego states: child, adult, and parent. Each ego state manifests itself in a different communication style. Figure 11.1 illustrates the three ego states of TA.

1. *The child.* The child manifests itself through childish use of verbal and nonverbal communication. The child uses coyness, naivete, charm and seduction, boisterousness, giggling, and whining and is spontaneous, irresponsible, and manipulative. Our childish ego state is playful and free of restraint.

2. *The adult.* The adult is rational and objective, uses logic and analysis, and exhibits sound decision making based on accurate perception and analysis. The adult is fair, responsible, sociable.

3. *The parent.* The parent incorporates feelings and behaviors learned from authority figures. The parent communicates the conscience of the person through words, actions, postures, behaviors, expectations, and the use of guilt or reward. The parent can be nurturing (protects, cuddles, and cares for) or critical (corrects and condemns).

According to Berne, when we communicate, our message is sent from one of our three ego states and is received by a specific ego state of another. Ideally, the ego state from which we send messages matches that of the person to whom we are talking. Thus, if we are speaking from our adult state to another person, that person should be receiving our message

Transactional analysis (TA)
Eric Berne's communication model based on three ego states — parent, adult, and child

nurturing, caring, helpful, loving — **Parent** — critical, condemning, unforgiving

rational, objective — **Adult** — analytical, complex thinker

adapted, compliant, malleable, seductive — **Child** — natural, spontaneous, wild, free, boisterous

Source: *Transactional Analysis in Psychotherapy*, by Eric Berne (New York: Grove Press, 1960).

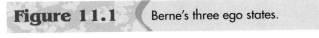

Figure 11.1 Berne's three ego states.

in his or her adult state. If this is not the case, a mismatch occurs. A mismatch is similar to the complementary message in Watzlawick, Beavin, and Jackson's metacommunication model. Mismatches between messages sent from one state and received by another can be a source of stress and sexual miscommunication.

Figure 11.2 illustrates a mismatch that occurs when we are talking to a peer and we use our parent ego state instead of our adult state. Our friend, receiving in an adult ego state, expects us to send an adult message. Instead, we send a parent message assuming we are sending to an assumed child ego state, which creates a mismatch and is a source of stress.

Figure 11.3 illustrates another mismatch between two lovers. One is in a playful mood and communicates a sexy message from his adult state. His lover, in an adult state, receives the message, is confused, and sends back a parent message. The critical nature of the message and the condemning tone send a stressful message that resonates within the partner's child state. Mismatches like this can cool the fires of desire if they are not cleared up.

FORMS OF COMMUNICATION

The basic forms of communication are one-way and two-way.

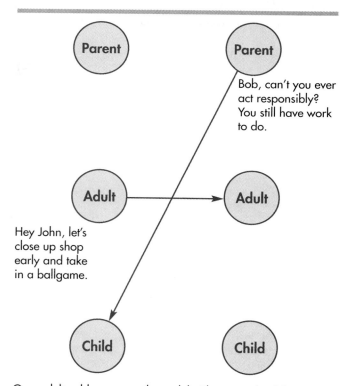

Bob, can't you ever act responsibly? You still have work to do.

Hey John, let's close up shop early and take in a ballgame.

One adult addresses another adult. The second adult receives the message in an adult ego state and responds as if to a child ego state.

Figure 11.2 Transactional mismatches.

One-Way Communication

One-way communication is an information-giving process that does not involve or rely on feedback. Speeches, lectures, movies, TV programs, concerts, and radio broadcasts are examples of one-way communication. One-way communication is a direct and powerful way to transmit information about sexuality. Much of what we learn about sexuality in our culture is disseminated through one-way communication.

Print and broadcast media use sexual themes in their programming and to sell their products. Movies, TV programs, and music videos weave visual sexual images into their plots. Song lyrics provide auditory sexual information. We absorb most of what we learn about the cultural context of sexuality through this passive transfer of sexual information through mass media. Mass media convey messages about how our culture views sex. Mass media communicate sexual information to entertain or sell products, not to inform and educate us. Although the impact of this exposure is powerful and conveys messages about sex, the portrayal is often shallow and inaccurate and doesn't offer the opportunity for a dialogue. It also doesn't afford the opportunity to personalize the information and explore how it relates to us as individuals.

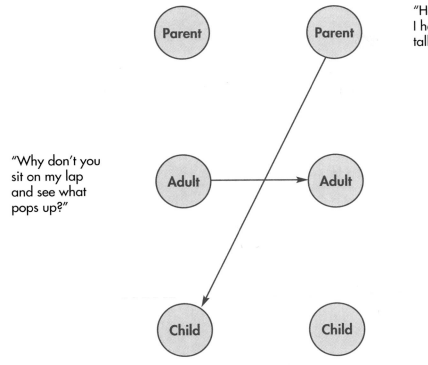

"How disgusting! I hate it when you talk dirty!"

"Why don't you sit on my lap and see what pops up?"

One person initiates from his adult state, using humor to signal his sexual interest. His partner responds sternly from her critical parent state, treating him like a child.

Figure 11.3 Sexual transactional analysis mismatches.

Two-Way Communication

Two-way communication goes beyond information-giving by including feedback. Feedback ensures a dialogue, the key component of two-way communication. It gives us the opportunity to share information, ask questions, seek clarification, and explore ideas and feelings that go beyond those initially presented. **Dialogue** represents a true exchange of information. This is why two-way communication is essential for communicating about sexuality. Two-way communication increases the likelihood that each person will express his or her needs and wants and will understand each other clearly. One way to explain two-way communication is through a circular model of communication.

A Circular Model of Communication

Effective communication is a circular process that involves sending and receiving coded messages, as illustrated in Figure 11.4. A sender, wishing to communicate, puts the idea and feeling of the message into a form that can be transmitted. This process of formulating a message, choosing appropriate words, symbols, tone, and expressions to represent it is called **encoding**.

Providing feedback is the key to creating a dialogue and establishing effective two-way communication.

Feedback
a verbal or nonverbal response sent from a person receiving a message to the person sending that message

Dialogue
exchange of information in communication

Encoding
selecting the signs, symbols, emotions, and words to transmit a message

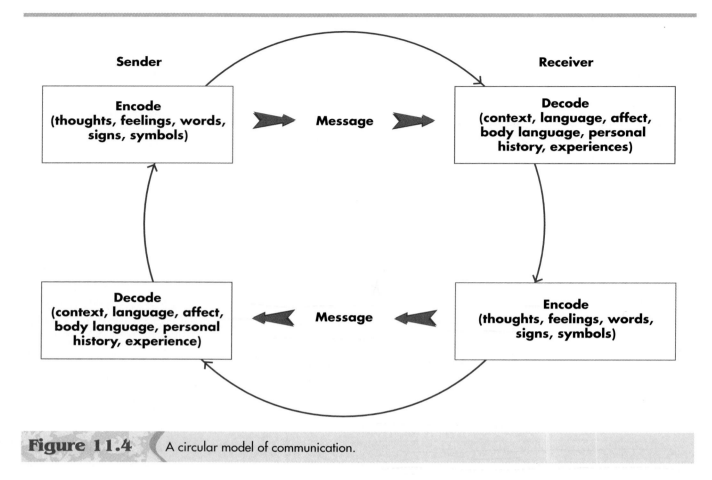

Figure 11.4   A circular model of communication.

Decoding
the use of knowledge, memory, language, context, and personal history and experience to interpret a message

The receiver perceives and translates the message using his or her personal storehouse of knowledge and experience in a process called **decoding**.

Communication Environment

Encoding and decoding take place within the context of the communicator's interpersonal and physical relationship. What is being said involves not only the actual message but also the physical environment of the communication as well as the relationship of the sender and receiver. A sender might alter the message depending upon whether the environment is friendly or unfriendly, familiar or unfamiliar, safe or unsafe, formal or informal.

In addition, a sender might send a different message in the same environment depending upon the nature of the relationship with the receiver. The message might be affected by whether the sender and receiver are friends or enemies, strangers or known to each other, peers or of unequal status. Communication involves sending and receiving both verbal and nonverbal messages. Each type of message is capable of transmitting information and is part of the encoding and decoding process.

Verbal Communication

Verbal communication is two-dimensional in that it involves transmitting both thoughts and feelings through words. The *cognitive* domain is concerned with communicating our thoughts about things. The *affective* domain involves putting our feelings into words. Many people find communicating cognitive information easier than expressing feelings.

Specificity

Specificity is crucial in effective verbal communication. The more specific the message, the more likely it is to be transmitted clearly. Vocabulary plays a big part in the specificity of our verbal communication. Having a large working vocabulary allows us to specify exactly what we want to say.

Sexual Vocabulary

One of the things that makes sexual communication difficult is the lack of a common sexual vocabulary. U.S. culture has no uniform set of agreed-upon

PERSPECTIVES

He Said/She Said

Do men and women communicate differently? Research about this subject over the past 20 years has yielded mixed results. Men and women are socialized differently, and many researchers believe this emerges in the way we communicate. Women are socialized to show their feelings, whereas men have been taught to keep their feelings hidden. In particular, men have been taught to keep their fears and doubts disguised, because showing these is considered a sign of weakness. Men are socialized to believe that admitting weakness is unmanly. These beliefs can affect the way we communicate with our partners. Wives send clearer and more emotional messages than their husbands.[1] Wives tend to frame their message in an emotional context, whereas husbands deemphasize affect and focus instead on issues and facts. Husbands send more neutral, less expressive messages that are harder to interpret.

Males and females also differ according to the nature of the relationship and the context of the communication. One study investigated the communication patterns of college students across four different contexts.[2] Students were asked how they communicate about their genitals and sexual behavior when talking with their partners, parents, and members of the same and opposite gender. Male and female students alike tended to be more formal when communicating with their parents and in mixed-gender groups. Men, however, were much more likely to use slang when communicating with other men or their female sex partners than women were. Female students tended to continue to use formal sexual language when communicating with other women and with their male partners.

Although the sexes clearly differ in the way they communicate, many of the differences are based on stereotypes. One common myth about communication is that women talk more than men.[3] A study of male/female communication patterns found that men both talk and interrupt more than women do.

Another myth about male/female communication patterns is that women are more open about their feelings and disclose more than their partners. A new ethic of openness, flexibility, and desire to communicate effectively is emerging within today's young people. It is gradually replacing the more rigid stereotypical communication patterns for men and women. Among college students involved in long-term relationships, both partners reported equal levels of disclosure concerning their thoughts and feelings.[4] A blending of more traditional male/female communication patterns allows men and women to share responsibility for communicating their thoughts and feelings.

1. Marital Communication," by P. Noller and M. A. Fitzpatrick, in *Contemporary Families: Looking Forward, Looking Back,* edited by A. Booth (Minneapolis: Council on Family Relations, 1991).
2. "Male and Female Sexual Vocabulary in Different Interpersonal Contexts," by R. Simpkins, *Journal of Sex Research,* 18 (1982) 160–172.
3. *Women's Language: Uncertainty or Interpersonal Sensitivity and Emotionality?* by J. McMillan et al., *Sex Roles,* 3 (1977), 545–560.
4. "Self-disclosure in Dating Couples: Sex Roles and Ethics of Openness," by Z. Rubin et al., *Journal of Marriage and the Family,* 42 (1981), 305–317.

What are your thoughts about how men and women communicate? Do you think men and women today are becoming more willing and able to describe their thoughts and feelings about sex? Do your sexual communication patterns differ if you are speaking to someone of the same or opposite sex?

words, phrases, and sexual language level. Often we are unsure of the proper terminology for sexual topics such as anatomy and physiology and sexual behaviors. Insecurity about sexual terminology, coupled with emotional discomfort, makes talking about sex difficult.

Language Level

The level of language we use also plays a part in effective verbal communication. The four levels of language are: childhood, street, everyday discourse, and scientific language.[5]

1. *Childhood language* is simple, cute, and fun and often is used to disguise embarrassment. Lovers have their own brand of childhood language. They may use it to describe their sexual anatomy and physiology, sexual desire, or need for pleasure. Pet names and phrases are part of this language. Lovers often use childhood language to refer to their genitalia or sexual desire. People also use childhood language when they make mistakes and seek forgiveness. "Ooops, sowwy about that," we might say in mock childhood tones.

2. *Street language* is tough, expressive, and emotional. Street language can be disarming and often is used to level the playing field when communicators do not share equal power or prestige. Tough talk can bestow power and superiority. Street language also serves to create bonds between members of subcultures by sharing a language that members of mainstream society do not understand. Rap music incorporates the power and raw sensuality of street language into a unique art form.

Listen to several rap songs. What is your reaction to the lyrics? What are your thoughts and feelings about them? How do you feel about using street language to talk about sexuality?

3. *Common discourse* is the language level of mainstream society. It is the generally accepted form of language with which most of us communicate. Most people use its words, expressions, and speech patterns in communicating information that is neither intimate nor scientific. It is the language taught in schools and used in most communications.

4. *Scientific/professional language* is the discourse of the work world and professional community. It is the language that professional peers use as they communicate about the subtleties of their chosen professions. Like street language, it usually is understood only by those who share its culture. Computer programmers, doctors, and other professions have unique vocabularies, complete with acronyms only they understand.

When we communicate with our partners, we must use the level of language with which they are most comfortable. Miscommunication can occur when the language levels of two communicators are not the same. A language level in common is a good starting point for effective sexual communication.

Nonverbal Communication

How we say things is just as important as *what* we actually say. **Body language** describes the nonverbal messages we send through posture, gestures, movement, and physical appearance, including adornment. Our body language intentionally or unintentionally sends messages to receivers.

Lovers use nonverbal communication to express feelings, ask for things, and reinforce pleasurable activities. A moan, a hug, a seductive look — these can speak a thousand words. Placing a partner's hand in the correct spot or squeezing it when you are being touched as you want can accomplish as much as explaining these things through words.

Body language
sending intentional or unintentional messages through body postures and movements

Body Language

Positive, or open, body language is demonstrated by a relaxed posture, steady eye contact, nods of the head, and an occasional smile or happy expression. These are cues that you are an approachable sender or a receptive receiver.

Negative, or closed, body language has visible signs of tension such as clenched fists or tight jaw muscles, a closed posture (arms folded, body shifted sideways and the like), and facial expressions ranging from anger to disbelief. Negative body language can indicate either apathy or disturbance about something.

Physical Appearance

Physical appearance can convey a variety of messages. A messy, sloppy, or ungroomed appearance may send encoded messages ranging from positive ("I'm comfortable enough in your presence to relax") to negative ("I don't care enough about you or myself to pay attention to my appearance"). Clothing and adornment might intentionally or unintentionally be erotic and seductive. This can affect both the encoding and the decoding process, as the sender might be trying to convey one message ("I'm trying to look my best") while the receiver may perceive another ("This person is trying to manipulate or come on to me sexually").

Silence

Silence is a form of nonverbal communication that can be either a source of stress or a sign of comfort. Silence also can be used to hurt and control people. Silence is a stressor when wordless pauses are perceived as signs of a breakdown in communication. Conversely, silence communicates comfort and acceptance between friends and lovers who understand that a loving bond is present despite a lack of conversation. Silence is a necessary part of effective communication that is often overlooked. We need time to listen, digest, and understand messages. Silence allows us time to reflect as we formulate our thoughts and words.

Silence allows us time to reflect as we formulate our thoughts and words.

Touch

A firm handshake, a reassuring touch on the arm, a gentle squeeze of the buttocks, the placing of a partner's hand on the genitals or breast — all convey messages without speaking a single word. Appropriately used, touch adds another dimension of communication that sometimes reaches deeper than mere words.

Often we find it easier to communicate our sexual desires through touch than words. For instance, a man might take his partner's hand and place it on his penis and squeeze it rather than ask, "Please squeeze my penis this hard." A woman might draw her partner's head upon her breast rather than ask, "Please suck on my nipples." A person might moan or groan rather than say "I like it when you suck on my penis like that" or "it feels good when you rub my clitoris like that."

When used inappropriately, however, the effects of touch can be devastating. A pat on the head can be a sign of endearment to a child but can embarrass or infuriate another adult. A squeeze on your friend's shoulder can show him you understand his problems and care about him. The same squeeze on your secretary's shoulder, however, can convey an entirely different meaning. A pat on a teammate's buttocks can show appreciation of a great play or an extreme effort. The same pat on a co-worker's buttocks can be perceived as sexual harassment.

When we are truly intimate with another person, we don't perceive silence as a threat.

Space

The space between sender and receiver also affects communication. Four space zones common to communication in North America are:[6]

- ◡ Intimate space (<18 inches) — space reserved for communication between intimate partners

- ◡ Personal space (18 inches–4 feet) — space appropriate for close relationships that may involve touching

- ◡ Social-consultive space (4 feet–12 feet) space for nontouching, less intimate relationships that may involve louder verbal communication

- ◡ Public space (>12 feet) — space used for formal gatherings such as addressing a large group.

Stress and sexual tension can arise when we violate these commonly accepted space parameters. For example, we find ourselves backing up to reclaim our violated space when a nonintimate person gets within the boundaries of our intimate space. Sometimes we place objects as barriers between us and other people to define our space and set allowable communication zones. Culture plays an important part in determining what is acceptable and unacceptable concerning space.

All communication involves three specific sets of skills: initiating, listening, and responding. Communicating about sex is the same, except that the subject is more intimate and sensitive.

Props such as a desk can help to establish our space boundaries.

INITIATING SKILLS

Initiating sexual communication is different for new and for established relationships. Initiating skills are critical in meeting new people. Initiating skills also are important for discovering what our partners desire, as well as for communicating our own wants and needs, likes and dislikes. Partners in established relationships have a history of intimacy and trust that foster communication. The context of their communication differs greatly from that of two people who are attracted to each other but have not established an intimate relationship yet.

Nonverbal Initiating Skills

Initiating communication starts with nonverbal messages. Think about how you act when you meet for the first time someone to whom you are attracted. You make eye contact and hold it a little longer than you would if you were not interested in meeting the person. Eye contact leads to a smile, a brush of the hair, followed by another look that signals approachability.

Take the case of John and Susan. They are in the same biology lecture class of 150 students. For a couple of weeks they have noticed each other and seem mutually attracted. Today Susan decides she wants to meet John.

PERSPECTIVES

Cultural Considerations in Communication

Communicating effectively requires awareness of, and sensitivity to, various cultural influences related to verbal and nonverbal communication. The following are a few examples of common cultural consideration to keep in mind.

Verbal Communication

Cultural groups and subcultures do not necessarily share a common language. Although English is the language that most people in the United States speak, at the common discourse level, this isn't always the case. For many people in the United States, English is a second language, and they do not always understand common discourse.

Certain cultures may find some subjects and forms of communication unacceptable. Unacceptable communication may range from discussing emotions and feelings to the use and focus of humor to the discussion of intimate sexual and other personal matters.

Nonverbal Communication

A variety of nonverbal factors also vary from culture to culture. Cultures differ in their norms for territoriality and personal space. In general, people of Arabic, Southern European, and African origins sit or stand relatively close to each other when talking. People of Asian, Northern European, and North American countries are more comfortable being farther apart when they are talking.[1]

Perception of time and the relationship of the past, the present, and the future also vary by culture. The predominant culture in the United States and Canada is time-urgent and future-oriented. Being aware of the present and doing something now to plan for the future (such as exercising now to prevent heart disease in the future) are commonly accepted. In daily life, people are oriented to specific times of the day, and strict schedules. Some other cultures are much less interested in the future and are not as oriented to specific schedules. Many American Indian homes do not even have clocks, as people of some tribes are more concerned about the present and live one day at a time.[2]

Body language varies significantly according to culture. The dominant U.S. culture places a high value on direct eye contact when speaking. In contrast, American Indians consider continuous direct eye contact to

She intentionally sits closer to him — about four seats down in the same row. She smiles at him as she takes her seat. She sees that he notices her and returns her smile. Buoyed by this, she glances over again, tossing back a long shock of hair while reestablishing eye contact — this time for a moment longer. She decides to approach John after class and initiate a conversation with him. If John hadn't noticed Susan, returned her glance, or maintained eye contact, she might have received a different message and decided not to pursue this any further.

Nonverbal communication between lovers in a long-term relationship is similar — but different because of their shared intimacy, comfort level, and experience together. Nonverbal messages are still important, though, to signal approachability and desire to communicate. They still need to establish eye contact, set the appropriate distance, and adopt a relaxed and approachable posture. Lovers can soften or strengthen their intentions with techniques such as a flirtatious look, lingering eye contact, a smile, or a serious look.

Initiating nonverbal communication also can involve props for both new and established lovers. Peering over the top of a book you are reading or the drink you are nursing provides a small security blanket. The feigned dropped handkerchief is the quintessential prop that heroines in classic movies use to gain the attention of their heros.

be insulting and disrespectful. Rules about eye contact also vary by gender in certain cultures. In Islamic cultures women are taught to avert the eyes, whereas eye contact is okay for men. The meaning and acceptability of a myriad of other nonverbal behaviors, such as pointing fingers, shaking hands, and other forms of touch, vary by culture.

The following general suggestions can be helpful in verbal and nonverbal communication with people from cultures different from one's own.

1. *Slow down.* People for whom English is a second language sometimes have a hard time keeping up with and understanding English when it is spoken too rapidly.

2. *Minimize nonverbal distractions.* Be conservative rather than flamboyant in your use of gestures, personal space, and other nonverbal communication.

3. *Look for feedback.* People who don't understand, can't keep up, or are uncomfortable with something you do or say often give nonverbal or verbal cues. These can be as overt as asking for clarification or as subtle as a turned head or lack of eye contact. Seek clarification of these cues.

4. *Avoid talking louder.* Sometimes, when we are not sure we are being understood, we raise our voice, assuming that the person can't hear us. Talking too loudly, however, can be perceived as threatening or condescending and is rarely helpful.

5. *Show respect.* Being humble and respectful of cultural differences conveys the message that you care and want to understand and improve communication.

6. *Use an interpreter.* If necessary, get someone to translate your message into the person's primary language.

1. *Fundamentals of Nursing*, by B. Kozier, G. Erb, and R. Oliver (Redwood City, CA: Addison Wesley/Benjamin Cummings, 1991), p. 747.
2. *Fundamentals of Nursing*, p. 748.

Leaving on the table a magazine opened to a story about sex is one way to send a message that you are interested in discussing the subject. Putting a sex manual on your coffee table or bedstand is a way to send messages of interest and approachability to your partner. Renting an erotic or romantic video is a way to introduce the topic of sex without saying a word.

Verbal Initiating Skills

Whether a person is trying to meet someone for the first time or to talk to a partner of 15 years about a sexual topic, he or she has to initiate the communication. Waiting and hoping that your partner or someone in whom you are interested will initiate is a sure way to end the communication before it begins.

A key to effective communication is to assume responsibility for clearing up misunderstandings.

Take the case of Susan and John again. Clearly, from his nonverbal messages, John is at least approachable. Susan now is responsible for initiating. Deciding what to say in first-time encounters can be excruciating. A simple rule of thumb is to be honest. Susan could simply say, "Hi, I'm Susan. I'm a little embarrassed, but I've noticed you for the past couple of weeks, and I'd like to meet you." It's now up to John to either reinforce his nonverbal display interest or to pass it up. Susan also could draw from their shared experience of the biology lecture. She might initiate by saying something like, "Hi — I'm Susan. I'm having trouble understanding something the professor just said. Can we talk?"

Four common initiating techniques that can be used in both first-time and long-time relationships are: open-ended questions, paraphrasing, declarative statements, and simple yes/no questions.

Open-ended Questions

Open-ended questions
sentences that require information from the other person

Open-ended questions are excellent for initiating a dialogue because they cannot be answered with a simple yes/no response. Imagine that you want to explore how your partner likes to be touched. You initiate using an open-ended question such as, "Tell me more about how you like to be touched," or "What else can I do to make you feel good?" Open-ended questions require information from the other person. Your partner can't respond with a simple yes/no answer. Open-ended questions will get your partner talking and draw out additional detail and emotion.

Paraphrasing

Paraphrasing
restating a message in one's own words

Paraphrasing means interpreting the meaning of a message and restating it in one's own words. Paraphrasing is another way to initiate a conversation and obtain additional information by getting a person to talk. Imagine that you want to follow up on something your partner said about sex last night. You could initiate a conversation by paraphrasing your partner's comments from the previous evening. For instance, in discussing last night's conversation about sexual technique, you might say, "I was thinking about what you said last night. What I heard you say was that you like it when I squeeze your scrotum firmly" or, "So, what you were saying last night is

Health Hint

Open-Ended Questions to Keep a Sexual Dialogue Flowing

Open-ended questions tend to begin with words that are different from close-ended questions, which usually can be answered with one- or two-word replies. Open-ended questions require the person to elaborate.

Close-Ended	Open-Ended
Are . . . ?	How . . . ?
Do . . . ?	Why . . . ?
Who . . . ?	In what way . . . ?
When, Where, Which . . . ?	

Examples of open-ended questions are:

- ⌣ "Can you tell me more about . . . ?"
- ⌣ "How do you feel about. . . ?"
- ⌣ "What are your thoughts about . . . ?"
- ⌣ "Can you explain that? I'm not sure I understand."
- ⌣ "What made you decide to do that?"

that you really enjoy it when I bite gently on your nipples" or, "I sense from last night that you don't like it when I put my tongue in your ear." Paraphrasing requires interpretation, or reading between the lines. Your partner usually will let you know if you are on target or off base in your interpretation of the initial message.

Simple Declarative Statements

Sometimes simple **declarative statements** about a sexual topic can initiate a dialogue. These are not as direct as the previous two techniques because they do not specifically require a response. They can be useful however, especially to test the waters to see how someone feels or what he or she thinks about some sexual topic. Imagine you just read some sexually provocative story in a magazine and are interested in discussing it with your partner. You could simply state this as a declarative sentence: "I just read a fascinating story in this magazine about what men desire most in sexual relationships." By tossing out this simple declarative statement, you could assess whether your partner wants to pursue the discussion and gauge his or her feelings about it. You might follow up with an open-ended statement or let it pass if your partner shows no interest.

Declarative statement
a verbal initiating technique that does not require a response to a message

Yes/No Questions

The weakest way to initiate a dialogue — and the way most of us start conversations — is to ask direct **yes/no questions**. These are questions that can be answered by a simple yes or no. They don't require explanation or embellishment in the way that open-ended statements and paraphrasing do. Although they are useful for verifying facts ("Do you like it when I touch you like this?" "Does this feel good?"), when they are overused, they can shut down a dialogue.

Yes/no questions
a verbal initiating technique involving a question that requires only a yes or no response

LISTENING SKILLS

There are two types of listening — passive and active.

Passive listening
one-way listening; provides no feedback

1. In **passive listening** the listener merely soaks in what the initiator of the message is sending. Passive listening is what we do when watching television, a movie, the radio, and so on. It is one-way communication. Although passive listening can be an effective way to receive sexual information, it is not the most effective form of listening to another person when trying to establish or maintain a dialogue.

Active listening
listening with understanding and providing feedback

2. **Active listening** is much better than passive listening for dealing with interpersonal communication because, by definition, it requires feedback. Active listeners show that they are listening by providing both nonverbal and verbal feedback. For this reason, active listening is demanding. It takes a lot of energy and concentration, and the listener can easily get distracted and lose interest.

Letting the sender know that the receiver is listening actively can be accomplished through a variety of nonverbal cues. First, the listener adopts a relaxed pose and maintains eye contact. Additional techniques include nodding the head and smiling. Simple verbal cues such as "uh huh," combined with eye contact and head nodding, are enough to let the speaker know the receiver is listening.

RESPONDING SKILLS

The message receiver reacts to the initiator's message and encodes some type of feedback using verbal or nonverbal communication. If the message was understood and no further clarification is necessary, the receiver can make a simple declarative statement, acknowledging the message with agreement, disagreement, or new information. If the receiver disagrees, or has problems, he or she can use **"I" language** to express opinions. An example is: "I hear what you're saying and I understand your point, but I disagree with that position. I see it differently."

"I" language
taking responsibility for feelings by saying "I feel . . ." versus "You make me feel. . . ."

Often, responding skills go beyond merely providing feedback and are used to get additional information needed to understand an issue or to solve a problem. Keeping the conversation going or requesting more information relies on being able to draw more information out of the initiator. Open-ended statements, paraphrasing, and simple yes/no questions, discussed earlier in the chapter, can be used to respond as well as initiate. An additional responding technique that can be powerful is mirroring.

Effective communicators use "I" language.

Open-ended Statements

The open-ended statement is an excellent responding technique because it provides feedback and also keeps the dialogue going. A response such as, "I hear what you're saying — tell me more about how you feel about masturbation" lets the sender know you are with him or her and want additional information.

Paraphrasing

Paraphrasing lets senders know you are listening but goes one step farther by giving them an idea of how you interpret their message. For instance, a response such as "What I heard you say is that you can accept masturbation as a form of sexual release in general but personally don't feel good about it" lets the sender know you are listening and also provides the opportunity for the sender to know what you think he or she said. The sender usually will let you know if your interpretation is accurate or if you missed the point.

Mirroring

A powerful technique for providing feedback and keeping a person talking is **mirroring**, restating the person's exact words while mimicking the body posturing. This is done intentionally for impact. Mirroring is useful when someone says something that has strong emotional connotations. The message was so powerful that you do not want to risk weakening or misinterpreting it. Let's say a friend tells you she was so angry at the lewd comments a stranger made to her as she walked by him that she felt she could kill him. You would mirror it by saying, "You were so angry you felt you could kill him!" This usually prompts the person to continue and go into the greater detail you desire.

Mirroring
restating the message exactly, including body language

Yes/No Questions

The weakest type of response in a dialogue — and the way most of us seek additional information about something — is to ask direct yes/no questions. Although these are useful for verifying facts ("Do you like it when I touch you like this?" " Does this feel good?"), they are easy to overuse, can make people feel defensive, and can shut down a dialogue.

Once the receiver encodes a response, the communication process shifts back to the sender. We have now come full circle from sender encoding, receiver decoding, receiver encoding, and providing feedback that now becomes information to be decoded by the sender. And the cycle begins all over again.

BARRIERS TO SEXUAL COMMUNICATION

Impediments to communicating sexually include failure to initiate, picking an inappropriate time or place, not being specific enough, lack of active listening and assertiveness, saying no when we mean yes, and failing to make requests.

Failing to Initiate

One of the biggest barriers to effective sexual communication is failing to initiate. Whether you want to meet someone or discuss a problem with something your long-term lover says or does, you are responsible for bringing it to the person's attention. Failing to initiate is the initiator's problem, not the receiver's.

The best time to address issues and problems is when they occur. Taking time to clear things up, before they are allowed to progress, can prevent problems from escalating. Often, however, situational constraints prevent this. Other people may be around, you're in the middle of something else, or you don't have enough time right now. In these cases, you should tell the other person you need some time alone with him or her to discuss something important. The two of you should be in a neutral territory where you feel safe and emotionally strong, with enough time so neither of you feels rushed. In the case of meeting someone new, initiators should wait until they can speak to the person alone, away from friends.

When using "I" language, communicators take responsibility for their feelings. This is especially important when discussing sexual concerns. For example, let's say your boyfriend has made fun of your outfit in front of three other mutual friends. Rather than blame your boyfriend by saying, "You really made me feel bad," you could say, "I felt bad when you criticized my outfit in front of our friends." Rather than blame your friend for what you are feeling, you own your feelings and state them in "I" language.

The situation and feelings about what happened should be stated in clear, simple terms. General statements like, "I hate it when you treat me like a sex object" or "I hate it when you do things like that" should be avoided. Good communicators specify exactly what the other person did that they dislike. It's better to say things like, "I don't like you to talk about my sexual behavior or level of desire in front of your friends," or "I really feel like a fool when you talk about my sexual needs in front of my friends." Specifying exactly *what* you dislike (talking about sexual needs) and the context (in front of your friends) clarifies the situation and leaves no room for misunderstanding.

Using "I" language when trying to meet others shows the other person that you are being responsible for your feelings and you really care: "Hi, I'm Rich. I find myself agreeing with a lot of your viewpoints about things. I really liked what you said in political science class today. Can we talk about it over a cup of coffee in the Student Center?"

Inappropriate Time and Place

Choosing the appropriate time and place to initiate a discussion about sexuality is important. To be able to relax, each person needs to feel safe and secure. This is important for establishing new relationships as well as strengthening existing ones.

In new relationships, talking in public, less intimate settings is sometimes better. A booth in a restaurant, a bench in the park, under a tree on campus all afford privacy, yet are public enough to ensure safety and security until you get to know each other better.

When dealing with problems or concerns in an established relationship, time should be sufficient to discuss the issues completely. Privacy and undisturbed time are ensured by shutting off the TV, putting the answering machine on the phone, closing the door to your room, and giving each other undivided attention. Some people prefer the privacy of their bedrooms when talking about sex. As one student explained, "I like to talk about sex in the bedroom — not when we're making love, but at other times. I like to close the door, prop up a few pillows, unplug the phone, and talk. Sometimes we'll have a glass of wine, relax, and let our feelings flow."

Other people prefer discussing sex outdoors. A student described it this way: " I like to get outdoors to talk to my wife about sex. We go for a long walk somewhere in the mountains or in a local park along the canal. There's something open but private about strolling slowly, hand-in-hand, and discussing our feelings. It works for us."

Lack of Specificity

Being critical of a partner's behavior at times is normal in any long-term relationship. Being critical of someone's behavior, however, is different from being critical of the person. A sure-fire way to sabotage an attempt to discuss sexual concerns is to criticize the partner rather than the behavior. It is important to criticize the behavior, not the person. People have to understand that the other still loves them but does not like a certain behavior. The partner probably is unaware of how the behavior affects the other. The more precision in describing exactly what a person did or said, the better is the chance of clearing up the problem without hurting the person's feelings. "I really feel hurt when you reject my sexual advances" is a lot easier to deal with than, "You're a jerk for rejecting me."

It is important to criticize the behavior, not the person.

Sexual messages are difficult to interpret clearly, even under the best of circumstances. People in long-term relationships are no exception. Mixed messages — contradictory messages — usually are a result of nonverbal cues not matching verbal messages or people saying something they don't really mean. For instance, if a partner asks, "Do you like it when I do this?" and the response is, "Yeah, sure" while the body is tight and the facial expression is pained, the message is mixed.

We send mixed messages for various reasons. In some cases, we are unsure where we stand or how we feel. The message is mixed because feelings are mixed. Sometimes we send mixed messages because we are unable or unwilling to be assertive and say no or tell the other person how we really feel. In the worst case, we send mixed messages because we play games and deliberately want to keep people off balance and unsure of our position. This may be linked to unhealthy sex-role stereotyping based on positioning for power and control in relationships.

The bottom line in mixed messages is that they impair the communication process, making it difficult to understand the true meaning of what is going on. Healthy sexuality revolves around effective communication, based on personal knowledge and the desire to communicate honestly.

Failing to Listen Actively

Many sexual communication problems, too, revolve around failure to listen actively.

Health Hint

How To Be a Better Listener

1. *Keep yourself in good mental and physical shape.* We listen better when we are mentally and physically alert.

2. *Keep eye contact with the speaker whenever possible.* This will assure the speaker that what he or she is saying is being heard.

3. *Listen actively rather than passively.* This means exerting energy and using body language to reflect what the speaker is saying. Nod in agreement, smile or laugh at the speaker's humor, and the like.

4. *Avoid distracting mannerisms.* Things such as hair twirling, fingernail inspecting, and similar behaviors convey boredom or uninterest.

5. *Ask questions* when you don't understand something the speaker is saying. Repeat what the speaker has said, in different words, to convey understanding.

6. *Resist the temptation to let your mind wander.* It's easy to do considering that a person can think much faster than he or she can speak.

The best listeners make the speaker feel like he is the only person in the world at that moment. By following the above tips, you can join the ranks of good listeners.

Instead of giving undivided attention and providing feedback, we get caught in a variety of bad listening habits that impair our ability to listen actively.

Lack of Assertiveness

Assertiveness
pursuing one's own needs and wants these without infringing on others

Aggressiveness
pursuing one's own wants and needs without regard for the rights of others

Assertiveness is a positive attribute, based on mutual respect and democracy in relationships. Assertiveness means understanding one's own wants and needs and pursuing these without infringing on others' ability to do the same. **Aggressiveness** on the other hand, means pursuing one's needs and wants without regard to how this affects the rights of the others. Often, aggressive people get their needs met at the expense of others. Nonassertive people fail to pursue their needs and wants while allowing others to meet theirs. Nonassertive people fail to stick up for their rights and allow others to take advantage of them, often denying what is going on.[8]

Assertiveness is important to effective communication. Many people are not assertive because they confuse assertiveness with aggressiveness. In an attempt to control what they perceive as aggressiveness, they act nonassertively and fail to meet their needs while allowing hostility and frustration to build up inside themselves, and weakening their communication and relationships.

Saying Yes When We Mean No

When people are nonassertive, they say "yes" to others' demands when they really want to say "no." They spend an inordinate amount of time pleasing others without being reciprocated. They forsake their sexual needs and wants while granting the partner's desires. Although sharing and sacrificing

Health Hint

Assertiveness Bill of Rights

The following "Assertiveness Bill of Rights" may help strengthen your resolve to speak up for yourself:

- You have the right to judge your own behavior, thoughts, emotions and to take responsibility for their initiation and consequences upon yourself.
- You have the right to offer no reason or excuses for justifying your behavior.
- You have the right to judge if you are responsible for finding solutions for other people's problems.
- You have the right to change your mind.

- You have the right to make mistakes and be responsible for them.
- You have the right to say, "I don't know."
- You have the right to be independent of the good will of others before coping with them.
- You have the right to be illogical in making decisions.
- You have the right to say, "I don't understand."
- You have the right to say, "I don't care."

Source: Terrap Treatment Centers, Menlo Park, CA, 1999. Reprinted with permission.

are important to relationships, this becomes a problem when this is always one-way and not reciprocated.

When people are nonassertive, they are filled with resentment and hostility towards their partner as a result. It's a vicious cycle. Originally, in an attempt to avoid conflict, discomfort, or hurting the partner's feelings, they say "yes" when they really mean "no." This temporarily relieves them from feeling guilty. Unfortunately, however, when they do this, they get trapped into doing things they really don't want to do. When this happens, they begin to feel miserable because they've lost control of their lives and lost their self-respect. Not only do they feel stressed because of this, but it also affects their sexual response. Desire and arousal are difficult when a person feels stressed and angry.

The only way to stop the cycle is to begin to say no. This brings us full circle to the same situation as the initial one: having to say no. If people are assertive to begin with, they can avoid the aggravation and stress.

Failing to Make Requests

Assertiveness is directly related to requesting things you desire and saying no to things you don't want to do. People have many reasons for not making explicit sexual requests. As we've already discussed, language poses a unique barrier. Feeling comfortable with sexual language is important and finding a comfortable language level helps. If sex has been a taboo topic of conversation while growing up, it may be difficult to talk about openly. People enter their first relationship without having had the benefit of knowing that talking about sex is okay. Shaking this taboo is sometimes difficult. You can become more comfortable by proceeding slowly, acknowledging your fears and discomfort, and allowing yourself to take chances and grow out of your old ways of thinking and feeling.

Another barrier is not taking responsibility for one's wants, needs, and feelings. First, the individual has to find out who he or she is as a sexual

Health Hint

Saying No

Saying no isn't always easy, but it is essential if you are to be assertive and reduce your stress. You have the right to say no. The following are clear guidelines.

1. Face the other person from a normal distance.
   - If you are too far away, you may appear timid.
   - If you crowd the person, you border on aggressiveness.
2. Look the person directly in the eyes.
   - Averting eye contact is a sure giveaway that you'll cave in.
3. Keep your head up and your body relaxed.
   - Don't be a shrinking violet.
4. Speak clearly and firmly, at a volume that can be heard clearly.
5. Just say no.
   - You don't have to clarify why.

6. Be prepared to repeat it.
   - Sometimes people are persistent. Be prepared to say it again.
7. Stick to your guns.
   - Don't give in. It gets easier with practice.

If you feel a need to explain why you are declining, here are a few tips for setting the stage:

1. Thank the person for the offer: "Gee, thanks, but *no*. I really can't [don't want to]. . . ."
2. Express appreciation: "I really appreciate the offer, but *no*. I'm not interested/too busy/don't want any. . . ."
3. Affirm your friendship: "I enjoy your company, and I'd like to do something together, but *no*. . . ."
4. Reject the offer, not the person: "Please don't take this personally. I like you, but *no*, I don't. . . ."

---

person. Then the person has to accept this. The third step is to share it with the partner. The partner can't know who the other is, what he or she needs, and how to please that person without the other person's taking responsibility to communicate this.

Our sexuality is continually growing and evolving. A married student expressed it this way in class:

Lack of assertiveness is a major factor in not having your sexual needs met.

> My wife is always saying that she shouldn't have to explain what she wants sexually. We've been together for ten years, and I should know how to please her and what her needs are. I have a hard time with this. My own needs change from day to day and from sexual encounter to sexual encounter. One day I may want her to take the lead and initiate sex and be dominant while I lie back and let her take me. The next time we make love, I might want to initiate. I know she's the same way, but I can't tell in advance without her communicating her desires to me.

We need to take responsibility for what we're feeling and make requests accordingly, using "I" language.

Gender and Cultural Considerations

Often, lack of assertiveness is based in religious, cultural or gender-role expectations and transcends lack of skill or desire to assert oneself. Some cultures require subjugating one's personal desires to those of the dominant partner in the relationship. In many cultures the male partner is the dominant member of the couple. Women are expected to put their needs behind those of their partner and behave in ways expected of them. Respecting the wishes of the partner and the culture is taught to be more important than one's own needs. The conflict between these traditional ways of behaving and U.S. cultural values focusing on the individual and self-actualization is a source of stress and sexual dissatisfaction for many women.

Do you know someone who has a cultural background different from the dominant U. S. culture? If so, has this presented any conflicts in communication? How might two people with different cultural or religious values enter a conversation about these differences? What techniques could you use to minimize difficulties?

Case Study

Sirahana

Sirahana was a senior with a major in Finance, enrolled in the Human Sexuality class to fulfill her free elective requirement and to learn more about herself. Normally an "A" student, Sirahana was having trouble with a couple of assignments that required her to write brief reactions about the influence of culture and religion on her sexuality.

She came to see me about this and explained that the assignments forced her to examine things about her life and culture that were painful to her. She had been able to avoid these subjects because she had lived away from home for the past 4 years and was able to hide them from her parents. In a couple of months, however, school would be ending and her parents expected her to move in with her Iranian family.

Sirahana would have to make some tough choices. She had a steady boyfriend, Sean, who was Irish Catholic. She had never told her parents about Sean because their relationship started out as a casual, lighthearted romance that neither thought would last. Little by little, it blossomed as their attraction for each other grew. She practically lived at his off-campus apartment and wanted to move in full-time once school would end in the summer. They had talked seriously about marriage, and eventually children, neither one wanting to let their religious beliefs stand in the way of their love.

Sirahana explained that she was feeling a tremendous amount of guilt over her desire to live apart from her family with Sean. Her parents, culture, and religion all expected her to follow tradition by living at home and ultimately marrying someone of her own faith. It was such a strong expectation that she felt utterly paralyzed at the thought of talking to her parents about it. She also knew that she loved Sean and wanted to start a new life with him. She didn't want to move back home.

She liked the freedom of her current life and felt less and less drawn by the covenants and traditions of her religion and culture. She also loved and respected her parents and deeply appreciated all they had done to put her through school and rear her. She wanted to talk to them, explain exactly what she was feeling, and help them understand, but she didn't know how or where to begin.

MODELS OF COMMUNICATION

Two models relevant to sexual communication are the DESC model and rational emotive therapy.

The DESC Model

A useful model that combines assertiveness and effective verbal communication is the DESC model.[9] It is a powerful tool that helps a person make requests, deliver criticism more effectively, and become more precise in assertiveness.

The DESC model has four parts:

- *D — describe*: Paint a verbal picture of the situation or the other person's behavior that is a source of stress. Be as precise as possible: "Honey, when you use language like, 'I'm feeling horny, lets fuck . . . .'"

- *E — express*: Express your feelings about the incident using "I" language: "I feel seedy and cheap" or "I feel very uncomfortable."

- *S — specify*: Be specific in identifying alternative ways that you would prefer the person to speak or behave: "I'd prefer you to soften your language and say, I'm feeling sexy; lets make love."

- *C — consequences*: Identify the consequences that will follow if the person does (pro) or doesn't (con) comply with your wishes: "In the future, if you do soften your language, I'll be much more likely to get in the mood and want to make love with you (pro)." "If you don't, and you continue to use such crude language, I can't guarantee that I won't be turned off and not feel sexy."

When using this model, precision is important in describing the other person's offending behavior or actions. Again, the offensive behavior, not the person, should be the object of criticism. And the person should take responsibility for his or her feelings and use "I" language when describing them. Rather than blaming the partner and saying, "'You make me feel cheap and seedy," the person should be clear and take responsibility by stating, "I feel cheap and seedy when you use those coarse words."

Rational Emotive Therapy (RET) and Irrational Thinking

Sometimes we fail to communicate clearly because our sexual thinking is irrational or illogical. Our sexual perspective, or belief system — as Albert Ellis, the father of rational emotive therapy (RET), calls it — is disordered. Ellis believes that our *perception* of our partners and specific sexual situations (not the actual person or situation) gives them meaning and determines whether they become a source of dissatisfaction and miscommunication.[10]

For instance, Khalid and Teri have been lovers for a year and have been happy with their sexual lifestyle. They make love about once a week and engage in a variety of sexual behaviors they find enjoyable. Last night, after they came home from the movies, Khalid wanted to make love and Teri didn't.

She was tired and wanted to get to bed early. Feeling rejected, Khalid began to have doubts about their sexual relationship, wondering, "What's wrong with her?" Teri should be in the mood when I am. What's wrong with our relationship?" In reality, nothing is wrong their relationship. They are happy, enjoy each other's company, and have a satisfying sex life together. The only problem is Khalid's perception of this specific situation.

In their clinical work with neurotic patients, Albert Ellis and Robert Harper identified a group of 10 commonly held irrational or illogical beliefs about life.[11] These beliefs form the basis of a belief system that gives one a distorted perspective for assessing potentially stressful situations. Using and understanding Ellis and Harper's theory can be simplified by grouping the 10 illogical/irrational beliefs into four categories:[12]

◡ *Awfulizing statements*: These exaggerate the negative aspects/impact of a situation.

◡ *Shoulds/musts/oughts*: These are beliefs that put illogical demands on oneself and others.

◡ *Evaluation-of-worth statements*: These imply that some people or things are worthless or a complete waste of time.

◡ *Need statements*: These are beliefs that set unrealistic, unattainable requirements for happiness.

We often blow things out of proportion, set unrealistic demands for our behavior and that of our partners, misinterpret sexual comments, or have irrational fears about discussing our wants, needs, desires, or problems with our partners. These illogical/irrational beliefs result in undesirable emotional, intellectual, physical, social, and behavioral consequences. Ellis and Harper use an ABC model to describe this interaction.[13] In this model, the presence of an activating event, A, triggers a series of irrational/illogical beliefs, B, about A. These illogical beliefs about A (not the activating event itself) are the cause of a variety of negative consequences, C. We'll illustrate the model again using Khalid and Teri:

A — *activating event*:

 Khalid wanted to make love with his girlfriend Teri when they came home from the movies, but she didn't. She said she wasn't in the mood and wanted to get to bed early.

B — *irrational/illogical beliefs*: negative self-talk

 "My girlfriend should always be in the mood."
 "My girlfriend should always be in the mood when I am."
 "Partners should always be sexually available."
 "People who are in love should always please their partners sexually."
 "She must not love me any more."
 "She must be having an affair with someone else."
 "I'm not good enough for her."

C — *Consequences*

Physical — muscle tension, upset stomach, tension headache
Emotional — anger, depression
Mental — irrational thoughts
Social — retreating into isolation, breaking off all physical touching
Behavioral — starting to drink to excess

Rational emotive therapy (RET) uses logical thinking and positive self-talk as an aid to reducing sexual problems.[14] Ellis and Harper's ABCDE technique attempts to help us understand our illogical beliefs and self-talk and learn to substitute more rational thoughts in their place.[15] The ABCDE technique builds upon Ellis's ABC model of **illogical thinking** by adding D (dispute) and E (evaluate). D involves disputing each illogical B and substituting a more logical belief in its place. When all of the illogical beliefs have been disputed, the effectiveness of the dispute in defusing the consequences is evaluated.

The ABCDE technique would work like this:

A — Khalid's girlfriend Teri rejecting his offer to make love.

B — Khalid's irrational beliefs about A:

"My girlfriend should always be in the mood."
"My girlfriend should always be in the mood when I am."
"Partners should always be sexually available."
"People who are in love should always please their partners sexually."
"She must not love me any more."
"She must be having an affair with someone else."
"I'm not good enough for her."

C — Consequences of B:

Physical — muscle tension, upset stomach, tension headache
Emotional — anger, depression
Mental — irrational thoughts
Social — retreating into isolation, breaking off all physical touching
Behavioral — starting to drink to excess

D — Dispute:

Khalid decides to tackle this problem by analyzing each of these illogical beliefs and substitute more rational thoughts in their place.

1. "It's irrational for me to think that Teri should always be in the mood."

2. "It's impossible for us both to always be in sync with our sexual desire."

3. "Each partner has the right to say no when he or she is not in the mood to make love."

Illogical thinking
thought based on inaccurate or irrational perception of information

4. "People can be in love but on any given day not feel sexually responsive."

5. "Teri's not wanting to have sex doesn't necessarily mean she doesn't love me."

6. "Her not wanting to have sex with me doesn't necessarily mean she's doing it with someone else."

7. "I'm great for Teri. This has nothing to do with that."

E — Evaluate:

As a result of working through the dispute and coming up with a more rational belief system concerning what happened, Khalid experiences the following changes: Physically, his muscles begin to relax and he can get to sleep again. His tension headache subsides. Emotionally, Khalid feels like a tremendous weight has been lifted from his shoulders. He feels he is thinking clearly again. Khalid stops drinking and asks Teri if she wants to snuggle and fall asleep while he reads his book.

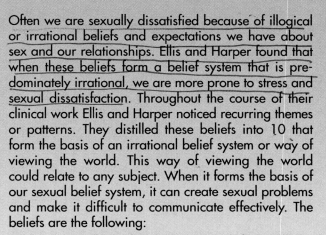

PERSPECTIVES

Ellis and Harper's 10 Irrational Beliefs

Often we are sexually dissatisfied because of illogical or irrational beliefs and expectations we have about sex and our relationships. Ellis and Harper found that when these beliefs form a belief system that is predominately irrational, we are more prone to stress and sexual dissatisfaction. Throughout the course of their clinical work Ellis and Harper noticed recurring themes or patterns. They distilled these beliefs into 10 that form the basis of an irrational belief system or way of viewing the world. This way of viewing the world could relate to any subject. When it forms the basis of our sexual belief system, it can create sexual problems and make it difficult to communicate effectively. The beliefs are the following:

1. You must have love or approval from all the people you find significant.

2. You must thoroughly prove adequate, competent, or achieving.

3. When people act obnoxiously or unfairly, you should blame and damn them and see them as bad, wicked, or rotten individuals.

4. You have to view things as awful, terrible, horrible, and catastrophic when you get seriously frustrated, treated unfairly, or rejected.

5. Emotional misery comes from external pressures, and you have little ability to control or change your feelings.

6. If something seems dangerous or fearsome, you must preoccupy yourself with it and make yourself anxious about it.

7. You can more easily avoid facing many life difficulties and self-responsibilities than undertake more rewarding forms of self-discipline.

8. Your past remains all-important and, because something once strongly influenced your life, it has to keep determining your feelings and behavior today.

9. People and things should turn out better than they do, and you must view it as awful and horrible if you do not find good solutions to life's grim realities.

10. You can achieve maximum human happiness by inertia and inaction or by passively and uncommittedly enjoying yourself.

Source: *Guide to Rational Living*, by A. Ellis and R. Harper (Hollywood, CA: Wilshire Book Company, 1998). Reprinted with permission.

WELLNESS SYNTHESIS

Healthy sexuality is based on good communication. All six components of wellness benefit from high-level verbal and nonverbal communication.

Physical Well-being

Good communication takes time and energy. Often we are too tired, too stressed, and too busy to communicate effectively. Sometimes when our energy level is low, we simply don't have the energy to think clearly and communicate well. Spending our energy on talking and active listening seems beyond our ability during times of low-energy.

Stress also robs us of energy, puts us on edge, and contributes to our being overly defensive. It's hard to communicate effectively when we are on edge. We don't listen effectively and have empathy when we are stressed out.

Sometimes we can combine good communication with physical activity. A walk or bike ride together provides a good opportunity to communicate, and to de-stress and energize at the same time.

Intellectual Well-being

Intellectual well-being can facilitate communication. Effective sexual communication involves three sets of skills: initiating, listening, and responding. Though each can be a source of miscommunication, a person can learn how to improve these skills. Countless books, self-help videos, and courses are available for improving communication skills. With training and practice, you can learn to formulate and express your thoughts and emotions regarding sexuality or any subject.

Emotional Well-being

Emotional well-being affects the ability to communicate clearly. Communicating effectively is difficult even under the best of circumstances. Communicating about sexuality poses unique challenges because of the sensitive nature of the topic. Even though people may want to communicate more effectively, emotions sometimes get in the way. They might feel embarrassed talking about their most intimate desires, thoughts, and feelings. They also might feel guilty about some of these things.

A first step in sexual communication is to identify how we are feeling and to take responsibility for owning these feelings. Once we assume ownership for our feelings, we can use "I" language to communicate them to our intimate partner.

Social Well-being

Communication has a social basis. It is not just about putting thoughts and feelings into words. It also is about the relationship between yourself and the person with whom you are communicating. Metacommunication proposes a framework for communicating based on symmetrical (equal) and complementary (confrontational) relationships. Symmetrical relationships foster good communication, whereas complementary ones discourage effective dialogue. People who are socially effective are able to communicate more easily because they take responsibility for strengthening their relationships and trust that they can withstand open, honest communication.

Spiritual Well-being

Sometimes our moral and ethical standards affect our emotions and impact negatively on our ability to communicate. We each have our own personal moral code with a unique set of values and ethics that develop over a lifetime. Taboos against behaviors ranging from masturbation to oral sex are often deep-seated and rooted in religious training. This can pose conflicts in communicating about some of these behaviors. A mismatch can be the basis of spiritual distress, which can interfere with effective sexual communication. Discussing these concerns with a spiritual advisor might be helpful. Or a college counselor might be a resource.

Environmental Well-being

Among the many barriers to effective communication, some are environmental in nature. Privacy, safety, and a nonthreatening, nondistracting environment are essential for effective sexual communication. Most people find that talking about intimate, personal issues in public places is somewhat threatening. A walk in the woods or along the beach or in a park sometimes can create a facilitative setting and mood for communicating about sexual matters.

WEB RESOURCES

Communication in Sexual Behavior
http://www.couns.msu.edu/self-help/behavior.htm
Michigan State University Counseling Center site with a wide range of topics to improve communications: asserting your interpersonal rights, improving communication skills, maintaining a relationship, communicating in sexual behavior, establishing sex guidelines, saying no without feeling guilty, criticizing others, blaming, and the self-defeating "should."

Manhattan College Counseling Center
http://www.mancol.edu/stntlife/relcom.html
Suggestions for improving communication skills in relationships. These hands-on exercises provide sentence-completion methods in which students complete statements with their partner.

University of Buffalo Communication Documents
http://ub-counseling.buffalo.edu/Relationships/Communication/sexcom.html
Communication documents by Counseling Center, including assertiveness, language of assertiveness, fighting the fair way, sexual communication, and problem solving. A search engine operates from the information from the counseling center.

Notes

1. C. L. Edelman and C. L. Mandel, *Health Promotion Throughout the Lifespan* (St Louis: Mosby-Year Book, 1994).
2. P. Watzlawick, J. H. Beaven, and D. D. Jackson, *Pragmatics of Human Communication* (New York: Norton, 1967).
3. Watzlawick et al.
4. *Transactional Analysis in Psychotherapy* (New York: Grove Press, 1960).
5. B. Mandel, "Communication: A Four Part Process," *Hotliner*, 1:4 (summer 1980/spring 1981), 6.
6. F. Hall, *The Silent Language* (Menlo Park, CA: Benjamin Cummings, 1973).
7. Edelman & Mandel.
8. J. C. Smith, *Creative Stress Management* (Englewood Cliffs, NJ: Prentice Hall, 1993).
9. Developed by S. A. Bower and G. Bower, *Asserting Yourself: A Practical Guide for Positive Change* (Reading, MA: Addison-Wesley, 1976); and utilized by G. Greenberg, *Comprehensive Stress Management* (Dubuque, IA: Brown/Benchmark, 1993).
10. "Reflections on Rational Emotive Therapy," *Journal of Consulting and Clinical Psychology*, 61:2 (1993), 199–201.
11. *Guide to Rational Living* (North Hollywood, CA: Wilshire Books, 1998).
12. S. Walen, R. DiGuisseppi, and R. Wessler, *A Practitioner's Guide to RET* (New York: Oxford University Press, 1980).
13. Ellis and Harper, 1975 (supra note 11).
14. Ellis, 1993 (supra note 10).
15. Ellis and Harper, 1975.

Student Study Questions

1. What makes communicating about sex different from communicating about other subjects?

2. Define metacommunication. What are the parts of a metacommunication model?

3. What four sets of skills are involved in two-way communication?

4. What is "I" language? Give examples of using "I" language.

5. How do we communicate about sexuality nonverbally? Is nonverbal sexual communication accurate?

6. What is the best thing to do if miscommunication becomes apparent? Whose responsibility is it? Why?

7. Give examples of four open-ended sexual statements.

8. What is the impact of language level on sexual communication?

9. What are three barriers to effective listening?

10. What are two barriers to correcting miscommunication?

11. What should you do if you reach a communication impasse?

Sexual Communication Satisfaction Questionnaire

This questionnaire assesses your satisfaction with your sexual communication with your partner. Use the following scale to indicate how strongly you agree or disagree with each statement:

1 = Strongly agree   4 = Disagree
2 = Agree   5 = Strongly disagree
3 = Neither agree nor disagree

_____ 1. I tell my partner when I am especially sexually satisfied.

_____ 2. I am satisfied with my partner's ability to communicate his/her sexual desires to me.

_____ 3. I do not let my partner know things that I find pleasing during sex.

_____ 4. I am very satisfied with the quality of our sexual interactions.

_____ 5. I do not hesitate to let my partner know when I want to have sex with him/her.

_____ 6. I do not tell my partner whether or not I am sexually satisfied.

_____ 7. I am dissatisfied over the degree to which my partner and I discuss our sexual relationship.

_____ 8. I am not afraid to show my partner what kind of sexual behavior I find satisfying.

_____ 9. I would not hesitate to show my partner what is a sexual turn-on to me.

_____10. My partner does not show me when he/she is sexually satisfied.

_____11. I show my partner what pleases me during sex.

_____12. I am displeased with the manner in which my partner and I communicate with each other during sex.

_____13. My partner does not show me things he/she finds pleasing during sex.

_____14. I show my partner when I am sexually satisfied.

_____15. My partner does not let me know whether sex has been satisfying or not.

_____16. I do not show my partner when I am sexually satisfied.

_____17. I am satisfied concerning my ability to communicate about sexual matters with my partner.

_____18. My partner shows me by the way he/she touches me if he/she is satisfied.

_____19. I am dissatisfied with my partner's ability to communicate his/her sexual desire to me.

_____20. I have no way of knowing when my partner is sexually satisfied.

_____21. I am not satisfied in the majority of our sexual interactions.

_____22. I am pleased with the manner in which my partner and I communicate with each other after sex.

Source: "Sexual Communication, Communication Satisfaction, and Solidarity in the Developmental Stages of Intimate Relationships," by Lawrence R. Wheeless, Virginia Eman Wheeless, and Raymond Baus, *Western Journal of Speech Communication*, 48:3 (1984), 224, Copyright © 1984 by Western Speech Communication Association. Reprinted by permission.

Sexual Dysfunction, Sex Therapy, & Sexual Enhancement

12

Major Topics

Physical/Medical Causes of
  Sexual Dysfunction
  Cardiovascular Disease
  Other Diseases
  Injuries
  Substance-induced Sexual
    Dysfunction
  Cautions
Psychological Causes of
  Sexual Dysfunction
  Prior Learning
  Immediate Causes
Types of Sexual Dysfunctions
  Sexual Desire Disorders
  Sexual Arousal Disorders
  Orgasmic Disorders
  Sexual Pain Disorders
  Survey of Sexual Dysfunction
Treating Sexual Dysfunctions
  Treating Sexual
    Dysfunction Related to
    Medical Conditions
  Treating Drug-induced
    Sexual Dysfunction
  Treating Psychosocially
    Based Sexual Dysfunction
Wellness Synthesis
  Physical Well-being
  Intellectual Well-being
  Emotional Well-being
  Social Well-being
  Spiritual Well-being
  Environmental Well-being

Student Learning Objectives

After reading this chapter, students will be able to:

❧ Describe the relationship between sexual dysfunctions and the phases of the sexual response cycle.

❧ Describe the key components of sexual desire disorders.

❧ Describe the key components of sexual arousal disorders.

❧ Describe the main elements of orgasmic disorders.

❧ Describe the main elements of sexual pain disorders.

❧ Describe the psychological causes of sexual dysfunctions.

❧ Describe the medical and pharmacological causes of sexual dysfunctions.

❧ Differentiate prior learning and immediate causes of sexual dysfunctions.

❧ Evaluate the effects of legal and illicit psychoactive substances on sexual dysfunction.

Sexual dysfunction
a disturbance or disorder in
desire, excitement, orgasm, or
resolution of the sexual response
cycle

According to the *Diagnostic and Statistical Manual*, **sexual dysfunction** is a disturbance or disorder in desire, excitement, orgasm, or resolution of the sexual response cycle.[1] As we discussed in detail in Chapter 7, the interaction of all five senses plays a key role in the sexual response: becoming sexually aroused, maintaining interest, having an orgasm, and feeling satisfied.

Sensory arousal combines with emotional arousal (limbic system) and conscious thought (cerebral cortex) as our sensing, feeling, thinking brain triggers and directs the organs, glands, and tissues that regulate our sexual response. Although something as common as developing and maintaining an erection seems like a fairly primitive response, in reality it is a complex result of many reactions within a complicated interdependent system.

Likewise, sexual dysfunction isn't always an all-or-nothing phenomenon. Levels of performance and satisfaction vary. Everyone experiences some level of dysfunction throughout the course of life. Sometimes it is produced by illness, stress, fatigue, or a variety of other causes. Dysfunction is not just a heterosexual issue either. Gay, lesbian, and bisexual people also experience sexual dysfunction.

Can you think of a time when your sexual desire was affected by troubling things going on in your life? Stress? Illness?

Our perception, gender role, and beliefs about aging all factor into determining whether a sexual problem is or is not a dysfunction. As we'll describe, one of the mediating factors in determining dysfunction is whether the "problem" causes emotional distress or relationship difficulties. One's perception of the issue plays a big part in determining if it is even a problem. If a person or partner does not perceive a sexual "problem" (premature ejaculation for instance) as troubling, is it a dysfunction, or even a problem?

Gender role also factors into the mix. For years women were taught that they were not supposed to initiate sex. Does a woman who wants sex but won't ask for it from her partner because she thinks this isn't the "proper" thing to do have a sexual dysfunction? What about our expectations of sex as we age? If we expect a decline in sexual performance and response because we view this as a normal part of aging, do these changes constitute a dysfunction? We'll address these and many other questions in this chapter.

If you recall from Chapter 7, sexual functioning combines physical, intellectual, emotional, social, spiritual, and environmental well-being. We need a minimum level of physical health to ensure that all of the component body parts and systems are able to perform the myriad tasks necessary for sexual response to occur. The health of our social relationships impacts on our ability to trust our partner, relax, and let the sexual response happen. Our emotional health contributes to our self-esteem, feeling good about ourselves, and feeling comfortable with our partner. Our intellectual health contributes to being able to understand and improve our sexual technique and to make informed choices about fertility control and protecting ourselves against STDs. Our spirituality helps us connect with our inner sexuality and others in a deeper way. And a healthy environment allows us to feel safe and comfortable in our sexual space. Sexual dysfunction can occur in any of these dimensions.

Most research on the causes of sexual dysfunctions centers on either the physical or psychological dimensions of health. Therefore, we will use these two domains as the basis for our discussion of the etiology of sexual dysfunctions.

PHYSICAL/MEDICAL CAUSES OF SEXUAL DYSFUNCTION

Research findings over the past decade concerning the causes of sexual dysfunctions have created a dramatic change in our understanding of these conditions and approach to their treatment. In the past, sexual dysfunctions (particularly **erectile dysfunction,** formerly known as "impotence") had been thought to be caused primarily by psychological factors. Most experts in the field now believe the exact opposite, especially regarding erectile disorder.[2] Sexual dysfunction can be caused by a host of physical causes, ranging from disease and injury to the side effects of legal and illegal drugs.

⊀ Erectile dysfunction
a disturbance or disorder related to obtaining an erection

Cardiovascular Disease

In a study of approximately 1,300 men in the Massachusetts Male Aging Study, nearly half of the subjects (all were between 40 and 70 years of age) had experienced erectile difficulties in the previous 6 months.[3] Further, men being treated for heart disease and high blood pressure were up to four

Vascular problems related to decreased blood flow are implicated in many instances of erectile disorder.

Aerobic fitness can reduce the risk for sexual dysfunction.

times more likely to be completely impotent than men without these conditions. These findings implicate vascular problems (blood flow) as the major culprit in erectile problems. All forms of cardiovascular disease rob the blood and body of adequate oxygen through circulation.

Behaviors that increase the risk for cardiovascular disease also can increase the likelihood of incurring erectile disorders. Smokers have been found to be four times more likely than nonsmokers to have severe erectile dysfunction.[4]

Other Diseases

Other physical causes of sexual dysfunction range from structural defects or changes (congenital abnormality of the penis or vagina, scar tissue, fibroids, tumors), to sexually transmitted disease, endocrine disorders, neurological problems, and spinal cord injury, to deficiency diseases (insufficient hormonal production, malnutrition, vitamin deficiency), to allergic reactions (say, to spermicide). These and other medical causes can affect any or all of the

Health Hint

Enhancing Male Potency by Increasing Wellness

Greg Gutfield summarized findings from studies documenting the effects of a healthy lifestyle on sexual potency. These findings show that many of the roadblocks to good sex can be removed through simple lifestyle changes aimed at improving overall health status.[1]

Three of the major culprits in sexual potency — heart disease, diabetes, and high blood pressure — often can be prevented by regular exercise and a healthy diet. Both of these also aid tremendously in weight management and controlling obesity, a major risk factor for all three conditions. The common denominator is *vascular health*. Impaired blood flow leads to poor sexual response. Increasing exercise and eating a healthy diet (low fat, high carbohydrate, moderate protein) enhances blood flow and vascular health.

Stress is another factor that can undermine sexual potency. Chronic stress can lower testosterone, the key hormone related to sexual desire. Less testosterone means less sexual desire. Stress also can make us angry. Men who respond to stressors by losing control and getting angry were much more likely to suffer from erectile disorder then men who were not angry. Of the men who scored highest on measures of anger, 35% reported moderate erectile disorder and 20%

complete erectile disorder. Stress management and relaxation will help moderate testosterone levels, reduce anger, and help restore potency.

Smoking increases the likelihood of erectile dysfunction and it is a major risk factor in cardiovascular disease.[2] Smokers are four times as likely as nonsmokers to develop complete erectile disorder. The negative effects of smoking can be reversed by quitting.

Use it or lose it. "The more erections you have, the more you're likely to have"[3] Having at least three erections per week can reduce the risk for erectile disorder. Erections improve blood flow to the penis. Frequent erections help promote circulation and bring oxygen-rich blood to the area.

To improve your erectile function, make these three simple lifestyle changes:

1. Exercise regularly.

2. Eat a balanced diet.

3. Stop smoking."

[1] Gutfield, "The Prescription for Male Potency," in *Prevention*, 46:11 (1994), 78–82.
[2] Gutfield, "Smoking Your Sex Life Away," by T. Heapes, in *Muscle & Fitness*, 55:4 (1994), 42.
[3] Gutfield.

phases of the sexual response cycle, resulting in a wide variety of sexual dysfunctions.

Injuries

Certain injuries also can cause erectile disorder and other forms of sexual dysfunction. An estimated 600,000 or more cases of erectile dysfunction are attributed to accidents and injuries to the underside of the penis.[5] Athletic injuries resulting from being kicked or struck in the groin can damage the area. Extensive bicycle riding (100-mile riders) can damage the blood vessels on the underside of the penis. Falls that crush the penis against an object (e.g., railing, fence) can damage the blood vessels that supply blood to the penis.

Table 12.1 summarizes some common physical/medical causes of sexual dysfunction and their effects.

Table 12.1 ▷ Effects of Select Medical Physical Conditions on Sexual Response

Condition	Effects of Sexual Response	
Cardiovascular disease	Men and women: sexual arousal disorder; loss of sexual desire	
Spinal cord injuries	Vary according to severity and location	
	Men:	often lose ability to have typical erections (may have "reflex" erections); often lose ability to ejaculate
	Women:	decreased vaginal lubrication; lose genital and orgasmic sensations
Multiple sclerosis and other neurogenic diseases	Men:	loss of erections and ejaculation
	Women:	orgasmic disorder
Diabetes	Men:	male erectile disorder; small % suffer from retrograde ejaculation and less intense ejaculation
	Women:	varies, some experience less lubrication and sexual arousal disorder; female orgasmic disorder
Cancer		
Breast	No physiological effects on sexual response (psychological distress can affect sexual desire and orgasmic capability)	
Cervix	Minimal if treated early (bleeding, discharge)	
Uterus	Vary according to amount of scarring; hysterectomy is sometimes related to sexual desire disorder in women who feel a diminished sense of femininity	
Prostate	Can cause sexual arousal disorder and orgasmic disorder	
Testicles	Infertility; no physiological changes but psychological distress is related to sexual desire disorder in some men who feel a diminished masculinity	
Anorexia	Sexual desire disorders, sexual arousal disorders	
Bulimia	Sexual desire disorder	

Sources: *Human Sexuality*, 5th edition, by W. H. Masters, V. E. Johnson, and R. Kolodny (New York: HarperCollins, 1996); *Handbook of Sexual Dysfunctions: Assessment and Treatment*, by W. O'Donohue and J. H. Geer (Needham Heights, MA: Allyn & Bacon, 1993); *Substance Abuse: A Comprehensive Textbook*, 2d edition, by J. H. Lowinson, P. Ruiz, R. B. Millman, and J. G. Langrod (Baltimore: Williams & Wilkins, 1992).

Substance-induced Sexual Dysfunction

Substance-induced sexual dysfunction can affect any stage of the sexual response cycle. The essential feature of this condition is the link between a clinically diagnosed sexual dysfunction and a specific substance, legal or illegal. The three diagnostic criteria of this condition are:

1. The sexual dysfunction causes marked distress or interpersonal difficulty.

2. Depending upon the substance involved, the condition may involve impaired desire, arousal, or orgasm, or sexual pain and is fully explained by the direct effects of the substance.

3. The dysfunction is not better accounted for by a dysfunction that is not substance-induced. A diagnosis of substance-induced sexual dysfunction represents a recurrent or persistent condition and should not be confused with the effects of episodic substance intoxication.

Both **psychotropic** (mind altering) **drugs** and **somatotropic** (body-altering) **drugs** can have side effects that can produce sexual dysfunction. In some cases, the use of drugs to influence sexual response is intentional (for instance, using alcohol to decrease sexual inhibitions). In other cases, the effects of drug use on sexual response are unintentional or unexpected (for instance, the contributing effects of prescription antihypertensive medications on male erectile disorders).

Prescription Drug Interactions

The effects of prescribed and over-the-counter drugs are many and varied. They range from decreased vaginal lubrication associated with antihistamines (over-the-counter use by allergy sufferers) to erectile dysfunction associated with certain forms of antihypertensive medication. The commonly prescribed antidepressant drug Prozac (fluoxetine) has been shown to cause erectile disorder and **anorgasmia** in small numbers of male and female users, respectively.[6] Table 12.2 outlines common medical drugs and their associated sexual dysfunctions.

Anyone who takes these drugs should have a thorough understanding of their potential sexual side effects. A potential complication associated with taking medications is the effect of combining two or more medications. The effects can range from a simple additive effect (the effect of one medication added to the effect of the other) to a **synergistic effect** (the effects of two or more drugs creating a third, enhanced and often unpredictable effect), which can be associated with sexual dysfunction. This can be especially troubling for people with chronic diseases who must take more than one medication regularly. They must guard against mixing over-the-counter medications with alcohol or illegal substances, as well as medically prescribed drugs.

Psychotropic Drugs

Mind-altering drugs, both legal and illegal, have the potential to affect sexual response. The complexity of our vascular, neurological, and endocrine interactions during sexual response makes us particularly susceptible to the

Psychotropic drugs
substances that are mind-altering

Somatotropic drugs
to substances that are body-altering

Anorgasmia
inability to achieve orgasm

Synergistic effect
an enhanced, unpredictable drug effect caused by combining two or more substances

effects of psychoactive substances. The sexually related side effects of psychoactive drugs are variable. As with all psychoactive drugs, the user's psychological well-being and environment can affect the outcome of the drug experience. A placebo effect can occur if a user has certain expectations for the drug.

Depressants

Tranquilizers, barbiturates, and alcohol are all central nervous system (CNS) depressants. They reduce, depress, or slow down brain and nervous system functioning. Although they are all classified as depressants, their intended use and effects are different. Barbiturates and alcohol have a more diffuse, less targeted effect on the nervous system. Benzodiazepines (the most frequently prescribed tranquilizers) selectively target neural receptors. In addition, tranquilizers and barbiturates are prescribed as medical drugs

Table 12.2 The Effects of Select Medical Drugs on Sexual Response

Drug	Medical Use	Effect on Sexual Response
Hormones Estrogen and Progesterone	Replacement therapy in menopause; birth control; prostate cancer prescription	May decrease sexual desire in women; sexual arousal disorder in men
Steroids Diannabol and others	Treatment for hypogonad disorder (deficiency in gonadal function) Promote growth Treatment for aplastic anemia	Men: atrophy of testicles; cessation of sperm production; growth of breasts; sexual desire disorder Women: masculization of clitoris; excessive facial and body hair
Hypertensive medications Diamox catapres Inderal Tanormin	Control high blood pressure	Loss of sexual desire; sexual arousal disorder; orgasmic disorders
Gastrointestinal drugs Tagament Librax	Treat gastrointestinal distress and similar problems	Decreased sexual desire; sexual arousal disorders
Antihistamines	Control allergic reactions, stop runny nose, itchy eyes	Inhibit lubrication; painful intercourse
Psychiatric medications (major tranquilizers)	Control psychotic episodes	Decreased sexual desire; sexual arousal disorders; orgasmic disorders

Sources: *Drugs and Society*, 3d edition, by W. Witters, P. Venturelli, and P. Hanson (Boston: Jones & Bartlett, 1992); *Sensual Drugs: Deprivation and Rehabilitation of the Mind*, by H. B. Jones and H. Jones (London: Cambridge University Press, 1977); *Human Sexuality*, 5th edition, by W. H. Masters, V. E. Johnson, and R. Kolodny (New York: HarperCollins, 1996); *Handbook of Sexual Dysfunctions: Assessment and Treatment*, by W. O'Donohue and J. H. Geer (Needham Heights, MA: Allyn & Bacon, 1993); *Substance Abuse: A Comprehensive Textbook*, 2d edition, by J. H. Lowinson, P. Ruiz, R. B. Millman, and J. G. Langrod (Baltimore: Williams & Wilkins, 1992).

for treating psychological disorders. Their social use is illegal. Alcohol is a legal, nonmedical drug whose primary use is social.

Tranquilizers originally were divided into two categories; minor (primarily used to treat anxiety and insomnia) and major (antipsychotic drugs used to treat severe mental illness such as schizophrenia). Benzodiazepines (Valium-like drugs) are the most frequently prescribed CNS depressants. The pharmacologic effects of benzodiazepines are so different from those of the antipsychotic drugs that the terms "minor" and "major" tranquilizers are rarely used today.

The primary medical use of Valium-like drugs is to reduce anxiety and treat neuroses. They work by depressing limbic functioning and thereby altering mood. Because these drugs can reduce anxiety and improve mood, they sometimes are used by people in an attempt to enhance sexual desire.

Barbiturates have a less specific, more diffuse sedative/hypnotic effect on depressing nervous system functioning. Barbiturates are used primarily as sedatives, to treat insomnia. Barbiturates are rarely used to treat anxiety these days, having been replaced by safer drugs (such as the benzodiazepines). In low doses, barbiturates can induce a lazy, sleepy state. Because of this, barbiturates sometimes are used incorrectly and illegally to enhance

Health Hint

Dealing with Side Effects of Drugs

Drugs have many different effects. The intended effect is the desired outcome of taking the product. The intended effect of hypertension medication, for instance, is to lower blood pressure.

Side effects are secondary outcomes that result from taking the medication. Some side effects are beneficial, such as regulation of the menstrual cycle when taking oral contraceptives. The drug is intended to prevent the release of an ovum, and as a side effect, it regulates the menstrual cycle. Many side effects however, are not beneficial for sexual response. A side effect of some hypertension medication, for instance, is a reduction in sexual desire.

All drug manufacturers are required by law to provide information about side effects concerning their products. Pharmacists also are required to discuss side effects with consumers.

Ultimately, you have the responsibility for making sense of it all. Here are some tips for understanding possible adverse side effects of prescriptions:

1. Make sure you know what disease or condition you have been diagnosed as having *before* you leave your health care provider.

2. Be sure you know the name of your medication and its intended effects.

3. Understand exactly how to take it (dosage schedule, contraindications, etc.).

4. Ask your health care provider, "What possible effects will taking this medication have on my sexual response?"

5. If the medication carries any potentially negative sexual side effects, ask, "What other medication can I take that will treat my disease (or condition) without affecting my sexual response?"

6. When you pick up your prescription, read the package insert. Ask the pharmacist to clear up any questions you have about the medication.

7. If you experience any negative side effects that detract from the quality of your life, go back to your health care provider.

PERSPECTIVES   Typical Prescription Drug Warning

PATIENT'S INSTRUCTIONS FOR USE

DOSAGE: Use only as directed by your physician.

WARNINGS: The action may last up to six hours and therefore it should not be used more frequently than recommended. Increasing the number or frequency of doses without consulting your physician can be dangerous. If recommended dosage does not provide relief of symptoms or symptoms become worse, seek immediate medical attention. Other medicines should be used only as prescribed by your physician.

sexual response by inducing a relaxed, less inhibited state of mind. In high, toxic doses, barbiturates can induce coma. Table 12.3 summarizes the most common barbiturates and their general effects.

The alcohol people drink is more precisely termed ethyl alcohol, also known as ethanol. **Ethyl alcohol** is available either in its pure form, grain alcohol, or more commonly as the active ingredient in a wide variety of alcoholic beverages. Alcohol is a strong central nervous system depressant.

Unlike the other categories of depressants (tranquilizers and barbiturates), alcohol is not a prescription medical drug with specific intended effects. Alcohol creates a sedative/hypnotic effect similar to that of barbiturates. Alcohol decreases the inhibitory centers of the brain and is used primarily for its ability to reduce inhibitions. Therefore, people often use alcohol to enhance sexual desire. In larger doses, alcohol has effects similar to those of other depressant drugs.

When a person consumes an alcoholic beverage, about 20% of the alcohol enters the bloodstream immediately through the stomach lining. The

Ethyl alcohol
a grain alcohol that is a central nervous system depressant

Table 12.3 ⟩ Common Barbiturates, Their Uses and Effects

Drug	Uses and Effects
amobarbital (Amytal)	Sedative with moderately rapid action.
pentobarbital (Nembutal)	Induces sleep; causes euphoria and excitation at first, so it is abused.
phenobarbital (Luminal)	A long-acting barbiturate particularly well-suited for treatment of epilepsy. Because of its long action, it is not often abused.
secobarbital (Seconal)	Short-acting sedative with prompt onset of action; is commonly abused to produce intoxication and euphoria by blocking inhibitions.
tuinal (50% amobarbital and 50% secobarbital)	Rapidly effective, moderately long-acting sedative.

Blood alcohol concentration (BAC) a measurement of percentage of alcohol in blood; also termed blood alcohol level (BAL)

remainder enters the body when the stomach's contents enter the intestines. Because the brain has a large blood supply, it absorbs a lot of alcohol. The measurement of alcohol content of blood in circulation is termed **blood alcohol concentration** (**BAC**). Physical and psychological effects on the body at different blood alcohol levels are shown in Table 12.4.

Small elevations in BAC are characterized by a "mellow" state, in which the body is relaxed and the person is less inhibited than usual. At this stage, sexual desire — and sexual performance — may be enhanced. With increased alcohol intake, though, the person's judgment rapidly becomes impaired, which impacts sexual decisions. Because alcohol is classified as a depressant, the initial "high" may be followed by a "low." Some drinkers become suicidal.

Physiological responses (including sexual performance) are compromised with increasing BACs. The person may have trouble walking a straight line and maintaining balance, and the speech may become slurred.

PERSPECTIVES

Mixing Alcohol and Medicines

Sometimes alcohol increases the effects and the risks of a medicine to potentially dangerous levels. About 100 prescription medicines can produce unwanted effects when mixed with alcohol. A few examples are:

Analgesic pain medication
- salicylates (aspirin)
- ibuprofen (Advil, Motrin)

Effects
stomach and intestinal bleeding, bleeding ulcers

Antidiabetic agents
- chlorpropamide (Diabinese)
- tolbutamide (Orinase)
- insulin

altered control of blood sugar, most often hypoglycemia

Barbiturates
- secobarbitol (Seconal)
- phenobarbital (Barbita)
- pentobarbital (Nembutal)

greater sedative effect, drowsiness, confusion

Benzodiazepines
- alprazolam (Xanax)
- diazepam (Valium)
- triazolam (Halcion)

greater sedative effect, impaired motor coordination (such as driving ability)

Monamine oxidase (MAO) inhibitors
- isocarboxazid (Marplan)
- phenelzine (Nardil)
- tranylcypromine (Parnate)

certain alcoholic beverages contain tyramine, which can cause severe high blood pressure; may be fatal

Adapted from National Council on Patient Information and Education, 666 Eleventh St. N.W., Suite 810, Washington, DC 20001. Reprinted with permission.

Some people use hallucinogens to improve their sexual response by enhancing the perception of touch and other sensations. Users also report a sense of time distortion; sexual activities seem to last longer.

Three of the best known hallucinogens are lysergic acid diethylamide (LSD), methylenedioxymethamphetamine (MDMA), and phencyclidine (PCP). Hallucinogens are illegal except as part of certain American Indian tribal ceremonies.

Marijuana

For many years, marijuana or cannabis, was classified as a mild hallucinogen. Most drug authorities now place marijuana and its variants (hashish and hash oil) in its own category because of the varied effects. The effects of marijuana are result in part from the varying amounts of the active ingredient, tetrahydrocannabinol (THC). High levels of THC can produce a mild hallucinogenic effect, which leads to changes in perception of sensory stimuli. Users report a heightened sensitivity to visual and auditory stimuli and an increased craving for certain kinds of foods.

The effects of marijuana on sexual response are variable. Many users report increased sexual pleasure because of enhanced sensations, as well as a distortion of space and time. This creates a "time warp" in which the sexual act seems to hang suspended.

Other users, in contrast, report that the same mildly hallucinogenic state creates a kind of paranoia that cancels out these same effects. The loss of control brought on by the distortion of perception of time and space is frightening and can diminish sexual pleasure and disorders in sexual response. Long-term marijuana use has been shown to lower testosterone (the sex hormone most related to sexual desire) and sperm levels.

Marijuana use is illegal except in two instances: (a) as an adjunct to glaucoma treatment (to relieve pressure within the eye), and (b) reduction of nausea symptoms associated with chemotherapy for cancer. In both instances, strict legal regulations control its use.

Narcotics

Narcotics drugs are pain killers. They work by diminishing the transmission of pain throughout the nerve pathway. The common opium-derivative narcotics are opium, heroin, and codeine. A common myth concerning heroin addicts is that they are sexually aggressive. To the contrary, one of the side effects of heroin addiction is a diminished interest in sex.

Cautions

Any illegal drug carries the potential for toxicity, overdose, and serious physical danger because illegal substances are not regulated or controlled. Therefore, a person has no idea where or how the substance was produced and there is no way to quantify the amount of the active ingredient in the drug or the presence of any additives. Marijuana, for instance, has varying amounts of THC and can be cured or mixed with a variety of other substances. Heroin and cocaine can be "cut" (diluting the original volume and pure form by adding ingredients to increase the volume) with anything ranging from talcum powder to rat poison.

Penalties for using illegal drugs are variable and far outweigh any perceived benefits associated with enhanced sexual response. Sexual response can be greatly diminished by spending the rest of one's life in prison.

All of the four categories of drugs (depressants, stimulants, hallucinogens, [including marijuana], and narcotics) have the potential to cause sexual dysfunction. Table 12.5 summarizes the effects of psychoactive drugs on sexual response.

Table 12.5 The Effects of Select Psychoactive Substances on Sexual Response

Drug	Chronic Use or Effects of Small Doses	High Dosage
Depressants		
Benzodiazepines		
Valium	Diminished anxiety and improved social	Loss of interest in sex
Librium	and sexual functioning	
Tranxene		
Barbiturates		
Amytal	Cerebral disinhibition; increased relaxation	Loss of desire; sexual
Nembutal		arousal disorders;
Luminal		loss of motor control
Seconal		
Tuinal		
Alcohol	Cerebral disinhibition; increased relaxation	After time, loss of desire; sexual arousal disorders; loss of motor control
Stimulants		
Amphetamines	Increased energy and interest in sex;	After time, loss of desire and
Cocaine	ability to prolong sexual activities;	interest; loss of control;
	"rush" similar to orgasm	orgasmic disorders
Hallucinogens		
Marijuana	Heightened awareness and sensations;	Decrease in testosterone;
LSD	time distortion (sex seems to last longer)	loss of desire
MDMA		
Narcotics		
Opium	Feelings of warmth; reduction in aggression;	Loss of desire; sexual
Heroin	sleepy/mellow state	arousal disorders; orgasmic
Morphine		disorders
Methadone		
Codeine		

PSYCHOLOGICAL CAUSES OF SEXUAL DYSFUNCTION

The two basic psychological causes of sexual dysfunction are (a) prior learning and (b) immediate causes.

Prior learning refers to factors related to childhood development. Immediate causes are factors that have their origins later than childhood learning.

Prior learning
factors relating to childhood development

Prior Learning

Most theorists agree that childhood learning shapes many of our fundamental attitudes, values, and beliefs about sexuality. Humans are capable of experiencing sexual and sensual pleasure from birth to death. Infants of both sexes seem to derive great pleasure from touching and rubbing their genitals against bedding and clothing. They also seem to thrive when physical bonding, breastfeeding, and other forms of intimate physical touch are established early in infancy.[8] When this seemingly innate sexual potential is thwarted through overt or covert childrearing practices, it plants the seeds of subsequent sexual problems in adulthood.

The messages we receive during childhood — particularly those from our parents and other primary caregivers — contribute heavily to healthy or unhealthy psychosexual development. Sex therapists widely report the relationship between severe anti-sex parenting and the development of sexual dysfunction in later life. Children who are reared in environments where nudity, masturbation, and childhood inquiry and discussion of sexuality are severely punished are more likely to develop sexual problems than their peers who are reared in more tolerant environments.

In one study, adults with the former childhood histories were less interested in sex, derived less pleasure from sexual relations, had more inhibitions about sexual expression, and had higher levels of shame, guilt, anxiety, and disgust than those with less rigid backgrounds.[9] The "sex-as-sin" message, and subsequent sexual problems came from a strict or orthodox religious orientation; the more rigidly orthodox, the greater the extent of dysfunction.

Another researcher warned about associating sexual dysfunction with religious orthodoxy. She notes the lack of suitable research designs and methodology associated with sex therapists' reports concerning the etiology of sexual dysfunction. Without suitable control groups, it is impossible to discern whether orthodoxy or some other factor is the problem.[10]

Even covert practices can sabotage the development of healthy sexuality. Parents who are uneasy about sexuality may choose to deal with this by ignoring the subject. Saying nothing still sends a strong message to children about sexuality. Omitting such an integral part of life from all discussion leaves a void that children clearly perceive. They learn early that something must be wrong, shameful, or dirty about sex if it doesn't ever come up as a topic of conversation. Students often report anecdotally in class their feelings that their parents must have made love only once

Not saying anything about sex sends a strong negative message about sexuality to kids.

Case Study

Lilian's Thoughts About Her Parents' Sexuality

Lilian is a 19-year-old freshman. She shared these feelings about her parents as sexual beings.

I never viewed my parents as sexual creatures. They never talked about sex once in my presence. My mom briefly explained menstruation to me, and what to expect when I get my period, but when I interrupted and told her we had already gone over that stuff in school, she abruptly stopped and seemed relieved.

My brothers told me that my mom and dad never talked to them about sex either. My parents are not very warm people. They never hug and kiss in public and very rarely express themselves physically.

I guess they love each other, because they seem to care about each other and respect one another's needs. It's just that they don't seem interested in sex at all. I'd never ask either of them about a sexual issue. My friend's mom kind of fills that role for me.

To tell you the truth, I can't even imagine my parents ever having sex. I guess they had to have it three times to conceive my brothers and me, but I can't even visualize it. It doesn't gross me out or anything. I just can't seem to create the picture. Funny, isn't it?

(for their conception) or as many times as they have siblings, because they never discussed sexuality, their desire for each other, or other sexual themes when the children were around.

Other messages about sexuality relate to gender role expectations. Males and females in U.S. culture often are reared with different sets of sexual standards and expectations. Rather than viewing sexual needs and expression as a human universal, they are reared with the belief that men and women have differing needs and wants that are gender-specific. Society also has different rules and codes of conduct concerning how to satisfy these needs. Men are expected to be more assertive and aggressive in pursuing their sexual needs. Women are expected to be more demure, to rely on men to pursue them and satisfy them.

These gender-role expectations can create anxiety, shame, guilt, and fear — all attributes that detract from sexual pleasure. As early as 1970, Masters and Johnson noted that rigid sex roles and a double standard concerning sexual expression was often at the root of much of their clients' sexual dysfunction.[11]

Fifteen years later another study found that nontraditional, less rigid gender roles were related positively to increased enjoyment with sex, greater levels of experimentation with sexual positions, oral sex, initiating sexual encounters, and asserting one's sexual needs and wants.[12]

Male sexual dysfunction is often related to performance anxiety stemming from rigid male gender-role socialization.[13] Many men grow up with an idealized picture of male sexuality that positions men as all-knowing, ever-ready, and being responsible for initiating sexual encounters and pleasing their partners. This puts tremendous pressure on men to live up to those expectations.

Immediate Causes

Immediate causes of sexual dysfunction were identified as:[14]

- ◡ Failure to engage in effective sexual behavior because of either ignorance or unconscious avoidance
- ◡ Anxiety related to performance, fear of failure, or perceived inability to please a partner
- ◡ Perceptual and intellectual defenses against erotic feelings
- ◡ Failure to communicate effectively with one's partner

Ignorance/Avoidance

Failure to engage in effective sexual behavior often arises from simple ignorance. Sexual dysfunctions related to the arousal and orgasm phase often are related to lack of knowledge concerning effective techniques for achieving optimal levels of stimulation. Ignorance is often compounded by shame and guilt related to sexual experimentation, assertiveness, and admission of what is arousing. These people unconsciously avoid exploration of the sensual and erotic and fail to take advantage of opportunities to explore sexual satisfaction.

Achieving sexual pleasure is a skill that can improve with better technique. If one perceives sexual activity as something that is learned rather than innate and allows oneself to pursue self-improvement, many sexual problems and dysfunctions can be remedied. All four phases of sexual response can be enhanced by improving technique. People can learn how to increase desire, enhance arousal, maximize plateau, increase the likelihood of orgasm (and multiple orgasms), and enjoy resolution and the refractory period.

Good communication can enhance technique, especially when practicing with a partner and discovering what works with him or her. But, as one man said, "The way I got to become such a good lover was that I practiced a lot by myself when I was at home." Through introspection, guided readings, practice activities, and a variety of other techniques, technique and performance can be enhanced.

Performance Anxiety

Sexual anxiety resulting from fear of failure, the demand for performance or excessive need to please one's partner can literally short-circuit sexual response. Any type of anxiety interferes with the ability to relax and allow vasocongestion and other sexual processes to occur. Anxiety can interfere with the level of sexual desire and ability to get aroused, and to create sufficient stimulation to trigger orgasm. Anxiety interferes with the ability to become fully involved in the moment, allowing one to be immersed in the sexual episode.

Anxiety related to a current sexual encounter is often rooted in past sexual episodes. Failure to become sufficiently aroused and maintain an erection in the past often leads to anxiety related to the present ability to perform satisfactorily. Being asked to perform sexually upon demand can create resentment and anxiety related to current functioning. In a sense, anxiety fosters the anticipation of failure.

Performance anxiety
fear, worry, or panic associated with one's perceived sexual behavior

Anxiety is perhaps the greatest psychological factor associated with erectile disorder.[15] Although **performance anxiety** is often characterized as a "male problem" because men usually are viewed as responsible for their partner's orgasm, women also suffer from this malady. The person worries over every facet of the sexual encounter: Am I attractive enough . . . sexy enough? Is my penis big enough . . . my breasts large enough? Is my underwear sexy? Will I be able to get (sustain) an erection? Will my technique work? What if he (she) asks me to do something I'm not comfortable with or know how to do? Will we "come" together?

These and countless other thoughts and concerns set up a expectation-anxiety-performance-feedback loop that initiates and perpetuates sexual problems. The expectation of failure or poor performance produces anxiety ranging from mild worry to panic. Anxiety creates physiological and psychological roadblocks that impair good performance, resulting in the kind of poor performance the person feared to begin with. In a sense, it creates a self-fulfilling prophecy. The fears are answered by, "I told you so," confirming the failure. This seals one's fate by making it twice as hard to correct the problem and improve performance.

Defenses

Spectatoring
becoming an outside observer of one's own sexual encounter while it is occurring

Anxiety also contributes to the perceptual and intellectual defense against erotic feelings called **spectatoring**. Spectatoring occurs when the person becomes an outside observer of his or her own sexual encounter. In a sense, the sexual encounter is reduced to an intellectual activity in which the participant steps away and critically analyzes his or her own behavior.

In spectatoring, a person becomes an outside observer rather than an active participant in the sexual experience.

Whether driven by narcissistic preoccupation with self, voyeurism, or performance anxiety, spectatoring turns the participant into an observer of his or her own sexual encounter. In a sense, the spectator examines the performance of self or partner rather than becoming fully involved in the sensations and experiences. This result is a lack of enjoyment in the experience, as well as dysfunction with any phase in the response cycle.

Do you ever find yourself spectatoring in your own sexual relations? How do you feel when you do this?

Communication Problems

We sometimes have trouble communicating our sexual desires, needs, and wants because of feelings of shame, guilt, or fear. Maybe we have learned that sex and sexual needs are a taboo subject.

Furthermore, we may be uncomfortable with the language of sexuality. Our culture does not have a common sexual language. This makes it difficult to understand, articulate, and communicate about sexuality with our partners.

Open communication between partners is essential for dealing with sexual difficulties.

Consequently, we suppress our needs and problems, anger and resentment build, and eventually this short-circuits the delicate balance between the neurological, vascular, and endocrine factors necessary in the sexual response.

Stress and Fatigue

Finally, stress and fatigue can precipitate sexual dysfunction. When associated with other aspects of life such as work, childrearing demands, money problems, and poor health, stress and fatigue can rob a person of vital energy and a zest for living. Stress and fatigue can affect all phases of the sexual response cycle.

When men are stressed, their testosterone levels drop. Testosterone, you may recall, is the hormone most related to the level of sexual desire. When these men participated in stress management activities, their testosterone levels and levels of sexual desire returned to normal.[16] Common sense tells us that when we are tired and stressed, the last thing we seem to be interested in is sex. For the sexual response to begin and orgasm to occur, people need to relax and let the body take over. This often is not possible if a person is feeling overwhelmed or just need a good night's sleep.

TYPES OF SEXUAL DYSFUNCTIONS

The American Psychiatric Association (APA) classifies sexual dysfunctions as the lifelong type, acquired type, generalized type, and situational type.[17] Lifelong disorders have been present since the onset of sexual functioning. Acquired disorders have developed after a period of normal functioning. Generalized dysfunctions are not limited to specific types of stimulation, situations or partners. Situational dysfunctions are limited to certain types of stimulation, situations, or partners.

The characterization of sexual dysfunctions below relates to the work of Helen Singer-Kaplan and Masters and Johnson in conceptualizing the phases of human sexual response: desire, excitement, orgasm, and resolution.

- The *desire phase* originates with fantasizing and thinking about engaging in sexual activities. Sexual dysfunctions that relate to this phase are called *sexual desire disorders*.

- The *excitement phase* is characterized by the build-up of sexual excitement and tension, manifested through vasocongestion. Penile tumescence and erection are physical evidence of desire in men. In women, vaginal lubrication and expansion and swelling of the vulva indicate arousal. Sexual dysfunctions related to this stage are called *sexual arousal disorders*.

- In the *orgasm phase*, built-up sexual tension is released. Followed immediately by psychological feelings of satisfaction and satiation. Sexual dysfunctions related to this phase are referred to as *orgasmic disorders*.

- The *resolution phase* is characterized by a physiologic return to the pre-desire stage. Sexual pain disorders may be present during intercourse or in the resolution phase.

Sexual Desire Disorders

Sexual desire disorders include hypoactive sexual desire disorder, and sexual aversion disorder.

Hypoactive Sexual Desire Disorder

Hypoactive sexual desire disorder is a dysfunction characterized by very low levels (or complete absence) of sexual desire. Individuals with this condition do not initiate sexual activity and may engage in sexual relations only begrudgingly at the insistence of their partner. They have little or no motivation to seek sexual stimulation and are increasingly undisturbed by this lack of opportunity.

Three APA criteria are necessary to diagnose hypoactive sexual desire disorder: (a) persistent or recurrent deficiency or absence of sexual fantasy or desire for sexual activity; (b) marked psychological or interpersonal distress attributable to the disorder; and (c) no other psychological disorder (such as major depression, post-traumatic stress disorder), medical condition, or direct physiological effects of a drug or medication.

The onset of hypoactive sexual desire disorder can be as early as puberty but usually begins in adulthood, after a period of adequate sexual interest. This dysfunction often is associated with chronic stress, interpersonal difficulties, and problems related to intimacy and commitment.

Although loss of sexual desire can be chronic or episodic, depending upon the underlying relationship and psychological problems, hypoactive sexual desire disorder is a chronic condition. Temporary loss of sexual desire is a common byproduct of recovery from depressive disorders.

Sexual Aversion Disorder

Sexual aversion disorder is characterized by disgust and active avoidance of any genital sexual contact with a sexual partner. People who have sexual aversion disorder report anxiety, fear, disgust, or revulsion when confronted

Hypoactive sexual desire disorder
a dysfunction characterized by very low or complete absence of sexual desire

Hypoactive sexual desire is chronic in nature.

Sexual aversion disorder
a disorder characterized by disgust and active avoidance of any genital sexual contact

Case Study

Hypoactive Sexual Disorder: The Case of Rhonda

Rhonda is a 45-year-old, part-time evening student. She has been married for 20 years and has three children, ages 19, 17, and 14. A homemaker for the past two decades, Rhonda has returned to school to earn a second degree in computer science (she already has a bachelor's degree in English). Rhonda met with one of the authors for counseling.

I'm not even sure why I came to see you. I've never discussed this with anyone before. We were discussing hypoactive sexual disorder in class today, and I think I have it.

I've been married to Ed over twenty years. We met in college in the seventies, fell in love, and were married in 1976. Our sex life was great for the first ten years of our marriage. Even with the pregnancies, the kids, staying home, and all, sex was always a strong part of our relationship. It all changed about ten years ago. Ed and I had been drifting apart a little. His career had taken off, and I was home with the kids. He felt we didn't have as much in common any more, and I was getting boring. It's hard when you're

raising three kids almost by yourself. Ed is on the road almost forty percent of the time, traveling all over the world for his job. One day he's in Japan, the next in Indianapolis. Meanwhile, I'm schlepping one kid off to soccer, another to band practice, and the third to the mall to work.

Anyway, we began to pull back from each other sexually. Sex became such a hassle. Half of the time Ed claimed he was too tired or busy with work. Other times he'd pop in, fresh from some exciting business trip to Europe or somewhere exotic and expect me to be Miss Bubbly, drop everything, and jump in the sack with him. I really resented that and just withdrew. Our sex life slipped from two or three times a week, when he was home, to two or three times a month. There were even some months when we didn't have sex at all.

It seems as though for the past two years I don't even care if we don't have sex at all. I'm not even sure if I miss it, but I know something is terribly wrong. I guess I thought these kind of feelings were inevitable after being together for twenty years.

with a sexual opportunity with a partner. The aversion may be to a specific aspect of sexual contact (such as genital secretions or vaginal penetration) or to all sexual stimuli including kissing and touching.[18]

People with this disorder may have extreme psychological distress, panic attacks, and physical symptoms such as dizziness, nausea, and breathing difficulties. These symptoms often are accompanied by impaired relationship functioning and unusual "covert" strategies to avoid sexual contact (immersion in work, going to sleep early, neglecting personal appearance, abusing substances, and so forth).

Dysfunction Versus Disinterest

When discussing sexual dysfunctions, we must recognize the normal continuum of sexual interest and desire in all people. Some people are much more interested in sexual activity than others. The level of interest, desire, and fantasy are variable and are not the only criteria for a diagnosis of sexual dysfunction. To qualify for a diagnosis of either hypoactive sexual desire disorder or sexual aversion disorder, the condition must: (a) be persistent and recurrent, (b) cause

Disinterest is not a sexual desire disorder if neither the person nor the partner is bothered by it.

marked distress or interpersonal difficulty, and (c) not be the result of another medical or physical condition. Little interest in sexual activity, low desire, and no fantasizing, aren't necessarily dysfunctional unless they are accompanied by the three diagnostic criteria. Individuals with low-levels of sexual desire still can be happy, productive, and sustain satisfying long-term relationships as long as their partners have similar sexual traits.

Rate your sexual desire on a scale of 1–10. Are you satisfied with this? If you have a partner, is this similar to your partner's level of desire?

Case Study

Sexual Aversion Disorder: The Case of Josh

Josh is a 25-year-old senior. He is single, an excellent student, and works for a large investment firm. He is finishing his degree in Finance. He grew up in a strict, conservative family, and remembers being severely punished for masturbating when he was a child. He came to the office of one of the authors to seek guidance concerning a sexual problem he had.

Josh began by saying, "I feel really strange talking to you about this, but you seem very understanding and I need to talk to someone."

After receiving some reassurances and permission, he began his story.

I met this wonderful woman, Suzanne, at work this semester. She is thirty years old, divorced with no kids, and is one of the stock traders for the company. She is gorgeous, funny, and bright. We hit it off immediately. I'm not a virgin, and I've been engaged in the past, but I'm hardly what you'd call sexually experienced. I like sex and all that, but I'm kind of conservative and not into any kinky stuff. Intercourse is okay, but oral sex repulses me. I start to get nauseous just thinking about it.

Anyway, Suzanne and I began dating, and from the start she was very passionate. She wanted to have sex on our first date, but I held off, told her I was tired

and needed to get up early the next day. I wasn't ready for her and needed time to get to know her. I was surprised she wanted to see me again, but she did, and we talked about my need to get to know her better before we began to have sex. She said she really liked me and it was okay — we wouldn't rush into a sexual relationship.

After about a month, we finally had sex. We went back to her place after dinner and a movie, and she had a glass of wine. We started to kiss and undress, and everything was great until she started to kiss me on the chest and stomach. I felt her head begin to go lower, and as she reached my penis, I began to stiffen up and push her away. I guess she thought I was teasing, because she persisted and even laughed. When I began to lose my erection, she knew something was wrong and stopped. I was so embarrassed I didn't know what to say.

She told me it was okay, that we'd try to work it out, but I just couldn't perform that night. I told her we'd have intercourse the next time, but I just couldn't enjoy oral sex. I really like her and want to make this relationship work. My fiancee broke our engagement because of this same issue three years ago, and I don't want to lose Suzanne.

Hypoactive sexual desire disorder should not be confused with voluntary celibacy or abstinence. Some people perceive celibacy as a sexual dysfunction because they believe it is "abnormal" and abstinence is "unnatural." Celibacy is not a sexual dysfunction. Not all celibate people lack sexual interest and desire. Most of us choose to be celibate and abstain from sexual activity at times in our lives, for a variety of reasons.

Sexual Arousal Disorders

Sexual arousal disorders differ from sexual desire disorders in that the latter are related to lack of desire and the former to the inability to achieve sufficient levels of arousal. The arousal phase of sexual response depends upon vasocongestion, which affects erection in men and vaginal lubrication and expansion and swelling of the external genitalia in women. Vasocongestion involves a complex interplay between psychological variables (desire, trust, affection), and physiological variables (unrestricted blood vessels, a healthy endocrine system). Similarly, the causes of sexual dysfunction related to vasocongestion can be psychological, physiological, or both.

Female Sexual Arousal Disorder

The major characteristic of this female dysfunction is the persistent or recurrent inability to attain or maintain sufficient vaginal lubrication and swelling to complete the sexual activity. Vasocongestion is impaired, and the vagina and external genitalia do not become fully engorged with blood. As a result, penetration is restricted, which may result in painful intercourse, avoidance of sexual relations and a disturbance of the relationship. Female sexual arousal disorder is often accompanied by a sexual desire disorder and female orgasmic disorder.

The three APA diagnostic criteria for female sexual arousal disorder are (a) persistent or recurrent inability to attain or maintain an adequate lubrication/swelling response, (b) marked psychological distress, and (c) not caused by another psychological condition (such as major depression), the effects of a medication or drug, or a general medical condition.

Women who have sexual arousal disorder simply do not become sufficiently aroused to have or enjoy sexual relations. This may result in painful intercourse, avoidance of sexual intercourse, and disturbance in sexual relations. Sexual arousal disorder often is accompanied by sexual desire disorders and female orgasmic disorder.

Male Erectile Disorder

Often called "impotence," male erectile disorder is the persistent or recurring inability to attain or maintain an adequate erection for the completion of sexual activity. This disorder has different patterns. Some men with the disorder are unable to attain an erection at all. Others are able to get an erection but lose it upon penetration. A third group of males are able to attain an erection and complete penetration but lose their erection during thrusting. Some men with this condition report having morning erections or being able to attain erection during masturbation. Others are unable to attain an erection through masturbation. Approximately 5% of men at age 40 are unable to get erections. This number climbs to 15% at age 70.

The three APA diagnostic criteria for male erectile disorder are: (a) marked distress or interpersonal difficulty, (b) no other coexisting psychological condition, and (c) no direct physiological effects of a substance or preexisting medical condition.

Most men occasionally are unable to obtain an erection.

Men who have male erectile disorder often are anxious, fear failure, and doubt their sexual performance. These psychological concerns often result in lack of sexual excitement and pleasure, avoidance of sexual intercourse, and disturbance in sexual and marital relationships.

Isolated episodes of inability to obtain an erection are almost universal among men. The reasons include, among others, stress, fatigue, overindulgence of food or drink, and adjusting to a new partner.[19]

Orgasmic Disorders

Orgasmic disorders
dysfunctions related to the orgasm phase of sexual response

Orgasmic disorders are dysfunctions related to the orgasm phase of sexual response. These disorders center on the inability of men and women to release pent-up sexual tension through orgasm. These people are interested in sexual relations and are able to become sexually aroused. Their problems relate to their inability to move to the next stage of sexual response, orgasm.

Female Orgasmic Disorder

Formerly known as "inhibited female orgasm," female orgasmic disorder is a persistent or recurring delay in or absence of orgasm following a typical excitement phase. Three specific APA criteria must be met to diagnose this condition: (a) the absence of orgasm following a "normal" excitement phase, (b) accompanying marked distress or interpersonal difficulty, and (c) not the result of another medical or psychological condition or direct physiological effects of a substance.

The "normal" excitement phase is highly variable. The clinician has to assess what is a normal excitement phase for any given patient. This assessment takes into account the woman's sexual experience, history, and level and adequacy of stimulation she receives. A normal excitement phase for one woman may be markedly different from that of another woman.

Because the female capacity for orgasm increases with age, female orgasmic disorder is more prevalent in younger women. As women experience more variety of sexual stimulation, become more knowledgeable about their bodies, and better communicate their needs to their partner, they tend to gain orgasmic facility. Most female orgasmic disorder is lifelong rather than acquired, as women who learn to be orgasmic rarely lose this capacity.

When orgasmic disorders are situational, they often are related to issues such as stress, fatigue, overindulgence of food or drink, or relationship problems such as poor communication and poor technique. Many, if not most, women do not receive enough direct clitoral stimulation through back and forth vaginal thrusting. Vaginal intercourse alone does not always provide enough clitoral stimulation for orgasm.[20]

Most women have temporary episodes of female orgasmic disorder.

Emphasis on intercourse (especially the man-on-top position) as the only acceptable sexual outlet for women can be the root of the problem. Often, women who are unable to achieve an orgasm through vaginal intercourse find that they can achieve it during cunnilingus or masturbation or with additional manual clitoral stimulation during coitus.

Some educators and therapists call women who never have had an orgasm as "preorgasmic," implying that all women are inherently capable of achieving orgasm. These professionals prefer to view the inability to orgasm as a developmental learning issue versus a dysfunction.[21]

Male Orgasmic Disorder

Formerly known as "inhibited male orgasm," this disorder is a persistent or recurrent delay in or absence of orgasm following a normal excitement phase. Like female orgasmic disorder, the three APA diagnostic criteria that must be met in making this diagnosis are: (a) absence of orgasm following a "normal" excitement phase, (b) marked distress or interpersonal difficulty, and (c) not the result of a preexisting medical or psychological condition or physiological effects of a medication or other drug.

In its most common form, men who have this condition cannot reach orgasm during intercourse. These men usually are able to reach orgasm if intercourse is accompanied by manual or oral stimulation of the penis. In

Case Study

Orgasmic Disorders: Christine

Christine is a 25-year-old college senior. She has been having sex with her boyfriend, Nick, for about 3 months and has not been able to have an orgasm yet.

I'm not sure whether I have a problem, but I've been having sex with my boyfriend, Nick, since the end of the spring semester — about three months — and haven't had an orgasm yet. He's a real nice guy, and I think I love him. I've been dating lots of guys since my boyfriend, Tom, and I broke up three years ago, and Nick is very special. I met him at the college gym, and we were instantly attracted to each other. He is in great shape, is very outgoing, a former athlete, and has a great sense of humor. In a way, he's a great big kid, always joking.

We started having sex from the first date and all spring made love about three to five times a week, but I never had an orgasm with him. Even though I don't come, sex with him is a lot of laughs. The only problem is that he kind of rushes through it and doesn't last very long. I haven't said anything because I kind of hoped he would get better with time.

During the summer, things cooled off because he had a summer house with a bunch of fraternity brothers and was at the shore every weekend (Friday to Sunday night) from Memorial Day to mid-September. I went down a few times but was really turned off because everyone did nothing but get drunk, act out, and sleep the days away.

Since September, we've picked up where we left off last spring, but I still can't come with him. When I masturbate by myself, I have satisfying orgasms, but not with Nick. I'm afraid that if I tell him, he'll get upset and maybe our relationship will suffer. The problem is that I like him a lot and would like the relationship to grow, but the sex is a real problem. I'm not sure what to do about the relationship. What would you suggest?

less common manifestations, the men are able to experience orgasm only after a substantial amount of noncoital stimulation. A smaller group of men with male orgasmic disorder are able to ejaculate only through masturbation or upon waking from an erotic dream.

Men who have male orgasmic disorder are able to experience pleasure during the excitement phase of sexual activity and enjoy the beginnings of a sexual encounter but rapidly lose interest. For these men, thrusting and prolonging sexual activity is a chore rather than a pleasure. Many men with male orgasmic disorder have a pattern of paraphiliac sexual arousal and are unable to experience orgasm without the object of their desire.

Another male orgasmic disorder is premature ejaculation, the persistent or recurring onset of orgasm and ejaculation shortly after penetration or before the man wishes it. The condition is diagnosed after the following three APA criteria have been met: (a) a clinician's estimation, a brief time between penetration and ejaculation, not the result of extenuating circumstances associated with the excitement phase, and consistent with associated expectations for the patient's age and level of sexual experience, (b) accompanying marked distress and interpersonal difficulty, and (c) not a result of the effects of a substance.

Occasional episodes of premature ejaculation are normal and don't pose a problem.

Sometimes premature ejaculation is related to the level of desire and excitement. An extremely high level of sexual arousal can trigger orgasm prematurely and does not represent the true disorder. Occasional episodes are common and are not a problem if they do not cause marked distress and interpersonal difficulty. Also, specific exercises can be practiced to delay orgasm.

With sexual experience and aging, most men learn to delay orgasm. As with women, this is related to learning from experience and better sexual communication. Some men continue to have premature ejaculation under all circumstances. Others incur this disorder only when they are with a new partner. Premature ejaculation can create tension and discord in sexual relationships and deter single men from dating and initiating new relationships because of fear and performance anxiety.

Sexual Pain Disorders

The most common sexual pain disorders are dyspareunia and vaginismus. Medical conditions also can result in pain during sexual intercourse.

Dyspareunia

Dyspareunia
genital pain associated with
sexual intercourse

Dyspareunia is genital pain associated with sexual intercourse. It may be present before, during, or after sexual intercourse and can affect both men and women. Symptoms range from mild discomfort to sharp pain.

Three APA diagnostic criteria must be met to diagnose this condition: (a) recurrent or persistent pain associated with sexual intercourse, (b) marked accompanying psychological distress or interpersonal difficulty, and

(c) not caused exclusively by vaginismus or lack of lubrication, a preexisting psychological or medical condition, and not the result of the direct effects of a substance.

Sexual pain disorders are not the result of insufficient excitement (which can account for insufficient lubrication and erection and tense muscles) or poor technique. Nor are they a result of medical conditions that affect sexual functioning (such as STDs, or scar tissue) or substance use. Sexual pain disorder is diagnosed when these other conditions are ruled out and the pain has no clear-cut physiological or medical basis.

Vaginismus

Vaginismus is the recurrent or persistent involuntary contraction of the perineal muscles surrounding the outer third of the vagina during attempted penetration with a penis, finger, tampon, or speculum. In some cases, even the anticipation of vaginal penetration can cause muscle spasms. Symptoms range from mild discomfort and tightness to severe contractions and cramping.

The three APA diagnostic criteria that must be met to diagnose this condition are: (a) recurrent or persistent involuntary spasm of the musculature of the outer third of the vagina upon insertion, (b) accompanying psychological distress or interpersonal difficulty, and (c) not caused by a preexisting psychological or medical condition.

Vaginismus usually is discovered upon first gynecological examination or onset of sexual intercourse. It is more common in young women than older women but can become chronic if it is not treated. It is a primary contributing factor to unconsummated marriages and can limit the development of relationships. Vaginismus is more common in women who have negative attitudes about sex, as well as females who have a history of sexual abuse or trauma.

Vaginismus
painful, involuntary contractions of the outer third of the vagina during attempted penetration

Sexual Dysfunction Caused by a General Medical Condition

The essential features of this disorder are pain, hypoactive sexual desire, male erectile dysfunction, or other types of sexual dysfunction that are direct physiological effects of an established medical condition. Medical conditions range from obvious sexual disorders such as sexually transmitted diseases to inapparent conditions such as atherosclerosis.

The three diagnostic criteria that must be met to establish the presence of this disorder are: (a) clinically significant sexual dysfunction resulting in marked distress or interpersonal difficulty, (b) medical history, physical examination, or laboratory findings fully explaining the dysfunction as the direct physiological effect of a general medical condition, and (c) not better accounted for by another mental disorder.

Survey of Sexual Dysfunction

At a 1999 meeting of the Office of Research on Women's Health, National Institutes of Health, the director of the Partnership for Women's Health at Columbia, Marianne Legato, reported that 43% of women and 30% of men have some sexual dysfunction. Figure 12.1 breaks down the various problems by gender. Many of these problems respond well to various treatments.

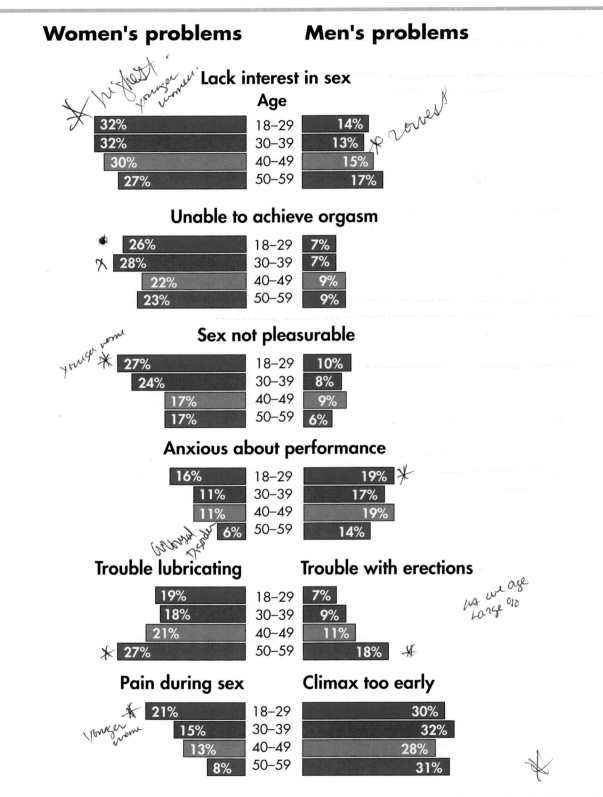

Source: National Health and Social Life Survey, 1992.

Figure 12.1 Sexual dysfunctions by gender and age.

TREATING SEXUAL DYSFUNCTIONS

Because the origin and nature of sexual dysfunction are multifaceted, diagnosis and treatment also are usually multifaceted. Treating impaired sexual functioning is complex, with many interdependent components. Sexual dysfunction can be caused by physical problems (for example, atherosclerosis, which impairs vasocongestion), emotional disorders, (excessive stress or negative emotions), spiritual distress (no longer being in love with a partner, lack of self-love), or simple ignorance (poor technique, inadequate stimulation). Often, sex therapy and enhancement involve all four components.

Sexual dysfunction is complex and is influenced by physical, social, and spiritual factors.

In 1959, Masters and Johnson developed a systematic approach to sex therapy that incorporated an extensive physical examination (to root out organic causes) and individual and couple counseling in the treatment of sexual dysfunction. Most sex therapists take an extensive medical history, and many incorporate a physical examination as part of the diagnostic work-up of their patients. The individual and couple approaches to counseling and treatment have many variations.

Treating Sexual Dysfunction Related to Medical Conditions

The first step in treating medically related sexual dysfunction is to properly diagnose the condition. A thorough medical examination, combined with a detailed sexual/medical history, guides the therapist in diagnosis. The overwhelming majority of cases of erectile disorder are caused by medical conditions and respond to medical treatment.

Viagra

Viagra, the trade name for sildenafil, a drug that went on the market in the United States in April, 1998, is revolutionizing the treatment of erectile disorder. The response to the drug by men who have erectile disorder has been staggering. After three weeks on the market, Viagra was being prescribed at a rate of at least 10,000 prescriptions a day.[22]

Much of the appeal of Viagra is its ease of use. Doctors recommend taking Viagra 1 hour before intercourse is desired. Unlike injectable drugs that produce an erection regardless of context, Viagra paves the way for the *possibility* of one. Viagra works with sexual desire in triggering erections. Once a user feels desire for his partner, Viagra allows erections to proceed.

The muscular and vascular changes of erection are controlled by a chemical called **guanosine triphosphate** (GMP). During sexual arousal, if the man feels sexual desire, GMP is released from cells in the penis that are stimulated by the brain and nervous system. The GMP triggers receptor cells in the spongy erectile tissue, allowing muscles there to relax and penile arteries to dilate. As the erectile tissue expands, it squeezes shut the veins responsible for removing the blood to the area. After orgasm, GMP is broken down by a normally occurring enzyme called phosphodiesterase 5 (PDE5).

Viagra
the drug, sildenafil, prescribed for the treatment of erectile disorder

Guanosine triphosphate
a chemical that controls the muscular and vascular changes of erection

Most men with erectile disorder don't produce enough GMP to override the ever-present PDE5. Their erectile tissue doesn't expand enough to squeeze the veins shut, and consequently the penis does not attain complete erection. Viagra works by suppressing the effects of PDE5, allowing even a limited amount of GMP to cause erections.

Viagra does not increase sexual desire. If a man is not interested in sex or has little sexual desire for a partner, Viagra will not increase his desire.[23] Viagra works for men who desire sex but can't get erections because they produce limited amounts of GMP.

Another important thing to know about Viagra is that more is not better. Viagra is prescribed in either 50 mg or 100 mg. tablets. The correct dose is the smallest needed to create the desired effect. The penis has a limited number of receptors for GMP, and the body can process only

With Viagra, more is not better.

so much of it. Taking a bigger dose of Viagra will not allow more GMP to be processed than the body can handle. Men who are not having problems with GMP production will not obtain any enhanced erectile effects from taking the drug because the body is already processing as much GMP as it can handle. Any enhanced erectile response reported probably is placebo effect rather than an effect of Viagra.[24]

Viagra has been tried with women, too, resulting in increased blood flow to the genital area, as in men. It may help a small group of women, such as those with nerve damage from multiplesclerosis. The overall conclusion to date, though, is that Viagra is no better than a placebo for most women.

Drug Injections

Prior to Viagra, most medically caused erectile disorder was treated with self-injections of a drug (alprostadil, a synthetic prostaglandin, is a common one) directly into the penis. The drug works by relaxing the muscles of the spongy erectile tissue, allowing the arteries to dilate and engorgement to occur. Men (and often their partners) were taught how to administer the injections using tiny needles similar to the ones diabetics use to inject insulin. The injections produce a pinprick sensation that patients usually tolerate well.

Unlike Viagra, injection treatment produces an erection without requiring the brain to initiate it through sexual desire. The injections lead to erections in approximately 15 minutes. The medication is premeasured in doses that will produce erections that last for approximately an hour.[25]

Another method of delivering alprostadil involves inserting tiny pellets of the drug directly into the urethra. A small plastic tube containing a plunger product is inserted about 1 inch into the urethra. When the plunger is pushed, it releases the drug, which resembles tiny rabbit-food pellets, into the urethra. Within 10 minutes the drug begins to take effect.

Vacuum Pumps

Prior to Viagra and injectable drug therapy, vacuum pumps and surgical implants were used to treat erectile disorder. The vacuum pump is a flexible plastic sleeve that is placed over the penis and secured at the base of the lubricated penis with an elastic band. Suction is applied to the sleeve, by mouth or a small hand pump, through a tube that connects at the other end.

The pump draws blood into the penis, filling the erectile tissue and thereby causing an erection. Once the man achieves a sufficient erection, the sleeve is removed and the band is kept in place to trap the blood for about half an hour.

Implants and Other Surgery

Implant treatment involves the surgical implantation of an inflatable penile prosthesis. The device consists of two hollow cylinders connected to a fluid-filled reservoir and a pump. The cylinders are implanted in the shaft of the penis, the reservoir in the abdomen, and the pump in the scrotum. When the man desires an erection, he activates the pump, which fills the cylinders and causes erection. After intercourse he turns a valve, which empties the cylinders back into the reservoir. Figure 12.2 depicts a penis pump.

Implant surgery is considered radical treatment and should be considered only if other forms of treatment fail. It can lead to permanent damage that could make a natural erection impossible.

Finally, some structural problems in sexual anatomy may have to be corrected with surgery. Examples are removing scar tissue and freeing adhesions that cause pain during intercourse.

Hormone Treatments

Certain medical conditions, particularly those of the endocrine system, respond to medication or hormone replacement therapy. Correcting a hormonal imbalance that might affect disorders of sexual arousal might

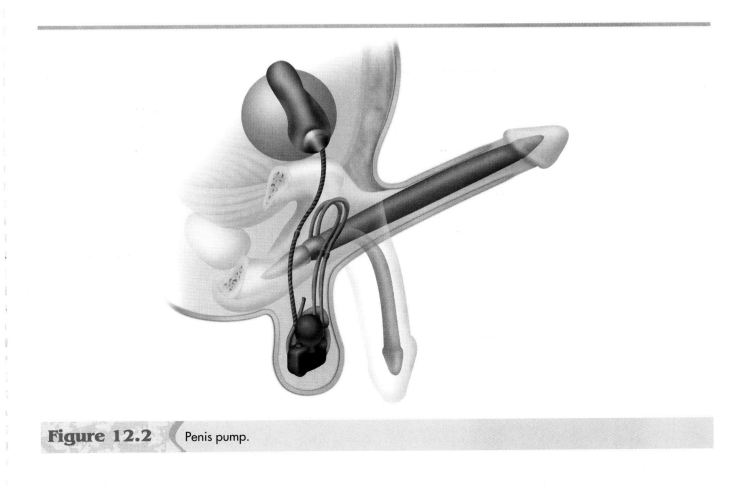

Figure 12.2   Penis pump.

best be treated through the oral administration of hormone replacement therapy. Sometimes endocrine glands need help in being stimulated to begin producing adequate amounts of sex hormones. Medications are available that activate endocrine glands to release their hormones.

Although testosterone is often considered a male hormone, both men and women have testosterone, and it is believed to have an important role in libido. As levels of this hormone decline with age, sexual interest may wane. Many women are helped by taking testosterone, in low enough doses to prevent any male secondary characteristics to develop. Also, estrogen improves vaginal lubrication in post-menopausal women.

Other Medical Treatments

Still other sexual dysfunctions are related to a disease that can be treated or cured with medication. Sexual pain disorders associated with STD infection, for instance, respond quite well to treatment or cure of the underlying disease condition. Sexual arousal disorders related to cardiovascular problems such as atherosclerosis often can be improved through medication designed to change blood biochemistry and improve the flow of blood and blood pressure.

Treating Drug-induced Sexual Dysfunction

Similar to treating organic-based sexual dysfunction, the treatment of drug-induced sexual dysfunction begins with a thorough sexual/medical history and medical examination. The assessment includes current drug use (licit and illicit). The specific drugs are analyzed for possible side effects and interactions to assess their role in the sexual dysfunction. The therapist examines the onset of the sexual dysfunction in relation to the onset of drug use.

Treatment of drug-induced sexual dysfunction begins with a thorough sexual/medical history and medical examination.

Many commonly prescribed medications, alone or in combination with other prescription or over-the-counter medications or psychoactive substances, have potential negative side effects related to sexual response. Sometimes treatment is as simple as changing the dosage of the medication or switching to a similar drug with different side effects. An example is provided by medication for controlling high blood pressure.

A common side effect of certain hypertension medications is erectile dysfunction. Changing the medication often relieves the erectile problem and still controls the patient's high blood pressure. In other cases, treatment consists of avoiding additional medications or substances that, when taken with the prescribed drug, results in sexual dysfunction. Patients often are unaware of the potentially troubling side effects of combining substances.

Treating Psychosocially Based Sexual Dysfunction

Several different sex therapy approaches can be applied when the origin of the dysfunction is psychosocial in nature. The four main variables in the therapeutic approach are:

1. The therapist's theoretical framework (psychoanalytic versus cognitive)

2. Duration and schedule of treatment

3. Individual versus couple or group approach

4. Use of surrogates.

Sex therapists come from a variety of backgrounds. Some are physicians with advanced training in psychiatry, sex therapy, psychoanalysis, or counseling. Others are psychologists, psychoanalysts, counselors, and social workers. No uniform credentials are required for sex therapists across the United States. Credentialing requirements vary from state to state.

Each of these professionals has a philosophical and theoretical framework regarding sex therapy that guides their work. Psychoanalysts, for instance take a psychodynamic approach to treatment that is grounded in the work of Freud. A basic element in their approach is helping the client gain insight into the origin of his or her problem.

Counselors using a behaviorist approach, in contrast, do not believe it is necessary to delve deeply into their clients' past to help them gain insight into the origin of their problem. Rather, the behaviorist focuses on the here-and-now and examines the nature of the problem, how the client perceives it, and how it directly affects the person's quality of life.

The therapist's theoretical framework is intimately related to the duration and schedule of therapy. A psychoanalyst might spend several sessions just getting to know the client and establishing trust while beginning to look back into his or her past. A Masters and Johnson trained therapist team would be finished with therapy by that time because the approach is to get right down to the business of treating the presenting problem in an intensive 2-week program.

Some sex therapists work only with individuals. Most however, believe that sexual dysfunction can be understood and treated only within the context of the relationship. Couples are seen together and individually, and treatment involves treating the couple as well as the individual. Carolyn Bundy of the National Institute of Child Health and Human Development says, "You don't want to bring one member of a couple back to health and ignore the other."

Still other therapeutic approaches incorporate group sessions in which people with similar problems come together to help each other work on getting better. And, finally, some sex therapists provide explicit help by using trained **sex surrogate** partners. These surrogates are sexually responsive trained professionals who serve as partners for clients. They help teach men and women with sexual dysfunction how to relax and perform sexually with a partner. The American Association of Sex Educators, Counselors and Therapists (AASECT), one of the leading professional groups charged with certifying sex therapists, does not recommend the use of surrogates for treating sexual dysfunctions.[26]

Sex surrogate
a person who acts as a substitute sex partner during therapy

What do you think of sex surrogates? Are they partners in the therapy process or just a type of paid sex worker?

Most sex therapy is eclectic, combining elements from various forms of psychotherapy, education, and medicine. Six common threads that seem to underlie the practice of sex therapy, regardless of the therapist's theoretical framework, are: (1) permission-giving, (2) limited information, (3) specific suggestions, (4) self-awareness, (5) communication training, and (6) use of masturbation.

Permission-Giving

Permission-giving is the unconditional support the therapist offers for becoming a fully self-actualized sexual being. Clients are given permission to explore any thoughts, feelings, desires, fantasies, and behaviors that might enhance their sexual pleasure. They also are given permission to not engage in behaviors and relationships that undermine their sexual and other well-being.

Information-Giving

Information-giving or education is a key element in all forms of sex therapy. Because most people receive little or no formal sex education, they often are misinformed about simple issues that can undermine their sexual enjoyment, such as penis size, level of sexual activity, and effects of aging. Often, providing information, along with permission-giving, is liberating enough to help people work their way out of some sexual dysfunctions.

Information-giving can include didactic sessions with the therapist related to the individual's specific concerns, guided reading (reading a prescribed set of materials), and viewing instructional videotapes. Providing limited information helps change negative attitudes, open lines of communication, and develop sexual skills necessary for enhancing performance and pleasure.

Specific Suggestions

Each person or couple has unique problems and needs that can be addressed through specific suggestions. The main technique in this regard is "homework assignments" with one's partner. The range of specific suggestions varies depending upon the nature of the problem and the specific individual or couple involved. Usually these homework assignments require the couple to practice activities and techniques that the therapist has discussed with them. These often are coupled with communication activities designed to help couples open up and share their feelings with each other.

Self-Awareness

Increased self-awareness is a natural outgrowth of the first two elements. Many of the specific suggestions prescribed as homework help individuals and couples focus on their sensual/sexual response. This is the first time many clients have spent focusing on their sexual response and specific techniques related to sensual and sexual arousal.

One commonly used activity is called **sensate focus.** In the early stages of sex therapy, the couple is instructed to refrain from sexual activity involving genital contact. This is designed to relieve performance anxiety and other forms of anxiety and to allow the couple to focus on nongenital pleasuring.

Sensate focus
nongenital pleasuring used to heighten sensuality without sexual activity

During the first phase of sensate focus (Figure 12.3), each partner is given a turn to explore the other's body. The breasts and genitals are off-limits. The intent is not to give sexual pleasure but, instead, to establish awareness of touch by paying attention to the textures, contours, and temperature of the partner, and to attend to what it feels like to touch and be touched.

The partner doing the touching is in control and is not driven by the needs of the person being touched. The initial stage is supposed to be conducted as silently as possible. The person being touched is allowed to convey (either verbally or nonverbally) when the partner's touch makes him or her uncomfortable.

During the second phase of sensate focus, touch is extended to include the breasts and genitals. The couple receive instructions similar to those in the first phase and are advised to gradually expand the touch to include the genitals. The purpose is still to experience the sensation of touch and to discover what types of touch are most pleasurable.

A simple technique called handriding (Figure 12.4) is used during this phase. This involves having one partner place his or her hand over the partner's and to guide it on an exploration of the other's body. The guiding hand nonverbally communicates by increasing or decreasing the pressure,

Figure 12.3 Sensate focus: first stage.

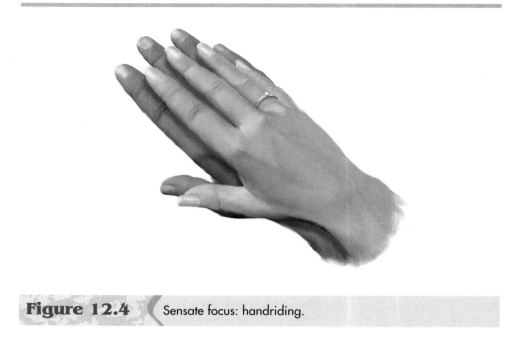

Figure 12.4 Sensate focus: handriding.

changing the speed or type of motion, and holding the hand to linger. The idea is to help the partner who is doing the touching understand the preferences of the partner being touched without controlling the action. The partner doing the touching is still in control but is guided along.

In the third phase of sensate focus, the couple are asked to explore each other at the same time. Rather than take turns, the couple doubles the amount of sensory input by mutual exploration. This simulates real-life touching and allows the couple the opportunity to get lost in the sensations of touch without the pressure to have intercourse.

In the last stage of sensate focus, the couple shift to the female-on-top position (Figure 12.5) without attempting full penetration of the penis. In this position the woman can rub her clitoris directly against her partner and stimulate his penis with her vulva and vaginal opening. This may or may not result in arousal and full erection in her partner. The purpose is not to cause full arousal and intercourse, but if an erection occurs, she can put the tip of the penis into her vaginal opening. The couple are instructed to continue to explore each other, using full body contact to explore the sensations of touch and arousal.

After the couple have worked through the stages of sensate focus successfully and is comfortable with it, the two of them usually are ready to experience full intercourse without difficulty.

Communication Training

Couples can learn how to communicate nonverbally through sensate focus and other awareness-building activities. Often, nonverbal communication — such as placing a hand or body part in a certain position or holding a partner to linger at what he or she is doing — can transmit information that will help treat sexual problems. Improving verbal communication — in

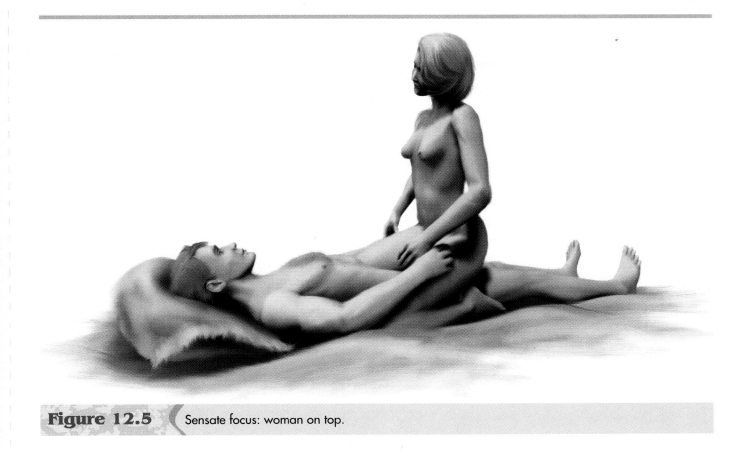

Figure 12.5   Sensate focus: woman on top.

particular, expressing needs and desires and communicating using "I" language instead of blaming one's partner — is integral to all forms of sex therapy. Communication building can occur during sessions with the therapist and as homework assignments.

Use of Masturbation

Sex therapy commonly includes masturbation, both individual and mutual. It can be used in sexual arousal disorders to help both partners explore the types, intensity, and duration of stimulation necessary for full arousal. It also can help the couple learn how to delay orgasm in cases of premature ejaculation.

A variation of masturbation used to treat premature ejaculation is the squeeze technique, illustrated in Figure 12.6. During manual stimulation of her partner, the woman is instructed to stop periodically and apply firm pressure for a few seconds to the frenulum and coronal ridge with her thumb and first and second fingers, respectively. This squeezing reduces her partner's urgency to ejaculate. She can continue to masturbate her partner, stopping periodically to squeeze. Through this technique her partner can learn to delay ejaculation.

Masturbation also can be used to treat female and male orgasmic disorder. Often these conditions are related to inadequate sexual stimulation.

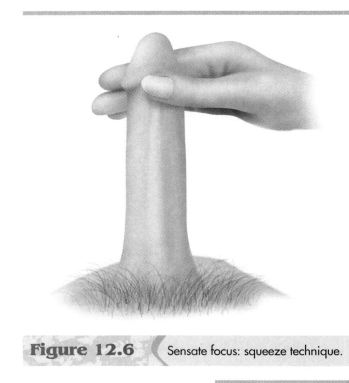

Figure 12.6 Sensate focus: squeeze technique.

Through permission-giving, sensate focus, and masturbation, men and women can learn the type, intensity, and duration of stimulation necessary for orgasm. Treatment progresses from individual masturbation, to masturbation in the presence of the partner, to being masturbated by the partner, to using masturbation as a prelude to intercourse.

Masturbation, coupled with the use of increasingly larger dilators (Figure 12.7), can be used to treat some cases of vaginismus. Women are taught to use permission-giving, self-awareness, and masturbation to initiate sexual arousal and to use the varying sizes of dilators for 10 to 15 minutes at a time to introduce objects into her vagina. The goal is to work up to a penis-size dilator and then make the transition to a real penis.

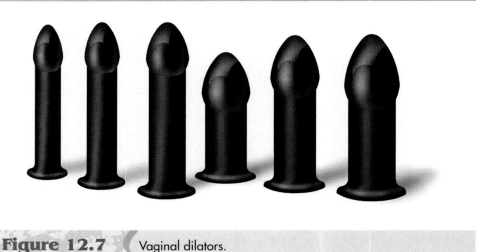

Figure 12.7 Vaginal dilators.

WELLNESS SYNTHESIS

When a person has a sexual dysfunction, every facet of wellness comes into play. Sexual therapy, therefore, focuses on the whole person.

Physical Well-being

High-level physical well-being can enhance sexual performance and satisfaction and lessen the risk for dysfunction. Physical well-being plays a crucial role in the desire and excitement phases of sexual response. Physical well-being is also linked to vasocongestion, as blood flow leading to engorgement of genital tissue and lubrication are affected adversely by obesity, atherosclerosis, and other physical health problems. Being fit (especially high levels of cardiovascular fitness) and maintaining recommended body composition promotes efficient vasocongestion.

Physical well-being also enhances body image and boosts self-esteem — which are related to sexual desire and performance. High-level physical well-being contributes to energy levels as well. Sexual interest, sexual desire, and sexual response all require energy. Most of us put in long, demanding workdays, and our lives are filled with many commitments that extend beyond the workplace.

Intellectual Well-being

Many sexual problems are based on ignorance, illogical thinking and irrational expectations, and poor technique. Intellectual well-being is fostered through knowledge, logical thinking, rational expectations, and improved sexual technique. Much of sex therapy revolves around relearning what good sex is and what being a good lover means. These things can be taught.

You can learn about sexual response and what to expect during lovemaking. You can learn to understand the factors that influence interest, desire, plateau, orgasm, and resolution and begin to set more realistic and logical expectations about lovemaking. You can learn techniques and practice your skills (by yourself or with your partner) and become a better lover. At a high level of intellectual well-being you are eager to learn, know where to get information and how to evaluate material and make informed choices that are right for you and your partner. You also know when you need additional help and where to find it.

Emotional Well-being

Emotions are related intimately to sexual response. All phases of the sexual response cycle are subject to the effects of emotions. Sexual interest and desire are fueled by positive emotions such as happiness, love, joy, respect, and trust. Negative emotions (especially directed at a partner), such as anxiety, anger, hate, fear, disgust, and mistrust, make interest and desire difficult at best and impossible for most. For the body to respond properly, the mind must let go and relax.

Arousal and orgasm also are affected by our emotions. The ability to prolong and enjoy sex are affected in part by emotions. Relaxing and becoming immersed in the sensuality of the plateau stage is difficult if we are feeling anxious, rushed, fearful, or angry. We just want to hurry up and get it over with. When we can relax, let down our guard, and allow our senses free rein, we can enjoy the plateau.

Orgasm is contingent on the build-up of tension through adequate stimulation. Orgasm is triggered when we give up mental control and allow our body to be swept along in the ecstasy of physical pleasuring. This is difficult if we are on guard, tense, angry, or resentful.

Resolution might be considered a thankful end to a resentful experience in which partners uncouple, roll over, and fall asleep. Or the resolution phase can be a special time. Lovers who are emotionally healthy can bask in the afterglow of loving time spent pleasuring each other.

Social Well-being

Sex with another person is a uniquely social experience that cannot be separated from the emotions the two people bring to the encounter. High-level social well-being revolves around healthy relationships. And healthy relationships are based on trust, respect, commitment, love, and affection. Good sex flows out of this safe and protected context.

When trust, respect, and affection are displaced by mistrust, disrespect, and fear, relationship problems ensue. Communication, which is central to good sex, often breaks down when couples are having relationship problems. When sexual needs and desires are not communicated clearly, sexual response suffers.

Spiritual Well-being

Sexual behavior and relationships have the potential to become deeply spiritual expressions of humanity. Spirituality, by definition, conveys a sense of connectedness to someone or something beyond the self. Being united with another human being in the flesh is a universal experience that transcends race, religion, national origin, and all other labels that separate us as a species.

Low levels of spiritual well-being are reflected in self-centeredness. Sex is something that revolves around their needs only. The partner is there to supply pleasure. A relationship is geared to what the other person can do. Intercourse is nothing more than masturbating within a vagina or masturbating with someone's penis in a vagina. When viewed this way, sex easily evolves into a dysfunctional activity. People who are spiritually healthy, by contrast, marvel at the transcendent power of sexual activity. They respect sex and use it to deepen the connectedness to the other person and appreciate it as a universal, unifying human force.

Environmental Well-being

Sexuality doesn't evolve in a vacuum. The environment influences, to some extent, the quality of our sexual life. The immediate environment offers the space, privacy, and safety that encourages good sex. Are the people who share our space respectful, supportive, loving? Do they communicate and interact in a sane, efficient way? How might your immediate environment be improved? Many people who have sexual problems learned how to be dysfunctional from their role models as children. Their sexual functioning, in addition to therapy, can improve if they surround themselves with roommates, fraternity/sorority members, and other people who are functional and come from more functional early environments.

WEB RESOURCES

Wellness Web Impotence Center

http://www.wellweb.com/impotent/chris/contents.htm

Detailed abstract about erectile dysfunction. An overview, anatomy of the penis and how the penis works, causes of impotence, effects of diseases and drugs. Peyronie's disease is also discussed. Links to health centers, nutrition, and fitness.

Mental Health Net

http://mentalhelp.net/sexual/

Net guide to mental health, psychology, and psychiatry; addresses the symptoms, online resources, and organizations concerning sexual problems of dyspareunia, exhibitionism, female and male orgasmic disorders, female sexual arousal disorder, fetishism, frotteurism, gender identity disorder, mail erectile disorder, premature ejaculation, sexual masochism and sadism, transvestic fetishism, vaginismus, and voyeurism.

Notes

1. American Psychiatric Association, *Diagnostic and Statistical Manual of Mental Illness,* 4th edition (Washington, DC: APA, 1994).
2. J. Buvat et al., "Recent Developments in the Clinical Assessment and Diagnosis of Erectile Dysfunction," *Annual Review of Sex Research* 1 (1990), 265–308; I. Goldstein et al., *Journal of Urology* (1994); L. A. Horvitz, "Can Better Sex Come with a Pill? The Nineties Impotence Cure," *Insight on the News,* 13:46 (1997), 38–40; J. Leland, "A Pill for Impotence?" *Newsweek,* 130:20 (1997), 62–68; J. D. Richardson, "Medical Causes of Sexual Dysfunction," *Medical Journal of Australia,* 155 (1991), 29–33.
3. Goldstein et al.
4. Goldstein et al.; T. Heapes, "Smoking Your Sex Life Away," Muscle & Fitness, 55:4 (1994), 42.
5. M. Parrish, "Up, Up, and Away," *Playboy,* 44:6 (1997), 92–99.
6. R. G. Rosen, "Alcohol and Drug Effects on Sexual Response," *Annual Reviews of Sex Research,* 2 (1991), 119–129.
7. R. Goldberg, *Drugs Across the Spectrum* (Englewood CO: Morton, 1997).

8. A. Montague, *Touching: The Human Significance of the Skin* (New York: Harper & Row, 1977).
9. S. Purcell, *The Relationship Between Religious Orthodoxy and Marital Sexual Functioning*, paper presented at annual meeting of American Psychological Association, August 25, 1985.
10. J. S. Hyde, *Understanding Human Sexuality*, 5th edition (New York: McGraw Hill, 1994).
11. *Human Sexual Inadequacy* (Boston: Little, Brown, 1970).
12. S. Kobilinsky and J. Palmeter, "Sex Role Orientation, Mother's Expression of Affection Toward Spouse and College Women's Attitudes Towards Sexual Behaviors," *Journal of Sex Research,* 20 (1984), 32–43.
13. B. Zilbergeld, *The New Male Sexuality* (New York: Bantam, 1992).
14. H. Singer-Kaplan, *The New Sex Therapy* (New York: Brunner/Mazel, 1974).
15. Singer-Kaplan.
16. Singer-Kaplan.
17. *DSM-IV,* 1994.
18. *DSM-IV.*

19. Masters and Johnson, *Human Sexual Inadequacy*; W. H. Masters, V. E. Johnson, and R. Kolodny, *Human Sexuality,* 5th edition (New York: HarperCollins, 1996).
20. A. E. Kinsey et al., *Sexual Behavior in the Human Female* (Philadelphia: Saunders, 1953; S. Fisher, *The Female Orgasm* (New York: Bantam Books, 1973); S. Hite, *The Hite Report* (New York: Dell 1977); M. Hunt, *Sexual Behavior in the 1970's* (New York: Dell, 1975).
21. L. Barbach, *For Each Other: Sharing Sexual Intimacy* (Garden City NY: Doubleday, 1982); B. Dodson, *Liberating Masturbation* (New York: Dodson, 1974).
22. B. Handy, "The Viagra Craze," *Time,* 151:17 (1998), 50–53.
23. Leland.
24. Handy.
25. Parrish.
26. *Ethical Guidelines for Sex Therapists* (Washington, DC: AASECT, 1998).

Student Study Questions

1. How do the categories of dysfunctions mesh with the stages of the sexual response cycle? Why are they set up this way?

2. What are two dysfunctions related to sexual desire?

3. When does low interest in sexual activity become a desire disorder?

4. What is the relationship between cardiovascular health and sexual arousal disorders?

5. What does the term "preorgasmic" mean?

6. What are three illness-related causes of sexual dysfunction?

7. What are three medication-related causes of sexual dysfunction?

8. Are isolated episodes of sexual dysfunction normal? If so, why?

Student Assessment

Are You an Addict?

Substance abuse is not only a risk factor for sexual dysfunction; it can destroy your life. This assessment is designed to help you assess whether your current drug use is considered addictive.

The following questions were written by recovering addicts in Narcotics Anonymous.

	Yes	No
1. Do you ever use alone?	☐	☐
2. Have you ever substituted one drug for another, thinking that one particular drug was the problem?	☐	☐
3. Have you ever manipulated or lied to a doctor to obtain prescription drugs?	☐	☐
4. Have you ever stolen drugs or stolen to obtain drugs?	☐	☐
5. Do you regularly use a drug when you wake up or when you go to bed?	☐	☐
6. Have you ever taken one drug to overcome the effects of another?	☐	☐
7. Do you avoid people or places that do not approve of you using drugs?	☐	☐
8. Have you ever used a drug without knowing what it was or what it would do to you?	☐	☐
9. Has your job or school performance ever suffered from the effects of your drug use?	☐	☐
10. Have you ever been arrested as a result of using drugs?	☐	☐
11. Have you ever lied about what or how much you use?	☐	☐
12. Do you put the purchase of drugs ahead of your financial responsibilities?	☐	☐
13. Have you ever tried to stop or control your using?	☐	☐
14. Have you ever been in a jail, hospital, or drug rehabilitation center because of your using?	☐	☐
15. Does using interfere with your sleeping or eating?	☐	☐
16. Does the thought of running out of drugs terrify you?	☐	☐
17. Do you feel it is impossible for you to live without drugs?	☐	☐
18. Do you ever question your own sanity?	☐	☐
19. Is your drug use making life at home unhappy?	☐	☐
20. Have you ever thought you couldn't fit in or have a good time without using drugs?	☐	☐
21. Have you ever felt defensive, guilty, or ashamed about your using?	☐	☐
22. Do you think a lot about drugs?	☐	☐
23. Have you had irrational or indefinable fears?	☐	☐
24. Has using affected your sexual relationships?	☐	☐
25. Have you ever taken drugs you didn't prefer?	☐	☐
26. Have you ever used drugs because of emotional pain or stress?	☐	☐
27. Have you ever overdosed on any drugs?	☐	☐
28. Do you continue to use despite negative consequences?	☐	☐
29. Do you think you might have a drug problem?	☐	☐

Are you an addict? This is a question only you can answer. Members of Narcotics Anonymous found that they all answered different numbers of these questions "yes." The actual number of yes responses isn't as important as how you feel inside and how addiction has affected your life. If you are an addict, you must first admit that you have a problem with drugs before any progress can be made toward recovery.

Human Reproduction

13

Major Topics

Student Learning Objectives

After reading this chapter, students will be able to:

◡ Describe the dynamics of conception.

◡ Describe normal developmental characteristics during the three trimesters of pregnancy.

◡ Assess the influence of a variety of negative personal behaviors (such as alcohol use) on prenatal development.

◡ Describe personal health behaviors that enhance pregnancy outcomes.

◡ Evaluate options for labor and delivery.

◡ Identify a variety of alternatives to traditional conception and parenting.

◡ Describe a variety of factors related to infertility.

◡ Identify options available to enhance fertility.

As a child, learning the "facts of life" or about "the birds and the bees" — getting an answer to, "Where did I come from?" — could make parents squirm a bit. Words would be carefully chosen, offering vague descriptions of sexual intercourse, followed by a brief summary of gestation, and ending with the birth at a hospital. Children asking this question today may receive answers that are far more complicated, as the ways in which babies are "made" and "born" have become more varied.

Imagine that a child asks her parents, "Where did I come from?" and gets the following answer:

> *Mom and Dad weren't able to have a child in the typical way, but we very much wanted to become parents. Since Mom's ovaries didn't work quite right, we went to the fertility bank, where we found an ova donor who was a lot like Mom. Her physical characteristics and interests seemed a close match.*
>
> *Dad found out that his body didn't make enough sperm, so he used the sperm directory and also found a good match. The laboratory was able to join the donated ova with the donated sperm, and then implanted the fertilized embryo into another woman's uterus. Nine months later we watched your birth and took you home!*

Even though one couple would not likely utilize all of this technology, each facet is possible today. Not even the U. S. legal system has been able to keep up with the rapid changes in reproductive technologies, with some very modern and difficult questions posed to the courts.

To date, individuals and couples alike have turned to the legal system for what sometimes seem Solomonesque decisions concerning their fertility and reproductive rights. In one divorce case the wife wanted the embryos as her only chance at a pregnancy, and the husband wanted them destroyed. The

PERSPECTIVES

Mary Beth Whitehead and Surrogacy

Among attempts to have a child, surrogate motherhood remains an option — albeit a controversial one. The case of Mary Beth Whitehead in 1986 brought the complicated issues of surrogacy to national attention.

Ms. Whitehead had signed a contract with a New Jersey couple and was artificially inseminated with the husband's sperm. After giving birth to a baby girl, Ms. Whitehead decided that she didn't want to give up the child for adoption. The courts became involved, and the story spread across the popular media. For a while the baby girl even had two names. The outcome of the court case was that the child was given to the adoptive parents, with Ms. Whitehead being granted visitation rights.

As a result of this case, a number of legal and ethical issues were brought to national attention. To some people, the use of surrogate mothers extends the array of reproductive options for infertile couples and allows potentially good parents that privilege. It represents a choice that is both private and not much different from traditional adoption. To others, it represents exploitation of women's bodies. Those who are able to pay hire women whose need of income may be paramount. The contractual elements, fees involved, and possible legal challenges all contribute to the debate over surrogate mothering.

court found that the frozen embryos were part of the property to be split in a divorce. The wife was awarded custody of the embryos. On appeal, the husband got "custody" of the embryos — and he destroyed them. Other cases have focused on unhealthy babies born from donors and large amounts of money having exchanged hands, leaving the "buyer" unhappy with his/her "purchase." Having babies indeed has moved from the bedroom and out into the medical, technological, legal, and business worlds.

U. S. courts are left to decide questions such as: Do gays and lesbians have the right to become parents? Should gays and lesbians be awarded custody of their children if they're already parents when they "come out?" Should gays and lesbians be allowed to adopt children? As a judge, how would you respond?

The Whitehead case highlighted class differences in the infertility and surrogacy realm, biological versus adoptive parents' rights, and the differences inherent in women "renting their wombs," in contrast to male sperm donors, who have limited involvement with the pregnancy. What is your position on surrogacy? Why?

TO PARENT OR NOT TO PARENT

The decision about whether to have children is one that individuals in the United States are free to make. As will be discussed in greater detail later, the term **family planning** refers to the conscious act of planning a family. Prospective parents can decide whether to have children, how many to have, when to have them, and how far apart to space them. With reproductive technologies becoming more familiar and accessible, prenatal screenings more widespread, and the availability of better prenatal care, prospective parents have the opportunity to improve the health and welfare of their babies. In addition, if biological parenthood is not possible, adoption opportunities — albeit at great personal, emotional and financial expense — exist both within and outside the United States.

Not everyone wants to be a parent. Not everyone has the physical capability to become a parent. And, certainly, plenty of evidence shows that not everyone is able to be a good parent. Too often, individuals are asked, "When are you going to settle down and get married?" and once in a committed relationship, "When are you two going to have children?" If individuals or couples respond that they don't want children, some people are taken aback, as if an offense has been committed.

Only recently has the language changed to be less judgmental. Couples without children now are referred to as "childfree," rather than "childless." In any case planning to become a parent rather than stumbling upon

Family planning
the conscious effort of deciding to have a family, including when to have children, how many, and how far apart to space them

PERSPECTIVES

Who Makes Appropriate Parents?

Society makes judgments about who would make appropriate parents. Young teens who become parents are part of the "teen pregnancy problem" in the United States. In 1997, a woman who had "tricked" a fertility program by claiming to be in her early 50s when she actually was in her early 60s subsequently gave birth to her first child at age 62. This prompted numerous editorials and angry letters to editors in newspapers across the country. How selfish for a woman to become a mother at that age! In contrast, when actor Tony Randall fathered his first child in his mid-70s, he was not subject to as much ridicule or outrage.

When lesbian and gay couples choose to parent, they often find themselves being judged by a culture that traditionally has placed parenthood within heterosexual couples' domain. Interracial and interfaith couples, too, may be seen as jeopardizing the health and development of their children. Couples who do not adhere to the traditional model are asked, "But what about the children? How will you rear them? Won't they suffer unfair treatment?" These questions have generated much debate.

impending parenthood has clear advantages. The wellness model provides a useful framework for assessing readiness for parenting.

THE MENSTRUAL CYCLE AND OVULATION

Fertilization/Conception
union of the sperm and ovum

Ovulation
release of an egg from the ovary

Understanding when a woman is fertile allows us to know when conception can take place.

A pregnancy begins with the union of an ovum (or ova) and a sperm, called **fertilization** or **conception**. For conception to take place, the sperm must get to the ovum within a 24-hour period after its release from the ovary, a process known as **ovulation**. Ovulation occurs 14 days before a woman's next menstrual cycle. Consequently, a woman who understands her menstrual cycle can predict when ovulation is most likely to occur. Although most women ovulate within 14 to 16 days from the beginning of the menstrual cycle, the timing depends on the length of the cycle itself — a piece of information not available until the cycle is over.

Couples have to try to predict when fertility is most likely. Women who have cycles that are 25 days long will ovulate closer to the first day of menstruation (the first day of the cycle). Women whose cycles are 31 days in duration will ovulate farther from the first date of the cycle. See Chapter 3, Figure 3.9 which illustrates the menstrual cycle and timing of ovulation. Understanding when a woman is fertile allows us to know when conception can take place.

Women who pay close attention to their body changes throughout the menstrual cycle may be more successful at predicting ovulation. The cervical mucus goes through changes: At ovulation it is clear and thin — sort of like egg white. Sometimes a discharge signals ovulation.

Changes in body temperature can be used to monitor ovulation. Women use a basal body temperature thermometer to determine slight fluctuations

Case Study

John and Luanne: A Case of Infertility

After 6 years of infertility treatments, John and Luanne Buzzanca turned to a laboratory that supplied donor sperm and ova, paid a surrogate, and finally became parents in San Francisco in April 1995. Shortly after the birth, John filed for divorce and refused to make child support payments on the grounds that he wasn't the baby's father in any true legal sense, despite having earlier signed a contract agreeing to the child's birth. The Superior Court agreed, claiming that baby Jaycee had been conceived in a petri dish, from anonymous donors, and carried and delivered by a surrogate mother with no genetic ties to her. Consequently, according to California law, not only was John not the father, but Luanne was not the legal mother. By California law, the child had no parents.[1]

A petition filed with the California Court of Appeals for the Fourth Circuit (March, 1998), however, resulted in the determination that both John and Luanne Buzzanca were the legal parents of Jaycee.[2] As a result of that ruling, individuals who use assisted reproductive technologies and intend to be considered the parents can finalize their parental rights before the child is born, regardless of whether they use a traditional or a gestational surrogate. Specific to this case, because John Buzzanca initially had consented to using donor sperm and a surrogate to produce a child, he was viewed as the father and, therefore, has financial responsibilities to Jaycee.

1. D. Foote, "And Baby Makes One," *Newsweek*, Feb. 2, 1998, pp. 68–70.
2. *Buzzanca v. Buzzanca*, Sup. Ct. No. 95D002992.

Source: A. W. Vorzimer, M. D. O'Hara, & L. D. Shafton, *Buzzanca v. Buzzanca: The Ruling and Ramifications*, http:/www.inciid.org/buzzancaease.

in temperature. Ovulation is marked by a few tenths of a degree drop, followed by an increase, in which the body temperature remains slightly elevated until the next menstrual cycle. The temperature must be taken first thing in the morning, before any activity, toothbrushing, or drinking of hot or cold beverages. Careful charting over a period of months is necessary to see individual patterns (see Figure 14.1, the basal body temperature chart, in Chapter 14).

In recent years the pharmaceutical industry has been producing ovulation kits, which purport to detect critical hormonal changes signaling that ovulation will occur within 1–2 days. The kits can be helpful, although frequent use could become costly. Couples who develop difficulties in conceiving should consult a medical specialist.

CONCEPTION

Conception results from the successful journey of a group of sperm to the outer third of the **fallopian tube**. After being deposited in the vagina, ideally close to the cervix, sperm must make their way into the uterus, over to and up the fallopian tube where the ovum is waiting. Some argue that conception is enhanced when sperm arrive "early" and wait for the ova to be released.

Fallopian tubes
conduits connected to the uterus through which the egg passes into the uterus during ovulation. Fertilization usually takes place at the outer third of the tube

A normal ejaculation usually contains between 250 and 500 million sperm. Although only one penetrates the membrane of the ovum at conception, millions are needed for conception. Sperm survive best in an alkaline environment, and many die when confronting the acidity of the male urethra and female vagina. Continued losses result from sperm not heading toward the correct tube (the two tubes alternate in egg production each month). Finally, the much smaller group reaches the ovum. Consequently, though the sperm count starts at millions, only a few thousand make it to the fallopian tube, and a couple hundred get close to the ovum.

Descriptions of conception have often left mental images of the valiant, strong, surviving sperm successfully attacking and breaking through the membrane of the ovum. The process is really more of the egg pulling in the sperm. Sperm secrete a chemical that enables them to penetrate the ova, dissolving a jelly-like substance that coats the ovum's surface. The ovum extends microvilli up from its surface, which hold down the sperm and

Health Hint

Ovulation Predictor Tests

Self-tests to determine ovulation are based on the sudden surge in the level of leutinizing hormone (LH) that precedes ovulation by about 1½ days and lasts from 1 to 3 days.

Several tests are available on the market today, ranging in price from $15 up to $40 or so, and sales are continuing to grow. The kits vary in reliability. A comparison of the more popular kits on the market follows.

Product	Type*	Test Time
Clearplan (5 tests)	In-stream	6 minutes
Conceive (5 tests)	Two-step	5 minutes
First Response	Multi-step	5–6 minutes
Ovukit (6 tests)	Multi-step	74 minutes**
OvuQuick Self-Test (6 tests)	Multi-step	9 minutes

* In-stream — urine is placed on the test stick during urination
Two-step — urine is collected in a cup and added to a test cassette
Multi-step — urine is collected in a cup and mixed with chemicals

** The control stick has to be prepared for an hour before using.

Consumer Reports Ovulation Kit Ratings

To use an ovulation predictor kit:

1. Know the duration of your normal menstrual cycle before using the product, to determine what day you should begin testing.
2. Always read the instructions provided with the kit. These vary according to the brand.
3. Check the expiration date on the box to be sure the test kit is still within the expiration date.
4. Use a clock or timer to produce the most accurate results.
5. Use first morning urine for accurate results. (If you don't have time to do the test immediately, you may store this urine in the refrigerator for up to 3 hours, but allow the urine to return to room temperature by leaving it out a half hour before using it for the test.)
6. If you are taking any other medication, it may interfere with the test results. Ask your doctor about this.
7. Because a color change on the test is what indicates the LH surge denoting impending ovulation, have someone else read the test if you are color-blind.

push other sperm away. Finally, the egg pulls the sperm inside toward its nucleus. This process and its aftermath are depicted in Figure 13.1.

The fertilized egg, beginning a process of rapid cell division, travels down the fallopian tube over 3 to 4 days and sometimes longer, reaching the uterus, where it will attach to the uterine wall in a process called **implantation**. During this time, cell division is occurring constantly. Once implanted, the fertilized egg, now referred to as an **embryo**, will be nourished through the remaining term of the pregnancy. After 8 weeks, the structure is referred to as a **fetus**. (Although much of the following discussion focuses on planning wanted pregnancies, not all pregnancies are wanted or planned. How individuals and couples respond to a pregnancy can range from feelings of joy and excitement to pain and extreme distress.)

The environment within the uterus is a highly protected. The fetus floats in, and is protected by, **amniotic fluid**. The **placenta**, an organ of interchange that attaches to the uterine wall, passes oxygen and nutrients through the umbilical cord to the fetus and passes waste products and carbon dioxide back to the mother. Unfortunately, as will be discussed later, numerous toxins may also cross the placenta and damage the fetus in a variety of ways.

Implantation
attachment of a fertilized egg to lining of uterus

Embryo
fertilized egg up to 8 weeks gestation

Fetus
fertilized egg from 8 weeks after conception to birth

Amniotic fluid
the transparent liquid contained in the amniotic sac that protects the fetus from injury and helps maintain an even temperature

Placenta
organ that attaches to the uterine wall and serves as a conduit for oxygen and nutrients to pass to the developing fetus

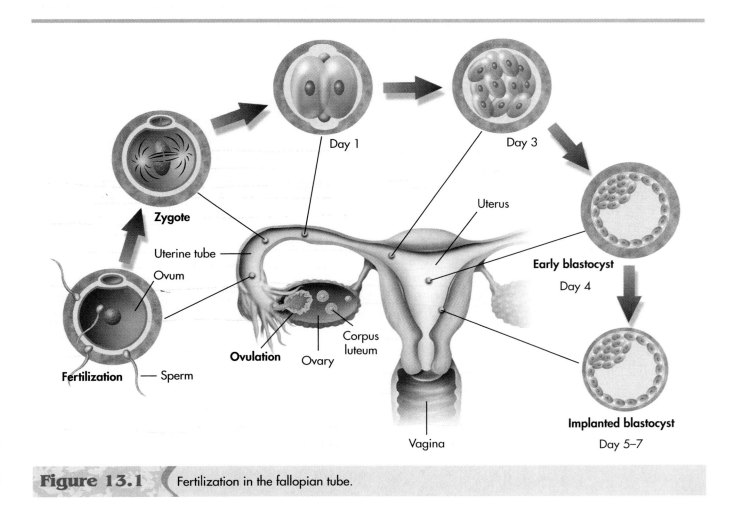

Figure 13.1 Fertilization in the fallopian tube.

INFERTILITY

Although pregnancy and childbirth are "natural" occurrences, they don't occur easily for all couples. One in every five to six couples in the United States is infertile.[1] Based upon surveys conducted by the National Center for Health Statistics (NCHS) in 1995, 6.1 million women between ages 15 and 44 had an impaired ability to have children; the number of infertile married couples was reported to be 2.1 million.[2]

Infertility is the inability to conceive or impregnate after 1 year of regularly engaging in sexual intercourse without the use of birth control. In approximately 40% of cases, the problem centers on the woman's body, in 40% of cases on the male's body, and the remaining 20% of unknown origin. On occasion, individuals may know or suspect that they may have difficulty or be unable to reproduce. For others the knowledge comes as a painful reality. In recent years, reproductive technologies have greatly expanded to enable couples to biologically become parents. The pregnancies that result, though, come at great physical, emotional, and financial cost and do not always result in a successful birth.

Individuals and couples have sometimes assumed mistakenly that they were infertile or even sterile. **Sterility** usually results from the purposeful action of being surgically sterilized through **vasectomy** or **tubal ligation**. Sterility also can result from disease. For example, if a woman's uterus is removed because of cancer or extensive fibroids, she will no longer be able to become pregnant. When chemotherapy is prescribed for men and women for the treatment of cancer, one common aftereffect is damage to the ovaries or testicles, impairing the ability to produce ova and sperm. We have sometimes heard young people describe themselves as "sterile" or "infertile." The explanation given is "I've been having sex for years, and I never use birth control. Since I never got pregnant, I just assume I'm sterile." Just because a couple have been lax in the use of contraception and has avoided unintended pregnancy, they should not assume infertility or sterility.

Individuals should not initially suspect infertility unless they are aware of specific health problems, congenital abnormalities, or environmental exposures that could impair the reproductive system. In women, infertility can be attributable to lack of ovulation, hormonal imbalances that impair endometrial functioning, scar tissue in the uterus and fallopian tubes resulting from advanced pelvic infections, endometriosis, habitual miscarriage, and production of antisperm antibodies. Other factors cited as causes of infertility include advanced age, cigarette smoking, drug use, and excessive dieting and exercise. The last two factors are related to body fat levels and the ability of the female body to store estrogen.

Male infertility focuses primarily on sperm production. Inadequate sperm production can be related to structural deformities, hormonal deficiencies, lifestyle habits including drug use, and sexual dysfunction. Problems generally focus on sperm being too few or none at all, slow movement of sperm present, or misshapen sperm. The cause of any problem has to be determined.

Numerous tests, with varying degrees of invasiveness, have been developed to determine the cause(s) of infertility. Males and females alike initially will have complete physical assessments, including a detailed medical

Infertility
inability to conceive after 1 year of unprotected intercourse

Sterility
permanent inability to reproduce

Vasectomy
surgical sterilization of the male that involves cutting and tying off the vas deferens

Tubal ligation
surgical sterilization of the female that involves cutting and tying off the fallopian tubes

and lifestyle history. The man will be asked to ejaculate into a sterile cup, after which his sperm will be tested for viability and motility. If problems are found with the sperm, correct diagnosis and treatment follow. These might consist of lifestyle changes, hormone treatment, surgery to remove a **varicocele** (an enlarged vein in the scrotum impairing blood flow), and artificial insemination with his sperm.

Tests for the female typically begin after months of first charting her menstrual cycle by taking her basal body temperature. Follow-up blood work can help determine whether she is ovulating. Endometrial biopsies can be performed to assess the readiness of the uterus to accept a fertilized egg. **Hysterosalpingograms** are tests that determine if the fallopian tubes are open. Laparoscopy and hysteroscopy are two tests that allow physicians to see any evidence of endometriosis and scar tissue. A post-coital test uses cervical mucus removed after intercourse to determine its interaction with sperm.[3]

If the infertility is suspected to result from absence of ovulation, women can be treated hormonally. Two common drugs are clomid and pergonal. One problem with medications is the increased possibility of multiple births — some of which receive a lot of media coverage and attention. Multiple birth babies, however, are almost always premature and frequently have health problems. Whereas normal gestation takes place over a 40-week period, multiple births usually do not go to term. Each additional fetus shortens the gestation period. When babies are born around the 32nd week of a pregnancy, for example, they weigh little more than 2 pounds and require weeks of treatment in a neonatal intensive care unit. Decades ago, these babies would not have survived. Today, more drugs and technology are available to keep these infants alive. The costs on many levels — physical, social, emotional, and financial — can be staggering.

Some women first undergo pelvic surgery to conceive and carry a pregnancy. Endometriosis, a condition in which endometrial tissue grows outside the uterus and in some cases literally wraps around and blocks off the fallopian tubes, can be treated with surgery. Myomectomy, a surgical procedure used to remove fibroid growths but preserve the uterus, can help women as well.

When a woman's fallopian tubes remain blocked, **in-vitro fertilization, IVF,** becomes an option. Her ovaries are first stimulated using hormones, so that more than one ovum matures each month. After surgically "harvesting" the eggs, they are joined with sperm in a laboratory. Often three or four **blastocysts** (pre-embryos) then will be placed directly into the woman's uterus. Approximately 27,000 IVF procedures are performed each year in the United States.[4] Success rates, defined as viable births, vary between 12% and 25%.[5] Generally, the more embryos that are transplanted, the higher is the rate of success.

Varicocele
an enlarged vein in the scrotum impairing blood flow

Hysterosalpingograms
tests that determine if the fallopian tubes are open

In-vitro fertilization (IVF)
procedure in which ova are removed from the woman's body and fertilized with sperm in a laboratory; the embryo is surgically implanted into her uterus

Blastocysts
spherical cluster of cells, also known as pre-embryos, that form shortly after conception

Could you be a sperm donor? Or could you be an ova donor? Could you imagine relying on a donor yourself to help create a pregnancy?

Some couples confront the reality that a pregnancy will result only from the use of donor sperm or donor ova. Fertility clinics can provide information to couples that allow them to choose donors who match them in physical appearance, background, and interests. Because college students are considered young and healthy, they may be approached as possible donors. For women in particular, the money offered is enticing and intended to compensate for the health risks involved. High doses of hormones are prescribed, which stimulate multiple ovulation. The ova are harvested and then retrieved surgically. Both hormone ingestion and surgery carry some risk to the woman's health.

Couples spend varying amounts of time, money, and certainly emotional energy being tested and evaluated for the causes of the infertility.

Case Study

Anthony's Story of Infertility

Looking back on it now, it all seems so distant. My wife and I married in September of 1989. We planned a perfect life together, filled with love and joy. We thought that most of this joy would come from the children we planned on having. Two years of enjoying ourselves together, and then it was time to have the children who would be an extension of our love.

I don't know whether it was the combination of my going back to college full-time and the pressures of conceiving or whether it just wasn't "God's time" (a phrase we held to that kept our faith), but getting pregnant just wasn't happening. At first we kidded about it. Then we decided to pay more attention to having sex around my wife's ovulation date. Purchasing and using the special thermometer that allowed us to take her basal body temperature was the beginning of a host of infertility treatments. We came to hate that word "infertility" as much as the constant advice to "relax."

One year passed, and no pregnancy. I thought about how my brother's infertility was remedied by an operation to remove a varicocele. Six months after his surgery, his wife became pregnant. The operation had helped his sperm count, which had been both low and with slow motility sperm.

Now it was my turn. I delivered more sperm samples to a variety of medical centers than I care to remember! I had such anxiety as I tried to ejaculate

into cups, being in public medical facilities with what seemed to be everyone knowing what I was doing. It was determined that I was a candidate for varicocele surgery. Finally our problems would be solved! I had the surgery and hoped to become a father soon. No such luck.

My wife was given two fertility drugs to improve our chances of children. Clomid didn't work. Serephene didn't work. She was scheduled for a laparoscopy to allow the doctors to see what was going on. It turned out that she had endometriosis, cysts on her ovaries, and one of her fallopian tubes was smaller than the other. All these problems were described as "fixable" and, paired with my problem, could have explained why we weren't getting pregnant. After the necessary surgery, we regained our hope.

Months and months of trying came and went. Negative pregnancy tests . . . trying again . . . waiting and hoping that she *wouldn't* get her period. Anger and sadness when her period came. And trying again. Lovemaking became a job. We were so upset that we were often no-shows at family christenings and children's birthday parties.

After a period of time, the doctor suggested artificial inseminations with my sperm. My wife would be put on fertility drugs to increase her chances of ovulation. I would provide a sample — legal masturbation,

Those who consider IVF can expect to pay more than $6,000 for each attempt. Class differences become readily apparent, as those with financial resources and better health insurance plans clearly have an advantage. When all the time and resources result in a healthy baby, however, those efforts pale in comparison to joy of new parenthood.

Should health insurance companies be required to cover the costs of infertility treatments? Should government-run Medicaid pay for infertility treatments? Give your reasons for the position you take.

as I called it — and the sperm would be injected into my wife using a long syringe. We agreed to the procedures. Each time we prayed and prayed, yet continued to get negative results.

Not being ready to consider adoption — people were kindly suggesting that to us — we enrolled at the Reproductive Clinic at a local hospital, known for its successes with infertile couples. I was now thirty-three years old, finished with college, and fortunately employed at a place with good health benefits. The doctors there suggested in-vitro fertilization. We agreed. I had to inject fertility drugs into my wife's buttocks for twenty-one straight days prior to "the day." Prayer got me through that. Retrieval of the eggs was successful, and we were told that there were seven excellent embryos. The doctors would put three back into my wife's uterus.

My wife had to be monitored daily at the hospital, giving blood and having ultrasounds. The egg retrieval was done on March seventeenth, Saint Patrick's Day. The embryos were put back on March twentieth, the first day of spring. We would have to wait fourteen days for the results. Those were the longest fourteen days of our lives.

On Easter Sunday we received the exciting news that she was pregnant! Tests conducted two weeks later confirmed that she was carrying triplets. We

were grateful . . . scared . . . overwhelmed. There was never a question that, despite the high risks associated with multiple births, we would keep all three babies.

After twenty weeks of bed rest and daily monitoring, my wife gave birth, with me at her side, to three beautiful girls. The road was long and bumpy. It took almost six years of trying. Although we had been angry, sad, and frustrated, we never lost our faith. We supported each other from start to finish. And now I live with the four most beautiful women in the world, all coming in "God's time."

Anthony's triplet girls.

PREGNANCY

Human chorionic gonadotropin (HCG)
a hormone secreted during pregnancy that shows up in the urine of pregnant women; the basis for determining pregnancy using home kits

Confirming a pregnancy used to mean that a woman had to see her physician, have a urine test, and wait for days for the results. Today, determining if a woman is pregnant is as simple as purchasing a home pregnancy kit at the local pharmacy. Home pregnancy kits are designed to detect the presence of **human chorionic gonadotropin (HCG)**, a hormone present in the urine of pregnant women. Because this hormone is secreted as the fertilized egg implants in the uterus, early testing can confirm a pregnancy. Many kits can be used reliably within a day or two of a missed period.

Although the specific procedure varies slightly with each brand, the basic test involves adding a small amount of morning urine (which has the highest concentration of HCG) to a sample of red blood cells coated with HCG antibodies. Other kits use a test strip, coated with the antibodies that is dipped into the urine. If the concentration of HCG is high enough, the women will test positive for pregnancy. If the test is done too early into the pregnancy, the test result could be a "false negative." That means the woman is pregnant but, because of too little HCG, the test showed her not to be pregnant. She should do a repeat test a few days later if she suspects she is pregnant.

Although home pregnancy tests are 85% to 95% accurate, medical laboratory tests are most accurate. False positives are extremely rare. When a woman has given birth recently, had a miscarriage, or is taking certain fertility drugs, a test may show that she is pregnant when she is not.

In all cases, the woman should follow up with a visit to a physician. A pelvic exam will indicate an enlarged uterus associated with pregnancy and also will allow the physician to estimate the duration of the pregnancy and project a birth date.

PERSPECTIVES
Common Questions About Home Pregnancy Tests

Consumers in the United States spend close to $200 million on home pregnancy kits. Here are the most common questions asked about them.

Q. How do home pregnancy tests work?

A. Pregnancy triggers release of the hormone HCG. Home pregnancy tests detect the presence of this hormone in the mother's urine.

Q. For the quick-stick type of pregnancy test kits that use absorbent tips, can I collect the urine in a cup instead?

A. Yes, this can be done if the cup or container is clean. But the absorbent tip must be immersed in the urine cup for the specified time.

Q. What is my next step if the test result is positive?

A. A positive test indicates the presence of HCG in the urine. You then should consult a health care professional to confirm the pregnancy.

Q. What if the test result is negative?

A. A negative test result means that HCG has not been detected. If the period has been miscalculated, though, you could still be pregnant. Wait a week, then repeat the test. If the test is negative again and your period still hasn't started, consult a health care professional.

Gestation

A pregnancy is measured from the first day of a woman's last menstrual period, with the expected period of **gestation** averaging 40 weeks. A normal birth will take place between the 38th and 42nd week. Deliveries before 38 weeks are considered premature, and after 42 weeks, the extended time may threaten the health of the baby, so labor may be induced. Pregnancies are divided into trimesters, each having unique characteristics. Figure 13.2 is a timeline showing features of each.

First Trimester

During the first trimester of the pregnancy, all structures and systems develop in rudimentary form. At the end of three months, the fetus has arms, legs, feet, toes, fingers, and the vital organs and body systems are functioning. The mother's taking drugs during the first trimester can have a particularly damaging effect on the fetus.

One overpowering argument for planning a pregnancy lies in the fact that without planning, the mother unintentionally may be taking medications with **teratogenic effects**, causing fetal malformations. At the end of the first trimester, the fetus is approximately 4 inches in length and weighs approximately 1 ounce.

Second Trimester

The second trimester is marked by growth and maturation of all the fetal systems. As the fetus grows in size and the uterus stretches, the mother's pregnancy becomes evident. During the fifth month of pregnancy, fetal movement is usually active enough for the mother to feel. By the end of the second trimester, the fetus is close to 12 inches long and weighs between 1 and 1½ pounds. The sex organs are apparent, as is bodily hair, including eyebrows and eyelashes. Neonatal intensive care units, equipped with the proper medications and technology, can help some babies born prematurely at the end of the sixth month of pregnancy to survive.

Third Trimester

During the third trimester the fetal systems continue to grow and mature. The last system to develop fully is the respiratory system. Without

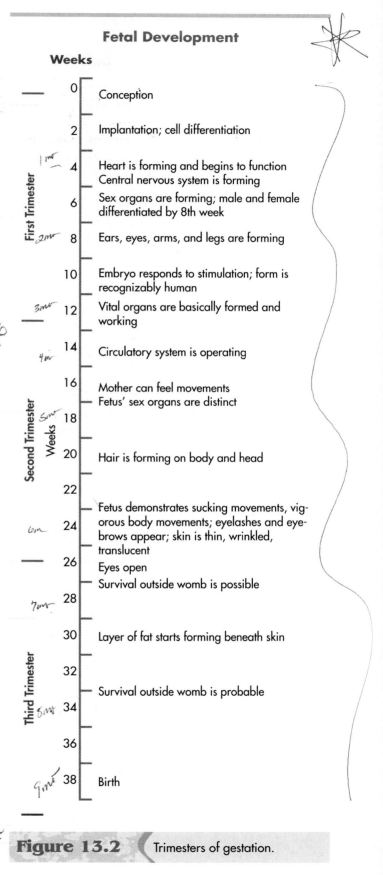

Fetal Development

Weeks

First Trimester

- 0 — Conception
- 2 — Implantation; cell differentiation
- 4 — Heart is forming and begins to function; Central nervous system is forming
- 6 — Sex organs are forming; male and female differentiated by 8th week
- 8 — Ears, eyes, arms, and legs are forming
- 10 — Embryo responds to stimulation; form is recognizably human
- 12 — Vital organs are basically formed and working
- 14 — Circulatory system is operating

Second Trimester / Weeks

- 16 — Mother can feel movements; Fetus' sex organs are distinct
- 18
- 20 — Hair is forming on body and head
- 22
- 24 — Fetus demonstrates sucking movements, vigorous body movements; eyelashes and eyebrows appear; skin is thin, wrinkled, translucent
- 26 — Eyes open; Survival outside womb is possible
- 28

Third Trimester

- 30 — Layer of fat starts forming beneath skin
- 32 — Survival outside womb is probable
- 34
- 36
- 38 — Birth

Figure 13.2 Trimesters of gestation.

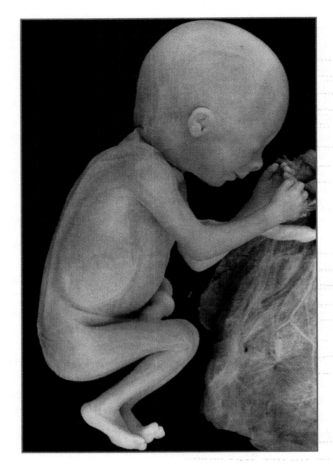

The fetus in the uterus at 24 weeks

Gestation
period of time representing pregnancy and development of fetus from conception to birth

Teratogenic effects
side effects of drugs and other substances that cause birth defects

Pheophylline
a drug used to relax the lungs and prevent bronchiospasm in preemie babies

proper lung function, the blood is not fully oxygenated, which can inflict damage to the fetus. The pharmaceutical industry has advanced treatments for babies born prematurely. Drugs such as survanta, which help the lungs expand and is being used for extremely tiny preemies, and **pheophylline**, which relaxes the lungs and prevents bronchiospasms, are being used in neonatal intensive care units to improve lung function and reduce the congenital problems associated with low birthweight babies.[6]

Health care costs associated with prematurity are high, and low-birth-weight babies are at risk for lasting health problems. At birth, most babies weigh between 6 and 9 pounds and are approximately 20 inches in length.

Physical, Psychological, and Social Effects of Pregnancy

Clearly, pregnancy has a powerful impact on health. The woman experiences a number of physical changes as her body responds to the physical demands of the pregnancy. Carrying an ever larger baby in the front of one's body puts demands on all the systems. Throughout pregnancy, women report varying degrees of fatigue, shortness of breath, heartburn, indigestion, nausea, gas, headaches, leg cramps, backaches, water retention, varicose veins, and difficulty sleeping.

As part of prenatal care, discussed below, the mother should be monitored for signs of hypertension and gestational diabetes. Pregnancy and childbirth may well be the greatest physical challenges in a woman's life.

Emotionally, fathers and mothers both respond to pregnancy in various ways. A planned pregnancy should connect to positive feelings — happiness, joy, excitement. Even so, periods of anxiety and fear about pending parenthood are normal. The high hormone levels in pregnancy affect women's moods and may result in their being weepy, irritable, and upset. As the projected date of birth gets closer and closer, pending parenthood, or the addition of another child to the family, becomes all the more real. Couples might have difficulty concentrating on anything but the soon-to-arrive baby.

Pregnancy may affect social relationships as well. Because the birth of a child, and having children, changes our lives in so many ways, some people report feeling awkward around those who have not had the experience of pregnancy. Once children are born, relationships may go through periods of additional strain. Couples with children are talking about their baby's smallest accomplishment or where to buy diapers at the lowest expense, whereas childfree couples may be discussing their latest vacation. Continuing to be able to relate to each other's lifestyle can test the bounds of friendship.

Relationships with family members also may change. Excited grandparents can be a tremendous source of support. Relations between adult children and their parents may improve as the new parents come to better understand the mother/father roles. In some situations, however, grandparents offer unsolicited advice and become controlling. Something as basic as naming a child and honoring relatives can be a source of tension.

Couples can manage the stresses associated with pregnancy, and later childrearing itself, by communicating openly. Private time to share what can be an intensely spiritual event becomes important.

Lovemaking During Pregnancy

Lovemaking can continue throughout a pregnancy, although males and females report changes in sexual desire at various stages. Many women have a progressive decline in sexual interest and activity, particularly by the third trimester.[7] Some women feel less attractive as their body becomes larger and larger and their nipples become darker and ultrasensitive, with stretch marks possibly forming. Other women feel sexy, attractive, and responsive throughout the pregnancy. Some males respond positively to their pregnant partners, and others fear hurting the developing fetus.

Many couples find massage and holding to be important sensual experiences during this time. Oral sex may be continued, although air should not be blown into the vagina. Couples do find the need to adjust positions when engaging in intercourse. The man-on-top position can be uncomfortable, if not difficult, as the pregnancy progresses.

If a pregnancy has been determined to be high-risk, a physician may advise modifications in lovemaking patterns. Women who are spotting, bleeding, at risk for premature labor, or in pain may be advised against sexual intercourse.

Prenatal Care

Creating a healthy environment for both the mother and developing fetus is the focus of prenatal care. Good prenatal care enhances the health of the mother and developing baby and reduces the possibility of congenital birth defects. The basic components of prenatal care are proper nutrition, exercise, medical monitoring, and, when medications are necessary for the mother's health, careful monitoring of those medications.

Nutrition

During pregnancy the mother should consume the proper amount of nutrient-dense foods. She must pay attention to her intake of all nutrients — protein, carbohydrates, fats, vitamins, minerals, fiber, and water. Pregnancy requires more calories and more protein. Because pregnant women also require more folic acid, iron, and calcium, a physician's prescription for vitamins and minerals may be needed.[8]

Appropriate weight gain for the mother remains controversial. The general recommendation is that women gain between 25 and 35 pounds. Recently, however, researchers are examining the type of weight gained rather than the precise amount; weight from fat and weight from fluid can have a different impact on the health of the baby. Other researchers are looking at the time within the pregnancy when the weight is gained, rather than the actual amount gained.[9]

Weight gains during pregnancy can range from 50 pounds or more to less than 15 pounds and still produce a healthy baby. What is certain is that women should gain weight and should not engage in a weight-loss diet during a pregnancy. Figure 13.3 shows the breakdown of weight for a 26.5-pound weight gain. Actual weight gain will be reflected in the weight of the baby and the other variables cited.

Health Hint

For Pregnant Women

To reduce complications during pregnancy, at delivery, and after delivery:

1. Begin prenatal care as soon as you know you are pregnant. If you cannot afford prenatal care from a private physician, it is available through your local public health department. Prenatal care is important for:

   a. consistent monitoring of the status of the mother and fetus.

   b. consistent monitoring of the mother's weight gain.

   c. consistent monitoring of the mother's nutritional needs.

2. Do not use any psychoactive substances, including tobacco and alcohol, during pregnancy. Drug use may cause problems in the pregnancy and damage the unborn baby.

3. Do not become pregnant without being certain that you have been immunized against German measles.

4. Schedule any of the fetal tests suggested by your health provider.

Exercise

Exercise during pregnancy is important although that area has been controversial as well. Exercise has been associated with fewer cesarean births. A woman's exercise routine should be consistent with her prepregnancy exercise levels and she should not begin a vigorous program to get in shape once she is pregnant. The American College of Obstetrics and Gynecology recommends that pregnant women not exercise strenuously for more than 15 minutes at a time. The body temperature should not rise above 100° F, and the heart rate should not rise above 140 beats per minute.

That too much exercise may cause miscarriage or harm the fetus is a myth.[10] Moderate exercise during pregnancy has the benefits of improving muscle tone and alleviating pregnancy-related discomforts such as backache, bloating, constipation, and swollen hands and feet. Whether pregnant or not, exercise relieves stress, gives the woman a sense of control of her body, and promotes relaxation.[11]

Baby	7.5	pounds
Placenta	1.5	pounds
Amniotic fluid	1.75	pounds
Uterine enlargement	2	pounds
Maternal breast tissue	1	pound
Maternal blood volume	2.75	pounds
Fluids in maternal tissue	3	pounds
Maternal fat	7	pounds
Average Total:	26.5	pounds

Note: Based on a 26.5-pound weight gain

Source: *What to Expect When You're Expecting*, by A. Eisenberg, H. Murkoff, and S. Hathaway (New York: Workman Publishing, 1984), p. 128.

Figure 13.3 Breakdown of weight gain during pregnancy.

Drug Use During Pregnancy

Because so many substances can cross the placenta, pregnant women are advised not to take any drug without first consulting a physician. In practical terms, however, that may not be possible, particularly given inadequate health-care services for many women. Public health messages have been created to make women aware of the dangers of consuming alcohol and smoking during pregnancy. Increasing awareness is the first strategy. Actually getting women to stop drinking and smoking is more difficult.

Smoking cigarettes and inhaling secondhand smoke both affect the health of the fetus negatively. Cigarette smoke reduces the amount of oxygen in the bloodstream, adversely affecting fetal growth. Babies born to smokers tend to have a lower birthweight and more breathing problems. Exposure to cigarette smoke also has been associated with spontaneous abortion/miscarriages.[12]

According to the Centers for Disease Control and Prevention, more than 8,000 babies are born every year with evidence of damage from alcohol. Because it is not known if there is a "safe" level of drinking, pregnant women are encouraged to abstain totally. The blood alcohol concentration (BAC) of the mother is the same as that of the fetus, so the impact to the fetus is greater. Some evidence indicates that binge drinking is the critical behavior to avoid, as it raises the BAC to dangerous levels. An occasional glass of wine or a beer will not have the same impact. Yet, the risk may not be worth taking.

Fetal alcohol syndrome (FAS) is a cluster of effects found in babies as a result of their mother's drinking. Children born with FAS have a small head, abnormal facial features, sleep disorders, short stature, a wide space

Fetal alcohol syndrome effects on embryo and fetus of pregnant woman's alcohol consumption; symptoms include facial abnormalities, mental retardation, and nervous system damage

between the eyes and between the nose and upper lip, hyperactivity, and mental retardation.

Women who abuse cocaine, heroin, and other opiates risk having babies addicted to the abused substance. What is less well known is that many other drugs can have damaging effects. Table 13.1 highlights commonly used substances and their potential risks. Table 13.2 lists common medications that can be used safely during pregnancy.

Prenatal Screening

Various screening procedures are available to help determine the health of the fetus. Certain diseases are hereditary — thalassemia and cystic fibrosis, among many others — and some prospective parents want to know whether they are carriers of a disease and their specific risks for having a baby with the disease.

For example, Jews of Eastern European descent are at risk for passing on the gene for Tay Sach's disease, an incurable neurological disorder that results in the degeneration of what appears to be a healthy baby, and death by age 5. Knowledge that the parents are carriers may influence their decision to reproduce or terminate a pregnancy that bears the fatal illness.

Common screenings during pregnancy include the following:

1. *Chorionic villus sampling (CVS)*. CVS is conducted between the 9th and 11th week of gestation. Cells from the chorionic membrane are removed, usually through the cervix, to screen for genetic abnormalities. Because of the early timing of the test, structural deformities — to legs, arms, and so on — cannot be detected. (An ultrasound can be conducted during the second trimester to identify structural anomalies.)

2. *Ultrasound*. Ultrasound uses high-frequency soundwaves to create a **sonogram**, a picture of the fetus. With advances in technology, more obstetricians are keeping the necessary equipment in their offices and

Sonogram
the picture of the fetus produced by an ultrasound screening

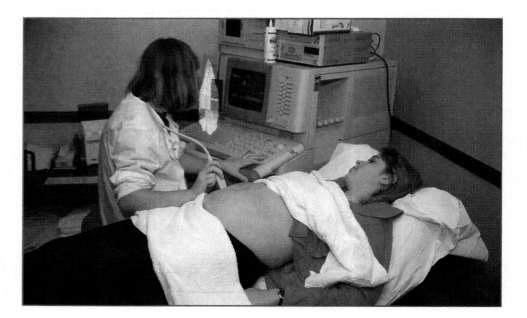

Ultrasound testing can determine position of the baby, any abnormalities, and often the sex.

Table 13.1 Impact of Selected Drugs and Other Substances During Pregnancy

Medication	Effects
Amphetamines (diet pills)	Heart defects; blood vessel malformations
Androgens	Genital abnormalities
Anticoagulants, such as warfarin (Coumadin) or dicumaro	Eye, bone, and cartilage abnormalities, including cleft lip, cleft palate; central nervous system defects
Anticonvulsants, such as valproic acid (Depakene), phenytoin (Dilantin), paramethadione (Paradione), and trimethadione (Tridione)	Neural tube defects; abnormal development; growth and mental retardation
Aspirin in large doses	Miscarriage; hemorrhage in newborn
Birth control pills	Arm and leg malformations; defects in internal organs; masculinization of females
Chemotherapeutic agents, such as methotrexate	Miscarriage; various fetal abnormalities
Cortisone	Various fetal and placental abnormalities, including cleft lip and stillbirth
Diethylstilbestrol (DES)	Numerous abnormalities in cervix and uterus of female fetuses; possible infertility in both males and females
Diuretics	Blood disorders; jaundice
Isotretinoin (Accutane)	Miscarriage; severe birth defects including heart defects, cleft palate, ear deformities
Lithium	Congenital heart disease
Nasal decongestant sprays	Reduce oxygen and nutrition to fetus by contracting blood vessels in placenta
Quinolones	Severe bone abnormalities
Tetracycline	Underdevelopment of tooth enamel; incorporation of tetracycline into bone
Thalidomide	Growth deficiency and other abnormalities
Chemical	
Lead	Miscarriage; stillbirths
Organic mercury	Brain disorders
Pesticides	Depends on specific chemical. Pregnant women should have someone else ventilate their home if extermination is necessary
Other	
Alcohol	Growth and mental retardation; fetal alcohol syndrome
Cat litter boxes	Toxoplasmosis
Herbs, including blue or black cohosh, pennyroyal, mugwort, tansy, slippery elm	Miscarriage
Illicit drugs	Numerous effects depending on the specific drug, including miscarriage, stillbirth, developmental abnormalities, growth and mental retardation, premature delivery, low birthweight, addicted newborns
Raw or undercooked meat	Toxoplasmosis
X-rays	Growth and mental retardation
Smoking cigarettes	Miscarriage, stillbirth, premature delivery, low birthweight, sudden infant death syndrome (SIDS). Smoking also increases the mother's risk of complications, including vaginal bleeding

Source: *The Harvard Guide to Women's Health*, by Karen J. Carlson, Stephanie E. Eisenstat, and Terra Ziporyn, Cambridge, MA: Harvard University Press, Copyright © 1996 by the President and Fellows of Harvard College. Reprinted with permission.

doing this test themselves. The sonogram outlines all structures in the fetus, showing the heart, kidneys, and liver as well as the full skeleton.

Amniocentesis
removal of the amniotic fluid

3. *Amniocentesis.* **Amniocentesis** involves removing some of the amniotic fluid and culturing the fetal cells that have sloughed off and are in the fluid. A complete genetic analysis then can be performed, identifying a number of potential diseases and conditions. The genetic analysis also yields the sex of the offspring, but couples are not given that information unless they want it. The test usually is conducted between the 14th and 18th week of gestation. Because an ultrasound is conducted prior to doing an amniocentesis, couples learn of the structural health of the fetus as well.

Amniocentesis is recommended particularly for women who become pregnant after age 35, because the rate of birth defects related to chromosomal abnormalities rises as women get older. Particular attention has been given to babies born with Down syndrome. At age 20, the risk of Down syndrome is 1 in 1667; at age 30 it is 1 in 952; and at age 35 it is 1 in 378. Rates associated with other chromosomal abnormalities also increase with maternal age.

4. *Alpha-fetoprotein (AFP) screening.* The AFP test involves taking a blood sample from the pregnant woman between the 15th and 18th

Table 13.2 ⟩ Medications That are Safe to Use Sparingly During Pregnancy

Symptom	Acceptable Medication	Comment
Pain or fever	Acetaminophen (Tylenol)	Avoid aspirin and nonsteroidal anti-inflammatory drugs except under a doctor's orders
Colds or coughs	Actifed, Sudafed, Co-Tylenol for congestion, or any Robitussin cough syrup	
Infections	Antibiotics such as penicillin and penicillin derivatives. Women allergic to penicillins can use erythromycin. Sulfa drugs (sulfonamides) are generally considered safe until the third trimester	Avoid tetracyclines, which can discolor the baby's teeth. Avoid Ciprofloxacin (quinolones), which can cause severe bone abnormalities
Constipation	Some stool softeners and laxatives including Metamucil, Milk of Magnesia, Peri-Colace, Colace, Senokot, Surfak	
Heartburn or indigestion	Antacids including Maalox, Mylanta, Riopan	
Diarrhea	Kaopectate or Pepto-Bismol	

Source: *The Harvard Guide to Women's Health*, by Karen J. Carlson, Stephanie E. Eisenstat, and Terra Ziporyn, Cambridge, MA: Harvard University Press, Copyright © 1996 by the President and Fellows of Harvard College. Reprinted with permission.

week of pregnancy. The fetal liver produces alpha-fetoprotein, and high levels in the mother's blood indicate neural tube defects. These defects include anencephaly, in which the upper portion of the brain and head is missing or underdeveloped, and spina bifida, in which the spinal cord is pushing through the spine. Most babies with anencephaly are stillborn or die shortly after birth, whereas babies with spina bifida, depending upon the extent of the disability, can live fairly functional lives.

Older mothers can have healthy pregnancies and babies and youth is not necessarily a protection against birth defects.

5. *Blood work.* The woman's blood may be tested at varying points throughout pregnancy. Blood testing has been encouraged especially to detect HIV-positive mothers. The rates of transmission of the virus from mother to fetus are variable. Not all children born to HIV-positive women become HIV-positive themselves. Treating women with the antiviral drug AZT has been shown to reduce the infant's chances of becoming HIV-positive.[13]

6. *Other tests.* Women with good prenatal care visit their obstetrician or nurse midwife monthly to ensure that the pregnancy is progressing normally and that no health problems are developing. A urine test is conducted at each visit. The presence of sugar in the urine may indicate gestational diabetes. A glucose tolerance test is needed for confirmation.

   At each visit the uterus is measured to ensure that the organ is expanding according to average measurements. The obstetrician or nurse midwife estimates growth of the fetus partly by measuring expansion of the uterus. Also, the woman's blood pressure is taken to watch for signs of hypertension. Each visit includes a weight measurement.

Some individuals and groups are opposed to prenatal screenings on religious and personal grounds. The implication is that results of a screening have to lead to action. Sometimes action is medical intervention during the pregnancy. Sometimes action means ending the pregnancy. Ethical, physical, financial, social, and emotional aspects have to be considered. At what point should decisions be made, and by whom?

CHILDBIRTH

Childbirth encompasses labor and delivery. Although the baby is born from the mother's body, the experience is increasingly viewed as one to be shared by the couple. Stories of experiences with childbirth vary from couple to couple, woman to woman, and birth to birth, even for the same woman.

For much of history, women helped women birth their babies. With the advent of "modern medicine," obstetricians began to deliver babies. Mothers left their other children at home, went to a hospital, and gave birth, while the fathers waited in the expectant fathers' waiting room. At the end of the 20th century, birthing has become an extended family event with much greater support and participation from partners, family, and friends.

Childbirth
labor and delivery

Depending to some extent on geography and the availability of health care providers, couples do have choices as to where and how their baby is born. Most babies in the United States are born in hospitals. Establishing a relationship with a private gynecologist/obstetrician, hospital clinic, or birthing center will determine where the baby is born. Although facilities share some fundamental aspects of delivery, they can have philosophical differences in practice and procedures. Being informed about the staff, facilities, and philosophy will enhance the birth experience. The type of health insurance, if any, that the couple has may be the driving force in making a choice.

The Childbirth Process

Childbirth is a three-phase process, shown in Figure 13.4, occurring over a 12–14 hour period on average. Some women have a rapid labor, delivering even before they can make it to the hospital. Others report long labors of 30 or more hours. Partly because of an appreciation of these women's exhaustion and partly because of the fear of malpractice, women today seldom are left to labor beyond 24 hours.

The first stage of labor is the longest; it also tends to be longer for a first delivery than subsequent births. A number of signs indicate that labor is beginning.

- The uterus begins to contract. As labor progresses, these contractions become more regular, closer together in time, and more intense.

- The thick mucous plug that has been covering the cervix, protecting the pregnancy, is dislodged. Because this mucus can be stained with blood, it sometimes is referred to as a "bloody show."

- Rupture of the amniotic membranes releases much of the amniotic fluid in the uterus that has protected the baby, and it trickles or gushes from the vagina. Not all women experience loss of amniotic fluid early in labor; it may happen later in the process. Other women may think their membranes have ruptured but actually be experiencing urinary incontinence from all the pressure. Because the risk of infection increases after the rupture of membranes, women who think their "water has burst" should get in touch with their healthcare provider.

First Stage

The first stage of labor is marked by dilation of the cervix to 10 cm. — the diameter needed for safe passage of the baby's head. Effacement, the thinning of the cervix, also takes place during this phase. The end of the first stage of labor, called transition, is marked by the most intense contractions, and some women experience chills, vomiting, and irritability. Women sometimes request medication during the first stage of labor.

Second Stage

The second stage of labor involves the actual birth. This is a short stage for some women — one to three pushes and the baby is out. Other women push for 1 or 2 hours and end up not only with a baby but also hemorrhoids, which aggravate the postpartum experience. Traditionally, women

Effacement
thinning of cervix during first stage of labor

are given an **episiotomy** to make more room for the birth. Nurse midwives have lower rates of episiotomies than physicians do, as the former use massage prior to and during labor to stretch the perineal tissues.[14]

Third Stage

The third stage of labor consists of delivery of the **afterbirth**. This includes the placenta, which had been attached to the uterine wall, and the umbilical cord, which has been cut at the baby's abdomen but remains attached to the placenta at the other end. During the third stage women may experience the rush of emotions associated with the birth itself and holding their newborn.

Episiotomy
surgical cutting of the perineum to facilitate childbirth

Afterbirth
the placenta, umbilical cord, which has been cut at the baby's abdomen but attached to the placenta and membranes expelled after the birth of a child

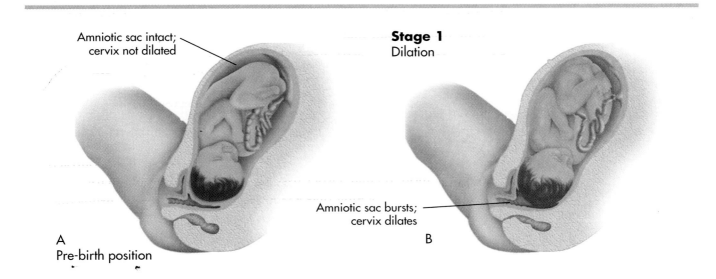

Amniotic sac intact; cervix not dilated

Stage 1
Dilation

Amniotic sac bursts; cervix dilates

A
Pre-birth position

B

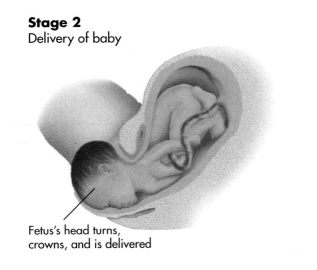

Stage 2
Delivery of baby

Fetus's head turns, crowns, and is delivered

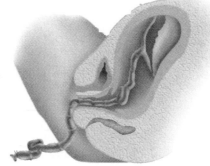

Stage 3
Delivery of placenta

Placenta separates from uterus and is delivered

Figure 13.4 〈 Stages of childbirth.

Delivery Options

Nowadays, delivery options include not only the traditional method but also birthing centers, home births, and cesarean deliveries.

Traditional Delivery

What has come to be viewed as traditional today is different from the traditional delivery of years ago. Both mother and father are often present at the delivery, which takes place in a hospital. Some fathers videotape and photograph their child's first minutes.

Some women come to their deliveries with a "coach," who is not necessarily the father of the child. Grandmothers and sisters may be present. Whatever the circumstance, most hospitals have modified their obstetrical practices to allow for one or more family members or designated friends to participate in the birth.

Hospitals have revamped the labor room/delivery room/recovery room/patient room/nursery arrangement in a variety of ways. Some of the changes resulted from women's voiced concerns for less of a "hospital" feel to the birth process. Some of the changes resulted from research that showed an improved labor experience as a result of being prepared, being flexible, and having support. Other changes undoubtedly have resulted from economic considerations.

Hospital births afford both mother and baby the availability of technology and monitoring. Some facilities also are known for their neonatal intensive care units, which become particularly important if the baby is at high risk — premature, physical deformities, infant in other than head-first position, blood incompatibility between mother and fetus, **toxemia**, multiple births, and so on.

Hospitals are set up to give women a lot of attention, with specialized nurses to care for the mother and the baby. During labor, women can be monitored with fetal heart monitors to detect fetal distress. Although this is comforting to some patients and is required by some physicians, it does limit the woman's movement during labor, requiring her to stay in bed. By contrast, walking around may reduce the length of labor.

Hospital births give women more options for managing pain. Although individuals may have decided beforehand what their philosophy of birth is, the true test comes during labor. Some women manage their pain well and find that the breathing techniques they learned in their childbirth classes prepared them well. Relaxation techniques and hypnosis also can be helpful in managing the discomfort associated with labor. Other women request a shot of demoral, a narcotic, that quickly reduces the pain but also can cross the placenta.

Increasingly popular in hospitals is the use of an **epidural anesthetic** during labor. The epidural can be administered once a woman has dilated to 5 cm. This numbs her abdominal area, removing pain and discomfort while allowing labor to progress. Women who have an epidural must remain in bed. Its advantage is that the dosage of the drug is monitored in such a way so that the woman regains the capacity to push the baby out at the time of delivery.

Toxemia
a highly dangerous condition during pregnancy when high blood pressure occurs

Epidural anesthetic
injection of a drug into the spinal cord during labor to dull pain

PERSPECTIVES

Lemaze —
A Natural Childbirth Method

One of the natural childbirth methods used today was developed in the 1950's by a French obstetrician named Dr. Fernand Lamaze after observing a technique used by Russian women in labor. Lamaze, as do other methods, focuses on the normal process of labor. The Lamaze method of delivery can help reduce the pain and fear of labor and birth. The majority of expectant parents attend Lamaze classes to prepare for childbirth.

Several key points utilized in the Lamaze technique are:

- ✺ Allows the woman to have control over her body and help her with labor management.
- ✺ The coach is very much involved.
- ✺ Controlled deep breathing.
- ✺ Light massage of the abdomen.
- ✺ Concentration on a focal point.

Even though hospitals maintain nurseries, the baby spends most of the time in the room with the mother. Hospitals have greatly eased visitation restrictions. Fathers have few limitations on the amount of time they can spend in the room, and some choose to sleep at the hospital. Siblings, too, can visit their newborn brother or sister. Gone are the days when the family looked at the new addition briefly behind glass windows.

Birthing Centers

Birthing centers gained in popularity with the growth of the women's movement in the 1970s. Women were taking an increased role in the birth of their babies and asking for changes to traditional delivery. Birthing centers were operated by nurse midwives who worked under the supervision of obstetricians, in close physical proximity to hospitals.

The unique feature of birthing centers is the belief that the woman, with the support of her partner, should have as much control over the birthing process as possible. They were the first places where the space for deliveries was "homey," utilizing birthing beds, wall-papered rooms, and rocking chairs. They also cut back on the use of fetal heart monitors so the woman could move around more easily during the first stage of labor. Women could take showers, eat lightly, and have family, including their other children, with them.

Women who deliver at birthing centers usually are screened to rule out high-risk cases. Multiple births, health conditions that warrant close medical monitoring — for example, diabetes and heart conditions — and being over 40 years of age are situations in which a hospital birth is encouraged or required.

As hospitals have increasingly embraced some of the offerings of birthing centers — leaving women to labor and deliver in one room, making those rooms more attractive and less stereotypically hospital-like, having nurse midwives on staff — free-standing birthing centers away from hospitals may be a less attractive option now. New Jersey, for example, has one free-standing birthing center and recently closed the birthing center that was housed within a hospital. One explanation for the closing was women's increasing desire to have epidural anesthesia rather than experience the first stage of labor more drug-free.

Home Births

Delivering babies at home may be a personal choice or may result from rapid labor. Lay midwives have delivered many babies at home. In the South, prior to changes resulting from the civil rights movement of the 1960s, segregation in medical care and minimal hospital facilities resulted in many Black women delivering their babies at home. Today, the attitude toward home birth is that it puts the life and welfare of both the baby and mother at risk. Because of the risk of charges of medical malpractice, obstetricians do not conduct home births, and only a select number of licensed nurse midwives will do so. In contrast, approximately 80% of the world's babies are born at home, particularly in nonindustrialized countries.

Cesarean Deliveries

Cesarean delivery, or **c-section,** is a surgical procedure done for a variety of reasons related to the health and survival of either the mother or the baby, or both. The 20% rate of cesarean births in the United States is high by contrast to that of other industrialized nations. Some argue that our

Cesarean delivery (c-section) surgical form of childbirth in which an incision is made through the abdomen and uterus to deliver the baby

Case Study

Kiesha's C-Section

When I listen to other women describe their child's birth, I sometimes feel a pang of jealousy. Why couldn't my baby have been born the "right way" — vaginally, that is. I never had true labor, nor do I know what it feels like to push your baby out into the world. But when I look down at my daughter and see that she's healthy and happy, I try to stay focused on what's truly important — and how happy I am that she's here.

George and I had attended childbirth classes for eight weeks, learning all about relaxation techniques, watching the video on the birth of the baby, and visiting the hospital. We felt very prepared for the birth, yet never really thought I'd become one of the women whose cervix wouldn't dilate and whose baby would be born by cesarean delivery.

As my due date came closer, my doctor examined me and said the baby would probably be late. She (we had discovered the sex from a recent sonogram) had not yet dropped into the pelvis, and my cervix had not begun to efface. When I went past my due date by more than a week, my obstetrician ordered a non-stress test. That test relies on a sonogram to determine if the baby is in any distress. Because the test showed little amniotic fluid, my doctor decided to induce me.

Being induced was no fun. A drug called pitocin was used to bring on contractions, and they were very strong. After many hours on pitocin, my baby still hadn't moved into the right position, and my cervix hadn't dilated much at all. My chart would later read "cesarean section due to failure to progress."

Having a cesarean performed today is very different than the way it was done years ago. My brother was born by c-section, and my mother was asleep for the delivery. I was awake through the whole delivery, and George sat next to me, holding my hand. When our daughter was lifted out, he was told to stand and take a look at her. So, while I didn't have a traditional labor experience, and I needed the surgical delivery, we were all there together and can remember the excitement of the birth.

improved methods of screening and prenatal care identify more problems that require surgical intervention. Others cynically claim that expectations of giving birth to the perfect child and the rise in medical malpractice lawsuits have changed the culture of childbirth to a point at which physicians do not want to take the risk of waiting for the outcome of a vaginal birth.

C-sections are generally done when the baby is in a **breech position** — feet or buttocks presenting first. Other indications for cesarean delivery are incompatibility between the baby's head size and size of the mother's pelvis, signs of fetal distress picked up by fetal heart monitors, weak contractions of the uterus and prolonged labor, or problems with the placenta and identified bleeding. If the surgery is performed under emergency conditions, such as a detached placenta, general anesthesia is administered. In other situations, where time allows, anesthesia can be given with an epidural, which allows the mother to remain awake and, in many hospitals, her partner to be present.

Breech position
birth position in which the buttocks or foot rather than the baby's head presents at the cervix

WELLNESS SYNTHESIS

Conception involves each of the six components of wellness. The pregnant mother in particular has to attend to all aspects of wellness.

Physical Well-being

Pregnancy and childbirth clearly have an impact on a woman's health, and parenting affects the health of all caregivers. The mere fact that pregnant women are advised to gain between 25 and 35 pounds to have a healthy baby can put a strain on many body systems. Blood pressure may increase. Respiration becomes more labored. Muscles and ligaments must stretch. Digestion may be compromised, manifested in heartburn and constipation. Nerves may be impinged upon by the developing fetus; sciatica is a common complaint. Maintaining a healthy pregnancy requires good prenatal care, focusing on nutrition, exercise, and monitored use of medication.

Intellectual Well-being

Becoming a parent has many intellectual challenges. Individuals find themselves thinking about their values, what is important, and how best to rear a child. College students may find that the challenges of college preclude time to take care of children. Particularly with young children, little time may be available to attend classes, read, study, and prepare papers. More and more colleges and universities are providing child care facilities, yet comprehensive care, including infant care, has limited availability.

Emotional Well-being

Becoming a parent requires emotional readiness. Some individuals say, "I'm just not ready to do this now." A fundamental question is whether becoming a parent is critical to one's emotional well-being. Could you be happy never having children? Do you think having children will make you happy?

The role of mother or father has been so idealized that reality comes as a major shock to many new parents. Finding no time for oneself, with another person so totally dependent upon the parent, is a new experience. The lack of sleep that accompanies new parenthood also takes its toll. When babies have colic and cry for what seems like months, can you be the patient, adoring parent that you envisioned being? How well are you able to put another's needs above your own?

Emotional/mental illnesses of their parents certainly have an impact on the welfare of the children. Television and newspapers often highlight the worst cases — stories of children physically and mentally abused or killed by parents who could not cope. The case of two college students from Wyckoff, New Jersey, accused of killing their newborn baby and leaving him in a motel dumpster made national news. Parenthood and care of a baby are not always "natural," positive experiences for which everyone is ready.

Social Well-being

Once children become a fact of life, notions of family expand and change. Relationships with parents, employers, and friends take on new dimensions and demands. Caring for children is a 24-hour job, not easily filled by one person. Will parenting responsibilities be shared? Who will take care of this child? What networks of support are in place? Will the mother work? Is child care available? Play groups? Recognizing what is required helps promote social health.

Spiritual Well-being

Parenthood can convey a sense of purpose and add meaning to life. Parents often discover new meaning in life/death issues as they become responsible for another human being. Parenthood brings with it an ongoing assessment of the relationship to one's child. Is the child like me? Does that matter? Can I love this child? Can I help him/her grow and be free to live her/his own life? What happens when parents die? If children die?

Environmental Well-being

When a woman becomes pregnant, the environment assumes different characteristics. Women in the workplace need to determine if their surroundings are free of toxins and other pollutants that may affect the fetus. Exposure to radiation can damage the fetus. Creating a safe environment in utero is a focus of prenatal care. Consequently, women are advised about both nutrition and drug use.

After a child is born, the environment in which the child lives must be safe. Poisonous substances must be out of reach, electric sockets must be covered, windows safely secured, and so on. Good parenting education may enable some parents to keep their home free of violence.

WEB RESOURCES

Atlanta Reproductive Health Centre

http://www.ivf.com/fert.html

A couples' guide to overcoming infertility. Articles on general information, ovulation and hormone disorders, male infertility, reproductive surgery and tubal infertility, advanced reproductive technology, miscarriage and recurrent pregnancy loss, adoption, egg donors, and internet resources.

International Council on Infertility Information Dissemination (INCIID)

http://www.inciid.org

A nonprofit organization committed to providing information about diagnosis, treatment, and prevention of infertility and pregnancy loss. The site accesses fact sheets and transcripts of auditoriums with renowned experts, more than 150 referrals and links to nonprofit organizations providing quality, sound infertility information, such as the American Society of Reproductive Medicine and the International Federation of Fertility Societies.

Infertility Resources

http://www.ihr.com/infertility/index.html

Offers extensive information about infertility organizations and clinics, IVF, GIFT, TET, ICSI, egg donor, financial issues, subject matter experts, sperm banks, Internet Newsgroups and mailing lists, research, journals, medications, infertility medical supplies, and adoption. The infertility educational articles offer diagnosis, male factor, treatment, drugs/medication, psychological and social issues, plus financial and legal information.

Online Birth Center

http://www.efn.org/~djz/birth/birthindex.html

A private center established to provide information and articles on issues concerning childbirth. Articles include fetal screening, physical violence and sexual abuse, HIV/AIDS, toxemia, cesarean section, complications of pregnancy, psychological complications, newborn, infant, and childhood problems, family planning, infertility, grief and loss.

Notes

1. R. Black, "Conception at Any Cost?" *Child*, June/July 1995, 79–81, 83; L. H. Burns, "An Exploratory Study of Perceptions of Parenting After Infertility," *Family Systems Medicine*, 8 (1990), 177–189.

2. NCHS, *Fastats/Fertility/Infertility*, www.cdc.gov/nchswww/fastats.

3. K. Carlson, S. Eisenstat, and T. Ziporyn, *The Harvard Guide to Women's Health* (Cambridge, MA: Harvard University Press, 1996), p. 322.

4. "In Vitro Fertilization — Embryo Transfer (IVF–ET) in the United States: 1990 Results from the IVF–ET Registry," *Fertility and Sterility*, 57:1 (1992), 15–24.

5. A. L. Cowan, "Can a Baby-making Venture Deliver?" *New York Times*, June 1, 1992, pp. C1, C4; E. Rosenthal. "Cost of High-tech Fertility: Too Many Tiny Babies," *New York Times*, May 26, 1992, C1, C10.

6. Personal conversation with D. Devine, a neonatal intensive care nurse, in 1998.

7. L. Bogren, "Changes in Sexuality in Women and Men During Pregnancy," *Archives of Sexual Behavior*, 20 (1991), 35–46.

8. Boston Women's Health Book Collective, *Our Bodies, Ourselves for the New Century* (New York: Simon & Schuster, 1998).

9. L. Beil, "Pregnancy Weight Gain Scrutinized," *Daily Record*, February 15, 1998, W2.

10. *Nutrition: Concepts and Controversies*, 7th ed., by F. Sizer and E. Whitney (Belmont, CA: West/Wadsworth, 1997).

11. Planned Parenthood, *All About Sex: A Family Resource on Sex and Sexuality* (New York: Three Rivers Press, 1997).

12. E. Ostrea, D. Knapp, A. Romero, M. Montes, and A. Ostrea, "Meconium Analysis to Assess Fetal Exposure to Nicotine by Active and Passive Maternal Smoking," *Journal of Pediatrics*, 124 (1994), 471–476.

13. V. B. Dole, "ACT in Pregnant Women with HIV: Risks and Benefits," *Neonatal Network*, 14:2 (1995), 62–63.

14. L. Locke, *Nurse Midwife Presentation* (Paterson, NJ: St. Joseph's Hospital, 1996).

Student Study Questions

1. When is the "right" time to have a baby? What are some of the considerations that go into this?

2. What happens in the process of fertilization and conception?

3. What major changes in the fetus are associated with each trimester?

4. What are the basic wellness guidelines to ensure a healthy pregnancy?

5. What tests and other technological advances are available to aid with pregnancy, labor, and delivery? How do these contribute to political debate?

6. What are the differences in hospital versus home (or birth center) births?

7. What is the role of the midwife?

8. What is cesarean birth? What is the rate of c-sections in the United States? What factors contribute to the high rate in the United States?

Assessing Readiness for Parenting

Using the wellness model, assess your readiness on each dimension. Issues that focus specifically on the pregnancy itself are weighted more toward the female parent. Nonetheless, for both males and females, parenthood touches on all dimensions of health and wellness.

Physical Well-being

● Are you physically healthy? Is your weight, blood pressure, and respiration within a normal range?

● Do you have any chronic illnesses that may impact your ability to conceive? Maintain a pregnancy? Experience childbirth?

● Are you taking any medications that may affect the normal growth and development of the fetus?

● Do you regularly use any drugs recreationally? Are you addicted to any substance? Could you stop using caffeine, alcohol, or other recreational drugs?

● What are your sleep patterns? How well do you function with interrupted sleep?

● Are you physically fit? Do you exercise regularly?

● Do you have any physical disabilities that may affect your ability to maintain a pregnancy? Go through childbirth? Take care of a child? Is so, do you have the resources to make pregnancy, childbirth, and caregiving manageable?

Intellectual Well-being

● Have you thought about the roles and responsibilities of being a parent?

● Have you thought about why you want to become a parent? Do they seem sound?

● Have you read any educational material on pregnancy, childbirth, and parenting skills?

● Have you assessed your financial readiness for parenthood?

● Do you have the financial resources to provide for a child — food, clothing, medical expenses?

Emotional Well-being

● Are you excited about becoming a parent?

● Are you comfortable with the person you are? Do you love yourself? Are you able to offer love to another?

● Do you handle frustration well? Anger?

● Are you currently struggling with any emotional problems that could interfere with your becoming a parent?

● Have you been diagnosed with any problems or mental conditions for which you take medication? Is so, would a pregnancy aggravate your condition? Would parenthood affect your condition in any way?

Continued

Student Assessment

Assessing Readiness for Parenting (cont.)

Social Well-being

- Is the quality of your relationship with your partner healthy?

- Are you considering being a single parent?

- What is the quality of your relationship with your family of origin? Will family members be involved as grandparents, aunts, cousins, uncles? Is that important to you?

- What is the quality of your relationship with the family of your partner? Will any of them be involved as grandparents, aunts, cousins, uncles? Is that important to you?

- Do you have other social support networks? Neighbors? Friends?

Spiritual Well-being

- Have you thought about the impact of parenthood on your life?

- Do you feel ready to be responsible for another? Nurture and love another? Put someone else's needs above your own?

- Do you and your partner share similar beliefs about religion? Would having a child bring to the surface any tensions and differences?

Environmental Well-being

- Are you currently living in a place where you can stay?

- What kind of living space will you provide for a baby? Is it safe, smoke-free?

- What kind of a community will you live in? Is the area safe? Can you easily get around (say, with a stroller)?

- Do you have access to medical care? For you? For a baby?

- Do you have access to a supermarket or other store for items such as baby food and diapers?

- Do you have access to transportation?

The answers to these questions can give you a sense of whether you are ready for parenthood. Keep in mind that no one is totally prepared for parenthood. It has too many unknowns, and the personal experience far exceeds your imagination and descriptions provided in books. Thinking about the issues, preparing for the possibilities, and being ready on many levels is part of good decision-making and planning.

Fertility Control

14

Major Topics

Student Learning Objectives

After reading this chapter, students will be able to:

- Differentiate the following terms: fertility control, contraception, birth control, family planning.

- Compare the theoretical effectiveness and the effectiveness of actual use.

- Determine personal level of risk for unintended pregnancy.

- Develop a personal plan for controlling fertility.

- Explain the different mechanisms of fertility control.

- Evaluate a variety of fertility control methods.

- Determine which methods work best for different types of users.

- Describe how fertility control requires change over the life cycle.

- Identify which methods work best in reducing the risks for STD and HIV infection.

- Evaluate the health aspects of various fertility control methods.

Many people use the terms *birth control*, *contraception*, and *family planning* interchangeably when referring to controlling fertility. Although the three terms are similar because they refer to strategies for preventing unintended pregnancy, they are vastly different in terms of their nature and scope. Although most people probably agree that avoiding unintended pregnancy is a good idea, how to accomplish this goal generates tremendous disagreement.

The terms birth control, contraception, *and* family planning *are often used interchangeably but are very different.*

Family planning
postponing children until the optimal point in one's life

Contraception
methods designed to prevent contraception

Birth control
broadest term covering all methods designed to prevent the birth of a child

Family planning implies the desire to have children at some point in time. Planning a family involves postponing childbearing until it is desired and also spacing subsequent births and avoiding pregnancy at other times. Family planning does not refer to specific methods or techniques to avoid unintended pregnancy.

Contraception refers to all methods designed to prevent conception or fertilization. Contraceptive methods work by preventing the sperm and egg from uniting to cause fertilization. These methods include noninsertive sexual activity, withdrawal, fertility awareness, barrier methods, hormonal contraception, and sterilization. How effective these methods are ranges from "not very" to almost complete, at the other end of the spectrum.

Birth control is a broad term encompassing all methods designed to prevent pregnancy and birth. Birth control includes all contraceptive methods and goes beyond them to include abortion and the use of IUDs and other techniques designed to disrupt pregnancy.

EFFECTIVENESS: THEORETICAL AND ACTUAL USE

One of the most important questions regarding any method of fertility control is, "How effective is it?" Effectiveness is measured two ways: theoretical use and actual use.

Although the differences in terms and their definitions might seem trivial, they form the basis of heated discussion and disagreement among people concerned with controlling fertility. Why might someone support one type of fertility control but strongly condemn another?

Theoretical effectiveness
the lowest expected percentage of women who will get pregnant while using a given contraceptive method

Theoretical Effectiveness

The **theoretical effectiveness** of any fertility control method estimates how it should work if it is used consistently and correctly. It is the ideal effectiveness of the method, determined through laboratory research and experimental studies. Theoretical effectiveness research designs attempt to control for as many variables as possible that may interfere with correct and consistent use. Failure of the method accounts for most of the ineffectiveness. Theoretical effectiveness is the lowest expected percentage of women who will get pregnant while using the method.

Actual-Use Effectiveness

The **actual-use effectiveness** of any fertility control method is how it actually works when real people use it under normal circumstances. This is the observed effectiveness of the method, determined by following a group of actual users for 1 year to see how many get pregnant. Actual-use studies are not subject to the same rigorous controls as most theoretical effectiveness studies. Because of this, user failure (failure to use the method consistently and correctly each time a couple has intercourse) largely accounts for the lack of effectiveness. Actual-use effectiveness is a combination of method and user failure, expressed as the percentage of women who get pregnant after 1 year of using the method.

> **Actual-use effectiveness**
> the percentage of women who get pregnant while using the method for 1 year

Theoretical and actual-use effectiveness studies traditionally were conducted using the Pearl index, an outdated research tool based on failures of the method per 100 women per years of exposure. This long-term methodology followed women (say, 10 women for 10 years each), and recorded the number of method failures each year using the lowest reported number to determine expected failures. This is misleading because research shows that failure rates normally decrease the longer a couple uses a method.[1]

Current studies base lowest and typical failure rates on the first year of observation. First-year data more accurately represent the risk of getting pregnant for someone using the method for the first time. Here, we will report data from studies that use first-year failure rates.

CHOOSING A METHOD

When contemplating which fertility control method to use, questions range from, "Is it safe and effective?" to "Does it go against my religion?" No contraceptive method is 100% perfect and without risk. Some methods might offer the level of effectiveness you want but lack aesthetic appeal. You may like a method but your partner hates it. A health care provider might recommend a method that looks ideal on paper but you might feel squeamish about using it. The self-assessment at the end of the chapter will help you examine your feelings about the various methods.

No contraceptive method is 100% perfect and without risk. The best contraceptive method is the one that a person or couple uses consistently and correctly.

Given this confusing array of things to consider, what is the best method of fertility control? The best method is the one the person or couple uses consistently and correctly. It is the one that those involved are happy with, that offers the level of protection desired, and that fits the needs of those involved at this point in life. Needs will change over time. Therefore, people would do well to review their fertility control needs periodically and make changes accordingly. Table 14.1 provides a summary of contraceptive methods.

MECHANISMS OF ACTION

Fertility control methods work in a variety of ways. The seven mechanisms of action related to fertility control methods are:

1. Provide non-penetrative sexual pleasure
2. Prevent sperm from reaching egg

Table 14.1 ▶ Summary of Birth Control/Contraceptives

Type	Male Condom	Female Condom	Spermicides Used Alone	Sponge	Diaphragm with Spermicide	Cervical Cap with Spermicide
Estimated Effectiveness	About 85%	An estimated 74%–79%	70%–80%	72%–82%	82%–94%	At least 82%
Risks	Rarely, irritation and allergic reactions	Rarely, irritation and allergic reactions	Rarely, irritation and allergic reactions	Rarely, irritation and allergic reactions; difficulty in removal; very rarely, toxic shock syndrome	Rarely, irritation and allergic ; reactions bladder infection; very rarely, toxic shock syndrome	Abnormal Pap test; vaginal or cervical infections;very rarely, toxic shock syndrome
Protection Against Sexually Transmitted Diseases	Latex condoms help protect against sexually transmitted diseases, including herpes and AIDS	May give some protection against sexually transmitted diseases including herpes and AIDS; not as effective as male latex condom	Unknown	None	None	None
Convenience	Applied immediately before intercourse; used only once and discarded	Applied immediately before intercourse; used only once and discarded	Applied no more than 1 hour before intercourse	Can be inserted hours before intercourse and left in place up to 24 hours; used only once and discarded	Inserted before intercourse; can be left in place 24 hours, but additional spermicide must be used if intercourse is repeated	Can remain in place 48 hours; not necessary to reapply spermicide upon repeated intercourse; may be difficult to insert
Availability	Nonprescription	Nonprescription	Nonprescription	Nonprescription	Prescription	Prescription

Source: *Personal Health: A Multicultural Perspective* by Patricia A. Floyd, Sandra E. Mimms, and Caroline Yelding-Howard (Englewood, CO: Morton Publishing, 1998), pp. 102–103.

Note: Abortion methods are not included in this summary.

3. Provide a barrier between the sperm and egg

4. Prevent release of the egg

5. Prevent implantation

6. Block egg or sperm transport surgically.

7. Terminate established pregnancy.

Nonpenetrative Sexual Release

Nonpenetrative activities are described in Chapter 5. They include massage, masturbation, outercourse, and the like. These activities provide sexual release but do not involve vaginal penetration.[2]

Oral Contraceptive Pill	Implant Norplant®	Injection Depo-Provera®	IUD	Fertility Awareness	Surgical Sterilization
97%–99%	99%	99%	95%–96%	Highly variable, perhaps 53%–85%	Over 99%
Blood clots, heart attacks and strokes, gall-bladder disease, liver tumors, water retention, hypertension, mood changes, dizziness and nausea; not for smokers	Menstrual cycle irregularity; headaches, nervousness, depression, nausea, dizziness, change of appetite, breast tenderness, weight gain, enlargement of ovaries and/or fallopian tubes, excessive growth of body and facial hair; may subside after first year	Amenorrhea, weight gain, and other side effects similar to those with Norplant	Cramps, bleeding, pelvic inflammatory disease, infertility; rarely, perforation of the uterus	None	Pain, infection, and, possible surgical complications in tubal ligation
None	None	None	None	None	None
Pill must be taken on daily schedule, regardless of frequency of intercourse	Effective 24 hours after implantation for approximately 5 years; can be removed by physician at any time	One injection every 3 months	After insertion, stays in place until physician removes it	Requires frequent monitoring of body functions and periods of abstinence	Vasectomy is a one-time procedure usually performed in a doctor's office. Tubal ligation is a one-time procedure performed in an operating room
Prescription	Prescription; minor outpatient surgical procedure	Prescription	Prescription	Instructions from physician or clinic	Surgery

Case Study

Charles: A Man's Perspective on Birth Control

Charles is a 21-year-old college junior. He has been in a monogamous relationship with Shannon, his current girlfriend, for the past 6 months. Prior to that, he had sex with about six different young women since becoming sexually active at age 17.

Charles and Shannon trade off the responsibility of fertility control every other month. Charles uses condoms and Shannon uses a diaphragm. Charles insisted on this arrangement. He explained it this way:

I don't understand what the big deal is. My father taught me that a man needs to be responsible for his behavior. Dad always believed that if you were old enough to have sex, you were old enough to be responsible for preventing pregnancy.

The first time Shannon and I had sex, I pulled out a condom. It was really funny. We'd been talking about starting to have sex for a while. We dated a couple of times and really liked each other. I was over at her apartment, and her roommate was away for the weekend.

We were making out and things got pretty involved when she got up to excuse herself. I asked her what was wrong and she said. "Nothing. I'm just going to put my diaphragm in."

I told her that she didn't have to if she didn't want to because I had a condom in my pocket. She kind of stared at me for a while, and I asked her what was wrong.

"Nothing, nothing at all," she said. "I guess I didn't believe you really would use a condom like you said you would."

She said it was a turn-on that I cared enough about her to actually think about bringing a condom. We decided after that night that we'd take turns being responsible for birth control from that point on. I really like the fact that we share the responsibility, but I'd have no problem if we didn't and we relied on condoms. As I said before, I always felt that a real man takes responsibility for his actions.

The actual-use effectiveness of sexual activities that do not involve vaginal penetration has not been established. Their effectiveness lies in their theoretical attributes. If vaginal penetration doesn't occur, no mechanism is available for live sperm to reach a mature ovum. Theoretical effectiveness, therefore, should approach 100%.

Unprotected anal intercourse is not included in this group because, although it doesn't involve vaginal penetration, the close proximity of the anus could allow migration of fluids across the perineum and into the vagina. Ejaculating near the vagina is discouraged for this reason.

Celibacy/Abstinence

The first category of nonpenetrative methods is celibacy and abstinence. As mentioned in Chapter 5, many people assume that celibacy and abstinence mean total avoidance of all forms of sexual release. This is not true. Celibacy and abstinence refer to avoidance of sexual intercourse. A person can be celibate or abstain from sexual intercourse but still masturbate or use other forms of nonpenetrative behaviors to release sexual tension.[3]

PERSPECTIVES

Mechanisms of Action

Although birth control methods can be grouped in a variety of ways, we've chosen the following seven categories according to their mechanisms of action.

1. *Provide nonpenetrative sexual pleasure.* This group of methods, sometimes called *outercourse*, provides options for the satisfaction of sexual desire and orgasm that do not involve the penis penetrating the vagina. Methods in this category include kissing, hugging/rubbing, massage, masturbation, use of sex toys, and oral-genital sexual contact.

2. *Prevent sperm from meeting egg.* These methods work either by withdrawing the penis prior to ejaculation or by predicting ovulation and avoiding unprotected intercourse during fertile times.

3. *Provide barrier between sperm and egg.* This group of methods is characterized by putting a mechanical or chemical device between the sperm and the egg (hence the term "barrier"). In either case, these methods prevent the sperm and egg from uniting in the fertilization process. Methods in this group include male condom, female condom,

diaphragm, contraceptive sponge, cervical cap, and spermicides.

4. *Prevent release of egg.* Ovulation is suppressed by altering the hormonal balance in the body. This prevents the pituitary gland from stimulating the release of hormones necessary to trigger the release of an egg from the ovary. Methods in this group include oral contraceptives and Norplant.

5. *Surgically block passage of sperm or egg.* Methods in this category work by sealing off the main egg and sperm transport routes (fallopian tubes and vas deferens, respectively). Female and male sterilization comprise this group.

6. *Prevent implantation.* Methods in this group work by preventing the implantation of a fertilized egg in the uterine lining. These methods encompass the variety of intrauterine devices (IUDs).

7. *Terminate an established pregnancy.* This group consists of methods that end an established pregnancy. Methods include abortion and RU-486.

Kissing

Kissing can provide intense sensual and sexual delight. The sucking, licking and rubbing, and tongue probing associated with kissing is pleasurable while imposing no risk for pregnancy.

Hugging/Rubbing

Kissing usually is associated with hugging and rubbing. Once commonly referred to as petting, these activities can take on new meaning when visualized as a viable form of fertility control. As discussed in Chapter 5, hugging and rubbing, even with the clothes on, can be intensely pleasurable and can be carried to the point of orgasm with no risk of pregnancy. With a little imagination, these safe sex activities can be erotic and provide a satisfying outlet for sexual desire by themselves or when other fertility-control methods are unavailable.

Massage

Nongenital massage is one of the greatest sensual delights that can be shared with a partner. As mentioned in Chapter 5, massage can be a standalone sensual activity or can be part of activities culminating with orgasm.

Masturbation

As described in Chapter 5, masturbation is an excellent way to share an orgasm with a partner without worrying about conception. Masturbation can offer a break from having to worry about who is supplying the contraception.

Sex Toys

As described in Chapter 5, sex toys come in a variety of shapes and sizes. They offer a safe, low pregnancy-risk sexual option.[4]

Oral-Genital Sexual Behavior

Oral sex is different from nonpenetrative sex because it can pose disease transmission risks.

The various forms of oral-genital sexual contact (fellatio, cunnilingus, anilingus) offer a sexual option with low risk for pregnancy. Unlike abstinence and nonpenetrative sexual behavior, however, oral-genital sexual contact can pose risks of disease transmission. We touched on this in Chapter 5 and will discuss these risks in detail in Chapter 17.

Preventing Sperm from Reaching Egg (Nonsurgical)

Sperm can be prevented from reaching the ova through coitus interruptus and fertility awareness methods.

Coitus Interruptus (Withdrawal; Pulling Out)

Coitus interruptus is one of the most commonly used and least understood of all the fertility-control strategies. Coitus interruptus is a Latin term, literally meaning interrupting intercourse by withdrawing the penis prior to ejaculation.

The actual-use effectiveness of coitus interruptus is 65%–70%. Three factors seem to contribute to the relatively low actual-use effectiveness: human error (not withdrawing the penis in time), method failure (sperm present in preejaculatory fluid), and using the method during peak fertility (mid-cycle versus other times during a woman's menstrual cycle).

More than half of the couples around the world use coitus interruptus as their primary method of fertility control.[5] Such heavy reliance on what most couples in the USA would characterize as a relatively ineffective method of fertility control is a testament to the effects of poverty and ignorance. Coitus interruptus is free, readily available, and perceived by users as a "natural," "effective" method of fertility control. In a sense, this is true. Coitus interruptus is free, it is always available, and it is relatively effective (65%–70% versus 5% for "hope and a prayer"). Let's look at a few ways to increase the effectiveness of coitus interruptus.

You'll remember from Chapter 4 that orgasm in men is a two-step process. The first step, ejaculatory inevitability, begins with the man feeling the contractions initiating the expulsion of semen that occurs during the next step, emission. Many couples, especially sexually inexperienced ones, overestimate the man's ability to withdraw his penis in time if he waits for ejaculatory inevitability. Timing the removal of the penis so closely sets the

Case Study

Bill and Joan: Nonpenetrative Methods

Bill and Joan are both 20 year-old juniors who have been dating ever since they met on campus as sophomores. They have been having sex for the past 6 months and use nonpenetrative forms of sexual activity as a way to prevent unintended pregnancy.

Bill: Joan and I take turns as far as who is responsible for birth control. I use condoms, and she has a diaphragm. We also like to do other things that don't involve using birth control.

Joan: Like massage and masturbation.

Bill: Sometimes Joan will give me a long massage and then bring me off using her hand. Sometimes I like that more than having intercourse.

Joan: I feel the same way. Sometimes I'm not in the mood to have sex but I like to please Bill. I've found that he likes this and will do the same for me when he really isn't in the mood.

Bill: Joan also has this vibrator or massager we use on each other. It's a little kinky, but she uses this and her hand and the sensations are intense.

Joan: It's funny because I bought the vibrator for me before I met Bill. I found that I could have really intense orgasms masturbating with it. I never figured Bill and I would have such a good time with it. It also takes off some of the pressure to always use birth control.

stage for method failure. This is difficult for sexually inexperienced men to do. A safe way to learn about this timing is to practice it with your female partner using a back-up method. This will allow you to practice withdrawal without excessive risk of unintended pregnancy.

Another way to do coitus interruptus is to withdraw prior to any sense of ejaculatory inevitability and finish with a nonpenetrative sexual method (such as masturbation) or oral-genital sex. This offers more variety in your sexual experience and reduces the risk of unintended pregnancy. You are able to enjoy vaginal intercourse while reducing the risk of pregnancy.

As a man becomes more sexually experienced, he usually develops greater ejaculatory control. He can sense when he is getting excited and beginning to lose control and can slow down (if desired) or remove his penis in time to avoid ejaculating into his partner. Married couples in their 30s and 40s seem to have the lowest failure rates with this method.[6]

The risk of pregnancy using coitus interruptus because of the possibility of live sperm being in preejaculatory fluid seems to be less than originally believed. Studies have demonstrated that the amount of live sperm present in preejaculatory fluid varies from none,[7] to an insignificantly small number (small clumps with a few hundred live sperm).[8] Residual sperm left behind from a prior ejaculation would most likely be washed out by the force of a normal urination.[9] Consequently, the presence of live sperm from a previous ejaculation (unless it was during the same interval of lovemaking) mixing with new preejaculatory fluid would be unlikely.

The presence of live sperm in pre-ejaculatory fluid is influenced by time since last ejaculation and urination.

Two factors influence the presence of live sperm in significant amounts: time since last ejaculation and urination prior to intercourse. The nearer the last ejaculation, the greater is the likelihood of live sperm being present in preejaculatory fluid. Sperm can live for 3 to 5 days. Theoretically, therefore, some still may be present if a man ejaculated within that time. Urinating, however, flushes the urethra with an acidic fluid that generally destroys sperm. If a man has urinated since his last ejaculation, he will flush out his urethra, killing any sperm that may remain.

We suggest that all men who intend to use coitus interruptus urinate before they initiate any sexual activity. Also, we recommend that during sexual arousal and plateau, the couple remove any existing pre-ejaculatory fluid (with a tissue, or orally) before intromission of the penis. This will remove some of the fluid.

The last thing to consider with coitus interruptus is your fertility status. One way to increase the effectiveness of coitus interruptus is to limit its use to less fertile times of the menstrual cycle. Avoiding intercourse during peak fertility times will increase its effectiveness.

With an actual-use effectiveness of 82%,[10] 18 in 100 women using this method in their first year will get pregnant. It offers no protection against transmission of STDs and HIV. This method usually is recommended for couples in disease-free, monogamous relationships who have greater tolerance for risk of an unintended pregnancy.

Fertility Awareness

Fertility awareness
natural family planning

Fertility awareness, also known as natural family planning and the rhythm method, is a strategy based on avoiding unprotected intercourse during peak fertility. Peak fertility can be estimated by combining knowledge about an individual woman's menstrual cycle with the latest scientific findings about egg and sperm viability. The four fertility awareness methods

---

PERSPECTIVES Enhancing Spiritual Well-being through Fertility Awareness

At its most fundamental level, fertility awareness is about making you more aware of the rhythms of life and nature that connect a female with all females. Fertility awareness teaches the cycles and rhythms of the body. Like the rhythms of nature, they are cyclic and predictable. They draw women into the web of life that connects all humans and other mammals.

Through awareness, exploration, and study, women can become more connected with the processes that govern the ability to create new life. They begin to view the body and fertility as something natural and under their control rather than something medical and governed by the health-care system.

Learning about fertility demystifies the ovarian and menstrual cycles. It puts them into the same perspective as night turning into day, movement of the tides, changing of the seasons. This sense of interconnectedness is the basis for spirituality, linking people with others and the environment, and to all humankind, past, present, and future.

Awareness of fertility also can slow women down and make them more introspective. It commands them to pay attention to their body, their life, their relationships. It connects them to the partner because they can't avoid talking, explaining how discussing sexuality connects to the body cycle. It opens up dialogue, discussion, negotiation. Fertility control is part of one's very being.

are: calendar, basal body temperature, cervical mucous, and combined. Each of these methods requires understanding of the specific woman's menstrual cycle and her fertile periods, discussed in Chapter 13.

Actual and theoretical use effectiveness data are available for individual fertility awareness methods and the combined method. Table 14.2 provides theoretical and actual-use data for the fertility awareness groups. As you can see, effectiveness increases markedly when two methods are combined. This allows cross-checking, in which, for example, body temperature changes are used to verify physical indications of ovulation.

Table 14.2	Theoretical and Actual-Use Effectiveness of Fertility Awareness Methods	
	Theoretical Effectiveness	Actual Use
Calendar	91%	80%
Mucous	97%	80%
Body basal temperature	93%	80%
Sympto-Thermal	94%	89%

Calendar Method The calendar method of fertility awareness uses the menstrual cycle history to estimate future ovulation. Once a woman can estimate the day she is likely to ovulate, she can build a **safe zone** around this day by factoring in how long an egg (1–2 days) and sperm (3–5) can live. This safe zone represents days prior to and after ovulation when the presence of live sperm could result in fertilization.

Steps involved in the calendar method are:

1. Keep a log of your menstrual cycle for 8 months. The first day of your cycle is the first day of menstrual bleeding. The last day of the cycle is the last day prior to the onset of bleeding.
2. Subtract 18 from your shortest cycle. This represents your first unsafe day.
3. Subtract 11 from your longest cycle. This represents your last unsafe day.
4. Avoid unprotected vaginal intercourse during your unsafe days.

Example:

Mary charted her menstrual cycles for nine months. Her longest cycle was 31 days. Her shortest cycle was 28 days. Thus:

28 − 18 = 10 (Day 10 is her first unsafe day).

31 − 11 = 20 (Day 20 is her last unsafe day).

During days 10–20 Mary should avoid unprotected vaginal intercourse.

Safe zone
a fertility awareness concept that factors ovulation and length of time sperm and eggs can live as a time to avoid intercourse

Cervical Mucous Method The cervical mucous method works by checking changes in cervical mucus during the menstrual cycle to predict ovulation. Mucus present in the cervix and vagina cause changes described as "wet" or "dry." In general, wet conditions represent fertile, unsafe days, and dry conditions designate infertile, safe days.

Menstruation masks mucous changes. Immediately following menstruation the cycle moves from infertile (dry) to fertile (wet), back to infertile (dry), and into menstruation. During infertile times of the cycle, cervical mucus is scanty and the vagina and vulva feel dry (some women report an absence of totally dry days). During fertile periods, cervical mucus is abundant, clear, and stringy (resembles the consistency of egg whites and will stretch if you try to pull it apart), and the vagina and vulva feel wet. Vaginal mucus should be checked a few times a day for a few months to observe how it changes. This can be done by inserting a finger and gathering mucus from the cervix and vaginal walls.

Once you are comfortable with interpreting these changes, you can:

- Check your cervical/vaginal mucus each time you urinate. Insert a finger and obtain a specimen or wipe a small amount from the vulva and examine it.

- Record the changes.

- Once you note the initial wetness, consider yourself fertile. The vagina should feel moist but not distinctly wet. Mucus should be thick, cloudy, and whitish.

- Notice, a few days later, that your vagina and vulva feel distinctly wet. The mucus becomes more profuse and is stringy and slippery. See if you can stretch a specimen between your thumb and forefinger. If you can do this, you are fertile.

- Continue checking your mucus. About 4 days after your wettest day, the mucus decreases and is no longer detectable. You should return to a drier state, indicating that ovulation has occurred. It is now safe to resume unprotected intercourse.

As a caution, production of mucus and vaginal/vulval wetness can be altered by antihistamines and other medications, douching, vaginal infection, contraceptive foam, jelly, and lubricants. For maximum effectiveness, this method should be combined with the calendar method to cross-validate the conclusion. For instance, if your calendar indicates that you are approaching mid-cycle and you don't feel the characteristic wetness, something may have altered your production of mucus. When in doubt, use a back-up method.

Basal Body Temperature To practice BBT, you will need a basal-body thermometer. This method relies on recognizing the slight, but measurable, change in **basal body temperature** associated with ovulation.[11]

The procedure is as follows:

- Each morning, immediately upon rising, take your temperature using the basal body thermometer. Do not eat, shower, smoke, or do anything else before taking your temperature. Do this every day for 3 months.

- Record your temperature on a special grid, as illustrated in Figure 14.1.

- After 3 months, note the changes in your cycle. Normally, between 12 to 24 hours prior to ovulation, a woman's basal body temperature will drop (the decrease varies from none to about .3 of 1 degree).

- Note the subsequent rise in temperature, indicating that ovulation has occurred. The pre-ovulatory drop in temperature is followed by a rise in

Basal body temperature (BBT) lowest body temperature of a healthy person during waking hours

temperature .4–.8 degrees F above her readings for about 6 days preceding the rise.

☾ Assume that unprotected intercourse is safe after 3 days of sustained temperature rise.

Because this method does not predict ovulation (it notes when ovulation occurs), sexual activity prior to temperature changes may result in unintended pregnancy. Therefore, this method is best used in combination with either the calendar or the cervical mucous method, which help predict ovulation. The temperature charts should match the calendar charting of safe and unsafe days and the characteristics of wet and dry mucus.

☀ **Sympto-Thermal Method** The sympto-thermal method designates the combination of basal body temperature and mucous methods. It also incorporates some signs indicating that ovulation is imminent or has occurred.

Providing Barrier Between Sperm and Egg

Barrier methods are among the oldest and most well-known of all methods used to control fertility. They are so named because they work by literally placing a barrier (mechanical, chemical, or a combination) between the sperm and the egg. Although these methods share the same mechanism of action, they differ in terms of how they are applied or inserted.

The mechanical devices use latex and polyurethane barriers to cover the penis (male condom), line the vagina (female condom), or protect the cervix

Barrier methods
nonsurgical contraceptive measures that prevent the sperm and egg from uniting

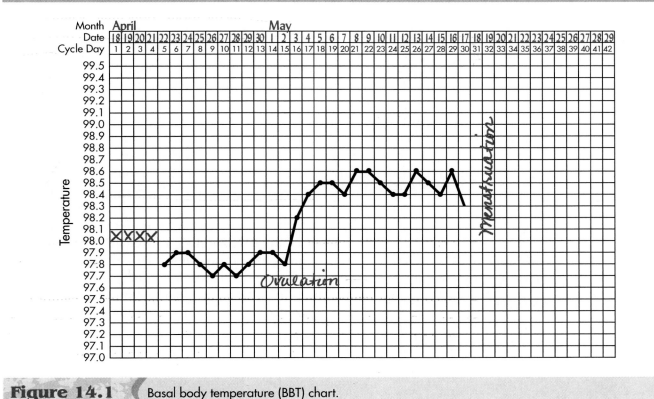

Figure 14.1 ❨ Basal body temperature (BBT) chart.

(diaphragm, cervical cap). The chemical devices provide either a stand-alone spermicidal barrier that covers the cervix (foam, suppositories, film) or are used in combination with a mechanical device (gel/diaphragm or cap, spermicide impregnated in sponge, spermicidal lubricant for condoms.

Male Condom

The male condom is one of the oldest known fertility devices. Two types of condoms are currently available in the USA: latex and natural lamb membrane. Each type is manufactured under stringent quality control, regularly inspected for leaks and other damage. For a batch of condoms to be legally sold, only four in 1,000 defects are allowed. If more than one defective condom is found, the entire batch is destroyed.[12]

The male condom works by covering the penis and trapping the ejaculate, thereby preventing it from being deposited in the vagina. It offers some protection against STD organisms that might be present in the ejaculate or in lesions on the penis.

Latex Condoms

Latex condoms come in a variety of shapes and colors. In the USA most condoms come in one size. Latex condoms come individually wrapped in foil or other sealed packets. They are rolled up to the size of a half-dollar or are folded.

Latex condoms can be lubricated (with either a spermicide or a non-spermicidal lubricant) or nonlubricated. Most nonlubricated latex condoms are dusted with powder or corn starch to facilitate putting them on an erect penis. Latex condoms come in a variety of shapes. The traditional shape is a long, uniform sheath, with a rounded end. Latex condoms also can be scented or unscented. The most recent addition to latex condom accoutrements is flavoring.

A variation of this shape comes with a reservoir tip. It also is a uniformly shaped sheath but has a small nipple that protrudes about 3/4 inch at the sealed end, to catch the ejaculate.

Form-fitting condoms generally mimic the shape of the penis. They are wider at the opening and taper to their narrowest dimension close to the end, where they flare out again in the shape of the glans of the penis. They tend to fit more snuggly than traditionally shaped condoms.

The theoretical effectiveness of condoms is 97%. Stringent manufacturing standards ensure uniformly high quality. Actual-use effectiveness is 88%. The disparity between actual use and theoretical effectiveness is attributed mostly to human error regarding storage and application. Figure 14.2 describes the steps involved in using a male condom properly.

All condoms offer the same amount of protection against unintended pregnancy, although they do not offer the same amount of protection against STDs (including HIV).

The proper latex condom combines personal taste and need. All condoms offer the same amount of protection against unintended pregnancy, although they do not offer the same amount of protection against STD (including HIV) transmission. If disease prevention is a concern, a latex condom with spermicidal lubrication offers the best protection. A person at low risk (see

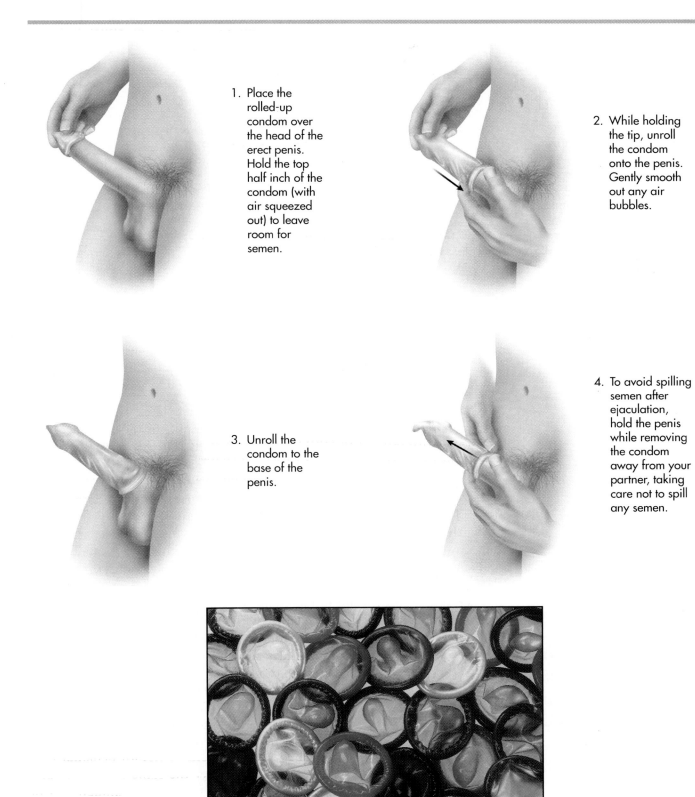

1. Place the rolled-up condom over the head of the erect penis. Hold the top half inch of the condom (with air squeezed out) to leave room for semen.

2. While holding the tip, unroll the condom onto the penis. Gently smooth out any air bubbles.

3. Unroll the condom to the base of the penis.

4. To avoid spilling semen after ejaculation, hold the penis while removing the condom away from your partner, taking care not to spill any semen.

Condoms come in different colors and shapes.

Figure 14.2   How to use a condom.

Health Hint

Choosing a Condom

Other than effectiveness and disease protection, condom selection is a matter of personal preference. Do you prefer a tighter or a looser fit? Natural lamb condoms tend to be slippery and allow more movement of the penis within the condom. Form-fitting latex condoms provide the opposite feel and allow little movement within the condom.

Do you prefer a scented condom? Do you (and your partner) like exotic, flavored, or colored condoms?

Do you like lubricated condoms or a dry, powdered feel?

Whatever your preference, keep in mind the purpose of using a condom and discuss the risks. Then try several types until you find the one(s) you like. Use them correctly and consistently every time you have intercourse.

Chapter 15 for evaluating STD risk) may choose either a nonspermicidally lubricated condom or a natural lamb membrane condom.[13]

Some men and women are allergic to latex and itch, become dry, burn, and develop a rash when exposed to it. These people may not be able to use latex condoms (or diaphragms). They are good candidates for natural membrane condoms or the female condom.

Natural Lamb Membrane Condoms Unlike their latex cousins, natural lamb membrane condoms are not uniformly manufactured from scratch. They are made from the intestines of commercially slaughtered lambs. They are shipped to the condom manufacturer, where they are cleaned and inspected prior to being cut and sealed at one end. Even though each condom is slightly different from the next, they all must pass safety inspections and are held to the same standards as latex condoms.

Natural membrane condoms tend to fit more loosely than latex condoms. Some secure themselves to the penis with the help of a small elastic band sewn into the base. Others are snugger and grip the penis much like a latex condom. Natural lamb condoms are wet. They are sealed in a foil or other pouch with more liquid than latex condoms to keep them from deteriorating. They are available either with or without spermicides.

Natural membrane condoms are not effective barriers against STDs.

Natural lamb condoms offer an entirely different feel than their latex cousins. They simulate human tissue as closely as is possible. The combination of the material (lamb membrane), its wetness, and the loose fit makes natural lamb condoms feel almost like the lining of the vagina, mouth, or rectum.

As a cautionary note, studies have shown that the surface of natural skin condoms contains small pores that permit the passage of viruses including the hepatitis B virus, herpes simplex virus, and HIV.[14] Sperm, however, are not able to penetrate these pores because sperm are much larger than viruses.

Female Condom

The female condom is a loose-fitting polyurethane pouch that is inserted into the vagina, covering its walls and protruding over the vulva.

The female condom works by containing a man's semen after he ejaculates into his partner's vagina. It also offers protection against STD germs that might be in the man's semen or emanating from penile lesions.

Female condoms are made from a polyurethane material that is similar to latex but is less penetrable. The female condom is also lubricated with a spermicide to enhance its fertility-control effectiveness. Unlike the male condom, it does not come in different shapes, sizes, colors, or flavors. Female condoms are uniform in size and have a ring at both ends. The rings help with insertion and ensure a proper fit. The ring at the closed end loops around the cervix, anchoring it in place in a way that is similar to a diaphragm (discussed next), although the female condom does not require a prescription. The female condom is inserted like a diaphragm. You first fold the ring in half, then insert it similar to the way a tampon is inserted and feel the inner ring notch against the cervix (see Figure 14.3).

A major advantage of the female condom is that it provides women a reliable source of nonprescription protection against both pregnancy and

Health Hint

Eroticizing Condom Use

Condoms have been making a steady resurgence as a contraceptive method, primarily because they reduce pregnancies. Many couples, however, still find condom use unacceptable, or not as desirable as making love without one. The following tips on eroticizing condom use might change your thinking about them.

1. It's all in your head (the one on your shoulders).
   — Start to examine your thoughts about condoms.
   — Don't buy into the myth that you can't have great sex if you use a condom.

2. Be prepared.
   — Keep a supply of condoms handy.
   — Distribute packets in the bedroom chest, living room end-table, downstairs and upstairs bathrooms, and other places where you might have intercourse.

3. Practice condom use by yourself.
   — Men: Masturbate using a condom (this will help you get used to the feel); practice putting one on under a variety of conditions (in the dark, with lights, one-handed, etc.)
   — Women: Practice putting a condom on a simulated penis (such as a vibrator); practice putting one on with your mouth.

4. Try several styles/brands.
   — Find a brand and style that feels right for you.

5. Use extra lubrication.
   — Smear some water-soluble lubricating jelly (*not* petroleum-based products) on the head of your penis before putting on the condom.
   — Smear extra jelly on the outside before penetration.

6. Make condom use (and penetration) just one part of lovemaking.
   — Read Chapter 8 about viewing lovemaking as a gourmet meal (you can enjoy a lot of erotic delights before even putting on the condom).

7. Don't rush to remove the condom.
   — Enjoy the afterglow of orgasm. After a while, hold the condom firmly against the base of your penis and pull out.

8. Take turns with birth control.
   — Trade off responsibility every month (condoms this month, spermicides or oral sex the next month, and so on), and you might find using a condom less objectionable.

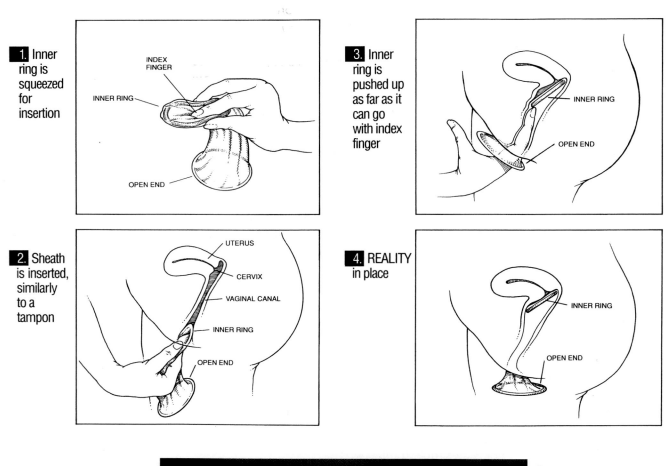

1. Inner ring is squeezed for insertion

INDEX FINGER
INNER RING
OPEN END

2. Sheath is inserted, similarly to a tampon

UTERUS
CERVIX
VAGINAL CANAL
INNER RING
OPEN END

3. Inner ring is pushed up as far as it can go with index finger

INNER RING
OPEN END

4. REALITY in place

INNER RING
OPEN END

Source: The Female Health Company, Chicago, IL. Reprinted with permission.

Figure 14.3   Inserting a female condom.

STDs. A woman does not have to rely on her partner for this protection; she can control the method. A disadvantage of the female condom is that it costs about three times more than a male condom. Like the male condom, it can be used only once.

The theoretical effectiveness of female condoms is 95%; Actual-use effectiveness is 79%.[15] It is considered at least as effective as the male condom in preventing transmission of STDs, including HIV.

Diaphragm

The diaphragm is a spring-loaded rubber or plastic dome that is inserted into the vagina and is anchored between the wall of the vagina and the cervix (see Figure 14.4). It is nonlubricated, so before insertion, spermicidal jelly must be placed around the rim and on the inside of the dome for it to work properly. It is not designed to form an impenetrable barrier against the cervix. It works by covering the cervix and thereby blocking access of most sperm to the egg. Any sperm that are able to get around the edge of the diaphragm are immobilized by the spermicide contained in the dome.

A diaphragm must be fitted by an experienced health-care professional. This person can determine the proper size to fit into your vagina so the diaphragm will rest comfortably between the cervix and the top portion of the vagina. Diaphragms should be refitted if you gain or lose more than 10 pounds, have an abortion, or have a full-term pregnancy.[16]

The theoretical effectiveness of diaphragms is 97%. Actual-use effectiveness is 82% — slightly lower than the male condom. As with condoms, the drop-off in effectiveness is primarily a result of human error associated with incorrect and inconsistent use. Like condoms, diaphragms are manufactured under strict quality assurance controls.

The steps in inserting a diaphragm are as follows.

1. Insert the diaphragm up to 2 hours before intercourse.
2. First smear spermicidal jelly (see later discussion for more detail) around the rim, and put about 1 tablespoon inside the dome.
3. Stand with one leg raised, supported on a chair or similar object.
4. Bend the diaphragm in half by moving it with the spring action.
5. Insert it as far into the vagina as possible.
6. Push it the remaining distance with your finger until you feel the rim notch behind your cervix.
7. Once you have finished having sex, leave it in place at least 6 hours (but no more than 24 hours).
8. If you continue to have sex, for each ejaculation insert an additional applicator of contraceptive foam or jelly. (Do not remove the diaphragm if you decide to have more than one act of intercourse.)
9. After 6 hours, remove the diaphragm by pulling it out with a finger.
10. Wash it off with clean, soapy water.
11. Dry it, dust it with corn starch, and put it into its case.
12. If you are uncomfortable touching yourself or want to get your partner involved, have your lover remove (or insert) the diaphragm.

Inserting the diaphragm:

1 Fold the diaphragm in half by pressing the middle of the opposite sides together between the thumb and fingers of one hand. Hold diaphragm with the dome down to keep cream or jelly in.

2 Hold the lips of your vagina open with your other hand. Gently slide folded diaphragm into your vagina, placing your index finger on the rim to guide it.

Aim toward the small of the back, as if inserting a tampon. You may feel the rim pass over the cervix.

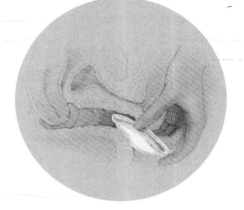

3 Use the index finger to push the front rim up behind the pubic bone.

To check if the diaphragm is in place:

A. Insert your index finger into your vagina and tough the dome. You should feel the cervix underneath and you may also feel folds in the surface of the dome.

B. Move your index finger to the front rim of the diaphragm and make sure it is firmly in place behind the pubic bone and the posterior rim is behind the cervix.

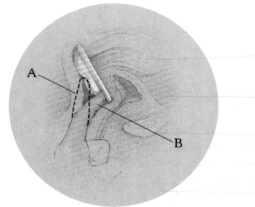

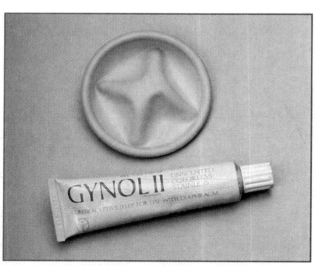

A diaphragm is always used with contraceptive jelly.

Figure 14.4   The diaphragm and how to insert it.

Cervical Cap

The cervical cap is a small, thimble-shaped plastic or rubber cap that fits snugly against the cervix through suction. It must be fitted by a health-care professional. It works in a fashion similar to the diaphragm. It blocks the passage of sperm and utilizes spermicidal jelly as a back-up to immobilize sperm that may enter around its rim.

The cervical cap differs from the diaphragm in these ways:

1. The cervical cap anchors to the cervix through suction rather than by pressing against the walls of the vagina and the cervix the way the diaphragm does.
2. The cap is much smaller and less conspicuous than the diaphragm.
3. The cap requires less spermicide (because of its smaller size).
4. The cap does not require additional spermicide with additional episodes of intercourse.

Theoretical and actual-use effectiveness data for the cervical cap are similar to that of the diaphragm. Actual-use effectiveness drops off to 82%, most of the decline being associated with user error. Effectiveness of the cervical cap is based on the cap being used in conjunction with spermicidal gel. The theoretical-use effectiveness is 95%.

To use the cervical cap:

1. Insert the cervical cap several hours before intercourse. Once inserted, leave it in place for at least 6 hours — as long as 24 hours if you wish.
2. Fill the cap with spermicidal jelly.
3. Using the thumb and forefinger, squeeze the cap and push it into the vagina all the way to the cervix.
4. Once it reaches the cervix, release it with a small twist, notching it in place.

The cervical cap must be fitted properly to be sure it will stay in place during intercourse.

Vaginal Contraceptive Sponge

The vaginal sponge is a soft, white, polyurethane sponge impregnated with spermicide. It works the same way as the diaphragm and cervical cap: It creates a double barrier (absorbent polyurethane sponge and spermicide) that blocks and absorbs sperm while chemically deactivating them.

Unlike the diaphragm and cervical cap, the sponge can be inserted up to 6 hours before intercourse and can be left in place for 24 hours. Once in place, no subsequent applications of spermicide are needed with each additional ejaculation. These features allow greater flexibility in planning a session of sexual activity without the need for using additional spermicides.

A major advantage of the sponge is that it is a nonprescription device. Sponges typically cost between one and two dollars each. Because one sponge can protect a woman for several episodes of intercourse in a 24-hour-period, this puts them in the price range of the average male condom. Like the diaphragm and the cervical cap, the vaginal contraceptive sponge provides a protective barrier against the cervix. Studies have shown that these female barrier methods also provide limited protection against most STDs.[17]

The vaginal contraceptive sponge is similar in effectiveness to the diaphragm and the cervical cap. Its theoretical effectiveness is 96%, and actual-use effectiveness is 84%.

PERSPECTIVES

Update on the Sponge

In March, 1994, Whitehall-Robbins Healthcare in Hammontown, New Jersey, stopped manufacturing the Today Sponge. At that time, Whitehall-Robbins was the only company producing contraceptive sponges. (The company also manufactured nasal sprays, ointments, and suppositories at the Hammontown facility.)

The company stopped production of the sponge after being cited by the FDA for unacceptable manufacturing standards. FDA inspectors cited the facility for failing to validate its microbiological test methods (thereby raising questions of reliability) and problems related to equipment sanitization. At no point did the FDA cite any problems associated with the sponge itself. The agency did not object to continued production as long as the facility would be brought up to acceptable manufacturing standards.

The company weighed the costs associated with bringing the facility into FDA compliance with the lost revenue anticipated from removing the sponge from the market while it upgraded the facility. Whitehall-Robbins announced that it would discontinue making

the sponge rather than lose the revenue (and contraceptive market share) associated with down time in the plant.

Whitehall-Robbins Healthcare since has resolved the problems in its Hammontown facility and resumed production of the Today Sponge. National distribution of the sponge resumed at the end of 1998.

A new competitor to the Today Sponge — the Proctectaid Contraceptive Sponge — was developed in Canada in 1996, by Axcan Limited, a division of Axcan Pharmaceuticals. It is similar to the Today Sponge in size, shape, use, and instructions. Its manufacturers claim that it offers a major advantage over the Today Sponge in that it has three active spermicidal ingredients: Nonoxynol-9, Benzalkonium Chloride, and Sodium Cholate.

The Proctectaid Sponge has the potential to offer a high degree of protection against STDs because two of its ingredients (Nonoxynol-9 and Benzalkonium Chloride) have been shown (in the laboratory) to have strong virucidal, fungicidal, and bactericidal actions.

To use the contraceptive sponge:

1. Moisten the sponge with 1 to 2 tablespoons of water.
2. Insert it into the vagina up to 6 hours prior to intercourse. Its smaller size makes insertion easier than the diaphragm.
3. Leave the sponge in place for at least 6 hours after the last ejaculation. (Once in place, a woman can have multiple episodes of intercourse without the need for additional spermicides.)
4. Remove the sponge by slipping a finger through the sewn-in-loop and pulling out of the vagina.
5. Dispose with regular trash. (Do not flush down toilet.)

Chemical Spermicides

A wide variety of chemical spermicides are available as stand-alone fertility control methods or to be used in conjunction with mechanical barriers as previously discussed. They all work by immobilizing and killing sperm though they vary in form and method of application. They are available as nonprescription fertility control devices at most drug stores. Laboratory studies have shown that nonoxynol 9 is the leading spermicide effective in killing the organisms that cause syphilis, gonorrhea, genital herpes, HIV/AIDS, and other STDs.[18]

The best known spermicides are foams, gels, and creams. These work by creating a chemical barrier suspended in either a shaving-cream-like foam, clear gel, or smooth cream. All three are inserted into the vagina, near the cervix, using a cylindrical applicator (see Figure 14.5) They create an immediate, effective chemical barrier against sperm.

These spermicides may be inserted no more than 30 minutes prior to intercourse. Instructions for using foams, gels, and creams are as follows.

1. Fill the applicator with the product.
2. While lying down, insert the applicator deep into the vagina, near the cervix.
3. Push the plunger until the contents are completely released against the cervix.
4. If intercourse proceeds longer than 30 minutes, stop and insert another applicator full of spermicide.
5. Insert a new application for each episode of intercourse.

Spermicidal film works the same way that foam, gel, and cream do. It is different, however, because it is not immediately effective. It takes about 15 minutes to transform from its original shape into an effervescent liquid once inserted into the vagina. Vaginal film comes packaged as a flat, 2"×2" sheet resembling a piece of camera lens tissue paper (see Figure 14.6).

These are the instructions for using film:[19]

1. Fold the film into a tentlike shape over your finger. Do not insert more than 30 minutes prior to intercourse.
2. Push all the way into the vagina.
3. Release from finger.

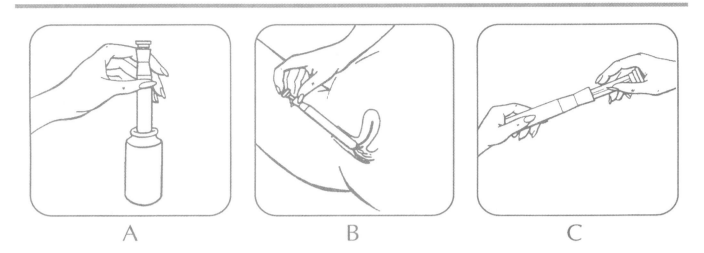

A B C

DIRECTIONS FOR USE:

1. SHAKE THE CONTAINER BEFORE EACH USE.
2. Remove the cap after the container has been shaken.
2. Place container upright on a level surface.
4. Place applicator on top of container. (See Illustration A.) Press applicator down gently to fill. Fill to the top of the clear barrel. See Note below.
5. Remove applicator from container to stop flow of foam.
6. The position for inserting the applicator into the vagina is on your back with the knees bent. Insert the applicator gently as far as it will go. Withdraw the applicator about one half (1/2) inch. Press plunger to release foam. (See illustration B.) After foam is released withdraw the applicator with plunger depressed. NOTE: Should the foam fail to come out at any time before

the container is empty, place the can under hot tap water for several minutes and then shake. Proceed to use as described above.
7. TO CLEAN THE APPLICATOR: Pull apart the applicator for easy cleaning. (See illustration C.) Wash the two parts with soap and lukewarm water... then dry. (DO NOT BOIL OR SOAK IN VERY HOT WATER.) Reassemble by gently pushing the plunger back into the barrel as far as it will go. It is now ready for reuse.
8. Wipe excess foam from container. Replace cap.
9. WHEN TO REPLACE THE CONTAINER: When the applicator fills more slowly than is normal and a sputtering sound can be heard, this means the container is almost empty. ALWAYS KEEP AN EXTRA CONTAINER ON HAND.

Source: © 1998 Apothecus Pharmaceutical Corp. Reprinted with permission.

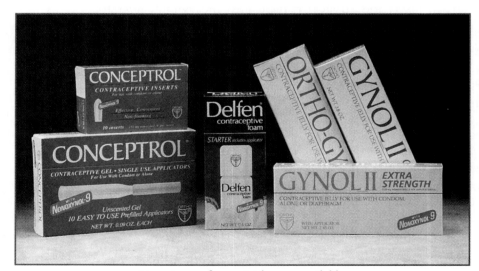

Many types of spermicides are available.

Figure 14.5 Selected spermicides and how to insert them.

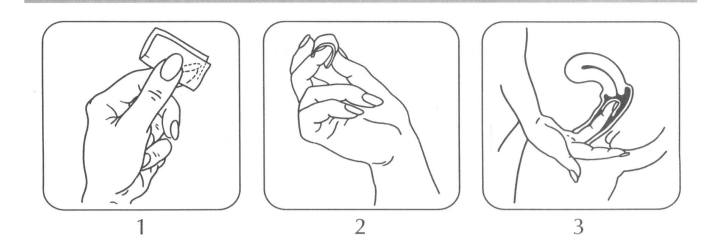

1   2   3

DIRECTIONS FOR USE:

1. Remove the square of film from the pouch and fold VCF in half.

2. With dry fingers place on second or third finger.

3. With one swift movement, place VCF high in the vagina against the cervix.

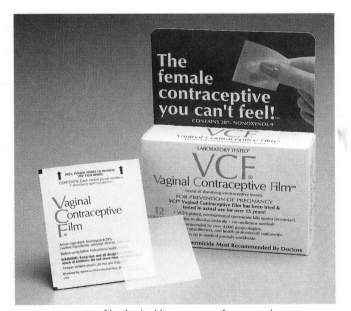

Contraceptive film looks like a piece of camera lens tissue.

Source: VCF® Vaginal Contraceptive Film ™ © 1998 Apothecus Pharmaceutical Corp. Reprinted with permission.

Figure 14.6 Contraceptive film and how to insert it.

4. Let dissolve for 15 minutes.

5. Use another application of film if intercourse lasts longer than 30 minutes or with each subsequent episode of intercourse.

Spermicidal suppositories are waxlike cylinders about the size of earplugs. They are applied in the same way as rectal suppositories, except into the vagina. Like film, the suppository requires about 15 minutes to liquefy after insertion into the vagina.

To use suppositories:

1. Put a suppository into the applicator.

2. Lying down, insert the applicator deep into the vagina near the cervix.

3. Release the applicator plunger.

4. Let dissolve for 15 minutes.

5. Use another application of suppositories if intercourse lasts longer than 30 minutes or with each subsequent episode of intercourse.

The effectiveness of vaginal spermicides is similar regardless of the specific type. Foam, gel, cream, film, and suppositories are much the same in outcome. The theoretical effectiveness of spermicides is 97%. Actual-use effectiveness is much lower at 79%. This presumably is mostly a result of incorrect and inconsistent use.

Preventing Implantation of Fertilized Egg

Implantation is prevented by various types of intrauterine devices (IUDs). IUDs are pieces of plastic that are inserted into the uterus. The two models currently available for use in the United States are T-shaped and covered with either a layer of synthetic progesterone or copper. Prior to 1990, several types of IUDs were available. Most were taken off the market after the Dalkon Shield was found to be associated with several serious side effects.[20]

PERSPECTIVES

The Dalkon Shield

Some of the original IUDs on the market were responsible for a variety of painful and deadly complications for early users. In the 1970s, the Dalkon shield was a commonly prescribed IUD. A significant number of users did not tolerate it. Because of its irregular shape and large size, the Dalkon shield triggered strong uterine contractions as the body attempted to expel it from the uterus. The contractions often resulted in the shield penetrating the uterus and creating other problems, including severe infection, that resulted in pain, hemorrhage, and sometimes death. The company that made the Dalkon lost a civil lawsuit brought by users and their families and subsequently took the product off the market and went out of business.

Many safe IUDs were discontinued because of the costs involved in litigation, even though the companies that produced these products were found innocent of any liability claims. Consumer fears and the costs of of litigation have driven most IUDs from the market. At the present time, only the Copper T and Progestesert IUDs, made by the Alza Corporation, are available in the United States.

No one is sure exactly how the IUD works, but it is generally believed to control fertility by causing an inflammatory response within the uterus that prevents implantation and by initiating an immune response that mobilizes white blood cells, which attack and immobilize sperm. The IUD also slows the movement of sperm, inhibiting their ability to reach the ovum while it is still viable. The presence of the IUD within the uterus triggers the inflammatory response, and the synthetic progesterone or copper are related to the biochemical changes within the uterus and fallopian tubes. Figure 14.7 shows an inserted IUD.

IUDs have to be inserted into the uterus by a trained health-care professional. Once inside the uterus, the IUD irritates and inflames the endometrial lining and slowly releases either copper or synthetic progesterone depending on the type of device. Once inserted, the IUD provides continuous protection with no further need for user to do anything except to check the strings daily to be sure they are in place. The user can insert one or two fingers into the vagina and feel for the string. If she feels the string, the IUD is in place. If she doesn't, she should see her health care provider immediately and consider herself fertile.

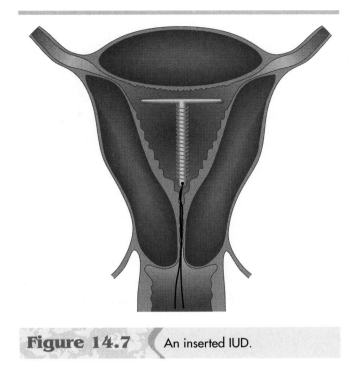

Figure 14.7 An inserted IUD.

The synthetic progesterone IUD has to be replaced annually. The copper-coated IUD can be left in place 4 years before being removed by a health care professional.

The IUD is best suited for a woman who already has had at least one child, as the uterus seems to tolerate it better than the uterus of a woman who has never experienced pregnancy or childbirth. Women who have never been pregnant have more severe cramping, as the uterus becomes accustomed to the presence of this device. Women who have never been pregnant, however, can still use the device and achieve the same high actual-use effectiveness as women who have had children.

All IUD users report heavier than normal menstrual flow. The IUD is not recommended for women with a history of pelvic inflammatory disease (PID), as they are eight times more likely than women who have never had PID to experience a second episode if they use an IUD. Also, women with a

Pelvic inflammatory disease (PID) a catch-all term used to describe infection of the uterus, fallopian tubes, or ovaries resulting in fever, malaise, pain, and other symptoms

Some potential IUD users face an ethical dilemma when considering the IUD as their method of fertility control. Because IUDs work in part by allowing fertilization but preventing implantation, many believe this is taking a life and would not be willing to use this method. What do you think?

history of STD or who have high-risk sexual lifestyles for STD are discouraged from using the IUD. If they become infected with an STD, they are 4 to 8 times more likely than low risk-women to develop PID while using the IUD. Because PID can cause infertility, women who desire to have children should be cautious about using the IUD.

Theoretical effectiveness and actual-use effectiveness of IUDs are similar. Theoretical-use effectiveness is approximately 99%. Actual-use effectiveness is 97%. Most of the failure associated with IUD use has to do with the body's attempt to reject the device through uterine contractions. Proper screening of potential users and vigilance in checking for strings can help reduce the failure rate.[21]

Women who are considering using an IUD should visit a health care provider experienced in inserting IUDs. The provider will measure the size and depth of the uterus by dilating the cervix and using special probes to measure it. This procedure, called "sounding," is necessary for the safe insertion of any IUD.

If the woman decides to use the IUD, the provider will insert the IUD using an insertion device. Once inserted, the provider pushes the IUD into place, and removes the device.

The provider locates the strings attached to the end of the IUD and trims them to a shorter length. These strings will pass through the cervix and hang into the vagina. The woman has to demonstrate that she can find these strings, as they let her know if the IUD is still in place. If the woman experiences bleeding or extreme cramping, or cannot find the strings, she must go back to the provider immediately.

Preventing Release of Ova

The methods that prevent the release of an egg are hormonal. Currently the three methods consist of oral contraceptives (birth control pills), surgically implanted time-release rods (Norplant), and Depo-Provera shots. All three work by altering the hormonal control of ovum development and release within the ovaries.

Oral Contraceptives

Oral contraceptives, are of two types: combination pills and minipills. Combination pills combine synthetic estrogen and progesterone. Minipills contain progesterone only.

Combination pills are the most commonly used oral contraceptives. The combinations and levels of hormones contained in birth control pills have been changing constantly since their introduction in the early 1960s. Pills that are currently available contain the minimum levels of hormones necessary to carry out their intended functions and are much lower than the original formulations. This has resulted in a safer pill with fewer side effects.[22] In fact, using the birth control pill is safer than carrying a pregnancy to term.

Combination Birth Control Pills Combination birth control pills work in several ways. The main action is to suppress ovulation by elevating estrogen

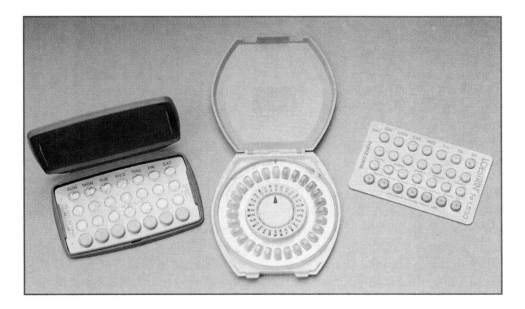

Birth control pills come in containers that are easy to use and allow you to see if you've missed any.

levels within the bloodstream. An abnormally high level of estrogen inhibits the secretion of follicle stimulating hormone (FSH), which is necessary for the release of an mature ovum.

Normally, levels of estrogen, FSH, and leutinizing hormone (LH) are low during the initial phases of the menstrual cycle. The hypothalamus senses this and triggers the pituitary gland to secrete estrogen, FSH, and LH just prior to midcycle. If there is no surge of these substances, there is no release of a mature ovum. Birth control pills create an artificially high level of estrogen, which floods the hypothalamus, keeping it from releasing more into the bloodstream, and thereby preventing ovulation.

Birth control pills prevent the estrogen surge necessary to trigger ovulation.

Progestin, the artificial progesterone in combination pills, provides additional protection by keeping the cervical mucus thick. This makes it harder for sperm to penetrate the cervix. In addition, progestin alters the composition of the endometrium, reducing the likelihood of implantation if the effects of estrogen fail and fertilization occurs.

Oral contraceptives are highly effective in controlling fertility. The theoretical effectiveness is >99%. Actual-use effectiveness is 97%. The drop-off associated with human error in failing to take pills consistently and correctly.

Birth control pills come packaged in either 21- or 28-pill containers. In the 28-pill packages, the last seven pills are placebos designed to help keep the woman on schedule and not to produce any contraceptive effect. With either prescription the woman begins taking the pills on the fifth day of the menstrual cycle, or on the first Sunday following the beginning of her period. If you remember from Chapter 3, the first day of bleeding is considered the first day of the cycle.

The woman takes a pill each day until she has consumed them all. With the 21-pill package, she will not take any pills for the last 7 days of the cycle and will begin the new package of pills on the fifth day of bleeding. With the 28-pill package, she takes one pill every day. When she runs out after the 28th day, she begins her new package of pills.

All women taking birth control pills are regulated automatically to a 28-day menstrual cycle. The presence of constant levels of estrogen and progesterone will standardize the cycle (even if the woman has been irregular in the past). Birth control pills frequently are prescribed for women with irregular periods to regulate them as well as to provide fertility control protection.

Consistent use is crucial for maximum effectiveness. The woman should try to take the pill at the same time each day. This will help to develop the habit of taking one pill each day, keep the same amount of hormones in the blood level, and ensure consistent use. Some women prefer to take the pill each morning as part of their ritual for getting ready for school or work. Others take it at night as part of a night-time sleep ritual. The time is up to her. Taking the birth control pill should become part of the lifestyle, just like brushing the teeth. The woman doesn't even have to think about it.

If a pill is missed, the woman should take two the next day. Missing one pill will not compromise the effectiveness of the method. Missing two pills, however, does reduce the effectiveness of oral contraceptives, and a back-up fertility control method will be necessary. If she misses two pills, she should take two immediately and two the next day. After that, she should continue to take one each day until they are all gone.

Progesterone-only Minipills Progesterone-only minipills are to be taken every day. The same precautions and instructions for missed combination pills apply to the minipill. Progestin, the same artificial progesterone used in combination pills, is taken by itself. Its action is identical to the way it works in the combination pill: It keeps cervical mucus thick and alters the composition of the endometrium, reducing the likelihood of fertilization and implantation.

Side Effects and Risks Some women experience side effects when taking oral contraceptives. The most common side effects of oral contraceptives mimic those attributed to pregnancy: nausea, breast tenderness, constipation, mild swelling, and skin rashes. Other common, mild side effects include weight gain or loss, increased vaginal secretions, and increased susceptibility to vaginal infections such as monilia (yeast).

Many of these effects can be minimized or eliminated by changing the formula or brand of pill. Combination pills differ slightly by manufacturer in the amounts of estrogen and progesterone. If the combination of these hormones in your present pill is causing unacceptable side effects, the health care provider can change the prescription and the woman can try a different formulation.

The amounts of estrogen and progesterone in different brands of birth control pills vary.

The birth control pill also can interact with other medications. In some cases, oral contraceptives lessen the effectiveness of the other medications. Or other medications can lessen the effectiveness of the pill. Table 14.3 details some of these interactions.

Table 14.3 ▶ Effects of Common Medications on the Pill

Interacting Drugs	Adverse Effects (Probable Mechanism)	Comments and Recommendations
Acetaminophen (Tylenol and others)	Possible decreased pain-relieving effect (increased metabolism)	Monitor pain-relieving response
Alcohol	Possible increased effect of alcohol	Use with caution
Anticoagulants (oral)	Decreased anticoagulant effect	Use alternative contraceptive
Antidepressants (Elavil, Norpramin, Tofranil, and others)	Possible increased antidepressant effect	Monitor antidepressant concentration
Barbiturates (phenobarbital and others)	Decreased contraceptive effect	Avoid simultaneous use; use alternative contraceptive for epileptics
Benzodiazepine Tranquilizers (Ativan, Librium, Serax, Tranxene, Valium, Xanax, and others)	Possible increased or decreased tranquilizer effects including psychomotor impairment	Use with caution. Greatest impairment during menstrual pause in oral contraceptive dosage
Beta-blockers (Corgard, Inderal, Lopressor, Tenormin)	Possible increased blocker effect	Monitor cardiovascular status
Carbamazepine (Tegretol)	Possible decreased contraceptive effect	Use alternative contraceptive
Corticosteroids (cortisone)	Possible increased corticosteroid toxicity	Clinical significance not established
Griseofulvin (Fulvicin, Grifulvin V, and others)	Decreased contraceptive effect	Use alternative contraceptive
Guanethidine (Esimil, Ismelin)	Decreased guanethidine effect (mechanism not established)	Avoid simultaneous use
Hypoglycemics (Tolbutamide, Diabinese, Orinase, Tolinase)	Possible decreased hypoglycemic effect	Monitor blood glucose
Methyldopa (Aldoclor, Aldoment, and others)	Decreased antihypertensive effect	Avoid simultaneous use
Penicillin	Decreased contraceptive effect with ampicillin	Low but unpredictable incidence; use alternative contraceptive
Phenytoin (Dilantin)	Decreased contraceptive effect Possible increased phenytoin effect	Use alternative contraceptive Monitor phenytoin concentration
Primidone (Mysoline)	Decreased contraceptive effect	Use alternative contraceptive
Rifampin	Decreased contraceptive effect	Use alternative contraceptive
Tetracycline	Decreased contraceptive effect	Use alternative contraceptive
Theophylline (Bronkotabs, Marax, Primatene, Quibron Tedral, Theor-Dur, and others)	Increased theophylline effect	Monitor theophylline concentration
Troleandomycin (TAO)	Jaundice (additive)	Avoid simultaneous use
Vitamin C	Increased serum concentration and possible increased adverse effects of estrogens with 1 g or more per day of vitamin C	Decrease vitamin C to 100 mg per day

Source: *Contraceptive Technology*, 16th edition, by R. Hatcher et al. (New York: Irvington Publishers, 1993). Reprinted with permission.

Health Hint

Who Shouldn't Use the Pill

High blood pressure, migraine headaches, blood clots and stroke have been associated with the use of birth control pills by selected groups of women. These risks can be minimized through careful scrutiny of a potential user's medical history before prescribing any type of oral contraceptives.

The following women should avoid using oral contraceptives:

- Women with a history of cardiovascular disease (high blood pressure, heart attack, stroke)
- Women with a history of diabetes or heart attack in family members (particularly women) under 50 years of age.

- Women with blood clots or a history of blood clots
- Women with diabetes
- Women with cancer (breast, vagina, uterus)
- Women with diseases of the liver, kidney, gall bladder
- Women older than 35 years of age.
- Women who smoke.

For these women, using the pill would increase their risk of life-threatening cardiovascular, liver, kidney, and other diseases.

Although the risks associated with oral contraceptives are serious and have to be considered, most of them can be reduced through proper screening of the woman by a health care professional. The benefits far outweigh the risks. Further, many of the side effects are protective and reduce other disease risks. Some of the health benefits of the pill are shown in Table 14.4, in terms of hospitalizations and deaths averted.

Another way to view the risks associated with use of the pill is to put them into a broader perspective. Most of us assume many risks in the course of a day without even thinking about them. A taken-for-granted activity such as driving a car puts us at a much higher risk of dying than does using the pill or other fertility control technique. We accept the risk because it is worth assuming. The activity (driving a car, for instance) adds so much to our daily quality of life that we accept the risk it entails. We also do whatever we can to decrease the risks associated with driving. We use seat belts, obey speed limits and other traffic laws, don't drink and drive, and so on.

Emergency Contraception Pill Commonly called the "morning-after" pill, newly marketed as Previn, the emergency contraception pill is a combination pill with higher than normal levels of estrogen and progesterone. Approved by the Food and Drug Administration (FDA), it is designed to be administered under medical supervision within 72 hours after unprotected intercourse. It works by preventing the release of an ovum, or slowing the movement of the ovum, or preventing implantation.

Table 14.4	Health Benefits of the Pill		
Disease	Rate of Hospitalizations Prevented per 100,000 Pill Users (U.S)	Number of Hospitalizations Prevented (U.S.)	Number of Deaths Averted (U.S)
Benign breast disease	235	20,000	—
Ovarian retention cysts	35	3,000	—
Iron-deficiency anemia	320	27,000	—
Pelvic inflammatory disease (first episodes)			
Total episodes	600	51,000	100
Hospitalizations	156	13,300	
Ectopic pregnancy	117	9,900	10
Endometrial cancer	5	2,000	100
Ovarian cancer	4	1,700	1,000

Source: *Contraceptive Technology*, by R. Hatcher, F. Guest, and, G. Stewart et al. (New York: Irvington, 1996), p. 239. Reprinted with permission.

Hormone Implantation

Another method of fertility control using hormones is to implant them under the skin in silicone tubes. The only product available at the present time, Norplant®, consists of six silicone rods filled with synthetic progesterone, which are inserted under the skin of the upper arm. The rods, each about the size of a wooden matchstick, slowly release synthetic progesterone into the bloodstream. The contraceptive effect is similar to that of the progesterone-only minipill.

Norplant is the most effective reversible fertility control method available. Its theoretical and actual use effectiveness are identical at >99%. Immediately after Norplant is inserted into the upper arm, it begins to exert its contraceptive effects. Once in place, the woman does not have to do or remember anything for 5 years. This accounts for the identical theoretical and actual use effectiveness ratings.[23] Even though the cost may seem high, at approximately $300, Norplant lasts for 5 years. Its side effects are similar to those of the pill. Some women report weight gains in excess of those women commonly experience while on the pill. Figure 14.8 illustrates the Norplant rods and their insertion.

Depo-Provera

Like Norplant, Depo-Provera® is a progestin-only hormonal contraceptive. Its action is the same as the minipill and Norplant. A major advantage of Depo-Provera over these other methods is the way in which it is administered. Depo-Provera is given by injection every 3 months. The injections can be administered in either the arm or the buttocks. A single injection provides 3 months' worth of protection.

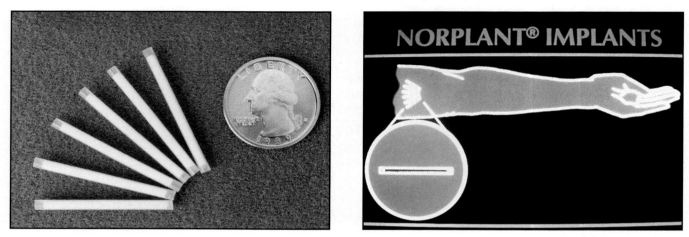

Source: Wyeth-Ayerst Laboratories.

Figure 14.8 Norplant rods and their insertion.

Depo-Provera has one of the highest actual-use effectiveness rates of all fertility control methods, at 97%. This can be attributed mostly to the nature of administering the product. There is no room for actual-use error. Once the shot is administered, the user doesn't have to remember to do anything.

Because Depo-Provera does not contain estrogen, it does not produce many of the side effects associated with combination pills. Nevertheless it does produce two noticeable side effects: weight gain and very light periods. Many women discontinue Depo-Provera because of predictable weight gain (5.4 pounds average during the first year; some women gain three times that). It also produces scanty menstrual flow and **amenorrhea** in some women.[24]

Amenorrhea
absence of menstruation at some time after a female has reached menses

Preventing Sperm from Reaching Egg (Surgical)

The surgical methods that prevent sperm from reaching the ova consist of vasectomy and tubal ligation, both **sterilization** techniques. Sterilization does not prevent sperm and ova from being released. It works by blocking the path of either the sperm or the egg as a result of surgical removal of a small section of the vas deferens (vasectomy) in the male or fallopian tubes (minilaparotomy and tubal ligation) in the female. The ends of the vas deferens and fallopian tubes are either folded back and sewn shut or cauterized.

Sterilization
techniques (vasectomy and tubal ligation) that prevent sperm from reaching ova

Sterilization should be considered a permanent procedure.

All sterilization procedures should be viewed as permanent, because once these structures have been surgically altered, there is no guarantee that they can be rejoined. Ova or sperm that are produced after sterilization cannot continue their journey, so they die, break down, and are excreted from the body as waste products.

Both male and female sterilization have theoretical and actual-use effectiveness rates of higher than 99%. Once the surgery has been performed, the user has to do nothing more to ensure safe, effective fertility control.

Of the two procedures, vasectomy is the simplest. Most vasectomies are performed as outpatient visits and last no longer than 20 or 30 minutes. Female sterilization often requires an overnight stay in the hospital, although some are performed as outpatient procedures. Female sterilization (minilaparotomy and tubal ligation) is relatively simple and usually takes under an hour to perform.

Both procedures require a presurgical conference with the husband and wife and the surgeon, to ensure that the couple understands the permanence of the procedure. Many physicians will not sterilize younger (under age 30) or single persons because of the possibility that they will desire children sometime later in life.

Vasectomy

No major preoperatory testing procedures are done for a **vasectomy**. During the initial consultation, patients are advised to bring an athletic supporter to wear home after the procedure.

The patient disrobes and lies on his back on the examination table. He is given a local anesthetic in the vas deferens and remains awake throughout the entire procedure (see Figure 14.9). The physician locates the vas deferens and makes a small incision in the scrotal sac. The physician isolates the vas deferens and cuts out a small piece. He or she then cauterizes or ties back the ends of the tubes and sutures the incision. The physician then performs the same procedure on the other vas deferens. The patient is instructed to rest for a short time, and is then free to leave. The entire outpatient stay is usually no more than an hour.

Patients normally are cleared to go back to work the next day but are advised to avoid strenuous activity. Often, patients rest the day following surgery as local soreness or swelling makes walking around uncomfortable. Patients can resume intercourse after a couple of days but are cautioned that the procedure is not considered complete until they have a negative sperm sample. If they have intercourse before then, they are advised to use a back-up fertility control method.

Because live sperm can still exist after 6 to 10 ejaculations, patients are instructed to bring a semen sample after that time to test for live sperm. If the test is negative, they can resume intercourse without a back-up method.

Side effects of a vasectomy are relatively mild. The most common are pain and tenderness. A small percentage of patients (about 5%), report swelling of the vas deferens or epididymis. This is related to the surgery and usually is easy to control with ice or heat, support, and rest, in some combination.

A small percentage of men report psychological problems after having a vasectomy. This seems to be a gender identity issue linking virility and potency to sex pleasure and performance. Counseling can

Vasectomy
a male sterilization procedure in which the vas deferens are cut and tied to block the transport of sperm

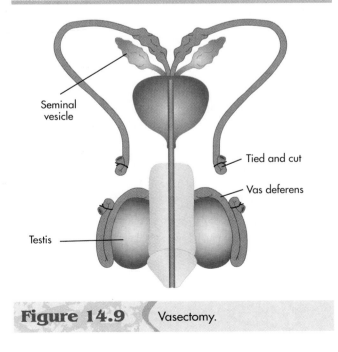

Seminal
vesicle

Tied and cut

Vas deferens

Testis

Figure 14.9 Vasectomy.

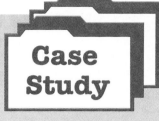

Case Study

Joe's Vasectomy

Joe is a 34-year-old married student with two children. He attended an evening class with one of the authors. This is his account.

"The best present I ever gave myself was my vasectomy. I belong to an HMO, and it cost me a dollar to have it done. I'll always feel it was the best dollar I ever spent. I guess I've used almost every method available with my wife, and my girlfriends before I got married. All these methods had one problem or another, so I promised myself that when the kids were born, I'd take responsibility and get a vasectomy.

"The week after my second son was born, I told my wife I wanted to have it done. She was glad that

we could stop using condoms and fertility awareness and supported my decision. The procedure was uneventful. I was in and out in one hour. The only glitch was that the anesthesiologist had to give me three shots of pain killer before they could make the incision.

"After about two weeks my follow-up tests were negative and we had sex for the first time without worry of my wife getting pregnant. The first time was in the shower. It was great. I can't remember the last time we made love in the shower. Getting the vasectomy was the biggest boost to our sex life in the past ten years!"

help resolve these issues. On the other hand, many men report an increase in sexual desire after being freed from the burden of birth control.

Female Sterilization

The two sterilization procedures used most often with women are minilaparotomy and tubal ligation. **Minilaparotomy,** the simpler of the two, usually can be performed under local anesthesia and as an outpatient procedure. **Tubal ligation** usually is done under general anesthesia and requires an overnight hospital stay.

Minilaparotomy The patient lies on her back on the examination table and receives an injection of anesthetic into her abdomen. Once the anesthesia has been administered and takes effect, a small incision is made in the abdomen, and a fallopian tube is pulled out. The tube is either cut and tied back or clipped and allowed to slip back into place. The incision is sutured. The same procedure is repeated with the other fallopian tube.

Tubal Ligation Once anesthesia is administered and it has taken effect, a small incision is made near the navel and a **laparoscope** is inserted to locate the fallopian tubes. A surgical instrument is threaded through the laparoscope. It is used to cut and tie back the tube (see Figure 14.10). In

Minilaparotomy
a female sterilization procedure in which the fallopian tubes are cut to block transport of the egg

Tubal ligation
a female sterilization procedure in which a surgical instrument is used to cut and tie back the fallopian tubes to block passage of the ova and thereby prevent fertilization

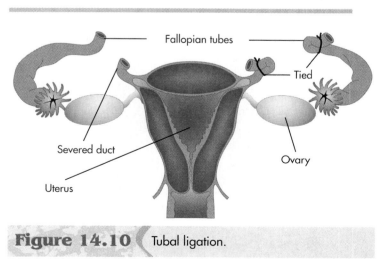

Figure 14.10 Tubal ligation.

some cases, the end of each tube is cauterized or plugged before being tied back. The same procedure is repeated with the other fallopian tube.

Side Effects Both procedures require several days to a week to heal. Mild abdominal pain or tenderness is common. Intercourse may be resumed when the sutures heal and pain subsides.

As with a vasectomy, side effects are relatively rare. A small percentage of women (1%–2%) experience surgery-related complications such as inflammation and infection.[25]

Laparoscope
a flexible surgical instrument with a cameralike attachment that can be inserted into the abdomen to view the fallopian tubes and other organs

Terminating an Established Pregnancy

Established pregnancies can be terminated through surgical and nonsurgical abortion. **Abortion** is defined as the termination, spontaneous or induced, of an established pregnancy and relates to **viability**. A viable fetus has attained a weight of at least 500 grams and/or an age of 24 weeks (gestational age starting at conception).

About one-third of all abortions are *spontaneous abortions*, or miscarriages. They result from a variety of conditions ranging from physical trauma to a breakdown of the uterine lining. *Induced abortions* account for the remaining two-thirds. Induced abortions involve removing the lining of the uterus after pregnancy has been established. This removes not only the endometrium but the placenta and embryo or fetus as well. Abortion procedures are of several types, related to the length of the pregnancy and other extenuating circumstances.

Induced abortions have been legal in the United States since 1973, when two U.S. Supreme Court decisions, *Roe v. Wade* and *Doe v. Bolton*, determined that the decision to have a first-trimester abortion need concern only a woman and her physician. States could not use legislation to deny a woman's choice of first-trimester abortions. The ruling did allow states the ability to set standards for second- and third-trimester abortions.

Abortion
termination of an established pregnancy through surgical or nonsurgical techniques

Viability
a gestational weight of the fetus of at least 500 grams and/or age of 24 weeks of age

Surgical Methods

Surgical methods include vacuum aspiration, dilation and curettage (D & C), dilation and evacuation (D & E), and hysterotomy.

Vacuum Aspiration **Vacuum aspiration** is the surgical method of choice for early abortions and those performed up to the 18th week of gestation. It can be performed as outpatient surgery under local anesthesia and does not require an overnight stay in a hospital.

A vacuum aspiration abortion usually can be performed in approximately 10 minutes. It is safe and usually causes few side effects. The cervix is dilated and a vacuum tube is inserted into the cervix. At the end of the tube is a **cannula**, which is attached to a vacuum pump (aspirator) used to suction off the contents of the wall of the uterus (endometrium, fetus/embryo, and placenta).

Dilation and Curettage (D & C) Dilation and curettage (D & C) is similar to vacuum aspiration and can be used for abortions up to 20 weeks'

Vacuum aspiration
induced abortion procedure in which uterine contents are removed by suction; used for early abortions

Cannula
a tapered, strawlike tube used in the vacuum aspiration method of abortion

Dilation and curettage (D & C)
surgical abortion procedure that removes the embryo and placenta from the uterus by scraping

Curette
a long-handled spoonlike instrument used to scrape off contents of uterus in an abortion

Dilation and evacuation (D & E)
abortion procedure in which the cervix is dilated and the fetus removed by suction

Hysterotomy
surgical procedure in which the fetus and placenta are removed surgically through an abdominal incision

gestation. D & C may require the use of general anesthesia and a hospital stay, which makes it more expensive than a vacuum aspiration. As with vacuum aspiration, the cervix is dilated and a vacuum tube is inserted into the cervix. Instead of being suctioned off, however, the contents of the uterus are scraped off using a **curette**. Figure 14.11 shows this procedure.

Dilation and Evacuation (D & E) **Dilation and evacuation** combines the two previously described techniques and can be used in abortions up to the fifth month of gestation. The cervix is dilated and most of the contents of the uterus are removed through suction. Because of the more advanced stage of fetal development, not all of the uterine contents can be removed through aspiration. A curette is inserted, and the remaining uterine contents are scraped out.

Hysterotomy **Hysterotomy** is a major surgical procedure used in second-trimester pregnancies. The procedure is similar to a cesarean section. An incision is made through the abdomen and uterus, and the fetus is removed and destroyed. This is considered major surgery and requires general anesthesia and a hospital stay of several days. It is not used very often.

Surgical abortions are very safe procedures. Surgical abortions have a lower death rate (4 per 100,000 women) than carrying a pregnancy to full term (14 deaths per 100,000) women. Since the legalization of abortion in 1973, the death rate for the procedure has dropped steadily.

In recent years the debate over a procedure unofficially called "partial-birth abortion" or "late-term abortion," a procedure known officially as dilation and extraction (D & X), has reached the highest branches of government. Having narrowly passed a congressional vote twice, President Bill Clinton vetoed the bill both times. His reasoning, and that of proponents in the hearings, was based on preservation of the life and health of the mother. The debate drew upon statements by national bodies such as the American Medical Association, as well as individual witnesses including women who had undergone the procedure.

The issue of the mother's "health" was most hotly debated. Should this include mental health? If so, how should mental health be measured? Should this procedure remain a federal issue, or should states be allowed to decide the matter in their own legislatures? Should it be proposed as a Constitutional amendment? How broadly or narrowly should the procedure be defined? Under what physical conditions is the mother's life in danger? What, if any rights, does the fetus have? Should weeks of gestation be specified in whatever definition is forthcoming?

Nonsurgical Abortions

Nonsurgical abortions can be induced by administering agents that work two ways: (a) by causing the uterus to contract and expel its contents, or (b) by initiating the breakdown of the endometrium, making it impossible to sustain the pregnancy.

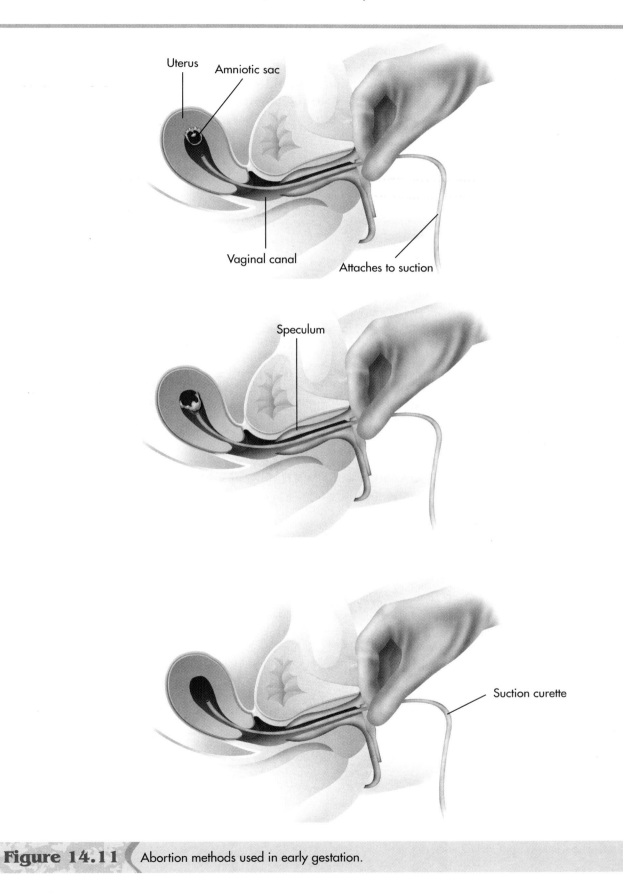

Uterus Amniotic sac

Vaginal canal

Attaches to suction

Speculum

Suction curette

Figure 14.11 Abortion methods used in early gestation.

Prostaglandins Prostaglandins, discussed in Chapter 3, are responsible for causing the uterus to contract during menstruation. They also can be used to induce an abortion. Prostaglandins can be administered either by injection into the amniotic fluid or inserted as vaginal suppositories. The prostaglandins initiate strong contractions, which dislodge the uterine lining and expel its contents.

Case Study

Mindy's Experience with Abortion

Mindy is a 29-year-old mother of one. A successful small business owner, she has been married to Bob about 5 years. This is the account of her decision to have an abortion.

I grew up in a small town and was raised to think that abortion was killing. I remember seeing those films about little babies being tossed out in the garbage after their mothers had abortions and all the posters and billboards with pictures of fully developed fetuses and the headings, "Abortion is murder." I couldn't imagine anyone ever having an abortion. But then I got pregnant and began to look at things differently.

I was away at college. I was a nineteen year-old sophomore and had been having sex with my boyfriend, Michael, for about six months. We were using my diaphragm for birth control and, to tell you the truth, I don't ever remember having any problems with it. I used it faithfully, every time we had sex.

I couldn't believe I was pregnant. I was frantic. I must have had five pregnancy tests until I finally accepted the fact. I couldn't have this baby! I cried for two days, and Michael was very supportive. Sometimes we cried together as we tried to figure out what to do. I knew in my heart that I wasn't ready to be a mother. I still had three years of school left, plus graduate school. I had no job, no time, and psychologically just couldn't handle it.

I went to a local abortion clinic. The people were great. They gave me all the information I needed, I took tests, and they assured me that because I was only three weeks pregnant, the procedure they would use was safe and relatively simple. I scheduled an appointment and went home to think about it.

It wasn't an easy decision, but I felt I had no acceptable choice. I didn't think I could handle being pregnant, having a baby, and then give it up for adoption or foster care. I didn't want to tell my parents. I wasn't sure how they'd react and didn't want to jeopardize my being away at school. They were paying for everything and I wasn't sure if they'd force me to drop out.

I guess the hardest thing for me was rationalizing what I considered the taking of a human life. I'm not a pacifist, and I do believe in capital punishment, so I guess I don't feel that human life is sacred under all conditions. This was different, though, because I wasn't talking about soldiers or prisoners. I was talking about a life that I carried within me. I always believed that life begins at conception. I vividly recall from biology how quickly embryos turn into fetuses and how the various body parts and systems grow. I really felt that I was carrying a life within me and that, regardless of the stage of my pregnancy, or "viability of life outside of the womb," aborting this 'fetus' was taking a life.

I felt sad for a few weeks after my abortion. I wished I hadn't gotten pregnant and didn't have to make the decision, but sometimes life doesn't always work out the way you plan. I got over it gradually, finished out the school year, and graduated on time two years later. Now, ten years later and the mother of a two-year-old girl, I know I never could have been the mom I am now. Although it was a tough decision, it was the right one for me.

Saline Solution Saline solution or urea acid is also used to induce non-surgical abortion. Either can be injected into the amniotic fluid. These substances are toxic to the fetus and cause fetal death. This triggers the uterus to induce contractions, slough off the uterine lining, and expel its contents.

RU-486 RU-486 (mifepristone) is an antiprogesterone drug that works by blocking the absorption of progesterone, the hormone necessary for continued viability of the endometrium. If progesterone is blocked, the uterine lining will no longer support fetal development.

RU-486 is administered by a physician up to the 49th week of gestation. After 2 days, a second drug, misoprostol (a type of prostaglandin), is administered. This induces uterine contractions, and the uterine lining (along with the products of conception) is sloughed off within 24 hours.[26]

Table 14.5 gives the relative risks of death for activities including fertility control methods. This puts contraception into perspective.

RU-486
known as "abortion pill"; mifepristone, a drug used to induce menstruation by blocking the absorption of progesterone and thereby preventing uterine lining from supporting embryo

Post-Abortion Syndrome

Post-abortion syndrome (PAS) is a term used to characterize the suggested long-term negative psychological effects of abortion. According to the National Right to Life Committee, "Post-abortion syndrome is a pattern of denial that may last for 5 to 10 years before emotional difficulties surface.[27] Women who have PAS may experience the following psychosocial effects: drug and alcohol abuse, personal relationship disorders, nightmares, sexual dysfunction, difficulty with communication, damaged self-esteem, and even suicide.

PAS activists are especially concerned about the possible negative psychological effects of RU-486. Unlike other abortion methods, which distance the woman from her aborted fetus, using RU 486 often results in the abortion occurring in a home setting in which the woman is confronted with having to dispose of fetal remains.[28]

The American Psychiatric Association does not recognize PAS, and PAS is not included in the most recent *Diagnostic and Statistical Manual (DSM)*, which characterizes recognized psychological illnesses. Critics claim that much of the available data on the purported syndrome has come from "expert witnesses" in congressional hearings and anecdotal reports from physicians, clinicians, and women who have incurred ill effects after having abortions.

Abortion follow-up includes referral for post-abortion counseling and group therapy for women who need these services to cope with their distress. Post-abortion counseling and support groups are viable options for women who have emotional distress related to their abortions.

The decision to have an abortion is not an easy one to make. It is a complex moral and ethical decision that most women (and men) who face it take seriously. The decision has both immediate and long-term consequences that the woman should take into account.

Post-abortion syndrome (PAS)
long-term negative psychological effects of abortion

Table 14.5 Relative Risks for Death from Various Activities Including Prevention of Pregnancy

Activity	Chance of Death in a Year
Risks per year for men and women of all ages who participate in:	
Motorcycling	1 in 1,000
Automobile driving	1 in 5,900
Power boating	1 in 5,900
Rock climbing	1 in 7,200
Playing football	1 in 25,000
Canoeing	1 in 100,000
Risks per year for women 15 to 44 years of age:	
Using tampons	1 in 350,000
Having sexual intercourse (PID)	1 in 50,000
Risks for women preventing pregnancy:	
Using oral contraceptives (per year)	
Nonsmoker	1 in 66,700
Age younger than 35 years	1 in 200,000
Ages 35–44	1 in 28,600
Heavy smoker (25 or more cigarettes per day)	1 in 1,700
Age younger than 35 years	1 in 5,300
Ages 35–44	1 in 700
Using IUDs (per year)	1 in 10,000,000
Using diaphragm, condom, or spermicides	None
Using fertility awareness methods	None
Undergoing sterilization:	
Laparoscopic tubal ligation	1 in 38,500
Hysterectomy	1 in 1,600
Vasectomy	1 in 1,000,000
Risk per pregnancy from continuing pregnancy	1 in 10,000
Risk from terminating pregnancy:	
Legal abortion	
Before 9 weeks	1 in 262,800
Between 9 and 12 weeks	1 in 100,100
Between 13 and 15 weeks	1 in 34,400
After 15 weeks	1 in 10,200

Source: *Contraceptive Technology*, by R. Hatcher, F. Guest, and G. Stewart, et al. (New York, Ardent Media, Inc., 1998), p. 230. Reprinted with permission.

WELLNESS SYNTHESIS

Fertility control truly embraces the six dimensions of wellness: physical, intellectual, emotional, social, spiritual, and environmental. Advances in this area are ongoing, so keeping up-to-date is vital.

Physical Well-being

Fertility control, first, is affected by one's level of physical well-being. Overall physical health influences the fertility methods available to you. For example, physical conditions such as hypertension and diabetes are contraindications for oral contraceptives. Having a history of pelvic inflammatory disease precludes using an IUD. Health status also affects *how* you use certain methods. For instance, gaining weight necessitates refitting of a diaphragm.

Consistent and proper use of fertility control methods can enhance physical well-being. Practicing fertility control carries less risk to a woman than getting pregnant and having a child. The risk of dying associated with pregnancy and childbirth is much greater than that for using fertility control.

Certain methods impart specific health-enhancing benefits. Hormonal contraception offers protective effects against a variety of diseases including ovarian cancer. Barrier contraceptives reduce the risk of cervical cancer, as well as some STDs. Fertility awareness can give women a greater understanding of vaginal health and how their bodies work.

Intellectual Well-being

Learning about controlling fertility is intellectually enriching. It provides opportunities to learn how you and your partner's bodies function. It teaches about anatomy, physiology, and biochemistry. The human body and health become less of a mystery.

Emotional Well-being

Correct and consistent fertility control can reduce fears and anxiety associated with unintended pregnancy and STDs. Sexual response is enhanced when these worries are reduced. Taking control of fertility is empowering. It promotes an internal rather than an external locus of control.

Social Well-being

Taking fertility control seriously means taking relationships seriously. Effective contraception requires open and ongoing dialogue between the partners, and the health care provider. Preventing unintended pregnancy and disease enhances relationships, and strong social relationships are a major health resource.

Spiritual Well-being

Spirituality plays a big role in how people evaluate fertility control methods and which ones they ultimately choose. Religions have various beliefs regarding fertility control.

From a broad perspective, all decisions about pregnancy relate to the underlying theme of interconnectedness. The decision to create a new life or to prevent the unintended creation of life is fundamentally a spiritual issue.

Environmental Well-being

Fertility control does not take place within a vacuum. On a national level, personal fertility control is influenced by legislation that ensures the availability of safe, tested contraceptive methods and unrestricted access to these methods for all users. In addition, governmental actions set the tone for the free and open discussion of fertility control. At the local level, users must feel safe in procuring medical care and fertility control. Medical and health care providers, clinics, drug stores, schools, and other outlets for fertility control information and services must be safe and accessible for all.

WEB RESOURCES

Alan Guttmacher Institute

http://www.agi-usa.org/home.html

Nonprofit institute protecting and expanding reproductive choices of women and men, including preventing unintended pregnancies, guaranteeing freedom to terminate unwanted pregnancies, protecting reproductive capacity and promoting wanted pregnancies, fostering women's health throughout pregnancy and childbirth, and promoting the birth of healthy infants. The site provides the latest statistics and the latest policy papers concerning the above.

Feminist Women's Health Center (FWHC)

http://www.fwhc.org/homemast.htm

A nonprofit organization that promotes and protects a woman's right to choose and receive reproductive health care, including keeping abortion safe, legal, accessible, and acceptable. Articles accessible on women's health, birth control, abortion, breast cancer, menopause, resources, and links.

Birthright International

http://www.birthright.org

Support organization to girls and women who experience distress from unplanned pregnancy. Provides alternatives to abortion, free pregnancy tests, legal, medical, financial and legal assistance, referral to social agencies, and maternity and baby clothes.

Successful Contraception

http://www.arhp.org/success/index.html

Site of Association of Reproductive Health Professionals, an interdisciplinary association composed of professionals who provide reproductive health services or education and conduct reproductive health research. This site link provides a survey for a profile of birth control options that seem best suited for you, based on your medical history and lifestyle; survey takes approximately 15 minutes to complete.

Notes

1. R. Hatcher, F. Guest, and G. Stewart et al., *Contraceptive Technology* (Atlanta: Printed Matter/Irvington Publishers).
2. P. McDonough, "The Safest Sex," *Psychology Today*, Sept./Oct. 1995, 47–49.
3. K. Norris, "Celibate Passion," *Utne Reader*, Sept. 1996, 51–53.
4. C. Davis, J. Blank, H. Y. Lin, and C. Bonillas, "Characteristics of Vibrator Use Among Women," *Journal of Sex Research*, 33:4 (1996), 313–321.
5. Hatcher et al.
6. Hatcher et al.
7. G. Ilaria, J. L. Jacobs, B. Polsky, B. Koll, P. Baron, C. MacLow, D. Armstrong, and P. N. Schlegal, "Detection of HIV-1DNA Sequences in Pre-Ejaculatory Fluid," *Lancet* 340:8833 (1992), 1469.
8. J. Prudney, M. Oneta, K. Mayer, G. Seage, and D. Andersen, "Pre-ejaculatory Fluid as a Potential Vector for the Transmission of HIV-1," *Lancet* 340:8833 (1992), 1470.
9. Hatcher et al.
10. Hatcher et al.
11. Hatcher et al., 1994.
12. "How Reliable Are Condoms?" *Consumer Reports*, May 1995, pp. 320–325.
13. E. J. Shaw and B. Rienzo, "Permeability of Latex Condoms: Do Latex Condoms Prevent HIV Transmission?" *Journal of Health Education*, 26:6 (1995), 372–376.
14. W. Cate and K. M. Stone, "Family Planning, Sexually Transmitted Diseases and Contraceptive Choice: A Literature Update — Part 1," *Family Planning Perspectives*, 24:2 (1992), 75–84.
15. Hatcher et al.
16. Hatcher et al.
17. Cate and Stone; Hatcher et al.
18. N. J. Alexander, in *Heterosexual Transmission of AIDS*, edited by N. J. Alexander, H. L. Gablenick, and J. H. Speiler (New York: Wiley-Liss, 1990; K. M. Stone, D. A. Grimes, and L. S. Magder. "Personal Protection Against STDs," *American Journal of Obstetrics and Gynecology*, 155:1 (1986), 80–188.
19. American Health Consultants, "VCF: Convenient Contraceptive, But It May Be Hard to Find," *Contraceptive Technology Update*, 13:11 (Nov. 1992), 1–2.
20. M. Klitsch, "Still Waiting for the Contraceptive Revolution," *Family Planning Perspectives*, 27:6 (1995), 246–253.
21. "On the Needless Hounding of a Safe Contraceptive," *Economist*, 336:7930 (1995), 75–77.
22. A. Glusker, "The Pill: What It's Done For Us, and To Us," *MS.*, Nov./Dec. 1995, 30–32.
23. P. D. Darney. "Hormonal Implants: Contraception for a New Century," *American Journal of Obstetrics & Gynecology*, 170:5 (1994), 1536–1543.
24. Hatcher et al.
25. H. Voherr, R. H. Messer, and D. Reid, "Complications of Tubal Sterilization: Menstrual Abnormalities and Fibrocystic Breast Disease," *American Journal of Obstetrics and Gynecology*, 145 (1983), 644–645.
26. Hatcher et al.
27. L. Levathes, "Listening to RU-486," *Health*, Jan/Feb 1995, 86–89.
28. Levathes.

Student Study Questions

1. What are the differences between birth control, contraception, and family planning?

2. What are the five mechanisms of action for fertility control methods?

3. What is an acceptable level of risk of pregnancy for a fertility control method? Why?

4. What are the risks associated with pregnancy and childbirth for the various fertility control methods?

5. What category of fertility control methods offers the best protection against STDs? What are differences in STD protection among the methods in this category?

6. How do hormonal contraception measures work?

7. What risks are associated with the pill?

8. How do a person's (or couple's) fertility control needs change over the course of a lifetime?

9. What key questions should you ask yourself when evaluating any fertility control method?

Is This The Right Method for Me?

It is important to choose a method of birth control that works well to prevent pregnancy. It is also important to choose a method you will like! Ask yourself these questions so you can judge carefully.

What type of birth control are you thinking about?_____

Have you ever used it before? _____ yes _____ no   If yes, how long did you use it? _____

_____

Circle your answer

Are you afraid of using this method?	yes	no	don't know
Would you rather not use this method?	yes	no	don't know
Will you have trouble remembering to use this method?	yes	no	don't know
Have you ever become pregnant while using this method?	yes	no	don't know
Will you have trouble using this method carefully?	yes	no	don't know
Do you have unanswered questions about this method?	yes	no	don't know
Does this method make menstrual periods longer or more painful?	yes	no	don't know
Does this method cost more than you can afford?	yes	no	don't know
Does this method ever cause serious health problems?	yes	no	don't know
Do you object to this method because of religious beliefs?	yes	no	don't know
Have you already had problems using this method?	yes	no	don't know
Is your partner opposed to this method?	yes	no	don't know
Are you using this method without your partner's knowledge?	yes	no	don't know
Will using this method embarrass you?	yes	no	don't know
Will using this method embarrass your partner?	yes	no	don't know
Will you enjoy intercourse less because of this method?	yes	no	don't know
Will this method interrupt lovemaking?	yes	no	don't know
Has a nurse or doctor ever told you *not* to use this method?	yes	no	don't know

Do you have any "don't know" answers? Ask your instructor or physician to help you with more information.
Do you have any "yes" answers? "Yes" answers mean you may not like this method. If you have several "yes" answers, chances go up that you might not like this method; you may need to think about another method.

Source: *Contraceptive Technology*, 17th edition, by Robert A. Hatcher et al. © 1998 Ardent Media, Inc., New York. Used with permission.

Sexually Transmitted Diseases (STDs)

15

Major Topics

Student Learning Objectives

After reading this chapter, students will be able to:

- Describe the four major STD trends of the past decade.
- Diagram and describe the Pyramid of Risk for STD/HIV infection.
- Explain how demographic variables are related to STD/HIV risk
- Describe how sexual orientation affects STD/HIV risk.
- Describe the characteristics of core transmitters of STD, including HIV.
- Evaluate the relationship between sexual/medical history and STD/HIV risk.
- Assess a variety of sexual lifestyles and the continuum of risk for STD that they represent.
- Evaluate the risks inherent in a variety of sexual behaviors.
- Develop a personal plan for reducing the risk for STD/HIV infection.
- Describe the major modes of STD/HIV transmission.
- Describe the major symptoms associated with STD/HIV infection.
- Describe the epidemiology of a variety of STDs.

Sexually transmitted diseases (STDs)
diseases that are spread from person to person through sexual contact

Sexually transmitted diseases (STDs) are infections that are almost always contracted through sexual contact. Although STDs theoretically can be transmitted via any form of sexual contact, vaginal and anal intercourse are much more efficient modes of transmission than is oral-genital sexual contact. Some STDs, such as HIV and hepatitis B, also are transmitted by contaminated blood through needle-sharing associated with injectable drug use.[1]

More than 12 million new cases of the 25 diseases categorized as STDs are reported each year in the United States. STDs represent 87% of the cases of the diseases reported to the Centers for Disease Control and Prevention. Five of the top ten most frequently reported diseases in the United States are STDs.[2]

Morbidity
the relative incidence of a disease

Mortality
the number of deaths during a specific time period

Incidence
the number of new cases of a disease during a specific time period

TRENDS

Beginning in the 1970s, four major trends related to sexually transmitted diseases (STDs) have been identified:

1. An overall increase in STD **morbidity** and **mortality**
2. Increasing **incidence** of STDs in adolescents
3. Increasing levels of infections in urban Blacks and Hispanics/Latinos
4. Epidemiological synergy (the effects of infection with multiple STDs).

Increased Morbidity

Epidemiologic
dealing with incidence, distribution, and control, as in STDs

Endemic
a 20% level of ongoing infection within a specific population

Gonorrhea
sexually transmitted disease caused by the bacteria *Neisseria gonorrheae*

Rates
a statistic calculated by dividing the number of cases of disease by the population at risk of infection

Epidemiologic trends over the past 20 years show an alarming increase in most STDs,[3] especially gonorrhea,[4] chlamydia,[5] syphilis,[6] and HIV/AIDS.[7] Although HIV/AIDS has received the bulk of the media attention involving STDs, these other diseases continue to increase, and some, such as chlamydia in college women, exist at **endemic** levels in some subpopulations.[8] Figure 15.1 shows the estimated incidence of various STDs.

Gonorrhea Infection

Gonorrhea is one of the most common STDs, with more than 300,000 cases reported annually.[9] It is under-reported by up to 50%.[10] Between 1975 and 1990, gonorrhea **rates** decreased by 37% nationally. Of that decline, 22% was between 1986 and 1989.[11] Those declines are credited largely to safer-sex behaviors by white gay men.[12]

While disease rates for an entire population can decrease, sub-groups can experience a rise in the number of cases.

One of the health status objectives for the nation (reducing gonorrhea rates to 225 cases per 100,000 people) is based on a projection of the continued decline in rates (see Figure 15.2). We will discuss the epidemiology of gonorrhea in greater detail later in the chapter.

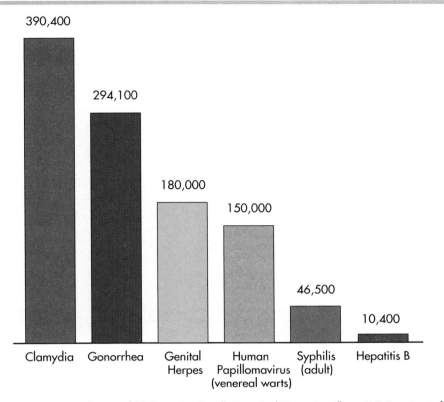

Source: Division of STD Prevention, Sexually Transmitted Disease Surveillance, U.S. Department of Health and Human Services, Public Health Service Atlanta: Centers for Disease Control and Prevention, Sept. 1998. *Morbidity and Mortality Weekly Report, 46:54 (Nov. 20, 1998)*.

Figure 15.1 ❬ Estimated incidence of some common STDs.

Chlamydia Trachomatis Infection

Chlamydia trachomatis (commonly called Chlamydia infection) is the most prevalent sexually transmitted bacterial pathogen in the United States. The estimated incidence is between 3,000,000 and 5,000,000 new cases annually (2,600,000 in women and 1,800,000 in men). Between 1987 and 1997 the chlamydia rate in the United States increased from fewer than 10 cases per 100,000 persons to close to 200 cases per 100,000.[13] Figure 15.3 shows the rapid climb in rates during that time.

Chlamydia trachomatis
most prevalent sexually transmitted bacterial pathogen, causing the STD chlamydia

Syphilis Infection

The incidence of **syphilis** declined by a dramatic 99% from the 1940s to the mid-1980s, primarily because of penicillin therapy, and the public health strategy of follow-up of sex partners. Public health officials prioritized syphilis control and insisted that all infected persons be interviewed and counseled about their disease. Their sex partners were followed up with preventive treatment for the disease.

The largest recent decline has been in gay men of all ages from 1983 to 1986, partly because of their adoption of safer-sex behaviors. From 1986 to

Syphilis
STD caused by the spirochete bacterium *Treponema pallidum*

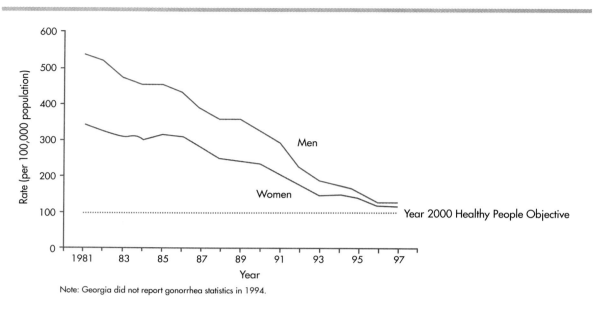

Note: Georgia did not report gonorrhea statistics in 1994.

Source: Division of STD Prevention, Sexually Transmitted Disease Surveillance, U.S. Department of Health and Human Services, Public Health Service (Atlanta: Centers for Disease Control and Prevention, Sept. 1998).

Figure 15.2   Gonorrhea rates by gender, United States, 1981–1997.

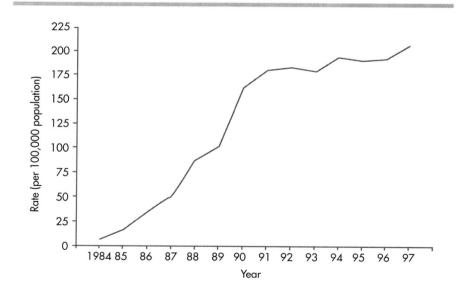

Source: Division of STD Prevention, Sexually Transmitted Disease Surveillance, U.S. Department of Health and Human Services, Public Health Service (Atlanta: Centers for Disease Control and Prevention, Sept. 1998).

Figure 15.3   Chlamydia rates, United States, 1984–1997.

1990, in an epidemic of syphilis throughout the United States, rates increased from 12 cases per 100,000 to 20 per 100,000.[14] This represented the highest level in the United States in 40 years. Figure 15.4 shows the trends by age in syphilis infection for males and females respectively.

Acquired Immunodeficiency Disease

As of June 1998, 665,357 persons had been diagnosed with **AIDS** in the United States. Of those, 60% (401,028) have died. Of the cumulative cases,

AIDS
acronym for acquired immunodeficiency syndrome, the end result of HIV

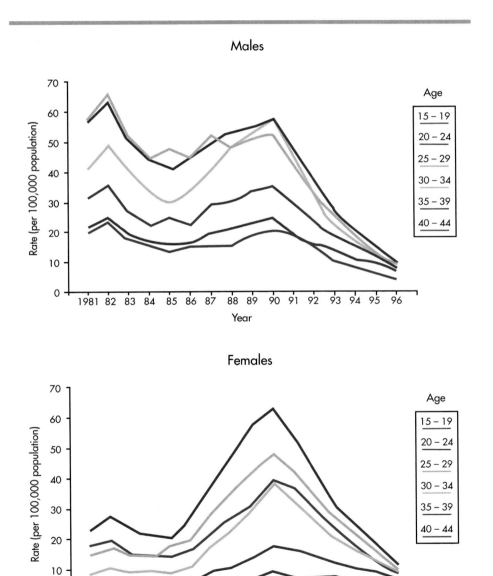

Source: Centers for Disease Control and Prevention, Atlanta, GA.

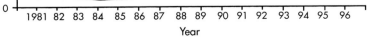

Figure 15.4 Age-specific syphilis rates among males and females 15–44 years of age, United States.

50,352 (7%) were reported during 1981–1987, 203,217 (32%) during 1988–1992, and 387,517 (61%) during 1992–1997. The new case definition, set forth in 1992, and more efficient reporting mechanisms, account for some of the surge in numbers. Since then, cases have started to decline, although AIDs remains a continuing problem of major public health significance.[15] Figure 15.5 shows the trend in AIDS cases over the years 1984–1996. Even though the overall morbidity and mortality rates are down in the United States, cases are increasing steadily in women and people of color.

Increased Infection in Adolescents

Probably the single greatest contributing factor to the increased incidence of STDs in adolescents is the change in adolescent sexual behavior. As we discussed in Chapter 5, the National Survey of Family Growth (NSFG) showed that the proportion of 15–19 year-old females initiating intercourse rose steadily in the 1970s and 1980s. By 1988, 25% of all 15-year-old and 75% of all 19-year-old girls had experienced intercourse.[16] CDC's National Youth Risk Behavior Surveillance Program in 1995 found that by 12th grade, 68% of all teenagers have had sexual intercourse.

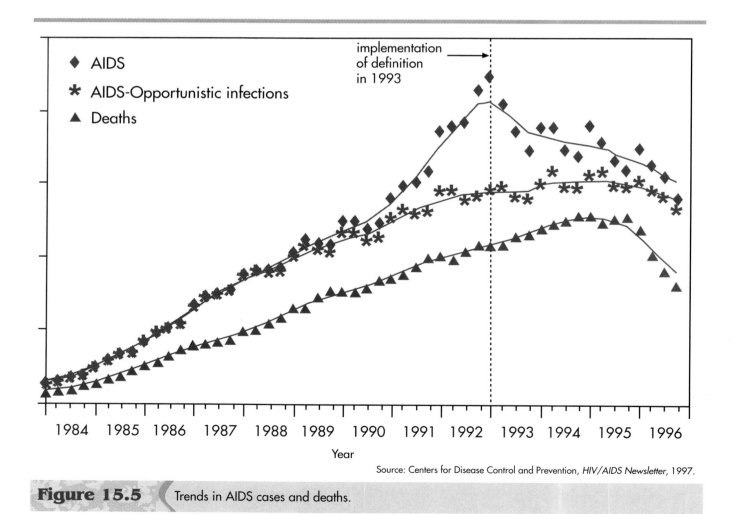

Source: Centers for Disease Control and Prevention, *HIV/AIDS Newsletter*, 1997.

Figure 15.5   Trends in AIDS cases and deaths.

Three STD-related considerations derive from these data:

1. The earlier the onset of intercourse, the longer is the interval of exposure to potentially different sex partners.

2. Individuals who initiate sexual activity earlier are more likely to have more sex partners over a lifetime (more than 25% of women initiating intercourse by age 15 had more than 10 lifetime sex partners, whereas only 6% of women initiating intercourse at age 20 or later had more than 10 sex partners).

3. The transformation zone in women (the end of the cervix, where cervical tissue meets vaginal tissue), is most exposed during adolescence, and this tissue is most susceptible to STD infection in general, and viral infection (cancer-causing) in particular.[17]

Sexually active teenagers have the highest rates of infection with almost all STDs. Trends in gonorrhea infection illustrate this the best. Teenage girls had the highest risk of becoming infected. Females in the 15–19-year-old age group were more than 20 times more likely to be infected with gonorrhea than females 30 years of age and older.[18]

Increased Risk in Blacks and Hispanics

Blacks and Hispanics have the highest rates of STD infection. Rates for almost all STDs are substantially higher for these groups than for Whites. Much of the disparity in STD rates and morbidity/mortality for all causes is attributable to class, not race. Although disease rates in general are higher for Blacks and Hispanics than Whites, racial/ethnic differences are really markers for social class and poverty.[19] Poverty, especially that which affects the urban poor, is the true risk factor. The increased problem of STDs in minority populations in inner cities may stem in part from the unequal distribution of poverty, not race or ethnicity.[20]

Epidemiological Synergy

Wasserheit coined the term **epidemiological synergy** to refer to the effects of infection with one STD on the transmission and development of complications of another.[21] Generally this works two ways;

Epidemiological synergy
the distribution of disease caused by the effects of infection with more than one condition

∿ Infection with one STD provides an entry-point where other STD pathogens can invade.

∿ Infection with one form of STD could weaken the body's immune system, making exposure to another infection more risky.

An example of the former is the synergistic effect between genital ulcer diseases such as chancroid, genital herpes, and syphilis and increased susceptibility to HIV infection. The ulcerative lesions caused by chancroid, genital herpes, and syphilis literally provide an entry-point for HIV.

Someone who has a genital ulcer and has sex with a person who is infected with HIV is more likely to become infected as a result. Genital ulcer disease may increase the risk of transmission per exposure 10 to 50 times in male-to-female transmission, and 50–300 times in female-to-male exposure.[22]

An example is infection with tuberculosis. Infection with HIV weakens the immune system and the body's ability to resist exposure to new disease-causing organisms. A person who is HIV-positive and is exposed to tuberculosis is at greater risk for acquiring the infection than a person who is not HIV-positive.[23] The coexistence of HIV with these other conditions also makes diagnosis, treatment, and follow-up much more difficult.

STD TRANSMISSION, SIGNS, AND SYMPTOMS

STDs can be grouped in several ways to study their transmission, symptoms, treatment, and prevention. Table 15.1 provides a summary of the transmission, symptoms, diagnosis, and treatment of the most common STDs.

One simple way to group STDs is by the nature of transmission. The main modes of STD transmission are:

- Direct sexual contact (sexual contact with someone's STD symptoms, such as genital ulcers) or sexual contact with someone's infected semen, vaginal lubricant, blood, and other body fluids

- Maternal transfer (mother to fetus during pregnancy or childbirth)

- Sharing contaminated needles through injectable drug use.

Minor STDs, such as crabs and scabies, can be passed through direct sexual contact with infected persons or, in rare cases, their contaminated bedding, items of clothing, and similar objects. Some STDs (such as HIV and hepatitis B) can be spread both by sexual contact and by injectable drug use.

During sexual exposure to genital ulcers or other symptoms (such as genital warts), the uninfected person is exposed to infectious organisms that are present in the **serous fluid** of the lesions. During sexual contact these pathogens are transmitted through the thrusting and grinding of sexual activity. The organisms are introduced into tiny breaks in the skin that commonly occur during sexual activity.

During sexual exposure to semen, vaginal lubricants, blood, and other body fluids, the infected partner passes the infection through unprotected vaginal or anal intercourse or oral sex. During sexual exposure to contaminated blood, STD organisms that live in the blood are passed between individuals as they exchange this body fluid. Blood is exchanged from person to person most commonly through (a) sexual contact with someone who has open lesions or ulcers that bleed during sex, (b) sexual contact that involves unlubricated anal intercourse and some vaginal intercourse.

STD microorganisms can be passed by maternal transfer two ways:

1. During pregnancy, STD microorganisms in the mother's blood pass through the placenta and enter the bloodstream of the fetus.

Serous fluid
a fluid that has the characteristics of serum

2. During labor and delivery, the newborn is exposed directly to disease-causing germs present in the birth canal.

Any type of shared injectable drug use is capable of transmitting blood-borne STDs. The transmission could be by an athlete shooting steroids and then passing the unsterilized needle to a friend to use, or it could be by a heroin addict doing the same. The risk is in the sharing, not the drug of choice.

In most cases, infestation with scabies and crabs occurs during sexual contact. A person whose genitals are infected with the lice pass on the crabs

---

Table 15.1 ⟩ Common STDs, Their Source, Symptoms, Diagnosis, and Treatment

Summary of Common Sexually Transmitted Diseases

Name	Mode of Transmission	Distinguishing Sign or Symptom	Diagnosis	Treatment
Chlamydia	bacterium	male: watery discharge from urethra; pains when urinating female: usually asymptomatic; sometimes a similar discharge; leading cause of PID*; can cause prostatitis in men	culture of discharge	antibiotics other than penicillin (cure)
Gonorrhea (clap)	bacterium	male: pus discharge from urethra, burning during urination; female: usually asymptomatic; can lead to PID*; sterility (in both)	culture of discharge	antibiotics (ceftriaxone) sodium (cure)
Genital herpes	virus	blisters in genital and rectal areas	presence of blisters and laboratory identification of virus in fluid of blister	Zovirax (acyclovir) (not a cure)
Venereal warts (HPV)	virus (HPV)	cauliflowerlike growths in genital and rectal areas;	presence of lesions	removal of lesions by laser surgery or chemicals (not a cure)
Syphilis	bacterium (spirochete)	primary: chancre secondary: rash latent: asymptomatic late: irreversible damage to central nervous system, cardiovascular system	blood test	penicillin or other antibiotic (cure)
HIV/AIDS	virus	asymptomatic at first; opportunistic infections	blood test; usually none in initial stages	AZT (now called ZDV) (not a cure)
Chancroid	bacterium (bacillus)	male: painful irregular chancre on penis; female: chancre on labia	smear/stain and microscopic identification	tetracycline
Pubic lice (crabs)	metazoan	intense itching of areas covered with pubic hair	presence of lice and nits (eggs) on pubic hair	prescription or OTC pediulocide shampoo (cure)

*PID = Pelvic inflammatory disease, a generic term describing inflammation of upper reproductive tract of females

or scabies during sexual contact with an uninfected sex partner. Lice also are able to live on clothing and bedding and, in rare cases, can be spread via these inanimate objects.

PREVENTION AND RISK REDUCTION

Personal health STD/HIV prevention programs focus largely on individual behavior as the basis for risk reduction. Many of these programs emphasize "safer sex" (using condoms consistently and correctly and verifying HIV status through testing) as the primary prevention approach. Others stress abstinence from sexual intercourse as the preferred preventive approach.[24]

Community health prevention programs emphasize public health interventions designed to stop the diseases from spreading. Examples of activities are political lobbying to establish needle-exchange programs, increased funding of STD/HIV services (for example, to allow expanded hours), free and confidential treatment, and socio-marketing to promote condom distribution and family planning services.

Pyramid of Risk for STDs/HIV

The problem with compartmentalizing STD/HIV risks is that it fails to acknowledge that personal and community risks have a synergistic effect. We propose a new way to conceptualize the relationship between community and personal risks as pyramidal in nature, consisting of various public and personal factors that build upon each other. Figure 15.6 illustrates this pyramid of risk.

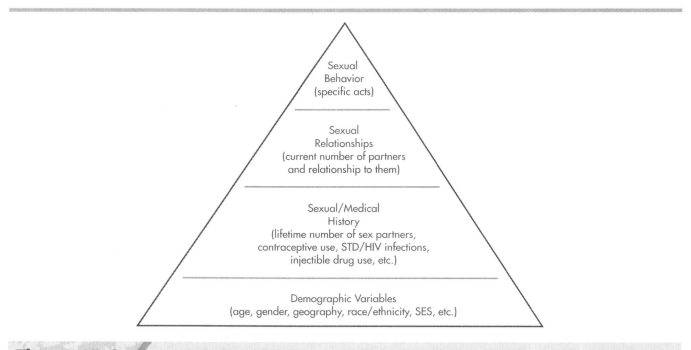

Figure 15.6 Pyramid of risk for STDs.

The foundation of the pyramid is made up of demographic variables that influence STD/HIV risk. These are generally beyond our individual control.

The next level of risk revolves around the sexual and medical history of ourself or our partner. Because these risks are part of a person's past, they also cannot be changed. They are the history that each of us brings to any sexual encounter.

The third level of risk represents a person's current **sexual lifestyle**. The last level of risk is the one most educators focus on: personal sexual behavior. Most risk-reduction pamphlets provide a laundry list of sexual behaviors that range from low risk to high risk. Although the four levels of factors influence STD/HIV risk independently, the interaction of levels can have a synergistic effect that can increase or reduce personal risk dramatically.

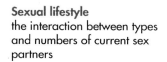

Sexual lifestyle
the interaction between types and numbers of current sex partners

Demographic Variables and the Distribution of STDs/HIV

Seven major demographic variables that contribute to STD/HIV risk are age, gender, sexual orientation, injecting drug abuse (IDA) (the clustering of injectable drug abusers in communities), geography, socioeconomic status (SES), and race/ethnicity.

Age Age is a major risk factor for infection with STDs/HIV. STDs are found most often among the adolescent segments of society. Because this age group has more STDs, the risk of acquiring an infection is greater if they have sex with persons from this age category (versus the 55+ age group, in which STD rates are much lower). The risk is associated with the likelihood that someone will interact sexually with a member of this subpopulation.

Case Study

Jim's Fear of STDs

Jim was a student in Dr. Blonna's Human Sexuality class. Jim came to see him after class about some concerns regarding STDs.

You've got to help me. I made a mistake, and I'm super-paranoid about what's going to happen to me. I was coming back to school last Friday night late, and I was cruising through Paterson [a large city adjacent to the town where the college campus is located]. I don't know what got into me, but I picked up a hitchhiker on Broadway and gave her a ride to the end of Paterson. She was really hot and offered to give me a blow job to thank me.

I said yes and she went down on me in the parking lot where she lived. I don't know how to describe how I felt afterward — part ashamed, part stupid, part afraid. I'm so worried that I got AIDS from her.

On Monday in class, you talked about demographic risks, and the whole things got me freaked. My girlfriend wanted to have sex last night, and I used a condom with her. She freaked out. She's on the pill, and we never use condoms. I broke down and had to tell her what I did. Am I going to die of AIDS?

For instance, a 15–25 year-old will more likely seek sex partners among people within this general range of ages than, say, a partner who is 45 years of age or older.

Age also is related to sexual lifestyle. Adolescents and young adults are more likely than older people to have multiple sex partners, engage in unprotected intercourse, abuse substances, and have risky partners.[25] When we are younger, we tend to take more risks in our sexual pairings, as well as our overall behavior.

The risk for STDs/HIV is different for men and women.

Sex The risk for STDs/HIV is different for men and women. Biological gender is a risk factor related to the genetic, anatomical, and physiological differences between men and women. Women face a greater risk than men for both acquiring a sexually transmitted disease and developing complications,[26] for several reasons:

- Heterosexual women are receptive sexually — vaginally, orally, and anally. This greatly increases their risks for initial infection by exposing a greater surface area of mucosal tissue.[27]

- Once infected with most STDs, heterosexual women tend to be asymptomatic more often than heterosexual men. Most heterosexual men notice initial symptoms of infection, whereas about half of women are asymptomatic.[28]

- Because of the asymptomatic nature of STDs in women, more women than men do not seek treatment during the initial stages of infection. This delayed access to treatment results in progression of the disease and a greater likelihood of developing complications. For example, about 15% of women develop complications associated with gonorrhea or chlamydia versus less than 1% of men.[29]

- Menstruation plays a role in facilitating the movement of pathogens from the lower reproductive tract (below the cervix) to the upper parts, facilitating the development of complications.

- Women face the added risk of passing on their infection to their developing fetus during pregnancy or newborn through childbirth.[30]

The likelihood of transmitting infections such as syphilis or HIV is greatly reduced if mothers attend routine trimester prenatal screening. Despite the availability of prenatal screening programs, the incidence of congenital syphilis in the United States has increased from four cases to 175 cases per 100,000 from 1983 to 1990.[31]

Sexual Orientation Risks Risks for STDs are affected by a person's sexual orientation. The risks that heterosexual women face accrue as a result of their anatomy and physiology, which facilitate exposure to disease agents. Sexual exposure results in infection without symptoms, and menstruation facilitates infection.

Gay and bisexual men have some of the risks that heterosexual women do. They are receptive sexually and tend to have asymptomatic infections. This facilitates the development and spread of disease. In addition, certain diseases, such as HIV and hepatitis B, exist in endemic levels in the gay community. These diseases are incurable and capable of causing death.[32]

Heterosexual men are at less risk than heterosexual women and gay men for a variety or reasons. First, their symptoms tend to be more obvious because these men usually are the insertive sexual partners and develop external symptoms. Early detection facilitates seeking prompt treatment and reducing complications. As an example, fewer than 1% of all heterosexual men infected with gonorrhea develop complications such as **epididymitis**.[33] Also, female-to-male transmission of STDs is more difficult because heterosexual men are not receptive sexually and vaginal fluids are less likely to transmit infection than is contaminated semen.[34]

Of the four groups, lesbian women have the lowest rates of infection. Gay women tend to have fewer sexual partners over the course of their lifetime, and they do not engage in vaginal or anal intercourse.[35]

IDA The risk for STD/HIV is becoming increasingly related to the prevalence of **IDA** (injectable drug abusers) in a community. Drug use is associated with increased STD/HIV risk in two ways.

1. Psychoactive drugs impair users' ability to make good decisions regarding sexual behavior. Therefore, engaging in safer sex becomes less likely when a person is using psychoactive drugs. And good choice of partner(s) is impaired by psychoactive drug use.

2. Injectable drug use often involves needle-sharing between users. This facilitates the transmission of bloodborne infections such as HIV and hepatitis B if one of the users is infected.

The drugs most often involved are crack cocaine and injectable heroin. A vicious cycle of drug abuse, exchanging sex for money or other resources, unsafe sex, and infection with a variety of genital ulcer diseases has occurred since the mid-1980s. This cycle is intimately related to the resurgence of syphilis and other diseases in urban America. The effects are most notable among young, urban, Black and Hispanic/Latino men and women.

Urban/Rural Differences STDs including HIV are disproportionately higher in urban areas than in rural or suburban locations.[36] "Core urban populations" may be a major contributing factor for higher STD rates in urban communities and disproportionately high personal risk, despite individual behavior. The rate of acquisition of gonorrhea, for instance, in core urban populations is as much as 300 times higher than in the rest of the population.[37] With a high level of infection and prevalence of deadly diseases, any sexual activity (even so-called safer sex) between or with members of this population carries a higher degree of risk than the same behavior with non-core group people.

Socioeconomic Status (SES) To a large extent, STDs mimic other chronic diseases. SES can either facilitate or hinder access to preventive and interventive STD health care. People of lower SES tend to lack enabling factors related to prevention and treatment of STDs such as health care insurance and access to treatment services. Even though free public clinics are available, they may not be utilized promptly because poor people often lack

Epididymitis
inflammation of the small oblong body that rests upon and beside the surface of the testes

IDA
acronym for injecting drug abuse

access to transportation, don't have sick days if they are employed, or are unaware of the availability of free care.[38]

Also, people of lower SES often do not perceive themselves to be at great risk for STDs/HIV, do not respond to symptoms promptly, and do not practice preventive behavior.[39] Poverty and lower SES, too, contribute to higher levels of drug use — a major risk factor for STDs/HIV.

Race/Ethnicity Much of the disparity in STD rates and morbidity and mortality stems from class, not race. Although disease rates in general are higher for Blacks and Hispanics/Latinos than Whites, racial/ethnic differences, in most cases, are markers for social class.[40]

A greater proportion of Blacks and Hispanics/Latinos live at or below poverty than Whites. High rates of infection in non-Whites relate more to SES than race or ethnicity. Therefore, SES is the true risk factor. Class differentials are larger than race differentials in morbidity. When studies control for social class, racial differences in disease distribution drop markedly. The problem of STDs in minority populations in inner cities is a result, in part, of the unequal distribution of class.[41]

PERSPECTIVES

Core Transmitters of STDs

STDs seem to be much more common in certain pockets of infection. These pockets occur mostly in urban areas among specific subpopulations of sexually active people called "core groups." The following factors are related to transmission of STDs in the core population.

- *Endemic levels of infection* (20% or more of the population infected).[1]

- *High concentrations of infected persons in small geographic areas.*[2] Only 5.9% of census tracts accounted for 51% of cases of STDs, and an additional 9 adjacent census tracts accounted for 72% of cases and 74% of sexual contacts).

- *High levels of inter-group sexual activity and socializing.*[3] Of those infected with STDs, 51% had picked up their sexual partners in the same location (only 2% of all the bars and clubs in town).[4]

- *High levels of repeat infections.* Small percentages of infected individuals accounted for large percentages of multiple infections.[5]

- *High levels of multiple STD infections* (coexisting infection with gonorrhea and chlamydia; syphilis and HIV; HIV and chancroid).[6]

- *Longer than average duration of infectivity* (because of a delay in seeking treatment) *and rate of asymptomatic infection among core group members.*[7]

- *High levels of substance abuse* and *higher levels of sex for drugs* than non-core group patients.[8]

1. G. P. Garnett and R. M. Anderson, "Core-Group Transmission of STDs," *Sexually Transmitted Diseases,* 20:4 (1996), 181–191.
2. J. J. Potterat, R. Rothenberg, D. E. Woodhouse, J. B. Muth, C. I. Pratts, and J. S. Fogle, "Gonorrhea as a Social Disease," *Sexually Transmitted Diseases,* 1 (1985), 25–32.
3. Garnett and Anderson.
4. Potterat et al.
5. H. Handsfield, "Old Enemies: Combatting Syphilis and Gonorrhea in the 90's," *Journal of the American Medical Society,* 264:11 (1990), 1452–1494.
6. W. Cates, "Sexually Transmitted Diseases," *Encyclopedia of Human Biology,* 6 (1991), 891-902.
7. T. Quinn and W. Cates, "Epidemiology of STDs in the 1990s," in *Sexually Transmitted Diseases,* edited by Thomas Quinn (New York: Raven Press, 1993).
8. R. A. Dunn and R. T. Rolfs, "The Resurgence of Syphilis in the United States," *Curr Opinions in Infectious Diseases,* 4 (1991), 3–11; Quinn and Cates.

Sexual/Medical History

The next level of risk on the pyramid is sexual medical history. This is something we cannot control because it has occurred in the past. Yet, a person's sexual and medical history can greatly influence the present level of risk for STDs/HIV. Sexual/medical factors most associated with the current risk for STDs/HIV are:

❧ *Lifetime number of sexual partners*. In general, the greater the number, the higher the risk. Threshold levels of "safe" sexual activity have been identified.[42] Once the threshold number of sexual partners is reached, the risk for disease increases exponentially.

❧ *Contraceptive use*. Barrier contraceptive users have the lowest rates of infection. They are followed by other contraceptive users and nonusers who have the highest risk.[43]

❧ *History of IDA*. Persons with a history of IDA (injectable drug use) have an increased incidence of infection with bloodborne diseases, particularly HIV and hepatitis B.[44]

❧ *Prior STD history*. Persons who have been infected with STDs in the past are more likely to become infected again than those who have never been infected.[45]

Sexual Relationships

"Sexual relationship" refers to the connections between people rather then the specific behaviors in which they engage. In general, the risk for STDs/HIV decreases as sexual relationships move away from multiple, anonymous, sexual encounters toward monogamous (with uninfected partner), trusting partnerships. STD/HIV sexual relationship risks are specifically related to overall numbers of partners and the quality of the relationship

Case Study

Yolanda: Assessing the Risk

Yolanda is a 22-year-old student in a Human Sexuality class. She expressed the following concerns about finding out about her sex partners' medical histories.

It looks like I'm going to have to spend a lot more time getting to know my sex partners before I take a chance of having sex with them without condoms. Up until today I thought I was a responsible lady of the nineties because I'm on the pill and take responsibility for my sexuality. I always thought the pill would protect me against STDs. Boy, was I wrong. I never realized that there was so much to find out about a guy before you could tell if he was a threat to you.

I used to try to sneak a look to see if he had any symptoms, but now you're saying there are lots of other things that are important about his sexual past that I need to know about. I'm not sure what I'm going to do, but I know I'll never let any guy in there bareback until I can answer all those questions about him.

(trust, understanding, and knowledge of one's partner. Figure 15.7 shows the continuum of risks for sexual relationships.

Two dimensions of lifestyle of "partner risk" are *familiarity risk* and *exclusivity risk*.[46]

Familiarity Risk Familiarity risk is synonymous with *anonymity*. Laumann and colleagues operationally defined extent of familiarity along a continuum that measured how long the study subjects knew their partners before having sex with them. Their findings confirmed that the less familiar one is with the sex partner (the greater the anonymity), the greater is the risk. Anonymity is a risk factor because it influences the ability to make an informed choice about the risk for STD/HIV.

Exclusivity Risk Laumann and associates called the second variable *exclusivity* — the quality of the sexual relationship. Exclusivity, they said, has to be examined for *both* partners. If one partner is monogamous but the other is not, the benefits of exclusivity are lost. Further, if an uninfected person is monogamous with someone who has an STD, exclusivity can actually increase the risk by increasing the extent of exposure. For exclusivity to work, both partners have to be uninfected and monogamous. Subjects (and partners) who were not sexually exclusive were at increased risk for acquiring an STD.[47]

The highest risks were associated with the "interaction of risky partners" (lack of exclusivity and familiarity) and many partners.[48] This sexual lifestyle, which combines multiple partners with anonymous sexual encounters, creates a deadly synergy that increases the risk exponentially.[49]

Sexual Behavior

At the top of the pyramid of risk is sexual behavior. In general, as illustrated in Figure 15.8, the risks increase as behaviors incorporate unprotected insertion and ejaculation. The lower-risk behaviors are nonpenetrative and do not involve an exchange of bodily fluids. As we move along the continuum of risk, the behaviors reflect attempts to utilize barrier protection

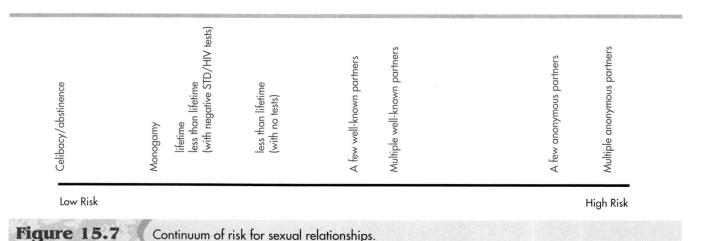

Celibacy/abstinence   Monogamy   lifetime less than lifetime (with negative STD/HIV tests)   less than lifetime (with no tests)   A few well-known partners   Multiple well-known partners   A few anonymous partners   Multiple anonymous partners

Low Risk   High Risk

Figure 15.7   Continuum of risk for sexual relationships.

against infectious agents. The highest-risk behavior is receptive anal penetration including ejaculation, which consists of unprotected ejaculation of
semen into the delicate, nonlubricated tissue of the rectum. This allows direct
access of infectious STD/HIV agents to the bloodstream. Theoretically, as Figure 15.8 illustrates, the risk for STD/HIV is greater for the receptive partner
of any sexual activity.

A Closer Look at Sexual Behaviors and STD Risk

Much remains to be known about the relative safety of various sexual
behaviors. For instance, a wealth of literature documents the degree of protection condoms provide in preventing STDs. Little, however, has been written concerning the effects of nonpenetrative sexual activity and withdrawal.
Some of these activities now are included in "safer sex" methods, instead of
"safe sex" behaviors because of the lack of adequate documentation on
their effectiveness.

The effects of some of the more bizarre techniques haven't been documented at all. Consider the recommendation of some safe sex educators of
the use of dental dams and clear-plastic food wraps to prevent the transmission of STDs through cunnilingus, fellatio, and vaginal intercourse. We do
not advocate these measures because they are untested and not intended for
those purposes. No evidence is available to suggest that they work. In fact,
the American Dental Association issued a disclaimer concerning using dental
dams (square pieces of latex designed to be used over the mouths of dental
patients) for any circumstances other than dental hygiene. Clear plastic
food wraps are an even more vivid example of safe sex gone mad. The
notion of covering one's genitalia with plastic wrap and then having intercourse or oral sex would be comical if the potential results weren't so
dangerous.

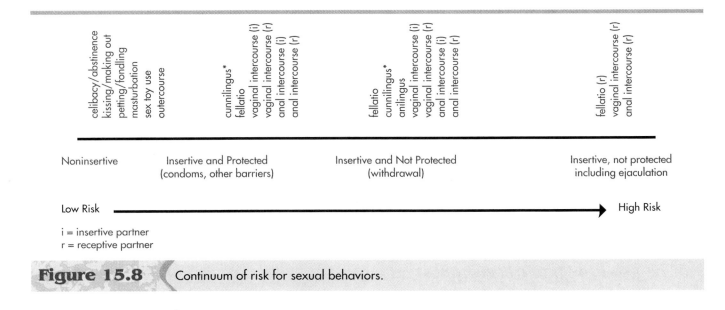

Figure 15.8 Continuum of risk for sexual behaviors.

Case Study

Lillie's Risk

Lillie is a 43-year-old continuing student. She made these comments in class:

Thank you! Finally, someone has said what I believed all along: It's not just sexual behavior that's the risk. It's the behavior in the context of a relationship that determines risk. I was always so annoyed and insulted when sex educators told me that I should always insist that my partner wear a condom and that any woman who is sexually active is at equal risk of becoming infected. I always felt that as long as I had one uninfected partner, and the two of us were monogamous, I was at low risk.

It's funny because even though I'm not married, my boyfriend (of three years) is less of a threat to me than my husband used to be. My ex-husband was always cheating on me and I was worried that even though I was monogamous, he'd bring something home to me.

I fully trust my current boyfriend. We've been monogamous (though unmarried) for three years, and I've never felt safer. We spent a lot of time building the trust and commitment in our relationship. I have great sex with him because I can fully relax and trust him, even though I've never gone down the list of things I need to know about his sexual past. We did talk about whether either of us ever had a viral STD, because viruses are forever.

For those who choose to have sexual intercourse, barrier methods provide the best protection. For those who do not want to have intercourse, a variety of nonpenetrative sexual activities offer close to 100% effectiveness against STDs.

Condoms

If worn properly and used consistently, condoms (both male and female) help protect the wearer against some STD infection by preventing direct contact between the penis and cervical, vaginal, rectal, or pharyngeal secretions or lesions. They also protect against exposure to penile lesions, discharges, and infected semen. Proper use for preventing STDs requires putting them on prior to any sexual contact, and they must remain intact throughout sexual activity.

Condoms are more effective against STDs such as gonorrhea and chlamydia, which are contained in semen (and therefore captured by the condom) than STDs such as genital warts and genital herpes. The organisms of the latter diseases and others live in outcrops of blisters and warts that could exist in areas that condoms do not protect.

In laboratory studies, latex condoms have been shown to block the larger bacterial pathogens (gonorrhea and chlamydia) and, to a lesser extent,

Natural membrane condoms should not be used for the prevention of STDs.

smaller viral organisms (such as HIV, HSV, and HPV).[50] Similar findings have not been found for natural membrane condoms. Although they block the passage of sperm, their pores are large enough to allow the passage of some STD organisms. Natural membrane condoms should not be used for the prevention of STDs.

In human studies, condoms also have been shown to be effective in reducing the risks for contracting STDs. Studies from all over the world, with diverse populations of users, have consistently documented that condoms reduce the risks for spreading STDs. Research as far back as the 1940s studied the use of condoms by troops in World War II and the Korean and Vietnam conflicts. In all three conflicts, soldiers and seamen using condoms had significantly lower rates of infection than their peers who did not use condoms.[51]

More recent studies of college men,[52] men and women attending STD clinics,[53] sex workers in Kenya[54] and Zaire[55] and many others document that condoms provide some protection against a host of STDs. Although use of condoms does not provide 100% protection against STDs, the studies we have mentioned have reduced risk by 50%–80% in actual users.[56]

Women-Centered Barriers

Although the male condom is the most reliable form of barrier protection against STDs/HIV, studies show that the women who stand to benefit the most do not use them consistently and correctly. The least consistent users of the male condom are adolescent women, women with a history of STD infection, and lower-SES women (who generally have less power and equality in their sexual relationships with men and have less negotiating skill).[57] This need not be a problem if more women were to use female barriers consistently and correctly.

In both laboratory and STD clinic studies, the following rates of effectiveness were reported for the sponge, diaphragm, and spermicides:[58]

❧ An overall reduced STD infection rate among barrier users compared to non-barrier users.

❧ Lower STD infection rates (87% lower) for women using barriers and attending HMOs (Health Maintenance Organizations) than nonusers.

❧ Lower STD infection rates (61% lower than nonusers) for women attending STD clinics who used barriers.

❧ Up to 70% effectiveness against gonorrhea when using barriers.

❧ Up to 40% effectiveness against chlamydia when using barriers.

Furthermore, in a study of 5,681 STD patients on the effectiveness of various contraceptive methods against STDs, not only was there a lower rate of infection among barrier users, but the lowest rates of infection were among sponge and diaphragm users. These rates were stable across all types of subjects, forms of sexual behavior, and STDs.[59]

Even though condoms have a higher rate of theoretical effectiveness against STDs, the women who need them the most use them less consistently and correctly. Woman-centered barriers, though theoretically less effective against STDs, provided greater actual effectiveness for women who used them instead of the male condom.

Nonpenetrative Sexual Behaviors

The effectiveness of nonpenetrative sexual activity in preventing STDs is relatively undocumented. Effectiveness in preventing STDs is generalized from the hypothesized ability of these methods to prevent unintended pregnancy by preventing the deposit of live sperm into the vagina. Because these methods exclude penetration and ejaculation, their ability to prevent pregnancy is very high (theoretically close to 100%).

Methods such as masturbation, use of sex toys, and even oral-genital sexual contact in preventing the transmission of STDs have not been scientifically studied and documented. Do these methods offer the same protection against STDs? No one knows for sure. When theorizing about their ability to prevent STDs, one can say that, because they do not involve penetration and ejaculation, they must offer a high level of protection against STDs as well. We are not as totally convinced of this as some other safer sex educators are.

The major difference in the ability of these activities to prevent STDs would be the presence or absence of genital symptoms that potentially could spread pathogens even in the absence of penile penetration and ejaculation. Also, STD organisms, in rare instances, could be passed from genital ulcers to the eyes via contaminated fingers. For instance, if a person who had genital lesions associated with herpes were to engage in mutual masturbation with his or her partner, and then rubbed the eyes, HSV could be spread to this site.

This is why we present sexual behaviors on a continuum of risk from low to high. No behavior except celibacy is completely risk-free. Viewing sexual activity in this way will allow you to examine the risk of specific behaviors in the context of other sexual activities. You also must evaluate any behavior within the context of the relationship you have with your partner. The less you know about your partner, the more risky any behavior becomes.

Using the Pyramid to Reduce Risks

The pyramid model presented earlier in the chapter shows that the risk for STDs/HIV combines personal lifestyle and behavior, past sexual history, and demographic factors. Focusing on just one set of factors and ignoring the others isn't enough. Though a person can never dismiss personal behavior as crucial to the success of prevention activities, other factors affect personal risk despite the most exemplary personal behavior.

For example, in certain core areas, individuals have 300 times more risk for acquiring infection simply by virtue of community risk factors.[60] Even if you are rather conservative in your behavior, if you live and interact sexually in such an area, engaging in any sexual activity carries a higher risk of becoming infected and engaging in risky sexual behavior may be life-threatening. This demographic influence might make risk-reduction measures much different from someone who lives in a lower-risk area.

The same dynamic can hold true for sexual/medical history. If the sex partner has a high-risk past (used injectable drugs and might be HIV positive, for instance), the other partner's personal behavior might be much different from that of someone whose partner has no history of infection. If the personal history includes a risk such as prior infection with gonococcal PID, for instance, a woman might take extra precautions against becoming infected with gonorrhea again as it could increase the risk for developing PID again.

Each individual has to develop a personal plan for STD risk reduction based on his or her (and the partner's) pyramid. Plans will vary according to the individuals involved. Although reducing risks this way takes a little more thought, it also respects individuality.

Health Hint

Reducing the Risk for STDs: Some Basic Guidelines

Although no universal solutions will work equally well for everyone, here are a few guidelines for reducing your risk for acquiring an STD.

1. *Become comfortable with your own sexuality.* Learn as much as you can about your sexuality. This will make you more accepting of who you are and what you need. You will be less likely to give in to doing something risky if you know and respect yourself. This includes choosing to abstain if that's what you desire.

2. *Check yourself for signs and symptoms of STDs.* This goes hand-in-hand with item 1. If you are comfortable with your body and your sexuality, you will be more aware of changes that signify possible STD infection. If you or your partner has the sores, rashes, discharges, itching, or pain associated with STDs, avoid sex.

3. *Develop a repertoire of low-risk sexual outlets.* Learn how to enjoy a low-risk sexual outlet. It's perfectly okay to say no to unprotected intercourse and yes to masturbation or massage.

4. *Work on your communication skills.* Practice how to initiate a dialogue about STD risk-reduction. You'll need to find out a lot about your partner to assess and reduce your personal risk. The only way to do this is to be able to talk openly about your sexual lifestyle. Practice now.

5. *Understand your demographic risks.* Find out about the area in which you live. You can get information about the level of STDs in your community from your local and state health departments.

6. *Know your partner's sexual/medical history.* Take time and care to find out the things you need to know about your partner, or develop the level of trust in the relationship that will allow you to make some judgments about your risk. In the meantime, if you choose to have sex with your partner, use condoms and nonintercourse options to reduce your risk.

7. *If you are at risk, seek regular check-ups.* If you have a very high-risk profile, go in for an STD check-up every three months. If you are in a lower risk category, go in at least twice a year. Most states have a list of free public clinics in your area.

8. *If you are not in a mutually monogamous, disease-free relationship, protect yourself.* Do not rely on your partner to look out for your health. All forms of sexual activity carry some degree of risk for spreading STDs. Gauge the level of risk you are willing to assume (see Figure 5.8).

9. *Strive to be in a mutually satisfying, disease-free relationship with one person.* If both you and your sex partner are monogamous and disease-free, you will not be at risk for STDs. Two mutually exclusive, uninfected partners can enjoy sex without fear of infection.

EPIDEMIOLOGY, DIAGNOSIS, AND TREATMENT

Syphilis

Spirochete
a mobile, flexible, corkscrew-shaped bacterium of the genus Spirocheta, one type of which causes syphilis

Much of what we know about the history of syphilis was discovered through the Tuskeegee Study of the 1960s. Syphilis is a bloodborne STD caused by infection with *treponema pallidum*, a corkscrew-shaped bacterium. A **spirochete** type of bacteria, the *Treponema pallidum* is easily killed by penicillin and other broad-spectrum antibiotics. The *Treponema pallidum* is unique among STD organisms because its corkscrew shape and motility facilitate its entry into the bloodstream.

PERSPECTIVES   The Tuskegee Study — It Couldn't Happen Here

In 1932, the U. S. Public Health Service (USPHS) embarked upon one of the most tragic experiments ever conducted by a government on its own people. From 1932 to 1970, in Macon County, Alabama, the USPHS conducted a study under the guidance of the Tuskegee Institute (which, ironically, is one of the nation's most prestigious Black academic institutions), on the history of syphilis in Blacks.

Syphilis, it was hypothesized, progressed differently in Blacks than Whites. The study originally was intended to be a short-term investigation (6 to 9 months' duration) but evolved into a 40-year project that followed the subjects well beyond the initial stages of their disease through latency into complications, and ultimately to their deaths. Much of what we know about the disease, how it spreads, its complications, and how it attacks the body and kills, comes from the Tuskegee Study.

The study followed 600 Black subjects (399 infected men and 201 uninfected controls) for 40 years. Treatment was withheld intentionally from these men, even after they were diagnosed with serious, life-threatening complications of the disease. None of them benefited from penicillin as the effective treatment of choice in 1951. The USPHS devised elaborate plans to keep track of these men (and continue to withhold treatment) even after they moved from Alabama to other states.

In 1966, Peter Buxtun, an investigator for the USPHS, brought the matter before the then-director of the Division of Venereal Diseases, Peter Brown. Given the moral climate and racial turmoil of the 1960s and the immorality of such an experiment, Buxtun pleaded that something be done. A special committee was empaneled within the USPHS to discuss the study. The committee ruled in favor of continuing the study to its natural end-point.

Buxtun's pleas went unheeded, and the experiment continued. Not until Buxtun leaked his story to an Associated Press writer and it broke on the front pages of the *Washington Post* in 1972 was something done.

In 1973, a special subcommittee of the U. S. Congress, chaired by Edward Kennedy (D. MA) began to investigate the matter. The committee found the USPHS culpable, the study was terminated, and special regulations concerning conducting government experiments were drawn up. These regulations now serve as guidelines for handling human subjects in any government-financed study. Surviving participants of the Tuskegee Study and their heirs filed a $1.8 billion class-action lawsuit. The government settled the suit out of court for $10 million.

How all of this was allowed to happen — the circumstances behind the massive cover-up and the racial bigotry that may have poisoned a legitimate scientific quest for knowledge and understanding — are all chronicled in the work of James Jones' 1993 book, *Bad Blood: The Tuskegee Study — A Tragedy of Race and Medicine*.

After exposure to the bacterium, it enters the body through breaks in the skin or by penetrating intact skin, and from there passes into the bloodstream. Once in the bloodstream, it can move freely throughout the body. The usual incubation period for syphilis is 3 to 4 weeks, but it can be as short as 10 days or as long as 90 days.

Symptoms

After the the incubation period, a **chancre** appears at the spot where the organism entered. The primary chancre is painless and disappears within 1–5 weeks without treatment. Often it is internal (inside the vagina, mouth, or rectum). Because of this, many people who become infected with syphilis don't realize it. An infected person's blood test will detect antibodies to the syphilis spirochete a short time after the the primary chancre appears.

About 6 weeks later a generalized rash appears. The rash varies from being highly noticeable, covering the entire trunk, to a mild eruption on the hands or feet. As with the chancre, the rash disappears without treatment after 2 to 6 weeks.[61]

In about 25% of the cases, a second rash appears and also goes away without treatment. At this point, those who are infected enter the latency period, during which time they are infected but have no symptoms. They are capable of transmitting the infection only by donating blood or by a mother passing the infection across the placenta to a developing fetus, resulting in **congenital syphilis.**

All blood in the United States is tested for syphilis, and no cases of disease have been detected this way in decades. Because the symptoms of syphilis can be so mild and varied, it has been dubbed the "great imitator." It can mimic a variety of dermatological conditions and often is mistaken for these less serious infections. In adults, untreated syphilis takes several years to develop into a serious illness. Because the spirochetes are traveling throughout the body, they can infect any organ or body system and cause major damage.

Chancre
painless, indurated primary lesion of early syphilis

Congenital syphilis
the disease acquired by the fetus in the womb and present at birth

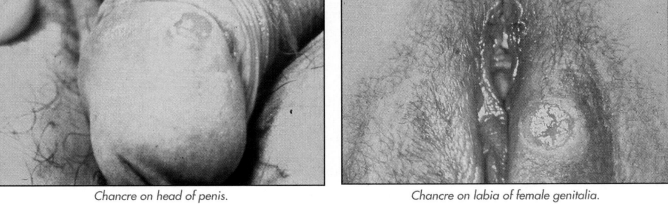

Chancre on head of penis.   Chancre on labia of female genitalia.
The typical chancre of primary syphilis is round, raised, and painless; it often is internal and goes unobserved.

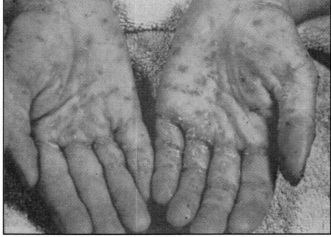

The typical rash associated with secondary syphilis is bilateral (both hands and/or feet), raised, and discolored.

In the United States, untreated syphilis going undetected for the decades required to develop life-threatening illness is unusual. Most Americans have a blood test for syphilis (e.g., for work, marriage, induction into the Armed Forces) at some point in their adult life. This also explains why disenfranchised people who live in poverty and are not in the mainstream are more likely to have undetected syphilis.

Treatment

Treatment of syphilis is relatively straightforward. Injections of penicillin are sufficient to treat most early cases of syphilis. One shot is administered to those who have been infected for less than one year. Those having infections more than one year are given three injections, each spaced one week apart. For individuals who are allergic to penicillin, 30 days of tetracycline or other antibiotics will cure most cases.

From the 1940s to the mid-1980s, morbidity from syphilis declined by 99%. Two factors weighed heavily in this decline:[62]

❧ The advent of penicillin therapy

❧ A national commitment to intensive follow-up of the sexual partners of infected persons.

The greatest recent decline in syphilis morbidity has been in gay men. In the 1970s–80s the ratio of male-to-female cases was almost 4:1 (for every case in women, there were four in men — an indicator of greater male-to-male transmission). In 1991, the ratio dropped to just slightly more than 1:1, signifying a drop in male-to-male transmission.

Since 1986, the level of infection has increased dramatically to its highest level in 40 years. Although overall rates for syphilis in the 1980s initially were heading downward, post-1985 gains resulted in an increase of 34% from 1981 to 1989 (from a rate of 13.7 cases per 100,000 persons to 18.4 cases per 100,000).

Factors related to the dramatic rise in all types of syphilis are:[63]

❧ An increased level of trading sex for drugs (crack cocaine in particular)

❧ An endemic level of disease in inner-city core populations

◡ A high level of intergroup sexual encounters (high-risk group members having sex with each other)

◡ The lack of safer sex behaviors

◡ A vicious cycle of poverty, poor education, unemployment, and inadequate health care, which leads to crime, prostitution, family disruption, unsafe sex, and despair.

Hardest hit with this increase in syphilis have been:[64]

◡ Major urban areas (where the rate jumped from 105 cases per 100,000 residents to 126 cases per 100,000 people)

◡ Heterosexual Blacks (whose disease rates were 39 times greater than those for Whites)

◡ Heterosexual Hispanics (whose rates were 9 times greater than those for Whites).

Congenital Syphilis

Related to the increase in early syphilis among urban, heterosexual people of color is a dramatic increase in congenital syphilis cases and rates. Reported cases of congenital syphilis increased from 158 in 1983 to 7,219 cases in 1990 (from 4.3 to 174.7 cases per 100,000).[65]

The risks of congenital syphilis are greatest among young, lower-SES, drug-abusing mothers.[66] These young women are much less likely than their older, more affluent, and better educated peers to seek and obtain adequate prenatal care. Many of these pregnant women fail to have the recommended three trimester visits with an obstetrician. A requirement of routine prenatal care is a blood test for syphilis. Most adult women with health insurance get this test early in their pregnancies. If it is positive, they can be treated. Treatment of the mother almost always results in treatment of her developing fetus.

A partial explanation for the dramatic rise in congenital syphilis was the adoption of a new case definition from the CDC.[67] Under this new definition, a case is defined as any infant whose mother was determined to be

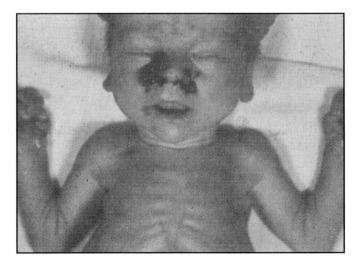

Congenital syphilis results from an infected mother passing the organism through the placenta to a developing fetus.

untreated or inadequately treated for syphilis, regardless of the presence/absence of symptoms in the baby.

Chancroid

Chancroid is often confused with syphilis because both present with an initial genital ulcer as the primary symptom. The ulcers associated with chancroid, however, are irregular in shape and painful (versus symmetrical and painless for syphilis).

The typical incubation period is 4 to 10 days, after which the ulcer appears. After their initial appearance, the ulcers progress to become beefy, granular, painful erosions. The ulcers are accompanied by painful, swollen, lymph glands in the groin.

Like syphilis, chancroid is diagnosed through the presence (or history) of symptoms and the results of a blood test. Chancroid is easily treated with antibiotics.

Chancroid
STD named for the irregular and painful genital lesions it produces, caused by bacterium *Haemophilus ducreyl*

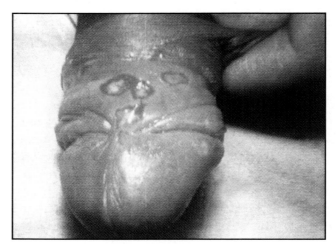

Unlike syphilis, the ulcers of chancroid are irregular in shape and painful.

Although chancroid is not common in the United States and other developed countries, it is endemic in some Third World countries and is considered a co-factor in the explosion of HIV infection in these nations. In the United States, the incidence of chancroid peaked in 1947 with 10,000 cases nationwide and steadily declined until 1981.

Since 1981, morbidity has increased slightly, with eight distinct outbreaks scattered around the country. These outbreaks all had the following commonalities:

- The introduction of infected individuals from outside areas (including merchant seamen and recent immigrants)
- Predominance in Black and Hispanic males
- Linkage to prostitution.

HIV/AIDS

HIV
acronym for human immunodeficiency virus, the infection that leads to AIDS

AIDS represents the end stage of **HIV**. Figure 15.9 traces the natural progression of HIV infection. As you can see, AIDS can develop within 2 years of exposure but typically takes longer.

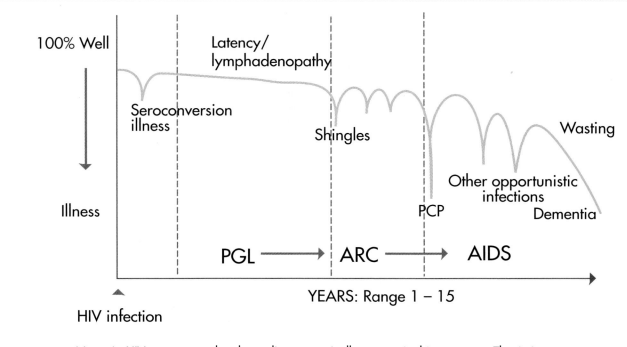

Note: As HIV progresses, the above diseases typically appear in this sequence. The timing, however, may range from 1 to 15 years.

Source: *HIV/AIDS Newsletter,* Centers for Disease Control and Prevention, Atlanta, 1992.

Figure 15.9   Natural progression of HIV.

HIV infection is caused by person-to-person transmission of the human immunodeficiency virus. The most common modes of transmission are (a) sexual contact (vaginal or anal intercourse are most efficient), (b) sharing contaminated needles (through injecting drug use), and (c) maternal-to-fetal transfer. Once the virus has been transmitted, it enters the bloodstream, where it incubates from 8 weeks to 6 months, when it will show positive on a blood test.

Diagnosis

A person who elects to take a blood test for HIV is given a screening test, called the ELISA (enzyme-linked immunosorbent assay), which detects the presence of antibodies to the HIV. If this test is negative, the person is counseled to come back for a second ELISA in a few months, to make sure the maximum incubation period has elapsed. If a person tests positive on the initial ELISA, he or she is given a second test, called the Western Blot, to confirm infection. If this test comes back positive, the person is diagnosed as having HIV infection.

HIV infection is essentially a disorder of the immune system. The virus weakens the body's immune system, making the person susceptible to other infections and chronic diseases. These are called **opportunistic infections** because they take advantage of the body's weakened state to attack and cause disease. When people with a fully functioning immune system come in contact with opportunistic organisms, they normally repel them.

Opportunistic infection
an infection that is able to develop as a result of the body's weakened immune status

Health Hint

Should You Take the AIDS Test?

The question about whether to get tested for HIV has concerned many individuals. When HIV infection and AIDS are concerned, clouds of fear, suspicion, and misunderstanding still loom large in many communities. Fears of being ostracized by family and friends, being kicked out of school, or losing a job have kept many people who suspect exposure to HIV from being tested. In some cases people simply cannot face the possibility of a positive test and do not want

to know. If you are considering having a screening test for HIV:

- Take your test anonymously in an alternative-site facility where you will be given a number and your name will not be used (some facilities do confidential, not anonymous testing).

- Make sure the testing site does counseling before and after the test.

Immunocompetence
the level of efficiency of
the immune system

People with HIV cannot fight off opportunistic infections and eventually die from them. Most people with HIV infection are completely free of symptoms for more than 10 years. Others deteriorate rapidly and develop symptoms and AIDS within 2 to 4 years.

Early symptoms of HIV infection stem from infections that begin to invade the body because of its weakened immune status. When the immune system begins to fail, the following symptoms begin to occur: fatigue, diarrhea, fever, night sweats, skin rashes, sudden weight loss, dry cough, swollen lymph nodes, and vaginal yeast infection. These symptoms can be present for weeks, months, or even years without opportunistic infections taking hold.

With treatment, many people with HIV can prevent these symptoms from ever occurring. And aggressive treatment can return symptomatic individuals to a symptom-free state. Although the medication doesn't kill the virus, it slows or stops viral replication and thereby boosts **immunocompetence**.

If an opportunistic infection does take hold, the person moves from being infected with HIV to being diagnosed as having AIDS. In 1993, the Centers for Disease Control and Prevention broadened the definition of AIDS to include 26 opportunistic infections. Infection with any one of these combined with being HIV-positive leads to a diagnosis of AIDS.

Treatment

HIV/AIDS treatment is not a cure, because viruses have no cure. The multitude of new antiviral drugs and combination drug treatment regimens do not kill all of the HIV as do antibiotics, such as penicillin, kill bacteria. Antiviral therapy prevents or slows the unchecked replication and growth of HIV, helping the infected person's immune system keep the virus in check. This prevents them from contracting opportunistic infections. Other treatments focus on killing the opportunistic infections that take hold.

Prior to 1995, most HIV antiviral treatment revolved around drugs that inhibited the activity of reverse transcriptase, an enzyme that HIV requires to transform its RNA (ribonucleic acid) genetic material into DNA (deoxyribonucleic acid) — the first step in viral replication. These drugs prevented the spread of HIV to new cells but did little to stop viral replication in cells that were infected already.

In 1995, the FDA approved a new group of antiviral drugs called **protease inhibitors**. These drugs act against an enzyme, HIV protease, whose function is to break down and reassemble the proteins that infectious viral particles require. When protease is inhibited in infected cells, a noninfectious virus results.

Protease inhibitors
a group of antiviral drugs used to prevent replication of HIV-infected cells

Current treatment regimens combine the older reverse transcriptase drugs with the newer protease inhibitors to attack the virus in two ways. First, these "AIDS cocktails" have been effective in halting the spread of the virus and, second, in reducing viral loads (the amount of HIV RNA in plasma, a direct measure of disease progression.[69]

These advances in treatment have enabled persons infected with HIV to live longer and also have changed the face of the AIDS epidemic. As people live longer with HIV, fewer people develop AIDS and die as a result of HIV infection. In a sense, HIV becomes more of a chronic disease. Nowhere is this more apparent than in the declining death rate for AIDS.

Epidemiology

The epidemiology of HIV/AIDS has changed considerably over the first 25 years of the epidemic. In the 1990s, for the first time in nearly two decades, the number of new cases and the death rate for AIDS began to decline. This represents a trend that has the potential to continue into the new century as more effective antiviral agents become available for use. Figure 15.10 shows the estimated number of people living in the United States with AIDS, 1992–1997. The figure graphs the data separately by gender, race/ethnicity, and region of the country.[71]

In 1997, Blacks accounted for 30% of adult AIDS cases and 53% of pediatric AIDS cases. In 1997, Hispanics represented 16% of the adult cases and 25% of the pediatric AIDS cases. Proportionately, blacks and Hispanics account for only 11.6% and 6.5%, respectively, of the U.S. population. The proportion of cases among whites decreased from 60% to 43% in 1997.[71]

In 1997, IDAs accounted for 26% of all AIDS cases, up from 14% in 1987. The proportion of heterosexually acquired cases increased from 3% to 10%.[72] Most heterosexually acquired cases involve sex with individuals who are injectable drug users.

The proportion of cases in women increased from 8% in 1981 to 18% in 1995. Although Black and Hispanic women make up only 19% of all U.S. women, they account for 72% of all female AIDS cases. AIDS is the number-one cause of death in Black women aged 25–44 and is the third leading cause of death for Hispanic women in this age group.[73] In 1993, AIDS was the seventh leading cause of death for all children aged 1–4 and the second for Black children.[74]

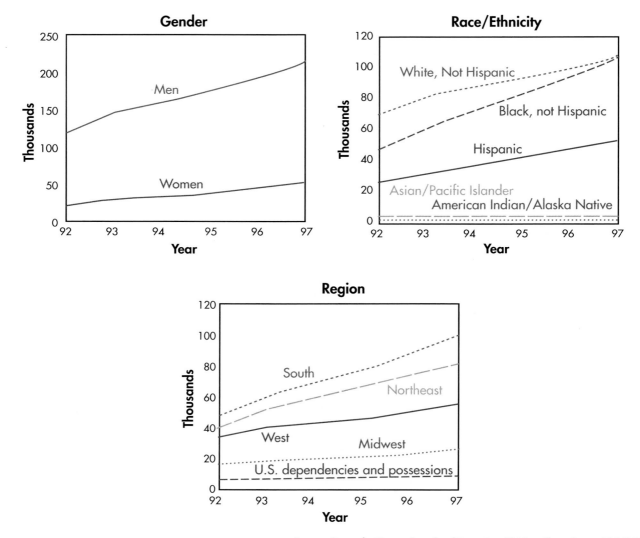

Source: Centers for Disease Control and Prevention, *HIV Surveillance Report*, 10:2 (1998).

Figure 15.10   Trends in reported AIDS cases by sexual orientation, gender, and race/ethnicity.

Hepatitis B Virus (HBV)

Hepatitis B Virus (HBV)
a disease caused by contact with infected blood; often associated with unprotected sex with multiple partners

Carriers
individuals who have a given disease and are capable of passing it on genetically but have no apparent symptoms

Hepatitis B virus (HBV) infection is another bloodborne disease capable of being transmitted sexually. Figures 15.11 shows the distribution of HBV cases in the United States between 1983 and 1993 for males and females, respectively. Table 15.2 shows the proportionate risk of all cases of hepatitis B in the U. S. since 1986. To most people, infection with hepatitis B is not clinically apparent. Between 10% and 68% of all cases are chronic **carriers**; the infected individuals have the disease and are capable of spreading it but have no noticeable symptoms. When they do notice their symptoms, they usually have jaundice, dark urine, fever, malaise, and moderate liver enlargement with tenderness. Chronic infection can lead to cirrhosis of the liver and liver cancer.

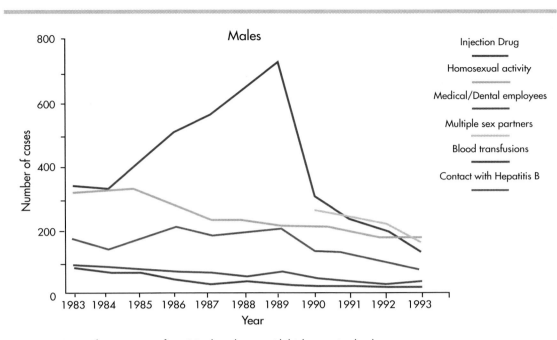

Note: These cases are from 15 selected states with high reporting levels.

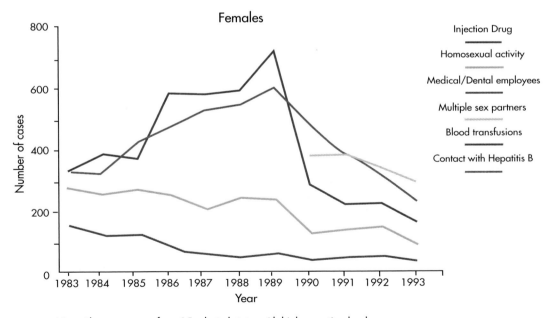

Note: These cases are from 15 selected states with high reporting levels.

Source: Viral Hepatitis Surveillance Programs, Centers for Disease Control and Prevention, Atlanta.

Figure 15.11 Trends in selected risk factors for male and female patients with Hepatitis B.

Table 15.2	Proportionate Risk of All Cases of Hepatitis B in U.S. Since 1986	
Population	<1986	>1986
Gay men	21%	9%
Heterosexual	18%	24%
Injecting drug users	15%	27%
Healthcare	5%	1%

(Remaining % from all other sources and no known source)

HBV infection has no cure because, like HIV, it is caused by a virus. Treatment consists of boosting the strength of the immune system to help the body keep the virus in check.

Genital Herpes Infection

Genital herpes
infection caused by exposure to the herpes simplex virus type 1 or type 2 through sexual contact

Genital herpes infection is caused by exposure to the herpes simplex virus type 1 (HSV 1) or herpes simplex virus type 2 (HSV 2) through sexual contact. HSV 1 initially was associated with oral infection and HSV 2 with genital infection. Over the past 25 years, however, the increased popularity of oral sex has led to an almost equal probability of contracting either form from the genital area. A 2 to 12-day incubation period follows transmission of the virus.

Health Hint

Self-Help for People with Genital Herpes

Most people with genital herpes are able to manage their infections and prevent spreading their infection to others. The following health hints will help you do just that.

1. If you are taking acyclovir or other herpes medication on a maintenance schedule and it helps to reduce recurring episodes of infection, continue taking the medicine as prescribed.

2. At the first hint of prodromal symptoms, consider yourself infectious and capable of spreading your infection. During this time, abstain from intercourse, or engage in nongenital sexual pleasuring, or use condoms.

3. Treat any outbreak as you would the flu (another viral infection), with bed rest and over-the-counter pain relievers.

4. Keep your genitals clean and dry. Take short baths, pat your genitals with a towel, and use a hair dryer to dry the area thoroughly.

5. Avoid panty-hose, tight underwear, and binding clothes until the blisters crust over and dry up. If you can, take a day or two off during the worst symptoms, stay in bed, and avoid wearing clothes.

6. Do not cover the blisters with petroleum jelly or other cream that blocks air from drying the area.

7. Minimize stress, as it delays healing.

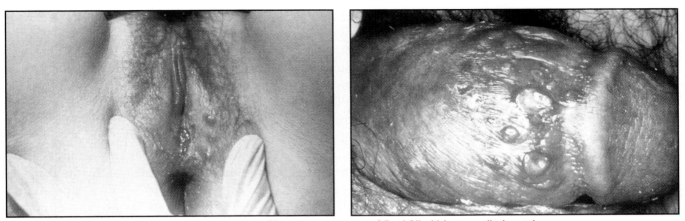

The primary symptoms of herpes are groups of fluid-filled blisters called vesicles which break open to form painful, highly infectious ulcers.

The initial symptoms (also known as the primary outbreak) start as discrete grouped **vesicles**. After a short time (a few hours to a few days), the vesicles break open, merge with each other, and form painful ulcers, which drain and crust over. The entire first episode takes 15 to 20 days. Often, a systemic, flulike syndrome accompanies the primary outbreak. The symptoms of this syndrome, known as the **prodrome**, include aches, fever, and malaise.

Recurring outbreaks occur in most sufferers on an average of five to eight times/year and last approximately 10 days per episode. Recurrences often are preceded by the same prodromal syndrome that accompanies the primary episode. The frequency and severity of recurring episodes diminish with time. Genital herpes tends to be a self-limiting, albeit painful, STD.

Vesicles
fluid-filled blisters

Prodrome
systemic, flulike syndrome that accompanies genital herpes infection

Case Study

Susan, an HSV Sufferer

Susan was a 23-year-old woman one of the authors met while conducting a self-help group for persons suffering with genital herpes. Susan had just found out that the ulcerative genital infection she had was caused by HSV. She came to the group to learn how to manage her disease.

I was shocked when my doctor told me I had herpes. I couldn't figure out how I got it, since I've been sexually involved with just my boyfriend for the past six months and he doesn't have any symptoms.

The doctor explained that my present boyfriend might not even have given it to me. [The doctor]

explained that since I had several other sex partners since beginning to have intercourse at 19 years old, any of those guys could have given it to me. He said I might not have had any initial symptoms or might have missed them because they were so mild.

Now, because I've been stressed out — a new job, graduate school, getting engaged, moving into a house — the herpes is coming back. He suggested that I come here and learn about how to cope with it if I keep getting recurrences.

I'm so stressed, but I know this is also the worst thing for me if I want to help my body keep it under control. Please help me!

Genital HSV infection has no cure. As with the other viral STDs, treatment focuses on slowing the replication of the virus and boosting the immune system. Treatment also includes techniques to speed drying and healing of the vesicles and blisters associated with the infection.

Initial consultations with private physicians for genital herpes increased from fewer than 25,000 in 1996 to about 175,000 in 1997 (see Figure 15.12). A similar increase in office visits (from 18,000 to 176,000) — a more accurate index of morbidity — was also noted.

Advances in antiviral therapies, such as acyclovir, have made drugs available that shorten the duration of outbreaks and reduce the number and likelihood of recurrent episodes.[75] An estimated 20 to 30 million people are presently infected with genital herpes in the United States. The estimated annual incidence is approximately 270,000 cases per year.[76]

Genital Warts (HPV)

Genital warts also known as venereal warts, are caused by infection with the **human papilloma virus (HPV)**. There are at least 46 known varieties of HPV. Of these, at least 12 are associated with genital infection. The virus is spread through direct contact with an infected person's genital warts during sexual contact.

The average incubation period for genital warts is 3 months from the time of exposure. The initial warts can be isolated or appear in clusters on the genitals and perianal area. The warts vary in size from ⅛ inch to considerably larger, and in some cases growths become so large that they cause deformity of genital structures. Growths can **autoinoculate** adjoining tissue.

Genital warts
an STD caused by the HPV or human papilloma virus

Human papilloma virus (HPV)
condition spread through direct contact with an infected person's genital warts during sexual contact

Autoinnoculate
to self-inflict the spread of disease from one body part to another

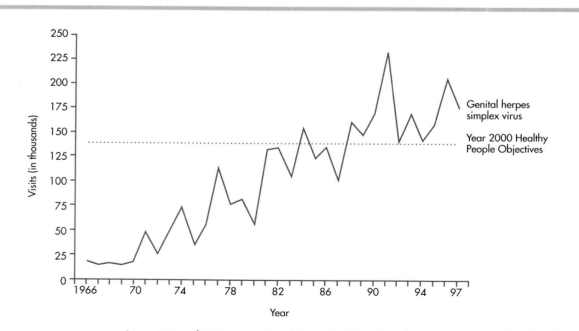

Source: Division of STD Prevention, Sexually Transmitted Disease Surveillance, U.S. Department of Health and Human Services, Public Health Service (Atlanta: Centers for Disease Control and Prevention, Sept. 1998).

Figure 15.12　Initial herpes consultations, United States.

The genital warts associated with HPV infection can grow very large and threaten to block the openings to the vagina, urethra, and anus.

These "kissing lesions" are often found on the labia or under the foreskin of uncircumcised men.

Estimates of infection with no symptoms vary from 10% to 45% of infected individuals.[77] Infection with warts is not painful, but continued growth can cause a painful obstruction of the vaginal, anal, or urethral opening.

The major concern associated with HPV is the increased risk for cancer. Cervical infection with HPV is associated with at least 80% of all cervical cancer cases.[78] Women with HPV infection of the cervix are 10 times more likely to develop cervical cancer than women without the infection.[79] As many as 10% of women with cervical HPV infections will develop **cervical interepithelial neoplasms (CIN)** within 1 year. HPV Types 16, 18, and 31 have been found in all types of genital cancers.

No medication is available to cure a person of HPV infection, as this is another viral condition. Various forms of treatment, however, are used to remove warts from the skin's surface. Warts do not disappear by themselves. They are removed by applying medications to the warts that dry them out. If this doesn't work, the warts are removed surgically by laser excision, through freezing, or by burning them off.

A 1992 estimate indicated that more than 12 million Americans had genital warts.[80] As with genital herpes, the rate of initial consultations for genital warts has increased, though it has shown some decline since 1986 (see Figure 15.13). Women and individuals in the 20- to 24-year-old age bracket constitute the bulk of the visits.

Routine testing of women for HPV in four locations yielded the following infectivity percentages:[81]

✺ 9% of women seeking routine Pap smears at ob/gyn facilities across the United States tested positive.

✺ Between 9% and 45% of women attending health services in a university health center had positive test results.

✺ 23% of women attending family planning clinics were positive

✺ 82% of street prostitutes in a select study had the virus.

Cervical interepithelial neoplasms (CIN) tumor or growth within the cervical membrane tissues

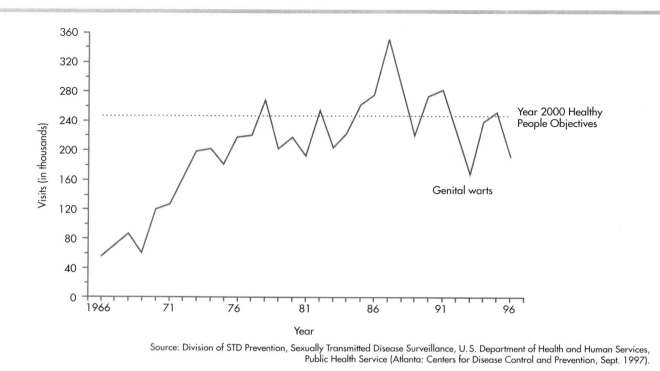

Source: Division of STD Prevention, Sexually Transmitted Disease Surveillance, U.S. Department of Health and Human Services, Public Health Service (Atlanta: Centers for Disease Control and Prevention, Sept. 1997).

Figure 15.13 Initial consultations for human papillomavirus (genital warts) — United States.

Chlamydia

Chlamydia is a sexually transmitted disease caused by the *chlamydia trachomatis* organism. Chlamydia trachomatis is transmitted through contact with infected semen or cervical mucus. It also can be passed through oral contact (usually fellatio) with infected mucus patches in the throat.

During sexual contact the organisms are passed by person-to-person contact with the infected ejaculate or mucous. Incubation is from 1 to 30 days. The initial symptoms of chlamydia in men are a scanty, clear to milky-white discharge from the penis, and burning upon urination. Approximately 25% of infected men have no symptoms. Women are usually asymptomatic (75% do not get symptoms). Some women notice a scanty, clear to milky-white discharge and irritation of the vulva.

Chlamydia infection is believed to be the most prevalent of all STDs, with an estimated annual incidence of between 3,000,000 and 5,000,000 new cases occurring each year. The rate of chlamydia in women is six times higher than that for men.[82] Most cases of nongonococcal urethritis infection (NGU) (an infection of the male urethra, discussed later in the chapter) are attributed to chlamydia trachomatis.

The highest rates of infection are in adolescent females (because of asymptomatic infection). Of inner-city adolescent girls attending STD clinics, 21% were infected with chlamydia, and 15% to 20% of inner-city adolescent boys attending similar clinics were infected with NGU (which usually is caused by chlamydia trachomatis). The rates were higher for Blacks, both boys and girls, than Whites.[83]

In the 1960s and 1970s, chlamydia infection was believed to be a relatively minor problem. Men with the infection were often referred to as having "nonspecific urethritis" and were not counseled extensively regarding the necessity to have their sexual partners examined. Chlamydia, however, was discovered to be a major source of **PID** (pelvic inflammatory disease). Up to 20% of all women with chlamydia trachomatis infection will develop PID.

PID can result in chronic pain, ectopic pregnancy, and sterility, and in rare instances is fatal. More than half of all PID is caused by chlamydia trachomatis. Infection in men rarely leads to major complications. Less than 1% of men infected with chlamydia trachomatis develop epididymitis.[84]

Chlamydia trachomatis infection is relatively easy to treat. The organism is destroyed by a number of antibiotics, and alternative treatments are available. Two weeks' treatment with tetracycline or other broad-spectrum antibiotics is effective for most infections.

PID
acronym for pelvic inflammatory disease, a generic term that can apply to any STD that produces the characteristic symptoms of infection

Gonorrhea

Gonorrhea is similar to chlamydia trachomatis clinically. Following sexual exposure, the organism incubates from 1 to 30 days. Most people who develop symptoms notice them within 1 to 3 days. The initial symptoms are the same as those associated with chlamydia. Discharge and burning upon urination are the most common symptoms in men. The difference is in the severity of symptoms. Gonorrhea symptoms usually are more severe — heavy discharge, yellowish-green in color, and severe burning. The symptoms usually are enough to cause men with the infection to seek treatment. Up to 20% of men have no symptoms. About 50% of women infected with gonorrhea are asymptomatic, and a small percentage will notice a discharge or have irritation of the vulva.

In women, gonorrhea often results in complications, the most common of which is PID (pelvic inflammatory disease) — in approximately 15% of all women with untreated gonorrhea. These women, as with those who develop PID from chlamydia, have an increased risk for chronic pain, ectopic pregnancy, sterility, and even death. Less than 1% of men with

Gonorrhea infection typically produces discharge that is thick, profuse, and yellowish/green in color. It can however present with milder symptoms that mimic chlamydia or be asymptomatic.

untreated gonorrhea develop disseminated gonococcal infection and/or epididymitis.[84] Like chlamydia, gonorrhea is easy to treat. Most infected individuals can be treated with tetracycline.

Approximately 1.2 million cases of gonorrhea are reported annually in the United States. Gonorrhea may be underreported by up to 50%.[85] Many clinicians diagnose it in their offices based on symptoms and medical history without need for a confirmatory laboratory test.

The number of cases of regular gonorrhea has decreased over the past decade while cases of penicillin-resistant strains have increased. Most of the overall dramatic declines in gonorrhea morbidity are associated with safer-sex behaviors by White gay men, supported by the steep declines in cases in White men.

Although gonorrhea has declined in general, cases in Blacks have actually increased. Gonorrhea rates in Blacks are 20 to 30 times higher than Whites. The explanation is similar to that used to explain the rise in syphilis cases discussed earlier in this chapter.

Nongonococcal Urethritis (NGU)

Nongonococcal urethritis (NGU)
infection in the urethra of males, usually caused by chlamydia bacteria

Nongonococcal urethritis (NGU) is diagnosed when neisseria gonorrhea is ruled out as the causative agent of discharge and burning in a male. In most cases, a negative lab test for gonorrhea and the presence of symptoms is enough to diagnose NGU. NGU is also a surrogate measure of chlamydia in men, as more than half of all cases of NGU are attributable to chlamydia trachomatis. In some cases, a test for chlamydia trachomatis is done.

NGU presents the same symptoms as chlamydia infection in men and is treated the same way. Approximately 3,000,000 cases occur annually in the United States.[86]

Pubic Lice

Pubic lice
phthirius pubis; small insects (metazoan) that infest the host's pubic hair,

Infection with **pubic lice,** commonly called crabs, is caused by infestation of *phthirius pubis.* The lice are transmitted during sexual contact from the infested pubic hair of one person to the other. In rarer instances, the lice are transmitted from contaminated bedding, clothing, and towels that people share.

Female lice lay eggs, called nits, which attach to the shaft of the pubic hair of the exposed individual. The incubation period for lice is between 24 and 48 hours, at which time the eggs hatch and another batch of lice spread throughout the pubic hair.

Symptoms of pubic lice are (a) visual confirmation of the lice, (b) intense itching of the pubic and perianal area, (c) skin irritation, and (d) secondary sores and erosions from scratching. Although infestation rarely leads to complications, persons with pubic lice sometimes develop secondary infections from their intense scratching.

Treatment of lice consists of special shampoos that kill the lice on the skin and hair. Bedding, clothing, and other contaminated articles must be washed thoroughly or dry-cleaned.

Scabies

Like crabs, **scabies** are caused by infestation with a mite. This mite, *sarcoptes scabies*, is transmitted in the same way as pubic lice. Symptoms are similar with one notable exception: Sarcoptes scabies actually burrows under the skin of an infected person and feeds on cellular matter.

Diagnosis usually consists of identifying the mite's burrows under the skin. Because of the burrowing, more than one application of the topical shampoo may be required.

Scabies
condition caused by the *sarcotes scabiei* parasite, which burrows under the skin and lays eggs

WELLNESS SYNTHESIS

Although physical well-being is the most obvious domain affected by STDs, each of the other components of wellness is involved as well. Environmental demographics especially, is a large factor.

Physical Well-being

High-level physical well-being will not do much to prevent the transmission of most STDs. It can play a part, however, in helping us manage chronic viral infections ranging from HIV to genital herpes. All viral conditions seem capable of being contained somewhat by the immune system once they have passed through the primary stage. Indeed, therapy for some conditions, such as hepatitis B and HSV, involves bed rest, stress management, and proper nutrition. Recent therapeutic plans for slowing the progression of HIV include exercise, stress management, nutritional supplementation, and other measures aimed at enhancing physical well-being.

Another facet of physical well-being is awareness of changes in the body that might indicate the presence of infection.

Intellectual Well-being

High-level intellectual well-being is the cornerstone of effective prevention of STDs. Knowing the risks and how to reduce them is critical to preventing STDs. This knowledge includes information about personal behavior and also about lifestyles and demographic risks. Intellectual well-being also fosters enhanced decision making. Reducing the risks for STD is all about personal choice.

Emotional Well-being

Because STDs are sexually transmitted, their prevention and control are more than just a medical matter. STDs involve our most intimate emotions. Knowing about prevention and seeking treatment are one thing. Working through the anxiety, fear, and guilt, and a host of other emotions that interfere with clear thinking about STDs is another thing. Emotional health can help us deal with the emotions that can cloud rational thinking. It also can help us, if we become infected, to accept the reality of the disease and seek proper care for ourselves and our partner.

Social Well-being

STDs used to be called "social diseases" because of the nature of sexual transmission. Social well-being is a major preventive strategy against STDs. Being in a mutually exclusive, monogamous, disease-free relationship is the best prevention against STDs. High-level social relationships are characterized by openness, honesty, caring, and trust — all key elements in preventing STDs. The same benefits of high-level social relationships we've talked about throughout the book hold true for preventing STDs.

Spiritual Well-being

Researchers and clinicians have studied the role of spirituality in treatment and management of disease. Probably the best known research is that related to cancer and other life-threatening diseases, in which spirituality has been shown to help prolong life, enhance treatment, and, at the very least, comfort those whose death is imminent. Spirituality has been shown to help those who have permanent disfigurement from disease and who are terminally ill. Developing spiritual well-being is an approach now being used with those who are HIV-positive. This includes imagery and other therapies to help the immune system keep the virus in check. In the case of AIDS, spirituality is a part of hospice care, helping those with AIDS to maximize their remaining time and prepare for their ultimate death.

Environmental Well-being

Environmental factors — demographic and other — contribute to an alarmingly high level of risk within a community, despite personal behavior. In the United States, the quality of one's environment seems to be directly proportional to SES. As SES rises, most Americans seek out safer, healthier communities, and safe communities carry much lower risk for STDs. High-risk/low-wellness communities should be targeted for STD prevention and treatment services and programs.

WEB RESOURCES

American Social Health Association (ASHA)

http://www.ashastd.org

A nonprofit organization dedicated to stopping sexually transmitted diseases and their consequences. The site offers excellent links and information to other ASHA programs. STD information, facts and questions, sexual health glossary, and support groups sections.

The Body

http://www.thebody.com/index.shtml

A compilation of organizations and experts that exchange ideas and information. The HIV/AIDS information resource lists many articles on what AIDS is, who gets it, HIV testing, safe sex and prevention, on learning one is HIV-positive, AIDS vaccines, dictionaries and drug glossaries, books on HIV/AIDS and additional resources.

Gay Men's Health Crisis

http://www.gmhc.org/

Nonprofit organization providing support services to men, women, children, and their families with AIDS in the New York City area, as well as education and advocacy nationwide.

Herpes Resource Center (HRC)

http://www.ashastd.org/herpes/hrc.html

Accurate information about herpes simplex virus infections. This site offers a wide selection of good herpes links. HRC provides questions and answers, how to tell your partner, when to tell your partner, and issues of herpes and pregnancy.

Notes

1. T. R. Eng and W. T. Butler, editors, "Summary," *The Hidden Epidemic: Confronting STDs* (Washington, DC: Academy Press, Institute of Medicine, 1997).

2. Centers for Disease Control and Prevention, Division of STD Prevention, *Sexually Transmitted Disease Surveillance 1995* (Atlanta: Public Health Service, 1996).

3. P. Piot, and M. Q. Islam, "Sexually Transmitted Diseases in the 1990's: Global Epidemiology and the Challenges for Control," *Sexually Transmitted Diseases*, 21:suppl 2 (1994), 7–13.

4. L. A. Webster, S. M. Berman, and J. R. Greenspan, "Surveillance for Gonorrhea and Primary and Secondary Syphilis Among Adolescents, United States, 1981–91," *Mortality and Morbidity Weekly Report*, 42 (SS–3) (1993), 1–10.

5. L. A. Webster, J. R. Greenspan, A. K. Nakashima, and R. E. Johnson, "An Evaluation of Surveillance for Chlamydia Trachomatis in the United States 1987–91," *Mortality and Morbidity Weekly Report*, 42 (SS-3) (1993), 21–27.

6. A. K. Nakashima, R. T. Rolfs, and M. L. Flock et al., "Epidemiology of Syphilis in the United States, 1941–1993," *Sexually Transmitted Diseases*, 23:1 (1996), 16–23.

7. Centers for Disease Control and Prevention, "Update: Trends in AIDS Among Men Who Have Sex with Men — United States, 1989–94," *Mortality and Morbidity Weekly Report*, 44, (June 2, 1995); CDC, "Preventing HIV Infection in Women and Children," *Mortality and Morbidity Weekly Report*, 44 (July 7, 1995); "HIV: Preventing the Spread of Opportunistic Infections," *Mortality and Morbidity Weekly Report*, 44 (July 14, 1995); "First 500,000 Cases of AIDS — United States," *Mortality and Morbidity Weekly Report*, 44 (Nov. 24, 1995); "The HIV/AIDS Epidemic: The First 10 Years," *Mortality and Morbidity Weekly Report*, 40:22 (1991).

8. T. Quinn, and W. Cates, "Epidemiology of STDs in the 1990s," *Sexually Transmitted Diseases*, edited by Thomas Quinn (New York: Raven Press, 1993).

9. Centers for Disease Control, Division of STD Prevention, *Sexually Transmitted Disease Surveillance 1994* (Atlanta: Public Health Service, 1995).

10. Quinn and Cates.

11. Webster, Berman, and Greenspan, 1993.

12. Winkelestein et al., "The San Francisco Men's Study," *American Journal of Public Health*, 84 (1988): 1933–1937; J. A. Yorke, H. W. Heathcote and A. Nold, "Dynamics and Control of the Transmission of Gonorrhea," *Sexually Transmitted Disease*, 2 (1978), 51–57.

13. Webster, Greenspan, Nakashima, and Johnson, 1993.

14. L. A. Webster, and R. T. Rolfs, "Surveillance for Primary and Secondary Syphilis, United States, 1991," *Mortality and Morbidity Weekly Report*, 42(SS–3) (1993): 13–18.

15. Centers for Disease Control and Prevention, *HIV/AIDS Surveillance Report*, 9:1 (1997), 1–28.

16. J. D. Forrest and S. Singh, "The Sexual and Reproductive Behavior of American Women 1982–88," *Family Plan Perspectives*, 22 (1990), 206–214.

17. Quinn and Cates, 1993.

18. Webster, Berman, and Greenspan, 1993.

19. R. J. Rice, P. L. Roberts, and H. H. Handsfield, "Sociodemographic Distribution of Gonorrhea Incidence: Implications for Prevention and Behavioral Research," *American Journal of Public Health*, 10 (1991), 1253–1257.

20. V. Navarro, "Race or Class: Mortality Differentials in the United States," *Lancet*, 336 (1990), 1238–1240.

21. J. Wasserheit, "Epidemiological Synergy," *Sexually Transmitted Diseases*, 2 (1992), 61–77.

22. R. J. Hayes, K. F. Schulz, F. A. Plummer, "The Co-factor Effect of Genital Ulcers on the Per-exposure Risk of HIV Transmission in Sub-Sahara Africa," *Journal of Tropical and Medical Hygiene*, 98, (1995), 1–8.

23. L. Finelli, J. Budd, and K. Spitalny, "Early Syphilis: Relationships to Sex, Drugs, and Changes in High-Risk Behavior from 1987–1990," *Sexually Transmitted Diseases*, 2 (1993), 89–95.

24. M. Howard, J. B. McCabe, "Helping Teenagers Postpone Sexual Involvement," *Family Planning Perspectives*, 22 (1990), 21–26.

25. CDC/DSTDP, 1996; Alan Guttmacher Institute, *Sex and America's Teenagers* (New York: AGI, 1994); W. Cates, "Sexually Transmitted Diseases," *Encyclopedia of Human Biology*, 6 (1991), 891–902; Quinn and Cates.

26. Cates, 1991; M. B. Kennedy, M. I. Scarlett, A. C. Duer, and S. Y. Chu, "Assessing HIV Risk Among Women Who have Sex with Women: Scientific and Communication Issues," in *Journal of the American Medical Women's Association*, 50 (1995), 103–107; American Medical Association, Council on Scientific Affairs, "Health Care Needs of Gay Men and Lesbians in the United States," *Journal of American Medical Association*, 275 (1996), 1354–1359.

27. Quinn and Cates, 1993.

28. S. Morse, A. Moreland, and S. Thompson, *Sexually Transmitted Diseases* (New York: Gower Medical Publishing, 1990).

29. Morse et al.

30. S. Smeltzer and B. Whipple, "Women and HIV," *Journal of Nursing Scholarship*, 4 (1991), 249–256.

31. R. A. Dunn and R. T Rolfs, "The Resurgence of Syphilis in the United States," *Curr Opinions in Infectious Diseases*, 4 (1991), 3–11.

32. M. Alter and H. Margolis, "The Emergence of Hepatitis B as a Sexually Transmitted Disease," *Medical Clinics of North America*, 6 (1990), 1529–1541; AMA, 1996.

Notes cont.

33. Morse et al.

34. Eng and Butler.

35. Kennedy et al.; AMA.

36. Rice et al.; H. Handsfield, "Old Enemies: Combatting Syphilis and Gonorrhea in the 90's," *Journal of American Medical Association*, 264:11 (1990), 1452–1454; J.J. Potterat, R. Rothenberg, D.E. Woodhouse, J.B. Muth, C.I. Pratts, and J.S. Fogle, "Gonorrhea as a Social Disease," *Sexually Transmitted Diseases*, 1 (1985) 25–32.

37. Rice et al.; G.P. Garnett, and R.M. Anderson, "Core-Group Transmission of STDs," *Sexually Transmitted Diseases*, 20:4 (1996), 181–191.

38. K. Donelan, R.J. Blendon, C.A. Hill, et al., "Whatever Happened to the Health Insurance Crisis in the United States? Voices from a National Survey," *Journal of American Medical Association*, 276 (1996), 1346–1350.

39. R. Ramos, R.N. Shain, and L. Johnson, "Men I Mess with Don't Have Anything to do With AIDS: Using Ethno-theory to Understand Sexual Risk Perception," *Sociology Quarterly*, 36 (1995), 483–505.

40. Rice et al.

41. Navarro.

41. Handsfield.

42. B.D. Dan, "Sex and the Singles Whirl: The Quantum Dynamics of Hepatitis B," *Journal of American Medical Association*, 256:10 (1996), 1344; W.W. Darrow, D. Barrett, K.J. McPhil, and M.A. Young, "The Gay Report on Sexually Transmitted Diseases," *American Journal of Public Health*, 71:9 (1981), 1004–1011.

43. M.J. Rosenberg, and E.L. Gollub, "Commentary: Methods Women Can Use That May Prevent Sexually Transmitted Disease, Including HIV, *American Journal of Public Health*, 82:11 (1992), 1473–1478.

44. Alter and Margolis.

45. Darrow et al.; Dan.

46. E.O. Laumann, J.H. Gagnon, R.Y. Michael, and S. Michaels, *The Social Organization of Sexuality: Sexual Practices in the United States* (Chicago: University of Chicago Press, 1994).

47. Laumann et al.

48. Laumann et al.

49. Dan.

50. D.A. Grimes and W. Cates, "Family Planning and Sexually Transmitted Diseases, in *Sexually Transmitted Diseases*, 2d edition, edited by K.K. Holmes, P.A. Mardh, P.F. Sparling, P. Wiesner, W. Cates, S.M. Lemon, and W.E. Stamm (New York: McGraw Hill, 1990), 1087–1094; M. Conant, D. Hardy, J. Sernatinger, D. Spicer, and J. Levy, "Condoms Prevent Transmission of AIDS-associated Retrovirus," *Journal of American Medical Association*, 255 (1986), 1706; G. Minuk, C. Bohme, and T. Bowen, "Condoms and Hepatitis B Virus Infection," *Annals of Internal Medicine*, 104 (1986), 584.

51. G. Hart, "Factors Influencing Venereal Infection in a War Environment," *British Journal of Venereal Disease*, 50 (1974) 68–72.

52. W.M. McCormack, Y. Lee, and S.H. Zinner, "Sexual Experience and Urethral Colonization with Genital Mycoplasmas: A Study in Normal Men," *Annals of Internal Medicine*, 78 (1973) 696–702.

53. W.W. Darrow, "Condom Use and Use-effectiveness in High-risk Populations, *Sexually Transmitted Diseases*, 16 (1989), 157–162; H. Austin, W.C. Louv, and W.J. Alexander, "A Case-control Study of Spermicides and Gonorrhea, *Journal of American Medical Association*, (1984) 2822–2826.

54. D.W. Cameron et al., "Condom Use Prevents Genital Ulcers in Women Working as Prostitutes: Influences of Human Immunodeficiency Virus Infection," *Sexually Transmitted Diseases*, 18 (1991) 188–194.

55. J. Mann, T. Quinn, and P. Piot et al., "Condom Use and HIV Infection Among Prostitutes in Zaire" (letter), *New England Journal of Medicine*, 316 (1987), 345.

56. W. Cates and K.M. Stone, "Family Planning, Sexually Transmitted Diseases and Contraceptive Choice: A Literature Update — Part I," *Family Planning Perspectives*, 24:2 (1992), 75–84.

57. Rosenberg and Gollub.

58. Rosenberg and Gollub.

59. Rosenberg and Gollub.

60. Potterat et al.

61. Centers for Disease Control and Prevention, "Sexually Transmitted Disease: Treatment Guidelines," *Mortality and Morbidity Weekly Report*, 42:RR14(1993), 56–66.

62. Dunn and Rolfs.

63. Handsfield; Dunn and Rolfs; Finelli, et al.

64. CDC, 1996; Dunn and Rolfs.

65. P. Zenker, "New Case Definition for Congenital Syphilis," *STDs*, 1 (1991), 44–45.

66. Cates, 1991.

67. Zenker.

68. Morse et al.

69. P.J. Ungvarski, "Update on HIV Infection," *American Journal of Nursing*, 97:1 (1997), 44–51.

70. CDC, *HIV/AIDS Surveillance Report*, 10:2 (1998).

71. CDC, 1991.

72. CDC, Http://www.cdcnpin.org/gene va98/trends/trends_5.htm

73. CDC, "Preventing HIV Infection in Women and Children," 1995.

74. CDC, "Preventing HIV Infection in Women and Children," 1995; V. Alexander, "Black Women and HIV/AIDS," *SIECUS Newsletter*, Winter 1990; Smeltzer and Whipple.

75. Morse et al.

76. W. Kessler and W. Cates, "The Epidemiology and Prevention of STDs, *Urologic Clinics of North America*, 19:1 (1992) 1–11.

77. Cates, "Sexually Transmitted Diseases," 1991.

78. National Institutes of Health (NIH), Consensus Development Conference Statement on Cervical Cancer, (Bethesda MD: NIH, 1996).

79. M.H. Schiffman, "Recent Progress in Defining the Epidemiology of Human Papillomavirus Infection and Cervical Neoplasia," *Journal of National Cancer Institute*, 84 (1992), 394–398.

80. Quinn and Cates, 1992.

81. Quinn and Cates.

82. Webster, Greenspan, Nakashima, and Johnson, 1993.

83. Quinn and Cates, 1993.

84. Morse et al.

85. Morse et al.

86. Quinn and Cates, 1993.

Student Study Questions

1. What are the various modes of transmission associated with STDs/HIV?

2. What are four major trends associated with STDs over the past two decades?

3. What is the underlying premise of the Pyramid of Risk for STDs?

4. How are demographic variables related to the risk for STD/HIV?

5. What are five important things to know about a potential sex partner's sexual history as related to STD/HIV risk?

6. How do sexual lifestyles and sexual behavior work together to increase or decrease risk?

7. What are the major signs and symptoms of STDs in men and women?

8. Why do gay men and heterosexual women have a similar risk profile?

Risk Assessment Form

Leland G. Wessell, M.D., M.P.H.

This form is confidential — it is not a permanent part of your medical record.

Many factors must be considered in assessing your health and fitness. Among these are: (1) your risk of acquiring or transmitting any sexually transmitted disease (STD) and (2) your use of psychoactive chemicals in connection with sexual activity, a practice that can increase your risk of acquiring an STD. STDs considered here include, but are not limited to: gonorrhea; syphilis; genital herpes; genital warts; chlamydia; hepatitis B; giardiasis; and infection with HIV, the virus that causes AIDS.

The first two questions are biographical in nature and are not part of the risk assessment score. They are intended to guide your provider in making the best possible appraisal of your health. The remaining 11 are the scored behavioral risk assessment. Please be honest in responding to the questions — we assure you that this document will be handled with the utmost confidentiality by you and your health care provider only. Please feel free to discuss the results with your provider. You may retain the survey for your own reference. *In any event, it will not be placed in your medical record.*

There are 11 questions listed below. Please check the one single answer that best describes your preferences or activities.

A)　How long have you been sexually active? _____

B)　Your most recent consistent sexual partner experience
　　　male _____ female _____ both male and female _____

1. How many sexual partners *per month* in the last year?
　　3 _____ 5 or more
　　2 _____ 2–4
　　1 _____ 0–1

2. How many partners *per month* in the year previous?
　　3 _____ 5 or more
　　2 _____ 2–4
　　1 _____ 0–1

3. The kinds of sexual contacts I have are:
　　3 _____ one-time or anonymous "tricks," "one night stands," groups, or prostitutes
　　2 _____ multiple times with two or more partners
　　1 _____ exclusively with one partner

4. I have sexual encounters or contacts most frequently
　　3 _____ in baths, bookstores, parties, "massage parlors," "spas," public restrooms, autos
　　1 _____ in my or my partner's home

Reprinted from the special report, "AIDS on the College Campus" (no longer in print) with permission from the American College Health Association, P. O. Box 28937, Baltimore, MD 20840-8937.

Continued

Student Assessment

Risk Assessment Form (cont.)

5. The frequency with which I use drugs or alcohol to enhance my sexual encounters:

   3 _____ frequently

   2 _____ occasionally

   1 _____ rarely/never

   Please circle drug used: "poppers" (amyl or butyl nitrates), alcohol, marijuana, hallucinogens (LSD, mushrooms), "angel dust" (PCP), amphetamines, barbiturates, quaaludes, ecstasy, eve, cocaine, crack or _____ (please fill in others)

6. I have injected myself with one or more of the above drugs in the past five years.

   4 _____ yes

   1 _____ no

7. I have sexual encounters most frequently in:

   3 _____ New York, Los Angeles, San Francisco, Miami, Washington, Dallas, Houston, Newark, Atlanta

   2 _____ other large urban areas (Boston, Philadelphia, St. Louis, Seattle, San Diego, etc.)

   1 _____ small cities, towns, rural areas

8. Those kinds of sexual activities I practice most frequently are (please circle specific activities):

   4 _____ vaginal or anal intercourse without a condom, oral-anal contact (rimming), direct fecal or urine contact (scat or water sports), or manual anal contact (fisting)

   3 _____ "protected" vaginal or anal intercourse (use of condoms and spermicides)

   2 _____ oral-genital contact (fellatio or cunnilingus)

   1 _____ masturbation, massage, body rubbing, kissing

9. My current sexual partner and I have discussed our previous sexual behavior and experiences with each other.

   4 _____ No

   1 _____ Yes

10. I negotiate with sexual partners for safer sexual practices.

    4 _____ No

    2 _____ Sometimes

    1 _____ Yes

11. I ask potential sexual partners about their use of drugs and steroids, especially their use of needles.

    4 _____ No

    2 _____ Sometimes

    1 _____ Yes

Continued

Student Assessment

Risk Assessment Form (cont.)

Add up the numbers from each question (1–11) and see the key below to determine your level of risk.

My score is _____.

If you answered "1" (the last option) for question 8, deduct 3 points.

Total adjusted score _____.

KEY:

17 or more: You appear to be at high risk for developing STDs, including HIV infection, and for possibly developing dependence on psychoactive substances. You should visit your health care provider immediately to discuss your risk of these dangers.

12–16 points: You appear to be at moderate risk for developing either an STD or chemical dependence and are encouraged to lower your overall risk by altering the behaviors that resulted in high scores on some of the questions. See your health care provider for any questions or concerns you may have regarding your risk.

11: You are at low risk for problems and are encouraged to continue your healthy behavior. Please feel free to contact your health care provider at any time for updated information regarding safer sex, AIDS, or any other issues.

This scoring system was designed to: (l) increase your awareness of STDs and the risk factors associated with acquiring or transmitting STDs, (2) stimulate self-evaluation of your health and your sexual lifestyle, and (3) encourage your taking responsibility for your health and the health of your sexual contacts. **This questionnaire is yours to keep and review. It will not go into your medical record even if you bring it to your health care provider.**

Sexual Coercion

Major Topics

Student Learning Objectives

After reading this chapter, students will be able to:

- Define sexual coercion and sexual victimization and the three forms highlighted in this chapter: harassment, rape, and child sexual abuse.

- Explain and give examples of the three conditions that constitute sexual harassment.

- Describe the dynamic of power over subordinates in determining sexual harassment.

- Define rape and differentiate it from other forms of sexual aggression.

- Describe the typical pattern of rape by a stranger and develop a personal plan to reduce the risk for this form of rape.

- Define acquaintance rape and identify the risks.

- Develop a personal plan for reducing the risk for date rape.

- Assess the impact of alcohol abuse in coercive sex.

- Describe the characteristics of rapists.

- Evaluate common myths associated with rape and rapists.

- Describe the preconditions of child sexual abuse.

- Evaluate ways to reduce the risks for child sexual abuse.

Coercive sex can take many forms. The commonality is the element of power and victimhood. In this chapter we focus on three forms: harassment, rape (also called sexual assault), and child sexual abuse.

Sexual coercion is defined as any nonconsensual sexual behavior that occurs as a result of arguing, pleading, and cajoling, in addition to force. In **sexual victimization**, a person is deprived of free choice and is forced to endure, observe, or comply with sexual acts. We will start our examination with a look at sexual harassment.

SEXUAL HARASSMENT

The issue of sexual harassment leaped onto the television screens and front pages of the United States in 1992 with the much publicized Clarence Thomas–Anita Hill sexual harassment hearings by the U. S. Congress, after President George Bush nominated Thomas to the Supreme Court. Thomas had been Hill's boss at the Equal Employment Opportunity Commission (EEOC). Hill came forward at the time of Thomas's nomination with claims of sexual harassment.

These hearings brought sexual harassment out of the closet and forced people to examine this dark side of human sexual behavior. Since then, the number of sexual harassment complaints filed with the EEOC more than doubled between 1990 and 1996, from 6,000 to 15,300.[1] U. S. Supreme Court rulings have made it easier to sue (and win) sexual harassment cases because victims no longer have to prove psychological harm, just that sexually inappropriate behavior took place.[2]

In regard to the Thomas–Hill hearings, what supporting evidence did each side bring to the debate? What were the major issues of contention? How have sexual harassment laws changed since the 1992 hearings?

According to the EEOC, sexual harassment consists of unwelcome sexual advances, requests for sexual favors, and other verbal or physical conduct of a sexual nature. These constitute **sexual harassment** when

(1) submission of such conduct is made explicitly, or implicitly a term or condition of an individual's employment or academic advancement, (2) submission or rejection of such conduct by an individual is used as the basis for academic or employment decisions affecting the individual, or (3) such conduct has the purpose or effect of unreasonably interfering with an individual's work or academic performance or creating an intimidating, hostile, or offensive working or educational environment.

Sexual coercion
any nonconsensual sexual behavior that occurs as the result of arguing, pleading, and cajoling and includes, but is not limited to, force

Sexual victimization
depriving a person of free choice and forcing him/her to endure, observe, or comply with sexual acts

Sexual harassment
unwelcome sexual advances, requests for sexual favors, and other verbal or physical conduct of a sexual nature in the workplace

Sexual harassment has two facets:

1. Unwanted sexual attention or advances.

2. A hostile environment (work or school) where the person faces daily stress and oppression because of the unwanted sexual attention.

The two facets of sexual harassment are unwanted sexual attention and a hostile environment.

Although the two often go together, they can exist independently.

Sexual harassment relates in part to how males are socialized. Men tend to interpret women's friendliness as a sign of sexual interest, as an invitation to pursue sexual involvement.[3] Men and women perceive sexual harassment differently. Men are much less likely to perceive certain behaviors as harassing then women are.[4] Thus, men have difficulty judging their behavior and its potential for harassment. The courts, too, have trouble determining whether certain actions cross the line between aggressive courting and sexual harassment.

PERSPECTIVES

The Clarence Thomas — Anita Hill Hearing

The Thomas–Hill congressional hearings in 1992 had effects far beyond the matter of deciding whether Clarence Thomas should sit on the U. S. Supreme Court. As a result of these hearings, the issue of sexual harassment came to the fore and led to a whole new zeitgeist of how people are to conduct themselves in the workplace. The hearings were also noteworthy in that this event involved two prominent Blacks — Thomas a judge and Hill a law professor at the time of the hearings — with opposing political ideologies.

In her testimony, Hill described her position as an employee of Thomas at the Equal Economic Opportunity Commission (EEOC). She claimed that, beginning in 1982, Thomas had pressured her to go out on dates and that he had made lewd comments to her, including references to a pubic hair on a coke can and the size of his penis. She stated that, because Thomas was well connected and could help her advance her career, she was reluctant to speak out at the time. She produced three witnesses who testified to Hill's having told them that she was being harassed, though they did not recall Hill's having accused Thomas by name.

Hill's critics charged that she waited too long (10 years) to speak of the harassment, and that she agreed to testify to members of committee only under condition of anonymity. Her detractors took this as an indication that she made the charges only to try to derail Thomas's chances to gain a Supreme Court

berth. They produced a number of witnesses who had worked for Thomas at the same time as Hill did and they testified that they had witnessed no evidence of harassment and were not harassed themselves. Finally, Hill's critics questioned why she had followed Thomas to another job subsequent to the alleged harassment.

Thomas denounced the charges as completely untrue and a "high-tech lynching." In a close vote, he was confirmed to the Supreme Court. Irrespective of the outcome, the legacy of the hearings was far-reaching and has an enduring symbolic value. Major changes include the recognition of sexual harassment in the workplace, its definition, and enactment of legislation making sexual harassment easier to prove. Monetary awards and settlements also increased dramatically. In 1990, sexual harassment awards handled through the EEOC totaled $7.7 million; by 1996, settlements had reached $27 million.

Awakened by the prospects of costly lawsuits, the public and private sectors alike have gone on the defensive. Sexual harassment training is becoming common. Formal policies now are the rule rather than the exception in the workplace. More women (and men) are filing suit and supporting the victims of harassment. As a result of the Thomas–Hill hearings, public attitudes and actions regarding sexual harassment were irrevocably changed.

Case Study

Linda and Beth:
Sexual Harassment Victims

Linda, a secretary for a medium-sized trucking company, is being harassed by her boss, John. He takes every opportunity to position himself around Linda to maximize the opportunity for physical contact. John leans over her desk, puts his arm around her chair, places himself in a doorway through which she must pass, and uses these opportunities to brush against Linda.

He has made comments about the size of her breasts, her shapely legs, and how he could really show her a good time in bed. Both John and Linda are married, and she has told him she is not interested in having an affair with him.

★   ★   ★

Beth is a driver for a local bus company, one of two women who work for this company. The other 48 drivers are men. All drivers report to the local garage, where the buses are parked. The garage has two locker rooms, restrooms, a cafeteria, and administrative offices. Beth has complained to her supervisor (a man) that the work environment is not conducive to her well-being and may even be hostile. The male drivers are fond of soft and hard-core pornography and have pinned-up pictures of naked women on the walls of the garage. They also leave these magazines out on the tables in the cafeteria.

Besides the print materials, the male drivers congregate in the cafeteria and tell sexually degrading jokes about women. They generally refer to women in derogatory terms when Beth is alone with them and when the other female driver is there. Although no one has made any direct advances toward her (she is living with her boyfriend and uninterested), she feels the work environment is hostile to women.

★   ★   ★

Both of these women are victims of sexual harassment — Linda, who is the victim of unwanted sexual advances from her boss, and Beth, who hasn't been personally confronted but is forced to work in a hostile environment created by her co-workers.

The whole issue of sexual harassment has many men and women confused over the new rules for flirting and attracting a partner. Where does one cross the line from flirting and teasing to harassing? How does harassment relate to the way men are socialized and their view of male-female relationships as inherently sexual.

Conditions of Sexual Harassment

Sexual harassment has three attributes that transcend individual perception and set the context for any interaction between individuals:

1. A power differential in the relationship
2. Inappropriate approach
3. Pressure after expression of disinterest.

A hallmark of sexual harassment is the use and abuse of power to secure sexual favors. Power differentials exist in the workplace and the

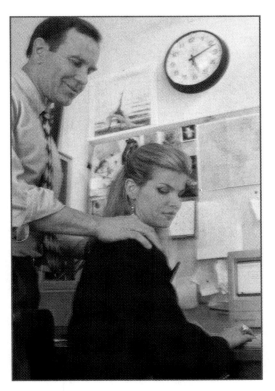

Placing a hand on a subordinate in the workplace is a form of harassment.

That's Entertainment?

Few things are as boring as most corporate meetings. In an attempt to liven up the presentations, an oil company brought a barely clad woman on a motorcycle to a regional meeting, according to a sexual-harassment complaint filed by a female supervisor for the company.

Moreover, she charged, when the corporation held a sales meeting at a restaurant, the entertainment was provided by strippers. And at a slide show held for employees, one slide featured the female supervisor's clothed rear end.

Was the Woman Harassed?

The Decision: The federal judge presiding over this case noted that the incidents were without question inappropriate but weren't "sufficiently severe or pervasive to constitute a hostile environment." That noted, he found that no harassment had taken place.

Is This Sexual Harassment?

The Expert Analysis: Surely there are other ways to entertain and inform employees, suggests Anthony M. Micolo, a human-resources representative with Eastman Kodak in New York City. As for the incidents in the case: "I would probably feel myself, as a man, uncomfortable with this stuff," he says.

More to the point is that while a "hostile environment" charge often needs more than one or two incidents to substantiate it, other judges might find episodes such as the preceding sufficient to establish a pervasive climate of harassment. Micolo points out that corporations need to consider what conduct will be deemed acceptable. "Above and beyond sales goals and operational goals, there have to be people goals," he says. "You have to view the work environment as one that's productive to employees, not oppressive to them."

classroom based on roles and responsibilities. The boss, supervisor, and professor have power over workers and students by the nature of their roles and authority. A boss or supervisor is responsible for evaluating work performance, giving assignments, and the like. A professor evaluates papers, tests, and exams and ultimately assigns a grade to students in the class.

When someone holds power over another by virtue of a "superior" role, the subordinate person has a harder time refusing the advances. The subordinates fear reprisal — in a poor performance review, no raise, undesirable work assignments, even termination. In a school environment, the students fear a less objective review of their work and lower grades. Also, being approached in a respectful, inquiring way is vastly different from being approached in a harassing way.

Finally, if the pursuing person stops the pursuit once the subordinate has expressed noninterest or displeasure, it's not harassment. Persistence and an attempt to pressure the other person into responding, however, is more likely to be considered harassment, especially if the first two criteria are also present.

Case Study

Hanna: A Victim of Sexual Harassment

Hanna is a 43-year-old continuing student. She returned to school to prepare for a new career after leaving a job in an insurance company, which she had held for 20 years. She gave this account of sexual harassment.

I guess it happened about fifteen years ago. I was married to my first husband at the time and was working for a large multinational insurance company and doing a lot of traveling. I had been there about ten years and was in an entry-level management position. I would travel to various branch offices of the company both in the United States and Canada. Sometimes I would accompany one or another of my bosses — who were all male. We stayed in separate rooms, but there was pressure to eat meals together and socialize after the work day. I was always cordial but usually returned to my room after dinner if there wasn't anything special planned with the client. Occasionally, people from the branch office would have something

planned, such as going to a hockey game. We'd go as a group, and it was fun. I discussed this after-work socializing with my husband, and we agreed that it was okay and a normal part of the job.

Things started to change after a couple of trips with my new boss, Charlie. He was about ten years older than me, married with two teenage sons, and with a twenty-five-year career with the company. On about the third trip, Charlie started pressuring me to "hang out" with him after the clients left or on evenings when no group activities were planned. He'd say things like, "It's okay — we work together" or, "We'll just have a couple of drinks and hang out at the bar."

I always refused because I didn't think it was right for a married woman to hang out with another man and have a few drinks. There was just something about the way he said it — his smile, the tilt of his eyebrows, his penetrating look. The other thing was that I don't like to hang out at bars. If I had the night

Sexual Harassment
Involving Children and Teens

One of the outcomes of the Thomas–Hill hearings and subsequent legislation is an attempt to define and prevent harassment at all levels. This has extended into all segments of society, including the elementary school.

Sexual Harassment in Elementary Schools

Sexual harassment in the schools goes way beyond mere teasing. Although poking fun and teasing can be emotionally painful and stressful, they do not constitute sexual harassment. In childhood, teasing peers of the other sex is a developmentally appropriate form of gender validation and, if not carried to an extreme, actually can strengthen the bonds little boys and girls have with their friends. Most of it is innocent and not discriminatory.

When the teasing is sexual in nature, it is a different matter. Uninvited sexual advances, lewd comments, ogling, and catcalls are different from simple put-downs ("Boys are better than girls," and vice versa) and nonsexual teasing. Even if they are not outright sexual acts directed at a child, they are capable of creating a climate of hostility that characterizes sexual harassment.

Often the focus of childhood teasing is sexual orientation. Children sometimes tease same- or opposite-sex peers with taunts of "queer," "homo,"

off and I was on the road, I liked to catch up on my reading or go to the hotel gym and work out.

He never touched me but got very close. A couple of times, he literally pinned me in my chair by leaning over me to ask about my evening plans. He was clearly disappointed when I said I was going back to my room and would let me know it with his facial expressions.

Everything kind of came to a head after our last trip. This was a long trip — five days — and I guess he figured I'd come across over the course of the week. On the next to the last day, he cornered me after work and asked if we could "get together" that night following dinner. He said that "a girl could get really far in this company if she were part of the team." He then read off a list of women who were "part of the team." I didn't ask him what team he was referring to but did ask what he meant by "get together."

He said, "You know, fool around after the clients leave."

I told him that I wasn't interested in fooling around and that I would see him in the morning. I would be eating in my room alone for the last night.

On the way to the airport the next day, Charlie was very brusque and told me, "I'm very disappointed in you. I really thought we could have a good time. I guess you're not very interested in getting ahead in this company."

I didn't respond and boarded the plane ahead of him.

He never said anything else to me about it. We didn't travel together any more. At the first opportunity, I transferred out of his unit and into a new division of the company. I'm not sure if my career has been short-circuited by my response, but I've progressed more slowly than the women who were "team players." My new male colleagues were totally different, and I didn't experience that kind of behavior from them during my continuing travels with the company.

"fag," "lesbo," "dyke," and the like. Whether the perception is accurate or not, it creates a hostile environment for these children, making daily interactions with peers painful.

Several noteworthy court rulings have been made regarding sexual harassment by elementary school students.[5] In Lexington, North Carolina, in 1966, 6-year-old Jonathan Prevette was suspended for kissing a classmate in an incident that the court ruled was sexual harassment. In response, the boy's parents threatened to sue if their son was not reinstated and the policy changed. The school board reviewed the case and agreed that the incident wasn't sexual harassment and the policy required retooling.

In another case, in New York, 7-year-old De'Andre Dearinge was charged with sexual harassment for kissing a student against her will and pulling a button off her skirt. Again, the school board intervened and reinstated the child.

What both of these examples illustrate is the difficulty in determining if specific incidents involving students constitute sexual harassment or represent something else. Obviously, singular, isolated incidents have to be evaluated differently from repeated acts that are more in keeping with creating a

---

Health Hint

Sexual Harassment: How to Fight Back

The following guidelines may be helpful in fighting back if you think you have been the victim of sexual harassment on campus or at work.

1. If the harassment includes rape or attempted rape, file criminal charges against the perpetrator.

2. If the act does not include rape or attempted rape, confront the person who is harassing you. Write a letter to the offender, and follow up with a meeting. Be as clear and specific about the offender's actions as possible. Be specific about the incidents, times, and dates. A history and pattern of events are important. Most harassers are repeat offenders.

   Describe exactly what happened, your feelings about the incidents, and how you reacted. Include a short statement indicating your desire for the harasser to stop. Sign and date the letter, and make duplicate copies. Send a copy to the perpetrator, and indicate that if the behavior doesn't stop immediately, you will press charges using the letter as evidence.

3. Seek support. Don't hide what happened. Talk to co-workers, fellow students, and people identified with the issue. This may help put pressure on the offender to stop. Contact a local support group, and talk to others who have experienced the same problem. Relate your incidents to your significant other.

4. If the behavior doesn't stop, meet with offender's supervisor. In a work setting, this is the offender's immediate supervisor. In a college setting, this person may be the department chairperson, the student center, sexual harassment panel, or Dean of Students. Discuss the incidents and give a copy of your letter to the supervisor.

5. Know your rights. Sexual harassment is against the law. You do not have to put up with it. Obtain the company's/school's sexual harassment policy. Read it thoroughly, and make sure you follow its guidelines for handling your case. Identify the administrative office and person responsible for handling sexual harassment violations in your workplace or school.

Although it may seem frightening, it's better to act quickly than to wait and see what happens. Harassers rarely stop their activities if they are not challenged.

Case Study

Marc: Learning That No Means No

Marc was a student in one of Dr. Blonna's Human Sexuality classes. He submitted a written assignment about how he learned the difference between yes and no.

I'm embarrassed to write this, but I think the story needs to be told. I grew up learning that when a woman said no, she really meant yes. My brother and his friends explained it to me by saying that women do this so they can remain ladies but still get laid. It made sense to me then, even though I now realize this kind of thinking is crazy.

I didn't encounter this with the first two women I had sex with. They both willingly went along. I went out with my second girlfriend for almost two years. When we broke up, I had to start dating again and didn't get anywhere with the first two girls I went out with. They didn't even let me get to first base.

The third woman was very sexy. I met her at a frat party, and she was hot. We danced a little and had a couple of beers, and then she wanted to leave. I walked her back to her room, and she invited me up. Her roommates had gone home for the weekend and we started making out on the couch. She was so sexy and I thought she really wanted to have sex. She let me feel her breasts and put my hand in her pants, but every time I tried to unzip her jeans, she pulled away and said no. I figured she was just teasing and really wanted me to continue, so I kept pushing the limit.

After about twenty minutes of this, she suddenly pushed me off of her and literally dumped me on the floor. She screamed at me, "Look, I told you 'no' five times. I don't want to fuck you, now get out before I call the campus cops."

I was shocked and very upset. I really didn't want to rape her, just push her until she gave in. I felt embarrassed and wanted to explain how I felt, but she told me if I didn't leave immediately, she'd call the police. I ran out of there zipping up as I left. I've seen her on campus, but she won't even look at me. I learned that no really means no!

hostile climate and failing to stop when the other person expresses a desire to halt the sexual overtures or remarks.

Some child development authorities think that most 6- and 7-year-olds like the ones publicized in North Carolina and New York are too young to understand the concept of sexual harassment. Their behavior might be better labeled as a form of bullying in which they use power over another inappropriately. Some child development experts view this as a sort of testing the waters, and children (both perpetrator and victim) need to be educated about how to handle the situation rather than take it out of their hands. By having the proper authorities (such as school officials) step in, the victim relinquishes the ability to develop a repertoire of assertive behavior that could be used to fend off future would-be harassers.[6]

Prosecutors would counter this defense by claiming that abuse of power is the first step in harassment. If a 6- or 7-year-old thinks he (or she) can kiss or pull a button off a skirt of a classmate, the next act might be more overtly sexual in nature, Also, by stepping in quickly, the school officials are bringing the issue to the students' (and parents') awareness.

In response to these and a host of other lawsuits being filed around the country, the U. S. Department of Education's Office for Civil Rights issued a new policy entitled "Sexual Harassment Guidance: Harassment of Students by School Employees, Other Students, and Third Parties." The document attempts to bring standards for determining sexual harassment in line with the guidelines used for evaluating adult cases. The policy defines the same two types of sexual harassment used in adult rulings: quid pro quo (say, sexual favors for advancement) and hostile environment.[7]

Sexual Harassment in College

Over the past decade, many colleges have instituted sexual harassment policies, in response to concerns of students, faculty members, and administrators. Most sexual harassment in college is between male professors and female students. Although the reverse can happen (female professor harassing a male student), it is much less common.

Between 15% and 50% of undergraduate and graduate-level college women report having been the victim of sexual harassment by a professor. Further, between 10% and 20% of male undergraduates have been the victims of sexual harassment.[8] This encompasses either unwanted sexual advances or the creation of a hostile environment.

Table 16.1 illustrates some of the findings of Benson and Thompson's classic study of sexual harassment at the University of California, Berkeley.

Case Study

Beth:
A Proposition from Her Professor

Beth is a 23-year-old college senior. She was having trouble with one of her classes and went to see her professor, a 35-year-old, married man.

When I went to see him, I was a little surprised that he shut the door. It was after our late-afternoon class, and there wasn't anybody around in his department. He had this weird little smile on his face when he asked me to sit down. I sensed something was wrong and should have left then, but I didn't. When I sat down, his first remark was about how good I smelled. I smiled and thanked him but thought to myself that the comment was totally inappropriate.

I explained to him that I was there because I was worried about my grade for the semester. I had gotten a "D" on the last test and didn't want to lower my grade below a "B–." He told me not to worry; he didn't like to see me so sad. Again I smiled but thought that this remark was also inappropriate. He said he'd take care of me, that I was one of his favorite students. With that, he slid his hand over the table and began rubbing my hand with his.

I was getting very uncomfortable by now and moved my hand away. He said, "Don't be so tense; let

me rub your shoulders." He started to get up, but I stood up and said, "I don't think that's necessary. I must be going."

He said "Sit down. I thought you wanted to talk about your grade."

I sat back down, and he proceeded to explain to me that he'd had his eye on me all semester and was hoping I'd come to visit him. He explained that other female students in the past had worked out "special arrangements" to boost their grades.

I asked him, "What kind of special arrangements?"

He said, "Come on now, Beth, don't be so naive. You're a very sexy girl. We could have lots of fun together."

At this point, I was so flustered that I got up quickly and excused myself. I had to beat him to the door because he got up as if to block my exit, but I already had opened the door. He smiled and told me not to do anything foolish. I didn't tell anyone because I was afraid he'd flunk me. He kind of ignored me the rest of the semester but did wind up giving me a higher grade than I thought I earned.

Table **16.1**	The Berkeley Study
Behavior	**Examples**
Verbal advances	Explicit sexual propositions
Invitations	For dates, to one's apartment
Physical advances	Touching, kissing, fondling breasts
Body language	Leering, standing too close
Emotional come-ons	Writing long letters
Undue attention	Too helpful
Sexual bribery	Grade offered in exchange for affair

Source: "Sexual Harassment on a University Campus: The Confluence of Authority Relations, Sexual Interest and Gender Stratification," by Donna J. Benson and G. E. Thompson in *The Society for the Study of Social Problems,* 29:3 (1981), p. 242. Reprinted with permission.

It shows the range of unwanted sexual attention expressed by a group of Berkeley students regarding sexual harassment by their professors. In the Berkeley study approximately one-third of female students reported at least one incident of sexual harassment on campus.[9]

RAPE

The dictionary definition of **rape** is "sexual intercourse without the consent of the man/woman and effected by force, duress, intimidation or deception as to the nature of the act."[10] The word *rape* comes from the Latin term *rapere*, which means to steal, seize, or carry away. Rape has been a common theme in literature, art, and popular culture throughout history.

Chilling examples of rape occur regularly in cartoons, comic strips, and other "children's entertainment." The caveman, replete with club and knuckles dragging the earth, is out and about to find a mate. When he spies the female he desires, he hits her with the club, knocks her out, and drags her away by her long hair (presumably to make her his wife).

More than 95% of rapes are committed by men against women or other men. Although 9 of 10 rapists are men, this does not mean that all men rape, nor are all men potential rapists. If you were to take a sample of 100 rapists, more than 90 would be men. If you were to take a random sample of 100 men, fewer than 10 would be rapists or potential rapists. The statistic does mean, however, that most of the rapes are committed by a small percentage of men who achieve power over women and other men by forced sexual aggression.

Rape is a form of **sexual aggression**, a broader term than rape, encompassing all forms of nonconsensual sexual behavior against men, women

Rape
illicit sexual intercourse without consent

Although nearly all rapes are committed by men, only a small percentage of all men are rapists.

Sexual aggression
any form of forced sexual contact, including but not limited to intercourse, without the person's consent

children, and gay people as victims.[11] It includes fondling, oral sex, and anal sex, as well as vaginal intercourse. Sexual coercion, the broadest term, covers all nonconsensual sexual behavior that results from arguing, pleading, and cajoling, in addition to force.

The term "victim" is gradually being replaced by words such as "target" and "survivor," in some contexts. This avoids further degradation of the person who was raped. The new terminology connotes the encouragement for survivors to reclaim control over their lives.

In most states, to be considered rape, the target's body (usually the vagina) has to be penetrated. Forced oral sex and the insertion of fingers and other objects into the vagina, anus, or mouth don't automatically qualify as rape. Although these sexually aggressive acts are still illegal and can result in prosecution, they are tried as less serious offenses than is rape.

Rape includes stranger rape, acquaintance rape (also known as date rape), marital rape, gang rape, and statutory rape. A last category of rape, male rape, usually is committed by men against other men but does occur, rarely, with women as the perpetrators.

PERSPECTIVES   A Historical Look at Rape

In *Against Our Will*, one of the most definitive works on the subject, author Susan Brownmiller describes the evolution of our current attitudes toward rape and the laws against it.* According to Brownmiller, rape has a long, sordid history. In antiquity, women were considered one of the spoils of war, objects to be taken and used in whatever way one wished. After a battle, the conquering army routinely rounded up all female survivors and had free rein to do what they wanted with them. Women who resisted were routinely slaughtered. Women who were spared were often sold off as slaves once their captors became bored with them.

Although rape seems to have been a part of all cultures, it has not always been considered a crime against a person. The earliest statutes against rape were laws related to property. Women were not considered persons. Instead, they were valued as property. They could provide labor and bear children — two important commodities in an agrarian economy dependent upon the availability of workers.

Under Hammurabi's Code (Babylonian law approximately 4,000 years old), a woman was not considered to be a free, independent human being. She was considered to be some man's (father's, husband's) property. Therefore, if someone violated the woman, he committed a crime against that man's property and was prosecuted accordingly.

Women also were categorized according to their marital status and virginity. Virgins were considered purer than nonvirgins in relation to sex-related crimes. The purest of all virgins were those engaged to be married. A man convicted of raping a betrothed virgin was put to death and his victim set free. A man convicted of raping a married woman also was put to death. His victim, however, also was put to death because she was considered a willing victim or accomplice in the crime. Presumably, the feeling was that she somehow led the rapist on or consented to the act. The two early beliefs about women and rape — that a woman is a man's property, and that rape cannot occur unless a woman somehow consents — still exist and form the foundation of much of the legislation and belief systems that people share about rape.

*New York: Simon and Schuster, 1975.

Stranger Rape

Stranger rape is rape by a person whom the target does not know. The overwhelming majority of rapes reported to the police and resulting in prosecution are stranger rapes. Although stranger rape can involve a premeditated assault with an anonymous assailant descending upon the victim totally without warning, statistics prove otherwise. Most cases of stranger rape seem to spring out of chance meetings that create the potential for assault. The assailant targets the victim in a park, a shopping mall parking lot, while driving in a car, and so on. The perpetrator initiates contact, appears friendly, "safe," and lulls the victim into relaxing her (usually) guard, allowing the perpetrator to strike. The assailant maneuvers the target to one or the other of their cars or lures the victim into an alley, stairwell, or other remote location, then commits the rape.

Stranger rapes are more likely to involve guns, knives and other weapons than other forms of rape.[12] Older persons are more likely to be raped in their homes than in public places, and the assailant often gains access by overpowering them or by posing as a delivery person, utility representatives, and the like.[13] A relatively recent type of stranger rape involves targeting women who are driving by themselves. The perpetrators intentionally rear-end the cars of their potential victims, forcing them to pull off the road, where they are assaulted when they leave their car to investigate the accident. Often the rape is combined with stealing the woman's car.

Stranger rape
forced intercourse by a person who is unknown to the target person

Acquaintance Rape

Many experts consider **acquaintance rape**, also known as date rape, to be the most common and least reported of all forms of rape. It is a form of rape defined as forced sexual intercourse by a dating partner. Women are often reluctant to report the incident because of their relationship with the perpetrator. Often, victims will even question if it was actually rape or if they are to blame. Male perpetrators often report that their actions don't constitute rape, that their dates came onto them and initiated, or at least consented to, the sexual activity. Most date rape is not planned. The sex may be planned, but the actual rape is not.

In recent years, date rape has become a serious issue to think about as young adults begin to explore intimate relationships with one another.

As many as 20% of all college women report having experienced date rape or attempted rape. The number of reports of other forms of sexual violation, including being touched and kissed against their will, are even higher.[14] Although some men report similar experiences, the occurrence of female-to-male date rape is rare.

Acquaintance rape
forced intercourse by a person, other than a spouse, whom the victim knows

Post-Traumatic Stress Disorder

Date rape can be traumatic, and targets feel particularly violated because in most cases the perpetrator was someone with whom they had developed some trust. Because of this, survivors often have **post-traumatic stress disorder** (PTSD). PTSD sufferers experience anxiety, sleeplessness, eating disorders, depression, and hyperactive neural functioning. Date rape victims

Post-traumatic stress disorder (PTSD)
a syndrome developing after exposure to an extremely traumatic event. Symptoms include anxiety, sleeplessness, eating disorders, depression, and hyperactive nervous system activity

also have considerable stress related to future dating and establishing trust within intimate relationships.

Drinking and Date Rape

Many college students use alcohol and other drugs to "fit in," cope with college stressors, and reduce inhibitions related to dating and sex. Unfortunately, alcohol consumption is often linked to sexual coercion and other forms of violence.

In a study of 1,500 undergraduate women in a large midwestern university in 1992, alcohol was implicated in a variety of problems.[15] Besides alcohol, another drug, **Rohoypnol**, has been implicated in date rape. Rohoypnol, also known as "roofies" or the "date-rape drug," is a depressant drug that is illegal in the United States. Besides having classic depressant drug characteristics (slowing central nervous system functioning), Rohoypnol causes loss of consciousness and memory loss. Because of this, women who have been raped while under the influence of Rohoypnol are unable to resist the rapist or recall any of the details concerning the incident. The assailant mixes Rohoypnol, a powder, into the drink of the unsuspecting woman, then takes advantage of her once the drug takes effect.

More prevalent is **binge drinking**. Bingeing on alcohol often becomes part of the social fabric of the college experience. Wechsler and colleagues studied the binge drinking behavior of more than 17,000 students on 140

Rohoypnol
a depressant drug also known as the "date rape drug," because it causes loss of memory and makes women vulnerable to uninvited sexual intercourse

Binge drinking
having four or more drinks at one sitting

Health Hint

Reducing Risks for Stranger Rape

Personal preparation

1. *Plan in advance.* Be aware of where you are, areas of possible trouble, and escape routes.

2. *Avoid dark and isolated areas.* Park in well-lit areas, as close to stores as possible. Avoid dark side streets, back roads, and the like, whenever possible. Jog and bicycle only in busy or public places.

3. *Arrange for an escort.* Have someone leave work, school, or an event with you and walk you to your car. Avoid empty stairwells and elevators unless you are accompanied by your escort.

4. *Use technology.* Carry an airhorn or whistle. If you can afford it, install automatic door locks and alarms in your car. Buy a cellular phone and carry it with you. Install your local police department number as a quick-dial memory number.

5. *Take a self-defense course.* Know how to defend yourself. A few simple techniques can make a difference.

6. *Remain vigilant.* Don't let your guard down. You are a potential victim any time you go anywhere by yourself.

What to do if you are attacked

1. *Run away if you can.*

2. *Resist if you can.* Be as active and loud as possible: Scream, curse, yell, cause a scene. If you have a whistle or horn, blow it.

3. *Fight back.* Kick, punch, bite, scratch, vomit, spit. Use your keys, umbrellas, rolled-up newspapers, and books to jab for the eyes, throat, and face. There are no rules, and fighting back may reduce the abuse you might sustain without increasing your risk of injury. Carry keys in your hand as a weapon.

4. *Stall for time.* If you can't fight back, talk to your attacker — by name if you know it. Express empathy. Get him talking. Try to escape at the first distraction.

four-year college campuses across the United States.[16] They found binge drinking to be associated with unplanned and unsafe sexual activity, physical and sexual assault, other criminal violations, physical injury, interpersonal problems, and poor academic performance.

The results confirmed what several smaller-scale studies of college drinking had uncovered.[17] About one in six (16%) of all the respondents were nondrinkers (15% of the men, 16% of the women). About two in five (41%) were drinkers but did not binge. Almost half (44%) of all the students were binge drinkers. About one in five (19%) were frequent binge drinkers (17% of the women and 23% of the men). These students had three or more binge drinking episodes within the past 2 weeks.

The consequences of binge drinking are many and varied. Binge drinkers were more likely than nonbinge drinkers and abstainers to engage in unplanned sexual activity, not use protection when having sex, get hurt or injured, damage property, argue with friends, miss classes, get behind in schoolwork, and do something they later regretted. Frequent binge drinkers were 10 times more likely than bingers to have unplanned and unprotected sex, get into trouble with campus police, and get injured or damage property. When asked to evaluate the seriousness of their bingeing and its repercussions, less than 1% of the binge drinkers designated themselves as problem drinkers.[18]

In the car

1. *Always drive with your doors locked.*

2. *Lock your doors immediately after you park.*

3. *Approach your car with your keys in your hand* (have them sticking out like brass knuckles) and check the back seat to make sure no one is hiding there before you let yourself in.

4. *If you break down, do not leave the car.* Tie a white rag to the antenna, lock yourself in, and wait for the police. If someone other than the police arrives, ask this person to call the police or a local garage. Don't open the door.

5. *If your car is hit from behind, don't leave the car.* Put your flashers on and wait for the police to arrive.

6. *Buy a cellular phone, if you can afford it.* It will enable you to call the police immediately.

At Home

1. *Don't list your name in the phone book, over the doorbell, or on the mailbox.*

2. *Install secure locks on all windows and doors.* Change locks if you lose your keys, move, or change your living situation (a roommate, husband, or boyfriend leaves).

3. *Install a peephole and safety chain and bar* on your door.

4. *Don't let people in your home unless you can verify who they are.* All service representatives (gas company, police, and so on), have identification. Request that they hold it in front of the peephole so you can see it. When in doubt, call the agency and verify who they are.

5. *Leave a light on near the entrance* when you know you will be returning home after dark.

6. *Organize or join a neighborhood watch program* for your block, building, or complex.

7. *Get a dog.* Perpetrators are less likely to attack you if you have a dog with you.

Health Hint   Reducing Risks for Date Rape

The following are specific strategies for women to reduce their risks for date rape:

- Arrange for your first date to be in a public place or as part of a larger group. Arrange your own transportation, or go with your friends.

- In the earliest stages of the relationship, suggest paying for yourself. This will derail any notion that your date thinks you owe him something. It also will give you an opportunity to assess his views about women.

- Pay attention to your date's attitudes and behavior. Is he controlling? Does he want to make all of the decisions?

- Avoid using alcohol and other drugs if you don't want to become involved in intimate sexual activities.

- Don't send mixed messages or anything that can be perceived as "teasing." If kissing is acceptable but you don't want to go any farther, state this clearly: "I'd like to hug and kiss, but I don't want to let things go any farther than this."

- If things begin to get out of control, resist. Use more and more emphatic verbal resistance: " I said, NO!!" If this doesn't work, use physical force: punch, slap, kick. Men are much more likely to believe you if you use physical force when you're saying no. Push him away, stand up, open the door, ask him to stop or leave. If this doesn't work, say, "This is rape. I'm calling the police."

- Run away. If he persists, escape. Get away. Go to a public place, and call the police.

Despite the overall decline in drinking in the United States, drinking on college campuses fails to show a corresponding drop-off. Drinking by college students often revolves around its social nature. College women perceive drinking as a way of being around others and seeking the acceptance of peers.[19] Alcohol is consumed more for social than for personal reasons.[20] Students reported using alcohol more for the purpose of meeting members of the other sex than for personal reasons, although alcohol did make them feel better about themselves.

Drinking behavior that elsewhere would be characterized as alcohol abuse is often socially acceptable and even desirable behavior on certain college campuses.[21] "Party schools" foster reputations and environments in which binge drinking is part of the fabric of college life. Conversely, institutions that do not have alcohol outlets within 1 mile of campus and colleges that prohibit alcohol use for everyone (even those older than 21 years of age) have lower rates of alcohol bingeing.

In "party schools," drinking is ingrained into the very fabric of college life.

Marital Rape

For many years, police were reluctant to investigate and prosecute marital rape. In a landmark case from 1978, Greta Rideout of Oregon filed charges against her husband for nonconsensual sex, bringing marital rape to national attention. Approximately 13% of married women had been raped by their husbands.[22] In most cases, the husband used force (84%) or the threat of

Health Hint

Helping a Friend Who Has Been Raped

Even though trained rape-crisis professionals are available in most communities, the first contact a survivor has is often a friend, roommate, or family member. If someone you care about has been raped, here are some tips to help you support them.

◡ *Accept her.* Be nonjudgmental about what happened. Tell her she is not to blame for the incident.

◡ *Listen.* Encourage her to tell you what happened. Listen actively and give her positive feedback.

◡ *Offer shelter and support.* Tell her you'll be there for her (and be sure you are). Offer her a safe haven until her ordeal is over. Care for her needs (food, clothing, a shoulder to cry on).

◡ *Have empathy.* Tell her you're sorry for what happened but glad she's alive and her injuries aren't worse.

◡ *Encourage action.* Tell her it's important that she report what happened to the police.

◡ *Accompany her to the police station.*

◡ *Keep your own feelings in check.* She will remain calmer if you do.

---

force (9%). The rape was an isolated incident for 31% of the victims. Another 31% reported being raped more than 20 times, and the rest fell somewhere in the middle.[23]

Perpetrators of marital rape share some of the same personality traits as other rapists — namely, anger, power, and sadism. Husbands who rape are also more likely to abuse their wives verbally, psychologically, and physically. More than 30% of wives who were raped also reported having been targets of physical abuse during their marriage.[24]

Verbal and psychological abuse often prove more damaging than physical abuse. The verbal and psychological abusers create an environment of endless criticism, suspicion, and torment. Abusers often undermine the confidence and self-esteem of their mates through constant criticism of everything from the way they look to their level of competence in performing simple household tasks. Abusers are extremely jealous and turn even the most casual remark or involvement with another person into suspicions of flirting or having an affair. This constant flow of criticism, insults, and accusations is tormenting and can result in a host of psychological problems.[25]

Survivors of marital rape suffer after-effects that are similar to those of women who have been sexually assaulted by someone they know (date rape). Because they know their assailants intimately and have an established history of trust, they feel especially betrayed, humiliated, and angry.

Statutory Rape

Statutory rape refers to sexual intercourse between a person older than the legal age of consent with a partner who is younger than legal age of consent.

Statutory rape
a person older than the legal age of consent having intercourse with a partner who is younger than the legal age of consent

In the eyes of the law, females under the age of consent established by each state are not considered legally capable of giving informed consent.

The legal age of consent in the states varies from 12 to 21 years of age. Traditionally, most states' original legal wording of definitions of statutory rape defined perpetrators as males and victims as females. Revised definitions of statutory rape are more gender-neutral and describe adult perpetrators and victims under the legal age of consent.

The recent high-profile case of 34-year old teacher Mary Kay Letourneau, convicted of the statutory rape of her 12-year-old student/lover, illustrates the importance of these revisions. Letourneau received national attention when the former elementary school teacher was convicted of having sex with (and becoming pregnant by) her former student. Even though the two claimed to be in love and the sex was consensual, the courts convicted her of statutory rape.

Case Study

Donna: A Saga of Spousal Abuse

Donna is a 33-year-old continuing education student. She is divorced and the mother of two daughters, 10 and 11 years of age. Donna related her story to one of the authors in a diary detailing her sexual development.

My father was an alcoholic. I didn't realize it as a young child, but by the time I was a teenager, I understood why my dad had lost his driver's license a couple of times, had a hard time holding down a steady job, and was so angry all of the time. Of course, by then it was too late. I loved him so much and felt so guilty about admitting to myself that he was an alcoholic. I blamed myself a lot for his behavior. "Maybe it's my fault Daddy drinks so much," I thought. "Maybe if I was a better daughter, he'd be okay."

Often Dad's anger was directed at Mom. He'd come home drunk after stopping off for "a few beers" after work and just be itching for a fight. The least little thing Mom would do would set him off, and he'd smack her with the back of his hand. My sister and I would run for our lives and dive under our bed or lock ourselves in the closet until he'd pass out. We'd hear Mom getting hit but would be too afraid to do anything.

Afterward mom would try to comfort us by saying that Daddy was really a "good man" and "cared"

about her but he just couldn't hold his liquor. She said that sometimes a woman has to stand by her man even when things weren't going well. I think about those words now, and I shudder.

Sometimes he'd turn on us if we tried to help Mom. He broke my arm once during one of these outbursts, and I had to go to the hospital to have a cast put on. To this day I can't believe that the hospital staff didn't know what was happening and intervene. Not only was my arm broken, but I had black-and-blue marks all over from where Dad hit me with his belt and his hand.

I ran away when I was 18. I guess it wasn't really running away since I was legally an adult, but to me it was because I wasn't leaving — I was escaping (at least I thought I was). I bounced around the country for a couple of years, in and out of jobs as well as relationships with men.

My first real love was a guy who reminded me a lot of my father. I guess I felt like a victim and was attracted to a guy who allowed me to be a victim. I needed to be punished to feel good, and he was up to the task. He'd treat me like dirt, constantly tell me I wasn't pretty and was terrible in bed, couldn't do anything right, and on and on. He drank, just like my dad, and beat me just like my dad beat my mom.

In statutory rape cases, consent of the under-age partner has little bearing in the case. In the eyes of the law, people under the age of consent are not considered legally capable of making an informed decision concerning their sexual behavior.

The whole notion of statutory rape brings up many vexing questions. Although the intent is to prevent older men from exploiting young women and girls, many sub-issues are troubling. For instance, should charges be brought against a 17-year-old boy who has sex with his 15-year-old girlfriend? Is it right for 16-year-old boys to be considered legally capable of making informed sexual choices but not girls of the same age? Should anyone under 16 years of age be considered capable of making informed choices?

Fate saved me from him, however. He was a real bad guy and was arrested for stealing a car and crashing it into a storefront. He was sent to jail for five years, and I wasn't into waiting around so I took off and wound up in a neighboring state.

I met my husband shortly after arriving. I was working as a barmaid, and he came into the bar late one night. I was very attracted to him and wound up going home with him that night. I moved in after about a month and got pregnant with my first child about six months later. He liked to drink, but it didn't seem to affect him at first. He was a pretty good guy until times got tough.

After the baby was born, we got married and he lost his job the next week. He couldn't find another job and had to go on unemployment for six months. He couldn't handle this and began to take it out on me. I was pregnant with our second child at the time. He started really abusing me for my size (I gained a lot of weight) and began hitting me. I almost miscarried one night after he hit me and knocked me down. When he sobered up, he felt really bad and apologized. He told me he'd never do it again. He said he loved me.

I felt trapped and didn't know what to do. I was pregnant, had a one-year-old baby, had no education, no real job skills, no money in the bank, and few real friends to turn to. I continued to live with him but

began to fear for my safety and that of the kids. I started to try to think of a way out. Something deep within me didn't want to wind up like my mother. He must have sensed it because he got very controlling. He tried to limit my involvement with any friends, checked my mail, scrutinized the phone bills. The beatings were coming more often, and he began to hit the kids more and more.

Things finally came to a head one night. After a particularly savage fight, a neighbor called the police. When the police arrived, they saw what he had done to me and locked him up. My children and I were examined, and I pressed charges for domestic and child abuse. To make a long story short, the kids and I found refuge in a battered women's shelter and he got three years in prison.

As soon as I was able, I filed divorce papers, went back to work, saved a few dollars, and left the state. I located my sister, also divorced with two kids, and we moved in together. We've both been working our way back slowly ever since — caring for each other and our kids, trying to put our lives back together. I'm in a support group for survivors of spousal abuse and have been dating a very nice man for about a year.

Incidence of Rape

The true incidence of rape in the United States is unknown. Federal estimates rely on reported cases. Critics have argued that a significant percentage of victims do not report the crimes to the police. Therefore, statistics that use reported incidents as their measure greatly underestimate the true incidence of rape. Further, this forces independent researchers to conduct survey research studies on smaller samples of women and extrapolate the findings to the population as a whole. Often these independent studies define rape differently, use differing methodologies, and mix incidence and prevalence measures, making meaningful comparisons of their data almost impossible.[26]

In 1991, the FBI reported 102,500 cases of rape. These are actual cases reported to the agency by various branches of law enforcement across the country. Two organizations conducted survey research in 1990, extrapolating their findings to estimate the number of rapes occurring in that year. The National Crime Survey reported 130,236 rapes in 1990.[27] The National Victim Center reported 683,000 victims of rape.[28]

Although the actual numbers of cases in these three sets of data are greatly disparate, most experts (police and civilian) agree that the actual number of rapes is probably much higher than the reported or estimated numbers that usually show up in reports or in the press. Rape is one of the least reported of all crimes in the United States. Between 10% and 50% of all rapes may go unreported to the police.[29] If we use the 1990 FBI reported

---

PERSPECTIVES

Myths About Rape

Myth: Rape is a sexual act, not a violent one.

Fact: Although the rapist achieves sexual gratification through his actions, the rape is first and foremost an act of violence. If sexual release were all that a rapist desires, he could achieve that by finding a willing partner, masturbating, or paying a prostitute for sex. The rapist seeks to dominate his victim, to exert power, and to humiliate by using threat and violence. In contrast, sex is a consensual act of pleasure, not a violent act of power.

Myth: Women secretly want to be raped.

Fact: Even though many men and women have rape fantasies, there is a world of difference between using fantasy to become sexually aroused and actually desiring to be assaulted, forced to submit to another's sexual onslaught, and humiliated or beaten in the process. In a fantasy, you control the situation, orchestrate the

script, create the happy ending. In a rape, someone assaults you and controls you. Women don't want to be raped.

Myth: A woman can't be raped if she really doesn't want to be.

Fact: The logic of this myth revolves around the difficulty surrounding inserting a penis into a vagina that is thrashing to and fro. Men who rape use force to hurt women, to injure them to the point of submission. They have been known to break her hip to stop it from moving. Rape is not about two lovers playfully teasing each other into submission. Rape is about force, domination, and pain.

Myth: Women ask for it by the way they act and dress.

Fact: Women don't dress provocatively to invite rapists. The idea of a woman wanting to attract a man and

cases as a baseline, that means that between 10,000 and 50,000 additional cases go unreported each year. Rape survivors are reluctant to report the crime for several reasons: fear of retaliation by the rapist, embarrassment or shame, fear of rejection by husband, boyfriend, or family, a desire to protect the rapist, and a lack of confidence in the judicial system.[30]

In a study of 246 rape victims, the following five variables were found to be related to whether a victim reports a rape:[31]

1. The relationship between the victim and the rapist
2. How the two came together
3. Threat of force
4. Use of force
5. Extent of injury
6. Use of medical treatment.

Victims were more likely to report when the rapist was a stranger or acquaintance rather than a friend or relative, had broken into her house, or had assaulted her in a public place (versus a party or other social situation), had threatened to use force (versus not threatening her), did use force (less likely to report if no actual force), had caused substantial injury (versus little physical harm), and had sought medical care for her injuries (versus not seeking medical care).

A close look at the variables related to more likelihood of reporting indicates that women are much more likely to report a rape when evidence

---

initiate a sexual liaison by acting in a sexy way is much different from the notion of a woman dressing in revealing clothing because she wants to be raped. If a woman intentionally acts and dresses provocatively to attract a man, that doesn't give any man the right to rape her.

Myth: No really means yes.

Fact: Where does the notion that *no* means *yes* come from? Is it a rationalization, made up by men, to justify their domination and overpower women into submission? Or is it a leftover piece of baggage from the Victorian era, reminding women that ladies are not supposed to enjoy sex? In that line of thinking, because a lady can't ask for sex, she has to say no even though she means yes. That way she can have it both ways: maintain her status as a lady and still have sex ("he did it to me"). Wherever this belief came

from, it's time to stop it and realize that *no* means *no*. When in doubt, don't continue.

Myth: Rape is justifiable under certain circumstances.

Fact: Rape is never justifiable. No one — husband, lover, boyfriend, father, or any man — ever has the right to force sex on anyone.

Myth: Most rapists are crazy.

Fact: Most rapists are not crazy. They are similar to the average man except for three distinguishing characteristics: (1) They are hostile toward women and have a harder time handling it, (2) they have more traditional beliefs about gender roles, and (3) they are more willing to use force to achieve their ends.

Myth: Women are responsible for preventing rape.

Fact: Everyone is responsible for preventing rape.

of the attack was available. This could consist of observable or clinical evidence of injury and the need for medical attention, when the woman clearly was not at fault (forced entry or a public place, didn't know the perpetrator or didn't know him well), and she felt emotionally distant from the rapist.

The variables found to be unrelated to the reporting of a rape were the victim's age, race, employment, living situation, the rapist's age, race, number of rapists, and place of assault.[32]

Perhaps more rape victims would come forth if they didn't feel that they were responsible for providing the burden of proof that the crime occurred. This attitude in part stems from the myths associated with rape that persist despite years of efforts to clear up misconceptions about the crime by individuals and organizations concerned about rape.

Characteristics of Rapists

Most of what we know about men who rape comes from research conducted on convicted rapists. It is estimated that less than 10% of all rapists are convicted of this crime. FBI statistics, in 1992, on convicted rapists are similar of those for perpetrators of other serious crimes: Most are under 25 years of age, are from single- or foster-parent homes, are marginally employed, have a low income, and have little formal education.

Because fewer than 10% of all rapists are ever convicted of their crimes, several researchers have studied populations of men who rape who have not been convicted or incarcerated. In one of the most comprehensive reviews of the literature, Cate and Lloyd identified seven characteristics of men who rape:

1. They are much more likely than their nonrapist peers to hold traditional beliefs about women and women's roles and female stereotypes. These beliefs range from nonsexual views concerning a woman's place (in the home) to sexual beliefs that men are the initiators during sex and that women want men to initiate.

2. They believe in rape-supportive myths — women secretly want to be overpowered during sex; they like it rough; *no* really means *yes* — and other stereotypical beliefs about women.

3. They use exploitative techniques such as coercing women into sex using alcohol and other drugs.

4. They accept the use of violence as a way to solve problems and dominate others.

5. They are more likely to vent their anger and express their need to dominate sexually rather than find other outlets for these feelings.

6. They devalue all that is feminine. They are hostile toward "feminine" personality attributes such as nurturance and collaboration and devalue traditional female pursuits such as child care and homemaking.

7. They are generally more sexually active than their peers who do not rape.

Malamuth and associates studied the sexual behavior of college men.[33] Using a large, representative sample (their sexual histories were unknown) instead of convicted rapists, Malamuth found four characteristics of men who rape:

1. *Hostility toward women.* Men who rape have a deep-seated hostility toward women and feminine traits. They devalue traits such as nurturance and equality and value dominance, power, and aggression.

2. *Hostile home environment.* Men who rape grew up in households where violence, battering, sexual abuse, and hostility between family members were the norm.

3. *History of delinquency.* Men who rape associate with peers who are delinquent and reinforce the same hostile, aggressive behaviors that were modeled in their homes and that contributed to their own delinquency.

4. *Sexual **promiscuity**.* Contrary to the perception that men who rape are sexually deprived, rapists generally are more sexually active than non-rapists but report much higher levels of dissatisfaction with their sex lives than their nonraping peers.

Promiscuity
frequent and indiscriminate change in sexual partners

Malamuth's and Cate and Lloyd's work seems to confirm Sanday's[34] findings concerning hostility toward women, stereotypical perceptions about women, and the devaluation of women and all things feminine as key attributes of rapists and societies that are "rape-prone."

Characteristics of Targets

Any female can be the target of rape. The woman can be young or old, attractive or unattractive, dressed provocatively or conservatively. Most targets tend to be under 30 years of age and single. Age and marital status may have more to do with the likelihood that these women travel, shop, walk, and live alone rather than some other factor.

Women who are the targets of rape are no different from nontargets in terms of personality attributes, lifestyle, or behavior. Attempts to characterize targets as being different from other women only serves to blame the victim rather than understand that it is the men who rape through their own actions.

CHILD SEXUAL ABUSE

Child sexual abuse is any sexual contact between an adult and a child under 18 years of age. Child sexual abuse runs the gamut from inappropriate fondling and touching, to masturbation, to oral sex, to penetration of the anus or vagina with fingers or a penis. These and other forms of sexual behavior are considered evidence of child sexual abuse despite the child's consent or sexual precociousness.

Child sexual abuse involving nonfamily members is generally referred to as **child molestation**. Child sexual abuse involving genetically related family members is called **incest**. Often, the perpetrators are adults who fall between the two forms, such as step-relatives, the mother's boyfriend, or a caregiver brought into the house to watch the children. As we discussed in Chapter 9,

Child sexual abuse
any sexual contact between an adult and a child who is under 18 years of age

Child molestation
abuse of a child by nonfamily members

Incest
child sexual abuse involving genetically related family members

a pedophile is an adult who is sexually aroused by children and initiates contact with them out of sexual desire. A nonpedophilic child molester is not motivated by sexual desire but, rather, by power, the desire to control, or out of affection.

Preconditions Related to Child Sexual Abuse

Preconditions related to child sexual abuse have been identified.[35] These are explored below.

Motivation to Abuse

Three key variables influence the perpetrator's motivation to abuse: emotional congruence, sexual arousal, and blockage of alternative forms of sexual arousal. Whereas adults typically are attracted to, and seek emotional connections with, other adults in emotional congruence, pedophiles are drawn to children for this fulfillment. This may be a result of the perpetrator's arrested emotional development, a need to feel powerful and in control, or a reenactment of his own childhood abuse.

Typically, adults are sexually aroused by other adults and find children's bodies immature and nonarousing. Pedophiles feel the opposite. They are sexually aroused by children and not by adults. In addition to the perpetrators' own modeling of sexual relations experienced in their youth or their own childhood trauma, it may be influenced by erotic portrayals of children in advertising and media or exposure to child pornography.

A subgroup of child sexual abusers are **sociopaths** or have **psychoses** or other forms of mental illness. These abusers obtain gratification not only from sexual activity but also from inflicting pain and suffering on their victims.

Blockage refers to child sexual abusers' inability to use other forms of sexual release and gratification. The abusers may be unable to form adult sexual relationships and be sexually naive. Their strict upbringing and sexual values may block their ability to use masturbation and fantasy as outlets for their sexual desire.

Internal Inhibitions Against Abuse

Child sexual abusers find ways to overcome **internal inhibitions** against adult-child sexual relations. Whereas other adults may be curious or fantasize about this activity, they stop short of actually doing it because of the strong cultural and social restrictions against such behavior. They have well developed impulse control. Child sexual abusers, however, lack these inhibitions. Further, they are more likely to use alcohol and drugs to overcome any inhibitions they do have.

External Inhibitions Against Abuse

External inhibitions against abuse include influences of family members, neighbors, friends, social connections, and household privacy. The greatest inhibitor of sexual abuse is the mother. Child sexual abuse is much more likely to occur in households where the mother is absent, neglectful, has emotional or physical problems, or is a victim of marital abuse.

Sociopath
a manifestly antisocial psychopath

Psychosis
severe form of mental disorder or disease affecting the total personality

Internal inhibitions
natural impulse control against adult-child sexual relations

External inhibitions
impulse control against abusing children, as influenced by surrounding people and environment

In cases where the mother herself was a victim of child sexual abuse or is disengaged from her husband, she will turn her back on, or even use, her daughter as a buffer between her and her husband.[36] This clears the way for the father, stepfather, mother's boyfriend, or other dominant man to gain access to the child.

Children who are socially isolated (having few close friends or neighbors) also are more likely to be victimized. Household sleeping arrangements and crowding, too, may create opportunities for abusers to gain ready access to victims.

Children's Resistance

Child sexual abusers prey on any perceived child weaknesses. They are canny in using coercion, threat, punishment, or force to overcome any resistance a child may use. Children who are emotionally insecure, deprived, needy, and unsupported are prime victims for the abuser's offers, pleas, bribes, and threats. Children who lack education about sexual abuse and do not have good communication skills and caring adult support systems are easier for the abuser to manipulate.

Risks for Child Sexual Abuse

In a study of approximately 800 college students conducted in 1984, eight risk factors were related to an increased likelihood of childhood sexual abuse:[37]

1. Have a stepfather
2. Ever lived with mother alone
3. Not close to mother
4. Mother never finished high school
5. Sex-punitive mother
6. No physical affection from father
7. Income under $10,000 a year (although low income by itself is not a risk)
8. Two friends or fewer in childhood.

The incidence of childhood sexual abuse was virtually nonexistent in subjects who did not have any of these risk factors. In contrast, two-thirds of the subjects reporting five or more of the risk factors were victims of childhood sexual abuse. The risk factor that was the greatest predictor of child sexual abuse was having a stepfather. This doubled a woman's risk of ever being abused. These findings confirmed those of Russel, who found that 1 in 40 victims of child sexual victims were abused by their biological fathers versus 1 in 6 from stepfathers.

The second greatest predictor was having a sex-punitive mother. This type of mother was likely to scold or punish her daughter for asking questions about sex or engaging in behavior such as masturbation.

Hyde speculated about child abuse as related to male psychosexual development.[38] She asserted that men are socialized to be sexually attracted to partners who are smaller and younger than they are, whereas women receive the opposite messages. Women usually are sexually involved with, and attracted to, partners who are larger and older than them.

Characteristics of Child Sexual Abusers

Child molester
one who makes indecent sexual
advances to children

Child sexual abusers tend to be shy, lonely, and have poor interpersonal skills with other adults.[39] They are conservative in their political and sexual beliefs, religious, and lack knowledge about sex.[40] **Child molesters** are more likely to be victims of child sexual molestation themselves, alcoholics, and have severe marital difficulties.[41]

Incidence of Child Sexual Abuse

In a national study of more than 2,500 adults, 27% of the women and 16% of the men reported being victims of child sexual abuse. Of these, one in four of the women and one in seven of the men reported being victimized by a family member.[42]

The actual number of cases of child sexual abuse is unknown. Further, the number of reported cases may represent just the tip of the iceberg regarding the actual incidence. National surveys estimate that between 20% and 33% of all girls and 10% to 16% of all boys in the United States have been victims of child sexual abuse.[43]

Like rape, child sexual abuse is often unreported for many reasons. Often sexual abuse starts off as normal hugging, kissing, and playful behavior. It then progresses to more intimate touching, manual and oral stimulation, and finally intercourse. The perpetrator often tells the child that he or she is not doing anything wrong but "don't tell anyone because they might not understand." The perpetrator often uses bribes and rewards to get the child to conceal the illicit behavior. Or physical threats or threats of desertion scare the child into silence. Children also may not report abuse because of fear and guilt. They sense that something is wrong but can't bear the shame of others finding out. Often, fear of reprisals from the perpetrator or other family member stands in the way of the victim's reporting abuse. In many cases, even when children report the behavior to a parent, they are not believed.

Effects of Child Sexual Abuse

Several factors have an impact on the future well-being of the victim. Four factors are related to the need for long-term treatment and the prognosis for the child.[44] The closer the victim's relationship to the perpetrator, the longer the abuse, the more violent the contact, and the more intrusive the relationship, the greater is the need for treatment and the poorer the hope for an effective outcome.

As adults, child sexual abuse victims report extremely sad, pain-filled childhoods. They recollect feelings of betrayal, fear, and loss of innocence, painting a picture of a lost childhood.[45] Victims of child sexual abuse often have difficulty forming intimate relationships as adults. They have feelings of shame and guilt, depression, a lack of trust and revulsion at being touched, and they often are alcohol and other drug abusers.[46] When victims are able to form relationships, they are often characterized by a lack of emotion and sexual interest and gratification.[47]

Megan's Law

More than 40 state legislatures have passed legislation similar to New Jersey's "**Megan's Law.**" The law is named after Megan Kanka, who was lured into the house of a neighbor, a known sex offender who raped and killed her. In May 1996, President Bill Clinton signed into law a federal version of the bill requiring all states who wish to continue to receive federal funding for law enforcement to enforce Megan's Law.[48] The law came under intense scrutiny from civil libertarian groups, who claimed it denies convicted sex offenders their constitutional rights to privacy and protection.[49]

The various versions of Megan's Law all contain provisions for identifying convicted sex offenders and ranking them on a three-tiered scale according to their likelihood to offend again. First-tier offenders are considered unlikely to molest again. Second-tier offenders are believed to be moderately likely to commit sexual assault again. Tier-three offenders are considered to be high risk. The level of community notification varies according to the offender's level. Tier-one offenders must register with local authorities, but their status is not released to the community. High-risk residents are notified of tier-two offenders (all day-care center operators, supervisors of Boy Scouts, Big Brothers, Big Sisters, and the like). All immediate neighbors and others likely to come in contact with tier-three offenders are sent registered letters notifying them of the presence of the offender in their neighborhood.[50]

Megan's Law
legislation requiring notification that a sex offender has been released and is residing in a community

Parents can help their children reduce their risks for becoming victims of sexual abuse by talking to them about ways to reduce their risks.

Critics of Megan's Law legislation claim that, in addition to being unconstitutional, it does not work. Just knowing that a sex offender lives on your street is not sufficient to protect your children.[51] Neighbors of Megan Kanka, for instance, knew that at least one sex offender (the roommate of Megan's killer) already lived on their street.[52]

There is no way to identify potential child abusers and isolate them from children. Preventing child sexual abuse must revolve around empowering children by teaching them the warning signs of inappropriate adult sexual behavior and the escape and communication skills necessary to protect themselves. Parents and other adult caregivers must convey to their children a sense of approachability. Children must feel free to discuss their concerns without fear of reprisal.

Strategies to Prevent Child Sexual Abuse

Parents, teachers, and other helpful adults might use the following strategies to help prevent child sexual abuse:

1. Provide sex education. One of the cornerstones of any good school-based sexuality education program is a child sexual abuse prevention component. The unit should be comprehensive and cover issues including self-esteem, communication skills, inappropriate adult physical contact, refusal skills, and escape skills. This unit should be presented early in the child's curriculum, as most sexual abuse begins before 8 years of age.

2. Become an approachable parent. Open lines of communication early with your children. Continually underscore the fact that your children can come to you with any question involving sex. Do not punish your children for asking questions.

3. Discuss inappropriate sexual behavior with your children. Let your children know that you do not approve of any adult-child sexual contact (explain kissing, hugging, and so forth). Tell them that you would never punish them for telling on another adult (no matter how close their relationship — stepfather, babysitter, coach). Differentiate "good touch" and "bad touch" while letting your children know that they have the right to want "no touch."

4. Let your children know they can decide how, when, and by whom they want to be touched. Do not force them to hug, kiss, or be affectionate with adults with whom they do not want to behave this way. This reinforces their trust in their intuition about other people's sexual behavior.

5. Discuss refusal skills. Have your children practice how to say no in an assertive way. Teach them how to refuse an offer to engage in any behavior in which they do not want to be involved.

6. Discuss escape skills. Teach your children how to escape from potentially dangerous or abusive situations. Tell them it is okay to yell, scream, hit, and run away from any adult who does not stop touching them when asked to. Help children identify trusted friends, neighbors, and family members with whom they can seek shelter.

7. Discuss telling. Your children have to understand that they absolutely must tell you if they have been approached or touched inappropriately by any adult, no matter how close that person's relationship is with you. Children need to understand that this isn't tattle-telling and is the best way to deal with the situation.

Case Study

Lucy: A Victim of Child Abuse

A 16-year-old girl was referred to the STD clinic by her high school nurse. The report showed a classic macular/papular rash on her hands and feet and a blood test confirming secondary syphilis. I saw these kids all the time. She probably used drugs, had a few boyfriends, and was a dropout candidate.

When I first interviewed Lucy, however, I knew from the start that this was not a cut-and-dried case. She was young, fresh-faced, and preppy-looking in her Catholic girl's school pleated skirt and white sox.

Lucy was quiet, almost sunken in her posture. She averted eye contact, obviously embarrassed. After my usual introduction, explaining why I needed to talk to her, I began to explain the nitty-gritty of sexually transmitted diseases and how they are spread. By the time I got around to asking her about her sexual contacts, she was on the verge of tears.

Lucy's initial response to my asking for the names of her sexual contacts was, "There's only one — my boyfriend, Hector."

When pressed for Hector's address and telephone number, Lucy hemmed and hawed, said she didn't know where he lived or went to school, and tried to move the interview along.

Finally I had enough and said, "Look, I know you're lying to me. What's going on here?"

It took but a second for Lucy to break down and the floodgates to open up, her tears pouring forth in a torrent followed by shakes, sobs, and near hyperventilation.

She couldn't contain herself any longer. Between gasps of air and bodywracking sobs, she told her story. There was no boyfriend Hector. Rather, there was a 45-year-old man, Luis. Luis was the boyfriend

of her mother, Maria. He mostly lived with them and had free rein to come and go. It seemed that he liked to come around when Maria was still at work and Lucy and her younger sister were home from school.

Luis started sexually abusing Lucy about five years ago. It started out with her sitting on his lap and his fondling her. It progressed to his exposing himself to her, demanding fellatio, and for the past couple of years, vaginal intercourse. When it began, Lucy was confused, but Luis told her not to say anything to her mother. Lucy thought her mother knew what was going on because there were times when Lucy didn't want to be left home with Luis but her mom made excuses for him and didn't let Lucy leave.

When Luis began to force fellatio and intercourse on Lucy, he warned her not to tell her mother or he'd leave them, or worse, hurt her mother and little sister. Lucy was beginning to worry about her little sister. She'd seen the way Luis was eyeing her sister lately, and Lucy didn't want her to have to go through the same thing that Lucy did.

I'm not sure how the story ended. I brought Lucy downtown to the child welfare agency that afternoon. I had to fill out forms and was still there when they returned with her little sister, afraid but unmolested. The social worker told me that they were removing Lucy and her sister from the home, arresting Luis and probably Maria, and would find a safe home for the girls. The last image I have of Lucy is her sitting on the wooden bench in the child welfare office, her arm around her little sister, smoothing the pleats on her school uniform, looking much older and more tired than her 16 years.

WELLNESS SYNTHESIS

All six domains have an impact on and are impacted by sexual coercion. Here, however, the emphasis is on emotional and social well-being.

Physical Well-being

Of all of the domains of health, physical well-being impacts the least on coercive sex. With the exception of organic brain damage, physical status exerts little influence on coercive sex. Men do use physical strength to threaten and overpower their female and youth victims; however, physical strength and coercive sex have no association.

Substance abuse poses a more immediate physical concern. Individuals who abuse substances (particularly alcohol) are more likely to engage in coercive sex than their nonabusing peers. Coercive sex is fairly common among college men who are binge drinkers. Of course, substance abuse is more than a physical health problem. Although the abuse of alcohol and other drugs undermines physical well-being, the effects of these drugs on intellectual and emotional functioning are the link to coercive sex.

High-level physical well-being may empower women and help prevent their becoming victims of coercive sex. Activities such as lifting weights to develop strength and practicing self-defense skills can help women repel would-be attackers. Feeling physically stronger and more prepared to fight might also send nonverbal messages to would-be attackers.

Intellectual Well-being

Sexual predators can be very smart. They develop elaborate plans for luring and trapping their victims. They observe and note their victim's behavior, patterns, and weaknesses. Their cognitive abilities, although they may be high-level, are without moral controls.

It is up to the rest of us to develop higher levels of intellectual well-being to protect ourselves and defeat sexual predators. This starts with fully understanding the range of coercive sex, from sexual harassment to child sexual abuse. It involves knowing all of the risk factors for coercive sex. Then we can begin to take steps for reducing these risks for ourselves and our children. We can lessen the likelihood of becoming victims by reducing or eliminating risks.

Intellectual well-being also involves knowing our rights and how to reduce our risks by demanding these rights. We have the right to safe and secure environments at work and school. We have the right to workplaces free from sexual harassment and discrimination. These rights are backed by the power of the courts.

We need to know how to protect ourselves, starting with protecting our privacy. We can learn how to reduce our invasion of privacy by doing things such as listing our telephone numbers using a first initial only, refusing to give our name and address over the internet or phone, and not allowing strangers in our home. We need to be able to fully utilize all of the information at our disposal to protect ourselves and our loved ones from sexual predators.

Emotional Well-being

People who engage in coercive sex exhibit low levels of emotional well-being. Men who rape usually have low self-esteem, harbor resentment and rage, and are not in control of their emotions. They do not understand their negative emotions and do not deal with them in socially acceptable ways. Rather, they vent their rage and hostility by attacking women.

Child abusers use power to exploit children. They do not have the usual adult sexual desires and lack the emotional maturity to sustain adult relationships. Often their emotional problems are exacerbated by substance abuse, which further reduces their ability to understand and control their feelings.

High-level emotional well-being can offer a protective effect by helping us understand our emotions and also others' emotional signals. When something doesn't "feel right" about a person or situation, we respect that intuition. Often we get cues about people and situations that tell us to walk away or refuse, or get help, or seek safer ground. As we develop higher levels of emotional well-being, we learn to trust our inner voice. These warnings work hand-in-hand with our intellectual functioning, the part of us that is able to think, process information, and solve problems.

Social Well-being

Sexual predators do not have strong social relationships. Starting with their dysfunctional relationships with their own parents, sexual predators have not developed mature, egalitarian relationships based on caring, respect, and tolerance. From those who harass, to those who rape, to those who abuse children, a common thread is immature, dysfunctional, unsatisfying social relationships.

Those who engage in coercive sex often have limited experience with relationships based on love and caring, trust, respect, mutuality, sharing, and commitment. Their relationships are exploitive, self-centered, and destructive. They use power differentials in relationships to take advantage and inflict pain and suffering. Their relationships are really not relationships at all. They are artificial arrangements set up to trap and abuse.

People with high-level social well-being can use it to protect themselves from becoming victims. High-level social relationships are based on trust and caring and mutuality. They don't develop overnight. A college student, for instance, is much less likely to be the victim of date rape if she takes time to get to know the person she is dating and observes his behavior across a variety of circumstances. And children can be protected from sexual abuse by developing a supportive social network to help watch over all neighborhood children through networks such as a "neighborhood watch."

Spiritual Well-being

High-level spiritual well-being cannot co-exist with coercive sex. Spirituality implies a connectedness with something or someone other than the self. It respects the goodness of all people and living things and seeks ways to develop stronger connections. It is based on faith in things we can't prove including faith in others — the belief that they will have our best interests in mind.

Sexual predators have the lowest level of spiritual well-being. They are unable to fuse morality and ethics with behavior. They act without a conscience. Often they use the very trust and faith others have in them to lure, trap, seduce, and abuse others. They are morally bankrupt.

Therefore, we must temper our faith and trust with reason and caution. We must resist the urge to treat all people the same until we get to know them better. If we are to protect ourselves and our loved ones, we must curtail our desire to connect with others until we get to know them better. We must learn to hold onto our faith while using common sense and the specific skills discussed in this chapter to reduce our risk for becoming a target of sexual coercion.

Environmental Well-being

High-level environmental well-being implies safety, security, and respect. A work environment with high-level environmental well-being is a place where workers co-exist without fear of abuse, discrimination, or harassment. Policies to guard against harassment and discrimination are in place and can be enforced if necessary.

A safe home environment includes appropriate parenting, setting boundaries for behavior, and getting help with emotional problems. A neighborhood that offers high-level environmental well-being is well-lit, policed, and has neighbors looking out for one another. The schools are safe and do not tolerate sexual harassment and discrimination. The community has safe playgrounds and parks that are well patrolled and not inviting for sex offenders.

A college that offers high-level environmental well-being is a microcosm of any community. It has policies and procedures in place for dealing with harassment and discrimination and offers safety and protection. Its students don't fear walking to their cars after class or attending social functions.

WEB RESOURCES

National Center for Victims of Crime

http://www.nvc.org/

Nonprofit organization providing resources and advocacy to victims of crime. The site offers safety strategies for victims of domestic violence and stalking, highlights of laws and public policy impacting crime victims at state and federal levels, information on crime victims, and finding a lawyer. Access to a virtual library with full-text publications, a directory of publications, recommended reading, bibliographies and a book review, plus links to victim-related sites.

National Organization on Male Sexual Victimization

http://www.malesurvivor.org

Started in 1988 by mental health providers who wanted to better understand and treat adult male survivors of childhood sexual abuse. Section on prevention and education talks about how to prevent abused boys from becoming abusive men.

Rape Abuse and Incest National Network (RAINN)

http://www.rainn.org

Nonprofit organization hotline providing 24-hour counseling service to survivors of sexual assault. Site also offers information, statistics, and a list of local crisis centers.

Sexual Assault Prevention

http://www.cc.ysu.edu/rape-prev-info

Site sponsored by University Counseling Center, Youngstown State University, Youngstown, Ohio. Provides information on prevalence, after-effects, and treatment of rape and sexual assault and links with a specific focus on higher education.

University of Illinois at Urbana-Champaign, Counseling Center

http://www.odos.uiuc.edu/Counseling_Center/friends.htm

Provides a guide for friends, family, and partners of sexual assault and abuse survivors. Articles address statistics, responses to recent sexual assault/abuse, phases, how to help the survivor, additional suggestions for romantic partner of survivor, feelings victim may experience, how to help oneself, books to read, and resources.

Notes

1. L. Kaufman, "A Report from the Front: Why It's Gotten Easier to Sue for Sexual Harassment," *Newsweek*, 129:2 (1997), 32.

2. Kaufman.

3. C. B. Johnson, M. S. Stockdale, and F. E. Saal, "Persistence of Men's Misperceptions of Friendly Cues Across a Variety of Interpersonal Encounters," *Psychology of Women Quarterly*, 15:3 (1991), 463–375; M. S. Stockdale, "The Role of Sexual Misperceptions of Women's Friendliness in an Emerging Theory of Sexual Harassment," *Journal of Vocational Behavior*, 42:1 (1993), 84–101.

4. T. S. Jones and M. S. Remland, "Sources of Variability in Perceptions of and Responses to Sexual Harassment," *Sex Roles*, 27:3–4 (1992), 121–142.

5. J. LeLand, "A Kiss is Just a Kiss: Where Should Schools Draw the Line Between Normal Childhood Behavior and Sexual Harassment?" *Newsweek*, 128:17 (1996), 71–72.

6. Leland.

7. C. M. Chmielewski, "Sexual Harassment Meets Title IX: New Federal Rules to Combat Sexual Harassment and Place Schools at the Battlefront," *NEA Today*, 16:2 (1997), 25.

8. D. Benson and G. Thompson, "Sexual Harassment on a University Campus: The Confluence of Authority Relations, Sexual Interest, and Gender Stratification, "*Society for the Study of Social Problems*, 29:3 (1991), 236–251; M. A. Paludi, "Sociopsychological and Structural Factors to Women's Vocational Development," *Annals of the New York Academy of Sciences*, 602 (1990), 157–168; K. Bursik, "Perceptions of Sexual Harassment in an Academic Context," *Sex Roles*, 27:7–8 (1992), 401–412; L. Rubin and S. Borgers, "Sexual Harassment in the Universities During the 1980's," *Sex Roles*, 23 (1990), 397–411.

9. Benson and Thompson.

10. W. Benton, *Websters New International Dictionary* (Toronto: Encyclopedia Britannica, 1996).

11. R. M. Cate and S. A. Lloyd, *Courtship* (Newbury Park, CA: Sage, 1992); C. L. Muehlenhard, I. G. Ponch, J. L. Phelps, and L. M. Giusti. "Definitions of Rape: Scientific and Political Implications," *Journal of Social Issues*, 48:1 (1992), 23–44.

12. C. W. Harlow, *Female Victims of Violent Crime* (Washington, DC: U. S. Department of Justice), (NCJ-126826)

13. D. Muram, K. Miller, and A. Cutler, "Sexual Assault of the Elderly Victim," *Journal of Interpersonal Violence*, 791 (1992), 70–76.

14. Cate and Lloyd.

15. Frintner and Robinson study summarized by C. G. Manisses, "Alcohol Strongly Implicated in Acquaintance Rape," *Brown University Digest of Addiction Theory and Application*, 13:4 (April 1994), 6–8.

16. H. Wechsler, A. Davenport, G. Dowdell, B. Moeykens, and S. Castillo, "Health and Behavioral Consequences of Binge Drinking in College," *Journal of American Medical Association*, 272:21 (1994), 1672–1677.

17. C. A. Presley, P. W. Meilman, and R. Lyerla, *Alcohol and Drugs on America's College Campuses: Use, Consequences, and Perceptions of the College Environment*, Vol. 1 (1989–1991 (Carbondale IL: Core Institute, 1993); L. D. Johnston, P. M. O'Mally, and J. G. Bachman, "Drug Use Among American High School Seniors, College Students, and Young Adults, 1975–1990," Vol. 2 (Washington, DC: U. S. Department of Health and Human Services, 1991). (ADM 91-1835)

18. Wechsler et al.

19. N. A. Gleason, "College Women and Alcohol: A Relational Perspective," *Journal of American College Health*, 42:6 (May 1994), 279–289.

20. R. L. Montgomery, J. A. Benedicto, and F. M. Hammerke, "Personal U. S. Social Motivation of Undergraduates in Using Alcohol," *Psychological Reports*, Dec. 1993, 960–962.

21. Wechsler et al.

22. D. E. H. Russel, *Rape in Marriage* (Bloomington, IN: Indiana University Press, 1990).

23. Russel, 1984.

24. I. H. Frieze. "Causes and Consequences of Marital Rape," *Signs*, 8 (1983), 532–553; C. R. Hanneke, N. M. Shields, and G. J. McCall. "Assessing the Prevalence of Marital Rape," *Journal of Interpersonal Violence*, 1 (1986), 350–362.

25. H. E. Marano. "Why They Stay: A Saga of Spouse Abuse," *Psychology Today*, 29:3 (1996), 56–66.

26. M. P. Koss, "The Measurement of Rape Victimization in Crime Surveys," *Criminal Justice and Behavior*, 23:1 (1996), 55–69.

27. D. Johnston, "Survey Shows Number of Rapes Far Higher Than Official Figures," *New York Times*, April 24, 1992, p. A9.

28. *Rape in America: A Report to the Nation* (Charleston, SC: Crime Victims Research and Treatment Center, 1992).

29. L. Williams, "The Classic Rape: When Do Victims Report?" *Social Problems*, 31 (1984), 459–457.

30. M. P. Koss, "The Underdetection of Rape: Methodological Choices Influence Incidental Estimates," *Journal of Social Issues*, 48 (1992), 61–75.

31. Williams, 1984.

32. Williams, 1984.

33. N. M. Malamuth, R. J. Sockloski, M. P. Koss, and J. S. Tanaka, "Characteristics of Aggressors Against Women: Testing a Model Using a National Sample of College Students," *Journal of Consulting and Clinical Psychology*, 59 (1991), 670–781.

34. P. Sanday. "The Socio-cultural Context of Rape: A Cross-cultural Study," *Journal of Social Issues*, 37:4 (1987), 5–27

35. D. Finkelhor, *Child Sexual Abuse: New Theory and Research* (New York: Free Press, 1984).

36. D. Browning and B. Boatman, "Incest: Children at Risk," *American Journal of Psychiatry*, 134 (1977), 69–72; K. Meisleman, *Incest* (San Francisco: Jossey Bass, 1978).

37. Finkelhor, 1984.

38. J. S. Hyde, *Understanding Human Sexuality,* 5th edition (New York: McGraw Hill, 1994).

39. R. Bauman, C. Kasper, and J. Alford, "The Child Sex Abusers," *Corrective and Social Psychiatry, 30* (1984), 76–81.

40. Z. Segal and W. Marshall, "Heterosexual Social Skills in a Population of Rapists and Child Molesters," *Journal of Consulting and Clinical Psychology,* 53 (1985), 55–63; Bauman et al.

41. S. Johnston, "The Mind of the Molester," *Psychology Today,* Feb. 1987, 60–63; G. Gaffney, S. Luries, and P. Berlin, "Is There Familiar Transmission of Pedophilia?" *Journal of Nervous and Mental Disease,* 172 (1984), 546–548.

42. D. Finkelhor, G. Hoatling, L. Lewis, and C. Smith, "Sexual Abuse in a National Sample of Adult Men and Women: Prevalence, Characteristics and Risk Factors," *Child Abuse and Neglect,* 14 (1990), 19–28.

43. D. Finkelhor, "Epidemiological Factors in the Clinical Identification of Child Sexual Abuse," *Child Abuse and Neglect,* 17 (1993), 67–70; "The International Epidemiology of Child Sexual Abuse," *Child Abuse and Neglect,* 18 (1994), 409–417; H. Guidry, "Childhood Sexual Abuse: Role of the Family Physician," *American Family Physician,* 51 (1995), 407–414; L. Williams. "Recall of Childhood Trauma: A Prospective Study of Women's Memories of Child Sexual Abuse," *Journal of Counseling and Clinical Psychology,* 62 (1994), 1167–1176.

44. R. Krugman, J. Bays, D. Chadwick, C. Levitt, M. McMugh, and J. Whitworth, "Guidelines for Evaluation of Sexual Abuse of Children," *Pediatrics,* 87 (1991), 254–260.

45. V. Felitti, "Long-term Medical Consequences of Incest, Rape, and Molestation," *Southern Medical Journal,* 84 (1991), 328–331; M. Koss, T. Dinero, C. Seibel, and S. Cox, "Stranger and Acquaintance Rape: Are There Differences in the Victim's Experience?" *Psychology of Women Quarterly,* 12 (1988), 1–24.

46. P. Frazier and B. Cohen, "Research on the Sexual Victimization of Women," *Counseling Psychologist,* 20 (1992), 141–158.

47. I. Jackson, K. Calhoun, A. Amick, H. Maddever, and V. Habif, "Young Adult Women Who Report Childhood Intrafamilial Sexual Abuse: Subsequent Adjustment," *Archives of Sexual Behavior,* 19 (1990), 211–221.

48. "Pointing the Finger at Megan's Law," *Economist,* 342:8004 (1997), 27–29.

49. A. Brooks. "Megan's Law: Constitutionality and Policy," *Criminal Justice Ethics,* 15:56 (1996), 51.

50. "Pointing the Finger at Megan's Law."

51. Brooks.

52. M. Bai, "A Report from the Front in the War on Predators: Years After Megan's Murder, Her Law is Still on Trial," *Newsweek,* 129:20 (1977), 67.

Student Study Questions

1. What sexual acts are covered by the umbrella term "coercive sex?"

2. What conditions are necessary to meet sexual harassment criteria?

3. What is a "hostile environment" in a sexual harassment case? Give an example of a hostile environment.

4. How does power over a subordinate factor into sexual harassment?

5. What are three variations of rape? Is it considered a sexual act? Why or why not?

6. What are three risk factors for acquaintance rape?

7. What are three ways to reduce the risk for acquaintance rape?

8. What are some personality characteristics of a typical child molester?

9. What is the difference between a child molester and a pedophile?

10. What is "Megan's Law?"

Temper Test

Directions: A number of statements that people have used to describe themselves are given below. Read each statement and then circle the appropriate number to indicate how you generally fee. Give the answer that seems to describe how you generally feel.

	Almost Never	Some-times	Often	Almost Always
1. I am quick-tempered.	1	2	3	4
2. I get annoyed when I don't receive recognition for doing good work.	1	2	3	4
3. I have a fiery temper.	1	2	3	4
4. I feel infuriated when I do a good job or study hard and get a poor evaluation or test score.	1	2	3	4
5. I am a hot-headed person.	1	2	3	4
6. I get furious when I'm criticized in front of others.	1	2	3	4
7. I get angry when others' mistakes slow me down.	1	2	3	4
8. I fly off the handle easily.	1	2	3	4
9. When I get angry, I say nasty things to anyone around me.	1	2	3	4
10. When I get frustrated, I feel like hitting someone.	1	2	3	4

Total Points: _____

Scoring

Add the points from each item (1–4) together to get your total score, somewhere between 10 and 40. A man who scores 17 or a woman who scores 18 is just about average. If you score below 13, you're well down in the safe zone. A score above 20 means you may be a hot-head — scoring higher than three-quarters of those tested. If these tendencies cause you to take out your anger on anyone else, professional help is advised.

Sex for Sale

17

Major Topics

Student Learning Objectives

After reading this chapter, students will be able to:

ꙮ Explain the major historical events that have shaped current attitudes and practices related to sex for sale over the past three decades.

ꙮ Describe the significance of Madonna, Calvin Klein, and Gary Hart in shaping the sexual climate of today.

ꙮ Differentiate pornography, erotica, and obscenity.

ꙮ Discuss how technological advances have combined with other historical trends to create a new commercialization of sex.

ꙮ Describe some of the problems inherent in policing the internet for sexual victimization and exploitation.

ꙮ Describe a variety of types of prostitution.

ꙮ Evaluate the effectiveness of blocking tools that parents can use to limit children's access to internet or television-based sexual material.

ꙮ Evaluate the effects of sexually explicit materials on sexual behavior.

Prior to the 1960s, sexual themes in mainstream advertising were mostly covert and reflected the mores of the times. Advertisers were subjected to much more stringent controls concerning issues such as the verbal content of advertisements, overt pictorial displays of nudity, and implied sexual themes. Modesty prevailed, as cleavage, bare midriffs, and other examples of exposing the human body were not allowed. Using sex in advertising was limited to full-bosomed "sweater girls" to promote cigarettes, appliances, and cars.

Besides the lack of overt sexuality in advertising, it was noticeably absent from other forms of entertainment and media. Few mainstream books, television shows, magazines, movies, and other media included sexual content. Although Kinsey's studies had been conducted and disseminated to the professional community, sexual information was not readily available to the general public.

CHANGES IN THE 1960S

This all began to change in the 1960s. The peace, prosperity, and contentment of the post-war 1950's began to give way to the rebelliousness of the baby-boom generation of the 1960s. Many social, economic, technological, and political forces came together to create a synergy that changed the course of history.

Nowhere was this more evident than in issues related to sexuality. Technological advances in contraception brought widespread availability of birth

In the 1950s, tight sweaters and a cigarette dangling from the corner of the mouth were considered risque.

control pills. This gave women newfound freedom and control regarding their fertility and enabled women to re-enter the workforce in ever increasing numbers.

Masters and Johnson released their breakthrough research regarding sexual response and sexual pleasure. Men and women learned about the clitoris and multiple orgasms. Other research followed when the interest in information about sexuality became an outcry. Popular magazines of the 1950s, such as *Playboy*, were joined by *Penthouse* and others to meet this need.

All of this helped spawn a **women's movement**, which began to question many longstanding cultural assumptions regarding the roles of men and women in society. The women's movement brought to the forefront issues such as equal rights, abortion, child care in the workplace, sexual assault, and a host of others. The ensuing debate forever changed the way men and women perceived themselves and their roles as citizens.

Women's movement
force to gain full educational, social, and economic opportunities and rights for women equal to those that men are traditionally understood to have

Styles, too, began to change. Men began to grow long hair and wear beads, and some women discarded their bras and exposed their midriffs. Attitudes and values about sexuality were changing faster than the society could adapt to the change.

One of the most telling legacies of the 1960s was the growing mainstream acceptance of sex as a topic of discussion. Books, films, magazines, newspapers, posters, and the evening news began to increase the level and realism of sexual content. Self-help books about sexuality proliferated. Academicians, feminists, and politicians began to seriously discuss the implications of sexuality and gender research for social policy and laws.

One of the most telling legacies of the 1960s was the growing mainstream acceptance of sex as a topic of discussion.

What do you think about the increase in sexual themes in the mainstream media? Would you prefer more restrained media coverage of sexual issues?

While this was going on, average Americans were beginning to discuss their own sexuality. One of the most interesting byproducts of the women's and sexual revolutions of the 1960s and early 1970s was how comfortable people became in discussing sex.

CHANGES IN THE 1970s AND 1980s

The 1970s and 1980s saw a continued increase of sexual themes in the media. Not only did the amount of sexual information increase, but the content, too, became more diverse. Subjects such as homosexuality, bisexuality, and interracial sex were becoming much more noticeable in mainstream media. This new wave of sexual permissiveness was marked by changing rules about what previously had been considered private information.

THREE ILLUSTRATIVE EXAMPLES

Three well known media figures serve as examples here: actress/singer Madonna, designer Calvin Klein, and 1988 Presidential candidate Gary Hart.

The Material Girl

Madonna ushered in a new era of mainstream hedonism and me-generation narcissism. Madonna's "material girl" embodied all of the elements of post-1960s sexuality: open acceptance of sexual desire, the pursuit of sex and passion, a focus on self-fulfillment, glorification of the human body as a sensual and sexual object, permission to explore bisexuality, interracial sex, and personal adornment and clothing that transcended gender conventional style.

PERSPECTIVES   Reactions to the Material Girl

Students' reactions to Madonna tend to be polarized. Love her or hate her, she is a current icon of a changing society.

"Madonna — wow, is she hot." (male, age 22)

"Madonna — I love her. She does what she wants, says what she wants. She's a real bitch, but cool." (female, age 21)

"She's hot, but I wouldn't screw her. She probably has AIDS" (male, age 22)

"I love her. She's definitely a nineties woman." (female, age 19)

" What a slut." (female, age 19)

"I wish I could be more like her. She's so confident and assertive. She knows what she wants and goes after it." (female, age 18)

"I think she's gross. She'd sleep with anybody." (female, age 29)

"I like her attitudes about sex. She's exploring all of the possibilities and apologizing for nothing. She's got guts." (female age 35)

" She's my ultimate fantasy lady, but I don't think I'd want to marry her." (male, age 23)

Madonna, the material girl,
took America by storm in the 1980s.

Madonna combined all of these things into one package and put that package on display in American living rooms. She represented the disparate elements of the tumultuous 1960s, the self-centered 1970s, and the androgynous 1980s into a synergistic, in-your-face assault on American sexual mores.

Madonna has been one of our most visible and identifiable symbols of the American sexual revolution of the past 30 years. She embodies all of the issues that many people have been struggling with most of our lives. She is part caricature, part best friend, part you or me. Almost anyone who identifies with any of the vast changes in U. S. sexual values of the past three decades can see something of themselves in Madonna.

 Is Madonna a good role model for young women? Why or why not?

Klein's Clothing Ads

Calvin Klein has been one of the most influential businesspersons in the United States, responsible for increased acceptance of homosexuality, bisexuality, and **androgyny**. Through his clothing and, more important, his advertising, Calvin Klein ushered in an acceptance of alternative sexual lifestyles without ever conducting a study, publishing research, or delivering a speech. Klein has pushed the limits of acceptability and taste to the maximum for 25 years.

Androgyny
exhibiting both male and female traits

Klein's clothing style almost singlehandedly transformed the boundaries of acceptable standards of dress for men. Klein ushered in denim-chic. His casual look helped men (and women) introduce the casual look into the social scene and the workplace. Today, we often see men in denim shirts or dress shirts and ties with jeans or a casual sport coat in the fanciest of locations — the ballet, opera, theater, and most restaurants and clubs. Klein-influenced attire is accepted in all but the most formal of workplaces. This represents a milestone in gender-role expectations for men. More and more, men are realizing that being a man doesn't have to include strict adherence to a dress code of the past.

Klein's advertising, however, had even more of an impact on the fabric of sexuality than his clothing did. From the start, Klein's ads pushed the advertising industry to the limits. He exposed flesh — exposed naked backs, buttocks, and breasts. He posed his models suggestively and flaunted the merchandising of products through sex. Even when he wasn't exposing flesh, he was emphasizing the allure of young, nubile bodies; the curve of a hip in skin-tight jeans, the slope of a neck from a denim shirt wide open at the collar, the span of a set of shoulders or the bulge of a bicep. All of these images are Klein trademarks.

Another of Klein's impacts was with his models. He imprinted first homosexuality, then bisexuality, and most recently androgyny onto the American advertising and marketing scene. Klein's male models of the

Calvin Klein's trademark ads reflect the merchandising of products through sex.

1970s were hunks — well-built, with bulging arms and chiseled abdomens. His men of the 1970s turned on male and female viewers alike. His eroticism was always double-edged: It mimicked the sex-role behavior of gay men, and was a turn-on to heterosexual women. Gay men admired Klein's hunks with their tight buns, broad shoulders, and clean-shaven, healthy look. Straight women admired them for the same look.

Klein's more recent group shots left lingering questions about who was cavorting with whom in the ads. Were the men cavorting with the women, the other men, or both? Were the women wistfully admiring the men or the other women, or both? It was clear who the men were and who the women were. The object of their affection, however, was in doubt.

One of Klein's more recent advertising themes is of a sort of emaciated androgyny. The men and the women are cast in muted tones — blacks, blues, grays. Most of the models look thin and in need of some personal grooming. This has been referred to as a "heroin chic" look.

A 1995 Klein campaign raised the ire of media watchdog groups that claimed he crossed the line from bad taste into harmful promotion of a life-threatening lifestyle and look. This advertising campaign used adolescent boys in various seductive poses amid backdrops reminiscent of someone's den. An anonymous voice in the background asked the boys, "Do you like to pose?" The campaign, critics claim, bordered on "kiddie porn" and smacked of pedophilia.[1] Whatever one feels about Klein and his various campaigns over the past two decades, his images and ideas undoubtedly helped shape American perceptions about what is sexy and sensual.

Monkey Business

A Presidential aspirant finishes our trilogy of symbols of an evolving American sexuality of the past 30 years. Gary Hart was a Democratic Party candidate for President of the United States in 1988. One of the front-runners in the campaign, he had a good chance to earn the Democratic Party endorsement for President. All of that changed on the fateful morning of May 3, 1987, when the headline of the *Miami Herald* read, "Miami Woman linked to Hart."[2]

Gary Hart — candidate for President, respectable Congressman, businessman, married, kids, All-American good looks, and charismatic personality — was caught by photographers with Donna Rice, his associate, sitting on his lap on the deck of the yacht, "Monkey Business." Reporters revealed that Rice had stayed overnight in Hart's Capitol Hill house.

This may not seem like a big deal today. As a culture, we seem to have been desensitized to such carryings-on. In 1988, however, it represented a tremendous change in the evolution of American sexual values and the way in which the media covered events and the lives of public figures. Prior to Hart's affair, the personal sex lives of political and other (such as sports) figures were off-limits. The media stayed away from sexual behavior, especially if this activity was out of public view. It was not allowed on air, in print, or as a subject of interview.

Stories that we read about today, such as the pro football player with the Dallas Cowboys drug/prostitution case and President Clinton's alleged affairs, never would have been aired in the past. We would not know about them. The unwritten rules of the game were that certain aspects of celebrities' lives were off-limits to the media and were not available to the public.

That all changed with the Gary Hart case. Leaking of the story and the subsequent in-depth coverage, complete with front-page photos, broke new ground. The rules had changed. One newspaper's decision about allowing the story to be printed changed the way the U.S. media would report the news from then on. It also set the stage for how information of that nature would be handled in the future.

 Should the media cover the private lives of public figures? Would this amount of scrutiny keep you from seeking public office or stardom?

It also opened the floodgates for a new way of sexual information to be disseminated to the American public. Sexual behavior, drug-use behavior, and the like began to be carried over the airwaves into every small town, big city, and suburban living room. This was the beginning of the in-your-face talk shows, news magazine programs, and shock-jocks that now are prominent on the American media landscape.

 The portrayal of beauty captured by Calvin Klein ads sets a standard for physical perfection for our society. How does a young woman capture the thin, almost emaciated look portrayed by a Kate Moss, for instance? Is this creating a risk for anorexia and bulimia? Do women seek physical interventions such as breast augmentation to seek an ideal perpetuated by unrealistic standards set through advertising?

THE IMPACT OF TECHNOLOGY

Madonna, Klein, and Hart broke new cultural ground by pushing sexual standards to the limit. They set the stage for allowable behavior and media coverage. What makes their emergence as sexual standard bearers different from those that came before them is timing. The sweeping changes they created in entertainment, advertising and media reporting came at a time when the United States was ushering in the first wave of massive technological changes. The 1980s and 1990s brought a new wave of information technology that included cable television, personal computers, and home video.

The 1980s and 1990s brought a new wave of information technology that included cable television, personal computers, and home video.

These new technologies were different from all those that had preceded them. The three qualities that set them apart from all the others were power, personal use, and low cost. Cable television brought the world into our living rooms. With more than 100 channels today, we are literally flooded with visual information and data from around the world. For the first time in history, with the Gulf War, we were spectators in one of our wars as we watched it unfold on television on real time as it actually happened. There were no time delays, no papers to read, nothing to mull over. We simply sat back and watched our country wage war, without editing or tape-delay as in Vietnam and previous conflicts.

In addition to the power of the media, these technologies ushered in a new era of personal accessibility. Cable television and personal computers are becoming as common as the telephone. Cable television made available pay-per-view movies, x-rated programming, and a host of other innovations that has the potential to bring sexual content along with other topics into our homes 24 hours a day.

Combined with the power of the home computer is the internet. The personal computer took the nation by storm in the early 1990s, and introduction of the internet offered Americans the opportunity to instantly connect with millions of users worldwide.

The sweeping acceptance of this technology and its sheer power in moving volumes of information and images into U.S. homes opened the floodgate to another wave of sexual communication. One positive aspect of this second wave is its ability to provide accurate, nonbiased information on sexuality.[3] The internet is so large and powerful that it is almost impossible to police. It brings graphic, sadomasochistic, live video clips into the living room. It connects 45-year-old pedophiles with potential victims through **chat rooms**.

These new technologies are not only available but now are relatively affordable, and they have established a strong foothold in the average U.S. household. Costs of electronic technologies have continued to plummet in our climate of competition. Also, many local libraries, school and college facilities, and worksites offer free internet access to people.

The number of people in the United States who subscribe to cable television has risen steadily over

Chat rooms
live e-mail discussion lines in which a person can communicate with others by typing messages

The cost of technology has dropped so low that it is within reach of most U.S. households.

the past few years. Cable television sales in 1996 reached the $2 billion mark — 15%–20% higher than 1995.[4] Home VCR costs have decreased markedly in the past decade. In 1996, more than 84% of all homes in the United States owned at least one VCR, and 39% owned two or more VCR units. The personal computer industry has grown more than 400% since 1990. In 1996, 40% of U.S. homes had at least one personal computer.[5]

Couple this technology with a much more permissive culture, and you have an entirely different sexual landscape than at any time in U.S. history. It is a no-holds-barred culture in which almost anything goes — and much of it goes into our living rooms via these new technologies. Although all of these things existed before 1990, now the cost has allowed Americans to be exposed to almost any sexual idea, theme, or image in the privacy of the home. Anything goes — especially if it sells (attracts viewers).

PORNOGRAPHY, EROTICA, AND OBSCENITY

One of the major concerns about the increasing availability of sexual information and images in the media and over the internet is the easy access to pornography, erotica, and obscene materials. In past decades, restricting access to this material was much easier. Keeping it away from minors, as well as adults who did not desire that type of exposure, was simple. Today it is much more difficult. The debate concerning what is pornographic, erotic, or obscene has reopened and intensified. Although *pornography*, *erotica*, and *obscenity* have been used interchangeably, these terms mean entirely different things.

Although the terms obscenity, pornography, *and* erotica *are used interchangeably, they mean entirely different things.*

Pornography

Derived from the its Latin roots *porne* (prostitute) and *graphos* (depicting), **pornography** literally means a depiction, in writing or pictures, of prostitutes or prostitution. It refers more commonly to any depiction of lewd material, or erotic behavior designed to cause sexual arousal. In U.S. culture, the connotation of pornography and pornographic materials is usually negative, even though most people admit they get sexually excited while viewing it.

Pornography
a depiction of lewd material or erotic behavior designed to cause sexual arousal

Erotica

Derived from the Greek word *erotikos* (love poem), **erotic** means devoted to or tending to arouse sexual love or desire. Erotic materials depict beauty, love, sensuousness, voluptuousness, and the like. In U.S. culture (and most others around the world) the depiction of erotica and erotic materials tends to be positive. This judgment is subjective, however. Some people do not distinguish pornography from erotica and lump them together.

Erotic
devoted to arousing sexual desire

In real life, separating some pornographic materials from erotica is difficult. Often, the context of the material helps to define it. For instance, one could view two films, an x-rated "porn" film and a "sex ed" video. Each film portrays a heterosexual couple having sex. Both films have graphic displays of nudity, masturbation, oral sex, and intercourse in various positions. What is the difference? Are the films pornographic or erotic?

The porno film makes little mention of love or expressions of caring. The relationship between the partners may be unknown or casual. The sexual acts may be forced or seemingly initiated by one partner for his or her own gratification. The genitalia are overemphasized with close-ups of the coupled genitalia. Most porn films end with a mandatory, degrading ejaculation in the face of the female.

The sex ed video emphasizes communication. The couple talk to each other. They ask what each desires, whether something feels good, and the like. They take their time. Their intent is mutual pleasuring. They equally participate and initiate. The narration describes what is happening. The partners proceed through the various acts and show their appreciation, caring, and kindness. These videos do not include genital close-ups and orgasm. They do not show "in-your-face" ejaculation.

One could almost use a continuum to evaluate sexually explicit materials. Pornographic materials would represent one extreme, and instructional sex-ed materials would be at the other end, with erotica in the middle. To complicate matters, one must also consider if the material is obscene.

Obscenity

Obscenity
material that is abhorrent to moral virtue and accepted norms of social behavior

Obscenity is derived from the Latin word *obscenus,* which means dirty, filthy, and disgusting. Obscene materials repel the senses and are abhorrent to morality, virtue, and accepted norms of societal behavior. In 1966 the U.S. Supreme Court defined obscene materials as meeting three criteria:

1. The dominant theme had to appeal to a purely erotic interest in sex.
2. The material had to be offensive to contemporary community standards.
3. The material had to be without serious literary, artistic, political, or scientific value.

This definition posed serious difficulties in interpretation, and numerous challenges have been brought to bear. In 1973 the Supreme Court reversed its ruling using the three original criteria. In *Miller* v. *California* the court decided that only one criterion was necessary to define obscenity: local community standards. Each community had to decide for itself whether specific materials were offensive by its standards. The producers, actors, distributors, and sellers of materials that a community defines as obscene are all subject to prosecution even if the materials were produced in another community. This criterion is still in effect today. It is troubling because it gives a vocal minority in a community the ability to declare anything from skimpy bathing suits to Michelangelo's Venus de Milo obscene.

The only criterion necessary to define obscenity is local community standards.

In general, materials described as erotic are not perceived as obscene and usually are not the target of prosecution. Obscene materials, in contrast are considered to be subcategories of pornography. The overwhelming majority of Americans believe that adults should have access to sexually explicit material, both erotic and pornographic, depicting sexual activity between consenting adults.[6]

Support for obscene materials is much less. These materials usually depict themes other than sexual activity between consenting adults. Materials that involve children, rape, sadomasochism, and similar themes are more often those that fail to meet community standards.

Some municipalities have attempted to control pornography by restricting the location of x-rated bookstores and clubs to areas no less than 1,000 feet from residential housing (even if the businesses are located on major highways). Opponents claim this will force many legitimate businesses to close. How would you vote on this issue if you were a member of City Council? What is your justification?

PROSTITUTION

Prostitution has been around since the dawn of civilization. The earliest written accounts are in the Bible. Jesus himself took time to protect a prostitute from a stone-throwing crowd who would persecute her. Prostitution is illegal in the United States except in Nevada, where it is regulated and limited to certain counties. In Nevada and other places where prostitution is legal, prostitutes are called sex workers, and they are employed in the sex worker industry. Prostitution is legal in many European, Asian, African, and South American countries, where it is considered a victimless crime.

Prostitution
the exchange of sexual services for money

What are the arguments for and against the legalization of prostitution? What restrictions, if any, should be written into laws regarding prostitution?

Small numbers of prostitutes in the United States have organized in an attempt to try to legalize it in all 50 states. Legalization, they believe, will help protect prostitutes, ensure better working conditions, extend benefits such as disability and social security, and help them reduce their risk for contracting a variety of sexually transmitted diseases including HIV.[7] It also will free police to spend more time on other forms of crime, relieve the courts of a tremendous burden, and allow women to use their bodies the way they want to.

Although people tend to assume that all prostitutes are women, men and women alike engage in exchanging sex for money, food, shelter, drugs, or other resources. They can be subcategorized.

Prostitutes who literally solicit clients off the streets are called *hookers* (females) and *hustlers* (males), although the labels could apply to either gender. These prostitutes also are known as streetwalkers. They generally are at the lower end of the social order of prostitutes. Street hustlers and hookers are frequently addicted to drugs, are runaways, or have other economic or personal problems that force them into the often violent world of streetwalking.

Case Study

Edgar: Paying for Sex

Edgar is 43, married, and has two children, ages 13 and 16. He is a middle-manager in an insurance company. Married for 20 years, he describes his relationship with his wife as intimate and committed but feels the passion in their relationship died several years ago. Although they have sex about once a week or every other week, it isn't very exciting and he wants more. He frequents massage parlors about twice a month, paying for a massage that includes masturbation and usually fellatio.

I guess you could say that sex for me has never been all that exciting. Except for the prostitutes I used to pay for when I was in Vietnam, I was sexually inexperienced. I didn't have sex until I enlisted in the army at eighteen and went to Vietnam. When I returned, I got a job in an insurance company and went to college at night.

I met my wife at the insurance company during the first month I worked there, and we got married about a year after that. The first year or so, things were okay. My wife wasn't very interested in sex, and we probably had intercourse about once a week that first year. She's pretty conservative and isn't into oral sex or anything kinky.

I really didn't know what to expect of married life. My dad never really talked about sex with me, and I was too embarrassed to talk to my friends about it in much detail. My first son was born after a year, and things slowed down a little more with my wife.

I was in New York for a training program for my current job. I guess it was about ten years ago. I remember walking around Times Square and going into the bookstores and bars. I passed a massage parlor, and the guy out front was passing out coupons for a special deal. I said "What the heck" and went in. I had been curious about these massage parlors and was feeling horny. No one there knew me, so I took a chance. I picked out my masseuse and went into our little room.

After undressing, she started to rub my back, and before long her touches became a lot more intimate. She asked if I wanted her to jerk me off, and I said yes. I had to pay her a little more but it was worth it. The next night I went into a different place and found out I could get a blow job for about twenty dollars. The masseuse there was unattractive, but boy could she give head. It reminded me of my experiences in Vietnam.

When I returned home to Virginia from my training program, I began to seek out massage parlors in Richmond and other places within a reasonable drive from my home. I've been doing this at least once a month more than ten years. My wife doesn't know, and the cost isn't too much. I'm basically happily married and love my kids. I wish I had more sex with my wife and she was into oral sex, but I don't think she'll change. She won't even talk about seeing a sex therapist, so I keep doing what I'm doing. I don't have a problem with it, and it probably keeps my marriage going.

It may not be the world's oldest profession, but prostitution has been around since the dawn of civilization.

Street prostitutes solicit customers who walk or drive by them. Street-walkers usually negotiate with their clients and then have sex with them either in their car or at a local hotel or motel where short-stay rooms are available at reasonable rates. Some hustlers and hookers solicit clients in truck stop parking areas and have sex with their clients in their rigs.

In urban areas, many street hookers and hustlers are runaways — adolescents who have run away from home or have been forced out by their parents or caregivers. Many have run away from abusive home environments and are willing to risk the dangers of the streets over the sure harm of the environments from which they escaped. Many of the gay youth hooking and hustling on the streets ran away from persecution for their sexual orientation.

Streetwalking has many unwritten rules, which concern respecting other prostitutes' work areas (also known as "turf"), outwitting undercover police officers, avoiding sadists and murderers, and trying to avoid STDs/HIV. Because of this, streetwalkers often work for pimps (a type of business agent) who help control some of these problems in exchange for a share of the profits.

Street pimps vary in their approach to working with hookers and hustlers. Some provide valuable protection and care for their workers to some extent. Others are thinly disguised sadists and criminals who dominate their hookers and hustlers through drugs, violence, and fear. In the netherworld of streetwalking, violence and death are never far away.

Sex in Our World: The HIV Highway

They call it the HIV highway. In reality, it is a transcontinental highway linking the several sub-Saharan African countries. It is more like a dirt road than a highway. It is a symbol of the old Africa, where time has stood still and traditions live on. The HIV highway got its name because of health officials' belief that it has been a main conduit of infection with the deadly virus. The highway has countless roadside stops where prostitutes ply their trade.

This is the same trade they have pursued throughout the history of the road. The main difference is that now most of them are infected with HIV. These factors make sex along the trans-Africa highway a deadly behavior:

1. Condom use by the truck drivers and the prostitutes is practically nonexistent.

2. Anal intercourse is common.

3. The coexistence of genital ulcer disease (STDs that cause genital ulcers such as chancroid and syphilis) is common in the women and their customers. A final tragic note is the reluctance of these men to use condoms with their wives once they have been notified of their HIV seropositivity. Many of them perceive condom use as both unmanly and a sure sign of promiscuity.

The governments of both nations have instituted a massive STD/HIV prevention program to try to combat the problem. They have literally set up prevention service on the road. They have worked with the prostitutes to try to have them organize and institute greater compliance with use of condoms. They have used educational strategies ranging from one-to-one counseling to massive governmental media campaigns.

Brothels

Brothel
house of prostitution

Prior to 1920, large **brothels** could be found in every major American city. Many were elegant facilities where customers (overwhelmingly male) could have a drink, eat dinner, play cards, socialize with peers and the prostitutes, and have sex. Typically, brothels were set up like hotels, with socializing downstairs and sex negotiated in upstairs rooms. Repeat business was the norm, and clients were generally recruited by word of mouth.[8] As a result of legislation and the sweeping moral reform of the early 1920s, most brothels were closed, driving prostitution into the streets or the massage parlors. Brothels still exist in Nevada and, on a much smaller scale, most major metropolitan areas.

Massage Parlors

Prostitutes who work in massage parlors are referred to as hookers and hustlers but also may be known as masseuses. Most massage parlors are fronts for houses of prostitution, where in addition to a massage, clients are able to receive masturbation, oral sex, and sometimes sexual intercourse.

Most clients of massage parlors walk in off the street and pay cash for a massage and either masturbation or oral sex. Their visit usually lasts 30 minutes and costs anywhere from $20 to $50. Massage parlors usually have procedures that help screen for potential undercover police activities. For example, they require that customers sign a form indicating that they are not police officers. Clients pay for the massage in advance, with no mention of sexual "extras" until the later stages of the massage. The overwhelming majority of prostitutes working in massage parlors are female.

Escort Services

In theory, escort services involve the legal practice of "escorting" a client to dinner, a show, a political affair, and the like for a fee. In reality, most escort services derive their primary business through "out-call" male and female prostitution. Escort services advertise in telephone books, newspapers, and magazines. Many clients are referred by other satisfied customers. Customers call and are matched with the type of "escort" they desire. Escorts come to the client's residence or hotel and negotiate sexual activity.[9]

Prostitutes who work for escort services are referred to as "call girls" or "call boys," as well as escorts. Escort services may be run by a pimp or madam who works the phones and arranges the meetings. Some escort services are run by groups of prostitutes who schedule appointments based on availability and referral. Many call girls and call boys work independently after they establish their own client base.

In general, call girls and call boys are at the top of the status hierarchy of prostitutes. They typically charge from $50 to $200 an hour, or between $500 and $1,000 a night. Call girls and call boys work through telephone calls, personal meetings, and referrals. Because they are not on the street, they are not subject to the control and fees associated with pimps. If call persons are not in business for themselves, they have a madam or pimp scheduling for them.

Periodically high-priced call girls are arrested and their high-profile clients make the headlines. The cases of Sydney Biddle-Barrows, the "Mayflower Madam," and Heidi Fleiss are two examples. In each case the "madam" was a well-educated, respectable woman of noble upbringing (well-heeled families from New York and Los Angeles, respectively). Both told of enterprising entrepreneurs who earned a living catering to the sexual needs of the rich and famous. The clientele included famous actors (and actresses), politicians, judges, businesspersons, and assorted celebrities.

EXOTIC DANCERS, STRIPPERS, AND LIVE SEX PERFORMERS

Bars and clubs dedicated to providing adult entertainment from dancers have proliferated in the 1990s. These may be bars (which have licenses to sell and offer alcoholic beverages and are open to the general public) or "gentlemen's" clubs (which do not have licenses to sell liquor and are open to members only). The activities of establishments licensed to sell liquor are regulated by agencies such as the Bureau of Alcohol, Tobacco and Firearms (AFT). These establishments usually are under a stricter code than clubs, which usually, are regulated by local ordinances. Because of this, clubs usually tend to offer more risque forms of entertainment ranging from totally nude dancing to lap and couch dancing.

About 2,500 gentlemen's clubs have been established around the United States. The industry has gotten so large that it has its own trade publication, *Stripper* magazine. The revenues generated from these clubs are staggering: from $500,000 a year for the average club to more than $5 million for a well-run club.

Once called go-go dancers, the entertainment provided by strippers and exotic dancers has changed in the 1990s. Go-go dancers and strippers of the past usually performed on a stage, or literally in a cage, separated from their customers. Appreciative customers sometimes threw money onto the stage or offered to buy the dancer a drink and offer a tip.

In the 1990s, dancers have come off the stage and cages and onto the bars, tabletops, couches, and laps of customers in these clubs. Nowadays exotic dancers typically dance along the bar, discarding items of clothing as they stop to tease customers, who are allowed to slip their tips (usually folded dollar bills) into the dancer's top or G-string (a skimpy thong covering her pubic area). Dancers (at least those desiring larger tips) usually

Case Study

Carina: Working Her Way Through College as an Exotic Dancer

I guess you could say I got into this line of work as a fluke. A couple of years ago, my boyfriend, John, talked me into entering a wet T-shirt competition at a local bar. The grand prize was one hundred dollars, some promotional clothing, and a case of the tequila that was the sponsor for the event. I didn't want to do it, but John said he'd be there to make sure nobody hassled me. The rest is history.

I won the contest, and the manager asked me if I was interested in exotic dancing. I really wasn't, but he told me the money was good — over one hundred dollars a night in tips alone — the bouncers would protect me, and there would be no sexual favors expected. Besides he said, John is a regular here, and he'll be around a lot.

I'll never forget the first night. I was very nervous and couldn't relax. The first set was a disaster. I didn't make eye contact with the customers and was very aloof. My dancing wasn't too hot either. I don't think I got more than five dollars in tips. I was worried that I'd get assaulted or something.

In about the middle of my next routine, however, I began to relax a little — having a couple of shots of tequila after the first set helped — and started to get into the music. That first night John was there, so I

danced for him. He told me to relax and fantasize that he was the only guy in the bar. It started to be quite a turn-on and I really got into the music and was quite sexy.

The customers loved it and couldn't wait to stuff dollar bills in my G-string. I must admit that I didn't — and still don't — like the customers feeling my breasts or ass as they slip their money into my bra or G-string. The manager and the bouncers, however, make sure that this doesn't get out of hand and the tips are good. I average one hundred dollars in tips on a weekend night.

I still get a little annoyed at the customers propositioning me — about one in five do — but I've learned how to smile, refuse their advances, and move on. Most of the customers are there to blow off some steam, have a few drinks, and fantasize about having sex with me or whatever, but they never make a pass. A lot of them are pretty timid and are not a problem at all.

I plan on stopping this summer. I'm graduating from college with a degree in small-business management and am looking forward to getting an entry-level job managing a restaurant. I'd like to own a restaurant and bar of my own someday.

allow customers to feel their breasts, buttocks, and vulva fleetingly while passing along their tips.

Most dancers earn between ten dollars and twenty dollars an hour and rely heavily on tips to make up the bulk of their earnings. Many of the larger gentlemen's clubs employ big-name, hard-core film actresses as feature performers. The nation's top five or six porn actresses can earn $15,000 to $20,000 per week (four shows a night) to dance at the larger clubs. The next half-dozen famous actresses earn about $8,000 to $15,000 to dance in these clubs. Club owners use film credits and magazine spreads to market their performers.[10]

Many states have laws regulating dancers' attire and may require her to wear panty hose and keep her top on, or at least hold it up against her breasts. Customers are not allowed to fondle the dancers, with the exception of inserting dollar bills into their G-strings or tops. Any sexual exchange between dancer and customer is not allowed, as this constitutes prostitution, and bars usually hire bouncers to ensure that neither customers nor dancers violate this rule.

Exotic dancers in clubs often leave the bar to dance one-on-one with customers. Lap dancers usually straddle a customer and dance suggestively against his crotch. Couch dancers usually take a customer to a private couch, where they kneel on top of him or over him and dance suggestively in a more private ambiance. The objective of lap dancing and couch dancing in many instances is to offer the customer the opportunity literally to be masturbated to the point of orgasm by the dancer's motions without her ever using her hand. Such dancing usually requires an extra fee ($20 and up) and is timed (if the customer hasn't "come" or wants more stimulation, he has to buy more time).

Live sex shows usually take place in a theater environment but often occurs in a bar or club. One or more couples literally have sex on stage, on the floor, or on the bar while the customers watch, often masturbating as they become aroused.

Although dancing and live sex shows are not the same as prostitution, the performers often are prostitutes and are willing to arrange sex for pay sessions with customers at a later time. Live sex shows now are available on the internet. A customer can sign on in Iowa and be a member of the audience in a live sex show in Amsterdam.

Live sex shows usually take place in a theater environment.

TECH SEX

Whereas prostitution entails sexual contact with a live person, tech sex — sexual activity that connects with some form of technology — is masturbatory sex. It is designed to excite and arouse, leading to release of tension through masturbation. The same technological innovations that make sexual information available have opened new outlets for purveyors of impersonal sex for sale. These include sex talk lines, interactive cable TV sex, interactive computer sex, and computer sex chat rooms. These differ from ordinary pornography and erotica because the customer connects to a live human being via the phone, television, or computer. It is the ultimate sex of the 1990's technological revolution.

Telephone Sex

Every night, between the hours of 9:00 p.m. and 1:00 a.m., approximately 250,000 people in the United States dial a commercial phone-sex number. The average call lasts 6 to 8 minutes and costs anywhere from 89¢ to $4 a minute. In 1996, Americans spent between $750 million and $1 billion on telephone sex."[11]

A customer buys telephone sex by dialing a 1–900 number. A new scam uses a free 800 number to mask a 900 pay-per-call service. When the 800 number is called, the caller is identified through caller ID and the 900 pay-per-call provider bills the incoming number for the call.[12]

In 1991, the Federal Communications Commission restricted the type of calls that could be made using 900 numbers. The FCC banned all domestic calls it titled "obscene communications for commercial purposes." Because the ban does not extend to overseas calls, however, this loophole has created a burgeoning foreign market for telephone sex. Phone sex calls are routed to out-of-the-way places such as Aruba, the Mariana Islands, Guyana, and the Dominican Republic, where operators are standing by to take your call and cater to your every whim.[13] In 1993, telephone companies earned nearly $900 million from international services. An estimated 90% of those revenues came from phone sex lines.[14] These foreign revenues are shared between the domestic American company, its foreign phone company, and telephone sex providers. Some small countries have started their own telephone companies to get a bigger chunk of the market.[15]

Once customers' connections are established, they are billed per minute to their telephone bill. A person can engage in heterosexual talk, homosexual talk, bisexual talk, group talk. It is anonymous, graphic, expensive — and an illusion. Phone sex practitioners are trained to keep customers talking, to cater to their every fantasy. Because it is impersonal and anonymous, they are tempted to say things that normally are taboo.

The typical telephone sex customer is a "lonely heart" seeking conversation. Often, the sexual content of the call is of secondary importance. Anyone, however, is capable of becoming hooked on phone sex. Most telephone "actresses" — as they are referred to — are housewives, accountants, secretaries, bank tellers, senior citizens, and various other women seeking to earn a little extra income.[16]

Although it is a seemingly innocent form of sexual contact, telephone sex has become a major problem. It is a difficult form of sexual exchange to control. Minors have easy access to these services, and the costs can add up. The media are full of stories of parents opening up their phone bills and being surprised by junior's 900-number bill for hundreds of dollars.

Also, pedophiles and other sex offenders often use internet access to identify and lure their victims. Further, they can gain access to potential victims by establishing relationships with phone-sex providers to illegally trace their victim's telephone numbers through caller ID.

Commercial Television

Two trends within commercial television programming are of note concerning the dissemination of sexually explicit material and messages: the relaxation of restrictions on presenting sexual themes (particularly regarding the spoken word) and the creation of music video.

Commercial television closely regulates overt visual sexual programming. Total frontal nudity and sexual behavior without clothes are prohibited. Partial nudity is regulated but has a much wider berth than it did 20 years ago. Shows such as Baywatch and the morning workout shows feature scantily clad lifeguards and athletes with bulging swimsuits and plunging tank tops. In soap operas, lovemaking is depicted but involves the participants in bed under the covers, or the camera cuts away as clothes begin to be shed. Although partial nudity is common, it is restricted to nongenital displays. In 1997, under pressure from the federal government, the entertainment industry proposed a set of voluntary standards to rate television programming.

The spoken word and sexual posturing while clothed are subject to much less regulation. Talk shows and soap operas are permitted to use all but the most graphic language ("fuck" is still banned, but "ball," and "screw," among others, are permissible). Participants on panel talk shows and audience participation programs bare their soul while discussing everything from adultery to zoophilia.

The most unique addition to prime-time commercial television sex is the music video. This medium combines the power of music with implied and overt sexual themes. Undulating bodies (many partially clad) combine with seductive melodies and lyrics to offer a powerfully erotic presentation. In other cases, music combines with a kaleidoscope of disjointed violent images ranging from smashing guitars to drive-by shootings.

The most unique addition to prime-time commercial television sex is music video.

PERSPECTIVES

Television Rating Guide

In response to the 1996 Telecommunications Law, a voluntary committee made up of executives from the television and movie industries was established. In December, 1997, the task force, led by chief of the Motion Picture Association of America (MPAA) Jack Valenti, presented a set of guidelines to rate television programs.

These guidelines have sparked controversy among children's and parents' rights groups. The groups' major complaint centers on the ambiguity of the ratings, which are age-, not content-based.

Valenti's group presented ratings that are remarkably similar to those used in evaluating motion pictures. These, and the proposed TV ratings, evaluate programming by age-appropriateness. Those contesting such a rating system prefer a more content-based rating system similar to that used in Canada. The Canadian system evaluates programming based on the strength of content using a 1 to 3 scale on V (violent content), S (sexual content and nudity), and L (adult language). A program could get mixed ratings (L–1, V–3, or S–1) for instance.

Sources: "Age-based TV Ratings Slated as First Planned," by A. Bash, *USA Today On-line*, Aug. 20,1997; "Television Ratings," by R.E. Kent, FCC-V-Chip Homepage (e-mail rekent@eecs.wsu.edu; "U. S. TV Ratings System Almost Finalized," *Toronto Star*, Nov 26,1996.

Illicit drug use is often thrown into the mix, creating a unique melange of sex, drugs, and music.

Cable Television and Videocassettes

A leading product that cable television subscribers request is pay-per-view and subscription sex services. The adult video market, personified by sex-on-cable providers such as *Playboy*, *Spice*, and the *Adam and Eve* channel, grew from $521 million in 1994 to $664 million in 1995, with projections for continued growth.[17]

> *The advent of cable television and home VCRs has almost single handedly caused the near-extinction of the "porno movie theater."*

The advent of cable television and home VCRs has almost single handedly caused the near-extinction of the "porno movie theater." Cable television has literally brought the world of soft-core and hard-core pornography into middle America's living room. Twenty years ago, viewing pornography entailed either a trip to the local x-rated movie house or threading a super-8 film into the old family projector, setting up the screen, and hoping kids (or the parents) won't discover you watching the movie.

Today, virtually every cable television service provider has at least one "soft-core" channel that serves up late-evening viewing of "nonpenetrative" (penetration and ejaculation scenes have been edited out) versions of x-rated films. Many of the larger metropolitan-area cable television companies also offer x-rated shows (penetration and ejaculation are shown) channels for home viewing. These channels typically are offered for an extra charge (premium) that rarely exceeds $15 per month, thereby ensuring access to nearly all markets.

Case Study

Robert: Watching X-rated Videos

Robert is a 20-year-old college junior in one of the author's Human Sexuality classes. His comments are in response to the author's queries concerning his exposure to x-rated videos as an adolescent.

The first time I ever saw an X-rated video was over at my friend Matt's house. Matt's dad was a real collector of those movies and hid them in a trunk in his basement. Matt had discovered them about six months before, and told me about them.

Matt had a sleepover with me and a couple of other guys, and when his parents went to bed, we snuck downstairs and watched one. I forget the title, but it was some four-hour marathon with about a hundred short clips. It showed everything — intercourse, oral, anal, group, and interracial sex.

It was kind of weird watching it with the guys. I mean, it was a turn-on, but we all kind of laughed and joked about it at the time. It sure made me horny. I borrowed it from Matt and watched it at home for a week or so. I must have masturbated about 10 times that week watching that video. It got a little boring after that.

I still like to rent X movies every once in a while. Sometimes my girlfriend and I watch them and get turned on. Other times I prefer to watch them and masturbate. I don't see any harm in that.

In 1996, the Federal Telecommunications Law was passed, limiting the hours for airing these channels to between 10 p.m. and 6 a.m. All companies also are required to provide devices that deny transmission without a code that can be entered to activate the service.

The cost of the average videocassette recorder (VCR) has dropped to well below $200, putting it in the range of affordability for most households. The boom in VCR sales of the 1980s and 1990s created a massive audience for marketing home movies. The fastest growing segment of the home videocassette market is the adult video consumer. The number of hard-core sex video rentals in the United States rose from 75 million in 1985 to 490 million in 1992. It reached an all-time high in 1996, with rentals of more than 665 million x-rated sex videos.[18]

Purchases of adult videos in the United States approached that of rentals over the past decade. The x-rated video segment of the film industry is one of the most profitable and reliable forms of film production. In California alone, more than 7,800 new hard-core video titles were released in 1996.[19]

This dramatic rise in home video rentals and purchases has shifted the focus of consumption of these products from the seedy adult movie houses of 20 years ago to the home. It also has provided easier access for adolescent viewers.

Case Study

Ed: A Father's Perspective

Ed, a 41-year-old continuing student, recalls his response to finding an x-rated video in the VCR in the family room after a sleepover his 14-year-old son had the night before.

    I was cleaning the basement family room. The VCR light was on, so I ejected the film and, much to my surprise, found an x-rated video in it. I figured my son and his friends had watched it the night before, so I talked with him about it when he came home from school.

    I asked him if it was his, and he said it was one of his friend's father's tapes. His buddy had brought it over for the guys to watch. I told him that I was more upset over him leaving it in the basement where his 10-year-old brother could have viewed it than the fact that he had seen it. I asked him what he thought of the movie and he told me that it was a real turn-on.

    I reemphasized to him that his mother and I still didn't want him to begin having intercourse until he

was older and found a girlfriend he cared about and it would be exclusive. I also reassured him that I understood his natural curiosity about sex and sexual behavior and that masturbation was an acceptable outlet. I also wanted to be sure that he understood that x-rated films are fantasy sex and that he shouldn't confuse what he saw on some of these tapes with reality. I explained that these tapes are designed to cater to our fantasies but that real sex between two people involves talking, negotiating, and caring.

    He said he understood and didn't really expect that sex would be like the film. He said that some of the stuff on the film was too kinky for him anyway.

    I sometimes worry that my approach is too casual, but Ed is a very responsible boy and seems to treat girls with respect. I feel that if I make too big a deal out of this, it will become a forbidden-fruit deal and he'll want to watch them even more.

Computer Sex

More than 40% of U. S. households own at least one personal computer and in 1996, 24.8 million Americans were internet users.[20] Most of these users are experienced PC owners who access the internet with their home computers. Web TV, a type of internet TV (not a personal computer) introduced in the U. S. market in 1998, is expected to add an additional 250,000–300,00 users in 1999. If this technology catches on, the average noncomputer-literate person will have access to the World Wide Web and internet.[21]

The world of personal computers has opened up two primary access points to sexually oriented materials and adult-oriented Web site connections via the internet and x-rated software.

The world of personal computers has opened up two primary access points to sexually oriented materials and adult-oriented Web site connections via the internet and x-rated software. Rimm's controversial study, "Marketing Pornography on the Information Superhighway," surveyed 917,410 sexually explicit pictures, descriptions, short studies, and film clips available on the internet.[22] Not only does the internet make downloading hard-core pictures, movie clips, and stories easy, but it also provides access to hard-to-find materials that aren't readily available and are often illegal. This cornucopia of sexually explicit materials includes pedophilia, bondage, sadomasochism, and sex with animals.[23]

Internet-based sexually oriented materials are difficult to supervise. With more than 40,000,000 sites (the number grows by thousands daily) and nearly universal access, the internet provides global access to sexually oriented material. A consumer who has an internet connection to the World Wide Web can access sexually oriented chat rooms, still pictures (x-rated stills of anything desired, including kiddie-porn), video-clips (short sections of sex films), and live sex shows (the viewer becomes part of the audience from his or her living room) that can originate from anywhere around the globe. A person can connect with a live sex show from Denmark, a sadist or masochist from Asia, or a housewife selling still pictures of herself engaging in fellatio with her husband in Australia. Although this may sound too good to be true to an adult who enjoys pornography, it can cause much concern for the average parent of a teenage son or daughter. Technology is available to block minors' access to adult internet sites. These barriers, however, work only if parents and other adults using home PCs install them and check up on them regularly. Problems remain, however, even with these technological aids in place.

Computer chat rooms share many of the characteristics of telephone sex lines.

Computer chat rooms share many of the characteristics of telephone sex lines. They allow intimate but nonpersonal interaction over telephone lines. Users of computer chat rooms sit at a keyboard and "chat" by typing in messages and sharing them with other users in the "room." The relative safety of sitting at a keyboard creates an environment in which "chatter" is often personal and graphic in its sexual content.[24]

If your partner were engaging in explicit sexual chat with another person online, would you consider this cheating, harmless fantasy sex, or something else? Do you think sexual chat rooms are harmless, destructive, or neutral?

Software

The production of computer software has undergone a renaissance over the past few years. The primitive, sexually oriented software of the 1980s, which featured cartoon like animation has given way to the crystal-clear CD ROM-based x-rated interactive software of the 1990s. The newest software features sound, color, lifelike graphics, and the ability to move the characters into a limitless variety of sexually explicit interactions. Software technology is increasing in sophistication and quality with such speed that, by the time this page is printed, the x-rated software on the shelves of your local computer or "adult" store will be outdated. X-rated and soft-core software is available in stores, through the mail, or can be downloaded directly onto a personal computer. It is a huge industry that is difficult to supervise. Innovative software peddlers market their wares through chat rooms on the internet, computer and sex magazines, and shareware (public-domain software that is exchanged without cost).[25]

Health Hint

Computer Blocking Software

Several blocking software packages are available for use with personal computers to selectively block internet sites that transmit sexual material intended for adults. These products average about $35 retail and must be installed on the computer's hard drive. Each works in a slightly different way.

PC Magazine rated seven products and found that no single screening tool will meet the needs of every user. The tools ranged from simple to complex to install and use. The more complex software seems to provide more comprehensive blocking capability, allowing parents to control Web sites, chat rooms, e-mail, and other applications. Some allow parents to control the amount of time children spend online and to monitor the sites visited.

All of the tested products performed well in their intended functions. *PC Magazine* found, however, that a foolproof blocking software product is impossible to develop because of the subjective nature of what parents consider objectionable and the everchanging nature of the internet.

Nonetheless, these products do offer a tool to help parents monitor their children's computer activity. As with all software applications, parents must continually upgrade and monitor the products to ensure that they are performing at optimal efficiency.

Sources: "Filtering Utilities," by K. Munro, *PC Magazine*, 16:7 (April 8, 1997), 235–238; "Is Your Kid Caught Up in the Web? How to Find the Best Parts and Avoid the Others," *Consumer Reports*, 65:5, (May1997), 27–32; "Guarding Young Web-surfers; Don't Count on Special Software to Protect Kid's Privacy," *Consumer Reports*, 62:9, (Sept. 1977), 17.

EFFECTS OF PORNOGRAPHY AND SEXUALLY EXPLICIT MATERIAL

As long as pornography has been available, there have been attempts to regulate it, citing that it leads to a variety of social maladies including rape, sexual harassment, degradation and exploitation of women, and weakening of the moral fiber of America.

Two presidential commissions on pornography and obscenity have been empaneled over the past 25 years to examine the effects of viewing such material. The first commission was paneled in 1970 by President Richard Nixon. The commission was charged with examining whether exposure to pornography could cause personal harm or lead to sexual violence. The

Case Study

Lisa: Addicted to Cyber Sex

Lisa is a 42-year-old continuing education student. She has been married for 22 years and is the mother of a 14-year-old daughter and 13-year-old son. She works part-time and is taking one of the author's Human Sexuality classes for personal enrichment.

I had a real problem with computer sex. I had to see a therapist because I was really addicted. My telephone and internet bills were getting huge and I was spending about three hours a night online. I've been in counseling for a couple of months and actually took this class to try to understand my sexuality a little better. I think my marriage was in jeopardy, and that scared me.

My addiction began innocently enough. I had a lot of time on my hands. My husband, whom I love very much, travels about half of the time. As the national sales manager for a small company, he is off on business at least two weeks a month. He earns a fabulous salary, and I don't have to work. The kids are both grown up and don't need me much except to drive them around. Other than my exercise class, I had no real time commitments.

We bought my son a new, powerful computer, with internet access, and he showed me how to go online and get into these chat rooms. I started to log-on and chat with people. Before long, I found my way into a couple of chat rooms that were sexually oriented. I mean, the primary purpose was to discuss sexual fantasies. It was quite a turn-on. I was getting into these intimate discussions with all kinds of men. It started out as kind of generic. We talked about our sex lives and what we liked to do in bed. Then it got personal — what we'd like to do to each other.

At first I didn't think it was a problem, and I didn't feel guilty, but after a while I found that I was getting really worked up about these calls. I'd masturbate after hanging up. Sometimes I'd even make myself come while online. That's when I started to worry. I never wanted to meet these guys face-to-face, but I started to feel like I was still having sex with them. I was also worried about my kids walking in and seeing me playing with myself.

It all came to a head when my husband saw one of the internet bills. It seems as though I used a toll number instead of one of the toll-free access ones, and the bill was over five hundred fifty dollars for the month. I had to explain the whole thing to him, and he freaked out. He felt like I cheated on him, and he considered separation. It took several weeks to restore his trust and convince him that I still loved him. We moved the computer into my son's room, and I promised not to go online again. We started seeing a family therapist, and I got a part-time job to get me out of the house a little. I'm taking this class to try to learn a little about my sexuality.

Health Hint

Safe Internet Use

The internet offers the world at your fingertips. It personifies the best and the worst of technological innovation. With a little common sense and some specific safeguards, it can be a great source of sexual information and materials. The following tips can help you surf safely.

1. Install site-blocking software. Some things on the internet are best kept away from children.

2. Monitor your family's use of the internet. Computers were never intended to take the place of live human interaction.

3. Establish online guidelines, and limit the amount of time children stay online.

4. Think of the computer as you would a television set. You don't want to (or want your family to) spend hours mesmerized in front of the screen. Take a walk, get some exercise, do something physical.

5. Never give out your real name and address over the internet, for any reason (especially on chat lines).

6. Never agree to unsupervised personal meetings with people you "meet" over the internet. Let them know you will meet them in a neutral public place and that you will be bringing a friend.

7. If you use online sex services (view erotic materials, chat, etc.), realize that this is fantasy sex. The reason it is a turn-on relates in part to the anonymity of the sex.

8. Like all fantasy sex, recognize that you may not want to actually experience what you discuss or view on the internet.

9. If someone you met on the internet has found out who you are and where you live and is trying to establish contact with you against your will, call the police immediately. Internet use is not illegal, but stalking is.

10. If you find yourself becoming addicted, disconnect, drop your online service, and get professional help.

commission found that exposure to pornography and obscene materials did not cause personal harm or contribute to sexual violence.

The second commission, empaneled by President Ronald Reagan in the early 1980s, had a similar charge. The commission found that exposure to nonviolent pornography was not harmful and did not lead to sexual aggression and violence.[26] A secondary finding of the commission, however, touched off a great deal of controversy among human sexuality professionals. This finding was the claim that the most prevalent forms of pornography were violent in nature, and that exposure to this material had a causal relationship to sexual violence.

These claims were instantly refuted by sex researchers and professional organizations.[27] Researchers argued that studies of the sexual content of samples of pornographic material revealed that between 4% and 16% contained violent themes or scenes depicting violence.[28] Professional organizations decried the supposed causal link between viewing violent pornography and sexual violence, citing the lack of substantiating evidence within the commission's report or in the professional literature.

WELLNESS SYNTHESIS

The fast pace of today's world requires that we have high-level wellness in all domains of wellness.

Physical Well-being

Although our changing sexual environment doesn't impact directly on our physical well-being, it does have an indirect effect by sending messages about what is sensual, beautiful, and sexual. This can set unrealistic standards of perfection or a physical ideal that is unattainable. One also could view this in a positive way. The newfound interest in lifting weights, exercising, and eating healthfully in part from images of physical beauty personified by models and popular media personalities (like Madonna), who promote these behaviors as contributing to their sexiness.

You can scarcely pass a woman's or men's magazine that doesn't portray the virtues of working out to sculpt a "sexy" body. In a sense, then, the fitness craze, which generally enhances physical well-being is fueled by the same sexual climate that has also produced many negative sexual images.

Intellectual Well-being

One positive outcome of greater accessibility to sexual resources coupled with the technological innovations of the past decade is the incredible explosion in information technology. Our ability to conduct research, gather information, process what we've found, and share resources has never been better. Average people working from home on a personal computer can tap into the greatest minds of our time without leaving home. This has the potential to greatly enhance our intellectual well-being. We have unprecedented access to information about any facet of sexuality, in the privacy of our own home.

Emotional Well-being

Not only is sexual information available in unprecedented amounts, but sexual counseling, therapy, and self-help also are within the average person's reach. As sex comes into the open, so does sexual healing. Online chat rooms, self-help groups, and other computerized services offer increasing opportunities for dealing with sexual concerns and problems.

Web sites are available catering to all people and interests. Gay people who need help to come out of the closet can find help and link up with others around the country or around the corner. Transgendered people no longer have to feel alone. They have their own web sites and referral networks a mere mouse-click away. Although electronic resources will never take the place of a live helping relationship, the technological innovations and resources available to the average person can greatly improve their emotional well-being by providing easy access to information and services that were not available a decade ago.

Social Well-being

Does the current climate concerning sexuality and the pervasiveness of sexual themes and availability affect our social well-being? Or does our social well-being affect the way we perceive and deal with this highly sexual social climate? Reality probably lies somewhere in the middle. The sheer volume of sexual messages, availability of sexual products and services, and the use of sex to market and sell everything influences our social well-being. Every social situation we experience and all of our social relationships take place within this highly charged sexual culture.

Our level of social well-being mediates how we interpret and react to sexual messages and availability emanating from the culture. Those who have high levels of social well-being, strong support systems, and loving relationships, respond to a highly charged sexual environment differently than most who do not.

Opponents argue that the current sexual climate impacts negatively on our social well-being. Everything from childrearing to productivity in the workplace, they say, becomes harder as parents, employers, and government have to compete against the lure and distraction of sexual availability. It is more difficult, they argue, to uphold standards of decency and social relationships in the face of a no-holds-barred societal attitude toward sex.

Others disagree. They argue that greater sexual freedom and availability of sexual information and services empowers people and fosters understanding of their sexuality. Social well-being, they say, is thereby enhanced because sexuality, a natural part of life, is allowed its full expression. This allows people to understand their sexuality better and develop higher levels of social well-being.

Spiritual Well-being

The effects of our cultural beliefs and behavior concerning sexuality on our spiritual well-being is closely aligned to those regarding our social health. The "moral fabric" of our nation is a term used to describe our standards as a society. It refers to our values, attitudes, and beliefs about moral issues that reflect our spiritual health. Issues such as the availability of pornography on the internet, some postulate, reflect our moral bankruptcy as a society. Our spirituality, they say, suffers when sex becomes a commodity instead of an intimate bond that connects people through love and commitment. Those who represent the opposing view cite the absence of evidence connecting greater sexual availability and permissiveness with moral decay.

Environmental Well-being

Our sexual environment has definitely changed over the past 30 years. Changes in standards of acceptability and permissiveness, coupled with advances in technology, have created an environment in which access to sexual information, products, and services is vastly different than at any other point in our history.

Some communities have organized to restrict sex-industry outlets to nonresidential sectors rather than eliminate x-rated bookstores, bars, and other establishments. Other communities have banned them outright. Home-based blockers allow parents to monitor and control the internet and pay television. This allows them to enjoy the service and at the same time to bar it from young children in the family.

It remains to be seen as to whether this is the beginning of a truly enlightened society that finally places sexuality in its rightful place or whether we have pushed the limits of good taste and decency too far and are beginning to suffer from our excesses. Communities have a way of determining these limits for themselves.

WEB RESOURCES

National Task Force on Prostitution
http://www.bayswan.org/NTFP.html
Prostitutes' Education Network site providing information about health, legislation, and other issues affecting prostitutes and sex workers.

Blue Ribbon Campaign for Online Free Speech
http://www.eff.org/blueribbon.html
Site sponsored by Electronic Frontier Foundation (EFF), a movement that opposes censorship on the web. There is a section on the latest news from the government with links for more information.

Sex, Censorship, and the Internet
http://www.eff.org/CAF/cafuiuc.html
The Electronic Frontier Foundation is a nonprofit, nonpartisan organization working to protect fundamental civil liberties and freedom of expression on internet. This site describes threats to academic freedom and use of the internet to disseminate sexual material. An outline of topics, *Policies and Experience, Academic Freedom, Two Types of Acceptable Use Policies,* and *Top Library Intellectual Freedom Policies.*

Notes

1. J. Martin, "Calvinism," *America*, Sept. 1995.
2. N. C. Bradlee, "The Bradlee Files," *Newsweek*, 126:13 (1997), 82–88.
3. M. Edwards, "The Net and the Web: Unlimited Potential to Communicate Sexuality Issues," *SIECUS Reports*, 25:1 (1996), 2–4.
4. J. McConville, "Cable Upfront Hits $2 Billion Mark," *Broadcasting & Cable*, 126:30 (1997), 7.
5. I. Lagnado, "Is the PC Party Really Over?" *HFN: The Weekly Network for the Home Furnishing Network*, 71:3, 10.
6. M. Diamond and J. E. Dannemiller, "Pornography and Community Standards in Hawaii: Comparisons with Other States," *Archives of Sexual Behavior*, 18 (1989), 6.
7. L. Shrage, "Prostitution and the Case for Decriminalization," *Dissent*, Spring 1996.
8. J. R. Petersen, *Playboy's History of the Sexual Revolution*; Part 1. *Playboy*, 43:12 (Dec 1996), 66.
9. M. O'Kane, "All in a Night's Work; Male Escorts" *Guardian*, (March 21, 1994), 2–4.
10. E. Schlosser," Pornography," *U.S. News & World Report*, Feb. 10, 1997, pp. 43–50.
11. Schlosser.
12. "Call for a Crackdown on the 900 Billing Charade" (editorial). *Business Communications Review*, 24:5 (1994), 12.
13. Schlosser.
14. "Heavy Breathing: Phone Sex", *Economist*, 332:7874 (1994), 71.
15. Schlosser.
16. Schlosser.
17. "Adult Video, Cable Market Surges," *Broadcasting & Cable*, 125:13 (1995), 47.
18. Schlosser.
19. K. Spicer, "The Talent of Max Hardcore," *Guardian*, May 19, 1997, T8–T10.
20. K. Richards, "PCs on the Web; Researcher Forecasts Sales Drive," *HFN: The Weekly Newspaper for the Home Furnishing Network*, 71:1 (1997), 79–81.
21. Richards.
22. M. Rimm, "Marketing Pornography on the Information Superhighway," *Georgetown Law Journal*, 83 (June 1995) 1849–1934.
23. P. Elmer-Dewitti, "'On a Screen Near You' Cyberporn," *Time*, July 1995; D. Hoffman and T. Novak, "A Detailed Criticism of 'On a Screen Near You.'" (http://www2000.ogsm.vanderbuilt.edu/novak/time.dewitt.html)
24. G. Topp, "Virtual Immorality," walraven@iadfw.net and http://web2.airmail.net/walraven/esquire.htm
25. L. Silberg, "Hot for your Home PC," *HFN: The Weekly Newspaper for the Home Furnishing Network*, 70:48 (1996), 47–49.
26. Attorney General's Commission on Pornography, *Report on Pornography and Obscenity* (Washington DC: Department of Justice, 1986).
27. Board of Directors of the Society for the Scientific Study of Sex, "SSSS Responds to the U. S. Attorney General's Commission on Pornography," *Journal of Sex Research*, 23:2 (1987), 284–285.
28. J. Slade, "Violence in the Hard-core Pornographic Film: A Historical Survey," *Journal of Communication*, 34:3 (1984), 148–163, J. Scott, "An Updated Longitudinal Content Analysis of Sex References in Mass Circulation Magazines, "*Journal of Sex Research*, 2293(1986), 385–392.

Student Study Questions

1. How are pornography, obscenity, and erotica different?

2. What is the significance of the Gary Hart scandal in establishing a new zeitgeist concerning the media and sexuality?

3. What impact has technology had on the availability of sexuality explicit material and services?

4. What are the arguments for and against legalization of prostitution?

5. What are some of the sexual problems associated with the internet, and how can they be addressed?

Private Lives of Public People

1. Do the media (or anyone) have the right to divulge a private citizen's personal sexual information under any circumstances?

    yes _____ no_____

2. Do the media (or any person) have the right to divulge a public (person running for office, sports figure, entertainer, etc.) figure's personal sexual information under any circumstance?

    yes _____ no_____

    If you answered yes to #1 or #2, please describe those circumstances.

3. Does a person's personal sexuality influence his/her professional behavior?

    yes _____ no_____

4. If you answered yes to #3, please describe how.

5. Should some sexual things be kept private regardless of the circumstances?

    yes _____ no_____

6. If you answered yes to #5, please describe these things and why you feel this way.

Select Bibliography

American Cancer Society. *Breast Self-Exam Guidelines*. Atlanta: ACS, 1993.

Anderson, K. N., et al. *Mosby's Medical, Nursing, and Allied Health Dictionary*, 4th ed. St Louis: Mosby, 1995.

Ballard-Barbash R., et al. "Body Fat Distribution and Breast Cancer in the Framingham Study." *Journal of the National Cancer Institute*, 82:24(1990), 1943–1944.

Berne, E. *Transactional Analysis in Psychotherapy*. New York: Grove Press, 1960.

Blank, J. Good Vibrations — Catalog and Home Page. Available http://www.goodvibes .com/guindex.html.

Blonna, R. *Coping With Stress in a Changing World*. St. Louis: Mosby, 1995.

Boston Women's Health Collective. *The New Our Bodies, Our Selves*. New York: Simon and Schuster, 1992.

Brownmiller, S. *Against Our Will: Men, Women, and Rape*. New York: Simon & Schuster, 1975.

Collum, C. S. *Co-parent Adoptions: Lesbian and Gay Parenting*, 1998, http://nac.adopt.org/ adopt/gay.

Dodson, Betty. *Sex for One: The Joy of Self Loving*. New York: Crown, (1996).

Dunham, C. Myers, F., McDougall, A., and Barnden, N. *Mamatoto: A Celebration of Birth*. New York: Penguin Group, 1992.

Eisenberg, A., Murkoff, H., and Hathaway, S. (1991) *What to Expect When You're Expecting*. New York: Workman Publishing, 1991.

Foote, D. "And Baby Makes One." *Newsweek*, February 2, 1998, pp. 68–70.

Freud, Sigmund. "Three Contributions to the Theory of Sex," in *The Basic Writings of Sigmund Freud*, edited by A. A. Brill. New York: Modern Library, 1938.

Haas, K., and Haas, A. *Understanding Sexuality*. St. Louis: Mosby, 1993.

Intersex Society of North America. *Recommendations for Treatment: Intersex Infants and Children*. San Francisco: ISNA, 1995.

Jemmott, J. B., Jemmott, L., and Fong, G. T. "Reductions in HIV Risk-associated Sexual Behaviors Among Black Male Adolescents." *American Journal of Public Health*, 32:3 (1992) 372–377.

Jouris, D. (1996) *All Over the Map*. Berkeley, CA: Ten Speed Press.

Kassman, Leon, & Weinstock, Alexander. "Self Acceptance and Intimacy." *SIECUS Report*, 25:5 (June/July/1997).

Lowinson, J. H., Ruiz, P., Millman, R. B., and Langrod, J. G. *Substance Abuse: A Comprehensive Textbook*, 2d edition. Baltimore: Williams & Wilkins, 1992.

Martin, A. *Same-sex Marriage and Parenting*, 1996, http://www.buddybuddy.com/martin-1.

Marx R., Aral, S., Rolfs, R., Sterk, C., and Kahn, J. "Crack, Sex, and STD." *Sexually Transmitted Diseases*, 2 (1991), 92–101.

Masters, W. H., and Johnson, V. E. *Human Sexual Response*. Boston: Little Brown, 1966.

Michaud, S. L., and Warner, R. M. "Gender Differences in Self-reported Responses in Troubles Talk." *Sex Roles: A Journal of Research*, 7–8 (Oct. 37), 527–541.

Moss, B. F., & Schwebel, I. A. "Marriage and Romantic Relationships: Defining Intimacy in Romantic Relationships." *Family Relations*, 42 (1993), 31–37.

Muehlenhard, C. L., Sympson, S., Phelps, J., and Highby, B. "Are Rape Statistics Exaggerated? A Response to Criticism of Contemporary Research." *Journal of Sex Research*, 31:2 (1994), 144–147.

Nilsson, L. *A Child is Born*. New York: Bantam Books, 1990.

Office of Public Health and Science (1997). *Federal Register*, 62:49 (March 13, 1997).

Perlman, Daniel, and Fehr, B. "The Development of Intimate Relationships," in *Intimate Relationships: Development, Dynamics, and Deterioration*, edited by D. Perlman and S. Duck. Newberry Park, CA: Sage, 1987.

Rosen, J. "The End of Obscenity." *New Republic* (July 15, 22, 1996), 6.

Schultz, D. P. *A History of Modern Psychology*. New York: Academic Press, 1969.

Sellers, T. A., et al. "Effect of Family History, Body Fat Distribution, and Reproductive Factors on the Risk of Postmenopausal Breast Cancer." *New England Journal of Medicine* 326:20(1992), 1323–1329.

Tannen, D. *You Just Don't Understand: Women and Men in Conversation*. New York: William Morrow, 1990.

Wheeless, L. R., Wheeless, V. E., and Baus, R. "Sexual Communication, Communication Satisfaction and Solidarity in the Development of Sexual Relationships." *Western Journal of Speech Communication*, 48:3 (1984), 224.

Willett, W., Hunter, D., and Stampfer, M., et al. "Dietary Fat and Fiber in Relation to Risk of Breast Cancer: An 8-year Follow-up" *Journal of the American Medical Association*, 268:15(1992), 2037–2044.

U. S. Department of Health & Human Services (USDHHS). "Preventing Risk Behaviors Among Students." *HIV/AIDS Prevention Newsletter*, 3 (1992), 1–2.

Suggested Readings

Barbach, Lonnie. (1991). *For Yourself: The Fulfillment of Female Sexuality*. New York: New American Library.
    One of the best women's self-help sexuality books; describes how to maximize sexual pleasure.

Barbach, Lonnie, (1984). *For Each Other: Sharing Sexual Intimacy*. New York: New American Library.
    A follow-up targeted to couples.

Comfort, Alex. (1994). *The New Joy of Sex*. New York: Crown.
    Similar in nature to The Joy of Sex, but targeted to sexual needs of gays and lesbians.

Rubin, David. (1999). *Everything You Always Wanted to Know About Sex: But Were Afraid to Ask*. New York. Harper Collins.
    First popular self-help book about sex; offers practical, nonthreatening answers to the most common questions about sexuality.

Silverstein, C. and Picano, R. (1993) *The New Joy of Gay Sex*. New York. Harper Collins.
    Updated edition targeted to gay and lesbian sexual activity.

Vatsyayana (1994) *The Complete Kama Sutra: The First Unabridged Modern Translation of the Classic Indian Text*, Alain Danielou (translator). Inner Traditions International Ltd.
    Available online, translated by Sir Richard Burton; timeless Indian sex manual that merges yoga, spirituality, and sex.
    http://www.bibliomania.com/NonFiction/Vatsyayana/KamaSutra

Westheimer, Ruth (1994). *Dr. Ruth's Guide to Good Sex*. New York: Warner.
    The famous Dr. Ruth at her best; witty, irreverent, warmly engaging, a fun book about good sex for everyone.

Resources on Human Sexuality

ALCOHOL AND DRUGS

Al-Anon Family Groups Headquarters
1600 Corporate Landing Park Way
Virginia Beach, VA 23454   800-356-9996

Nonprofit agency providing a 12-step program for family members and friends who have been affected by another's alcoholism.

Alcoholics Anonymous
Grand Central Station
PO Box 459
New York, NY 10163   212-870-3400
http://www.alcoholics-anonymous.org

Nonprofit agency offering support services to alcoholics.

Narcotics Anonymous
World Service Office
PO Box 9999
Van Nuys, CA 91409   818-773-9999
http://www.na.org

A 12-step recovery program for those with drug addictions.

National Association for Children of Alcoholics
11426 Rockville Pike, Suite 100
Rockville, MD 20852   888-554-2627
http://www.health.org/nacoa

Nonprofit organization offering educational information and advocacy for children of alcoholics.

National Clearinghouse for Alcohol and Drug Information
PO Box 2345
Rockville, MD 20847-2345   800-487-4890
http://www.health.org

Media support service for spokespersons; data and information on substance abuse and related issues.

National Council on Alcoholism and Drug Dependence
12 West 21st Street, 8th Floor
New York, NY 10010   800-622-2255
http://www.ncadd.org

Nonprofit organization providing referrals to addiction services and information on the treatment and prevention of alcoholism.

Rational Recovery
PO Box 800
Lotus, CA 95651   530-621-2667
http://rational.org/recovery

Alternative resource to Alcoholics Anonymous.

Stop Teenage Addiction to Tobacco
Northeastern University
360 Huntington Avenue
241 Cushing Hall
Boston, MA 02115   617-373-7828
http://www.stat.org

Training, advocacy and research for tobacco prevention among young adults.

GENDER IDENTITY AND CROSS-GENDERISM, GAY MALES, LESBIANS, AND BISEXUALS

Bisexual Resource Center
PO Box 400639
Cambridge, MA 02140   617-424-9595
http://www.biresource.org

A nonprofit organization providing research and education about bisexuality to the general public.

Children of Lesbians and Gays Everywhere (COLAGE)
3543 - 18th Street #17
San Francisco, CA 94110   415-861-5437
http://www.colage.org

An autonomous program of the Family Pride Coalition that provides education, support, and community for families with transgendered members, advocating for their rights and acceptance.

Family Pride Coalition
PO Box 34337
San Diego, CA 92163   619-296-0199
c/o Gay Fathers of Toronto
PO Box 187, Station F
Toronto Ontario, Canada M4Y 2L5
http://www.familypride.org

Coalition providing advocacy, education, and support for gay, lesbian, bisexual, and transgendered persons.

Gay and Lesbian Alliance Against Defamation (GLAAD)
1825 Connecticut Avenue NW, 5th Floor
Washington, DC 20009   202-986-1360
http://www.glaad.org/glaad

National organization dedicated to promoting fair, accurate, and inclusive representation of individuals and events in the media as a means of challenging discrimination based on sexual orientation or identity.

Gay, Lesbian, and Straight Education Network
121 West 27th Street, Suite 804
New York, NY 10001   212-727-0135
http://www.glsen.org

National organization dedicated to ending the cycle of bigotry by teaching the lesson of respect for all in public, private, and parochial K-12 schools.

Harry Benjamin International Gender Dysphoria Association
C/O The Program in Human Sexuality
1300 South 2nd Street, Suite 180
Minneapolis, MN 55454
http://www.tc.umn.edu/nlhome/m201/colem001/hbigda/

Professional organization devoted to the understanding and treating gender identity disorders; established Standards of Care for treatment of gender identity disorders.

Ingersoll Gender Center
1812 East Madison Street
Seattle, WA 98122   206-860-6064
http://www.ingersollcenter.org

Nonprofit service agency promoting awareness of gender identity and expression for transsexual, transvestite, and transgendered community.

International Gay and Lesbian Archives

PO Box 69679
West Hollywood, CA 90069   310-854-0271

http://www.usc.edu/Library/oneigla

Oldest ongoing gay/lesbian organization in the western hemisphere houses the world's largest research library on gay, lesbian, bisexual, and transgendered heritage and concerns.

Intersex Society of North America (ISNA)

PO Box 31791
San Francisco, CA 94131

http://www.isna.org/

A peer support, education, and advocacy group established for intersexuals (individuals born with anatomy or physiology different from cultural ideals of male and female).

Kinsey Institute for Research in Sex, Gender, and Reproduction

Morrison 313
Indiana University
Bloomington, MN 47405   812-855-7686

http://www.indiana.edu/~kinsey/

Supports interdisciplinary research, scholarship, and study in the field of human sexuality, gender, and reproduction

National Black Lesbian and Gay Leadership Forum

1612 K Street NW, Suite 500
Washington, DC 20006   202-483-6786

http://www.nblglf.org

Forum that advocates on behalf of black lesbigaytrans people in United States.

National Center for Lesbian Rights

870 Market Street, Suite 570
San Francisco, CA 94102   415-392-6257

http://www.nclrights.org

National legal center committed to advancing the rights and safety of lesbians and their families through a program of litigation, public policy advocacy, free legal advice and counseling, and public education; also provides representation and resource to gay men and bisexual and transgendered individuals on key issues that significantly advance lesbian rights.

National Latino/a Lesbian and Gay Organization Incorporated

1612 K Street NW, Suite 500
Washington, DC 20006   202-466-8240

http://www.llego.org

Nonprofit network of lesbian and gay Latinos/as; maintains a database and directory of resources and hold yearly conferences.

National Gay and Lesbian Task Force (NGLTF)

1700 Kalorama Road, Suite 101
Washington, DC 20009   202-332-6483

http://www.ngltf.org

Civil rights organization that supports grassroots organizing and advocacy for lesbian, gay, bisexual, and transgendered rights.

National Lesbian and Gay Health Association

1407 S Street NW
Washington, DC 20009   202-939-7880
Association devoted to assisting the needs of lesbians and gay men.

Out Proud!

The National Organization for Gay, Lesbian, Bisexual and Transgendered Youth
369 Third Street, Suite B-362
San Rafael, CA 94901-3581   415-460-5451 fax

Infor@outproud.org

http://www.outproud.org/

Organization serving the needs of young people by providing advocacy, information, resources, and support.

Outreach Institute of Gender Studies

126 Western Avenue, PMB #246
Augusta, ME 04330   207-622-7618

http://www.cowart.com/outreach/

Program that strives to advance understanding of gender identity and role development, with particular focus on alternative gender lifestyles.

Parents, Families and Friends of Lesbians and Gays (PFLAG)

1101 Fourteenth Street NW, Suite 1030
Washington, DC 20005   202-638-4200

http://www.pflag.org/

National nonprofit organization supporting parents, families, and friends of lesbians and gays; provides resources and literature to assist in coping and to educate society toward ending discrimination and secure equal civil rights.

The Renaissance Transgender Association

987 Old Eagle School Road, Suite 719
Wayne, PA 19087   610-975-9119

http://www.ren.org/

Provides comprehensive education and support to transgendered persons and to those close to them; offer programs and resources for crossdressers, transvestites, and transsexuals.

Society for the Second Self

C/O Beta Gamma Chapter, Tri-Ess
PO Box 49522
Minneapolis, MN 55449

http://www.triess.com

Family-oriented organization that provides support to the heterosexual crossdresser, their partners. Its focus is on affirming crossdressers and their partners and in supporting their social needs and their desire to improve themselves in the areas of crossdressing.

HOTLINES

CDC National AIDS Hotline

PO Box 13827   800-342-2437
Research Triangle, Park NC 27709-3827   800-344-7432 (Spanish)
          800-243-7889 (TTY)

CDC National STD Hotline

          800-227-8922
          800-243-7889 (TTY)
Hours: 8 a.m. - 11 p.m. (EST) weekend

Childhelp USA Hotline

          800-422-4453
          800-222-4453 (TTY)
(largest and oldest organization in the treatment, prevention and research of child abuse and neglect servicing United States, Canada, Virgin Island, Guam, and Puerto Rico)

National Domestic Violence Hotline

800-799-7233   800-787-3224 (TTY)

Men's Health Network and Men's/Father's Hotline

807 Brazos, Suite 315
Austin, TX 78701   512-472-3237
(crisis line for men and fathers; caller is referred to local, state, or national assistance programs)

National Herpes Hotline

PO Box 13827   919-361-8488
Research Triangle Park, NC 27709   800-230-6039
(provides an up-to-date literature, counseling, and informational material on promoting social health)

Rape Abuse and Incest National Network (RAINN)

252 Tenth Street NE
Washington, DC 20002   800-656-HOPE (4673) (24-hours/day)
http://www.rainn.org

MEN'S HEALTH AND FAMILY ISSUES

American Coalition for Fathers and Children

1718 M Street NW, Suite 187
Washington, DC 20036   800-978-3237
http://www.acfc.org
Coalition that promotes father's and grandparent's rights to be involved in the family and with children after divorce.

The Institute for Responsible Fatherhood and Family Revitalization

1146 Nineteenth Street NW, Suite 800
Washington, DC 20036   202-293-4420
http://www.responsiblefatherhood.org
Home-based grassroots nonprofit organization encouraging fathers to become involved in their children's lives.

Men's Health Network

PO Box 75972
Washington, DC 20013   202-543-6461
http://www.menshealthnetwork.org/
Information and educational organization that recognizes men's health as a specific societal concern and is committed to promoting issues affecting men's health.

National Center for Fathering

PO Box 413888
Kansas City, MO 64141-3888   800-593-3237
http://www.fathers.com
Conducts research on fathers and fathering and develops practical resources to prepare dads for all situations.

ORGANIZATIONS (Miscellaneous)

Administration on Aging (AOA)

330 Independence Avenue NW
Washington, DC 20201   202-619-0724
http://www.aoa.dhhs.gov/
Develops and supports comprehensive in-home and community services that create opportunities for active older persons and meets the needs of older persons at risk of losing their independence.

Alliance of Genetic Support Groups

4301 Connecticut Avenue NW, #404
Washington, DC 20008-2304   800-336-4363
Nonprofit organization founded as a national coalition of consumers, professionals and genetic support groups to state common concerns of children, adults, and families living with, and at risk for, genetic conditions.

American Association on Mental Retardation (AAMR)

444 North Capitol Street NW, Suite 846
Washington, DC 20001-1512   800-424-3688
http://www.aamr.org
Promotes global development and dissemination of progressive policies, research, practices, and universal human rights for people with intellectual disabilities.

American Association of Sex Educators, Counselors, and Therapists

PO Box 238
Mount Vernon, IA 52314   319-895-6203 (fax)
http://www.aasect.org
Promotes sexual health by developing and advancing the fields of sex therapy, counseling, and education.

American Cancer Society (ACS)

1599 Clifton Road NE
Atlanta, GA 30329   800-227-2345
http://www.cancer.org
Provides information and research on cancer.

American Diabetes Association

1660 Duke Street
Alexandria, VA 22314   800-342-2383
http://www.diabetes.org
Leading nonprofit organization providing diabetes research, information, and advocacy.

American Foundation for the Blind

11 Penn Plaza, Suite 300
New York, NY 10001   212-502-7661
http://www.afb.org
Nonprofit organization serving people who are blind or have visual impairment.

American Heart Association (AHA)

7272 Greenville Avenue
Dallas, TX 75231   214-373-6300
http://www.americanheart.org
Provides education and information on fighting heart disease and stroke.

Arthritis Foundation

1330 West Peachtree Street
Atlanta, GA 30309   800-283-7800
http://www.arthritis.org
Provides information and referral for arthritics disease.

Center for Disease Control and Prevention (CDC)

1600 Clifton Road
Atlanta, GA 30329   800-311-3435
http://www.cdc.gov
Agency promoting health and quality of life by preventing and controlling diseases, injury, and disability; complies and publishes relevant data.

Foundation for the Scientific Study of Sexuality (FSSS)

PO 970 Peck Slip Station
New York, NY 10272-0970
http://www.ssc.wisc.edu/ssss
Nonprofit organization supporting scholarly activities related to advancement of scientific study of sexuality; provides funding for individuals and organizations that conduct scientific research to further understanding of sexuality.

Lambda Legal Defense Education Fund

120 Wall Street, Suite 1500
New York, NY 10005   212-809-8585
http://208.178.40.104/cgi-bin/pages/

National organization committed to achieving full recognition of civil rights of lesbians, gay men, and people with HIV/HIVS by impacting litigation, education, and public policy work.

National Hemophilia Foundation

116 W 32nd Street, 11th Floor
New York, NY 10001   212-328-3700
http://www.hemophilia.org

Supports and promotes research leading to finding cures for hemophilia and other bleeding disorders.

National Hospice Organization

1901 N Moore Street, Suite 901
Arlington, VA 22209   703-243-5900
http://www.nho.org

Nonprofit organization devoted to hospice care by maintaining quality care for terminally ill persons and their families.

National Institute of Health (NIH)

Bethesda, MD 20892
http://www.nih.gov/icd

One of eight health agencies of the U. S. Department of Health and Human Services; consists of 25 separate institutes and centers, including National Institute of Drug Abuse and National Institute of Alcohol and Alcohol Abuse.

Sexuality and Developmental Disability Network

Sex Information and Education Council of Canada (SIECCAN)
850 Coxwell Avenue
Toronto, Ontario, Canada M4C 5RI   416-466-5304

Sexuality Information and Education Council of the United States (SIECUS)

130 West 42nd St, Suite 350
New York, NY 10036   212-819-9770
http://www.siecus.org

National nonprofit organization, that promotes comprehensive education about sexuality and advocates rights of individuals to make responsible sexual choice; details information on sexuality, contraception, sexual abuse, and assault.

REPRODUCTIVE HEALTH, CONTRACEPTION, FERTILITY, AND WOMEN'S HEALTH

Access to Voluntary and Safe Contraception

79 Madison Avenue, 7th Floor
New York, NY 10016   212-561-8000
http://www.avsc.org

International nonprofit organization dedicated to making reproductive health care accessible to women and men around the world; also provides programs for voluntary family planning and reproductive health services, including health care for sexually transmitted diseases, postpartum care, and post-abortion care.

Advocates for Youth

1025 Vermont Avenue NW, Suite 200
Washington, DC 20005   202-347-5700
http://www.advocatesforyouth.org

Offers teen education and advocates in areas of HIV prevention, peer education, sexuality, and teen pregnancy prevention, plus helps activists implement local and state policies about teen health initiatives and policies.

Alan Guttmacher Institute

120 Wall Street, 21st Floor
New York, NY 10005   212-248-1111
http://www.agi-usa.org

Nonprofit organization providing research and policy analysis for family planning and reproduction rights.

American Medical Association — JAMA Woman's Health Information Center

515 North State Street
Chicago, IL 60610   312-464-5000
http://www.ama-assn.org/special/womh/womh.htm

Source for physicians and other health professionals produced under direction of editorial review board of leading women's health authorities; this site has large selection of readings and information including in-depth articles from major professional sources, abstracts from major articles published in JAMA clinical guidelines, resources for contraception information, plus a collection of Web links.

Association for Voluntary Surgical Contraception

79 Madison Avenue, 7th Floor
New York, NY 10016   212-561-8000
Provides information on sterilization and other contraceptive methods.

Center for Women Policy Studies

1211 Connecticut Avenue NW, Suite 312
Washington, DC 20036   202-872-1770
http://www.centerwomenpolicy.org

Independent, national multiethnic and multicultural feminist policy research and advocacy organization for women and AIDS, violence against women and girls, welfare reform, access to health care, educational equity, work/family and workplace diversity policies.

Human Resources and Service Administration Women's Health

5600 Fishers Lane, Room 14-25
Rockville, MD 20857   301-443-8695
http://www.hrsa.gov/womenshealth

Provides leadership to increase access to primary and preventive health care for women and girls who are medically underserved.

Healthy Mothers/Healthy Babies Coalition (HMHB)

121 N Washington Street
Alexandria, VA 22314   703-836-6110
http://www.hmhb.org

A forum for a collaborative partnership of public and private organizations, employers, policymakers and consumers to promote and improve culturally and linguistically appropriate, community-based services that foster healthy mothers, healthy babies, and healthy families.

International Childbirth Education Association (ICEA)

PO Box 20048
Minneapolis, MN 55420   612-854-8660
http://www.healthy.net/pan/cso/cioi/ICEA.HTM

Unites people who support family-centered maternity care and believe in freedom of choice based on knowledge of alternatives.

International Council on Infertility Information Dissemination (INCIID)

PO Box 6836
Arlington, VA 22206   703-379-9178
http://www.inciid.org

Nonprofit organization that provides information regarding diagnosis, treatment, and prevention of infertility and pregnancy loss; site accesses fact sheets and transcripts of auditoriums with renowned experts, more than 150 referrals and links to nonprofit organizations providing quality, sound infertility information, such as American Society of Reproductive Medicine and International Federation of Fertility Societies.

La Leche League International

1400 N. Meacham Road
Schaumburg, IL 60173   847-519-7730
http://www.lalecheleague.org
Provides information and encouragement, mainly through personal help, to all mothers who want to breast-feed their babies.

Midwives Alliance of North America

888-923-6262
http://www.mana.org
Promotes interprofessional relations with doctors, nurses, and other health care providers; provides guidelines for midwifery education and expand communication among midwives.

National Abortion Rights Action League (NARAL)

1156 15th Street NW, Suite 700
Washington, DC 20005   202-973-3000
http://www.naral.org/choice/index.html
A political action organization working for productive freedom and dignity for women choosing abortion.

National Organization for Women (NOW)

1000 16th Street NW, Suite 700
Washington, DC 20036   202-331-0066
http://www.now.org
Feminist activists organization striving to bring about equality for all women.

National Right to Life

419 Seventh NW, Suite 500
Washington, DC 20004   202-626-8800
http://www.nrlc.org/
The pro-life organization promoting rights of unborn child.

National Women's Health America

429 Gammon Place
Madison, WI 52725   800-222-4767
http://www.womenshealth.com/hotline.html
Health organization providing information and education about pre-menstrual syndrome (PMS), menopause, natural hormone replacement therapy (HRT), and other women's health concerns.

National Women's Health Resource Center

120 Albany Street, Suite 820
New Brunswick, NJ 08901   877-986-9472
http://www.healthywomen.org/index.html
Nonprofit organization offering a national clearinghouse and information resource for women's health information.

North American Menopause Society

PO Box 94527
Cleveland, OH 44101   216-844-8748
http://www.menopause.org
Multidisciplinary, nonprofit organization that provides a forum for many scientific disciplines and an interest in human female menopause.

Planned Parenthood Federation of America

810 Seventh Avenue
New York, NY 10019

800-230-7526
connects to affiliate in caller's service area.
800-829-7732 National Office

http://www.plannedparenthood.org
Family planning organization that provides reproductive health care, family planning services, and sexuality education including contraception, abortion, sterilization, and infertility services.

Population Institute

107 Second Street NE
Washington, DC 20002   202-544-3300
http://www.populationinstitute.org
Provides leadership in creating national and international awareness of social, economic, and environmental implications of rapid population growth.

RESOLVE, The National Infertility Association

1310 Broadway
Somerville MA 02144   617-623-0744
http://www.resolve.org/
Provides help, support, and information to individuals experiencing infertility through advocacy, and public education.

Sudden Infant Death Syndrome (SIDS) Alliance

1314 Bedford Avenue, Suite 210
Baltimore, MD 21208   800-221-7437
http://www.healthy.net/pan/cso/cioi/SIDSA.HTM
Nonprofit organization providing counseling, support, public education, and medical research to families affected by SIDS.

U.S. Public Health Service' Office on Women's Health

Department of Health and Human Services
200 Independence Avenue SW, Room 730B
Washington, DC 20201   202-690-7650
http://www.4woman.gov
Agency that redresses the inequities in research, health care services, and education that have placed the health of women at risk; coordinates women's health research, health care services, policy, and public and health care professional education.

Zero Population Growth

1400 - 16th Street NW, Suite 320
Washington, DC 20036   202-332-2200
http://www.zpg.org
Nonprofit group working to slow population growth and achieve sustainable balance between earth's people and its resources.

STDs HIV/AIDS, AND SAFER SEX ORGANIZATIONS

AIDS Policy Center (APC) for Children, Youth, and Families

918 - 16th Street, NW, Suite 201
Washington, DC 20006   202-785-3564
http://www.hivdent.org
Outgrowth of the Public Policy Committee of National Pediatric HIV Resource Center; serves service providers and persons living with HIV/AIDS (PLWAs); assures health care and psychosocial needs of HIV-affected children, youth, women, and families; they conduct policy research and analysis, legal and policy training, and technical assistance to pediatric, adolescent, and family service providers throughout U. S.

American Civil Liberties Union (ACLU)

AIDS Project
125 Broad Street, 18th Floor
New York, NY 10004   212-549-2500
http://www.aclu.org/issues/aids/hmaids.html
Advocate of individual rights and litigating and educating the public on issues affecting individual freedom in United States.

American Social Health Association (ASHA)

PO Box 13827
Research Triangle Park, NC 27709   919-361-8400

http://www.ashastd.org

Nonprofit organization dedicated to stopping sexually transmitted diseases and their consequences.

CDC National Prevention Information Network

PO Box 6003
Rockville, MD 20849-6003   800-458-5231

http://www.cdcnpin.org

Provides information and referrals on AIDS/HIV, STD, and TB prevention.

Elizabeth Glaser Pediatric AIDS Foundation

2950 - 31st Street, #125
Santa Monica CA 90405   310-314-1459

http://www.pedaids.org/

Nonprofit organization that funds and conducts research impacting the diagnosis, treatment, and prevention of HIV/AIDS in children.

Women Organized to Respond to Life

414 - 13th Street, Second Floor
Oakland, CA 94612   510-986-0340

http://www.womenhiv.org

Provides support and information to women with HIV/AIDS and their friends, family, and loved ones; educates and inspires women to advocate for themselves, each another, and their communities to promote public awareness of women's HIV/AIDS issues. World offers retreats, maintains a speakers' bureau and an information hotline, as well as information, and referrals, and publishes a monthly newsletter.

SINGLE PARENTS

Parents Without Partners

401 N. Michigan Avenue
Chicago, IL 60611   312-644-6610

http://parentswithoutpartners.org/index.htm

International, nonprofit, educational organization devoted to interests of single parents and their children.

Single Mothers by Choice

PO Box 1642
Gracie Square Station
New York, NY 10028   212-988-0993

http://www3.parentsplace.com/readroom/smc/index.html

Provides information and support to single mothers as well as those contemplating or trying to achieve single motherhood.

VICTIMIZATION

American Professional Society on Abuse of Children

407 S. Dearborn Street, Suite 1300
Chicago, IL 60605   312-554-0166

http://www.apsac.org

Professional society whose mission is to ensure that everyone affected by child maltreatment receives the best possible professional response.

Association for the Treatment of Sexual Abusers

10700 SW Beaverton-Hillsdale Highway, Suite 26
Beaverton, OR 97005-3035   503-643-1023

http://www.atsa.com

Nonprofit interdisciplinary organization founded to foster research, facilitate information exchange, further professional education, and provide for advancement of professional standards and practices in the field of sex offender evaluation and treatment.

Childhelp USA

15757 N. 78th Street
Scottsdale, AZ 85260   480-922-8212

http://www.childhelpusa.org

Organization dedicated to meeting physical, emotional, educational, and spiritual needs of abused and neglected children; focuses on treatment, prevention, and research and operates a child abuse hotline.

National Center for Victims of Crime

2111 Wilson Boulevard, Suite 300
Arlington, VA 22201   703-276-2880

http://www.nvc.org/

Nonprofit organization providing resources and advocacy to victims of crime.

National Coalition Against Domestic Violence

119 Constitution Avenue NE
Washington, DC 20002   202-544-7358

http://www.ncadv.org

Private nonprofit organization providing a network of shelter and support centers for battered women and their children.

Prevent Child Abuse America

200 S. Michigan Avenue, 16th Floor
Chicago, IL 60604   312-663-3520

http://www.childabuse.org

Nonprofit agency that strives to prevent child abuse; provides statistics, information, and publications relating to child abuse.

National Council on Child Abuse and Family Violence

1155 Connecticut Avenue NW, Suite 400
Washington, DC 20036   202-429-6695

http://www.nccafv.org

Nonprofit corporation that provides public education materials, program and resource development consultation, technical assistance and training to agencies and volunteers.

National Organization on Male Sexual Victimization

PO Box 20782
West Palm Beach, FL 33416   800-738-4181
PO Box 3582
Windsor, Novia Scotia Canada B0N 2T0

http://www.malesurvivor.org

Started in 1988 by mental health providers who wanted to better understand and treat adult male survivors of childhood sexual abuse.

Parents United International

615 - 15th Street
Modesto, CA 95354   209-572-3446

Supervised self-help group for families impacted by sexual abuse; chapters throughout United States.

Survivors of Incest Anonymous

PO Box 21817
Baltimore, MD 21222   410-282-3400

http://www.siawso.org

A 12-step recovery program for men and women. For information, send a self-addressed envelop with two postage stamps to the above address.

Glossary

A

Abstinence self-restraint or self-denial, as in not engaging in sexual activity

Abortion termination of an established pregnancy through surgical or nonsurgical techniques

Active listening listening with understanding using appropriate body language, and providing feedback

Actual-use effectiveness the reliability of a contraceptive expressed as percentage of women who get pregnant while using the method for 1 year

Adhesions spiderweblike bands of scar tissue that painfully bind internal organs to each other or the abdominal wall

Adolescence time period representing the psychosocial transition from childhood to young adulthood; teenage years

Aggressiveness pursuing one's own wants and needs without regard for the rights of others

AIDS acronym for acquired immunodeficiency syndrome, the end result of HIV

Amenorrhea absence of menstruation at some time after a female has reached menses

Amphetamines a central nervous system stimulant that is administered by ingestion, injection, snorting, or inhalation

Androcentrism a position of viewing the world with the male at its center

Androgens a group of naturally occurring steroid hormones produced by both men and women

Androgyny expressing characteristics and traits considered stereotypically male and female

Anilingus licking and sucking the anus

Annular refers to hymen with a ring-shaped opening in the center

Anorgasmia inability to achieve orgasm

Anus opening of the bowel, through which fecal matter is eliminated from the body

Areola brownish or pink ring of tissue surrounding the nipple of the breast.

Assertiveness pursuing one's own needs and wants without infringing on others' needs and wants

Associational brain functions connecting together individual sensory inputs

Autoeroticism a sexual desire or gratification experienced by a person without the direct participation of another person

Autoinnoculate to self-inflict the spread of disease from one body part to another

Autonomic nervous system the part of the peripheral nervous system that is automatic and involuntary

Aversion therapy a behavior modification technique that pairs a negative stimulus with the behavior targeted for change

B

Balanitis inflammation of the glans penis

Barrier methods contraceptive measures that prevent the sperm and egg from uniting

Bartholins glands small glands adjacent to the vaginal opening that secrete a mucous-like lubricant during arousal

Basal body temperature (BBT) lowest body temperature of a healthy person during waking hours

Behaviorism a stimulus-response theory grounded in the belief that human personality evolves as a result of the interaction between exposure to stimuli and the responses that this exposure evokes in the person. Watson is credited with the theory, expanded later by Skinner

Biological essentialism the position that biology is destiny and biology explains human nature

Biological/anatomical sex categorizing individuals as male or female based upon their reproductive organs, chromosome make-up, and hormone levels

Biological immaturity incomplete anatomical and physiological development associated with early adolescence or preadolescence

Birth control broadest term covering all methods designed to prevent the birth of a child

Bisexuality forming sexual relationships with both men and women

Blood alcohol concentration (BAC) a measurement of percentage of alcohol in blood; also termed blood alcohol level (BAL)

Body composition the fat and nonfat components of the human body, important in assessing recommended body weight

Body language sent intentional or unintentional messages through body postures and movements

Bonding close physical and emotional attachment that develops between infants and their primary caregiver(s)

Breech position birth position in which buttocks or foot rather than baby's head presents at the cervix

Brothel house of prostitution

C

Cannula a tapered, strawlike tube used in the vacuum aspiration method of abortion

Carriers individuals who have a given disease and are capable of passing it on genetically but have no apparent symptoms

Celibacy abstaining from sexual intercourse

Central nervous system (CNS) the brain and spinal cord

Cervical interepithelial neoplasm (CIN) tumor or growth within the cervical membrane tissues

Cervix neck of uterus, which extends into inner end of vagina

Cesarean delivery (c-section) surgical form of childbirth in which an incision is made through the abdomen and uterus to deliver the baby

Chancre painless, primary lesion characteristic of early syphilis

Chat room live e-mail discussion lines in which a person can communicate with others online by typing messages

Chancroid STD named for irregular and painful genital lesions it produces, caused by bacterium *Haemophilus ducreyl*

Child molester one who makes indecent sexual advances to children

Childbirth labor and delivery

Chylamydia trachomatis most prevalent sexually transmitted bacterial pathogen, causing the STD chylamydia

Cilia hairlike projections lining the fallopian tubes

Circumcision surgical removal of foreskin of penis

Clitoral hood fold of skin that covers glans of clitoris

Clitoris small, highly sensitive organ located at top of labia minora; site of female orgasm

Cohabitation living together without being married

Coitus vaginal intercourse

Communication process by which information is exchanged between individuals through common system of symbols, signs, and behaviors

Companionate love feelings that include deep attachment, commitment, and intimacy

Complementary relationships relationships based on differences rather than similarities

Conception *see* **Fertilization**

Congenital syphilis disease acquired by fetus in the womb and present at birth

Connective tissue tissue that supports or binds other tissue

Contraception/contraceptives methods designed to prevent conception

Corpus luteum the follicle after it has released its ova and begins to produce progesterone

Covert sensitization a type of behavior modification in which an aversive fantasy is paired with paraphiliac fantasy in an attempt to extinguish it

Cowper's glands bulbourethral glands, located below seminal vesicles, which produce preejaculatory fluid that lubricate vas deferens and urethra and protect sperm that are being ejaculated

Cremaster muscle a layer of muscle tissue that covers spermatic cord

Cribiform type of hymen with many small perforations

Cryptorchidism undescended testicle(s)

Cunnilingus licking and sucking the vulva

Curette a long-handled spoonlike instrument used to scrape off contents of uterus in an abortion

Cystoscopy direct visual examination of interior of urethra, urinary bladder, and kidneys by inserting a cystoscope (optical viewing tube) into the urethra

Cysts an abnormal condition of fluid-filled sacs that can burst and cause pain and scarring

D

Decoding use of knowledge, memory, language, context, and personal history and experience to interpret a message

Declarative statement a verbal initiating technique that does not require a response to a message

Dialogue exchange of information in communication

Dilation and curettage (D & C) surgical abortion procedure that removes the embryo and placenta from the uterus by scraping

Dilation and evacuation (D & E) abortion procedure in which the cervix is dilated and the fetus is removed by suction

Dysmenorrhea painful menstruation

Dyspareunia genital pain associated with sexual intercourse

Dysuria burning upon urination

E

Ectopic pregnancy implantation of egg outside the womb; usually poses danger to pregnant women

Effacement Thinning of cervix during first stage of labor

Ego rational, analytical facet of human mind, according to Freudian theory

Ejaculatory inevitability first step in male ejaculation; beginning of smooth-muscle contractions that trigger release of ejaculate

Electromyographic refers to measurement of muscle tension through electrical sensors at skin surface

Embryo fertilized egg up to 8 weeks' gestation

Emission release of secretions from various organs and glands that produce male ejaculate

Emotional well-being component of wellness that refers to being in touch with one's feelings, having the ability to express them, and being able to control them when necessary

Endometrium inner lining of uterus

Encoding selecting the signs, symbols, emotions, and words to transmit a message

Endemic a 20% level of ongoing infection within a specific population

Endometriosis a condition in which pieces of the endometrium migrate to the fallopian tubes, ovaries, or abdominal cavity

Environmental well-being a component of wellness that reflects our ability to function in our immediate environment, such as home, school, and work, as well as being able to deal with the world at large

Epidemiologic dealing with incidence, distribution, and control, as in STDs

Epidemiological synergy distribution of disease caused by effects of infection with more than one condition

Epididymis comma-shaped structure that sits along top of each testicle and serves as storage chamber for immature sperm

Epididymitis inflammation epididymis

Epidural anesthetic injection of a drug into the spinal cord during labor to dull pain

Episiotomy surgical cutting of perineum to facilitate childbirth

Epidural injection of a drug into the spinal cord during labor to dull pain

Erectile dysfunction a disturbance or disorder related to obtaining an erection

Erection filling of the penile spongy tissue with blood during vasocongestion, resulting in a hard, erect, penis

Erogenous capable of producing sexual excitement

Erotic devoted to arousing sexual desire

Ethyl alcohol a grain alcohol that is a central nervous system depressant

Exhibitionism deriving sexual pleasure from exposing one's genitals to unsuspecting strangers

External inhibitions those who, through their influence, block natural inhibitions against child sexual abuse

F

Fallopian tubes two conduits, each of which is connected to uterus, through which egg passes ovulation.

Family planning the conscious effort of deciding to have a family, including when to have children, how many, and how far apart to space them

Feedback verbal or nonverbal response from the person receiving a message to the person sending the message

Fellatio licking and sucking of the penis

Female climacteric a syndrome experienced by women between 45 and 55 years of age as a result of declining levels of estrogen production associated with menopause

Fertility awareness natural family planning

Fertilization union of the sperm and ovum

Fetal alcohol syndrome (FAS) effects on embryo and fetus of pregnant woman's alcohol consumption; symptoms include facial abnormalities, mental retardation, and nervous system damage

Fetishism deriving sexual pleasure from inanimate objects

Fetus fertilized egg from 8 weeks after conception to birth

Fibroadenomas benign, solid tumors associated with fibrocystic breast disorder

Fimbriae fingerlike projections at the end of the fallopian tubes, which surround the ovary

Follicle egg sac in the ovary

Frotteurism deriving sexual pleasure from rubbing up against unsuspecting and unwilling victims

G

Gametes the reproductive cells — sperm and ova

Gender dysphoria condition wherein one's anatomy is inconsistent with one's gender identity

Gender identity one's personal perception and sense of being male, female, or blended

Gender polarization belief that males and females are fundamentally different, with mutually exclusive gender scripts

Gender role the ways we express our gender identity — including appearance, clothing, movement, and life choices

Genital herpes infection caused by exposure to herpes simplex virus type 1 or type 2 through sexual contact

Genital warts an STD caused by human papilloma virus (HPV)

Gestation period of time representing pregnancy and development of fetus from conception to birth

Glans penis end of corpus spongiosum, which comprises head of penis and urethral opening

Gonads ovaries and the testicles

Gonads the primary endocrine glands in men (testes) and women (ovaries) that influence sexuality

Gonorrhea sexually transmitted diseases caused by bacteria *Neisseria gonorrhea*

G-spot an area in the upper, rear section of the vagina named after Ernest Grafenberg, who claimed it to be an erogenous zone

Guanosine triphosphate a chemical that controls muscular and vascular changes of erection

Gynecomastia enlargement of one or both breasts in men

H

Hallucinogen a class of drugs that distort the perception of reality by altering the perception of all sensory inputs

Health state of complete mental, physical, and social well-being, not merely the absence of disease

Healthy sexuality the safe and open exploration and development of our potential as human beings

Hemispheres the two halves of the cerebrum; each controls the functions of the opposite side of the body

Hepatitis B Virus (HBV) a disease caused by contact with infected blood; often associated with unprotected sex with multiple partners

Heterosexuality forming sexual relationships with members of the other sex

HIV acronym for human immunodeficiency virus, the infection that leads to AIDS

Holistic health optimal functioning across the physical, intellectual, emotional, social, and spiritual dimensions

Homologous structures body parts that develop from the same embryonic tissue (for example, the female clitoris and male penis)

Homosexuality forming sexual relationships with members of the same sex

Hormonal releasing factors chemicals secreted by hypothalamus that trigger the pituitary to release specific hormones

Human chorionic gonadotropin (HCG) a hormone secreted during pregnancy that shows up in the urine of pregnant women; the basis for determining pregnancy using home kits

Human chorionic gonadotropin (HCG) a hormone secreted during pregnancy that shows up in the urine of pregnant women; the basis for determining pregnancy using home kits

Human papilloma virus (HPV) condition spread through direct contact with an infected person's genital warts during sexual contact

Humanism a theory of personality development proposing that personality is shaped by innate desire and need for maximizing personal growth

Hydrocele accumulation of fluid in a sac, cavity, or duct

Hymen membrane that lines the introitus and serves as a barrier to the vagina

Hypoactive sexual desire disorder a dysfunction characterized by low or complete absence of sexual desire

Hypothalamus part of the brain that correlates between the nervous centers and the pituitary gland

Hypoxyphilia deriving sexual pleasure from activities that involve oxygen deprivation

Hysterectomy surgical removal of uterus. In practice, a hysterectomy often is accompanied by surgical removal of fallopian tubes, and sometimes the ovaries as well

Hysterotomy surgical procedure in which the fetus and placenta are removed surgically through an abdominal incision

I

"I" language taking responsibility for feelings by saying "I feel . . ." versus "You make me feel. . . ."

Id pleasure-seeking, guilt-free facet of human mind, according to Freudian theory

IDA acronym for injecting drug abuse

Illogical thinking thought based on inaccurate or irrational perception of information

Immunocompetence level of efficiency of the immune system

Implantation attachment of a fertilized egg to lining of uterus

Implants migrating pieces of endometrial tissue associated with endometriosis

Incidence the number of new cases of a disease during a specific time period

Infantilism deriving sexual pleasure from being treated like an infant

Infertility inability to conceive after 1 year of unprotected intercourse

Intellectual well-being a component of wellness referring to the ability to process information effectively and rationally

Internal inhibitions well-developed impulse control against adult-child sexual relations

Intersexual refers to an individual possessing some degree of both male and female internal or external reproductive structures; the preferred term, replacing earlier labels of hermaphrodite and pseudohermaphrodite

Intimacy connectedness to another person characterized by mutual caring, openness, self-disclosure, honesty, attentiveness, sharing, commitment, trust, empathy, and tenderness

Introitus vaginal opening

In-vitro fertilization (IVF) procedure in which ova are removed from the woman's body and fertilized with sperm in a laboratory; the embryo is surgically implanted into her uterus

L

Labia majora the larger, outer vaginal lips

Labia minora the smaller, inner vaginal lips

Lactation the process of producing and secreting milk from the breasts

Laparoscope a flexible surgical instrument with a cameralike attachment that can be inserted into the abdomen to view the fallopian tubes and other organs

Leydig (interstitial) cells endocrine cells within the testicles that produce hormones

Lymph nodes the main drainage and filtration sites in the lymph system

M

Male climacteric a syndrome experienced by about 5% of men in their 40s and 50s, characterized by diminished interest in sex, loss of appetite, fatigue, and inability to concentrate

Mammary glands glands within the breasts that produce milk for lactation

Masturbation manual stimulation of the genitals to provide sexual pleasure

Megan's Law Legislation requiring notification that a sex offender has been released and is residing in a community

Metacommunication communicating about communication

Minilaparotomy female sterilization procedure in which fallopian tubes are cut to block transport of the egg

Mirroring restating a message exactly, including body language

Monogamy married to only one person at a time

Morbidity relative incidence of a disease

Mortality number of deaths from a specific cause during a specified time period

Motor relating to nerve impulses going out to muscles

Myomectomy surgical procedure that removes fibroid tumors without removing uterus

Myometrium muscular, middle layer of uterus

Myotonia involuntary skeletal muscle contractions

N

Nongonococcal urethritis (NGU) infection in urethra of males, usually caused by chlamydia bacteria

Nontraditional relationships any relationship other than a monogamous, legal marriage between a man and a woman

Nuclear family a family made up of the mother, father, and their children

O

Obscenity material that is abhorrent to moral virtue and accepted norms of social behavior

Oedipal complex a psychoanalytic term (named after Oedipus in Shakespeare's play) that describes the internal struggle that 3- to 4-year-olds face as they begin to identify more with their opposite-sex parent

Open-ended questions sentences that require information from the other person, not just a yes or no response

Opportunistic infection an infection that is able to develop as a result of the body's weakened immune status

Orgasm stage of sexual response characterized by ejaculation in males and involuntary muscular contractions followed by relaxation in both males and females

Orgasmic disorders dysfunctions related to the orgasm phase of sexual response

Ovarian cycle a three-phased period of time covering maturation of a follicle, release of ovum, and secreting role of corpus luteum

Ovaries two almond-shaped structures that contain and release ova and secrete the hormones estrogen and progesterone

Ovulation release of an egg from the ovary

P

Paraphilia an unusual or atypical sexual behavior that becomes the focal point for an obsessive preoccupation or need

Paraphrasing restating a message in one's own words

Passionate love feelings characterized by intense longing for another, infatuation, ecstasy when reciprocated, and emptiness when not shared by the other

Passive listening one-way listening; provides no feedback

Pedophilia engaging in sexual activity with, or fantasizing about, prepubescent children

Pelvic inflammatory disease (PID) a catch-all term used to describe infection of uterus, fallopian tubes, or ovaries, resulting in fever, malaise, pain, and other symptoms

Performance anxiety fear, worry, or panic associated with one's perceived sexual behavior

Perimetrium outer lining of uterus

Peripheral nervous system all nerves coming off of the spinal cord

Perineum erogenous area of skin extending from base of testicles to anal opening

Perineum area of muscle and skin between vagina and anus

Peritoneum cavity membrane covering entire abdominal wall

Personality collection of values, attitudes, and behavior that make us who we are

Pheromones body chemicals that attract potential sexual partners

Phimosis a tight foreskin that cannot be retracted fully

Physical well-being a component of wellness reflected in how well the body performs its intended functions

Post-abortion syndrome long-term negative psychological effects of abortion

Prior learning factors relating to childhood development

Placenta organ that attaches to uterine wall and serves as a conduit for oxygen and nutrients to pass to the developing fetus

Pornography a depiction of lewd material or erotic behavior designed to cause sexual arousal

Primary sex characteristics growth of the sex organs

Prodrome systemic, flulike syndrome that accompanies genital herpes infection

Promiscuity frequent and indiscriminate change in sexual partners

Prostate gland chestnut-sized gland in males, connected to neck of bladder and vas deferens, which secretes alkaline fluid and enzymes that are part of ejaculatory fluid

Prostaglandins hormones that can cause muscle contractions and have been associated with menstrual pain

Prostatitis irritation and inflammation of prostate gland

Prostitution exchange of sexual services for money

Protease inhibitors group of antiviral drugs used to prevent replication of HIV-infected cells

Psychoanalytic theory also known as Freudian theory (after its founder, Sigmund Freud), describes personality development as outgrowth of interaction of id (pleasure-seeking, guilt-free), superego (the conscience, influenced by society and parents), and ego (rational, analytical mind driven by logical thinking)

Psychoses severe form of mental disorder or disease affecting the total personality

Psychosexual development the blending of sexual aspects of one's development with other psychological factors

Psychotropic drugs substances that are mind-altering

Puberty biological transition from childhood to young adulthood

Pubic lice *Phthirius pubis;* small insects (metazoan) that infest the host's pubic hair

R

Raphe midline of testes, representing fusion of embryonic tissue

Rate a statistic calculated by dividing the number of cases of disease by the population at risk of infection

Refractory period the time from last orgasm to the next beginning of excitement

Reproductive readiness pubertal development resulting in full growth of genitalia and onset of fertility

Role model a person whose behaviors are imitated by others

RU-486 known as "abortion pill"; mifepristone, a drug used to induce menstruation by blocking absorption of progesterone and thereby preventing uterine lining from supporting embryo

S

Safe zone a fertility awareness concept that factors ovulation and length of time sperm and eggs can live as a time to avoid intercourse

Scabies condition caused by the *Sarcotes scabiei* parasite, which burrows under the skin and lays eggs

Scrotum a double-chambered pouch of tissue that hangs loosely from the base of the penis, containing the testicles

Secondary sex characteristics physical traits that develop during puberty and signal sexual maturity; examples are developed breasts in females, coarse facial hair on males, armpit and pubic hair in both

Seminal vesicles small structures connected to vas deferens, which release fluids that nourish and buffer sperm as they are ejaculated

Seminiferous tubules small, coiled structures within the testes where sperm production occurs

Sensate focus nongenital pleasuring used to heighten sensuality without sexual activity

Sensuality experiencing things through all five senses

Sensory relating to nerve messages coming into the brain

Septate type of hymen in which opening is separated by a thin septum (membrane wall)

Serous fluid a liquid that has the characteristics of serum

Sex surrogate person who acts as a substitute sex partner during therapy

Sexologists professionals who study sexuality using rigorous research methodologies. Sexologists come from a variety of disciplines such as psychology, biology, medicine, nursing, and health

Sexual assault broadest term applying to forms of sexual aggression against a target

Sexual aversion disorder a dysfunction characterized by disgust and active avoidance of any genital sexual contact

Sexual differentiation the processes by which the embryo/fetus develops into a male or a female; internal and external genitalia develop in distinct ways, as does the brain

Sexual dysfunction a disturbance or disorder in desire, excitement, orgasm, or resolution of the sexual response cycle

Sexual orientation one's propensity for romantic and erotic attachments. Heterosexuality refers to attaching to a partner with different anatomy; homosexuality refers to a same-sex partner; bisexuality refers to attaching to both men and women

Sexual lifestyle the interaction between types and numbers of current sex partners

Sexual masochism deriving sexual pleasure from being humiliated or forced to suffer pain

Sexual sadism deriving sexual pleasure from inflicting pain or humiliation

Sexuality a broad term referring to all aspects of being sexual

Sexually transmitted diseases (STDs) diseases that are spread from person to person through sexual contact

Social well-being a component of wellness that involves connection to others through various types of relationships

Sociopath a manifestly antisocial psychopath

Somatic nervous system the part of the peripheral nervous system under voluntary control

Somatotropic drugs substances that are body-altering

Sonogram the picture of the fetus produced by an ultrasound screening

Spectatoring becoming an outside observer of one's own sexual encounter while it is occurring

Spermatic cord a structure connecting the inguinal muscles in the abdomen with the testis; contains the vas deferens, blood and lymph vessels, and nerves

Spermatogenesis sperm production

Spiritual well-being a component of wellness that involves feeling connected to something beyond oneself

Spirochete a mobile, flexible, corkscrew-shaped bacterium of the genus Spirocheta, one type of which causes syphilis

Sterility permanent inability to reproduce

Sterilization techniques (vasectomy and tubal ligation) that prevent sperm from reaching ova

Superego the conscience, influenced by society and family, according to Freudian theory

Symmetrical relationships relationships based on equality

Synergistic effect an enhanced, unpredictable drug effect caused by combining two or more substances

Syphilis STD caused by the spirochete bacterium *Treponema pallidum*

T

Teratogenic effects side effects of drugs and other substances that cause birth defects

Testes two almond-shaped male gonads responsible for sperm and hormone production

Testosterone main male hormone associated with sexual desire

Thalamus part of the brain that relays all inputs to the cerebral cortex

Theoretical effectiveness the lowest expected percentage of women who will get pregnant while using a given contraceptive method

Thriving pattern of normal weight gain, neuromuscular development, and other developmental attributes of infants

Tubal ligation a female sterilization procedure in which a surgical instrument is used to cut and tie back the fallopian tubes to block passage of ova and thereby prevent fertilization

Transactional analysis (TA) Eric Berne's communication model based on three ego states — parent, adult, and child

Transudation the production of vaginal lubrication because of sweating of vaginal tissue engorged with blood during vasocongestion

Transgendered preferred term to describe individuals whose gender identity and ender role encompasses both masculinity and femininity; previous labels were transvestite and transsexual

Transsexualism (a gender identity disorder) a strong and persistent cross-gender identification

Transvestic fetishism deriving sexual pleasure from wearing women's clothing

Tubal ligation surgical sterilization of the female that involves cutting and tying off the fallopian tubes

Tunica dartos thin layer of connective and muscle tissue covering the testes

Tunica vaginalis a small, closed sac that covers the testes

T-zone transformation zone of cervix, where columnar epithelial tissue of uterus meets with squamous tissue of vagina

U

Urethra tube that transports urine and ejaculate through penis

Urethritis inflammation and irritation of urethra

Uterine fibroid tumors noncancerous solid growths on endometrium

Uterus womb

V

Vacuum curettage induced abortion procedure in which uterine contents are removed by suction; used for early abortions

Vagina tubular organ connecting to the uterus, which serves both reproductive and erotic functions

Vaginismus painful, involuntary contractions of outer third of the vagina during attempted penetration

Vaginitis inflammation and irritation of vagina

Vas deferens a tube extending from testicles to prostate gland, where it converts into urethra; responsible for transporting sperm and other ejaculatory fluid

Vasectomy a male sterilization procedure in which the vas deferens are cut and tied to block the transport of sperm

Vasocongestion movement of blood flow into the genitals at a resulting in a variety of responses including erection in men and lubrication in women

Vesicles fluid-filled blisters

Vestibular bulbs spongy tissue underlying vulva

Vestibule area within the labia minora that includes hymen, introitus, and urethral opening

Viability a gestational weight of the fetus of at least 500 grams and/or age of 24 weeks of age

Viagra the drug sildenafil, prescribed for treatment of erectile disorder

Voyeurism deriving sexual pleasure from observing unsuspecting individuals undressing or engaging in sexual activities

Vulva external female genitalia

W

Wellness the state of optimal health and well-being

Widowhood period of time between loss of spouse and remarriage

Women's movement force to gain full educational, social, and economic opportunities and rights for women equal to those which men are tradtionally understood to have

Y

Yes/no questions a verbal initiating technique that requires only a yes or a no response